Studies in the Economics of Aging

A National Bureau
of Economic Research
Project Report

Studies in the Economics of Aging

Edited by David A. Wise

The University of Chicago Press

Chicago and London

DAVID A. WISE is the John F. Stambaugh Professor of Political Economy at the John F. Kennedy School of Government, Harvard University, and the area director for Health and Retirement Programs at the National Bureau of Economic Research.

The University of Chicago Press, Chicago 60637
The University of Chicago Press, Ltd., London

© 1994 by the National Bureau of Economic Research
All rights reserved. Published 1994
Printed in the United States of America
03 02 01 00 99 98 97 96 95 94 1 2 3 4 5
ISBN: 0–226–90294–3 (cloth)

Library of Congress Cataloging-in-Publication Data

Studies in the economics of aging / edited by David A. Wise.
        p.   cm.—(A National Bureau of Economic Research project
report)
        Includes bibliographical references (p.   ) and index.
        1. Old age—Economic aspects—Congresses.   2. Aging—Eco-
nomic aspects—Congresses.   3. Retirement—Economic aspects—Congresses.
I. Wise, David A.   II. Series.
HQ1061.S844   1994
305.26—dc20   94-16196
                                                                    CIP

Relation of the Directors to the
Work and Publications of the
National Bureau of Economic Research

1. The object of the National Bureau of Economic Research is to ascertain and to present to the public important economic facts and their interpretation in a scientific and impartial manner. The Board of Directors is charged with the responsibility of ensuring that the work of the National Bureau is carried on in strict conformity with this object.

2. The President of the National Bureau shall submit to the Board of Directors, or to its Executive Committee, for their formal adoption all specific proposals for research to be instituted.

3. No research report shall be published by the National Bureau until the President has sent each member of the Board a notice that a manuscript is recommended for publication and that in the President's opinion it is suitable for publication in accordance with the principles of the National Bureau. Such notification will include an abstract or summary of the manuscript's content and a response form for use by those Directors who desire a copy of the manuscript for review. Each manuscript shall contain a summary drawing attention to the nature and treatment of the problem studied, the character of the data and their utilization in the report, and the main conclusions reached.

4. For each manuscript so submitted, a special committee of the Directors (including Directors Emeriti) shall be appointed by majority agreement of the President and Vice Presidents (or by the Executive Committee in case of inability to decide on the part of the President and Vice Presidents), consisting of three Directors selected as nearly as may be one from each general division of the Board. The names of the special manuscript committee shall be stated to each Director when notice of the proposed publication is submitted to him. It shall be the duty of each member of the special manuscript committee to read the manuscript. If each member of the manuscript committee signifies his approval within thirty days of the transmittal of the manuscript, the report may be published. If at the end of that period any member of the manuscript committee withholds his approval, the President shall then notify each member of the Board, requesting approval or disapproval of publication, and thirty days additional shall be granted for this purpose. The manuscript shall then not be published unless at least a majority of the entire Board who shall have voted on the proposal within the time fixed for the receipt of votes shall have approved.

5. No manuscript may be published, though approved by each member of the special manuscript committee, until forty-five days have elapsed from the transmittal of the report in manuscript form. The interval is allowed for the receipt of any memorandum of dissent or reservation, together with a brief statement of his reasons, that any member may wish to express; and such memorandum of dissent or reservation shall be published with the manuscript if he so desires. Publication does not, however, imply that each member of the Board has read the manuscript, or that either members of the Board in general or the special committee have passed on its validity in every detail.

6. Publications of the National Bureau issued for informational purposes concerning the work of the Bureau and its staff, or issued to inform the public of activities of Bureau staff, and volumes issued as a result of various conferences involving the National Bureau shall contain a specific disclaimer noting that such publication has not passed through the normal review procedures required in this resolution. The Executive Committee of the Board is charged with review of all such publications from time to time to ensure that they do not take on the character of formal research reports of the National Bureau, requiring formal Board approval.

7. Unless otherwise determined by the Board or exempted by the terms of paragraph 6, a copy of this resolution shall be printed in each National Bureau publication.

(Resolution adopted October 25, 1926, as revised through September 30, 1974)

Contents

Acknowledgments   xi

Introduction   1
David A. Wise

I. DEMOGRAPHIC TRANSITION AND THE FEDERAL BUDGET

1. **The Impact of the Demographic Transition
   on Government Spending**   13
   John B. Shoven, Michael D. Topper, and
   David A. Wise
   Comment: Michael D. Hurd

II. DEATH RATES AND LIFE EXPECTANCY

2. **Methods for Projecting the Future Size and
   Health Status of the U.S. Elderly Population**   41
   Kenneth G. Manton, Eric Stallard, and Burton H.
   Singer

3. **Longer Life Expectancy? Evidence from
   Sweden of Reductions in Mortality Rates at
   Advanced Ages**   79
   James W. Vaupel and Hans Lundström
   Comment (chaps. 2 and 3): Peter Diamond
   Comment (chaps. 2 and 3): Michael D. Hurd

III. RETIREMENT SAVING

   4. 401(k) Plans and Tax-Deferred Saving   105
   James M. Poterba, Steven F. Venti, and
   David A. Wise
   Comment: Jonathan Skinner

   5. Some Thoughts on Savings   143
   Edward P. Lazear
   Comment: Jonathan Skinner
   Comment (chaps. 4 and 5): B. Douglas Bernheim

IV. RETIREMENT BEHAVIOR

   6. Pension Plan Provisions and Retirement:
   Men and Women, Medicare, and Models   183
   Robin L. Lumsdaine, James H. Stock, and
   David A. Wise
   Comment: John Rust
   Comment: James P. Smith

V. DEMOGRAPHIC TRANSITION AND HOUSING VALUES

   7. Demographics, the Housing Market, and
   the Welfare of the Elderly   225
   Daniel McFadden
   Comment: N. Gregory Mankiw

VI. INTERNATIONAL COMPARISONS

   8. Aging in Germany and the United States:
   International Comparisons   291
   Axel Börsch-Supan
   Comment: N. Gregory Mankiw

   9. Saving, Growth, and Aging in Taiwan   331
   Angus S. Deaton and Christina H. Paxson
   Comment: Jonathan Skinner

VII. LONG-TERM CARE

   10. Forecasting Nursing Home Utilization of
   Elderly Americans   365
   Andrew Dick, Alan M. Garber, and Thomas A.
   MaCurdy

11. Policy Options for Long-Term Care   395
David M. Cutler and Louise M. Sheiner
Comment (chaps. 10 and 11): Jonathan Feinstein

Contributors   443

Author Index   447

Subject Index   451

Acknowledgments

This volume consists of papers presented at a conference held at Caneel Bay, St. John, U.S. Virgin Islands, May 7–9, 1992. It is part of the National Bureau of Economic Research's ongoing project on the economics of aging. The majority of the work reported here was sponsored by the U.S. Department of Health and Human Services, through National Institute on Aging grants P01-AG05842, R37-AG08146, and T32-AG00186.

Any opinions expressed in this volume are those of the respective authors and do not necessarily reflect the views of the National Bureau of Economic Research or of the sponsoring organization.

Introduction

David A. Wise

This volume contains papers presented at a National Bureau of Economic Research conference on the economics of aging in May 1992. This is the fourth in a series of volumes associated with the NBER's ongoing project on the economics of aging. The preceding volumes, also published by the University of Chicago Press, are *The Economics of Aging* (1989), *Issues in the Economics of Aging* (1990), and *Topics in the Economics of Aging* (1992). The goal of the economics of aging project is to further our understanding of the consequences for older people and for the population at large of an aging population. The papers in this volume deal with death rates and life expectancy, saving for retirement, retirement behavior, demographic transition, international comparisons, and long-term care.

Demographic Transition and the Federal Budget

An older age distribution of the population will affect many parts of the economy. Two important areas are considered in this volume: government spending and the housing market. In chapter 1 John B. Shoven, Michael D. Topper, and David A. Wise explore how government spending on a wide range of programs is likely to change with a different age distribution of the population. Since many programs are targeted to specific age groups in society, without change in program provisions demographic change will affect both the relative cost of these programs and the combined cost. In providing an indication of the magnitudes of the effects that might be expected, the paper serves

David A. Wise is the John F. Stambaugh Professor of Political Economy at the John F. Kennedy School of Government, Harvard University, and the area director for Health and Retirement Programs at the National Bureau of Economic Research.

to underscore the importance of the issues raised in the subsequent papers in this volume.

Shoven, Topper, and Wise focus on 22 government programs for whom the beneficiaries could be identified. The programs account for about 40 percent of all government expenditure, and they include Social Security, Medicare, Medicaid, education, and a range of income support, welfare, and work-related programs. In determining the cost of these programs, the study accounts for federal, state, and local government expenditures. To isolate the implications of demographic change, Shoven, Topper, and Wise assume no change in the real cost of each program for individuals of any given age. Thus the analysis is independent of any future policy changes, relative price changes, economic transitions, or economic growth.

The authors find that a high concentration of government spending on these programs is directed to older people. For example, single men between the ages of 15 and 44 receive an average of less than $1,000 from these programs, while single men over age 65 receive an average of over $10,000 from these programs. With the projected aging of the population, the total inflation-adjusted cost of the programs is estimated to increase from $669 billion in 1990 to $1,106 billion in 2040. This 65 percent increase in real expenditures compares with a total population growth of only 27.5 percent. The two largest increases are in Social Security expenditures, which would increase 103 percent from $203 billion to $412 billion, and Medicare expenditures, which would increase 125 percent from $78 billion to $176 billion. (The Social Security increases are likely to be smaller than this projection, owing to the change in normal retirement age from 65 to 67, but, based on current trends, the Medicare increases may well be larger, because the projection assumes no increase in the relative price of medical care.)

The results demonstrate the extent to which demographic changes are likely to exacerbate the existing budgetary pressures faced by the government. Even though many of the programs in this study are considered "entitlements," the authors anticipate strong pressure to cut benefits. They also anticipate that new government initiatives will be crowded out by the growing expense of existing programs.

In addition, the paper illustrates the effect of alternative demographic changes, about which there is great uncertainty, on government spending. As an alternative to the Social Security Administration's "best guess" population projections, the authors consider the effects of the "optimal" projections discussed by Kenneth G. Manton, Eric Stallard, and Burton H. Singer in chapter 2. Based on the Social Security Administration forecasts, per capita program outlays will increase by 37.7 percent between 2000 and 2040, but based on the admittedly optimistic estimates of Manton, Singer, and Stallard, the increase would be 126.5 percent.

Death Rates and Life Expectancy

As demonstrated in chapter 1, our ability to predict future life expectancy has important implications for public policy. The future cost of Social Security and Medicare, for example, depends directly on the number of older people receiving benefits from these programs. While the government routinely makes population projections, two studies reported in this volume suggest that there may be a lot more uncertainty about future mortality than we typically assume. In particular, people may live considerably longer than widely used projections anticipate, so that there could be many more older people than the projections recognize.

In chapter 2, Manton, Stallard and Singer model mortality as a function of risk factor histories prior to death. They note that part of the decline in mortality at older ages has resulted from improvements in these risk factors over time. For example, smoking, cholesterol level, and hypertension among the elderly have declined over the past two decades. The authors suggest that further improvements can be expected as the result of continued reductions in smoking, increased education, and adoption of healthier lifestyles (such as more exercise and improved nutrition). Thus the objective of their paper is to estimate the future size of the elderly population, using alternative assumptions about how the risk factors which affect mortality may change in the future.

The results suggest that improvements in behavior (and in the resulting risk factors) could dramatically reduce mortality at older ages and lead to an older population much larger than that estimated by the Census Bureau. For example, the *highest* Census Bureau estimate of the elderly population in 2040 is 82.6 million people over age 65, and 17.9 million over age 85. By controlling risk factors to their "optimal" level, however, Manton, Stallard, and Singer project that there would be 138.1 million people over age 65, and 63.7 million over age 85. While the authors do not suggest that risk factors will be controlled to this level, the results demonstrate an enormous amount of uncertainty in current population projections.

This uncertainty is also apparent in chapter 3, by James Vaupel and Hans Lundström. This chapter attempts to distinguish between two contradictory views of how life expectancy will change in the future. One view is that there is a natural limit to longevity of about 85 years, that mortality rates rise dramatically approaching this age, and that improvements in mortality will simply lower the variance in life spans around this natural limit. The other view is that mortality rates rise smoothly to very advanced ages and that reductions in mortality rates will be achieved at all ages, even at 90, 100, or older. The controversy between the "limited-life-span" and the "mortality-reduction" paradigms has not been resolved, because there has been little reliable data available on mortality among the oldest old. Vaupel and Lundström use data from Sweden from 1900 to 1990 to address the issue.

This chapter finds that mortality rates have declined at all ages after 60 for both men and women and that this decline has accelerated, particularly in the older age categories. In 1945, for example, single-year mortality rates for women rose above 12.5 percent at age 81, and above 25 percent at age 89. By 1990, single-year mortality rates of 12.5 and 25 percent did not occur until ages 87 and 94, respectively. Vaupel and Lundström suggest that one interpretation of this change is that an 87-year-old Swedish female in 1990 was as healthy (at least in terms of probability of death) as an 81-year-old Swedish female in 1945. If these historical rates of progress continue, newborn children today will have a life expectancy of 90 years. And if progress accelerates, life expectancies may rise to 100 years or more. Thus the oldest-old population of the future may be far larger than most current projections suggest.

Retirement Saving

Low rates of saving have aroused concern among economists both from a macroeconomic perspective, where the concern is about aggregate saving and inadequate capital accumulation, and from a microeconomic perspective, where the concern is about older households with little or no retirement saving. Two studies reported in this volume address the issue of saving but deal with quite different aspects of the issue: one with the prospects for individual retirement saving in the future and the other with the low national saving rate.

Chapter 4 deals with 401(k) plans, which are tax-deferred retirement savings plans sponsored by employers. These plans were the fastest growing saving program of the 1980s and thus have the potential to significantly affect the financial status of elderly households in the future. In chapter 4, James M. Poterba, Steven F. Venti, and David A. Wise note, for example, that the number of workers eligible to participate in 401(k) plans rose from 7.1 million in 1983 to 27.5 million in 1988, that the number of participants increased from 2.7 million in 1983 to 15.7 million in 1988, and that total contributions reached almost $40 billion in 1988 and are much larger now. The comparison with Individual Retirement Accounts (IRAs) is particularly striking, because participation rates among those eligible to participate are far higher for 401(k) plans (about 60 percent) than for IRAs.

An important finding of the study by Poterba, Venti, and Wise is that most 401(k) saving appears to represent new saving, rather than the transfer of assets from other forms of saving. It appears that 401(k) contributions neither displace IRA contributions nor substitute for other financial assets. The authors make this case by comparing financial assets of similar households after different durations of 401(k) eligibility and by comparing the assets of those eligible for 401(k) participation and those who are not eligible.

Poterba, Venti, and Wise also look at the differences in 401(k) plan provisions across employers. The most important of these differences is the employer matching rate. For about 35 percent of 401(k) plan participants in the Survey of Consumer Finances, for example, the employer matches the employee contribution at least dollar-for-dollar. About 25 percent of plan participants face match rates between 10 and 100 percent, and about 40 percent of participants face match rates below 10 percent. Higher employer matching may induce more participation among employees and higher contributions among those who participate, but the high participation rates are apparently due primarily to payroll deductions and other aspects of the employer sponsorship of the plans that facilitate saving in this form.

For many households, 401(k) plans represent more than half of their financial asset savings. Thus Poterba, Venti, and Wise conclude that 401(k) plans are likely to play a very important part in the economic security of retirees in the future.

In chapter 5, Edward P. Lazear argues that low savings rates may be no more than an expression of "tastes." It may not matter, therefore, that the saving rate is lower in the United States than in Japan or that the saving rate is lower today than at other times in U.S. history. In fact, Lazear argues, tastes seem to be the only way to reconcile the difference in saving rates between Japan and the United States. Lazear suggests that rather than making cross-national comparisons or historical comparisons, the relevant issue is whether the saving rate accurately reflects the intertemporal preferences of people today. Stated differently, if there were no tax distortions or other externalities, any government intervention to promote additional saving would lower social welfare. Lazear's discussion provides a quite different view of national savings than most studies present. Indeed, the comments on this chapter present a contrasting view.

Retirement Behavior

A series of studies by Robin L. Lumsdaine, James H. Stock, and David A. Wise has demonstrated the dramatic effect of pension plan provisions on retirement behavior. Because the value of pension plans to employees varies significantly by age and service tenure, there are financial incentives to keep working at some ages and to retire at other ages. Using an economic model that accounts for these financial incentives in pension plans, Lumsdaine, Stock, and Wise have been able to predict, with considerable accuracy, retirement rates by age for employees of a Fortune 500 company. The models were even successful in predicting the retirement behavior that would result from a temporary "window" plan, using only information about employee decisions before the window plan took effect. Because firm pension plans typically contain financial incentives to retire even before Social Security eligibility, they are likely to have a substantial influence on the overall labor-force participation of older people.

Chapter 6 is the most recent study in this series. Most of the prior studies had used the pension plans and employment experience of one Fortune 500 company to understand the relationship between pension provisions and retirement behavior. The study in this volume extends this work to a second company with similar results. Again, retirement rates by age are predicted accurately based on the financial incentives in the pension plan both during normal periods and during a period when a temporary window plan was in effect. Lumsdaine, Stock, and Wise also explore several other issues. For example, they find little difference between the retirement behavior of men and of women. They find that the simpler "option value model" of retirement is just as effective in predicting retirement behavior as a more complex stochastic dynamic programming specification, consistent with their prior findings. And they explore briefly the high rates of retirement at age 65 and the potential role of Medicare eligibility in explaining retirement at this age. A compelling estimate of the effect of Medicare eligibility, they conclude, will have to await more appropriate data.

Demographic Transition and Housing Values

In chapter 7, Daniel McFadden explores the effect of demographic change on housing prices. In particular, he focuses on how the capital gains associated with home ownership have been (and will be) distributed across various generations of U.S. households. The issue has particular importance for older people, because a large percentage of the wealth of most elderly households is invested in housing. And for the current generation of elderly, much of the value of this housing asset resulted from capital appreciation.

McFadden's study is based on past and projected changes in the population and the resulting changes in the demand for housing. He finds that the real price of housing is likely to decline for an extended period in the future. People born between 1880 and 1910 achieved a real rate of return on their housing investment of about 3 percent per year. McFadden estimates that real housing returns will decline to about 1 percent (annually) for people born around 1915, to zero percent for people born around 1930, to -1 percent for people born around 1945, and to -3 percent for people born between 1960 and 1990. Despite the significant variation in capital appreciation (or depreciation) across generations, McFadden argues that real income growth over time has a far larger effect on the relative welfare of different generations. For example, a reduction of 0.2 percent in the lifetime income of people born between 1920 and 1940 would, according to McFadden, fully offset their housing appreciation relative to people born in 1950. Nevertheless, the capital gains to be expected from homeownership in the future appear to be dramatically lower than in the past.

International Comparisons

This volume contains two chapters focusing on aging issues in other countries, one comparing aging-related policies in Germany and in the United States and one on aging and saving in Taiwan. In chapter 8, Axel Börsch-Supan looks at the policies influencing retirement, saving, and elderly housing decisions in Germany and compares them with the policies in effect in the United States. Germany offers an interesting comparison, because the age composition of the population in Germany today is similar to the age composition expected in the United States two decades from now. Thus an analysis of the policies in effect in Germany today may provide insights that can be used to shape policy for an aging population in the United States.

Börsch-Supan finds that differences in behavior between Germany and the United States are largely consistent with differences in policy incentives. Retirement policies in Germany, for example, contain stronger incentives to retire at particular ages, leading to a more uniform retirement age in Germany than in the United States, where policies are more age neutral and more varied in their incentive effects. Housing policies in Germany provide subsidies to elderly renters equal to about one-quarter of the rental cost of housing. The result is that more older people in Germany rent their homes than is the case in the United States, where the subsidies are toward home ownership. Housing mobility among the elderly is much lower in Germany than in the United States, which Börsch-Supan attributes to the tenant protection laws. These laws restrict rent increases, even when market rates are rising more rapidly. Thus differences in retirement and housing behavior in the two countries can be partially explained by differences in policy incentives. Börsch-Supan also discusses the policies affecting saving in Germany and the United States, though the relationships between these policies and the higher rates of saving in Germany are less obvious. Why is it, for example, that more than half of the elderly population in Germany has an annuity income that exceeds expenditures?

In chapter 9, Angus S. Deaton and Christina H. Paxson consider trends in saving behavior in Taiwan and relate those trends to economic and demographic changes. The study provides four broad observations. First, gross national saving as a fraction of GNP is very high and is increasing in Taiwan—from an average of 19 percent between 1961 and 1965 to over 32 percent between 1976 and 1990. Second, Taiwan has experienced rapid per capita economic growth, averaging almost 7 percent annually since 1970. Third, fertility rates in Taiwan have decreased dramatically from 6.1 in 1958 to 1.9 in 1985. Fourth, life expectancies have increased substantially. High growth, declining fertility, and increasing life expectancy all affect saving behavior, and these relationships are explored in this study using household survey data on income and consumption in Taiwan.

An important methodological component of the study is the separation of age effects and cohort effects, using repeated cross-section data. For each year of data, Deaton and Paxson identify the variables of interest, by age, and then track people with the same birth year from one survey year to the next. Although each survey year has different respondents, the authors generate many of the benefits of a longitudinal sample using this methodology. Though presented with skepticism by the authors, the main conclusion of the paper is that household saving behavior in Taiwan is broadly consistent with traditional life-cycle explanations of saving.

Long-Term Care

The largest users of nursing home services are the oldest old. Because of the enormous population growth anticipated at the oldest ages (close to double in the next 30 years), there is a great deal of concern about the future demand for nursing home care, the cost of this care, and the extent of public funding and insurance for long-term care. Two papers in this volume address nursing home utilization, one estimating the probability and duration of nursing home residency and one exploring the variation in nursing home use that results from alternative long-term care policies.

In chapter 10 Andrew Dick, Alan M. Garber, and Thomas A. MaCurdy combine information from two nationally representative data files to more accurately estimate the likelihood of a nursing home admission, the likelihood of multiple nursing home admissions, and the distribution of how long people stay in nursing homes after an admission. These probabilities are important, because they influence insurers' decisions about how to structure and price long-term care insurance policies; government decisions about how to structure public health programs for nursing home care; and individual decisions about whether to purchase long-term care insurance, how much to save for the possibility of future nursing home expenses, and what type of living arrangements to choose at older ages.

The results suggest that most people will spend little or no time residing in a nursing home but that a substantial minority of people will have extended nursing home residency. Beginning at age 65, about 35 percent of individuals will have at least one nursing home admission, 10 percent will have more than one admission, and less than 1 percent will have more than four admissions. The median age of a first nursing home admission is 81 for men and 84 for women. Of the individuals with some nursing home utilization, almost 25 percent spend a total of one month or less, and only half have more than six months of accumulated nursing home residency. However, almost one-quarter of those with some nursing home residency have lengthy stays, of three or more years, and this minority of the population accounts for a large fraction of total nursing home utilization.

Dick, Garber, and MaCurdy conclude that the small probability of lengthy nursing home residency suggests the desirability of long-term care insurance. This conclusion, however, depends on the extent to which long-term care insurance induces additional nursing home use. At least some of the hesitancy to enact a comprehensive long-term care policy is based on this possibility. In chapter 11, David M. Cutler and Louise M. Sheiner examine the effect of government nursing home policies on nursing home use. While the extent of policy variation is limited, Cutler and Sheiner use variation across states in both the generosity of Medicaid spend-down rules and the price differential between Medicaid reimbursement rates and private market rates.

Cutler and Sheiner conclude that there is indeed a large moral hazard effect in subsidizing long-term care. For example, states with more generous Medicaid spend-down rules or higher Medicaid reimbursement rates (relative to market rates) have more nursing home utilization. Higher Medicaid reimbursement rates (relative to market rates) also change the composition of nursing home residency, as poorer people have greater access to nursing home care. Cutler and Sheiner find that in states with more generous Medicaid policies, nursing home care is substituting for care from children or other helpers, rather than for independent living. Thus the elderly are less likely to receive help from their children, and more likely to live in nursing homes, when there is a greater government subsidy for long-term care.

I   Demographic Transition and the Federal Budget

1 The Impact of the Demographic Transition on Government Spending

John B. Shoven, Michael D. Topper, and David A. Wise

1.1 Introduction

The goal of this research is to determine the impact on government budgets of predicted changes in demographic structure in the United States over the next 90 years. A major part of the demographic shifts is due to the aging of the post–World War II baby-boom generation. Another important factor is the decrease in the age-specific mortality rates that has occurred and is predicted to continue. Many government programs are targeted to specific age groups in our society, and therefore we feel that the impact of the population's changing age structure on these programs' budgetary costs is an interesting research question. We were motivated to look at this issue to help address the question of the ability of governments to sustain programs already in place and to implement new ones, within the general scale of government of the recent past.

Our basic approach identifies those government programs for which beneficiaries can be distinguished. Some of these are traditional transfer programs, but others (such as retirement programs and education) are often not characterized as such. We calculate the cost to taxpayers of maintaining the 1986 level of age/family-structure-specific payments for each of 22 government programs for which we could identify beneficiaries. We estimate these costs for 1990, and at 20-year intervals from 2000 to 2080. These programs include Social Security, Medicare, Medicaid, education, and a range of income support, welfare, and work-related government programs. Our estimates include payments

John B. Shoven is the Charles R. Schwab Professor of Economics and dean of the School of Humanities and Sciences at Stanford University and a research associate of the National Bureau of Economic Research. Michael D. Topper is assistant professor of economics at the College of William and Mary. David A. Wise is the John F. Stambaugh Professor of Political Economy at the John F. Kennedy School of Government, Harvard University, and the area director for Health and Retirement Programs at the National Bureau of Economic Research.

made by federal, state, and local governments. In total, the programs we examine account for about 40 percent of all government expenditure. We find that maintaining the benefit levels for each age-specific family type would require quite dramatic increases in the total funds allocated to these programs.

1.2   Population Projections

The projected number of males and females in different age cohorts between 1990 and 2080 are shown in table 1.1. The data are based on Social Security Administration (SSA) population projections used to forecast the future income and expenditures of the Social Security system. The baseline for the projections is an estimate of the Social Security Area[1] population in 1987 by age, sex, and marital status and of the pattern of existing marriages by age of husband and wife. Finally, population projections for future years are simulated based on assumptions about future birth rates, death rates, marriage and divorce rates, and net immigration rates. The SSA considers three separate population projections. The data in table 1.1 are based on the intermediate "best guess" projection of the SSA.[2] We adopt this projection as a working hypothesis about population growth.

There is a great deal of uncertainty about the demographic projections contained in table 1.1. The SSA recognizes this uncertainty by producing three alternative scenarios, including an "optimistic" and a "pessimistic" forecast in addition to the "best guess" numbers we have used here. In contrast, Manton, Stallard, and Singer (chap. 2 in this volume) provide an alternative approach to handling the uncertainty about demographic trends, particularly that due to the uncertain evolution of age-specific mortality rates. They estimate the effect of 10 different risk factors (e.g., smoking, cholesterol level, pulse rate) on mortality and compute the age-specific death rates for people who optimally control these risk factors. They find that control of these risk factors can have a major impact on mortality and, hence, on the future age structure of the population.

Our basic calculations utilize the "best guess" demographic projections of the SSA. The population of different age cohorts with these forecasts are depicted in figures 1.1 and 1.2 for 1990–2080. Several important demographic changes are evident in these figures. First, the population aged 15–44 remains roughly constant between 1990 and 2080. Because of our constant payout assumption, government programs such as AFDC that focus on these age cohorts will experience little growth in total outlays. Similarly, the population aged 45–64 increases between 1990 and 2020 but then levels out and remains

1. The Social Security Area comprises residents of the 50 states, the District of Columbia, Puerto Rico, Virgin Islands, Guam, American Samoa, armed forces and armed forces dependents overseas, and other citizens overseas.
2. Described in U.S. SSA (1989). We use "alternative II," the middle case of the three developed by the SSA.

Table 1.1   **Population Projections (millions)**

	Age Cohort								
	15–24	25–34	35–44	45–54	55–64	65–74	75–84	85+	Total
Year 1990									
Single females	14.35	7.74	4.82	3.29	3.45	4.67	4.47	2.03	44.82
Single males	16.81	10.35	4.97	2.45	1.87	1.69	1.07	.43	39.64
Married females	4.00	14.61	14.42	9.89	7.98	5.47	1.83	.32	58.52
Married males	2.31	12.80	14.50	10.51	8.68	6.52	2.74	.46	58.52
Total	37.47	45.50	38.71	26.14	21.98	18.35	10.11	3.24	201.50
Year 2000									
Single females	14.66	6.49	6.44	5.48	4.01	4.47	4.97	2.77	49.29
Single males	17.09	9.17	7.42	4.57	2.19	1.74	1.36	.55	44.09
Married females	3.74	12.59	16.19	13.59	8.65	5.59	2.54	.42	63.31
Married males	2.13	10.63	15.58	14.30	9.76	6.72	3.49	.70	63.31
Total	37.62	38.88	45.63	37.94	24.61	18.52	12.36	4.44	220.00
Year 2020									
Single females	14.48	7.12	5.21	5.23	7.24	7.19	5.47	3.80	55.74
Single males	17.05	9.93	6.45	5.64	5.58	3.41	1.60	.81	50.47
Married females	3.97	13.26	14.27	14.07	14.34	9.13	3.14	.62	72.80
Married males	2.24	11.33	13.59	13.70	15.21	11.12	4.54	1.07	72.80
Total	37.74	41.64	39.52	38.64	42.37	30.85	14.75	6.30	251.81
Year 2040									
Single females	14.87	6.82	5.09	5.70	5.89	7.02	9.29	6.51	61.19
Single males	17.47	9.55	6.61	6.23	4.82	4.11	3.55	1.58	53.92
Married females	4.03	12.78	14.46	14.93	12.87	9.64	5.68	1.35	75.74
Married males	2.30	10.93	13.54	14.63	13.59	11.05	7.53	2.17	75.74
Total	38.67	40.08	39.70	41.49	37.17	31.82	26.05	11.61	266.59

Source: U.S. SSA (1989).

roughly constant between 2020 and 2080. Thus, employment-related programs that target the labor-force population will experience little growth in outlays beyond 2020.

Second, the aging of the postwar "baby boomers" is evident throughout the period of our analysis. Between 1990 and 2000, the 45–54 age cohort grows by 45 percent. Between 2000 and 2020, the 55–64 cohort grows by 72 percent, and the 65–74 cohort by 66 percent. Between 2020 and 2040, the 75–84 cohort grows by 77 percent, and the 85+ cohort by 84 percent. Beyond 2040, population growth remains roughly constant except for the 85+ cohort.

Third, the fraction of the adult population over age 65 grows in both absolute and relative terms. Table 1.2 shows the percentage of men and women over age 65, over 75, and over 85, relative to the adult population of men and women. Between 1990 and 2040, the fraction of adults over 65 relative to total adults increases from 18 to 29 percent for women and from 13 to 23 percent for men. The increase is even more dramatic for the "very old." Between 1990 and 2040, the fraction of adults over 85 relative to all adults increases from 2 to 6 percent

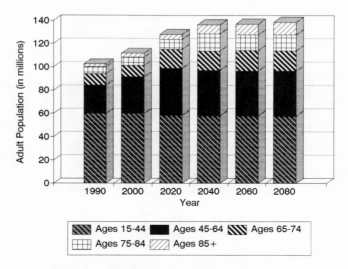

Fig. 1.1   Projected female population shares by age cohort

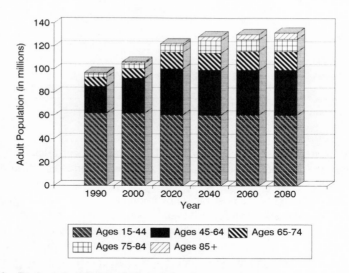

Fig. 1.2   Projected male population shares by age cohort

for women and from 1 to 3 percent for men. Thus, government programs that provide services for older individuals will experience substantial upward pressure on costs.

As an extreme alternative assumption, we can examine the implications of the Manton, Stallard, and Singer (hereafter MSS; chap. 2 in this volume) model in which people adopt optimal control of risk factors after 20 years (i.e., their

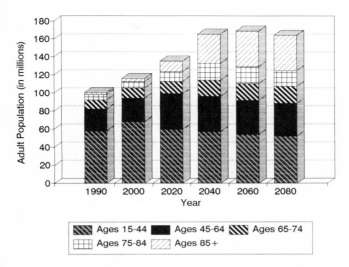

Fig. 1.3   Projected "optimal" female population shares by age cohort

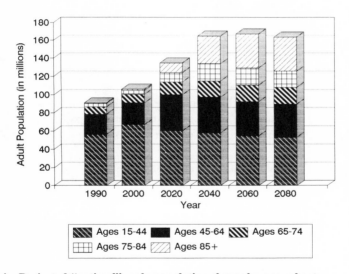

Fig. 1.4   Projected "optimal" male population shares by age cohort

behavior dramatically changes 20 years from now). The resulting population projections are shown in figures 1.3 and 1.4. Comparisons with figures 1.1 and 1.2 show dramatic differences, particularly for the very advanced ages. For example, whereas the middle SSA forecast projects a population of 11.1 million women aged 85 or older in 2080, the MSS forecast with optimal risk factor control is 39.7 million. The difference between the two types of forecasts is even more dramatic for elderly males. The point of presenting the MSS numbers is not to suggest that they may represent the actual outcome but to illustrate how sensitive demographic projections are to the control of risk factors.

1.3 Expected Program Payments

Expected program payments from the government to households are shown in table 1.3 by age of household head, household marital status, and program category. These data are for 1986 and are expressed in dollars per household. The numbers thus combine participation probabilities with average receipt conditional on participation. Large values can arise from high program participation rates and/or large payments to program participants. Government transfer payments were grouped into eight categories: (1) Social Security, (2) other retirement income—includes federal civil service pensions, railroad retirement income, and pensions from state and local governments, (3) Medicare, (4) Medicaid, (5) work-related programs—includes workers compensation and state and other unemployment compensation, (6) welfare and income support programs—includes AFDC, WIC, food stamps, Supplemental Security Income, general assistance, and other welfare programs, (7) military programs—includes military retirement pensions, veterans' compensation, and GI bill benefits, (8) education—includes public provision of elementary and secondary schooling and federal, state, and local support of higher education. Appendix A contains a brief description of each program. Appendix B presents the expected transfer program data disaggregated by individual program.

The primary source for these estimates was 1986 data from the Survey of Income Programs and Participation (SIPP; U.S. Bureau of the Census 1986). Program participation rates and average payments per participant for Social Security, other retirement income, work-related programs, welfare programs,

Table 1.2   **Adult Population over Age 65 (%)**

	Age		
	Over 65	Over 75	Over 85
Year 1990			
Females	18	8	2
Males	13	5	1
Year 2000			
Females	18	10	3
Males	14	6	1
Year 2020			
Females	23	10	3
Males	18	7	2
Year 2040			
Females	29	17	6
Males	23	11	3

Source: Derived from table 1.1.

Table 1.3   **Expected Government Payments per Household by Program Category in 1986 (1986 $)**

				Age Cohort				
	15–25	25–35	35–45	45–55	55–65	65–75	75–85	85+
Single males								
Social Security	49.01	70.00	136.02	356.04	1,231.72	5,190.20	5,257.96	5,197.11
Other retirement	0.00	4.79	0.00	34.32	298.15	1,650.04	1,571.71	1,631.98
Medicare	5.58	19.00	39.25	152.00	282.06	1,785.21	2,648.10	3,128.68
Medicaid	94.93	118.47	162.70	184.02	203.53	294.64	700.66	1,742.00
Welfare	29.22	92.32	231.97	182.13	234.48	250.89	147.10	96.23
Work-related	58.35	182.97	271.32	224.50	116.53	1.26	0.00	0.00
Military	12.93	26.88	106.49	646.25	864.01	1,206.04	186.02	11.45
Total	250.02	514.43	947.75	1,779.25	3,230.48	10,378.28	10,511.55	11,807.45
Single females								
Social Security	43.22	82.88	296.7	340.7	1,426.83	4,590.14	4,647.54	4,279.27
Other retirement	0.00	1.63	13.68	183.9	575.44	989.36	992.31	470.00
Medicare	7.06	25.11	49.44	148.98	272.33	1,637.97	2,456.49	2,851.89
Medicaid	213.13	472.53	611.37	327.33	211.91	294.64	700.66	1,742.00
Welfare	320.80	1,121.65	1,744.98	954.82	298.12	283.83	232.82	286.65
Work-related	23.15	75.48	191.03	108.04	81.91	10.35	0.00	0.00
Military	5.92	13.18	37.21	118.43	177.76	146.96	95.12	93.45
Total	613.28	1,792.46	2,944.51	2,182.20	3,044.29	7,953.25	9,124.94	9,723.26
Married couples								
Social Security	11.79	44.87	105.55	437.76	3,064.57	9,237.4	8,847.57	8,582.22
Other retirement	0.00	5.1	51.36	301.77	1,741.77	2,202.79	2,471.99	1,242.88
Medicare	0.00	3.96	21.44	94.60	217.91	3,513.87	5,142.88	5,928.77
Medicaid	263.82	270.29	317.92	354.07	407.15	568.68	1,254.32	3,246.84
Welfare	247.7	266.72	250.38	123.99	107.36	97.62	164.97	708.81
Work-related	268.4	341.02	215.55	236.11	203.13	27.92	0.00	0.00
Military	66.12	82.15	208.26	756.57	800.14	705.47	132.72	149.54
Total	857.83	1,014.11	1,170.46	2,304.87	6,542.03	16,353.75	18,014.45	19,859.06

Note: Cell entries are expected program payments per household derived from the SIPP (U.S. Bureau of the Census 1986). Age cohort for married couples based on age of husband.

and military programs were obtained by averaging across all SIPP households in each age/marital-status class. In the averaging process, we utilized the population weight for each household in the survey. SIPP data on program participation rates in Medicare and Medicaid were supplemented by Health Care Financing Administration (HCFA) data on average age-group-specific Medicare and Medicaid payments.[3] Expected program payments for these seven categories were expressed on a per household basis.

The concentration of transfer payment receipts among the older age cohorts is evident in the "total" rows in table 1.3. For example, on average, single males aged 15–44 receive less than $1,000 from these transfer programs. Single

3. Medicaid payments obtained from data in U.S. Department of Health and Human Services (1989). Medicare payments obtained from U.S. Department of Health and Human Services (1986).

males over age 65 receive an average of over $10,000. Obviously, a change in the distribution of the population toward the more elderly age cohorts will cause current age-specific programs to become more expensive, if maintained.

The final category of program payments is education. The education data include expenditure for elementary, secondary, and higher education by the federal, state, and local governments. These data were obtained from the *Statistical Abstract of the United States, 1987* (U.S. Bureau of the Census 1988) by dividing government educational expenses by the number of children in the relevant age groups.[4] Expected per child education payments in 1987 were $2,875 for ages 5–9, $3,079 for ages 10–14, $2,326 for ages 15–19, and $1,501 for ages 20–24.

We have not been able to assign all government expenditure to specific households. The list of unallocated government expenditure includes such major categories as national defense, agricultural policies, interest, capital outlays, police and fire protection, public parks and land management, and general administration. While the programs that we do consider include most transfer programs, they do not include all, because of limited data availability. The largest missing transfer program is public housing; information on it is not available from the SIPP data source.

1.4   The "Constant Average Deal" Modeling Approach

Our modeling approach is to calculate the cost to taxpayers of maintaining program payments at 1986 levels as the demographic structure of the population changes. That is, we assume that the "average deal" that a household of a particular type receives in 1986 is a predictor of the average deal a household of the same type will receive in future years. Thus, there are two reasons that total outlays change in our calculations. First, there is general population growth. The SSA projects that the total adult population over age 15 will increase from 201.5 million in 1990 to 266.6 million in 2040, an increase of 32 percent. In the absence of any changes to the age structure of the population our assumption of a constant average deal would suggest that total program payments would also increase by 32 percent. In fact, as described in section 1.2, the relative number of older individuals is expected to increase throughout the period. Second, for those government programs where the pattern of payouts varies by age, the shift in the age distribution provides an additional source of change in total outlays.

---

4. We make the simple assumption that total elementary/secondary expenditures were evenly distributed across children aged 5–17 and that total higher education expenditures were evenly distributed across children aged 18–24. This provided an estimate of total educational expenditure for four age groups: ages 5–9, ages 10–14, ages 15–19, and ages 20–24. Per capita education payments were then calculated by dividing age-group total expenditures by the total 1987 population in each age group.

This modeling approach essentially assumes that there is no behavioral response on the part of either the government or households as population growth and demographic shifts alter the level and distribution of total outlays. That is, we assume that program funding levels are maintained in real terms at 1986 levels and that a household in a specific age/marital class in each future year is identical to a household in that age/marital class in 1986. Thus, this procedure provides a simple baseline for evaluating the consequences of maintaining program benefits in the face of dramatic demographic changes. We certainly are not forecasting that government budgets will evolve along the time path that our numbers indicate. Rather, our approach is the standard "what if" approach, which is useful in debating the appropriate responses to the changing demographic and economic environment.

1.5   Estimates of Future Government Payments

We calculate the total payments for each program to each family structure/age cohort in future years by multiplying the 1986 expected program payment matrix by the population matrix in each year. The results of this procedure for each forecast year are shown separately for each age/family-structure group in Appendix C. Table 1.4 aggregates these data across age cohorts and family structures. With the SSA population forecasts, the total cost of all of the programs is projected to grow from $669 billion in 1990 to $1,106 billion in 2040. This 65.4 percent increase in cost compares with the anticipated 32.2 percent growth in the age 15+ population and an increase of 27.5 percent in the total population. Clearly the expected changes in the age structure of the population have large cost consequences. We can examine the projected cost changes by major program category.

1.5.1   Social Security

Table 1.4 indicates that the Old Age, Survivors, and Disability portion of Social Security accounts for about $209 billion of the $437.4 billion increase in the total cost increase of maintaining age-specific benefits. That still leaves the other programs accounting for 52 percent of the expenditure increase. Contrary to our assumption, the SSA does not intend to maintain its age-specific deal. In particular, the age of eligibility for full retirement benefits will gradually increase from 65 to 67. This will provide a relatively small offset against the increasing costs faced by this program.

1.5.2   Medicare

Medicare costs show a significantly higher growth rate than Social Security costs and contribute almost $100 billion to the increase. The more rapid rate of increase in Medicare costs is due to its higher concentration of benefits

Table 1.4   Projected Total Payments by Program Category (billion 1986 $)

Category	1990	2000	2020	2040	2060	2080
Social Security	203.41	229.39	337.75	412.44	428.34	442.97
Other retirement	59.34	67.32	99.33	114.86	117.76	120.83
Medicare	77.94	89.86	128.84	175.50	183.07	192.57
Medicaid	50.55	57.95	69.49	86.34	90.10	95.22
Welfare	44.03	49.78	52.61	55.44	55.87	56.44
Work-related	20.05	22.10	23.62	23.32	23.24	23.25
Military	33.29	39.82	53.32	54.56	55.69	56.00
Education	180.18	189.29	183.83	183.93	183.93	183.09
Total	668.80	745.52	948.79	1,106.38	1,138.00	1,170.37

Sources: Alternative II from U.S. SSA (1989); U.S. Bureau of the Census (1986).

among the elderly. Recall that Social Security includes disability benefits and survivor benefits, which are often received by the nonelderly.

Our calculation assumes that the age-specific cost of Medicare remains at 1986 levels. Therefore, we do not project that the relative cost of medical care will increase (even though most forecasters would predict that), and we implicitly assume that the average health status of individuals of a particular age will remain constant. Both assumptions are made for simplicity and to provide a baseline for discussion. However, both are open to question and may not be realistic. The relative cost of health care has been increasing at something like a 4 percent rate for at least a decade, and that trend is likely to continue. Part of the reason is that new and more expensive treatment procedures are constantly being developed. Second, one might think, for example, that the average 75-year-old male will be healthier in 2040 than in 1990, corresponding to his increase in life expectancy and improvements that can be anticipated in medical technology. However, the improvement in medical technology cuts both ways in terms of the average health status of elderly individuals. While it is reasonable to assume that some elderly will be healthier and have health status equivalent to that of younger individuals in the previous generation, others may survive into the older age cohorts because of improved medical technology, but their health status may still be relatively poor for their age. There is some evidence (Poterba and Summers 1987) that the two tendencies offset each other and that the average age-specific health status remains constant even as the life expectancies of men and women increase.

1.5.3 Medicaid

Medicaid is a state-administered, largely federally funded, program of health insurance for those in poverty. As displayed in table 1.3, the expected payments do not differ dramatically by age, with the exception of the two oldest age categories, 75–85 and 85+. Medicaid pays for a great deal of the long-term care for many of the institutionalized elderly. The costs of institutionalized care are such that if you are not in poverty at the time of admission, you may well be after a period of residence. The result of Medicaid's high expected payments to the very old and of the projected growth in the number of people in these age cohorts is a 70.8 percent increase in the cost of Medicaid between 1990 and 2040.

1.5.4   Education

Federal, state, and local expenditure on education remains roughly constant at $180–$190 billion between 1990 and 2040. This is a direct consequence of the projection that the number of children aged 5–19 will change very little during this period. Some observers have noted that reduced spending on education will partially offset increases in government spending for the elderly. Our projections suggest that educational spending will remain stable and will not offer such an offset. We do find that projected growth in spending for programs like Social Security, Medicare, and Medicaid will reduce education's share of total government outlays between 1990 and 2040.

1.5.5   Other Programs

Welfare and work-related programs show slower growth rates than Social Security and the medical programs, with spending on welfare growing by 25 percent and spending on work-related programs growing by 16 percent between 1990 and 2040. The largest expected welfare payments are received by single female heads of household aged 25–45. The largest expected work-related payments are received by married couples and single male heads of household aged 25–65. Because these groups are not projected to grow as rapidly as the population over age 65, welfare and work-related programs do not have a major impact on the overall trend in government spending. In 1990, total payments for Social Security were 4.6 times greater than total payments for welfare and 10.1 times greater than total payments for work-related programs. By 2040, the gap between Social Security and the other programs widens; Social Security payments are 7.4 times greater than welfare payments and 17.7 times greater than work-related payments. These trends suggest that even major cutbacks in welfare and work-related programs will do little to stem the projected increase in government program payments to households.

The results of table 1.4 are illustrated in figure 1.5. The graph highlights the importance of Social Security, Medicare, and Medicaid in the "constant-deal" cost growth between 1990 and 2040. The three programs account for $343 billion of the total increase of $437 billion.

The potential for even larger increases in the cost of these three programs if elderly populations exceed the SSA's "best guess" forecast is shown in table 1.5 and also in figure 1.6, which show the implications of the Manton, Stallard, and Singer "optimal risk factor" population projections. Reiterating the caveat that these are extreme upper bounds of what might happen, one sees that the cost of the programs examined goes from $651.4 billion in 1990 to almost $1.8 trillion by 2040. Both population forecasts imply that the cost of these pro-

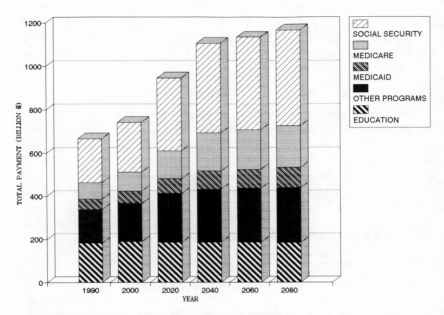

Fig. 1.5   Projected total payments by program category

Table 1.5   Projected Total Outlays Using "Optimal" Population Projections
                       (billion 1986 $)

Category	1990	2000	2020	2040	2060	2080
Social Security	193.603	227.551	407.986	707.589	770.832	759.473
Medicare	73.586	89.200	182.868	360.909	403.388	398.329
Medicaid	49.628	59.573	100.413	180.567	202.319	200.398
Welfare, work-related, and military	154.443	176.882	251.845	335.974	347.857	340.258
Education	180.176	189.294	183.834	183.927	183.931	183.092
Total	651.436	742.499	1,126.946	1,768.967	1,908.329	1,881.551

Sources: "Optimal" population projection from U.S. SSA (1989); U.S. Bureau of the Census (1986).

grams levels off after 2040, but there is no projected reduction in the required total outlays.

Tables 1.6 and 1.7 show the projected per capita outlays in each forecast year for the two alternative population projections. The per capita basis in both tables is the projected number of adults between the ages of 20 and 64. In table 1.6, based on the SSA's "best guess" population forecasts, per capita outlays grow 37.7 percent between 2000 and 2040. The per capita expenditure grows "only" 6 percent in the 40 years from 2040 to 2080. The jump in per capita

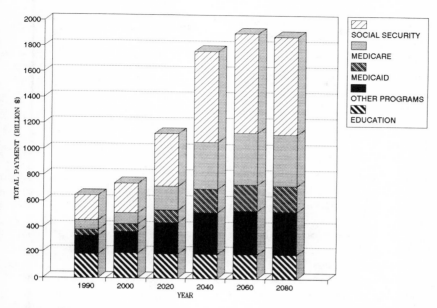

Fig. 1.6   Projected total payments by program category for "optimal" population projection

Table 1.6   **Projected per Capita Outlays by Program Category (1986 $)**

Category	1990	2000	2020	2040	2060	2080
Social Security	1,340	1,388	1,862	2,316	2,418	2,494
Medicare	513	544	710	985	1,033	1,084
Medicaid	333	351	383	485	509	536
Welfare, work-related, and military	1,033	1,083	1,262	1,393	1,426	1,444
Education	1,187	1,146	1,014	1,033	1,038	1,031
Total	4,406	4,512	5,232	6,212	6,423	6,589

Note: Projected per capita outlays were calculated by dividing projected total outlays from table 1.4 by the total population between ages 20–64 in each year.

costs is much sharper with the Manton, Stallard, and Singer numbers, growing 126.5 percent between 2000 and 2040 and 15 percent thereafter (between 2040 and 2080).

1.6 Summary

The U.S. federal government has found it impossible to balance its budget in recent years. Our conclusion is that the budgetary pressure caused by the

Table 1.7   **Projected per Capita Outlays by Program Category Using "Optimal"
Population Projection (1986 $)**

Category	1990	2000	2020	2040	2060	2080
Social Security	1,349	1,368	2,279	4,044	4,607	4,692
Medicare	513	536	1,022	2,063	2,411	2,461
Medicaid	346	358	561	1,032	1,209	1,238
Welfare, work-related, and military	1,076	1,063	1,407	1,920	2,079	2,102
Education	1,255	1,138	1,027	1,051	1,099	1,131
Total	4,538	4,463	6,296	10,110	11,404	11,623

Note: Projected per capita outlays were calculated by dividing projected total outlays from table 1.5 by the total population between ages 20–64 in each year.

aging of the population over the next 50 years will exacerbate this problem. The ability of the government to embark on new spending programs will undoubtedly be impeded.

We have purposely made the unrealistic assumption that the age-specific per capita cost of government health programs will remain constant. Even with that assumption and with the relatively conservative demographic assumptions in the SSA's "best guess" population forecasts, we calculate a 65.4 percent ($437 billion) increase in the cost of the programs we examine, by 2040. With the extreme "optimal risk factor" population projections, the total cost of our programs grows by well over $1 trillion in the next 50 years. Clearly, with either scenario, these projections have serious consequences. First, the constant age-specific generosity of these programs will be difficult to maintain. There will be strong pressures to cut the benefits of these programs, many of which are referred to as "entitlements." Second, new initiatives with budgetary costs will be crowded out by the growing expense of the existing programs.

The growth in expenditures of these programs is dominated by Social Security, Medicare, and Medicaid. Even if age-specific costs can be contained for these programs (a big "if"), their total costs will grow enormously as a result of the aging of our society. While it is conceivable that economic growth will permit us to afford these programs, most, if not all, of the fiscal dividend provided by growth over the next 50 years will have to be devoted to financing these programs. If we do not contain age-specific costs or if we do not experience robust economic growth, then the pressures to curtail these government programs will be overwhelming.

Appendix A
Government Transfer Program Descriptions

Name[5]	Description
Social Security Income	Federal: old age, survivors, and disability benefits; based on prior earnings and payroll contributions
Other retirement income Federal civil service pensions	
Railroad retirement income	For retired railroad workers
State government pensions	
Local government pensions	
Medicare	Federally administered subsidized health insurance; most hospital and medical costs for persons over 65 or disabled
Medicaid	State administered; federal grants made to states; health-care coverage to persons receiving federally supported public assistance; AFDC families automatically eligible
Work-related programs Workers' Compensation	State-administered compensation for injured workers, also for some work-related illnesses, notably black lung disease; composed of cash, medical, and rehabilitation benefits; total 1986 compensation = \$17.8 billion
State unemployment compensation	State administered; eligibility based on past earnings and work experience; each state has broad discretion; funded by payroll tax
Other unemployment compensation	
Welfare and Income Support Programs AFDC	State administered with federal matching shares; on average, burden is 55 percent federal, 40 percent state, and 5 percent local

5. Community health centers, Department of Veteran Affairs health-care system, Indian Health Service, low-income housing, and social service block grants are excluded from this analysis.

Special Supplemental Feeding Program (WIC)	Food and food vouchers for low income, pregnant, and postpartum women and for children up to age 5
Food stamps	Federally funded; households receive monthly allowances of food stamps based on income and household size; other food programs include child and elderly nutrition (such as school lunch program) and distribution of surplus food
Supplemental Security Income	Federal program for poor people aged 65 and over, blind, or disabled; means tested
General Assistance	Means-tested state programs for the poor; concentrated in big cities; combination of cash, medical, and hospital benefits; large variance across states
Foster childcare payments	Federal program channeled through the states for all foster-care children meeting AFDC eligibility
Child support payments	
Other welfare	
Military-related programs	
Military retirement pensions	Paid to veterans or survivors with annual income below a certain level, and over 65 or disabled; total 1988 payments = $4.3 billion
Veterans' Compensation	Compensation for injury, disability, or death paid to veterans or survivors; received by one-thirteenth of veterans; total 1988 cost = $8.7 billion
GI Bill Benefits	Educational assistance for veterans; 1989 total = $511 million
Education	Federal, state, and local spending for education, including elementary, secondary, and postsecondary education

Appendix B
Expected Transfer Payments in 1986 (1986 $)

Table 1B.1   **Single Females**

	Age Cohort							
	15–25	25–35	35–45	45–55	55–65	65–75	75–85	85+
AFDC	174.8	447.41	413.54	189.35	16.81	1.02	2.39	0
Social Security	43.22	82.88	296.7	340.7	1,426.82	4,590.14	4,647.54	4,279.27
Railroad retirement	0	1.35	0	0	12.03	139.88	126.99	100.22
Supplemental Security	30.81	91.23	85.69	222.9	169.95	237.26	196.68	267.86
State unemployment compensation	14.72	70.69	143.07	58.82	59.44	0.23	0	0
Veterans' compensation	2.65	10.82	37.31	106.05	170.6	112.25	69.51	93.45
Workers' compensation	8.43	4.5	47.26	49.22	22.47	10.12	0	0
General assistance	13.6	32.75	71.8	45.81	27.02	3.71	0	0
Foster childcare	0	0	0.67	0	2.29	0	0	0
Other welfare	4.85	12.86	8.51	5.69	0	12.59	6.93	1.76
Food stamps	67.2	253.79	313.24	216.25	75.57	29.25	26.82	17.03
Child support payments	18.7	276.4	847.84	273.42	6.48	0	0	0
Federal civil service pensions	0	0	13.68	146.78	272.31	369.4	301.83	206.86
Medicare	7.06	25.11	49.44	148.98	272.33	1,637.97	2,456.49	2,851.89
Medicaid	213.13	472.53	611.37	327.33	211.91	294.64	700.66	1742
Military retirement	0	0	0	12.38	7.16	34.71	25.61	0
State government pensions	0	0	0	35.63	237.42	382.02	258.29	128.68
Local government pensions	0	0.28	0	1.49	53.68	98.06	305.2	34.24
GI Bill benefits	3.27	2.36	0	0	0	0	0	0
WIC	10.84	7.21	3.69	1.4	0	0	0	0
Other unemployment compensation	0	0.29	0.7	0	0	0	0	0

Table 1B.2   Single Males

	Age Cohort							
	15–25	25–35	35–45	45–55	55–65	65–75	75–85	85+
AFDC	1.1	6.97	29.46	22.58	4.96	0	0	0
Social Security	49.01	70	136.02	356.04	1,231.72	5,190.2	5,257.96	5,197.11
Railroad retirement	0	0	0	0	11.76	248.28	331.45	486.79
Supplemental security	20.54	48.51	88.21	108.73	163.07	213.76	125.03	87.13
State unemployment compensation	48.07	123.03	172.61	119.1	81.88	1.26	0	0
Veterans' compensation	1.06	10.31	78.7	215.5	397.64	558.09	101.62	11.45
Workers' compensation	10.28	59.94	98.71	105.4	34.65	0	0	0
General assistance	3.46	19.45	37.71	15.06	42.07	10.49	0	0
Foster childcare	0	0	0	4.13	0	0	0	0
Other welfare	0.54	0.42	0	0	0.58	0	0.62	0
Food stamps	2.83	12.14	42.52	31.63	23.8	26.64	21.45	9.1
Child support payments	0.75	4.83	34.07	0	0	0	0	0
Federal civil service pensions	0	4.79	0	0	170.6	877.48	594.2	958.04
Medicare	5.58	19.00	39.25	152.00	282.06	1,785.21	2,648.10	3,128.68
Medicaid	94.93	118.47	162.7	184.02	203.53	294.64	700.66	1742
Military retirement	1.53	0	9.69	414.94	466.37	647.95	84.4	0
State government pensions	0	0	0	24.19	84.59	273.61	396.55	179.22
Local government pensions	0	0	0	10.13	31.2	250.67	249.51	7.93
GI Bill Benefits	10.34	16.57	18.1	15.81	0	0	0	0
WIC	0	0	0	0	0	0	0	0
Other unemployment compensation	0	0	0	0	0	0	0	0

Table 1B.3   **Married Couples**

	15–25	25–35	35–45	45–55	55–65	65–75	75–85	85+
				Age Cohort				
AFDC	105.3	63.63	58.56	30.47	10.04	6.92	0	0
Social security	11.79	44.87	105.55	437.76	3,064.57	9,237.4	8,847.57	8,582.22
Railroad retirement	0	1.95	0	5.33	174.88	357.04	181.12	175.65
Supplemental security	0	10.73	26.61	21.4	61.6	75.45	129.86	689.04
State unemployment compensation	189.64	231.93	174.35	141.19	88.86	12.62	0	0
Veterans' compensation	27.39	45.09	59.1	89.84	326.53	190.87	78.7	149.54
Workers' compensation	76.84	107.88	36.7	87.59	114.17	15.3	0	0
General assistance	3.64	10.44	6.68	8.14	8.83	0	2.89	0
Foster childcare	3.37	10.54	5.23	7.29	3.65	0	0	0
Other welfare	0.47	0.63	10.73	1.82	0.44	3.17	14.29	0
Food stamps	86.28	74.82	53.52	42.37	20.49	12.08	17.93	19.77
Child support payments	23.97	88.41	87.22	12.27	2.19	0	0	0
Federal civil pensions service	0	0	17.31	98.52	801.23	979.51	938	1,067.23
Medicare	0.00	3.96	21.44	94.60	217.91	3,513.87	5,142.88	5,928.77
Medicaid	263.82	270.29	317.92	354.07	407.15	568.68	1,254.32	3,246.84
Military retirement	24.56	7.21	128.98	656.43	468.37	514.6	54.02	0
State government pensions	0	3.15	25.3	145.45	564.54	601.67	1,029.28	0
Local government pensions	0	0	8.75	52.47	201.12	264.57	323.59	0
GI Bill benefits	14.17	29.85	20.18	10.3	5.24	0	0	0
WIC	24.67	7.52	1.83	0.23	0.12	0	0	0
Other unemployment compensation	1.92	1.21	4.5	7.33	0.1	0	0	0

Appendix C
Total Transfer Payments (billion $)

	Under 25	25–35	35–45	45–55	55–65	65–75	75–85	85+	Total
				Year 1990					
Social Security	1.47	1.94	3.64	6.60	33.82	90.44	50.60	14.90	203.41
Other retirement	0.00	0.13	0.81	3.86	17.65	21.77	12.88	2.24	59.34
Medicare	0.20	0.44	0.74	1.86	3.36	33.58	27.88	9.88	77.94
Medicaid	5.26	8.34	8.37	5.25	4.64	5.58	7.31	5.79	50.55
Income	5.67	13.05	13.19	4.89	2.40	2.38	1.65	0.95	44.19
Work-related	1.93	6.84	5.39	3.39	2.26	0.23	0.00	0.00	20.05
Military	0.45	1.43	3.73	9.93	9.18	7.32	0.99	0.26	33.29
Education	180.18	0.00	0.00	0.00	0.00	0.00	0.00	0.00	180.18
Total	195.16	32.18	35.88	35.78	73.31	161.32	101.32	34.02	668.95
				Year 2000					
Social Security	1.50	1.66	4.56	9.76	38.33	91.66	61.13	20.79	229.39
Other retirement	0.00	0.11	0.89	5.48	19.96	22.10	15.70	3.08	67.32
Medicare	0.20	0.38	0.94	2.86	3.84	34.06	33.76	13.82	89.86
Medicaid	5.31	7.03	10.09	7.70	5.27	5.65	8.81	8.08	57.95
Income	5.73	10.96	16.85	7.84	2.76	2.36	1.93	1.35	49.78
Work-related	1.91	5.79	6.60	5.00	2.57	0.24	0.00	0.00	22.10
Military	0.45	1.21	4.28	14.42	10.41	7.50	1.19	0.37	39.82
Education	189.29	0.00	0.00	0.00	0.00	0.00	0.00	0.00	189.29
Total	204.39	27.13	44.22	53.06	83.13	163.57	122.53	47.50	745.52
				Year 2020					
Social Security	1.49	1.79	3.86	9.79	63.80	153.42	74.05	29.56	337.75
Other retirement	0.00	0.12	0.77	5.29	32.32	37.23	19.18	4.43	99.33
Medicare	0.20	0.41	0.80	2.93	6.86	56.94	41.05	19.65	128.84
Medicaid	5.30	7.61	8.56	7.60	8.86	9.45	10.65	11.46	69.49
Income	5.70	11.93	14.00	7.73	5.10	3.98	2.26	1.92	52.61
Work-related	1.93	6.22	5.68	5.07	4.33	0.39	0.00	0.00	23.62
Military	0.45	1.29	3.71	14.63	18.27	13.01	1.42	0.52	53.32
Education	183.83	0.00	0.00	0.00	0.00	0.00	0.00	0.00	183.83
Total	198.90	29.37	37.37	53.05	139.54	274.42	148.60	67.54	948.79
				Year 2040					
Social Security	1.53	1.72	3.84	10.57	55.98	155.64	128.43	54.73	412.44
Other retirement	0.00	0.11	0.77	5.68	28.49	38.07	33.40	8.34	114.86
Medicare	0.20	0.40	0.80	3.18	5.93	57.67	70.93	36.40	175.50
Medicaid	5.43	7.31	8.50	8.19	7.76	9.56	18.44	21.15	86.34
Income	5.85	11.44	13.81	8.40	4.35	4.10	3.93	3.56	55.44
Work-related	1.98	5.99	5.69	5.47	3.80	0.39	0.00	0.00	23.32
Military	0.47	1.24	3.71	15.77	16.09	13.78	2.54	0.95	54.56
Education	183.93	0.00	0.00	0.00	0.00	0.00	0.00	0.00	183.93
Total	199.38	28.22	37.12	57.25	122.40	279.21	257.68	125.12	1,106.39
				Year 2060					
Social Security	1.51	1.70	3.95	10.20	56.15	169.95	118.30	66.59	428.34
Other retirement	0.00	0.11	0.78	5.50	28.56	41.64	30.90	10.27	117.76

				Age Cohort					
	Under 25	25–35	35–45	45–55	55–65	65–75	75–85	85+	Total
Medicare	0.20	0.39	0.82	3.06	5.94	62.97	65.48	44.22	183.07
Medicaid	5.38	7.18	8.73	7.91	7.79	10.44	16.97	25.71	90.10
Income	5.79	11.22	14.24	8.00	4.34	4.45	3.55	4.28	55.87
Work-related	1.96	5.91	5.84	5.29	3.82	0.42	0.00	0.00	23.24
Military	0.46	1.23	3.80	15.28	16.26	15.19	2.32	1.15	55.69
Education	183.93	0.00	0.00	0.00	0.00	0.00	0.00	0.00	183.93
Total	199.24	27.73	38.16	55.23	122.86	305.06	237.50	152.22	1,138.00
Year 2080									
Social Security	1.50	1.70	3.92	10.06	57.71	166.77	122.34	78.96	442.97
Other retirement	0.00	0.11	0.78	5.42	29.33	40.87	32.04	12.28	120.83
Medicare	0.20	0.39	0.82	3.01	6.11	61.83	67.75	52.45	192.57
Medicaid	5.35	7.21	8.67	7.79	8.01	10.24	17.53	30.43	95.22
Income	5.75	11.26	14.13	7.83	4.46	4.29	3.63	5.08	56.44
Work-related	1.95	5.93	5.80	5.22	3.93	0.41	0.00	0.00	23.25
Military	0.46	1.23	3.78	15.10	16.76	14.92	2.40	1.35	56.00
Education	183.09	0.00	0.00	0.00	0.00	0.00	0.00	0.00	183.09
Total	198.30	27.85	37.89	54.42	126.32	299.34	245.70	180.55	1,170.37

References

Poterba, James M., and Lawrence H. Summers. 1987. Public policy implications of declining old-age mortality. In *Work, health, and income among the elderly*, ed. Gary Burtless. Washington D.C.: Brookings Institution.

U.S. Bureau of the Census. 1986. *Survey of income programs and participation (SIPP)*. Washington, D.C.: Government Printing Office.

———. 1988. *Statistical abstract of the United States, 1987*. Washington, D.C.: Government Printing Office.

U.S. Department of Health and Human Services. Health Care Financing Administration. Office of Research and Demonstrations. 1986. *Medicare/Medicaid data book*. Baltimore: Department of Health and Human Services.

———. 1989. *Health Care Financing Review* 10, no. 4 (Summer).

U.S. Social Security Administration (SSA). 1989. *Social Security area population projections: 1989*. Washington, D.C.: Government Printing Office, June.

Comment   Michael D. Hurd

It can be useful to think of total government spending as a weighted average of per capita spending with weights given by the population that draws on the programs. This is particularly true for a range of entitlement programs such as Social Security, because the rules roughly fix individual benefits and the sys-

Michael D. Hurd is professor of economics at State University of New York at Stony Brook and a research associate of the National Bureau of Economic Research.

tem passively accepts total spending as determined by the number who qualify. This leads to a natural decomposition of change in spending into change per capita and change in population weights. Shoven, Topper, and Wise calculate part of this decomposition: the change in government spending on transfer programs that will result from changes in the age distribution of the population, holding constant per capita spending on each program.

The age distribution is expected to change rather dramatically, so we should expect rather large changes in government spending because of the importance of age-related programs. Indeed, Shoven, Topper, and Wise find that "the cost increase per adult is projected to be about 25%." Almost all of this is due to the increased costs of programs that benefit the elderly: about half comes from Social Security benefits and the rest from Medicare and Medicaid and from other federal government retirement programs (primarily civil service and military pensions). Shoven, Topper, and Wise conclude that "these projections have serious consequences. First, . . . there will be strong pressures to cut the benefits of these programs. . . . Second, new initiatives with budgetary costs will be crowded out by the growing expense of the existing programs."

I agree with their conclusion, but not because of their analysis. In fact, with a small modification, their analysis leads to optimistic conclusions. The modification is to allow income growth, which they exclude from their calculations. Suppose, for example, real GNP grows by 1 percent per year per capita. Then Social Security benefits as a percentage of GNP will fall from 5.0 percent in 1990 to 4.8 percent in 2020, so that the burden of transferring Social Security benefits through the tax system will decrease, not increase. Because the Medicare, Medicaid, and federal retirement programs increase at about the same rate as Social Security benefits, they will similarly decline as a percentage of GNP and, therefore, so will total government spending on these programs as a percentage of GNP.

Expert Panel Projections

The rest of my comments will be based on a report published by the 1991 Advisory Council on Social Security (1991). The council convened an expert panel to study the implications of the demographic change on income security and health-care expenditures. The panel produced a number of spending projections to 2020. I will take some examples from the panel's report and compare them with some results of Shoven, Topper, and Wise.

Table 1C.1 shows several categories of expenditures and transfers. The projection of Social Security benefits is based on a detailed projection model of the Office of the Actuary of the Social Security Administration. Health-care expenditures are the percentage of GNP spent on health care regardless of payment source. The projection is a modification of that of Shoven, Topper, and Wise: it reflects age-composition changes and per capita GNP growth. It is an aggregate of 18 kinds of health-care expenditures by age; an example is inpatient care in community hospitals, which varies by age. The projection of

Table 1C.1   **Current and Projected Expenditures (% of GNP)**

	1990	2020
Social Security retirement benefits	4.6	5.8
Health care	12.2	13.7[a]
Federal government purchases	7.7	6.2
State and local education	5.2	4.5
Total	29.7	30.2

Source: Advisory Council on Social Security (1991).
[a]Based only on changes in age composition and per capita GNP growth.

federal government purchases is based on expert judgement. The method of projecting educational expenses is similar to the method of Shoven, Topper, and Wise. Educational expenses fall because of the decline in the fraction of school-age population. The expert panel considered other uses of GNP, such as investment, but they are not sensitive to the age distribution, so I have not listed them.

The table shows a modest rise in the total. The conclusion is that at least until 2020 the change in age distribution is manageable. Between 2020 and 2030, the fraction of the population over age 65 increases further, but the same overall conclusion remains.

Table 1C.1 allows no change in per capita health-care expenditures except from income growth. However, over the past 20 years real per capita health-care expenditures have risen at an annual rate of 4.4 percent, which is much greater than the rate of GNP growth. A continuation of such rates of growth will have major impacts on Medicare and Medicaid and on the economic status of the elderly.

At the request of the expert panel, the Health Care Financing Administration (HCFA) constructed four scenarios for future health-care expenditures. The projections are based on forecasts of 18 kinds of health-care use. Expenditures on each kind can change because of demographic changes, changes in frequency of use, changes in intensity of use, and medical inflation in excess of general inflation.

Table 1C.2 gives an outline of the scenarios and the percentage of GNP spent on health care under each scenario. The expert panel focused on scenarios 2 and 3. Both show an increase in the percentage of GNP spent on health care that completely dominates any changes associated with demographic shifts (scenario 4). Both require a very large shift in the composition of total consumption from 12.2 percent of GNP in 1990 to 31.5 percent or 22.7 percent. Under scenario 2, all of the personal income growth between now and 2020 would be spent on health care, and under scenario 3, 69 percent of it would be.

It is hard to believe that health-care expenditures will grow from 12.2 percent of GNP to 22.7 percent or possibly even 31.5 percent; yet, it is difficult to

Table 1C.2   Four Scenarios of Health-Care Expenditures in 2020

	Scenario			
	1	2	3	4
Growth rates (%)	Same real growth per capita as last 10 years (4.7)	Modest reductions in growth rates; per capita growth same as last 20 years (4.4)	Moderate reductions in growth rates; per capita growth = 3.1	Demographic and GNP growth only
Expenditures (% of GNP)	36.0	31.5	22.7	13.7

Source: Advisory Council on Social Security (1991).

identify the mechanisms that will prevent such growth. One possibility is that a substantial fraction of the population will, because of costs, have limited access to the health-care system. In 1990, the elderly paid about 17 percent of their median income on medical expenses.[1] Under scenarios 2 and 3, this is expected to rise to 30 percent and 23 percent, respectively. Real per capita payments by private health-care insurers are projected to increase by factors of 3.2 and 2.3, which will threaten employment-based health-care coverage because of the expenses to employers.

The results of Shoven, Topper, and Wise, when normalized by GNP growth, show a fall in the tax burden; but according the HCFA projections, the per capita cost will substantially increase the tax burden. In 1990, the federal government's share of Medicare (HI and SMI) amounted to 4.4 percent of the taxable Social Security payroll. Under scenarios 2 and 3, this is expected to increase to 17.6 percent and 12.5 percent, respectively. Either of these is, of course, a very large increase in the tax burden.

Conclusion

The effects of population aging through 2020 seem manageable: the increase in transfers through the Social Security system are within historical variation; health-care costs associated with the demographic change do increase but not alarmingly; although not discussed here, the private pension system should be able to pay for the greater number of retirees. By far the most important problem is the escalation of health-care costs. This is associated with the demographic change because of an interaction effect: the elderly consume health-care services much more intensely than the nonelderly. The force driving the escalation, however, is not the age distribution of the population. The large projected increases in health-care costs come from inflation of medical

---

1. This figure includes payments for SMI premiums but not for any privately purchased health insurance.

costs in excess of general inflation, increased use per person, and increased intensity (higher cost per use). The expert panel concluded that immediate action is required to contain costs and that increasing costs will reduce the access of many to the health-care system.

Reference

Advisory Council on Social Security. 1991. *Income security and health care: Economic implications 1991–2020.* Washington, D.C.: Government Printing Office.

II Death Rates and Life Expectancy

2 Methods for Projecting the Future Size and Health Status of the U.S. Elderly Population

Kenneth G. Manton, Eric Stallard, and Burton H. Singer

2.1 Introduction

Reform of the U.S. health-care system has focused on payment systems and insurance for the elderly, a high consumption group, and for 36 million uninsured and 60 million underinsured, younger U.S. residents. For these efforts, forecasts of the consequences of public health programs are needed, as well as of the effects of population risk factor trends and diagnostic and treatment innovation (Blackburn 1989). Because actuarial projections (e.g., Spencer 1989; Wade 1987) do not use information on health change prior to death, their use in designing service delivery, acute and long-term care (LTC) insurance, and reimbursement systems is limited, as is their ability to anticipate "turning" points in population growth and health (Myers 1981). Health forecasts are also needed to design interfaces for private insurance and Medicare and Medicaid coverage and for long-term market planning by drug and medical equipment manufacturers.

Changes in the size and health of the U.S. adult population are determined by chronic disease morbidity and mortality. Lifestyle and behavior (e.g., physical activity, smoking, and diet) influence the natural history of many chronic diseases. Improvements in the population distribution of risk factors and treatment have reduced U.S. mortality of those above age 65 (Blackburn 1989). After plateauing from 1982 to 1988, mortality of persons aged 85+ declined 8.6 percent from 1989 to 1991 (National Center for Health Statistics [NCHS]

Kenneth G. Manton is research professor of demographic studies at Duke University. Eric Stallard is associate research professor of demographic studies at Duke University. Burton H. Singer is professor of epidemiology economics and statistics at Yale University.

Support for this research was provided by NIA Grant 5-R01-AG01159 and 1-R37-AG7025 (Manton and Stallard) and NIA Contract N01-AG02105 (Singer). The authors are grateful to Peter Diamond, Alan Garber, James Poterba, and David Wise for helpful comments on an earlier draft.

41

1992). To anticipate changes, health and mortality time-series data must be used. In this chapter we (i) introduce integrated models of risk factor dynamics and mortality processes, calibrated from longitudinal data, to forecast preventive and curative intervention effects; (ii) compare actuarial forecasts with those based on multivariate stochastic processes; and (iii) introduce models integrating disability dynamics with mortality processes, as a step toward integrating the dynamics of multiple biological levels (Lipsitz and Goldberger 1992).

In section 2.2, we review (2.2.1) the rationale of model specifications and introduce (2.2.2), time-inhomogeneous, multidimensional physiological variable processes. The dependency of mortality on the diffusion processes is defined in subsection 2.2.3 as a quadratic function of physiological variables multiplied by an exponential term representing "senescence." Dependent competing risks for multiple-cause mortality are discussed in subsection 2.2.4, where dependence is represented by risk factor trajectories generated by the diffusion process. In subsection 2.2.5 we introduce Grade of Membership (GoM) concepts to identify profiles of disabilities as vertices of a unit simplex within which individual disability dynamics operate as bounded diffusion processes. Positions in the simplex are defined by "scores" (i.e., coordinates in the convex space) representing the "degree of similarity" of an individual's traits to each "vertex" (i.e., profile of disabilities). Finally, we present discrete time approximations in subsection 2.2.6 for estimation and forecasting.

Section 2.3 presents projections based on scenarios about health interventions. We then discuss active life expectancy (ALE) projections and exogenous economic and social interventions. In section 2.4, we briefly discuss research needed to extend and refine models.

2.2 Methodology

2.2.1 Overview

We model mortality as influenced by the temporal dynamics of physiological (or, more generally, "state") variables. The mortality rate is expressed as a product of a quadratic function of measured physiological variables and an exponential function of age. The quadratic implies that there is an increasing risk of death with the movement of one or more physiological variables from an optimum homeostatic value (the minimum point of the function). The restriction to quadratic—as opposed to more complex—surfaces recognizes that data will seldom be sufficient to statistically discriminate between quadratic and higher-order polynomial surfaces. The exponential term, $\exp(\theta \text{ age})$, is interpreted as the contribution to mortality of "senescence." By "senescence" we mean the age-specific average effect of currently "unknown" factors on mortality; senescence does not include any of the measured variables in the quadratic hazard. Although senescence is discussed in most theories of aging (e.g., Medvedev 1990) as a decline in one or more biological functions, it has not been mathematically rigorously defined.

Evolution of physiological (state) variables in the quadratic hazard is assumed to be governed by stochastic differential equations with linear drift, i.e., dynamics are "Markovian." Although state variable processes may exhibit non-Markovian dependence, we assume that they can always be respecified to represent cumulative experience to approximate a Markovian process.

Forecasts using the stochastic differential equations focus on

1. The mean vector and covariance matrix of state variables at times/ages beyond the limits of data used to estimate parameters. Forecasts can be based on functional extrapolation assuming parameters do not change. Alternatively, parameters can be altered to represent scenarios about different interventions.

2. Life expectancy at birth, and specific ages, as measures of the effect of interventions on state dynamics and mortality.

3. Life tables for a range of interventions.

Total mortality is represented as a sum of "crude" cause-specific mortality rates, each operating in the presence of (i.e., competing with) all other causes (Yashin, Manton, and Stallard 1986). The mortality rate for a cause is correlated with rates for other causes through a vector of common physiological processes which represent the dependence of risks. Computational details are in subsection 2.2.4.

Mortality can also be modeled as a function of disability—both physical and cognitive—whose excursion from levels of performance associated with the lowest mortality risk are associated with the underlying state processes *causing* disability (see Manton, Stallard, and Singer 1992a). We use Grade of Membership (GoM) concepts to construct profiles of disabilities whose co-occurrence is biologically plausible. The profiles define fuzzy partitions using individual scores to represent the degree of similarity to each profile. The disability dynamics are modeled by a stochastic differential equation operating in the unit simplex whose vertices are the disability profiles. Mortality at a given age/time is represented by a quadratic function of the time-varying "scores," i.e., solutions for the stochastic differential equations in the simplex. In this formulation, high mortality rates are associated with excursions of the score vector away from $(0, \ldots, 0, 1, 0, \ldots, 0)$, where 1 is associated with the profile having "mild" (or no) disabilities (i.e., the "origin" of the space is a priori specifiable as the "state" having no "dis"-ability). Senescence is the average effect of unobserved variables at a given age. The hazard is $Q(\mathbf{g}) \exp(\theta \cdot age)$ where $Q(\mathbf{g})$ is a quadratic function of the score vector, $\mathbf{g}$.

Ideally, the hazard would contain both physiological variables and disabilities. A model for a comprehensive set of state variables representing multiple levels of biological organization is beyond this paper's scope. We do illustrate a model where exogenous factors are allowed to influence the disability dynamics. For a discussion of issues in creating multilevel models, and their use in forecasting, see Manton (1993).

2.2.2 Physiological Dynamics

Assume a vector of J variables, $\mathbf{x}(t)$, is governed by stochastic differential equations

(1) $$d\mathbf{x}(t) = \mathbf{a}(t, \mathbf{x}(t))\, dt + \mathbf{b}(t, \mathbf{x}(t))\, d\mathbf{W}(t),$$

where $\mathbf{W}(t)$ is a J-dimensional Brownian motion process independent of initial values $\mathbf{x}(0)$, $\mathbf{b}(t, \mathbf{y})$ is a bounded matrix-valued function whose entries are scale factors governing the size of random fluctuations around $\mathbf{y} = \mathbf{x}(t)$, and $\mathbf{a}(t, \mathbf{y})$ is a vector governing drift in the neighborhood of $\mathbf{y} = \mathbf{x}(t)$. Equation (1) describes dynamics for a cohort; hence, age and time are confounded. To unconfound age and time, $\mathbf{a}$ and $\mathbf{b}$ must be parameterized by age or, equivalently, by birth cohort, c, with age $= t - c$, where t is calendar time. Values of $\mathbf{x}(t)$ are deviations (excursions) about an optimal (minimum) risk vector of state variable values.

For the current example, we restrict $\mathbf{a}(t, \mathbf{y})$ to be

(2) $$\mathbf{a}(t, \mathbf{y}) = \mathbf{a}_0(t) + \mathbf{a}_1(t)\mathbf{y},$$

where $\mathbf{a}_1(t)$ is a restoring ("homeostatic") effect. We assume $\mathbf{b}$ depends on age/time and *not* on the level, $\mathbf{y} = \mathbf{x}(t)$. Equation (1) reduces to

(3) $$d\mathbf{x}(t) = [\mathbf{a}_0(t) + \mathbf{a}_1(t)\mathbf{x}(t)]\, dt + \mathbf{b}(t)\, d\mathbf{W}(t).$$

2.2.3 Mortality

Let T be a random age/time-at-death variable, with survival, conditional on T,

(4) $$P(T > t \,|\mathbf{x}(s), 0 \leq s < t) = \exp\left[-\int_0^t \mu(s, \mathbf{x}(s))\, ds\right],$$

where

(5) $$\mu(s, \mathbf{x}(s)) = \left[\mu_0(s) + \mathbf{b}^{\mathrm{T}} \cdot \mathbf{x}(s) + \frac{1}{2}\mathbf{x}^{\mathrm{T}}(s)\, \mathbf{B}(s)\, \mathbf{x}(s)\right] e^{\theta s}.$$

Here $e^{\theta s}$ is senescence. The quadratic describes mortality risk due to excursions of state variables away from values with minimum risk, e.g., x_0. The dynamics for an individual evolve according to the diffusion process (3) for a random length of time, T, where conditional survival is governed by equations (4) and (5). If the initial vector, $\mathbf{x}(0)$, is Gaussian, then the Gaussian property propagates to $\mathbf{x}(t)$ for all $t > 0$, even with mortality selection (Woodbury and Manton 1977). When $\mathbf{a}_0$, $\mathbf{a}_1$, and $\mathbf{b}$ are constants, then (3) is the Ornstein-Uhlenbeck process, a unique time-homogeneous Gaussian diffusion process.

2.2.4   Cause-Specific Mortality and Competing Risks

Let $c_1, \ldots, c_K$ be causes of death, and $T_1, \ldots, T_K$ random variables representing ages/times at death from $c_1, \ldots, c_K$; $T =$ age/time at death $=$ min $(T_1, \ldots, T_K)$. With the joint survival function $S(t_1, \ldots, t_K) = P(T_1 > t_1, \ldots, T_K > t_K)$, observe that $S(t) = P(T > t) = S(t, \ldots, t)$. The *net* hazard for c_k in the absence of other causes is $\lambda_k(t) = -\dfrac{dP(T_k > t)}{dt}\bigg|P(T_k > t)$. The crude hazard for c_k in the presence of other causes is

(6) $$\mu_k(t) = -\frac{1}{S(t, \ldots, t)} \frac{\partial S(t_1, \ldots, t_K)}{\partial t_k}\bigg|_{t_1 = \cdots = t_K = t.}$$

The rate $\mu(t) = -\dfrac{d}{dt} S(t, \ldots, t)/S(t, \ldots, t)$ is the sum of crude hazard rates, $\mu_k(t)$, by the definition of the total differential; i.e.,

(7) $$\mu(t) = -\frac{d}{dt} S(t, \ldots, t)/S(t, \ldots, t) =$$
$$-\frac{1}{S(t, \ldots, t)} \sum_{k=1}^{K} \frac{\partial S(t_1, \ldots, t_K)}{\partial t_k}\bigg|_{t_1 = \cdots = t_K = t} = \sum_{k=1}^{K} \mu_k(t).$$

The survival function, $S(t) = P(T > t)$, is

(8) $$S(t) = \exp\left[-\int_0^t \mu(s)\, ds\right] = \exp\left[-\sum_{k=1}^{K} \int_0^t \mu_k(s)\, ds\right] =$$
$$\prod_{k=1}^{K} \exp\left[-\int_0^t \mu_k(s)\, ds\right].$$

If we assume $T_1, \ldots, T_K$ are independent, then

(9) $$S(t) = \prod_{k=1}^{K} P(T_k > t) = \prod_{k=1}^{K} \exp\left[-\int_0^t \lambda_k(s)\, ds\right];$$

i.e., net and crude mortality rates are equal, assuming independence.

We can represent dependence among $T_1, \ldots, T_K$ generated by state processes, $\{\mathbf{x}(t), t \geq 0\}$. Let X_0^t be the history of the process $\mathbf{x}(s)$ over $0 \leq s < t$. More formally, X_0^t is the minimal σ-algebra generated by $\mathbf{x}(s)$ for $0 \leq s < t$. We assume that, conditional on X_0^t, $T_1, \ldots, T_K$ are independent. Then

(10) $$P(T > t|X_0^t) = \prod_{k=1}^{K} P(T_k > t\, |X_0^t).$$

Conditional independence of $T_1, \ldots, T_K$, given X_0^t, means, that the process $\mathbf{x}(t)$ accounts for ("explains") the unconditional dependence of $T_1, \ldots, T_K$. If we assume independence of $T_1, \ldots, T_K$ conditional on X_0^t, conditional net and crude rates are equal. The conditional survival function is

$$(11) \qquad P(T_k > t|X_0^t) = \exp\left[-\int_0^t \sum_{k=1}^K \mu_k(s| X_0^s)\, ds\right],$$

where $\mu_k(s \mid X_0^s)$ is the crude mortality rate conditional on the history of the process to s. Forecasts in section 2.3 assume that $\mu_k(s \mid X_0^s) = \mu_k(s, \mathbf{x}(s))$; i.e., only current values of $\mathbf{x}(s)$ are informative. This is plausible if components of $\mathbf{x}(s)$ can include measures of the effect of past history to s. For specifications involving more complex dependence on process history, see Yashin, Manton, and Stallard (1986).

We parameterize $\mu_k(s, \mathbf{x}(s))$, analogous to equation (5), as

$$(12) \qquad \mu_k(s, \mathbf{x}(s)) = [\mu_{0,k}(s) + \mathbf{b}_k^T \cdot \mathbf{x}(s) + \frac{1}{2} \mathbf{x}^T(s)\, \mathbf{B}_k \mathbf{x}(s)]\, e^{\theta s}.$$

Thus each μ_k is a quadratic function of J state variables. Senescence has a common value of θ for all c_k; i.e., senescence is the age-specific average effect of unknown factors on death. The unconditional survival function is

$$(13) \qquad P(T > t) = \exp\left[-\int_0^t \sum_{k=1}^K \bar{\mu}_k(s)\, ds\right],$$

where

$$(14) \qquad \bar{\mu}_k(t) = E[\mu_k(t, \mathbf{x}(t)) \mid T > t]$$

(see Yashin et al. 1986). Here equation (14) is the unconditional crude hazard for T_k. To see, in a simple scalar case with $J = 1$, how the $\bar{\mu}_k(t)$ are related by $\mathbf{x}(t)$—i.e., the explicit form of dependence—suppose that $\mu_k(t, \mathbf{x}(t)) = h_k(t)\mathbf{x}^2(t)$. Then, after manipulation, it can be shown (Yashin et al. 1986) that

$$(15) \qquad \bar{\mu}_k(t) = h_k(t)[\mathbf{m}^2(t) + \gamma(t)],$$

where

$$\mathbf{m}(t) = E[\mathbf{x}(t) \mid T > t]$$

and

$$\gamma(t) = \text{Var}[\mathbf{x}(t) \mid T > t].$$

These quantities satisfy the system of ordinary differential equations

$$(16) \qquad \frac{d\mathbf{m}(t)}{dt} = [\mathbf{a}_0(t) + \mathbf{a}_1(t)\mathbf{m}(t)] - 2\gamma(t) \sum_{k=1}^K h_k(t)\mathbf{m}(t),$$

$$\frac{d\gamma(t)}{dt} = 2\mathbf{a}_1(t)\, \gamma(t) + \mathbf{b}^2(t) - 2\gamma^2(t) \sum_{k=1}^K h_k(t).$$

To generate forecasts with cause elimination, one sets $h_k^0(t) \equiv 0$ when cause c_k^0 is eliminated. Observe that $\mathbf{m}(t)$ and $\gamma(t)$ depend—via equation (16)—on all other rates, $h_k(t); k \neq k^0$. The dependence of $\mu_k(t)$ on state variables is—for $\mu_k(t, \mathbf{x}(t)) = h_k(t) \, \mathbf{x}^T(t) \cdot \mathbf{x}(t)$—through $\mathbf{m}(t)$ and $\gamma(t)$ in equation (15). Although more general specifications (e.g., eq. [12]) are more complicated than equation (15), the dependence of competing risks still operates through differential equation systems for $\mathbf{m}(t)$ and $\gamma(t)$.

2.2.5   Disability and Grade of Membership (GoM) Models

Survey-based assessments of disability yield vectors of discrete responses, **x,** for each individual. Commonly, among the elderly, many individuals have multiple disabilities—but no specific combination occurs with high frequency. The distribution of disabilities in a population is best described by constructing empirically (and biologically) defensible profiles of co-occurring disabilities to be the vertices of a unit simplex. Each individual is associated with a point, $\mathbf{g}_i$, in the simplex. Components of $\mathbf{g}_i = (g_{i1}, \ldots, g_{iK})$ are convex weights (where $g_{ik} \geq 0$ and $\sum_{k=1}^{K} g_{ik} = 1$) representing the "degrees of similarity" of individuals to each profile (or distances to each vertex). For example, a person with $\mathbf{g}_i = (0, 1, 0, \ldots, 0)$ has disabilities only found in the second profile. A person with $\mathbf{g}_i = (2/3, 1/6, 0, \ldots, 0, 1/6)$ has some disabilities from profiles 1, 2, and K; however, more of his conditions are in profile 1 (the score of 2/3) than in profiles 2 and K (i.e., scores of 1/6).

The use of the g_{ik} is related to incidental parameter estimation problems discussed by Neyman and Pearson, Neyman and Scott, and others. Resolution of the problem requires imposition of a "smoothing" operator on incidental parameters (e.g., Kiefer and Wolfowitz 1956). In GoM, the statistical properties of the g_{ik} are derived from theorems due to Weyl (1949) on polyhedra. Specifically, such models are identifiable and parameters consistently estimated, because once J discrete variables are selected, a space of potential responses, say M, constructed from $\sum_{j=1}^{J}$ basis vectors (i.e., containing only 0s or 1s) is fixed. The probabilities calculated from score estimates (g_{ik}), vertex coordinates (λ_{kjl}), and observed responses define a linear parameter space, L_B, bounded by M. The intersection $L_B \cap M$ yields the simplex, B, whose vertices define the profiles (i.e., λ_{kjl} coordinates) and whose faces define the half-spaces for the g_{ik} (Woodbury, Manton, and Tolley 1994). The convex constraints imposed on the g_{ik} by M mean that all individuals are represented on the boundary, or in the interior of B, and that each individual's coordinates are uniquely defined (given his responses) because of the definition of vertices, λ_{kjl}, by $L_B \cap M$. This differs from multivariate continuous variable models where coordinate systems are constructed to represent central mass points (equivalent to centers of gravity) of specific multivariate distribution functions. It also differs from contingency tables (Bishop, Fienberg, and Holland 1975) and latent class models (LCM; Lazarsfeld and Henry 1968) used for discrete variables. In those procedures, the g_{ik} must be 0 or 1. In contingency tables, each person's group is observed (i.e., which $g_{ik} = 1.0$ is known) so that only the λ_{kjl} (for each of K observed groups) are estimated—under the constraint that groups are discrete (i.e., g_{ik} can only be 0 or 1). In LCM, groups are not observed, so that the g_{ik} must be estimated. Again the groups are discrete, so the state variable scores, g_{ik}, can only be 0 or 1, though the probability of being in a group (i.e., $p_{ik} = P(g_{ik} = 1.0)$ is what is typically estimated. In GoM there is an additional within-group heterogeneity component, due to the continuous scaling of the g_{ik}, not represented in LCM. However, LCM is nested within GoM, so likelihood ratio tests of model specification can be made. In forecasting, the process is generally restricted to the unit simplex B. In forecasting using LCM, cases can only fall on the vertices, with all transitions being discrete. B imposes constraints on the forecasts, although, if well-specified functions relate exogenous factors to the λ_{kjl} and g_{ik}, it is possible to use those functions to predict changes in the unit simplex; e.g., new variables can become relevant, changing the space M.

To formalize this, response vectors are modeled as

$$(17) \qquad P(\mathbf{X} = l) = \int_{S_K} P[\mathbf{X}^{(\mathbf{g}_i)} = l | \mathbf{g}_i = \boldsymbol{\gamma}_i] \, d\mu(\boldsymbol{\gamma}_i) \,,$$

where $\mathbf{X}^{(\mathbf{g}_i)}$ is a random response vector for an individual with score vector, $\mathbf{g}_i$, and $\mu(\boldsymbol{\gamma}_i)$ is a probability measure on the unit simplex with K vertices, S_K. Dependence among coordinates in the response vector is modeled assuming: (i) conditional on g_i, coordinate variables are independent; i.e.,

$$(18) \qquad P[\mathbf{X}^{(\mathbf{g})} = l \mid \mathbf{g}_i = \boldsymbol{\gamma}_i] = \prod_{j=1}^{J} P[X^{(\mathbf{g}_i)} = l_j \mid \mathbf{g}_i = \boldsymbol{\gamma}_i] \,;$$

and (ii) the conditional marginal frequencies, $P[X_j^{(\mathbf{g})} = l_j \mid \mathbf{g}_i = \boldsymbol{\gamma}_i]$, are convex combinations of profile frequencies for the same variable; i.e.,

$$(19) \qquad P[X_j^{(\mathbf{g})} = l_j \mid \mathbf{g}_i = \boldsymbol{\gamma}_i] = \sum_{k=1}^{K} \gamma_{ik} \, P[Y_{ij}^{(k)} = l_j] \equiv \sum_{k=1}^{K} \gamma_{ik} \, \lambda_{kjl_j}.$$

Here $Y_{ij}^{(k)}$ is a random variable describing responses to j by i with the characteristics of k.

Equations (17)–(19) describe the distribution of individuals at a fixed age/time. Disability dynamics are modeled as a diffusion process in B; i.e., the evolution of the g_{ik} are described relative to a fixed set (or a fixed set conditional on exogenous factors) of K profiles. For $K = 2$, scores evolve according to a diffusion process on an unit interval. With $\mathbf{g}_i = (g_{i1}, g_{i2}) \equiv (g_{i1}, 1 - g_{i1})$, the stochastic differential equation is

$$(20) \qquad dg_{i1}(t) = [a_0(t) + a_1(t)g_{i1}(t)] \, dt + c \sqrt{g_{i1}(t) \, [1 - g_{i1}(t)]} \, dW(t),$$

where $W(t)$ is standard Brownian motion, to describe dynamics within the unit interval. If we assume that $\{0\}$ and $\{1\}$—points identified by two profiles—

are "reflecting" boundaries, then transition probabilities governing equation (20) in the closed interval [0, 1] are given by the "fundamental" solution of

$$\frac{\partial u}{\partial t} = c^2 x(1 - x)\frac{\partial^2 u}{\partial x^2} + [a_0(t) + a_1(t)\,x]\frac{\partial u}{\partial x}, \quad \text{for } (x, t) \in [0,1] \times$$

$$[0, +\infty)\,, u(0, x) = f(x) \in C^2[0, 1],$$

subject to

$$(21) \qquad\qquad \frac{\partial u}{\partial x}\bigg|_{x=1-} = \frac{\partial u}{\partial x}\bigg|_{x=0+} = 0\,,$$

i.e., reflecting boundary conditions.

The "local" variance (diffusion-term) specification, $c^2 x(1 - x)$, implies that variance in the region of $g_1 = x$ is the same as for Bernoulli trials. The age/time-dependent coefficient, $a_1(t)$, defines drift either toward or away from profile 1, depending on its sign. Forecasts in section 2.3 are high-dimensional generalizations of equations (20)–(21). The discrete-time analogue of the process used for estimation is in subsection 2.2.6. For a more extensive discussion of GoM, see Manton et al. (1992b), Woodbury et al. (1994), Berkman, Singer, and Manton (1989), or Singer (1989).

Mortality, influenced by disability, is represented by the survival function

$$P(T > t|\mathbf{g}(s), 0 \le s < t) = \exp\left[-\int_0^t \mu(s, \mathbf{g}(s))\,ds\right],$$

where

$$(22) \qquad\qquad \mu(s, \mathbf{g}(s)) = [\frac{1}{2}\,\mathbf{g}^\mathrm{T}(s)\,\mathbf{B}\,\mathbf{g}(s)]e^{\theta s}\,.$$

Thus, mortality is governed by excursions of $g_{ik}(s)$ and the family of quadratic functions defined by (22), together with the average age-specific effect (θ) of unobserved factor(s).

2.2.6   Discrete-Time Approximations, Likelihood, and Forecasting Algorithms

Since the data used to estimate parameters in equations (3)–(5) are often collected in multiwave panel designs, observations on physiological variables and disabilities are of the form $\mathbf{x}(t_l)$, $l = 1, 2, \ldots$, (number of assessments), where t_l denotes the lth survey date. The discrete-time analogue of equation (3) is

$$(23) \qquad\qquad \mathbf{x}_{t+1} = u_t + R_t\,\mathbf{x}_t + \mathbf{e}_t\,,$$

where $R_t - I$ is the analogue of $\mathbf{a}_1(t)$, $\Sigma_t = E(\mathbf{e}_t\,\mathbf{e}_t^T)$ corresponds to $\mathbf{b}(t) \cdot \mathbf{b}^T(t)$, and $\{\mathbf{e}_t\}$ are independent, Gaussian distributed vectors with mean $\mathbf{O}$ and covariance matrix Σ_t. For estimation we generalize equation (23) to identify individuals in specific cohorts; i.e.,

(24)
$$\mathbf{x}_{t+1} = \mathbf{u}_0 + \mathbf{u}_1 \ \text{age}_t + \mathbf{R}_1 \ \mathbf{x}_t + \mathbf{R}_2 \ \mathbf{x}_t \ \text{age}_t + \mathbf{R}_3 \cdot \mathbf{z}_t + \mathbf{e}_t \ (\text{age}_t)^d ,$$

where age_t means "age of the individual at calender time t," $\mathbf{z}_t$ is a vector of exogenous variables, and $\mathbf{u}_0$ is a vector of genetically determined levels on J physiological variables. The age/time-dependent mortality rate is

(25)
$$\mu(\text{age}_t, \mathbf{x}_t) = (\mu_0 + \mathbf{b}^\mathrm{T} \cdot \mathbf{x}_t + \frac{1}{2} \mathbf{x}_t^\mathrm{T} \ \mathbf{B} \ \mathbf{x}_t) \exp (\theta \ \text{age}_t) .$$

The time scale for equations (23)–(25) is the intersurvey interval. This is reasonable when the time between surveys is "small" relative to the time required for "substantial" change on state variables. Alternatively, if observations are made at time points that are widely spaced relative to rates of change in underlying processes, then one must evaluate how well discrete time observations can be embedded in a continuous-time diffusion process, equation (1) (see Singer and Spilerman 1976; Frydman and Singer 1979, who discuss the problem for finite-state Markov chains). This is a substantive issue about the model specification used to estimate parameters of the theoretical process of interest given available data—and about its limitations. Two approaches are useful for this problem. First, if there is variation in the time of assessment (i.e., it is triggered by changes in health—as may be the case in studies of LTC delivery systems), then the process can be divided into the smallest possible time unit (e.g., a month), and, for GoM, the $g_{ik \cdot t}$ can be assumed to be unchanged until a new assessment is made (i.e., until there is a jump in information). Then the $g_{ik \cdot t}$ are recalculated. The vertices (λ_{kjl}) are assumed constant over all time, so that the $g_{ik \cdot t}$ at any time are comparable. Then the monthly process, which more accurately approximates continuous time, may be used. This was used to evaluate the performance of Social/Health Maintenance Organizations (Manton et al. 1994). Since an assessment is done (in theory) as often as health changes, the approximation of the continuous time process should be good. A second strategy can be used for surveys with list samples (e.g., the National Long-Term Care Survey [NLTCS]), where administrative records provide partial information on the continuous time process. This was done using the 1982 and 1984 NLTCS where mortality occurring within 3, 6, or 12 months of assessment could be defined. Changes in the mortality rate over, say, five years can be compared, for GoM, with the $g_{ik \cdot t}$'s relation to mortality over three or six months. Changes in mortality over five years gives ancillary information on likely aggregate changes in disability using maximum likelihood estimates of the mortality disability relation for shorter intervals (Manton, Stallard, and Woodbury 1991).

The likelihood, based on equations (24) and (25), using the time scale defined by intersurvey periods, is

$$L = \prod_{i=1}^{I} \{ \phi(\mathbf{x}_{it_0} | \text{age}_{it_0})$$

$$(26) \qquad \times \prod_{t=t_0+1}^{T_i} \phi(\mathbf{x}_{it} | \mathbf{x}_{it-1}, \text{age}_{it-1}, \delta_{it-1} = 0) \exp(-\mu(\mathbf{x}_{it-1}, \text{age}_{it-1}))$$

$$\times \exp(-\mu(\mathbf{x}_{1T_i}, \text{age}_{iT_i}))^{(1-\delta_{iT_i})} [1 - \exp(-\mu(\mathbf{x}_{iT_i}, \text{age}_{iT_i}))]^{\delta_{iT_i}} \}.$$

In equation (26) $\mathbf{x}_{it}$ and age $_{it}$ are observed $(T_i + 1) - t_0$ times for person i. At $t + 1$ survival is assessed: $\delta_{it} = 1$ if i dies before $t + 1$; $\delta_{it} = 0$ otherwise. Initial conditions are the distribution of $\mathbf{x}_{i0}$, conditional on age ($\phi(\mathbf{x}_{i0} | \text{age}_{i0})$), assuming random sampling. If sampling is nonrandom within age or if the model is applied to a new population, $\phi(\mathbf{x}_{i0} | \text{age}_{i0})$ can be reweighted to eliminate bias (Dowd and Manton 1990). Second (and subsequent) observation(s) on a person define the second term in equation (26)—a multivariate time series, where $\phi(\mathbf{x}_{it} | \mathbf{x}_{it-1}, \text{age}_{it-1}, \delta_{it-1} = 0)$ is the density of $\mathbf{x}_{it}$ conditioned on $\mathbf{x}_{it-1}$, age_{it-1}, and $\delta_{it-1} = 0$; I = number of persons in the population. One can see that the likelihood varies from that in standard time-series models (e.g., Box Jenkins) where mortality selection is not modeled.

Cohort life tables, and forecasts of their parameters beyond the bounds of the data, are based on recurrence formulas. First we set $l_t = P(T > t)$, then

$$(27) \qquad l_{t+1} = l_t |\mathbf{I} + \mathbf{V}_t \mathbf{B}_t|^{-1/2} \exp\left[\frac{\mu_t(\boldsymbol{v}_t) + \mu_t(\boldsymbol{v}_t^*)}{2} - 2\mu\left(\frac{\boldsymbol{v}_t + \boldsymbol{v}_t^*}{2}\right)\right],$$

where $\mu_t(\cdot)$ is the mortality rate, (25), with the exponential term absorbed into μ_{0t}, $\mathbf{b}_t$, and $\mathbf{B}_t$; $\boldsymbol{v}_t$ and $\mathbf{V}_t$ are the mean vector and covariance matrix, respectively, of state variables at t; $\boldsymbol{v}_t^*$ and $\mathbf{V}_t^*$ are adjusted for survival to $t + 1$. $\boldsymbol{v}_t$ and $\mathbf{V}_t$ satisfy

$$\boldsymbol{v}_t^* = \boldsymbol{v}_t - \mathbf{V}_t^* (\mathbf{b}_t + \mathbf{B}_t \boldsymbol{v}_t),$$

$$(28) \qquad \mathbf{V}_t^* = (\mathbf{I} + \mathbf{V}_t \mathbf{B}_t)^{-1} \mathbf{V}_t,$$

$$\boldsymbol{v}_{t+1} = \mathbf{u}_t + \mathbf{R}_t \boldsymbol{v}_t^*,$$

$$\mathbf{V}_{t+1} = \mathbf{R}_t \mathbf{V}_t^* \mathbf{R}_t^{\mathrm{T}} + \Sigma_t,$$

where

$$\mathbf{u}_t = \mathbf{u}_0 + \mathbf{u}_1 \text{age}_{t-1},$$

$$\mathbf{R}_t = \mathbf{R}_1 + \mathbf{R}_2 \text{age}_{t-1},$$

and, for the Framingham data,

$$\mathbf{R}_3 \equiv \mathbf{O}.$$

For analysis of disability, we used $\mathbf{R}_3$ to model the effects of income and education on disability transitions. Equation (28), for physiological variables, ensures that $\mathbf{X}_{t+1}$ is normally distributed with mean vector $\boldsymbol{v}_{t+1}$ and covariance matrix $\mathbf{V}_{t+1}$—i.e., $N(\boldsymbol{v}_{t+1}, \mathbf{V}_t)$—given that $\mathbf{X}_t \overset{L}{\longrightarrow} N(\boldsymbol{v}_t, \mathbf{V}_t)$. Furthermore, $\mathbf{X}_t \overset{L}{\longrightarrow} N(\boldsymbol{v}_t^*, \mathbf{V}_t^*)$ is the conditional distribution of $\mathbf{X}_t$ given survival to $t + 1$. For a derivation of these relations, see Woodbury and Manton (1983) and Manton, Stallard, and Woodbury (1986). For disability, the process is not Gaussian due to constraints on $\mathbf{B}$. Diffusion (Σ_t) is a time-dependent variable with variance related to that of Bernoulli trials.

To represent multiple causes of death, we use the crude mortality rate for c_k at t, $u_{kt}(\mathbf{x}_t) = \mu_{0k} + \mathbf{b}_k^T \cdot \mathbf{x}_t + \frac{1}{2} \mathbf{x}_t^T \mathbf{B}_k \mathbf{x}_t) \exp(\theta \text{ age}_t)$ and, using $\mathbf{B}_{kt} = \mathbf{B}_k \exp (\theta \text{ age}_t)$, observe

(29)
$$\bar{\mu}_{kt} = E[\mu_{kt}(\mathbf{x}_t) \mid T > t] = 2 \mu_{kt}[(\boldsymbol{v}_t + \boldsymbol{v}_t^*)/2] - [\mu_{kt}(\boldsymbol{v}_t)$$
$$+ \mu_{kt}(\boldsymbol{v}_t^*)]/2 + \frac{1}{2} \ln |\mathbf{I} + \mathbf{V}_t \mathbf{B}_t| \text{ tr } [\mathbf{V}_t \mathbf{B}_{kt}] / \text{tr}[\mathbf{V}_t \mathbf{B}_t]$$

(see Manton, Stallard, et al. 1992), with life tables generated by

(30)
$$l_{t+1} = l_t \exp \left(-\sum_{k=1}^{K} \bar{\mu}_{kt}\right).$$

To represent the effects of l_t of eliminating cause k in the dependent competing risk framework, we set the force of mortality for the kth cause, μ_{kt}, equal to zero in

$$\mu(\text{age}_t, \mathbf{x}_t) = (\mu_0 + \mathbf{b}^T \cdot \mathbf{x}_t + \frac{1}{2} \mathbf{x}_t^T \mathbf{B} \mathbf{x}_t) \exp (\theta \text{ age}_t),$$

where

$$\mu_0 = \sum_{k=1}^{K} \mu_{0k}, \quad \mathbf{b} = \sum_{k=1}^{K} \mathbf{b}_k, \quad \text{and } \mathbf{B} = \sum_{k=1}^{K} \mathbf{B}_k.$$

For disability dynamics, instead of equation (26), parameters are obtained by maximizing the conditional (on the g_{ik}) likelihood

(31)
$$L = \prod_i \prod_j \prod_l \left(\sum_k g_{ik} \cdot \lambda_{kjl}\right)^{x_{ijl}}.$$

Here

$$x_{ijl} = \begin{cases} 1 & \text{if individual } i \text{ has response } l \text{ on variable } j, \\ 0 & \text{otherwise,} \end{cases}$$

and $\mathbf{g}^{(i)} = (g_{i1}, \ldots, g_{iK})$, where $g_{ik} \geq 0$ and $\sum_{k=1}^{K} g_{ik} = 1$. For a discussion of computation, see Manton and Stallard (1988).

With multiple $g_{ik \cdot t}$ for each individual (i.e., eq. [31] is expanded by disaggregating individual observations into episodes based on assessment at each t), and λ_{kjl}s fixed over t, the discrete time analogue of diffusion in B is

(32) $$\mathbf{g}_{i(t+1)} = \mathbf{C}_t \mathbf{g}_{it} + \mathbf{e}_{i(t+1)},$$

where $\mathbf{C}_t$ is—for each t—a $K \times K$ matrix of coefficients which are functionally equivalent to regression coefficients subject to constraints that each $\mathbf{C}_t$ be a stochastic matrix and $g_{ik(t+1)} \geq 0$, $\sum_{k=1}^{K} g_{ik} = 1$. For $h \neq k$, c_{hkt} is the movement in B—away from profile k and toward h during $[t, t+1]$. Similarly, $1 - c_{kkt}$ is the total age/time-dependent movement from k during $[t, t + 1]$.

2.3   Forecasts

2.3.1   Data

The first analysis uses as state variables physiological risk factors measured in the Framingham Study (Dawber 1980) for 2,336 males and 2,873 females aged 29–62 years in 1950. The risk factors, measured biennally, were age (years), sex, diastolic blood pressure (DBP; mm Hg), pulse pressure (PP; mm Hg), serum cholesterol (SC; mg/dl), vital capacity index (VCI; cl/m²), hemoglobin (Hb; dg%) or hematocrit (Ht), smoking (CIG; cigarettes per day), body mass index (BMI; hg/m²), blood sugar (BLDS; mg%), ventricular (heart) rate (VRATE), and left ventricular hypertrophy (LVH).

Disability assessments were obtained from the 1982, 1984, and 1989 National Long-Term Care Surveys (NLTCS). Twenty-seven disability measures, listed in table 2.1, were obtained from all chronically disabled persons interviewed in the two community samples of the 1982 and 1984 NLTCS ($N = 11,535$). These were used in a GoM analysis to produce a six-profile solution defined by the λ_{kjl} in table 2.1. The 1989 NLTCS is used to confirm forecasts based on 1982 and 1984.

The profiles in table 2.1 may be interpreted as follows:

- 1 is "healthy" with few chronic impairments,
- 2 has no Activities of Daily Living (ADL) and few physical impairments but has Instrument Activities of Daily Living (IADL) impairments associated with cognition (e.g., phoning, managing money, and taking medication),
- 3 has no ADL and few IADL impairments but moderate physical limitations (e.g., climbing stairs and holding, reaching for, and grasping objects),
- 4 has problems with bathing, several IADLs, and more physical functions,
- 5 has several ADL and IADL impairments (but not involving cognition, cf. profile 2; profile 4 had more upper body impairment), and
- 6 is highly impaired on multiple ADLs and IADLS.

Thus, the profiles describe different dimensions of function, e.g., cognitive impairment (profile 2), upper (profile 4) and lower body function (profile 5), and mixed or combined disability and frailty. There is a rough tendency for disability to increase across profiles.

Table 2.1 Estimates of Response Profile Probabilities ($\lambda_{kjl} \times 100$) for the Combined 1982 and 1984 NLTCS Sample (11,535 complete detailed interviews)

Variable	Observed Frequency	Healthy (1)	Moderate Cognitive Impairment (2)	Mild Instrumental and Physical Impairment (3)	Serious Physical Impairment (4)	Moderate ADL and Serious Physical Impairment (5)	Frail (6)
ADL—Needs help:							
Eating	6.1	0.0	0.0	0.0	0.0	0.0	46.2
Getting in/out of bed	26.3	0.0	0.0	0.0	0.0	76.7	100.0
Getting around inside	40.6	0.0	0.0	0.0	0.0	100.0	100.0
Dressing	19.8	0.0	0.0	0.0	0.0	0.0	100.0
Bathing	44.0	0.0	0.0	0.0	42.0	100.0	100.0
Using toilet	21.3	0.0	0.0	0.0	0.0	41.5	100.0
Bedfast	0.8	0.0	0.0	0.0	0.0	0.0	5.3
No inside activity	1.4	0.0	0.0	0.0	0.0	0.0	9.8
Wheelchair-fast	3.4	0.0	0.0	0.0	0.0	0.0	23.0
IADL—Needs help:							
With heavy work	76.8	24.1	100.0	100.0	100.0	100.0	100.0
With light work	24.2	0.0	0.0	0.0	0.0	0.0	100.0
With laundry	46.1	0.0	100.0	18.2	100.0	45.3	100.0
With cooking	33.0	0.0	100.0	0.0	0.0	0.0	100.0
With grocery shopping	63.3	0.0	100.0	0.0	100.0	100.0	100.0
Getting about outside	63.5	0.0	52.7	55.1	100.0	100.0	100.0
Traveling	61.6	0.0	100.0	0.0	100.0	100.0	100.0
Managing money	29.7	0.0	100.0	0.0	0.0	0.0	100.0
Taking medicine	24.6	0.0	93.3	0.0	0.0	0.0	100.0
Making telephone calls	17.5	0.0	83.0	0.0	0.0	0.0	96.0

Function limitations—
How much difficulty do you have:

Climbing (one flight of stairs)

None	15.8	45.3	20.3	0.0	0.0	0.0	0.0
Some	28.9	54.7	79.7	22.1	0.0	0.0	0.0
Very difficult	33.0	0.0	0.0	77.9	53.1	67.1	7.0
Cannot at all	22.3	0.0	0.0	0.0	46.9	32.9	93.0

Bending (e.g., putting on socks)

None	41.4	100.0	100.0	0.0	0.0	100.0	0.0
Some	28.5	0.0	0.0	100.0	0.0	0.0	0.0
Very difficult	19.0	0.0	0.0	0.0	100.0	0.0	0.0
Cannot at all	11.1	0.0	0.0	0.0	0.0	0.0	100.0

Holding a 10 lb. package

None	26.4	77.4	45.2	0.0	0.0	0.0	0.0
Some	17.8	22.6	54.8	21.0	0.0	22.9	0.0
Very difficult	16.7	0.0	0.0	79.0	0.0	0.0	0.0
Cannot at all	39.0	0.0	0.0	0.0	100.0	77.1	100.0

Reaching overhead

None	54.0	100.0	100.0	0.0	0.0	100.0	0.0
Some	21.8	0.0	0.0	100.0	0.0	0.0	37.6
Very difficult	14.7	0.0	0.0	0.0	77.5	0.0	0.0
Cannot at all	9.5	0.0	0.0	0.0	22.5	0.0	62.4

Combing hair

None	69.8	100.0	100.0	0.0	0.0	100.0	0.0
Some	17.1	0.0	0.0	100.0	35.1	0.0	37.4
Very difficult	7.6	0.0	0.0	0.0	65.0	0.0	0.0
Cannot at all	5.5	0.0	0.0	0.0	0.0	0.0	62.6

Washing hair

None	53.4	100.0	100.0	0.0	0.0	100.0	0.0
Some	15.2	0.0	0.0	100.0	0.0	0.0	0.0
Very difficult	10.0	0.0	0.0	100.0	100.0	0.0	0.0

(continued)

Table 2.1   (continued)

Variable	Observed Frequency	Profiles					
		Healthy (1)	Moderate Cognitive Impairment (2)	Mild Instrumental and Physical Impairment (3)	Serious Physical Impairment (4)	Moderate ADL and Serious Physical Impairment (5)	Frail (6)
Cannot at all	21.4	0.0	0.0	0.0	0.0	0.0	100.0
Grasping an object							
None	64.8	100.0	100.0	0.0	0.0	100.0	27.3
Some	20.8	0.0	0.0	100.0	0.0	0.0	33.6
Very difficult	10.5	0.0	0.0	0.0	94.4	0.0	10.8
Cannot at all	3.9	0.0	0.0	0.0	5.6	0.0	28.3
Can you see well enough to read a newspaper?	73.1	100.0	0.0	100.0	71.3	100.0	46.4
Mean scores ($\bar{g}_k \times 100$)		33.7	11.9	13.5	9.0	16.5	15.2

We reanalyzed the 27 items, using the 16,485 respondents to the combined 1982, 1984, and 1989 NLTCS. The λ_{kjl} for the three surveys are in table 2.2. There is a high degree of similarity in the six profiles between the two solutions; i.e., B_{82-84} (table 2.1) and B_{82-89} (table 2.2) are similar. The primary difference is fewer IADL impairments involving outside mobility for profile 3 in table 2.2. Variables whose coefficients are on the boundary of B(i.e., $\lambda_{kjl} = 1.0$ or 0.0) are highly stable because the solution, given the constraints of M, is "hyper"-efficient. Thus, B is not changed much by the extension to 1989. The trait-weighted prevalence of the six profiles, 1982–89, at the bottom of table 2.2 for both solutions, also shows a high degree of similarity.

Finally, national population counts, together with growth rates, r_t, in year t, were derived from census estimates for ages 30–100 for 1986. Projections of the population aged 30–31 between 1988 and 2080 (Spencer 1989) determined the size of new cohorts at they "age in."

2.3.2   Risk Factor Projections/Simulations

For projections, we need initial conditions, descriptions of two-year changes in risk factors (24), and hazard rates for cancer, cardiovascular disease, and "other" causes ($K = 3$). In table 2.3 we present sex-specific life-table parameters for selected ages, for dependent *and* independent "elimination" of CVD generated using equation (28).

Under independence, age-specific risk factor means do *not* change. With dependence, means change due to decreased *selection* of persons with adverse CVD risk factor values. For males aged 90, mean BLDS rose to 115.0 (from 111.9) because CVD elimination allows diabetics to live longer. Mortality for causes dependent on the same risk factors increase. Thus, independence overstates the effect of eliminating CVD, with bias increasing as l_t decreases. By age 90, the bias for males is 39 percent (i.e., 3.1 vs. 4.3 years); 17.6 percent for females.

If there were no mortality change, the male population aged 85+ would grow 75 percent (to 1.4 million) by 2080 (the female population, 71 percent to 3.6 million) because of increased cohort size. This is less than the 9.8 million in the lowest Census Bureau Series 19 projection (mortality changes are 50 percent of the middle variant). Series 19 uses low, and Series 23 uses middle, fertility/immigration assumptions. We used fertility/immigration assumptions from Series 23. Life expectancy at age 30 (table 2.3) is similar to the United States in 1986 (i.e., males 43.8 vs. 43.9 and females 49.0 vs. 50.0). In 2080 the no mortality change scenario for the population aged 65+ is 19 percent lower than Census Bureau Series 23 (49.7 vs. 60.9 million). The relative difference for persons aged 85+ is larger (54 percent; 5.0 vs. 10.9 million). The Series 19 projections and the forecast with no mortality change are similar for the 65+ population (49.5 vs. 49.7 million).

Mortality is declining for the U.S. population aged 65+ and for those 85+ (i.e., for those aged 85+ it declined 8.6 percent from 1989 to 1991; NCHS

Table 2.2   Estimates of Response Profile Probabilities ($\lambda_{kjr} \times 100$) for the Combined 1982, 1984, and 1989 NLTCS ($N = 16,485$)

Variable	Observed Frequency	Profiles					
		Healthy (1)	Moderate Cognitive Impairment (2)	Mild Instrumental and Physical Impairment (3)	Serious Physical Impairment (4)	Moderate ADL and Serious Physical Impairment (5)	Frail (6)
ADL—Needs help							
Eating	7.0	0.0	0.0	0.0	0.0	0.0	55.2
Getting in/out of bed	39.9	0.0	0.0	0.0	0.0	100.0	100.0
Getting around inside	39.9	0.0	0.0	0.0	0.0	100.0	100.0
Dressing	19.4	0.0	0.0	0.0	0.0	0.0	100.0
Bathing	43.1	0.0	0.0	0.0	0.0	100.0	100.0
Using toilet	21.7	0.0	0.0	0.0	0.0	48.9	100.0
Bedfast	0.8	0.0	0.0	0.0	0.0	0.0	5.5
No inside activity	1.5	0.0	0.0	0.0	0.0	0.0	10.2
Wheelchair fast	7.0	0.0	0.0	0.0	0.0	19.9	25.8
IADL—Needs help							
With heavy work	71.9	14.5	100.0	100.0	100.0	100.0	100.0
With light work	22.6	0.0	35.5	0.0	0.0	0.0	100.0
With laundry	41.5	0.0	100.0	0.0	100.0	36.4	100.0
With cooking	29.8	0.0	100.0	0.0	0.0	0.0	100.0
With grocery shopping	56.9	0.0	100.0	0.0	100.0	100.0	100.0
Getting about outside	59.1	0.0	61.9	0.0	100.0	100.0	100.0
Traveling	52.9	0.0	100.0	0.0	100.0	100.0	80.3
Managing money	26.8	0.0	100.0	0.0	0.0	0.0	100.0
Taking medicine	23.5	0.0	100.0	0.0	0.0	0.0	100.0
Making telephone calls	16.0	0.0	87.3	0.0	0.0	0.0	85.5

Function limitations—How much difficulty do you have:

Climbing (one flight of stairs)							
None	18.6	53.5	0.0	0.0	0.0	0.0	0.0
Some	29.1	46.6	88.5	33.8	0.0	0.0	0.0
Very difficult	31.4	0.0	11.5	66.2	50.7	73.0	10.9
Cannot at all	21.0	0.0	0.0	0.0	49.3	27.0	89.1
Bending (e.g., putting on socks)							
None	43.5	100.0	100.0	0.0	0.0	100.0	0.0
Some	27.9	0.0	0.0	100.0	0.0	0.0	0.0
Very difficult	18.0	0.0	0.0	0.0	100.0	0.0	0.0
Cannot at all	10.6	0.0	0.0	0.0	0.0	0.0	100.0
Holding a 10 lb. package							
None	29.6	84.2	0.0	0.0	0.0	0.0	0.0
Some	18.1	15.9	58.6	38.9	0.0	24.9	0.0
Very difficult	15.9	0.0	41.4	61.1	0.0	30.3	0.0
Cannot at all	36.4	0.0	0.0	0.0	100.0	44.7	100.0
Reaching overhead							
None	56.1	100.0	100.0	0.0	0.0	100.0	0.0
Some	21.2	0.0	0.0	100.0	0.0	0.0	34.3
Very difficult	13.9	0.0	0.0	0.0	76.8	0.0	14.1
Cannot at all	8.8	0.0	0.0	0.0	23.3	0.0	51.6
Combing hair							
None	71.6	100.0	100.0	0.0	0.0	100.0	0.0
Some	16.0	0.00	0.00	100.0	42.77	0.00	33.68
Very difficult	7.0	0.00	0.00	0.00	57.23	0.00	11.54
Cannot at all	5.4	0.0	0.0	0.0	0.0	0.0	54.8

(*continued*)

Table 2.2   (continued)

		Profiles					
Variable	Observed Frequency	Healthy (1)	Moderate Cognitive Impairment (2)	Mild Instrumental and Physical Impairment (3)	Serious Physical Impairment (4)	Moderate ADL and Serious Physical Impairment (5)	Frail (6)
Washing hair							
None	55.8	100.0	100.0	0.0	0.0	100.0	0.0
Some	14.8	0.0	0.0	100.0	0.0	0.0	0.0
Very Difficult	9.4	0.0	0.0	0.0	100.0	0.0	0.0
Cannot at all	20.0	0.0	0.0	0.0	0.0	0.0	100.0
Grasping an object							
None	66.0	100.0	100.0	0.0	0.0	100.0	24.6
Some	20.3	0.0	0.0	100.0	0.0	0.0	34.3
Very Difficult	10.1	0.0	0.0	0.0	95.5	0.0	14.8
Cannot at all	3.6	0.0	0.0	0.0	4.5	0.0	26.3
Can you see well enough to read a newspaper?	74.3	100.0	0.0	100.0	100.0	100.0	45.4
Mean scores ($\bar{g}_k \times 100$)							
1982–84 NLTCS[a]		33.7	11.9	13.5	9.0	16.5	15.2
1982, 1984, and 1989 NLTCS		34.4	11.6	13.1	9.1	16.7	15.3

[a]From table 2.1.

Table 2.3   Observed (baseline) and Cause-Elimination Life-Table Values Assuming Independence and Dependence of Competing Risks: CVD Elimination for Male and Females, Framingham Heart Study (20-year follow-up)

	age,	e_t	PP	DBP	BMI	SC	BLDS	Hb	VCI	CIG
					Males					
Baseline	30	43.9	45.0	80.0	260.0	215.0	80.0	145.0	140.0	14.0
Dependence		53.9								
Independence		54.8								
Baseline	50	25.7	47.7	83.3	276.0	241.1	83.7	149.6	127.4	12.9
Dependence		34.9	47.7	83.4	276.1	241.2	83.7	149.6	147.4	13.0
Independence		35.8								
Baseline	70	10.8	63.0	82.8	266.1	223.0	98.5	150.7	100.8	4.9
Dependence		17.7	63.3	83.0	265.7	223.4	99.0	150.7	100.2	5.2
Independence		18.8								
Baseline	90	2.9	77.3	80.8	250.3	204.7	111.9	151.9	78.0	0.0
Dependence		6.0	79.4	81.7	242.3	205.6	115.0	151.3	73.3	0.0[a]
Independence		7.2								
Baseline	110	1.1	88.0	78.5	254.0	188.9	120.7	155.7	70.4	0.0
Dependence		1.8	96.2	80.5	225.8	199.0	133.3	154.4	53.1	0.0
Independence		2.7								
					Females					
Baseline	30	50.0	45.0	75.0	235.0	200.0	80.0	125.0	115.0	8.0
Dependence		56.9								
Independence		57.3								
Baseline	50	30.4	48.9	80.0	256.0	246.2	81.9	135.4	105.7	10.1
Dependence		38.0	48.9	80.0	256.1	246.3	81.9	135.4	105.7	10.1
Independence		38.5								
Baseline	70	13.7	68.8	83.0	252.5	255.9	94.2	141.8	78.1	6.8
Dependence		20.3	68.9	83.0	252.7	256.1	94.3	141.9	77.8	6.9
Independence		20.8								
Baseline	90	3.6	86.9	83.9	234.7	263.6	105.1	146.1	53.5	1.1
Dependence		7.0	88.2	84.7	233.4	262.7	106.1	146.5	51.0	1.4
Independence		7.6								
Baseline	110	1.1	99.6	80.2	220.1	275.6	113.0	148.3	41.4	0.0
Dependence		1.8	105.9	84.3	210.6	271.2	118.8	149.2	29.4	0.0
Independence		2.3								

[a]Cigarette smoking was fixed at zero to prevent negative values.

1992). Declines are due, in part, to observed risk factor trends from 1960 to 1987, where smoking, cholesterol and hypertension among the U.S. elderly (age 65–74) population declined (e.g., Popkin, Haines, and Patterson 1992). Further improvement can be expected due to smoking reduction (Fiore et al. 1989), increased education (Feldman et al. 1989), and adoption of healthier life styles (e.g., more physical activity and improved nutrition) by elderly cohorts.

For our projection we had to establish "optimal" risk factor values for total mortality. The total mortality function is generated as the sum of three cause-specific functions because certain risk factors (e.g., SC) had different relations with different causes (e.g., with CVD and cancer; Neaton et al. 1992). The cause-specific relations of risk factors is important in assessing "population" versus "high-risk" public health interventions. Indeed, "population" intervention for SC may increase mortality for a portion of the population (Frank et al. 1992). There have been questions raised about the evidence demonstrating the efficacy of SC reduction (Ravnskov 1992). There is less controversy about controlling SC by diet and exercise (which affects other metabolic parameters) than about the population use of SC-lowering drugs—especially those affecting liver enzymes (Oliver 1991). Consequently, we used the quadratic mortality model to determine the values that would increase life expectancy most, based on the 34-year Framingham follow-up. These are presented in table 2.4. Differences between the 20-year and 34-year data suggest what effects are like at the latter ages observed in the 34-year data.

There are differences between the optimal profiles for the 20-year and 34-year data on SC. This is because the quadratic surface for SC has a flat interior region due to the relations of SC to different diseases (Frank et al. 1992; Neaton et al. 1992). The additional 14 years of follow-up decreases the "optimal" male cholesterol value. The female cholesterol value remains higher (Epstein 1992). Part of the reason for the variability is the strong correlation over time of metabolic parameters. For example, BLDS, BMI, and VCI increased for males when SC declined.

The consequences of risk factor interventions, using parameters estimated from 20-year and 34-year Framingham data are in table 2.5. The mean and variance for CIG for smoking elimination are fixed at 0.0. This only modestly increases the population, because few smokers survive to age 80. Second, risk factor means were fixed at "optimal" levels for each cohort in 2006 (e.g., interventions for persons aged 30 in 1986 were introduced at age 50 in 2006, for those aged 50 in 1986 at age 70 in 2006, etc.). Life tables were calculated with ν_{30} set to "optimal" risk factor levels, $\hat{\mathbf{x}}_{it}$ and $\mathbf{R} = \mathbf{I}$, $\mathbf{u}_t = \mathbf{O}$, and $\Sigma = \mathbf{O}$. $\mathbf{V}_{t_0}$ was not changed. The male population in 2040 increased from 21.6 to 36.0 million at age 65 and from 1.6 to 9.8 million at age 85. Next, we partially (50% or 75%), or completely, eliminated variance by pre- and post-multiplying $\mathbf{V}_{t_0}$ by a diagonal matrix; Σ is recalculated. The male population aged 65+ increased to 62.1 million by 2040. Males aged 85+ increased to 25.4 million by 2040, and to 36.0 million in 2080. Females had similar increases (i.e., 28.5 million in 2040 and 37.9 million in 2080). Projections based on the 20-year and 34-year optimal risk factor profiles are similar.

In table 2.6, the highest census projections (Series 9) are presented along with "optimal" projections based on 34-year data (profile 3, table 2.4).

In the "optimal" case, of 177 million persons aged 0–44 in 1986, 61 percent of females and 33 percent of males survive to age 85 in 2080. The male population aged 65+ is projected to be 74.6 million in the optimal case versus 52.5

Table 2.4   **Risk Factor Means and Optimal Means (for eight variables, 20-year follow-up, and for ten variables, 34-year follow-up, Framingham data sets) Used in Projections**

Variable	Males				Females			
	Profile 1 (20-year)	Profile 2 (34-year)	Profile 3 (34-year)	Observed Means at Age 30	Profile 1 (20-year)	Profile 2 (34-year)	Profile 3 (34-year)	Observed Means at Age 30
1. PP (mm Hg)	32	35.5	27.8	45 (13.7)	59	47.2	46.8	45 (15.5)
2. DBP (mm Hg)	82	74.4	80.5	80 (12.5)	71	78.0	78.0	75 (12.3)
3. BMI (hg/m²)	227	254.5	257.5	260 (34.4)	274	267.3	267.6	235 (44.7)
4. SC (mg/dl)	260	211.8	172.8	215 (41.4)	257	222.0	221.7	200 (42.9)
5. BLDS (mg%)	58	57.5	101.8	80 (29.6)	107	124.9	124.4	80 (22.1)
6. Ht (%)[a]	–	46.8	47.5	47 (3.1)	–	44.6	44.6	44 (3.0)
Hb (dg%)	152	–	–	145 (10.2)	133	–	–	125 (10.2)
7. VCI (cl/m²)	152	145.9	160.1	140 (18.9)	100	121.7	121.6	115 (17.0)
8. CIG (cigarettes per day)	0	0.0	0.0	14 (11.5)	0	0.0	0.0	8 (8.1)
9. LVH	–	0.0	0.0	0.06 (0.0)	–	0.0	0.0	0.1 (0.0)
10. VRATE (per minute)	–	61.3	67.4	77.0 (11.8)	–	55.6	55.5	77.0 (11.6)
e_{30}		70.9	82.5			73.2	73.5	

Notes: Standard deviations in parentheses.

[a]Hermatocrit value used in 34-year projections.

million in Series 9. The optimal male population aged 85+ is 38.3 million versus 13.9 million according to Series 9. Similar results occur for females aged 85+ (i.e., 39.7 vs. 20.0 million). Comparison of Series 5 and 9 projections showed that fertility/immigration produced 10 percent of the age 85+ and 18 percent of the age 65+ population increase in Series 9.

Projections of persons aged 85+ for 2040 by Guralnik, Yanagishita, and Schneider (1988), assuming a 2 percent per year mortality decline, are a third higher than Series 9 projections (i.e., 23.5 vs. 17.9 million). Ahlburg and Vaupel (1990) projected 72 million persons over 85 in 2080—similar to our optimal case (78.0 million). Their projections use a 2 percent per year mortality reduction and high fertility and immigration rates. Using middle fertility/

Table 2.5   **Alternative Projections (in millions of Persons) for 2040, 2060, and 2080: 20-Year and 34-Year Framingham Data**

	2040	2060	2080
	Males		
Age 65+			
20-Year data			
Baseline[a]	21.6	21.6	20.7
Smoking eliminated	23.5	23.6	22.7
Reduction of profile 1[b] risk factor variance by:			
0%[c]	36.0	36.8	35.8
50%	51.5	55.5	54.3
75%	58.7	66.3	65.0
100%	62.1	72.0	71.0
34-Year data			
100% Reduction in variance (profile 2[b])	63.3	72.9	71.7
Age 85+			
20-Year data			
Baseline[a]	1.6	1.3	1.4
Smoking eliminated	1.7	1.5	1.6
Reduction of profile 1 risk factor variance by:			
0%[c]	9.8	9.8	10.0
50%	17.7	21.9	22.2
75%	22.9	30.4	30.8
100%	25.4	35.3	36.0
34-Year data			
100% Reduction in variance (profile 2)	26.4	36.2	36.7
	Females		
Age 65+			
20-Year data			
Baseline[a]	30.2	29.8	28.9
Smoking eliminated	31.4	31.1	30.2
Reduction of profile 1 risk factor variance by:			
0%[c]	43.9	45.1	44.1
50%	56.8	61.2	59.9
75%	62.1	68.9	67.7
100%	65.4	74.3	73.3
34-Year data			
100% Reduction in variance (profile 2)	67.3	74.4	73.3
Age 85+			
20-Year data			
Baseline[a]	3.8	3.3	3.6
Smoking eliminated	4.1	3.7	4.0
Reduction of profile 1 risk factor variance by:			
0%[c]	13.3	14.5	14.8
50%	21.8	26.3	26.5
75%	25.8	32.8	33.0
100%	28.5	37.5	37.9
34-Year data			
100% Reduction in variance (profile 2)	31.2	37.8	37.9

[a]See table 2.3.

[b]Optimal values for 20-year and 34-year data are presented in table 2.4.

[c]Changes in risk factor means only.

Table 2.6　Comparison of Population Projections Based on Control of Multiple Risk Factors and on the High Census Bureau Variant (millions)

Age	Males					Females					Total				
	1990	2010	2040	2060	2080	1990	2010	2040	2060	2080	1990	2010	2040	2060	2080
Risk Factor Control[1] *(20-Year Delay)*															
65+	13.0	24.9	68.1	75.6	74.6	18.9	26.5	70.0	77.5	76.3	31.9	51.4	138.1	153.0	151.1
85+	0.9	4.6	31.1	37.8	38.3	2.3	5.8	32.6	39.5	39.7	3.2	10.4	63.7	77.3	78.0
Surviving to age 85 from 65[a] (%)	(6.7)	(18.5)	(45.7)	(50.0)	(51.3)	(12.2)	(21.9)	(46.6)	(51.0)	(52.0)	(10.0)	(20.2)	(46.1)	(50.5)	(51.6)
Census Bureau Highest Variant (Series 9)[2]															
65+	11.8	18.1	37.1	43.1	52.5	17.5	24.4	45.5	51.7	61.4	29.3	42.5	82.6	94.8	113.9
85+	0.8	2.2	6.6	10.0	13.9	2.1	4.9	11.2	15.7	20.0	2.9	7.2	17.9	25.6	33.9
Surviving to age 85 from 65[a] (%)	(6.8)	(12.2)	(17.8)	(23.2)	(26.5)	(12.0)	(20.1)	(24.6)	(30.4)	(32.6)	(9.9)	(16.9)	(21.7)	(27.0)	(29.8)

Sources: For risk factor control, Duke University, Center for Demographic Studies; for Census Bureau highest variant, Spencer (1989).
[a]Figures in parentheses are percentage of persons over age 65 that are age 85+.

immigration assumptions, the 2 percent mortality decline projects 58 million persons aged 85+ in 2080. Thus, the optimal projections produce mortality declines averaging more than 2 percent per year. The 2 percent assumption generates a life expectancy of 100 years in 2080. "Optimal" interventions project life expectancies 3–12 years higher.

In the "optimal" case, senescence is assumed unchanged (θ is not altered) and no diseases are "cured." The Gompertz in equation (5) (θ is 8.05 percent for males, 8.12 percent for females) limits the life expectancy for persons with optimal risk factor profiles. Without using the 10 risk factors in the mortality function, the θ for the 34-year data was 9.4 percent for males and 10.0 percent for females. Thus, the 10 risk factors significantly reduced (by 14.4 percent and 19.0 percent) the effects (θ) of unobserved variables on the age dependence of mortality. Since θ is a nonlinear parameter, the proportion of the age dependence explained by the 10 risk factors is much higher than the decline in θ; about 62 percent of male and 69 percent of female age dependence of mortality was due to the risk factors.

Without θ, the coefficients of the mortality function are not only biased, but do not represent the age variable equilibrium of the process (e.g., Manton 1988) because the risk factors contain "age" effects that bias them away from the true homeostatic point. Since more persons survive to advanced ages, and with improved risk factor profiles, the probability of an individual living to ages higher than currently observed increases.

2.3.3   Projections Based on Disability Dynamics

Equations (31) and (32) in section 2.2.6 represent cohort changes in disability with age and mortality after an index age (e.g., $t_0 = 65$). To project the distribution of the disabled population to a future time, multiple cohort projections are needed. Specifically, for, say, 2020 we might consider the active life expectancy (ALE) for all persons aged 65+ at that date. To do this, we need to evaluate life-table equations for a cohort aged 65 in 1990 (i.e., the 1925 birth cohort), a cohort ages 67 in 1990 (i.e., the 1923 birth cohort), and so forth, up to the oldest age (e.g., the cohort aged 115 in 1990, or the birth cohort of 1875). The cohort life-table parameters weighted by its size in 1990 can, for the appropriate age and date, be assembled to form the cross-sectional population. Specifically, cohort calculations must be made from age-specific start points in, say, 1990 and run to 2020 using equations (27) and (28). For the population aged 65 in 1990, life-table calculations (population weighted) must be run from age 65 (in 1990) to age 95 (in 2020). In 2020, the ratio l_{95}/l_{65}, generates the number of persons surviving to 2020. Multiplying by $v_{k(95)}$, the mean of scores on profile k, generates the number of survivors aged 95 in 2020 in each disability class. For the population aged 70 in 1990, l_{100}/l_{70} generates the number of survivors to age 100 in 2020; multiplied by $v_{k(100)}$, this produces the number in each disability class. Similar calculations are performed for other age groups. These are summed to get the total population aged 65+ in a given disability state at a given date.

In interpreting the projections, it is important that individual membership in disability states are graded and multidimensional. This stabilizes projections but means that "counts" are sums of the g_{ik}, not the number of individuals with nonzero scores. If the average score among persons with nonzero g_{ik} is, say, .5, then the projected count is 50 percent of the number of such persons. Alternatively, two persons, each with 50 percent disability, are equivalent to one person with 100 percent disability; i.e., counts are weighted by traits associated with each profile. Since the k profiles form partitions for each individual, the sums of the g_{ik} partition the projected population.

Additionally, we do not want parameters for cross-sectional life tables. We need to simulate a current cohort's future experience. Estimates from the 1982, 1984, and 1989 NLTCS suggest that the proportion of the elderly population remaining nondisabled increased. The population aged 65+ grew 10 percent from 1984 to 1989, while the disabled population grew 6.8 percent (Manton, Corder, and Stallard 1992). The problem is to modify $\mathbf{C}_t$ to reflect a reasonable cohort scenario. The scenario is implemented by altering sample weights to reflect assumptions about cohort disability changes. In our cohort scenario, we assumed that half of 80 percent of the transitions to a disability state from the nondisabled, screened population were prevented and that two-thirds of 20 percent of that population with changes had disability prevented. The two adjustments, implemented by adjusting sample weights, imply 53 percent of the disability occurring in the younger nondisabled population is prevented. By imposing interventions in the screened, nondisabled population we simulated the prevention of disability in a population that (*a*) is younger than the NLTCS (Medicare-eligible elderly disabled) population on average, (*b*) has not had disability for a long time, i.e., it must be newly incident, and (*c*) tends to be at a relatively low level of disability. This produces a life table that matches the Social Security Administration (SSA) cohort life expectancy projected for persons age 65 in 1984 (Social Security Administration [SSA], 1983). Since the second NLTCS was done in 1984, the scenario produced results very close to the SSA projections. The cohort life expectancies also match period life tables projected by the SSA (1989) for the approximate midpoint (i.e., 2005) of the projection interval. The intervention produced dynamics ($\mathbf{C}_t$) (see eq. [32]) consistent with the monthly disability dynamics estimated from the Medicare component of the Social/Health Maintenance Organization (S/HMO) evaluation. Thus, the scenario accurately reflects short-term disability changes.

Projections can be altered by modifying the $g_{ik \cdot t}$ and generating new $\mathbf{C}_t$. Thus, the effects of disease intervention on disability may be forecast. In the projections, we did not change disease prevalence, but we assumed that the income and education distribution for persons aged 65–69 would be applied for persons at all ages in the cohort life table.

Table 2.7 contains sex-specific life-table parameters for selected ages for (*a*) cohort simulations, (*b*) the forecasting model calibrated with the 1982, 1984,

Table 2.7   Simulation, Baseline Cohort Life Tables, and Age-Specific Meaning $g_{ik} \times 100$

Age		l_t	ΔC/S[a] ΔI/S	e_t	Profiles 1	2	3	4	5	6	Institutional
				Males							
65	Simulation	100,000		15.4	92.7	0.7	1.1	0.8	2.2	1.5	1.0
	Cohort	100,000	0.0%	15.6	92.2	4.0	0.7	0.7	1.1	1.0	0.3
	Income and education	100,000	0.0%	16.8	92.7	0.7	1.4	0.9	1.9	1.7	0.7
75	Simulation	66,272		10.7	91.6	1.3	1.1	0.7	1.9	1.7	1.8
	Cohort	68,956	4.1%	10.3	85.4	8.5	0.8	71.1	1.8	1.3	1.2
	Income and education	68,958	4.1%	12.2	90.2	2.1	1.2	0.6	2.4	2.0	1.5
85	Simulation	32,587		6.6	78.5	4.6	2.0	1.7	3.9	4.2	5.1
	Cohort	32,886	1.0%	6.1	73.1	12.1	1.3	2.6	3.5	2.4	5.1
	Income and education	37,374	14.7%	8.1	75.7	6.2	2.1	1.5	5.5	4.8	4.2
95	Simulation	7,061		4.4	65.3	6.0	2.7	1.4	6.5	7.3	10.9
	Cohort	6,262	-11.3%	3.2	56.8	12.6	1.6	5.6	6.6	5.8	11.1
	Income and education	10,894	54.3%	5.8	63.6	7.4	2.9	1.3	7.9	8.1	8.9
105	Simulation	655		3.5	68.1	6.0	2.7	1.3	6.3	6.6	9.0
	Cohort	198	-69.8%	2.2	50.0	19.1	0.2	4.8	12.6	3.3	10.0
	Income and education	1,780	171.8%	4.8	65.2	7.3	2.9	1.2	7.9	7.7	8.0

Females

Age											
65	Simulation	100,000		20.5	91.2	0.9	1.7	2.2	1.4	1.4	1.1
	Cohort	100,000	0.0%	20.6	92.1	3.4	2.0	0.7	1.2	0.8	0.8
	Income and education	100,000	0.0%	23.7	91.8	0.9	1.7	1.7	1.5	1.3	1.2
75	Simulation	80,560		14.2	87.6	1.5	2.3	1.8	2.7	1.7	2.5
	Cohort	82,201	2.0%	13.9	84.0	7.8	1.3	1.1	2.2	1.4	2.2
	Income and education	84,340	4.7%	17.3	83.4	3.7	2.6	1.6	3.3	3.2	2.2
85	Simulation	53,931		8.5	68.8	4.4	3.6	2.5	5.3	4.0	11.5
	Cohort	54,235	0.6%	8.4	65.1	12.1	2.2	2.7	5.5	3.4	9.0
	Income and education	59,797	10.9%	11.9	65.1	7.2	3.0	2.0	6.1	7.0	8.0
95	Simulation	18,192		5.5	46.8	8.2	4.1	3.1	5.9	8.3	23.4
	Cohort	18,757	3.1%	4.9	48.8	10.6	1.8	4.6	5.8	6.1	22.4
	Income and education	26,725	46.9%	8.9	52.2	10.1	3.7	2.5	5.7	11.8	14.0
105	Simulation	2,916		4.5	49.6	8.5	4.3	3.2	6.1	8.6	19.7
	Cohort	2,246	−23.0%	3.6	50.0	9.9	1.2	4.4	4.9	5.0	24.5
	Income and education	8,111	178.2%	7.5	53.2	10.7	3.9	2.6	5.8	12.3	11.6

Source: 1982 and 1984 NLTCS.

[a]For each pair of numbers in this column, the top is the percentage increase in survival (l_i) for 1982–89 cohort relative to simulation, and the bottom is the percentage increase in survival for income and education adjustment relative to simulation.

and 1989 data, and (c) the cohort simulation with the income and education distribution adjusted.

The six profiles are augmented with an "Institutionalized" group to represent the entire U.S. Medicare-eligible population aged 65+. Life expectancy (e_t) for the cohort simulation is higher at age 65 than in the 1986 U.S. cross-sectional life tables produced by the U.S. Bureau of the Census (Spencer 1989; e.g., for females, 20.5 years vs. 19.0 years, and for males, 15.4 years vs. 14.8 years). Mortality decreases at later ages (from that observed in the period life table) because nondisabled persons have lower mortality. Overall, the life expectancy is nearly identical to that of the 1919 cohort (i.e., persons aged 65 in 1984) life tables prepared by the SSA (i.e., for males, 15.3 vs. 15.4 years, and for females, 20.6 vs. 20.5 years; SSA 1983). In table 2.7 we also present life tables calculated using the declines in disability observed from 1982 to 1989 (with mortality followed from 1982 to 1991; with Bayesian unit weights applied to each year's sample). The projected life expectancy at age 65 is again close for males (i.e., 15.4 vs. 15.6 years) and females (20.5 vs. 20.6 years). The simulations are similar to the 1982–89 life tables for males to age 85 and for females to age 95. The fact that the simulation provides a higher life expectancy at later ages than the 1982–89 data is because (a) the 1982–89 life tables do not reflect disability declines after 1989 and (b) since we weighted each survey year equally (a conservative approach), the θ for the 1982–84 interval is smaller because of the shorter interval (i.e., $\theta_M = 4.0$ percent and $\theta_F = 3.6$ percent) than for the 1982–89 estimates (i.e., $\theta_M = 5.5$ percent and $\theta_F = 4.4$ percent). This is because there are more unobserved disability transitions in the five-year interval 1984–89. We also show the effect of controlling income and education using the simulated cohort as the base. This increases life expectancy 1.4 years for males and 3.2 years for females. The life expectancy trajectories of the three scenarios are presented in figure 2.1.

Disability represents an actual loss of function for a person, rather than a risk factor out of range. Thus, it is a better predictor of mortality (see Grand et al. 1990; Campbell et al. 1985). For example, 92 percent of the age dependence of mortality for males, and 94.5 percent for females, is explained by functional level (compared to 62 and 69 percent for the risk factors). However, disability is not only an outcome of disease processes. Often, loss of function (implying decreased activity and worsened nutrition) is an etiological factor in mortality at advanced ages; e.g., 56 percent of deaths in one autopsy series were due to CHF, pulmonary embolism, or pneumonia, all of which are stimulated by lack of activity and poor nutrition. Only recently have mechanisms underlying the effect of functioning on health been specified. It was discovered, for example, that impaired heart muscle produced enzymes down-regulating the activity of skeletal muscle to keep them within the range of activity supportable by the remaining cardiac function (Drexler 1992). Many metabolic parameters are affected by activity—even to extreme ages (e.g., age 107 in Lindsted, Tonstad, and Kuzma 1991). Likewise, higher education and higher income not only

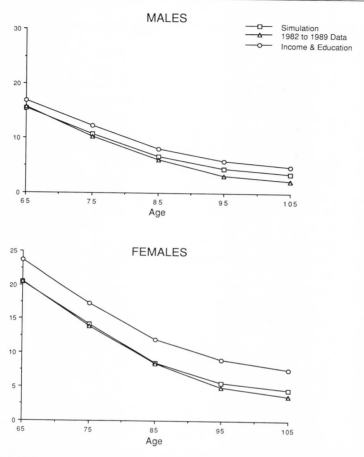

Fig. 2.1   Life expectancy at selected ages for males and females under three different scenarios: cohort simulation, 1982–89 life tables; and income and education adjustment of cohort simulation

imply improved access to medical care but also better lifestyle and higher expectations about health and functioning at later ages.

In addition, we can examine the distribution of frailty at each age. The value for $\bar{g}_1$ represents ALE at a given age. For males this declines more rapidly in the 1982–89 data (e.g., to 56.8 percent by age 95). For females the level of ALE is about the same at each age. In general the group that increases most rapidly in the 1982–89 data is the second group with mild cognitive impairment. For females, income and education greatly reduce the institutional population.

In table 2.8 we present cross-sectional distributions of males and females in each disability state for 1990 and 2020 and changes in the size of those populations (based on cohort simulations).

Table 2.8   **Distribution of Persons in Each Disability State, 1990 and 2020 (thousands)**

Age Group	Profile						Institutional
	1	2	3	4	5	6	
Males							
Baseline: 1990							
65+	11,047.41	184.75	173.79	109.99	305.40	280.60	255.44
85+	617.95	40.73	19.36	11.01	47.49	44.95	65.50
Baseline: 2020							
65+	20,490.82	352.32	316.48	202.72	592.51	522.48	545.93
85+	1,511.63	104.99	50.49	27.73	121.37	114.76	166.61
Variance control: 2020							
65+	20,479.09	375.91	336.81	225.83	635.87	604.89	721.86
85+	1,416.83	107.02	52.70	32.35	129.78	140.02	258.59
Females							
Baseline: 1990							
65+	15,228.11	343.02	437.46	352.48	513.50	396.42	722.42
85+	1,298.12	109.68	84.70	64.38	125.97	116.39	330.76
Baseline: 2020							
65+	26,037.34	679.84	790.24	634.12	940.28	784.75	1,535.03
85+	2,912.99	298.53	206.44	157.22	307.05	323.71	903.86
Variance control: 2020							
65+	25,915.74	679.66	803.76	661.15	959.60	865.16	2,009.09
85+	2,702.47	285.19	201.36	166.21	299.58	368.13	1,288.55

Source: 1982 and 1984 NLTCS.

The baseline population change from 1990 to 2020 reflects the growth of the age 85+ population. The changes for 2020 with, and without, variance control reflect increases in the size of the most disabled populations when disability heterogeneity is eliminated; i.e., this reflects what projections with discrete groups (e.g., using LCM categories, $g_{ik} = 0.0$ or 1.0) would produce. The effects are considerable at advanced ages; e.g., at ages 85+ in 2020 the institutional population increases 55 percent for males and 43 percent for females with variance control. The most fundamental problem is that age trajectories of disability are distorted by the use of homogeneous categories.

The variance control intervention shows that the effect of reduced mortality is eventually overwhelmed by mortality selection (i.e., reversing the mortality differentials). This demonstrates that the average age trajectory of risk factors (i.e., for an average individual) is not the same as the age trajectory observed for a heterogeneous population. In a population, mortality "prunes" the tails of the risk factor distribution, leaving a residual subpopulation with lower risks. The variance control intervention collapses the tails of the distribution to a single point mass, eliminating the effects of selection from the projections.

2.4   Discussion

We modeled mortality as a function of risk factor histories prior to death. The diffusion process describing the evolution of state variables and history-dependent mortality rates are used to forecast means and covariances of state variables and life tables and life expectancies for several scenarios. This is different from demographic forecasts (Spencer 1989; Wade 1987; Alho and Spencer 1990a, 1990b), which use only terminal-state information—i.e., age and cause of death. An advantage of the diffusion models is that one can ascertain the time scale and role of intermediate health processes prior to death. Methods that use only terminal-state information can assess interventions only when their effects on mortality are already manifest.

We also introduced a model of disability dynamics and mortality based on profiles of disabilities identified with the vertices of a unit simplex. Individual disability dynamics are represented via a diffusion process for score vectors, whose components are interpreted as the "degrees of similarity" of an individual's response to each profile of conditions. With mortality rates constructed in terms of g_{ik}, we produced history-dependent mortality rates which reflect physical and cognitive functioning of individuals prior to death. Ideally, both physiological and disability variables would be represented in a model. However, an integrated model, involving multiple levels of biological organization, lies in the future.

We forecast population size and health using the diffusion mortality processes with physiological variables. Changes in population produced by risk factor interventions were simulated. A stochastic limit to life expectancy was imposed by representing senescence in the mortality function. Risk factor values were not assumed to change until 2006. No change in case fatality or aging rates was assumed. Large population increases above age 85 resulted.

Federal population projections, useful for many purposes, do not make health forecasts. Models based on health processes sometimes make unrealistic assumptions, e.g., that risk factors operate independently (Tsevat et al. 1991). Multivariate stochastic process models, calibrated with longitudinal data, represent the interaction of risk factors, age, and mortality and may anticipate "turning points" that, without a model, may take years to identify (Myers 1981). Past mortality declines were presaged by risk factor changes in the population between 1960 and 1987. The projections illustrate (a) risk factor–based forecasts, (b) estimates of upper bounds to future population growth based on risk factor effects, and (c) variation of forecasts. They also show that Census Bureau projections are achievable by controlling known risk factors. In Census Bureau projections, however, mortality improvements are "front-end" loaded (they decline to an ultimate rate in 2012). We assumed no improvement in the first 20 (or 30) years.

The risk factor projections also suggest that uncertainty in the growth of the U.S. elderly population and changes in its health are greater than currently envisioned. To understand how uncertainty propagates in forecasts, research is needed on: (1) integration of multiple data sources with different error structures (e.g., superpopulation sampling models; Cassel, Sarndal, and Wretman 1977), (2) data with long-term follow-up and more experience at advanced ages, (3) biologically realistic models of health processes, (4) effects of error of parameter estimates, and modes of reducing it, on forecast uncertainty, and (5) effects of functional impairment on mortality.

In addition, the analyses identified risk factor dynamics important for mortality at late ages. For example, reduction of SC and BMI at later ages may be due to a significant prevalence of malnutrition (Williams 1992). Popkin et al. (1992), in analyzing risk factor trends, showed that the population aged 65–74 responded to public health initiatives. However, those initiatives emphasize risk factor avoidance appropriate to middle-aged persons—goals that may not be optimal at later ages. What is needed are recommendations of positive actions specifically for elderly persons. This model is one way to assess the content of public health programs designed specifically for the elderly. For example, forecasts of risk factor means to very advanced ages show nonlinear trajectories due to the interaction of state dynamics and mortality. Specifically, at some advanced age the mean of a risk factor must start moving to more optimal values because of the exponential increase in the force of mortality due to unobserved factors represented by the Gompertz. When sufficient numbers of risk factors are represented that θ is "small," the cross-temporal covariances of observed risk factors will describe optimal trajectories.

Using disability assessments from the NLTCS, we produced projections of ALE for males and females. Disability was represented by scores describing multiple dimensions of disability. The use of a dynamic model with graded scores predicted a very different distribution of disability in 2020 than if discrete disability groups are used. Specifically, variance within disability categories tended to increase mortality risks—especially for the most highly disabled groups. At the same time, it reduced the average $g_{ik\text{-}t}$ for high disability dimensions, so that the mortality in later years declined. This is why variance "control" initially increased life expectancy (i.e., at ages 65 and 75) and then decreased it (i.e., at ages 85 and above).

We also investigated an intervention whereby certain disability transitions (to low levels, at early ages among persons with no prior impairment) were modified to simulate a cohort. The cohort scenario focused on short-term changes in incidence. This is an area requiring further substantive and methodological research. Specifically, the NLTCS detects disability of 90+ days duration at two points in time. To take point prevalences as fixed to calculate disability effects may overestimate the length of disability episodes and underestimate the number of persons experiencing disability. The number of short-term stays, and the likelihood of disability reversal, may be underestimated. To deal with data limitations, a model accurately describing continuously changing disability states, their interaction with mortality, and time of observation is needed.

References

Ahlburg, D. A., and J. W. Vaupel. 1990. Alternative projections of the U.S. population. *Demography* 27:639–52.

Alho, J. M., B. D. Spencer. 1990a. Effects of targets and aggregation on the propagation of error in mortality forecasts. *Mathematical Population Studies* 2:209–27.

———. 1990b. Error models for official mortality forecasts. *Journal of the American Statistical Association* 85:609–16.

Berkman, L., B. Singer, and K. G. Manton. 1989. Black/white differences in health status and mortality among the elderly. *Demography* 26(4): 661–78.

Bishop, Y. M., S. E. Fienberg, and P. W. Holland. 1975. *Discrete multivariate analysis: Theory and practice.* Cambridge: MIT Press.

Blackburn, H. 1989. Trends and determinants of CHD mortality: Changes in risk factors and their effects. *International Journal of Epidemiology* 18, Suppl. 1:S210–S215.

Campbell, A. J., J. Reinken, C. Diep, and I. McCosh. 1985. Factors predicting mortality in a total population sample of the elderly. *Journal of Epidemiology and Community Health* 39(4): 337–42.

Cassel, C.-M., C.-E. Sarndal, and J. H. Wretman. 1977. *Foundations of inference in survey sampling.* New York: Wiley.

Dawber, T. R. 1980. *The Framingham study: The epidemiology of arteriosclerotic disease.* Cambridge: Harvard University Press.

Dowd, J. E., and K. G. Manton. 1990. Forecasting chronic disease risks in developing countries. *International Journal of Epidemiology* 19(4): 1018–36.

Drexler, H., S. U. Reide, T. Munzel, H. Konig, E. Funke, and H. Just. 1992. Alterations of skeletal muscle in chronic heart failure. *Circulation* 85:1751–59.

Epstein, F. H. 1992. Low serum cholesterol, cancer and other noncardiovascular disorders. *Atherosclerosis* 94:1–12.

Feldman, J. J., D. M. Makuc, J. C. Kleinman, and J. C. Huntley. 1989. National trends in educational differentials in mortality. *American Journal of Epidemiology* 129:919–33.

Fiore, M. C., T. E. Novotny, J. P. Pierce, E. J. Hatziandreu, K. M. Patel, and R. M. Davis. 1989. Trends in cigarette smoking in the United States: The changing influence of gender and race. *Journal of the American Medical Association* 261:49–55.

Frank, J. W., D. M. Reed, J. S. Grove, and R. Benfante. 1992. Will lowering population levels of serum cholesterol affect total mortality? Expectations from the Honolulu heart program. *Journal of Clinical Epidemiology* 45(4): 333–46.

Frydman, H., and B. Singer. 1979. Total positivity and the embedding problem for Markov chains. *Mathematical Proceedings of the Cambridge Philosophical Society* 86:339–44.

Grand, A., P. Grosclaude, H. Bocquet, J. Pous, and J. L. Albarede. 1990. Disability, psychosocial factors and mortality among the elderly in a rural French population. *Journal of Clinical Epidemiology* 43:773–82.

Guralnik, J. M., M. Yanagishita, and E. L. Schneider. 1988. Projecting the older population of the United States: Lessons from the past and prospects for the future. *Milbank Quarterly* 66:283–308.

Kiefer, J., and J. Wolfowitz. 1956. Consistency of the maximum likelihood estimator in the presence of infinitely many parameters. *Annals of Mathematical Statistics* 27:887–906.

Lazarsfeld, P. F., and N. W. Henry. 1968. *Latent structure analysis.* Boston: Houghton Mifflin.

Lindsted, K. D., S. Tonstad, and J. W. Kuzma. 1991. Self-report of physical activity and patterns of mortality in Seventh-Day Adventist men. *Journal of Clinical Epidemiology* 44:355–64.

Lipsitz, L. A., and A. L. Goldberger. 1992. Loss of "complexity" and aging. *Journal of the American Medical Association* 267(13): 1806.

Manton, K. G. 1988. Measurements of health and disease, a transitional perspective. In *Health in an aging America: Issues on data for policy analysis.* NCHS Vital and Health Statistics, series 4, no. 25. USHDDS Pub. no. (PHS) 89-1488. Public Health Service. Washington, D.C.: Government Printing Office, pp. 3–38.

———. 1993. Biomedical research and changing concepts of disease and dying: Implications for long-term health forecasts for elderly populations. In *Forecasting the health of elderly populations,* ed. K. G. Manton, B. H. Singer, and R. M. Suzman, 319–66. New York: Springer.

Manton, K. G., L. S. Corder, and E. Stallard. 1993. Estimates of changes in chronic disability and institutionalization in the U.S. elderly population from the 1982, 1984, and 1989 National Long Term Care Survey. *Journal of Gerontology: Social Sciences* 47(4):S153–S166.

Manton, K. G., R. Newcomer, G. Lowrimore, J. C. Vertrees, and C. Harrington. 1994. Social/Health Maintenance Organization for fee-for-service outcomes over time. *Health Care Financing Review.* Forthcoming.

Manton, K. G., and E. Stallard. 1988. *Chronic disease modeling: Measurement and evaluation of the risks of chronic disease processes.* London: Charles Griffin.

Manton, K. G., E. Stallard, and B. H. Singer. 1992. Projecting the future size and health status of the U.S. elderly population. *International Journal of Forecasting* 8:433–58.

Manton, K. G., E. Stallard, and M. A. Woodbury. 1986. Chronic disease evolution and human aging: A general model for assessing the impact of chronic disease in human populations. *Mathematical Modelling* 7:1155–71.

———. 1991. A multivariate event history model based upon fuzzy states: Estimation from longitudinal surveys with informative nonresponse. *Journal of Official Statistics* (Statistics Sweden, Stockholm) 7(3): 261–93.

Manton, K. G., M. A. Woodbury, L. S. Corder, and E. Stallard. 1992b. The use of grade of membership techniques to estimate regression relationships. In *Sociological Methodology, 1992,* ed. P. Marsden, 321–81. Oxford: Blackwell.

Medvedev, Z. 1990. An attempt at a rational classification of theories of aging. *Biological Reviews of Cambridge Philosophical Society* 65:375–98.

Myers, G. C. 1981. Future age projections and society. In *Aging: A challenge to science and society,* ed. W. M. Beattie, J. Piotrowske, and M. Marois. Vol. 2, part 2, *Social sciences and social policy,* 248–60. Oxford: Oxford University Press.

Neaton, J. D., H. Blackburn, D. Jacobs, L. Kuller, D. J. Lee, R. Sherwin, J. Shih, J. Stamler, D. Wentworth, and Multiple Risk Factor Intervention Trial Research Group. 1992. Serum cholesterol level and mortality findings for men screened in the Multiple Risk Factor Intervention Trial. *Archives of Internal Medicine* 152:1490–1500.

National Center for Health Statistics (NCHS). 1992. Births, marriages, divorces, and deaths for October 1991. *Monthly Vital Statistics Report* 40(10): 1–24.

Oliver, M. F. 1991. Might treatment of hypercholesterolaemia increase non-cardiac mortality? Viewpoint. *Lancet* 337:1529–31.

Popkin, B. M., P. S. Haines, and R. E. Patterson. 1992. Dietary changes in older Americans, 1977–1987. *American Journal of Clinical Nutrition* 55:823–30.

Ravnskov, U. 1992. Cholesterol lowering trials on coronary heart disease: Frequency of citation and outcome. *British Medical Journal* 305:15–19.

Singer, B. 1989. Grade of membership representations: Concepts and problems. In *Festschrift for Samuel Karlin,* ed. T. W. Anderson, K. B. Athreya, and D. Inglehardt, 317–34. Orlando, FL: Academic Press.

Singer, B., and S. Spilerman. 1976. The representation of social processes by Markov models. *American Journal of Sociology* 82(1): 1–54.

Social Security Administration (SSA). 1983. *Life tables for the United States: 1900–2050.* SSA Publication no. 11-11536. Baltimore: U.S. Department of Health and Human Services.

———. 1989. *U.S. life functions and actuarial functions.* Machine copy. Baltimore: U.S. Department of Health and Human Services.

Spencer, G. 1989. *Projections of the Population of the United States, by Age, Sex, and Race: 1988 to 2080.* Current Population Reports, Population Estimates and Projections, series P-25, no. 1018. Washington, D.C.: Government Printing Office.

Tsevat, J., M. C. Weinstein, L. W. Williams, et al. 1991. Expected gains in life expectancy from various coronary heart disease risk factor modifications. *Circulation* 83:1194–1201.

Wade, A. 1987. *Social security area population projections: 1987.* Social Security Administration, Office of the Actuary, Actuarial Study no. 99, SSA Pub. no. 11-11546. Baltimore.

Weyl, H. 1949. The elementary theory of convex polyhedra. *Annals of Mathematics* 24:3–18.

Williams, T. F. 1992. Serum albumin, aging and disease. *Journal of Clinical Epidemiology* 45:205–206.

Woodbury, M. A., and K. G. Manton. 1977. A random walk model of human mortality and aging. *Theoretical Population Biology* 11:37–48.

———. 1983. A theoretical model of the physiological dynamics of circulatory disease in human populations. *Human Biology* 55:417–41.

Woodbury, M. A., K. G. Manton, and H. D. Tolley. 1994. A general model for statistical analysis using fuzzy sets: Sufficient conditions for identifiability and statistical properties. *Information Sciences,* forthcoming.

Yashin, A. I., K. G. Manton, and E. Stallard. 1986. Dependent competing risks: A stochastic process model. *Journal of Mathematical Biology* 24:119–40.

3

Longer Life Expectancy? Evidence from Sweden of Reductions in Mortality Rates at Advanced Ages

James W. Vaupel and Hans Lundström

Life expectancy at current mortality rates in Western Europe, the United States, Canada, Australia, New Zealand, and Japan exceeds 75 years; in Japan and the Scandinavian countries (and in some states of the United States, such as Hawaii and Minnesota) life expectancy for women is around 80 years. Many demographers, gerontologists, and others believe that life expectancy will continue to rise slowly until it reaches an upper limit of perhaps 85 years. Fries (1980) has helped popularize this idea, but as adumbrated below, numerous others have contributed to it. Demeny (1984), in making long-term population forecasts for the World Bank, assumed that even by the year 2100 there would be no country with a life expectancy above 82.5 years.

Other researchers are skeptical about the existence of an upper limit to life expectancy, at least at an age as early as 85. They foresee continuing and perhaps even accelerating progress in reducing mortality rates at all ages, including the most advanced ages (Manton, Stallard, Tolley 1991). Some projections suggest that the life expectancy of the current generation of children in the United States might be 100 years or more, if progress in reducing mortality rates continues over the next century (Vaupel and Gowan 1986; Guralnik, Yanagishita, and Schneider 1988.)

If life expectancy remains at about current levels, demographers can make fairly long-term forecasts of the future size of the elderly population with reasonable accuracy. Everyone who will be more than 60 years old in the year 2050 has already been born; if age-specific death rates remain more or less constant and if migration rates are low or predictable, then the current popula-

James W. Vaupel is professor of medical demography and health policy at Odense University Medical School in Denmark and senior research scientist at the Center for Demographic Studies, Duke University. Hans Lundström is a senior research associate at the Bureau of Demographic Analysis, Statistics Sweden.

tion can be projected forward to estimate the population of the elderly up through the middle of the next century.

Suppose, however, life expectancy rises so that children alive today live 100 years on average, instead of 75 years. The elderly population will increase dramatically in size and the oldest-old population of those above age 85 will explode in number (Ahlburg and Vaupel 1990).

Hence, theory and evidence concerning the prospects for longer life expectancy are of fundamental relevance in assessing the impact of population aging. In particular, major issues in the economics of aging hinge on projections of the old and oldest-old populations. These issues include trends in (1) healthcare demand and costs, (2) the financial soundness of social security systems and pension plans, (3) individual, corporate, and governmental decisions about the age of retirement, and (4) the nature and extent of intergenerational transfers of resources.

A major biomedical uncertainty lies at the core of the disagreement between those who foresee life expectancy leveling off at about 80 or 85 years and those who predict more radical increases to a century or more. Does the force of mortality (i.e., the age-specific hazard of death) (1) sharply and inexorably rise for the typical individual to extremely high levels around age 85 or (2) increase after age 85 at about the same rate or even at a slower rate than before age 85, with the likelihood that the rate of progress being made in reducing the force of mortality among the very old will be of the same order of magnitude as the rate of progress being made among the younger old?

The first perspective implies that life spans are limited. Individuals may differ somewhat in their maximum potential life spans, with some individuals having a potential of 100 years and others a potential of 75 years. On average, however, the typical individual's longevity is unlikely to exceed the natural limit of 85 years or so that has prevailed for millennia. Most of those who adhere to this perspective believe that continued progress in reducing mortality rates up to age 75 or so is likely to be made, so that death before age 75 will become rare. Consequently, life expectancy will approach the length of the typical maximum life span, i.e., about 85 years. Eventually, some extraordinary breakthroughs may be made that permit humans to live beyond their natural life spans, but when such breakthroughs will occur, if ever, is uncertain.

This general point of view is often illustrated with diagrams showing an increasing rectangularization of survivorship curves or showing bell-shaped distributions, centered around age 85, of what Fries (1983) describes as "natural death (due to senescent frailty)." Such survivorship curves and distributions of deaths imply that little or no progress can be made in reducing death rates after age 80 or so.

The second perspective implies that the force of mortality rises fairly smoothly to very advanced ages exceeding 100 years or more—there is no sharp increase for the typical individual around age 85, and there may even be some gradual lessening of the rate of increase after age 90 or so (as implied by the power function or the logistic function used, instead of an exponential function, in some models of mortality). Furthermore, there is no discontinuity around age 85 in the rate of progress that is likely to be made in reducing the force of mortality, so that substantial reductions in mortality rates will probably be achieved at all ages. Consequently, life expectancy will continue to gradually but steadily increase and may rise to 90, 95, or even longer by the year 2050. Major biomedical breakthroughs are likely over the course of the next century, although the exact nature and significance of these breakthroughs cannot now be foreseen: these breakthroughs may result in some acceleration in the rate of progress made in reducing the force of mortality, so that a life expectancy of well over 100 years, less than 100 years from now, cannot be ruled out. In contrast to the limited-life-span paradigm, this might be called the mortality-reduction paradigm.

Given the current state of knowledge, no judicious researcher can claim to know for sure which of these two paradigms is more correct—or whether some combination of them or some entirely different perspective will eventually prove to be true. Furthermore, each of the two paradigms has numerous variants that have not yet been conclusively shown to be inconsistent with reliable empirical evidence.

Broadly speaking and with many caveats, the limited-life-span paradigm can be associated with the stream of research done by Pearson (1923), Pearl (1923), Clarke (1950), Bourgeois-Pichat (1952, 1978), Comfort ([1964] 1979), Ryder (1975), Hayflick (1977, 1980), Sacher (1977), Keyfitz (1978), Kohn (1982), and their colleagues. The most prominent recent advocate and popularizer of this general perspective is Fries (1980, 1983, 1984; Fries and Crapo 1981; Fries, Green, and Levine 1989); useful reviews are also provided by Rosenfeld ([1976] 1985) and Gavrilov and Gavrilova (1991). These researchers generally assume that there are biological barriers to longer life expectancy; in contrast, Olshansky, Carnes, and Cassel (1990) stress practical barriers that may effectively limit life expectancy to values less than 85 years or so. Whether the barriers are practical or genetic is, however, rarely explicitly addressed: in much of the gerontological literature it is simply accepted as a stylized fact that natural or senescent death implies that mortality rates cannot be substantially reduced at advanced ages. Harman (1991) and Lohman, Sankaranarayanan, and Ashby (1992) provide two recent examples of the strength and persistence of this point of view.

The possibility that the mortality-reduction paradigm may be more correct is implied by most of the process models of mortality developed from Gompertz (1825) onward. This viewpoint has been cogently argued by Manton (1982; Manton and Soldo 1985; Manton and Woodbury 1987; Myers and Manton 1984; Manton et al. 1991) and is supported either explicitly or implicitly by Schatzkin (1980), Schneider and Brody (1983), Peto, Parish, and Gray (1986), Vaupel and Owen (1986), Vaupel and Gowan (1986), Schneider and Guralnik (1987), Poterba and Summers (1987), and Rowe and Kahn (1987).

The key reason that the controversy between the limited-life-span and mortality-reduction paradigms has not been resolved is that there is relatively little reliable data on mortality rates over age, time, and sex among the oldest old (i.e., those over aged 85). Indeed, it is remarkable how little is known, considering the rapidly increasing population at advanced ages and the high life-table probability, approaching 50 percent for females in some countries, of survival past age 85.

Very few published human life tables extend past age 85, and the population and death counts that are available for the oldest old tend to be suspect. As reviewed (and bewailed) by numerous demographers (including Shryock and Siegel 1976; Mazess and Forman 1979; Rosenwaike 1981; Horiuchi and Coale 1983; Spencer 1986; Coale and Kisker 1986, 1990; Kannisto 1988), various kinds of gross errors are common in reported age-specific deaths and population sizes above age 85. These errors—such as age heaping caused by rounding off of ages to the nearest age divisible by five or ten, the tendency of some older people to exaggerate their ages, the fact that a relatively few errors in misclassifying younger people as very old people can swamp actual counts of very old people, or failures to remove the deceased from population registers so that the dead appear to survive eternally—may represent systematic biases across populations. Hence it may be impossible to reduce these errors by the usual statistical expedient of examining many data sets and either formally or informally averaging them. It is consequently essential that large, reliable databases on oldest-old human mortality be assembled and analyzed.

The most reliable data on mortality rates up to the most advanced ages over a long period of time pertain to Sweden. Excellent data exist for Sweden since 1750; superlative data have been archived since 1895. The published Swedish data that are readily available are highly accurate, but even these data have some deficiencies at advanced ages. In particular, much of the published data is smoothed by actuarial methods after age 90 or so, and the most widely available mortality rates are based on aggregated data on several years of age and time rather than on single years of age and time. Furthermore, the data, once published, have not been revised as new information (from censuses or cohort death counts) has become available.

Using unpublished information in the archives of Statistics Sweden, one of us (Lundström) is in the process of meticulously verifying, correcting, and computerizing the death counts and population counts needed to estimate mortality rates at advanced ages in Sweden from 1750 to 1992. For this article, we made use of a nearly completed version of the Lundström database for 1895 to 1990. A few minor changes may be made to a few of the death and population counts in this database, but the version we used is undoubtedly extremely close to the final version.

3.1   Force of Mortality at Ages 85, 90, and 95

Figure 3.1 plots the force of mortality for Swedish females at ages 85, 90, and 95, from 1900 through 1990. Other ages between 80 and 100 show similar patterns.

The force of mortality, also known as the hazard or intensity of death, is a measure favored by demographers to capture the level of mortality. It is defined, at age x and time y, by

$$\mu(x) = -\frac{ds(x,\,y)/dx}{s(x,\,y)}, \quad y = y_0 + x,$$

where $s(x,\,y)$ is the proportion of the cohort born x years ago that is surviving at time y, and y_0 is the time the cohort was born. The Swedish data are available by single years of age and time, so a discrete approximation must be used to estimate μ. We used the standard approximation

$$\mu(x,\,y) = -\ln(1 - D(x,\,y)/N(x,\,y)),$$

where $D(x,\,y)$ represents the number of deaths among the cohort of people who were between exact ages $x - 1$ and x on January 1st of year y, and $N(x,\,y)$ represents the number of people in this cohort on January 1st. Note that the

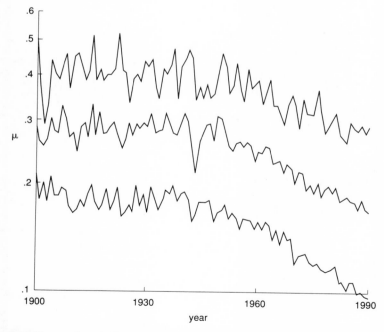

Fig. 3.1   Force of mortality for females, ages 85, 90, and 95: Sweden, 1900–90

members of this cohort attain exact age x (i.e., celebrate their xth birthday) over the course of year y. Also note that in-and-out migration is ignored: net migration is negligible in Sweden after age 80.

Population sizes are small, especially at age 95, so the trajectories in figure 3.1 show considerable random fluctuation. The overall trends, however, are clear. There was little progress in reducing the force of mortality at advanced ages before 1940 or 1950. Afterward, the force of mortality declined considerably, even at age 95. At age 85, the force of mortality declined from about .2 to about .1. At age 90, the decline was from a level of about .3 to about .2. An absolute decline on the order of magnitude of .1, from about .4 to about .3, is also apparent at age 95.

As shown in figure 3.2, the trends for Swedish males are roughly similar, although less dramatic. It is clear that the force of mortality for very old males in Sweden was substantially lower in 1990 than it was in 1900, although the reduction was less than for females and the levels of mortality are higher for males than for females. At each age, the absolute decline for males was on the order of magnitude of .05, in contrast to the decline of roughly .1 for females.

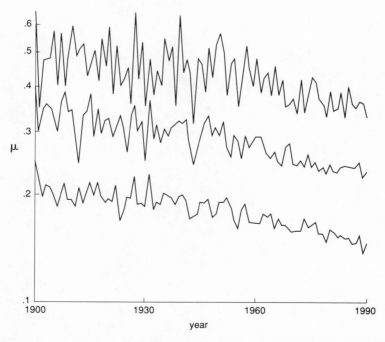

Fig. 3.2   Force of mortality for males, ages 85, 90, and 95: Sweden, 1900–90

3.2   Average Annual Rates of Progress in Reducing Mortality Rates

To summarize the overall pattern of reduction, table 3.1 presents average annual rates of progress in reducing the force of mortality for Swedish females and males over successive 20-year time periods and for people in their 60s and 70s as well as octogenarians, nonagenarians, and centenarians.

For males and for females, the average level of the force of mortality over a decade of time and age was calculated as follows:

$$\bar{\mu}(x_0, y_0) = \frac{\sum\limits_{y=y_0}^{y_0+9} \sum\limits_{x=x_0}^{x_0+9} \tilde{N}(x)\, \mu(x, y)}{\sum\limits_{y=y_0}^{y_0+9} \sum\limits_{x=x_0}^{x_0+9} \tilde{N}(x)}.$$

The $\tilde{N}$s are used to standardize the age composition of the population: we calculated the $\tilde{N}$s from the population of Sweden in the 1980s:

$$\tilde{N}(x) = \sum_{y=1980}^{1989} N(x, y).$$

The values of $\mu(x, y)$ were calculated as described above. If the death count equaled the population count, then the standard approximation $\mu = 2$ was used. Occasionally, at ages greater than 100, it was impossible to estimate μ for some specific year, because no one was alive at that age and year. In such cases, the μ term was dropped from the numerator and a corresponding correction was made in the denominator. The average annual rate of progress in reducing the force of mortality was then calculated using

$$\rho(x_0, y_0) = -\left[\left(\frac{\bar{\mu}(x_0, y_0 + 20)}{\bar{\mu}(x_0, y_0)}\right)^{.05} - 1\right].$$

Table 3.1   **Average Annual Rates of Progress in Reducing Mortality Rates by Age Category and Time Period**

		Time Period			
Sex	Age Category	1900–09 to 1920–29	1920–29 to 1940–49	1940–49 to 1960–69	1960–69 to 1980–89
Male	60–69	.50	.44	.28	.62
	70–79	.37	.20	.19	.62
	80–89	.36	.13	.36	.53
	90–99	.27	.11	.36	.56
	100+	1.76	−1.07	.97	.18
Female	60–69	.24	.61	1.88	1.63
	70–79	.18	.22	1.25	2.08
	80–89	.19	.10	.78	1.64
	90–99	.13	.03	.60	.94
	100+	.23	.41	.80	.49

Table 3.1 indicates that progress has been made in Sweden in reducing the force of mortality at all ages after 60 for both males and females. Estimated rates of progress fluctuate erratically for centenarian males, probably because there are so few observations for this category, but even so the general trend is toward a reduction in mortality rates. For females and for younger age categories, the picture is clear: mortality rates among the elderly are declining in Sweden and at a faster pace in recent decades than in the first decades of the century.

For males in the most recent time period, the rate of progress is roughly the same—about half a percent per year—for men in their 60s, 70s, 80s, and 90s. For females in the most recent time period, the rate of progress is about 2 percent for women in their 70s and half as much for women in their 90s. Note, however, that the rate of progress for women in their 80s is the same, 1.6 percent, as that for women in their 60s.

If rates of progress in the first 20 years of the century are compared with the most recent 20-year period, it is apparent that there has been a considerable acceleration of rates of progress. The acceleration is greater for females than for males. The acceleration is also greater in older age categories than in younger ones, at least in the age categories, below age 100, where there are substantial numbers of observations.

The overall acceleration in rates of progress and the greater acceleration at older ages may reflect actual changes on the individual level: the elderly today may be healthier than in the past, and they may be receiving better health care. A supplemental explanation was suggested by Vaupel, Manton, and Stallard (1979). Progress in reducing mortality rates at younger ages makes it more difficult to make progress at subsequent ages if the persons whose lives are saved are frail and vulnerable. In effect, progress in reducing cohort mortality rates at younger ages masks the true rate of progress (controlling for compositional changes) at older ages. However, as mortality rates in an age category decline, this effect diminishes in importance, resulting in an apparent acceleration in rates of progress.

3.3 Lexis Maps of Force of Mortality

Another way to summarize data concerning a surface of demographic rates over age and time is to present a Lexis map, i.e., a shaded contour map of the surface (Vaupel, Gambill, and Yashin 1987). Figure 3.3 displays a Lexis map of the force of mortality for Swedish females at ages 80–111 from 1900 through 1990. Figure 3.4 displays a corresponding map for Swedish males.

The data available to us include death counts by year of birth as well as by current age and year. Furthermore, the data include population counts of those attaining a specific age in some year (e.g., the number of those who celebrated their 85th birthday in 1970) as well as counts of the number of people at a given age on January 1st of a given year. Hence it is possible to estimate the

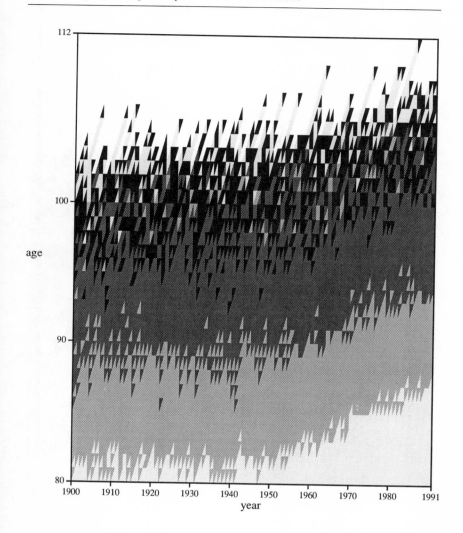

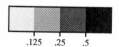

.125   .25   .5

Fig. 3.3   Force of mortality for females 80–111: Sweden, 1900–90

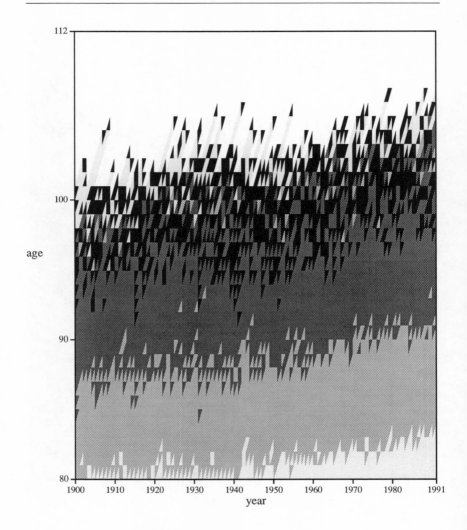

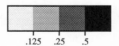

Fig. 3.4   Force of mortality for males 80–111: Sweden, 1900–90

force of mortality for triangular categories of age and time. Let $q = D/N$ be the ratio of the death count to the population at risk, in one of these triangles. To convert this into an annual probability of death, let

$$q^* = 1 - (1 - q)^2 .$$

Then, analogous to the formula used earlier, the force of mortality can be estimated by

$$\mu = -\ln(1 - q^*).$$

The four shades of gray in figures 3.3 and 3.4 represent four levels of this estimated force of mortality. The light gray tones along diagonals above age 100, terminated by a black triangle, generally represent cohorts with one remaining member: the force of mortality is zero until this person dies.

Consider the age at which the force of mortality for females crosses the level of .125, as shown in figure 3.3. Until 1945 or so, this age is around 81; by 1990, the age is up around 87. One interpretation of this is that an 87-year-old Swedish female in 1990 was as healthy (at least in terms of probability of death) as an 81-year-old Swedish female in the first four decades of the twentieth century. The age at which the force of mortality for females crosses the level of .250 increases by about five years from a level fluctuating around 89 to a level of 94. Despite substantial statistical noise, a shift upward is also apparent at the level of .5, and there is also a clear increase in the maximum age attained. The record longevity is 111 years, attained by the grandmother of an employee of Statistics Sweden.

For males, as shown in figure 3.4, the surface of mortality rates is higher than for females. Furthermore, the upward shift is less substantial at the .125, .25, and .5 levels and in the maximum age attained. Nonetheless, it is clear that there has been a definite shift, on the order of three years or so. As noted above, this can be interpreted as the result of a downward shift in mortality curves or, alternatively, as a delay in the aging process: elderly Swedish males in 1990 can be considered to be three years "younger" (in terms of their risk of death) than Swedish males of the same age in the first part of this century.

3.4   Remaining Life Expectancy

A final perspective on the decline in oldest-old mortality rates in Sweden is presented in table 3.2. For the various decades from 1900 until 1990, the table gives, for males and females, the age at which remaining life expectancy is two years and the age at which remaining life expectancy is five years.

The numbers given are based on decennial life tables for each decade. The age-specific mortality rates, for single years of age, that form the basis of these life tables were calculated using the following standard formula:

Table 3.2   Age at Which Remaining Life Expectancy is Two Years or Five Years

	Two Years Left		Five Years Left	
Period	Males	Females	Males	Females
1900–09	93.9	95.3	80.5	81.7
1910–19	94.1	95.7	80.7	81.8
1920–29	95.3	96.1	81.2	82.0
1930–39	94.4	95.4	80.9	81.5
1940–49	95.0	96.9	81.6	82.3
1950–59	95.9	97.3	81.8	82.9
1960–69	96.3	99.0	82.5	84.0
1970–79	97.6	99.7	83.2	85.8
1980–89	98.1	100.1	83.7	86.7

$$q(x, y_0) = \frac{\sum_{y=y_0}^{y_0+9} D(x, y)}{\sum_{y=y_0}^{y_0+9} N(x, y)},$$

where, unlike above, $D(x, y)$ now represents the number of deaths within a year of time of people who attained exact age x in year y, and $N(x, y)$ represents the number of people who attain age x in year y.

Note in table 3.2 that, for both males and females and when remaining life expectancy is either two years or five years, there was little net change between the decade 1900–09 and the decade 1930–39. From the 1930s to the 1980s, however, the shifts were substantial. For males, the age at which two years of life expectancy are left increased by almost four years, from 94.4 to 98.1. For females, the corresponding shift was close to five years, from 95.4 to 100.1. The age at which remaining life expectancy is five years increased for males by almost three years, from 80.9 to 83.7. For females, the increase was five years, from 81.5 to 86.7.

As suggested earlier, one interpretation of these shifts is that the process of aging has been slowed or delayed in Sweden such that elderly Swedish men are effectively three or four years "younger" than they used to be and elderly Swedish females are five years younger. Caution is required because these figures are based entirely on mortality statistics, with no information about morbidity or disability. Nonetheless, treated judiciously, this perspective suggests that certainly mortality, and perhaps health more generally, is plastic even at the most advanced ages. It has been possible, at least in Sweden, to lower the force of mortality and to significantly postpone death even among the oldest old.

3.5 Discussion

Swedish life expectancy has been among the very longest in the world for many decades. If progress can be made in Sweden in lowering mortality rates at advanced ages, then the contention that oldest-old mortality rates cannot be significantly reduced seems questionable. Using highly reliable data, we presented four perspectives on mortality changes in Sweden since 1990 among the elderly. As shown in figures 3.1 and 3.2, the force of mortality at ages 85, 90, and 95 has substantially declined, especially since 1945 or so, and more for females than for males. As shown in table 3.1, rates of progress in reducing mortality rates among the elderly have accelerated over the course of the century and from the 1960s to the 1980s ran at an average annual rate of 1–2 percent for females and half a percent for males. As shown in figures 3.3 and 3.4, the ages at which the force of mortality attains the levels of .125, .25, and .5 have shifted upward substantially since 1945 or so, by about five years for females and three years for males. Finally, as shown in table 3.2, the ages at which remaining life expectancy reaches two years or five years have also shifted upward, by about five years for females and three or four years for males. These four perspectives are consistent with each other. They indicate that the belief that oldest-old mortality rates cannot be significantly reduced is incorrect.

A variety of other strands of evidence, reviewed by Manton et al. (1991), point in the same direction. Most of this evidence pertains to small special populations followed for short periods of time or is based on the results of sophisticated mathematical modeling. The evidence from Sweden is highly reliable, pertains to a sizable national population followed since 1900, and is so straightforward that it does not have to be smoothed or filtered through a statistical model.

The available evidence, taken together, suggests that, if historical rates of progress in reducing mortality rates continue to prevail in the future, newborn children today can expect to live about 90 years on average. If, as health and biomedical knowledge develops, progress accelerates so that age-specific mortality rates come down at an average rate of about 2 percent per year, then the typical newborn today in developed countries will live to celebrate his or her 100th birthday.

Whether progress in reducing mortality rates will continue at historical levels or even accelerate is, of course, an open question. Even more uncertainty envelops an equally important question: if our children survive to become centenarians, what will their health be like during their extra life span? Will the added years be active, healthy years or years of decrepitude, disability, and misery? The answer to this question is central to forecasting the impact of population aging on health and social needs and costs, on retirement decisions and policies, and on other questions in the economics of aging, but very little is currently known about what the answer might be.

References

Ahlburg, D. A., and J. Vaupel. 1990. Alternative projections of the U.S. population. *Demography* 27:639–52.

Bourgeois-Pichat, J. 1952. Essai sur la mortalité "biologique" de l'homme. *Population* 7:381–94.

Bourgeois-Pichat, J. 1978. Future outlook for mortality declines in the world. Population Bulletin of the United Nations, no. 11. New York: United Nations.

Clarke, R. D. 1950. A Bio-actuarial approach to forecasting rates of mortality. In *Proceedings of the centenary assembly of the Institute of Actuaries.* Cambridge: Cambridge University Press.

Coale, A. J., and E. E. Kisker. 1986. Mortality crossovers: Reality or bad data? *Population Studies* 40:389–401.

———. 1990. Defects in data on old age mortality in the United States: New procedures for calculating mortality schedules and life tables at the highest ages. *Asian and Pacific Population Forum* 4(1):1–36.

Comfort, A. (1964) 1979. The biology of senescence, 3d ed. New York: Elsevier.

Demeny, P. 1984. A perspective on long-term population growth. *Population and Development Review* 10:103–26.

Fries, J. F. 1980. Aging, natural death, and the compression of morbidity. *New England Journal of Medicine* 303:130–35.

———. 1983. The compression of morbidity. *Milbank Memorial Fund Quarterly/ Health and Society* 61:397–419.

———. 1984. The compression of morbidity: Miscellaneous comments about a theme. *Gerontologist* 24:354–59.

Fries, J. F., and I. M. Crapo. 1981. Vitality and aging: Implications of the rectangular San Francisco: W. H. Freeman.

Fries, J. F., L. W. Green, and S. Levine. 1989. Health promotion and the compression of morbidity. Lancet 1:481–83.

Gavrilov, L. A., and N. S. Gavrilova. 1991. The biology of life span. Chur, Switzerland: Harwood Academic Publishers.

Gompertz, B. 1825. On the nature of the function expressive of the law of human mortality, and on a new mode of determining the value of life contingencies. *Philosophical Transactions of the Royal Society of London,* Series A 115: 513–85.

Guralnik, J. M., M. Yanagishita, and E. L. Schneider. 1988. Projecting the older population of the United States: Lessons from the past and prospects for the future. *Milbank Quarterly* 66:283–308.

Harman, D. 1991. The aging process: Major risk factor for disease and death. *Proceedings of National Academy of Sciences, USA* 88:5360–63.

Hayflick, L. 1977. The cellular basis for biological aging. In *Handbook of the biology of aging,* ed. C. E. Finch and L. Hayflick, 159–86. New York: Van Nostrand Reinhold.

———. 1980. The cell biology of human aging. *Scientific American* 242:58–65.

Horiuchi, S., and A. J. Coale. 1983. Age patterns of mortality for older women: Analysis using the age-specific rate of mortality change with age. Paper presented at the annual meeting of the Population Society of America, Pittsburgh.

Kannisto, V. 1988. On the survival of centenarians and the span of life. *Population Studies* 42:389–406.

Keyfitz, N. 1978. Improving life expectancy: An uphill road ahead. *American Journal of Public Health* 68:954–56.

Kohn, R. R. 1982. Cause of death in very old people. *Journal of American Medical Association* 247:2793–97.

Lohman, P. H. M., K. Sankaranarayanan, and J. Ashby. 1992. Choosing the limits to life. *Nature* 357:185–86.

Manton, K. G. 1982. Changing concepts of mortality and morbidity in the elderly population. *Milbank Memorial Fund Quarterly* 60:183–244.

Manton, K. G., and B. J. Soldo. 1985. Dynamics of health changes in the oldest old: New perspectives and evidence. *Milbank Memorial Fund Quarterly* 63:177–451.

Manton, K. G., E. Stallard, and H. D. Tolley. 1991. Limits to human life expectancy: Evidence, prospects, and implications. *Population and Development Review* 17(4): 603–37.

Manton, K. G., and M. A. Woodbury. 1987. Biological models of human mortality and the limits to life expectancy. Paper presented at the annual meeting of the Population Association of America, Chicago, April 29–May 2.

Mazess, R. B., and S. H. Forman. 1979. Longevity and age exaggeration in Vilcabamba, Ecuador. *Journal of Gerontology* 34:94–98.

Myers, G. C., and K. G. Manton. 1984. Compression of mortality: Myth or reality: *Gerontologist* 24:346–53.

Olshansky, S. J., B. A. Carnes, and C. Cassel. 1990. In search of Methuselah: Estimating the upper limits of human longevity. *Science* 250:634–40.

Pearl, R. 1923. *The rate of living*. New York: Knopf.

Pearson, K. 1923. *The chances of death, and other studies in evolution*. London: Arnold.

Peto, R., S. E. Parish, and R. G. Gray. 1986. There is no such thing as aging, and cancer is not related to it. In *Age-related factors in carcinogenesis*, ed. A. Likhachev et al. Lyon: International Agency for Research on Cancer.

Poterba, J. M., and L. H. Summers. 1987. Public policy implications of declining old-age mortality. In *Work, health, and income among the elderly,* ed. G. Burtless. Washington, D.C.: Brookings Institution.

Rosenfeld, A. (1976) 1985. *Prolongevity,* 2d ed. New York: Knopf.

Rosenwaike, I. 1981. A note on new estimates of the mortality of the extremely aged. *Demography* 18:257–66.

———. 1985. *The extreme aged in America: A portrait of an expanding population.* Westport, Conn.: Greenwood.

Rowe, J. W., and R. L. Kahn. 1987. Human aging: Usual and successful. *Science* 237:143–49.

Ryder, N. B. 1975. Notes on stationary populations. *Population Index* 41(1): 3–28.

Sacher, G. A. 1977. Life table modification and life prolongation. In *Handbook of the biology of aging,* ed. C. E. Finch and L. Hayflick, 582–638. New York: Van Nostrand Reinhold.

Sacher, G. A. 1980. Theory in gerontology, part I. *Annual Review of Gerontology and Geriatrics* 1:3–25.

Schatzkin, A. 1980. How long can we live? A more optimistic view of potential gains in life expectancy. *American Journal of Public Health* 70:1199–1200.

Schneider, E. L., and J. A. Brody. 1983. Aging, natural death, and the compression of morbidity: Another view. *New England Journal of Medicine* 309:854–56.

Schneider, E. L., and J. Guralnik. 1987. The compression of morbidity: A dream which will come true someday! *Gerontologica Perspecta* 1:8–13.

Schneider, E. L., and J. D. Reed. 1985. Life extension. *New England Journal of Medicine* 312:1159–68.

Shryock, H. S., and J. S. Siegel. 1976. *The methods and materials of demography.* New York: Academic Press.

Spencer, G. 1986. The first-ever examination of the characteristics of centenarians in the 1980 census. Paper presented at the annual meeting of the Population Association of America, New Orleans.

Vaupel, J. W., B. A. Gambill, and A. I. Yashin. 1987. Thousands of data at a glance: Shaded contour maps of demographic surfaces. Laxemburg, Austria: International Institute for Applied Systems Analysis.

Vaupel, J. W., and A. E. Gowan. 1986. Passage to methuselah: Some demographic consequences of continued progress against mortality. *American Journal of Public Health* 76:420–22.

Vaupel, J. W., K. G. Manton, and E. Stallard. 1979. The impact of heterogeneity in individual frailty on the dynamics of mortality. *Demography* 16:439–54.

Vaupel, J. W., and J. M. Owen. 1986. Anna's life expectancy. *Journal of Policy Analysis and Management* 5:383–89.

Comment on Chapters 2 and 3   Peter Diamond

When David Wise invited me to discuss these two papers, he said that he wanted me to think about the policy implications of the findings. He said the same to Michael Hurd. Mike and I have divided up the policy world. He will talk about the relationship to Old Age and Survivors Insurance (OASI). I will talk about the relationship to Disability Insurance (DI). Since there are two other chapters about long-term care (LTC), we will not relate chapters 2 and 3 to that topic.

First, a simple overview of what these papers are about. Let $M(a,t)$ be the aggregate mortality rate as a function of age and time. We are interested in (at least) three things. How would you project M into the future? How would you examine the impact of medical interventions on M? How might you relate M to other issues such as the demand for LTC, the supply of DI recipients, the supply of labor?

There are two ways to go about projections. One is to examine aggregate statistics, whether for M or for mortality by cause, examine the history of trends, and think about extrapolation on that basis. This is what the Vaupel and Lundström chapter (chap. 3) is about. The second is to estimate mortality hazards on individual data and simulate to produce an aggregate projection. This is what the Manton, Stallard, and Singer chapter (chap. 2) is about.

One can interpret a major part of the Vaupel and Lundström paper as asking the following question. If one wants to project $M(a,t)$ based on selecting a functional form and estimating the parameters on aggregate data, what is a sensible (a priori) form for M? In particular, is it sensible to have a form consistent with declines in M at all ages that do not have an asymptotic minimum level of M bounded away from zero? The alternative is to assume that M stays

Peter Diamond is professor of economics at the Massachusetts Institute of Technology and a research associate of the National Bureau of Economic Research.

very large at ages within the range we currently observe, that the asymptote, should the projection be extended indefinitely into the future, should not be zero.

The primary evidence brought directly to bear on this question is the presence of a trend in mortality rates at advanced ages. If there is an asymptote, it would appear that we are not sufficiently close to it for it to show up in the data, and therefore for it to play a role in functional form selection for estimations which are then used for projections out to the moderate term (100 years?).

The second topic in chapter 3 is the review of the basis for thinking that the mortality function should have an asymptote with a sharply rising section in the mid-90s. I have not read any of the literature being discussed. Without that background, I would hope that argument would be spelled out.

The Manton, Stallard, and Singer paper is of the micro simulation sort. It relates to Vaupel and Lundström's chapter in two ways. One is that disaggregated (by cause and individual) death rates should aggregate up to be consistent with our best sense of the shape of the aggregate mortality function. Second, the debate on functional form for the aggregate function is also relevant for the selection of functional form for disaggregated estimation. Unfortunately, in my reading of the Manton et al. paper, I could not tell how time entered in the functions to be estimated, so I could not tell how it related to the Vaupel and Lundström paper.

The methodology of chapter 2 involves two forms of disaggregation, if I have this right. One is by cause of death. The second comes from using individual data and introducing additional health variables into the estimation process. For example, if one has data on blood pressure at various times, one could estimate the stochastic time interdependence of blood pressures and the (lagged) stochastic structure of the relationship between blood pressure and mortality rates by cause. This is an extremely attractive way to proceed, since it opens up a way to address the additional questions I identified at the start. Disability is also identified as a powerful forecasting variable.

For example, if one wanted to consider the possible effects of a continued improvement in blood pressure and in the incidence of heart attacks in the population, one would proceed in different ways with the two different simulation models at hand. One might simply make an assumption on the extension of the trend in heart attack mortality. One would need to make some assumption (such as no effect) on the implication of the projected trend on other death rates. Alternatively, one could have an estimated relationship between blood pressure and different mortalities by cause and age and so derive the impact of blood pressure decline on all of the mortality rates by cause. Of course, one would then be making a different assumption: namely, that the interactions associated with the intervention are like those of the historical trend. That is, lowering blood pressure further is similar in its effects to previously caused improvements. If one is seeing improved dietary habits spreading to more of the population, this may be more plausible than if one is projecting a new drug which may have side effects or other differences in effects from the historically given decline. That is, if the historical decline is diet driven, then the effects of diet on mortality by cause that do not go through blood pressure will be partially captured by blood pressure and partially captured by trend. The projection will be implicitly picking up some of this.

This is part of a familiar tension. Both macro- and micro-based projections involve assumptions, differently described assumptions. Which basis is more reliable for projection depends in part on the quality of the different assumptions. That is why it will remain useful for research to project in parallel on both macro and micro levels.

What about the relation of chapter 2 to DI? One might have a database that allowed estimation of DI receipt as a function of health variables. If these same health variables were part of this mortality estimation, one could then derive a DI-receipt simulation model. (It would also be necessary to recognize that varying administrative interpretations of DI standards have been a major cause of fluctuations in disability rates.) One would also need the mortality of DI recipients, which might use the basic model or might recognize that DI receipt was a variable of independent econometric value in predicting mortality. (One would also want a model of return to the labor force which is additional.) Getting more ambitious, one observes that retirement is often related to health variables. Combining this relationship with both the health evolution model and the mortality model, one has a potentially improved basis for projecting labor force and OASI benefits. More generally, I find this approach very attractive.

What about DI policy and the sense of the findings coming from Manton et al.'s paper? For this, I need to back up and talk about the place of DI in our panoply of programs. (In part I am drawing on my paper with Sheshinski [Diamond and Sheshinski, in press].) We have lots of programs to provide income to people with low earnings. There are welfare programs. There is UI. There is SSI. There is OASI. There is DI. There are also private programs (soup kitchens) that provide some benefits to the destitute. What is a potentially useful pattern here, and how do demographic changes affect how we might want to combine these programs as well as structure them? That is, changing demographics might call for changing the parameters of an individual program (thought of in isolation). For example, if health and labor supply improve "in proportion" to life expectancy, then one might want to simply change the parameters of OASI by changing, in proportion to life expectancy, the "normal retirement age," the age of eligibility for early benefits and, the age of eligibility for benefits independent of earnings. If life expectancy, health, and labor supply do not change in proportion, then one might contemplate a different pattern of change in the parameters.

Similarly, the desired relationship between programs might change because of demographic changes. We have programs that are universal (along the lines of a negative income tax). We have programs that are targeted at a group with a relatively easy to measure target variable (age as a basis for OASI, at least after the start-up period, so that documentation of age happens well before eligibility). We have programs that are based on difficult to measure variables (such as DI based on the ability to work). Programs also differ in the cost of verification. Akerlof (1978) has written about the improved trade-off between distributional goals and disincentive costs that come from such targeted programs. But targeted programs are subject to both type I and type II errors. Stern (1982) has written about the choice between a targeted and a universal program as a function of the disincentives elements and the magnitude of the errors. Diamond and Sheshinski (in press) have written about combining both types of programs, incorporating awareness of both types of errors and disincentives in the choice of parameters for the two programs.

Workers become eligible for OASI at age 62. Workers remain eligible for DI until age 65. Thus there is a three-year overlap period during which workers are eligible for both programs. With the delay in the normal retirement age (but not the age of eligibility for OASI), the overlap period will grow. The overlap period is an accident of legislative history. Moreover the relative parameters of the two programs are a result of the adaptation of the parameters of the retirement program to generate a disability program, not the result of a conscious optimization over both programs. This should probably change. In particular, growing life expectancy together with health and labor supply improvements, which, I think, will not improve in proportion, will increase the range of differences in outcomes across people and so increase the importance of coordinating both programs. However, such a move is in the opposite direction to pressures in the United States and in many other countries.

In particular, following the Chilean example, there is a move toward forced savings programs that do not provide insurance for variation in the length of working life. Provision of such insurance is likely to have increased importance in the future, with growing life expectancy at older ages. The extent to which this is important is related to the impact on life expectancy of the sort of events that lead to early retirement. It would be wonderful to have a full-fledged estimation of the parameters of such interaction along the lines of Manton et al.'s chapter. Longer life expectancy, labor supply held constant, is a source of relatively lower living standard and so, on utilitarian lines, a reason for the receipt of income redistribution. The link with disability is more complicated because of the correlation with life expectancy. That is, recognizing that the groups of people who are more likely to receive disability are more likely to die young is relevant for designing programs which have given ex ante redistribution elements. I think that a detailed calculation of the conditional probabilities is important for design of disability programs relative to retirement programs. A similar approach may be a fruitful basis for design of LTC insurance as well, but that is a separate subject.

References

Akerlof, G. 1978. The economics of tagging as applied to the optimal income tax, welfare programs, and man power planning. *American Economic Review* 68:8–19.

Diamond, P., and E. Sheshinski. In press. Economic aspects of optimal disability benefits. *Journal of Public Economics.*

Stern, N. 1982. Optimum taxation with errors in administration. *Journal of Public Economics* 17(2): 181–211.

Comment on Chapters 2 and 3   Michael D. Hurd

Understanding the determinants of the mortality risk of the elderly and how those determinants will change over time is important for public policy. For example, the future costs of the Social Security retirement program depend directly on length of life following retirement: an underestimate of life expectancy at age 65 of, say, 10 percent translates directly into an underestimate of costs of 10 percent in steady state.

Because the elderly consume medical services at about four times the rate of the nonelderly, the amount we spend on health care depends in an important way on the life expectancy of the elderly, although the link is complicated because of the bunching of medical expenditures just before death. Trends in medical expenditures make this particularly important: health-care consumption rose from 9.1 percent of GNP in 1980 to 12.2 percent in 1990, because of sustained inflation in medical services in excess of CPI inflation and because of sharp increases in age-specific use per capita. Future increases in medical prices and in age-specific use will interact with demographic changes in a way that can produce very large increases in total consumption of medical services and, of course, in the costs of the Medicare and Medicaid programs.

In this comment I will focus on the variability of forecasts. I will use the forecasts of Manton, Singer, and Stallard (chap. 2), official forecasts from the Social Security Administration, and results from the Vaupel and Lundström paper (chap. 3) to argue that our uncertainty about the course of mortality risk is great, in the sense that the range of mortality outcomes spanned by the forecasts implies a wide range of tax and transfer outcomes.

Uncertainty in Population Forecasts.

The Office of the Actuary of the Social Security Administration forecasts both the elderly and nonelderly populations from assumptions about the future course of age-specific mortality rates, rates of immigration, and fertility rates. The rates are based on expert opinion: they are not based on a theoretical

Michael D. Hurd is professor of economics at State University of New York at Stony Brook and a research associate of the National Bureau of Economic Research.

model that has been fitted to historical data. Table IIC.1 has forecasts of the elderly population in 2040, life expectancy at age 65, and the elderly dependency ratio (the ratio of the number of elderly to the number aged 20–64) for three alternative assumptions about the course of mortality rates.[1] Alternative II is considered to be the best estimate, and it typically is used as the basis for forecasts of the cost, revenues, and balances of the trust funds. It embodies a 27 percent decline in age-specific mortality rates by 2040. Alternatives I and III are based on mortality rate declines of 13 and 40 percent, respectively, and forecasts of the trust funds that use these alternatives are often thought to bound the possible outcomes.

Alternative I has 7.5 percent fewer elderly in 2040 than the baseline (alternative II), and alternative III has 8.6 percent more. Under alternative III, life expectancy is 11–13 percent higher than under alternative II, so that in steady state costs would be 11–13 percent higher.

The baseline forecast of Manton et al. gives 51.7 million elderly in 2040 (table 2.5). I do not know of any way to analyze the causes of the difference between this number and the Social Security baseline (69.6 million); rather I would like to focus on the variation in forecasts. The forecast of Manton et al. is substantially outside the interval bounded by alternatives I and III. Furthermore, Manton et al. give simulations in which their risk factors are controlled. If the mean of each risk factor is put at its optimum but the variance is not changed, many individuals will have risk factors that are far from optimal. Nonetheless, controlling the mean in this way will increase the number of elderly to 79.9 million by 2040 (table 2.5), an increase of 54 percent over baseline. If, in addition, the variance of the risk factors is put to zero, so that the risk factors of each individual are at their optima, Manton et al. forecast 127.5

Table IIC.1   Number of Elderly, Life Expectancy, and Elderly Dependency Ratio

Year and Alternative	Mortality Reduction (%)	Number (millions)	Life Expectancy at Age 65		Dependency Ratio
			Male	Female	
1990	na	31.9	15.0	18.8	.21
2040					
I	13	64.4	15.6	19.4	.33
II	27	69.6	17.2	21.2	.39
III	40	75.6	19.3	23.5	.47

Source: OASDI Board of Trustees (1990).

1. The table has the Social Security area population, which differs slightly from the U.S. population because it includes some additional geographic areas such as Puerto Rico. The alternatives differ by assumptions about fertility and immigration as well as mortality rates, but variation in the fertility and immigration assumptions will have only marginal effects on the elderly population in 2040.

million elderly by 2040, an increase of 246% over baseline (table 2.5). These give, of course, enormous variation in the number of elderly compared with the forecasts of the Office of the Actuary.

A way to judge the importance of the variation is in terms of its effects on Social Security tax rates. The Trustees' Report has a sensitivity analysis, which gives the ceteris paribus change in net trust fund income resulting from a change in mortality assumptions. Moving from alternative I to alternative III, which increases the elderly population by 17 percent, requires that taxes increase by about 0.85 percent of taxable payroll each year from now to 2039 (OASDI Board of Trustees 1990, table B2, 50-year balance). Taking the baseline of Manton et al. and assuming a constant response of payroll taxes to percentage changes in the elderly population, I estimate that under the first forecast of Manton et al. (mean risk factors at their optimum) the tax would have to be 2.7 percent of taxable payroll greater than under baseline; under the forecast that puts the variance of risk factors to zero, the tax would have to be 7.3 percent of taxable payroll greater. The latter figure is rather large, about a 50 percent increase in the payroll tax. While the former figure, an increase of 2.7 percent, may seem moderate, it should be kept in mind that it is only moderate because it is levied over each of the next 50 years: if the tax is not levied until the baby-boom generation begins to retire, it will be much greater. Furthermore, it is greater by a factor of 3.2 than the variation in the tax rate between alternatives I and III.

Although Vaupel and Lundström have no population forecasts, the basic point of their paper is the same as that of Manton et al's: our uncertainty about the upper bound of the future elderly population is great. If the Fries hypothesis is correct, life expectancy can increase but not much beyond those figures given in my table IIC.1 under alternative III. Vaupel and Lundström argue that Fries is wrong and that there is no theoretical limit to life expectancy: even if the risk factors in Manton et al. are put to their optima, their population forecasts could be too low. In this event, the effects on the Social Security retirement system and the health-care system would be practically devastating.

Population Forecasts and Changes in Risk Factors.

In the forecasting model of Manton et al., the actual population could differ from the forecast population for at least two reasons: the choice of the level and variance of the risk factors used in the simulations could be different from actual future risk factors, or the model of mortality risk may not give the right change in mortality risk for a change in risk factors because it is incorrectly specified. The preceding section discussed how the forecasts vary as the risk factors vary. In this section, I will give an example that shows how difficult it is to find a correctly specified model. If the model is not correctly specified, we should be even more uncertain about the future elderly population because, even if we know with certainty the future course of the risk factors, we would still be uncertain about the course of mortality risk. The example will consider the relationship between mortality rates and exercise.

Suppose, as in Manton et al., we want to use epidemiological (nonexperimental) data such as the Framingham data to find the effects of exercise and cholesterol on mortality rates. Following them, we would fit a vector ARMA to the risk factors (exercise and cholesterol) and a mortality hazard which would depend on the risk factors and possibly on their past levels. Other risk factors such as age, sex, and marital status would also be used, but they are not necessary for this example. This system could be used to forecast values of exercise and cholesterol and, hence, mortality rates, and, therefore, it could forecast the population. We could get good forecasts if other unobserved determinants of risk factors and mortality evolve as they have in the past.

Now suppose we want to forecast the response to a change in a risk factor, say, exercise. As in Manton et al. this would involve changing a risk factor and, through simulation, finding the new forecast population. To illustrate the range of outcomes, I introduce two health models.

In health model A, exercise does affect mortality risk because it affects unmeasurable healthiness, which, in turn, affects mortality risk. People choose exercise levels by whim. In model B, exercise has no effect on healthiness or on mortality risk. However, individuals with differing levels of healthiness face differing costs of exercise: exercise is unpleasant or even painful for unhealthy individuals, and they would tend to exercise less. We would, therefore, observe a negative correlation between exercise and mortality under either model, but, of course, the effects in the population of requiring everyone to take up exercise would be completely different: under model A mortality risk would decline; under model B it would be unchanged.

A statistical method for controlling for unobserved healthiness can be based on panel data: the individual effect (healthiness) can be accounted for in a number of ways, such as by taking deviations from individual means in a linear model or by modeling the distribution of the individual effect in a nonlinear model. For simplicity, take the case of a linear model. Then, model parameter estimates will depend on variation in the time path of exercise at the individual level and any associated mortality events. Under model A, those individuals who decrease their exercise level will eventually have higher mortality rates, whereas individuals who do not decrease their exercise levels will have unchanging mortality rates. If healthiness is static, under model B any variation over time in exercise would not be associated with any variation in mortality rates. The two models predict different relationships between the time paths of exercise and mortality. That difference can be used to identify the true model, which will lead to the correct prediction about the effects of changing exercise on mortality risk.

However, the point of the model of Manton et al. is that risk factors evolve, and it surely follows that healthiness also changes over time. Under model A, mortality risk would vary as healthiness varies, but, on average, individuals who choose declining levels of exercise would have increasing mortality rates. Under model B, individuals whose healthiness fell would reduce exercise, and their mortality rates would also rise. Thus, the empirical outcomes would be the same under either model A or B: unchanging exercise is associated with unchanging mortality rates; falling exercise is associated with increasing mortality rates. Without further specification of what would amount to a structural model, no empirical methods could separate the models, and so we should not have much confidence that changing exercise in the population will have an effect on mortality risk.

This example is a gross simplification of the model of Manton et al., but it does, I believe, illustrate why I have reservations about their assessment of the effects of altering risk factors. I do not mean to be overly critical because this is the same kind of empirical problem economists face with nonexperimental data, and everyone knows how difficult it is to find convincing results.

Conclusion

The paper by Manton, Singer, and Stallard, the paper by Vaupel and Lundström, and the population forecasts by the Social Security Administration should lead practically anyone to the conclusion that the actual future elderly population could well be very different from the forecast population. The difference is large as measured by the variation in the impact on the Social Security retirement system. Although I have no quantitative measures, I am sure the effects on health-care expenditures and on the Medicare and Medicaid programs vary in a similar way. How policy should react to the uncertainty is not at all obvious, but because it will be practically catastrophic to the retirement and health-care financing systems should the actual population reach the upper levels of the forecasts, we should be thinking now of policies to cover those cases. Of particular importance is reducing the rate of growth in medical costs, because of the interaction of medical costs with the elderly population.[2]

Reference

OASDI Board of Trustees. 1990. 1990 annual report of the federal OASDI trust funds. OASDI Trust Funds. Washington, D.C.: Government Printing Office.

2. See my comment on Shoven, Topper, and Wise's chap. in this volume.

III Retirement Saving

4   401(k) Plans and Tax-Deferred Saving

James M. Poterba, Steven F. Venti, and David A. Wise

Tax-deferred 401(k) saving plans were the fastest-growing employee benefit during the 1980s. Since there are penalties for early withdrawal of assets in 401(k) accounts, the contributions to these plans are likely to remain invested until workers retire. The growth of 401(k) plans therefore has the potential to significantly affect the financial status of future elderly households.

Tax-deferred saving accounts, including 401(k)s, have become an increasingly significant channel for personal saving in the United States. This trend began with the Economic Recovery Tax Act of 1981, which dramatically expanded eligibility for Individual Retirement Accounts (IRAs) and allowed individuals who were also covered by employer pension plans to contribute to these accounts. By 1985, more than 15 percent of all taxpayers made IRA contributions totaling more than $38 billion, or nearly one-third of personal saving in the United States. More than 25 percent of all families had IRAs, even though not all of them made contributions in 1985. The 1986 Tax Reform Act limited the scope for tax-deductible IRA contributions. These changes prompted a sharp decline in the number of IRA contributors, from 15.5 million in 1986 to 7.3 million (6.8 percent of tax returns) in 1987. Total IRA contributions declined from $38 to $14 billion.

Like IRAs, 401(k) plans are deferred compensation plans for wage earners,

James M. Poterba is professor of economics at the Massachusetts Institute of Technology and director of the Public Economics Research Program at the National Bureau of Economic Research. Steven F. Venti is professor of economics at Dartmouth College and a research associate of the National Bureau of Economic Research. David A. Wise is the John F. Stambaugh Professor of Political Economy at the John F. Kennedy School of Government, Harvard University, and the area director for Health and Retirement Programs at the National Bureau of Economic Research.

The authors are grateful to Andrew Samwick for assistance with Survey of Consumer Finances computations, and to the National Institute of Aging, the James Phillips Fund (Poterba), the Rockefeller Research Fund at Dartmouth College (Venti), and the Hoover Institution (Wise) for research support.

but unlike IRAs, they are provided by employers. The plans were formally established by the Revenue Act of 1978, but were rarely used until the Treasury Department issued clarifying rules in 1981. If provided by the employer, the 401(k) plan permits the employee to contribute before-tax dollars to a retirement account. Taxes are deferred on the part of income that is contributed to the plan. The participant also benefits from tax-free accumulation of the 401(k) investment, just as with IRAs, and may obtain additional benefits if the employer matches part of the employee contribution. Taxes are paid when funds are withdrawn from the account. The Tax Reform Act of 1986 reduced the annual limit on 401(k) contributions from $30,000 to $7,000 and added nondiscrimination provisions to prevent plans from providing benefits exclusively to high-income employees. The $7,000 contribution limit has been indexed since 1988 and is $8,475 for the 1991 tax year.

The availability of 401(k)s and participation in them expanded rapidly after the 1981 clarifying rules. In 1983, total employment at firms with 401(k) plans totaled 7.1 million; by 1988, the number of workers eligible to participate had increased to 27.5 million. The number of participants increased as well, from 2.7 million in 1983 to 15.7 million in 1988. Almost $40 billion was contributed to 401(k) plans in 1988, with an average employee contribution of about $2,500. Most large firms now have 401(k) plans. A Hewitt Associates (1990) survey of 902 major U.S. employers found plans at 92 percent of the firms in 1989. The recent adoption of 401(k)s has been fastest, however, at small firms: a Massachusetts Mutual Life Insurance Company (1988) survey shows that the number of small firms offering these plans increased from 8 percent in 1984 to 36 percent in 1988.

This chapter provides a systematic analysis of the nature and significance of 401(k) plans. It is divided into five sections. Section 4.1 describes the structure of 401(k) plans, their eligibility rules, contribution limits, and typical balances. It presents summary information on 401(k) eligibility and participation decisions, with particular attention to participation patterns for those with and without IRA accounts. Section 4.2 considers the characteristics of 401(k) plans in more detail and includes preliminary evidence on employer matching rates and withdrawal provisions. Section 4.3 focuses on the overlap between IRA and 401(k) eligibility, directly addressing the extent of substitution between 401(k) and IRA saving and the correspondence between actual saving patterns and "rational" patterns. Section 4.4 examines the extent to which 401(k) contributions represent new saving. The analysis is based on changes over time in total assets of 401(k) participants, and on differences between the net worth of households eligible for and ineligible for 401(k) plans. The results suggest that 401(k) plan contributions represent a net addition to saving, rather than transfers from other stores of wealth or displacement of other forms of saving. Section 4.5 is a brief conclusion.

4.1   401(k) Plan Eligibility and Participation

The probability that an individual contributes a given amount to a 401(k) plan can be factored into the product of three probabilities: the probability of contributing that amount conditional on participating in a 401(k) plan, the probability of participating given that a plan is available, and the probability of being eligible to participate. We analyze each of these probabilities in turn.

The basic data are from the 1984, 1985, and 1986 panels of the Survey of Income and Program Participation (SIPP). Each panel comprises eight interview waves administered over two and one-half years. Data from wave 4 of the 1984 panel cover September–December 1984. Wave 7 of the 1985 panel and wave 4 of the 1986 panel cover the period January–April 1987. The same set of questions about income, assets, and personal retirement saving programs were asked of each panel, with one exception: the 1984 panel did not ask for the balance held in 401(k) accounts. We present nominal values from each of these surveys below. The consumer price index rose 5.9 percent during the twenty-eight-month period separating these surveys.

Five categories of financial assets are distinguished in our analysis: 401(k)s, IRAs, all other financial assets (excluding 401(k)s and IRAs), total financial assets, and debt. Other financial assets include all liquid assets such as bank saving accounts as well as stocks and bonds, although in some cases, we present results excluding stocks and bonds. Total financial assets equal the sum of IRAs, 401(k)s (when available), and other financial assets.

The unit of observation is the household reference person and the reference person's spouse, if present. For a family to be included in our sample, the household reference person had to be between 25 and 65 years of age, at least one member of the family had to be employed, and no member of the family could report self-employment income. The last restriction is necessary because in most cases neither IRAs nor 401(k)s are feasible options for the self-employed.

The SIPP data are supplemented with data from two additional sources. The May 1983 and 1988 Current Population Surveys (CPS) provide data on 401(k) eligibility and participation and on IRA contributions. The 1989 Survey of Consumer Finances (SCF) provides information on the characteristics of 401(k) plans at the end of the 1980s. In addition, we have used IRA contribution data from the Internal Revenue Service.

4.1.1   Eligibility and Participation in 401(k) Plans

At the beginning of the 1980s, 401(k) plans were virtually nonexistent. By 1987, however, one in eight families participated in a 401(k) plan, and one in five families were eligible for a plan through an employer. The top panel of table 4.1 reports the age and income characteristics of persons eligible for and participating in 401(k) plans in 1984 and 1987. The proportion of families contributing to a 401(k) plan increased by 62 percent between 1984 and 1987, from 7.7 to 12.5 percent. The percentage whose employers offered such plans

Table 4.1   401(k) Eligibility and Participation by Age and Income, 1984 and
                 1987 (%)

	401(k) Eligibility	401 (k) Participation Given Eligibility	401(k) Participation	IRA Participation
Total population				
1984	13.3	58.1	7.7	25.4
1987	20.0	62.6	12.5	28.8
1987 Income categories (thousand $)				
<10	3.9	49.3	1.9	8.3
10–20	10.3	49.8	5.1	12.3
20–30	16.7	54.9	9.2	22.7
30–40	24.1	61.8	14.9	31.9
40–50	31.9	64.6	20.6	41.1
50–75	35.8	68.0	24.3	56.1
>75	33.2	83.9	27.8	66.6
1987 Age categories				
25–34	18.3	53.3	9.7	16.3
35–44	22.2	63.3	14.1	25.1
45–54	21.3	66.9	14.3	37.4
55–64	17.6	72.0	12.7	48.1

Source: Authors' tabulations from the SIPP, as described in the text.

and who were thus eligible to contribute increased from 13.3 to 20.0 percent. Perhaps the most striking feature of these plans is the high participation rate of those who are eligible, 58.1 percent in 1984 and 62.6 percent in 1987.[1]

The 401(k) participation rate of eligible families is more than twice as high as the participation rate in the IRA program, for which virtually all wage earners were eligible through the 1986 tax year.[2] For example, 25.4 percent of families had IRA accounts in 1984, and 28.8 percent had these accounts in 1987. In fact, the difference in participation rates is greater than these data suggest; the "rates" are not precisely comparable. A family is counted as "participating" in a 401(k) if it contributed to a plan in the year of the survey. But a family need only *have* an IRA account to be classified as participating in the IRA program. Thus the IRA rate overestimates the proportion of families currently contributing to an IRA. This difference is especially important after the 1986 restrictions on IRA eligibility.

Several factors may account for the higher 401(k) participation rate, includ-

1. Throughout this paper we view 401(k) participation as a voluntary employee choice. Some employers make contributions to their employees' 401(k) accounts even if the employees choose not to make contributions. Only 24 percent of all 401(k) plans, and 5 percent of the plans at large employers, have this feature (see U.S. General Accounting Office [GAO] 1988a).

2. The 1987 data are for the months January–April. IRA contributions made during this period are generally for the 1986 tax year. Thus 1987 IRA data from the SIPP typically reflect the tax rules in effect through 1986.

ing attractive employer matching, some degree of encouragement for worker participation from employers, or the presence in some plans of "hardship withdrawal" provisions that make 401(k)s somewhat more liquid than IRAs. In addition, 401(k) contributions are usually made through payroll deductions, which may serve as a form of self-control and ensure that a saving plan is adhered to. Once the payroll deduction form has been signed, saving is further removed from day-to-day competition with consumption; salary reductions never appear as spendable earnings.

The two lower panels of table 4.1 report the income and age characteristics of families eligible for and participating in 401(k)s in 1987. The third column of the middle panel reveals that 401(k) participation is closely related to income. Among families with incomes less than $10,000, about 2 percent participate in a 401(k). For higher income families, the participation rate exceeds 25 percent.

The relationship between income and 401(k) participation that is graphed in figure 4.1 reflects both the relationship between income and 401(k) eligibility and the correlation between income and contributions conditional on eligibility. While only about 4 percent of families with annual income less than $10,000 work for employers who offer 401(k) plans, almost 35 percent of those with incomes above $50,000 are eligible for such plans.[3] The 401(k) participation rate conditional on eligibility also rises as income rises, from about 50

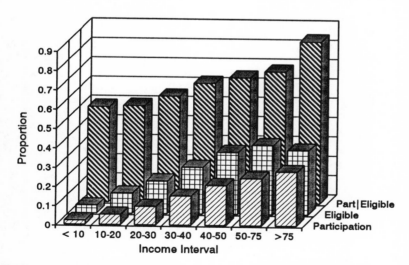

Fig. 4.1   401(k) rates of participation, eligibility, and participation given eligibility, 1987 (by income)

3. Eligibility shows only a weak relationship to age, however. Given eligibility, more than 50 percent of families in almost every age-income group participate in 401(k) plans.

percent for families with income less than $10,000 to 84 percent for families with income over $75,000.

The increase in participation as income rises is much less pronounced than the corresponding pattern for IRAs. IRA participation is only about 8 percent for families with income less than $10,000 but increases to 67 percent for those with income above $75,000.

4.1.2   401(k) Balances

Table 4.2 shows that in 1987, the *mean* balance in 401(k) accounts was $1,237 for all households. The mean IRA balance was $2,836. Among those who had 401(k) accounts, the mean 401(k) balance was $9,862 in 1987, almost the same as the mean IRA balance of families who had IRAs, $9,841. Among

Table 4.2   **Mean and Median Balances in 401(k) and IRA Accounts, 1987**

Income (thousand $)	Participants[a]		All Households	
	Median	Mean	Median	Mean
401(k) Balances				
All	4,000	9,862	0	1,237
<10	1,000	1,628	0	31
10–20	1,000	4,328	0	222
20–30	2,000	4,510	0	413
30–40	4,000	7,856	0	1,168
40–50	4,000	9,021	0	1,861
50–75	6,300	13,584	0	3,304
>75	11,560	20,350	0	5,660
IRA Balances				
All	8,000	9,841	0	2,836
<10	6,000	7,538	0	628
10–20	4,500	6,955	0	859
20–30	5,024	7,247	0	1,645
30–40	7,000	9,016	0	2,876
40–50	7,550	9,112	0	3,748
50–75	10,000	11,690	2,200	6,555
>75	13,600	15,175	7,500	10,107
IRA + 401(k) Balances				
All	18,000	24,208	0	4,073
<10	12,500	10,530	0	659
10–20	7,045	11,453	0	1,081
20–30	11,000	14,777	0	2,058
30–40	14,856	17,666	0	4,044
40–50	13,000	19,535	400	5,609
50–75	22,000	26,893	4,200	9,859
>75	31,518	37,295	10,000	15,767

Source: Authors' tabulations from the SIPP.

[a]Participation in a 401(k) or IRA defined as a balance greater than zero in that plan. Participation in IRA + 401(k) defined as balances greater than zero in *both* plans.

participants, however, the *median* 401(k) balance is half the median IRA balance. There are fewer very large IRA account balances than there are very large 401(k) balances because of the lower legal contribution limit for IRAs. Table 4.2 also reports the distribution of 401(k) and IRA balances by income. For low income groups, the mean 401(k) balance was about 20 percent of the IRA mean, and for high income groups, about half of the IRA mean. Conditional on participating in a 401(k), however, the mean 401(k) balance for high income households actually exceeds that in IRAs.

That the relationship of 401(k) assets to income is stronger than that of IRA assets, given participation, is probably the result of two effects. First, contributions to 401(k) plans, unlike IRA contributions, are typically specified as a percentage of salary. This applies to both employer and employee contributions. Thus high-income employees tend to contribute more than their low-income counterparts. Second, the contribution limits to the two plans are different. The IRA limit is typically $2,000. The 401(k) limit was $45,475 before 1982, $30,000 before the 1986 Tax Reform Act, and $7,000 thereafter. Thus there is much more latitude for 401(k) contributions to increase with income.

A large fraction of the financial assets of most families was in the form of IRAs or 401(k)s. Table 4.3 reports median financial total and other assets, 401(k) account balances, and IRA balances, for families in 1987 classified by 401(k) and IRA participation. Even families that had only 401(k)s had a large fraction of their assets in this form—$2,800 versus $2,149 in other financial assets. Families with both 401(k)s and IRAs typically had more in these accounts than in other financial assets—$18,000 versus $14,350. Families with both 401(k)s and IRAs had much larger balances in both accounts together than families with only IRAs had. The large share of assets held in 401(k) accounts will in all likelihood rise over time, as households continue to contribute to these accounts. It is particularly striking in light of the relatively short time that these plans have been available.

4.2   Characteristics of 401(k) Plans: Preliminary Evidence

This section presents descriptive evidence on characteristics of 401(k) plans that may affect the degree to which they are viewed as substitutes for other tax-deferred saving vehicles. These plan characteristics should also feature prominently in future work on 401(k) participation decisions.

4.2.1   Employer Matching Rates

A 1988 U.S. General Accounting Office (U.S. GAO 1988b) survey of 401(k) plans suggested that participation rates are much higher in plans with some employer matching of worker contributions. Table 4.4 presents summary tabulations from the GAO survey. While the employee participation rate in plans without any matching was less than 50 percent, the rate exceeded 75 percent in plans with employer matching. The increase in participation rates

Table 4.3   Median and Mean Asset Balances by 401(k) and IRA Participation, 1987

Asset	Households with IRA	Households with 401(k)	IRA-*Only* Households	401(k)-*Only* Households	Households with Both	All Households
			Median			
Total financial assets	22,300	17,100	19,300	7,299	38,276	2,849
Total financial assets excluding stocks and bonds	18,600	14,300	16,000	6,061	32,499	2,250
Non–IRA-401(k) assets	10,025	5,600	9,483	2,149	14,350	1,750
Non–IRA-401(k) assets excluding stocks and bonds	6,699	3,500	6,100	1,500	8,188	1,250
IRA	8,000	0	7,359	0	9,000	0
401(k)	0	4,000	0	2,800	6,000	0
IRA and 401(k)	8,997	7,500	7,359	2,800	18,000	0
Debt	500	1,000	500	1,200	700	650
			Mean			
Total financial assets	40,456	36,693	35,605	16,567	59,224	16,299
Total financial assets excluding stocks and bonds	29,856	26,614	26,413	11,819	43,177	11,845
Non–IRA-401(k) assets	27,901	21,645	26,062	9,702	35,016	12,227
Non–IRA-401(k) assets excluding stocks and bonds	17,300	11,566	16,869	4,954	18,969	7,772
IRA	9,841	5,186	9,544	0	–	2,836
401(k)	2,714	9,862	0	6,865	–	1,237
IRA and 401(k)	12,555	15,048	9,544	6,865	24,208	4,073
Debt	3,575	3,298	3,581	3,071	3,552	3,041

Source: Authors' tabulations based on the SIPP.

Table 4.4   401(k) Participation Rates by Employer Match Rate, 1986

Match Rate (%)	Participation Rate (%)	Average Contribution/Salary (%)
0	49.5	3.5
0–25	75.3	3.8
25–50	75.6	3.8
50–75	81.0	3.8
75–100	64.5	4.2
100	98.6	7.0
>100	88.1	8.6

Source: U.S. GAO (1988b).

as the firm match rate rises is less clear, but the nearly 90 percent participation rate for plans with more than dollar-for-dollar matching suggests there may be some incremental effects.

The data in table 4.4 also suggest that employees tend to contribute a higher fraction of their salary when employer match rates are more generous. Conditional on participating, employees at firms with no matching provisions contribute 3.5 percent of their salary. Those with plans matching more than dollar-for-dollar, however, contribute an average of 8.6 percent of salary.

We also investigated the importance of matching using the 1989 SCF, which includes information on both the employer match rate and the amount of employee contribution. Table 4.5 shows that nearly 40 percent of 401(k) participants in the SCF face match rates less than 10 percent, while one-quarter are matched more than dollar-for-dollar by their employers. For these employees, 401(k)s are clearly superior to IRAs, even when the IRA contribution is tax-deductible. The U.S. GAO (1988a) tabulations show that 51 percent of the firms sponsoring 401(k) plans matched employee contributions. As in the SCF, the GAO found that the majority of plans with matching provisions involved dollar-for-dollar matching. The similarity between the GAO and SCF results is encouraging, because the underlying sampling rules are different. The GAO results weight each *plan* equally, while our SCF tabulations average across households and therefore weight plans in proportion to their number of contributors.

Table 4.6 displays the distribution of *employee* contribution rates, as a share of salary, for those who reported 401(k) participation in the 1988 CPS. Most employees contribute 3–9 percent of their salary to the 401(k) plan. These results are similar to those from the 1989 SCF, although many more SCF participants (10.3 percent) indicated zero employee contributions to the plan.

4.2.2   Other Plan Provisions

Employer matching rates are probably the most important dimension along which 401(k) plans differ, but there are many other features of these plans that

Table 4.5   **Employer Match Rate for 401(k) Plan Contributions, 1989**

Match Rate (%)	Percentage of All 401(k) Plan Participants (%)
0–10	39.3
10–20	1.6
20–30	3.2
30–40	6.9
40–50	13.3
50–100	9.8
>100	25.7

Source: Authors' tabulations from the 1989 SCF.

Table 4.6   **Share of Employee Salary Contributed to 401(k) Plan, 1988**

	Percentage of All 401(k) Participants (%)	
Share of Salary (%)	Percentage	Cumulative
0	1.0	1.6
1	4.2	5.8
2	7.5	13.3
3	9.0	22.3
4	7.7	30.0
5	19.6	49.6
6	16.1	65.7
7	4.6	70.3
8	5.8	76.1
9	1.6	77.7
10	11.8	89.5
>10	9.4	100.0

Source: Authors' tabulations from the 1988 CPS.

can affect their attractiveness as saving vehicles. Table 4.7 presents descriptive information on the plans surveyed by the GAO in 1987. The table describes four plan provisions and yields no strong evidence on the link between these provisions and participation rates.

Participation rates are slightly higher in plans that preclude employees from borrowing against their accumulated balances, making their own investment choices, or making hardship withdrawals of their own contributions. While the differential participation rates are relatively small in all three cases, the pattern is surprising, since employees appear more likely to participate in plans that reduce their financial flexibility. These data are an invitation to further work, since the bivariate tabulations do not control for match rates or characteristics of the firm or workers covered by these plans.

4.3 Are 401(k)s and IRAs Substitutes?

A central issue in evaluating the net saving effects of tax-advantaged saving plans is the extent to which these plans serve as substitutes for other forms of saving. The net saving effect of 401(k) plans depends both on the extent to which individuals treat them as substitutes for traditional saving vehicles, and on the extent to which 401(k) plans substitute for other tax-advantaged saving plans such as IRAs.

Focusing on household behavior with respect to only one saving incentive program may yield misleading inferences about the consequences of changing the provisions of that program. For example, an increase in the IRA contribution limit is typically viewed as affecting the opportunity set of an individual

Table 4.7   **401(k) Participation Rates by Various Plan Characteristics, 1986**

Plan Characteristic	Participation Rate (%)	Average Contribution/Salary (%)
Loan provision?		
Yes	69.3	4.6
No	81.7	4.9
Hardship withdrawals for employee contributions?		
Yes	71.3	4.5
No	75.6	6.8
Hardship withdrawals for employer contributions?		
Yes	86.9	5.3
No	50.1	3.5
Self-directed investments?		
Yes	69.9	5.4
No	73.1	4.0

Source: U.S. GAO (1988b).

who is making the maximum possible IRA contribution. However, this may be incorrect if the IRA contributor is also participating in a 401(k) plan but not contributing up to the 401(k) limit, since this person's *total* tax-deferred saving is not constrained. If 401(k) and IRA accounts are treated as perfect substitutes, then changing the IRA limit should not affect the saving of such a household.

In contrast, a high-income worker who is not eligible to make a tax-deductible IRA contribution might change her saving if an employer 401(k) plan became available to her. If she contributed the 401(k) maximum, then changes in this limit would directly affect her saving. A "rational" saver should *never* contribute less than the maximum to a 401(k) and also make a non-deductible IRA contribution, since raising the former and reducing the latter would reduce her current tax liability with no change in net worth.

A few high-income households make limit contributions to both a 401(k) plan and an IRA.[4] If these households do no further saving through taxable channels, then changes in the IRA contribution limit or the 401(k) limit will almost surely affect their total saving. If these households save through taxable channels, then all tax-deferred saving might be thought of as inframarginal. If individuals treat all forms of saving as perfect substitutes, then changing either contribution limit would not affect net saving. A central issue in evaluating the net saving effects of IRAs is the degree to which IRAs and other forms of

---

4. Two-thirds to three-quarters of all IRA contributions are at the contribution limit. Only about 3 percent of all 401(k) contributions are at the post-1986 legal contribution limit. However, about 40 percent of firm 401(k) plans place additional limits on the contributions of some highly paid employees to comply with "nondiscrimination" tests for pension plans. See U.S. GAO (1988a) and Hewitt Associates (1988).

saving are treated as substitutes.[5] To illuminate the pattern of substitution between IRA and 401(k) saving and the correspondence between actual saving patterns and "rational" patterns, this section presents data on the interaction between IRA and 401(k) saving.

4.3.1   The Overlap between 401(k) and IRA Saving

Table 4.8 presents evidence on the overlap between IRA and 401(k) saving. The data show the percentage of persons who make 401(k) contributions who also participate in IRAs. The SIPP, the source for these tabulations, indicates whether a family has an IRA account in each year but does not report whether a contribution was made in that year. Even in the early years of the IRA program, the percentage of families contributing in a given year was less than the percentage with an account. In later years, particularly following the Tax Reform Act of 1986, the two percentages diverged as families that were once regular participants stopped contributing. In 1987, for instance, more than twice as many families had accounts as contributed.

To provide information on IRA contributions as well as accounts, therefore, we present data from the CPS, which reports the percentage of persons making an IRA contribution in the 1982 and 1987 tax years. Because the 1987 CPS data pertain to the 1987 tax year, they reflect the eligibility restrictions imposed by the Tax Reform Act of 1986. In 1987, 47 percent of 401(k) *contributors* also had IRA accounts. The CPS data for 1987 reveal that only 17 percent of 401(k) contributors also made an IRA contribution, a substantial decline from 37 percent in 1982.

4.3.2   401(k)s and the Post-1986 Fall in IRA Contributions

It is tempting to conclude that, as 401(k)s became more widely available, they displaced IRAs because employer matching made them more attractive. A large fraction of 401(k) contributors became ineligible for the full tax advantages of the IRA after 1986, however, and this may have induced a decline in IRA contributions even *without* any 401(k) substitution. This view is supported by the similarity between the decline in IRA participation among households

Table 4.8   **Overlap of 401(k)s and IRAs, 1982–87**

	1982 CPS	1984 SIPP	1987 SIPP	1987 CPS
Percentage of 401(k) contributors who:				
Have an IRA	–	41.1	47.1	–
Contribute to an IRA	37.0	–	–	17.4

Source: Authors' tabulations using surveys as indicated.

5. This is the focus of empirical work by Feenberg and Skinner (1989), Gale and Scholz (1994), and Venti and Wise (1986, 1990a, 1990b, 1992).

that are eligible, and those that are ineligible, for 401(k)s. The proportion of *all* tax filers making IRA contributions rose from 12.6 to 15.9 percent between 1982 and 1986, and then fell to 6.8 percent in 1987. The decline in IRA participation for 401(k) participants thus mirrors the population reduction, suggesting that tax reform and not the diffusion of 401(k)s explains the IRA decline.

The sharp decline in IRA contributions after 1986 was common to all income groups. Table 4.9 shows the percentage of persons who contributed to an IRA, by 401(k) eligibility status and by income interval, in 1982 and 1987. The data suggest several important conclusions that are made clear with the aid of figure 4.2. First, controlling for income, the percentage of 401(k) eligibles who contributed to an IRA in 1982 was very close to the percentage of ineligibles who contributed. The contribution rates are significantly different only for the less than $10,000 and greater than $75,000 income groups, for which the percentage of 401(k) eligibles contributing to IRAs is *higher* than the percentage of ineligibles.[6] If IRAs and 401(k)s were viewed as close substitutes, then IRA accounts would be less prevalent among those eligible for a 401(k). These data consequently cast doubt on either standard assumptions about saving behavior or the assumption that IRAs and 401(k)s are perfect substitutes.

Second, the decline in IRA contributions after 1986 is not consistent with a high degree of substitution between IRAs and 401(k)s. The Tax Reform Act of 1986 phased out the tax deduction for IRA contributions for higher-income taxpayers—married filing units with incomes above $40,000 and single filers with incomes above $30,000—provided they were also covered by an employer-sponsored pension plan. Approximately 73 percent of all tax filers

Table 4.9   **Percentage Contributing to an IRA by 401(k) Eligibility and Income**

Income (thousand $)	1982 Not Eligible for 401(k)	1982 Eligible for 401(k)	1987 Not Eligible for 401(k)	1987 Eligible for 401(k)
<10	11.9	20.9	7.2	12.8
10–20	16.1	18.5	9.6	12.2
20–30	24.3	22.9	15.8	14.0
30–40	36.8	39.2	18.3	17.5
40–50	50.5	46.3	24.2	15.3
50–75	59.2	55.2	26.5	19.6
>75	64.5	85.4	37.2	28.7
All	19.9	26.0	12.9	15.3

Source: Authors' tabulations based on 1983 and 1988 CPS.

6. App. A presents estimates of standard errors for the levels and differences in participation rates for various income groups.

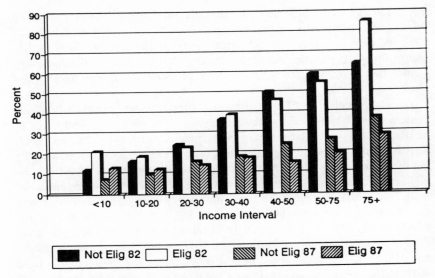

Fig. 4.2   IRA contribution percentage by 401(k) eligibility, 1982 and 1987

were unaffected by the changes. Given these changes, one would have expected little change in IRA contribution behavior at low income levels and the greatest response among high-income households that were eligible for a 401(k) plan.[7] In fact, the percentage contributing to IRAs fell dramatically for all income groups after 1986, and it was largely independent of 401(k) eligibility. Only for the greater than $75,000 income group was the *fall* in the contribution rate for 401(k) eligibles significantly greater than the fall in the contribution rate for the 401(k) ineligibles. Thus the availability of the 401(k) option cannot explain the drop in IRA contributions.

Figure 4.3 presents IRA contribution rates for 1985 and 1988, by income interval, without accounting for 401(k) eligibility. The data used to construct these figures are from the IRS Statistics of Income series. Actual rates are shown in figure 4.3A, and the percentage decline between 1985 and 1988 is presented in figure 4.3B. Families that lost the up-front tax deduction virtually quit contributing after the 1986 legislation. Close to 70 percent of families with incomes greater that $50,000 made IRA contributions before 1986. But after the legislation, the proportion fell by almost 90 percent, to less than 10 percent. Families with incomes between $40,000 and $50,000—the interval over which the up-front deduction was phased out—reduced their contribution

---

7. An alternative view is that the Tax Reform Act of 1986 lowered marginal tax rates and thus made the IRA tax deduction less attractive. But IRA contributions fell even for low-income families that experienced little change in marginal tax rates because of the 1986 legislation (see Hausman and Poterba 1987).

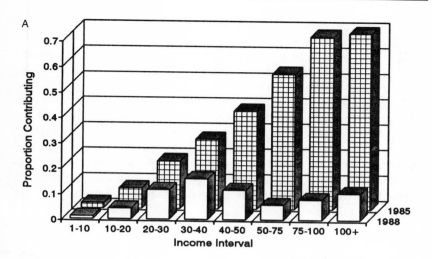

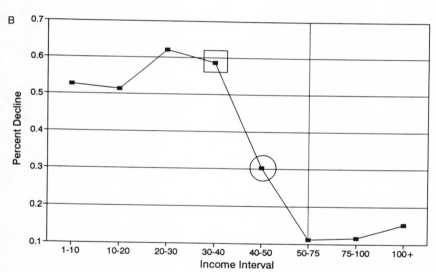

Fig. 4.3 *A,* **IRA contribution rate by income interval, 1985 and 1988.** *B,* **Decline in IRA contribution rate by income interval, 1985–88.**

rate by 70 percent. Even lower-income families unaffected by the legislation reduced their contributions by between 40 and 50 percent.

The across-the-board reduction in the IRA contribution rate was undoubtedly due in part to a misperception of the 1986 legislation, especially among lower-income families. Higher-income families may also have misunderstood the legislation, thinking that both the up-front deduction and the tax-free accumulation of returns had been eliminated. The systematic decline in IRA contributions also suggests that the promotion of these accounts may have been an important determinant of their widespread use.

Third, the pattern of IRA contribution rates in 1987 suggests only a modest relationship between IRA contributions and 401(k) eligibility. The rates for 401(k) eligibles are significantly lower than the rates for ineligibles in income categories above $40,000. At lower income levels, however, there is little relationship between IRA participation and the availability of a 401(k) plan. Indeed, the rate for eligibles is significantly higher than the rate for ineligibles in the two lowest income intervals. This suggests that, for households that remained eligible for tax-deductible IRAs after the 1986 tax reform, 401(k) saving did not displace IRA saving. Taken together, the results suggest that IRA contributions were curtailed as a result of the 1986 tax reform but were not displaced by 401(k)s.

4.3.3   IRA and 401(k) Saving by 401(k) Eligibles

Table 4.10 provides information on the saving behavior of all families *eligible* for 401(k)s in 1987. The first column, based on SIPP data, pertains to *families* and indicates whether the family has an IRA *account* in 1987. The second column, based on CPS data, pertains to *individuals* and indicates whether the individual *contributed* to an IRA in 1987. Only about one-third of 401(k) eligibles saved in neither a 401(k) nor an IRA. Among those eligible for a 401(k), 40 percent have an IRA account and 10.4 percent have only an IRA; 15.5 percent contribute to an IRA and 5.1 percent contribute only to an IRA. The IRA contribution rate for those eligible to make 401(k) contributions exceeded the IRA contribution rate for all tax filers in 1987, but this is because of the higher income of 401(k) eligibles. Controlling for income, there is little difference between the two groups except at higher income intervals, as shown in table 4.9.

4.3.4   IRA Limit Contributors and 401(k) Saving

The overlap between 401(k) and IRA saving for families making maximum possible IRA contributions in 1984 is shown in table 4.11. It might be pre-

Table 4.10	Retirement Plan Use by Families Eligible for 401(k)s (%)	
	1987 SIPP	1987 CPS
Neither a 401(k) nor an IRA	27.1	35.5
Only an IRA	10.4	5.1
Only a 401(k)	33.1	49.0
Both a 401(k) and an IRA	29.5	10.4

Source: Authors' tabulations from the CPS and the SIPP.

Note: The 1987 SIPP data pertain to families and to IRA accounts. The 1987 CPS data pertain to individuals and to IRA contributions.

Table 4.11   **IRA Limit Status versus 401(k) Participation**

	IRA Participants	IRA Limit Contributors	All Households
Probability of 401(k) participation (%)	16.2	17.2	11.5
Probability of 401(k) participation if eligible (%)	65.8	66.1	56.0

	401(k) Eligibles	401(k) Participants	All Households
Probability of IRA limit contribution (%)	20.6	24.3	16.3
Probability of IRA contribution (%)	26.2	30.8	21.9

Source: Authors' tabulations based on merging waves 4 and 7 of the 1984 SIPP Panel. A household is defined to be an IRA contributor in a year if the change in the IRA balance over the one-year interval exceeded $500. A household is defined to be a limit contributor if the change in the balance exceeded $2,000.

sumed that persons at the IRA limit are constrained by the limit and thus would like more tax-deferred saving. Indeed, 66 percent of families at the IRA maximum make additional contributions to a 401(k) plan if they are eligible for such a plan. The significant fraction that does not take advantage of the 401(k) is striking, because employer matching typically makes a 401(k) plan more attractive than an IRA. Perhaps some families are only motivated to make an IRA contribution to shelter income at the time of tax filing and do not consider the role of IRAs in an ongoing saving plan. This is consistent with the finding that one-third to one-half of all IRA contributions are made between the end of the tax year and the April 15 filing deadline (Summers 1986; Skinner 1992).

Among families who were eligible to participate in a 401(k), 26.2 percent made an IRA contribution. Of those who made a 401(k) contribution, 31 percent also contributed to an IRA. Although the data do not indicate whether the 401(k) contributors who made IRA contributions were at the 401(k) limit, it is likely that most were not. This pattern is also surprising, since for many households 401(k)s probably yield higher returns, inclusive of employer matching, than IRAs.

The results in this section cast doubt on the assumption that all forms of saving, and particularly saving in 401(k)s and IRAs, are treated as perfect substitutes. They also raise doubts about the extent to which all households are "rational" savers, basing saving decisions on economic return criteria only. The relationship between 401(k) eligibility and IRA saving is weak, and a substantial proportion of families save in IRAs even though they could make additional 401(k) contributions. Understanding why some households save through dominated saving instruments is an important issue for future work.

4.4   The Saving Effects of 401(k) Plans

To investigate whether 401(k) contributions represent "new saving," one could compare the total non-401(k) saving of 401(k) contributors to the total non-401(k) saving of noncontributors. Contributors save more in non-401(k) forms than do noncontributors, even after controlling for differences in income, and thus the total saving of 401(k) contributors exceeds the total saving of noncontributors. This does not necessarily mean that 401(k)s increased total saving, because the comparison of contributors to noncontributors ignores individual-specific saving effects. Some families are "savers" and some families are "nonsavers," and the former are likely to save more in all available forms. Convincing evidence on the net saving effect of 401(k)s therefore requires a more subtle test.

We use two simple approaches to consider the saving effect of 401(k)s, both intended to control for individual-specific saving effects. The first considers two demographically similar random cross sections of "like families" that have been "exposed" to 401(k) plans and IRAs for different periods of time. Since age, income, and other characteristics of the two cross sections are similar, one would expect saving balances also to be similar. However, the 1984 sample has had only about two years (1982–84) to accumulate 401(k) and IRA balances, but the more recent sample has had about five years. The central question is whether longer "exposure" to these plans results in higher levels of saving.[8] Our second approach relies on the natural experiment that is provided by the largely exogenous determination of 401(k) eligibility. It considers whether eligibility is associated with higher levels of total saving, holding income constant. This approach views 401(k) eligibility as the "treatment" in a "natural experiment" to evaluate the effect of tax incentives on saving.

4.4.1   Changes in Assets of "Like Families": 1984 versus 1987

In this subsection we compare two independent samples of households that contribute to 401(k)s. The samples are randomly chosen and thus are similar with respect to age, income, and other economic and demographic characteristics. One sample is from 1984, and the other is from 1987. In principle, we are comparing a typical person aged, say, 40 in 1984 to another person aged 40 in 1987. Both persons are at the same point in the life cycle and would presumably have accumulated similar levels of assets, abstracting from possible aggregate effects due to asset appreciation rates between 1984 and 1987.

---

8. An issue that cannot be controlled for with this approach is the possibility that the persons who took up the 401(k) option were those who were about to *change* their saving behavior, that the 401(k) just happened to be available at the opportune time, and that it was used as the saving vehicle for the reborn saver who would have increased saving in another form, had it not been for the 401(k) option. The second approach (below) tends to minimize the potential confounding of effect of this possible coincidence. This issue is discussed in more detail, with respect to IRAs, in Venti and Wise (1992).

There is one important difference, however. The 401(k) contributor in 1984 had roughly two years over which contributions could be made; the 401(k) contributor in 1987 had roughly five years. If 401(k) contributions represent asset transfers, then the total asset balances of the 1984 and 1987 contributors should be roughly the same—additional 401(k) contributions made by the 1987 contributor would replace saving that would have been done in other forms. If 401(k) contributions represent new saving, however, then the total financial assets—including 401(k)s—of the 1987 contributor should exceed the total assets of the 1984 contributor by the amount contributed to 401(k)s between 1984 and 1987.

The assets of families that had only 401(k) plans are shown in the first panel of table 4.12. The financial assets of these families in 1987 data are shown in the second and fourth columns. The median of total financial assets was about $6,100 excluding, and $7,300 including, stocks and bonds. We would like to know how much financial wealth families like these had in 1984. Was it about

Table 4.12   **Median IRA and 401(k) versus Other Financial Asset Balances by Type of Asset Held, 1984 and 1987**

Group	Excluding Stocks and Bonds		Including Stocks and Bonds	
	1984	1987	1984	1987
Families with 401(k) only				
Total assets	–	6,061	–	7,299
Other than 401(k)	1,800	1,500	3,000	2,149
401(k)	–	2,800	–	2,800
Debt	1,000	1,200	1,000	1,200
Families without 401(k)				
Total assets	1,500	1,500	1,949	2,000
Families with IRA only				
Total assets	13,000	16,000	16,170	19,300
Other than IRA	6,550	6,100	9,400	9,483
IRA	4,500	7,400	4,500	7,400
Debt	500	500	500	500
Families without IRA				
Total assets	650	754	800	960
Families with IRA and 401(k)				
Total assets	–	32,499	–	38,276
Other than IRA or 401(k)	8,499	8,188	13,000	14,350
IRA	5,000	9,000	5,000	9,000
401(k)	–	6,000	–	6,000
IRA and 401(k)	–	18,000	–	18,000
Debt	500	700	500	700
Families with neither IRA nor 401(k)				
Total assets	600	550	750	700

Note: Entries are in nominal dollars for 1984 and 1987.

the same as in 1987, suggesting no net saving effect, or did it increase, suggesting a net addition to saving? We assume that the families that participated in 401(k) plans in 1987 are like those that participated in such plans in 1984, except that the 1987 families were able to make plan contributions for two or three more years. The data for 1984 are not complete, however, because the SIPP did not obtain 401(k) asset balances in that year. Thus both 401(k) and total financial asset balances are missing.

It is nonetheless possible to make rough judgements about the net saving effect of the 401(k) contributions. No change in non-401(k) asset balances would suggest no substitution of 401(k) for other forms of saving, and thus that 401(k) balances represented net new saving, no matter what the magnitude of the 401(k) saving. The data, however, show a small decline in the median of other—non-401(k)—assets between 1984 and 1987, about $850 including stocks and bonds and about $300 excluding stocks and bonds. Median debt increased by about $200. Thus, we would like to compare this decline with the increase in 401(k) assets.

The increase in the median 401(k) balance was undoubtedly substantial, but we can provide only a rough approximation of the amount of the increase. About 40 percent of the families that had plans in 1987 did not have them in 1984. The typical 401(k) contribution is well above $2,000 (actually about $2,500). Thus, as a rough approximation, assume that the 401(k) balances of employees who had accounts in 1984 increased about $5,000 between 1984 and 1987. Again as a rough approximation, assume that the increase for those who began to contribute after 1984 was about $2,500 on average. The average increase would then be about $4,000 (0.4 × $2,500 + 0.6 × $5,000). If these 401(k) contributions replaced saving that would otherwise have occurred in other forms, the non-401(k) assets of the contributors should have fallen by about the same amount as the increase in 401(k) assets. But the decline in other assets was much smaller than the probable increase in 401(k) assets. This suggests that, in large part, the 401(k) contributions represented net new saving.[9] In contrast to the substantial increase in the financial assets of families with 401(k)s, families without 401(k)s had about the same median wealth in both years—exactly the same excluding stocks and bonds, and $1,949 in 1984 versus $2,000 in 1987 if stocks and bonds are included.

A similar comparison can be made between families that had only IRA accounts in 1987 and families that had only IRA accounts in 1984. These data are shown in the second panel of table 4.12. This comparison is more complete and probably more accurate than the comparison for 401(k) participants, however, because total assets are known in both years and because the sample size is much larger than the sample of families with 401(k)s only. Consider families

---

9. The approximations used in this paragraph relate more directly to means than to medians. Table 4.12 is reproduced in App. table 4B.1, but means rather than medians are reported. The basic conclusions are the same.

that had IRA accounts in 1987. Again, we assume that the families that had IRA accounts in 1987 are like those that had such accounts in 1984, except that the 1987 families were able to make IRA contributions for two or three more years. Indeed, the 1987 families had $2,859 more in IRA accounts than the 1984 families. If additional IRA contributions replaced saving that would otherwise have occurred in other forms, however, total assets of the 1987 sample should have been about the same as the total for the 1984 sample. But the median total financial assets of the 1987 families were in fact $3,130 larger than the total financial assets of the 1984 families. There was essentially no change in the nominal value of other financial asset balances ($9,400 in 1984 vs. $9,483 in 1987). In addition, there was no change in median debt. This suggests that the IRA contributions did not replace other saving. The basic pattern is the same whether stocks and bonds are included or excluded from the measure of other financial assets. These results are similar to those in earlier studies of IRA contributors (see, e.g., Venti and Wise 1990a, 1990b, 1992) and are directly comparable to the results in Venti and Wise (1992), based on Consumer Expenditure Survey data.

Comparable data for families that had both IRA and 401(k) accounts in 1987 and families that had both accounts in 1984 are shown in the bottom panel of table 4.12. By 1987, families with both accounts had a median balance of $18,000 in the two together, approximately half the median balance in total financial assets. Like the data for the 401(k)-only group, the data for this group are incomplete, because 401(k) balances were not obtained in the 1984 survey, but the basic inference is the same. IRA and 401(k) contributions were not offset by reduced saving in other financial asset forms. If they had been, the 1987 families would have accumulated fewer assets in other forms, because when they started to contribute to IRAs and 401(k)s they would have saved less in other forms.

The data show that the 1987 respondents had somewhat larger balances in non-401(k)-IRA financial assets than the 1984 respondents had, and their median debt was only slightly larger ($700 in 1987 vs. $500 in 1984). These data also suggest little substitution between IRA and 401(k) saving. The IRA balance for this group increased by $4,000—$1,000 more than the increase in the IRA balance for those with IRAs only.

4.4.2   Asset Balances by 401(k) Eligibility

This section relies on the natural experiment that is provided by the essentially exogenous determination of 401(k) eligibility to explore the effect of 401(k) contributions on total saving. Eligibility is determined by employers. If household saving behavior is independent of individual characteristics related to the probability of working at firms with 401(k) plans, an assumption which is unlikely to be completely accurate, then comparison of the net worth of families with and without 401(k) eligibility can be used to infer the saving effect of these plans. If there are no net saving effects of 401(k)s, then families who have the 401(k) option should have similar net worth, but less non-401(k) assets, than those families without 401(k) eligibility.

Median financial asset balances by 401(k) eligibility and by income interval are shown in table 4.13 for 1987 and 1984. We stratify by income because 401(k) eligibility increases with income. If, given income, eligibility is determined exogenously, then the data allow strong inferences about the saving effect of 401(k) plans. Figure 4.4 presents information from this table in graphical form. Figure 4.4A shows that families whose employers offered 401(k) plans had substantially greater total financial assets in 1987 than did families whose employers did not provide such plans. For example, the median level of financial assets of families with incomes between $50,000 and $75,000 who were eligible for a 401(k) was $25,343, whereas the median for families who were not eligible was only $14,650. If when families became eligible for 401(k) plans they reduced saving in other forms, the typical family eligible for a 401(k) in 1987 should have less accumulated wealth in other financial assets than the typical family who had not been eligible for a 401(k). Figure 4.4B shows that this was not the case. There was little difference in the other financial assets between families who were and those who were not eligible for a 401(k). Indeed, the eligible families had somewhat higher levels of other financial assets.

Table 4.13   **Median Asset Balances by 401(k) Eligibility and Income, 1984 and 1987**

Group	Income (thousand $)							
	<10	10–20	20–30	30–40	40–50	50–75	>75	All
1987								
Not eligible for a 401(k)								
All financial assets	22	400	1,366	4,000	6,630	14,650	30,900	1,870
Other assets	20	350	1,052	2,800	4,245	8,737	21,200	1,300
IRA	0	0	0	0	0	2,000	6,000	0
Eligible for a 401(k)								
All financial assets	1,090	1,190	4,000	9,205	12,650	25,343	58,119	10,330
Other assets	361	305	1,250	3,250	5,800	11,200	25,500	4,000
IRA	0	0	0	0	0	2,500	11,204	0
401(k)	0	0	150	1,000	1,000	1,500	8,500	1,000
1984								
Not eligible for a 401(k)								
All financial assets	34	458	1,768	3,950	7,150	15,870	19,000	1,850
Other assets	30	400	1,400	3,000	5,138	11,000	21,950	1,400
IRA	0	0	0	0	0	2,000	4,000	0
Eligible for a 401(k)								
All financial assets[a]	–	–	–	–	–	–	–	–
Other assets	25	509	1,749	3,740	5,049	11,500	30,400	3,740
IRA	0	0	0	0	0	0	0	0
401(k)[a]	–	–	–	–	–	–	–	–

[a]401(k) assets are not available for 1984. Entries are in nominal 1984 and 1987 dollars.

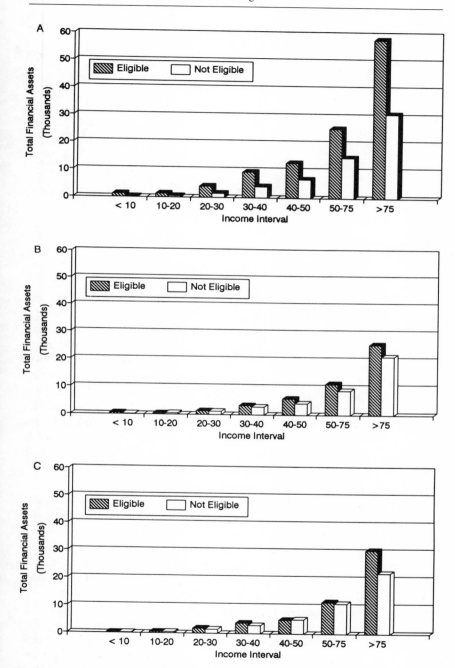

Fig. 4.4   Assets by 401(k) eligibility. *A,* **Total financial assets of all families, 1987.** *B,* **Other financial assets of all families, 1987.** *C,* **Other financial assets of all families, 1984.** *D,* **Other financial assets of 401(k) eligibles, 1984 and 1987.**

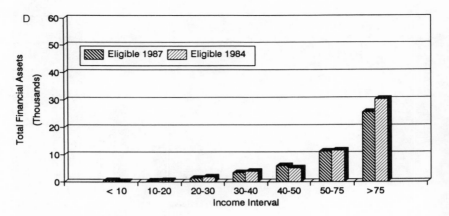

Fig. 4.4   (continued)

The data also show that, in 1984, eligible and ineligible families had virtually the same levels of other financial assets. Figure 4.4C suggests that 401(k) contributions did not substitute for other financial asset saving.[10] Moreover, other financial assets of eligible families in 1984 were about the same as the other financial assets of eligible families in 1987, as shown in figure 4.4D, again suggesting that 401(k) assets did not substitute for other financial assets.

Table 4.14 also distinguishes families on the basis of 401(k) eligibility, but the data pertain to families—eligible or ineligible for a 401(k)—that had IRA accounts. The conclusions are the same as those suggested by table 4.13 and figure 4.4. Eligible families have greater total financial wealth, but other financial assets of eligibles are virtually the same as those of ineligibles, in both 1987 and 1984. There was virtually no difference between the nominal holdings of other financial assets by eligibles in 1984 and 1987.

Our analysis relies on the exogenous determination of 401(k) eligibility status, given income. It could be that the eligible group is composed disproportionately of savers, who save more than the typical person, in all forms. There is little evidence, however, for this type of heterogeneity in saving behavior. As shown above, eligible and ineligible families had about the same level of other financial assets in 1987 and 1984. Thus the eligible group had not been saving more than the ineligible group, in other assets, as they would have if they were disproportionately high savers, saving more in all forms. Moreover, those who were eligible for a 401(k) in 1984 had about the same level of other assets as those who were eligible in 1987. In addition, among IRA savers, other assets do not differ by 401(k) eligibility status. Whereas 401(k) eligibility

10. The 1984 data do not show 401(k) asset balances, however, so that total assets of eligible and ineligible families can not be compared in that year.

Table 4.14   **Median Asset Balances for Families with IRAs by 401(k) Eligibility and Income, 1984 and 1987**

Group	<10	10–20	20–30	30–40	40–50	50–75	>75	All
				Income (thousand $)				
				1987				
Not eligible for a 401(k)								
All financial assets	13,249	10,800	12,487	18,748	19,000	28,050	48,550	19,646
Other assets	5,000	4,000	5,900	9,630	10,000	16,200	30,990	9,700
IRA	6,000	4,500	5,000	7,320	8,000	10,000	12,500	7,500
Eligible for a 401(k)								
All financial assets	5,820	9,400	15,228	21,000	24,700	36,400	68,500	30,600
Other assets	2,100	2,300	4,500	8,400	9,000	15,500	29,292	12,000
IRA	2,000	6,000	5,900	6,700	6,500	10,000	15,000	8,000
401(k)	0	300	1,000	2,000	2,316	4,000	10,000	2,900
				1984				
Not eligible for a 401(k)								
All financial assets	7,200	9,749	10,500	16,230	17,401	25,600	43,529	16,250
Other assets	2,525	5,000	5,700	9,300	10,600	17,400	33,529	9,450
IRA	3,000	3,800	4,000	4,500	4,700	6,000	7,500	4,500
Eligible for a 401(k)								
All financial assets[a]	–	–	–	–	–	–	–	–
Other assets	3,100	2,249	6,500	10,605	6,950	17,500	38,200	11,500
IRA	4,000	3,000	3,400	4,000	4,224	6,530	8,250	4,500
401(k)[a]	–	–	–	–	–	–	–	–

[a]401(k) assets are not available for 1984. Dollar magnitudes are measured in current-year dollars for 1984 and 1987.

status may be determined exogenously, IRA status is chosen by individuals. Within either eligibility status, families with an IRA have substantially greater total financial assets than those without an IRA. This may reflect, in part, an individual-specific saving effect. Like other assets, however, IRA assets do not differ much by 401(k) eligibility status, as shown in figure 4.5.[11] Thus these data suggest that 401(k) status is indeed largely independent of overall saving propensity, given income.

An additional source of information on the extent of substitutability between 401(k), IRA, and other forms of financial saving is the *change* between 1984 and 1987 in median asset balances, *not* controlling for income interval. The idea is to consider whether the non-401(k)-IRA assets—"other assets"—of families with 401(k)s and/or IRAs declined between 1984 and 1987, as they would if the tax-advantaged saving substituted for other saving. The data are summarized in table 4.15. The main point of the data is that there was no change in the other assets of 401(k)-eligible families—whether or not they contributed to an IRA. For example, the amount of total financial assets of all

11. This seems to suggest little substitution between 401(k) and IRA saving, consistent with the data in the previous sections that were graphed in fig. 4.2.

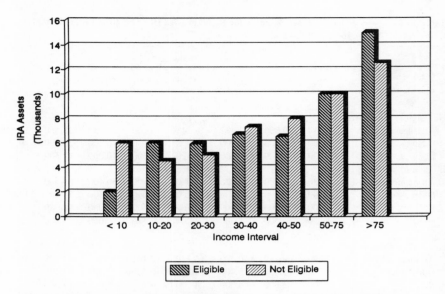

Fig. 4.5   IRA assets by 401(k) eligibility for families with an IRA, 1987

families eligible for a 401(k) in 1984 was $5,000 (excluding 401(k) assets); families eligible in 1987 had $10,330.[12] But there was almost no change in other financial assets of eligible families—a slight increase from $3,740 to $4,000. In contrast, the total (and other) financial assets of families not eligible for a 401(k) remained essentially unchanged over this period.

The message is the same for 401(k)-eligible families with an IRA and for those without an IRA: although total financial assets increased, other financial assets were essentially the same in 1984 and in 1987. The data reveal no hint of substitution. Among those not eligible for a 401(k), only those with an IRA experienced an increase in total assets—from $16,250 to $19,646—and for this group there was virtually no change in other assets. There was essentially no change in the assets of those without an IRA.

Finally, the increase in IRA assets—for families with these accounts—did not depend on 401(k) eligibility status. The increase for those not eligible for a 401(k) was from $4,500 to $7,500. For those who were eligible, the increase was from $4,500 to $8,000. Both the fact that both eligibility groups had the same level of IRA assets in 1984 and the almost identical increases suggest little substitution between 401(k) and IRA assets.

Throughout this section, we have focused on *median* asset levels, rather than on means, because the very large financial assets of a few families lead to mean

12. The median 401(k) balance in 1987 was $1,000, and the median 1984 balance was probably less than this.

Table 4.15   **Median Asset Balances for All Income Groups by 401(k) Eligibility and IRA Status, 1984 and 1987**

Group	1984	1987
All families		
Not eligible for a 401(k)		
All financial assets	1,850	1,870
Other assets	1,400	1,300
IRA	0	0
Eligible for a 401(k)		
All financial assets[a]	5,000	10,330
Other assets	3,740	4,000
IRA	0	0
401(k)	–	1,000
Families with an IRA		
Not eligible for a 401(k)		
All financial assets	16,250	19,646
Other assets	9,450	9,700
IRA	4,500	7,500
Eligible for a 401(k)		
All financial assets[a]	19,200	30,600
Other assets	11,500	12,000
IRA	4,500	8,000
401(k)	–	2,900
Families without an IRA		
Not eligible for a 401(k)		
All financial assets	700	623
Other assets	700	623
Eligible for a 401(k)		
All financial assets[a]	2,072	3,900
Other assets	1,774	1,923
401(k)	–	225

[a]Does not include 401(k) assets in 1984. Entries are measured in current dollars in 1984 and 1987.

asset levels that are much greater than the asset levels of the typical family. For example, the median of total financial assets of families not eligible for a 401(k) is $1,870, whereas the mean is $13,480. The median has the disadvantage, however, that medians of individual assets do not sum to the median of total assets, as means do. For example, the medians of the individual assets of all 401(k)-eligible families with incomes over $75,000 sum to $45,204, but the median of the total is $58,119. Mean values analogous to the medians in table 4.13 are presented in Appendix table 4B.2. The basic conclusions do not differ from the conclusions drawn from the median values. In fact, the difference in the means between the two groups is close to the difference in the medians.

4.5 Conclusions

Our results suggest that 401(k) plans are a significant and increasingly important component of retirement saving in the United States. Unlike IRA contributions, which fell by over 70 percent after the Tax Reform Act of 1986, 401(k) contribution levels have risen throughout the last decade. For many households, assets held through 401(k)s represent more than half of their financial wealth. The high participation rate of those eligible for 401(k)s, coupled with the tendency for most households to reach retirement age with few financial assets other than Social Security and employer-provided pension benefits, suggests that these accounts will play a very important part in the economic security of retirees in coming decades.

Our findings suggest several important conclusions. First, the high 401(k) participation rate of families whose employers offer 401(k) plans suggests that payroll deduction and emulation of other employees may be important determinants of saving decisions. While only about 16 percent of all tax filers made IRA contributions at the height of their popularity, over 60 percent of persons eligible for a 401(k) contribute to the plan. Even in the lowest income groups, the participation rate is close to 50 percent.

Second, the data reveal little substitution of 401(k) saving for either IRA saving or saving through traditional saving vehicles. The data actually show substantial IRA saving even when 401(k) saving would appear to offer a higher rate of return. This casts doubt on the usual assumptions that all forms of saving are treated as perfect substitutes and that all savers make "rational" saving decisions.

Third, the virtual cessation of IRA contributions by persons who lost the upfront tax deduction after the Tax Reform Act of 1986 suggests that such "attention getters" have an effect on saving that goes beyond the strict economic value of the deduction. The importance of promoting saving is suggested by the finding that, after the 1986 legislation, even unaffected persons reduced their contributions by almost 50 percent.

Fourth, the results suggest that 401(k) saving largely represents net new saving. This conclusion rests on the comparison of the financial assets of 401(k)-eligible and 401(k)-ineligible families and on the comparison of the assets of a random sample of 401(k) households in one year with the assets of a random sample of such households in a later year.

This paper sets the stage for further, more formal analysis of 401(k) saving. A behavioral model of household contributions to 401(k)s can in principle be used to simulate the effects of changes in the tax rules governing these plans or of changes in employer match rates. In some circumstances, for example at the firm analyzed in Kusko, Poterba, and Wilcox (1994), employer match rates change substantially from one year to the next. Economic conditions and other factors that affect these rates may therefore have an important influence on household saving as 401(k) plans become a more significant saving channel.

Another important question regarding the rapid rise of 401(k) plans concerns the extent to which these plans have replaced *previous* retirement saving plans. The 1988 GAO survey found that more than half of all firms with 401(k) plans also offer other saving vehicles, such as profit-sharing plans. At 61 percent of the firms in the GAO survey, the 401(k) plan was introduced as a new plan. For 29 percent of the firms, however, the 401(k) replaced a previous profit-sharing plan, and in the remaining cases, it replaced other pre-existing saving arrangements (see U.S. GAO 1988b). In 1987, the 401(k) was the primary plan of only 26 percent of participants (see Andrews 1992). Unfortunately, the published survey results provide no guidance on the number of workers who experienced plan replacements or on the extent to which 401(k) saving is simply a relabeling of saving that previously was channeled to other types of retirement plans.

Appendix A
IRA Contribution Rates by 401(k) Eligibility

We estimate two ANOVA specifications, one to provide estimates of the change in the IRA participation rates between 1982 and 1987 and the other to provide estimates of the difference in the rates for 401(k) eligibles versus ineligibles in 1982 and 1987. The first specification, for the change in participation rates, is of the form

(A1) $C = y_i + y(87)_i + e_i + e(87)_i + \varepsilon.$

This equation is estimated using data for individual persons, with $C = 1$ if the person contributes to an IRA and 0 otherwise. We denote different income intervals with subscript i, corresponding to the income groups in table 4.9. For each group, y is the base rate for ineligibles in 1982, $y(87)$ is the 1987 effect, e is the eligibility effect, and $e(87)$ is the eligibility effect in 1987. For each income group, the IRA contribution rates by year and 401(k) eligibility status—shown in table 4.9—are then given by

	1982	1987
Ineligible	y	$y + y(87)$
Eligible	$y + e$	$y + e + y(87) + e(87)$

The results are shown in table 4A.1. The $e(87)$ estimate of -0.2950 for the highest income interval indicates that the fall in the IRA contribution rates for the eligibles was 0.2950 larger than the fall for the ineligible group, and the *t*-statistic of -2.8 indicates that this difference is statistically significant at standard levels of significance.

The second specification, for the difference in contribution rates between 401(k) eligibles and ineligibles, is of the form

Table 4A.1   **IRA Contribution Rates by 401(k) Eligibility Status (estimates of eq. [A1])**

Variable	Parameter Estimate	Standard Error	t-Statistic
y_1	0.1186	0.0048	24.5
y_2	0.1607	0.0049	33.0
y_3	0.2427	0.0064	38.2
y_4	0.3679	0.0102	36.2
y_5	0.5046	0.0177	28.5
y_6	0.5924	0.0211	28.0
y_7	0.6446	0.0292	22.0
e_1	0.0904	0.0232	3.9
e_2	0.0238	0.0165	1.4
e_3	−0.0133	0.0173	−0.8
e_4	0.0239	0.0268	0.9
e_5	−0.0420	0.0436	−1.0
e_6	−0.0402	0.0554	−0.7
e_7	0.2092	0.0958	2.2
$y(87)_1$	−0.0464	0.0079	−5.9
$y(87)_2$	−0.0644	0.0073	−8.9
$y(87)_3$	−0.0849	0.0091	−9.3
$y(87)_4$	−0.1848	0.0136	−13.6
$y(87)_5$	−0.2625	0.0228	−11.5
$y(87)_6$	−0.3269	0.0269	−12.1
$y(87)_7$	−0.2721	0.0412	−6.6
$e(87)_1$	−0.0345	0.0298	−1.2
$e(87)_2$	0.0021	0.0199	0.1
$e(87)_3$	−0.0044	0.0205	−0.2
$e(87)_4$	−0.0321	0.0299	−1.1
$e(87)_5$	−0.0472	0.0479	−1.0
$e(87)_6$	−0.0297	0.0602	−0.5
$e(87)_7$	−0.2950	0.1036	−2.8

Source: Authors' estimates using the 1983 and 1988 CPS. See text for further description.

(A2) $$C = y(82)_i + y(87)_i + e(82)_i + e(87)_i + \varepsilon,$$

where $y(82)$ is the rate for ineligibles in 1982, $y(87)$ is the rate for ineligibles in 1987, $e(82)$ is the addition to the rate for eligibles in 1982, and $e(87)$ is the addition for eligibles in 1987. In this case the IRA contribution rates by year and 401(k) eligibility status are given by

	1982	1987
Ineligible	$y(82)$	$y(82) + e(82)$
Eligible	$y(87)$	$y(87) + e(87)$

The estimates are shown in table 4A.2.

Table 4A.2   **IRA Contribution Rates by 401(k) Eligibility Status (estimates of eq. [A2])**

Variable	Parameter Estimate	Standard Error	t-Statistic
y_1	0.1186	0.0048	24.5
y_2	0.1607	0.0049	33.0
y_3	0.2427	0.0064	38.2
y_4	0.3679	0.0102	36.2
y_5	0.5046	0.0177	28.5
y_6	0.5924	0.0211	28.0
y_7	0.6446	0.0292	22.0
e_1	0.0904	0.0232	3.9
e_2	0.0238	0.0165	1.4
e_3	−0.0133	0.0173	−0.8
e_4	0.0239	0.0268	0.9
e_5	−0.0420	0.0436	−1.0
e_6	−0.0402	0.0554	−0.7
e_7	0.2092	0.0958	2.2
$y(87)_1$	0.0722	0.0062	11.6
$y(87)_2$	0.0963	0.0054	17.9
$y(87)_3$	0.1578	0.0066	24.0
$y(87)_4$	0.1831	0.0091	20.2
$y(87)_5$	0.2421	0.0144	16.8
$y(87)_6$	0.2655	0.0167	15.9
$y(87)_7$	0.3725	0.0291	12.8
$e(87)_1$	0.0558	0.0187	3.0
$e(87)_2$	0.0259	0.0112	2.3
$e(87)_3$	−0.0177	0.0109	−1.6
$e(87)_4$	−0.0082	0.0133	−0.6
$e(87)_5$	−0.0892	0.0198	−4.5
$e(87)_6$	−0.0700	0.0237	−2.9
$e(87)_7$	−0.0858	0.0394	−2.2

Source: Authors' estimates using the 1983 and 1988 CPS. See text for further description.

Appendix B

Table 4B.1   **Mean IRA and 401(k) versus Other Financial Asset Balances by Type of Asset Held, 1984 and 1987**

	Excluding Stocks and Bonds		Including Stocks and Bonds	
Group	1984	1987	1984	1987
Families with 401(k) only				
Total assets	–	11,819	–	16,567
Other than 401(k)	5,851	4,354	8,259	9,702
401(k)	–	6,865	–	6,865
Debt	3,014	3,071	3,014	3,071
Families without 401(k)				
Total assets	8,942	9,729	12,239	13,375
Families with IRA only				
Total assets	23,725	26,427	32,954	35,617
Other than IRA	17,695	16,886	26,925	26,076
IRA	6,030	9,542	6,030	9,542
Debt	3,938	3,580	3,938	3,580
Families without IRA				
Total assets	4,343	4,553	5,815	6,519
Families with IRA and 401(k)				
Total assets	–	43,177	–	59,224
Other than IRA or 401(k)	19,063	18,969	33,606	35,016
IRA	6,305	10,992	6,305	10,992
401(k)	–	13,216	–	13,216
IRA and 401(k)	–	24,208	–	24,208
Debt	3,551	3,552	3,551	3,552
Families with neither IRA nor 401(k)				
Total assets	4,245	3,808	5,656	5,488

Note: Entries are measured in nominal 1984 and 1987 dollars.

Table 4B.2   Mean Asset Balances by 401(k) Eligibility and Income, 1984 and 1987

Group	Income (thousand $)							
	<10	10–20	20–30	30–40	40–50	50–75	>75	All
1987								
Not eligible for a 401(k)								
All financial assets	3,334	5,022	8,492	13,923	19,590	31,961	61,077	13,480
Other assets	2,714	4,149	6,843	11,087	15,800	25,410	51,947	10,960
IRA	620	874	1,649	2,836	3,790	6,551	9,130	2,520
Eligible for a 401(k)								
All financial assets	5,369	5,696	12,652	18,435	22,021	44,472	85,116	27,550
Other assets	3,748	2,811	8,548	10,578	12,532	28,672	55,972	17,285
IRA	819	730	1,626	3,003	3,660	6,562	12,077	4,092
401(k)	802	2,155	2,477	4,854	5,830	9,239	17,066	6,172
1984								
Not eligible for a 401(k)								
All financial assets	2,799	5,109	7,545	13,443	20,174	31,304	72,398	12,310
Other assets	2,517	4,477	6,469	11,602	17,598	27,268	67,175	10,844
IRA	282	632	1,076	1,841	2,576	4,036	5,222	1,466
Eligible for a 401(k)								
All financial assets[a]	–	–	–	–	–	–	–	–
Other assets	2,813	4,984	5,588	10,356	14,302	24,755	73,081	14,989
IRA	459	598	791	1,469	2,215	4,482	5,864	2,037
401(k)[a]	–	–	–	–	–	–	–	–

[a]401(k) assets are not available for 1984. Dollar magnitudes are measured in nominal 1984 and 1987 dollars.

References

Andrews, Emily S. 1992. The growth and distribution of 401(k) plans. In *Trends in pensions 1992*, ed. J. Turner and D. Beller. Washington, D.C.: Department of Labor.
Feenberg, Daniel, and Jonathan Skinner. 1989. Sources of IRA saving. *Tax Policy and the Economy* 3:25–46.
Gale, William G., and John Karl Scholz. 1994. IRAs and household saving. *American Economic Review.* Forthcoming.
Hausman, Jerry A., and James M. Poterba. 1987. Household behavior and the tax reform act of 1986. *Journal of Economic Perspectives* 1, no. 1 (Summer): 101–19.
Hewitt Associates. 1988. *What's new in 401(k) administration and experience.* Lincolnshire, Ill.: Hewitt Associates.
———. 1990. *Salaried employee benefits provided by major U.S. employers in 1989.* Lincolnshire, Ill.: Hewitt Associates.
Kusko, Andrea, James Poterba, and David Wilcox. 1994. Employee decisions with respect to 401(k) plans: Evidence from individual-level data. NBER Working Paper no. 4635. Cambridge, Mass.: National Bureau of Economic Research.
Massachusetts Mutual Life Insurance Company. 1988. 401(k) survey report, 1988. Springfield, Mass.: Massachusetts Mutual Life Insurance Co.
Skinner, Jonathan. 1992. Individual retirement accounts: A review of the evidence. *Tax Notes* 54(2): 201–12.
Summers, Lawrence. 1986. A reply to Galper and Byce on IRAs. *Tax Notes* 31 (10): 1016.
U.S. General Accounting Office. (GAO). 1988a. *401(k) plans: Incidence, provisions, and benefits.* Washington, D.C.: General Accounting Office.
———. 1988b. *401(k) plans: Participation and deferral rates by plan features and other information.* Washington, D.C.: General Accounting Office.
Venti, Steven F., and David A. Wise. 1986. Tax-deferred accounts, constrained choice and estimation of individual saving. *Review of Economic Studies* 53:579–601.
———. 1990a. Have IRAs increased U.S. saving?: Evidence from the Consumer Expenditure Surveys. *Quarterly Journal of Economics* 55, no. 3 (August): 661–98.
———. 1990b. The saving effects of tax-deferred retirement accounts: Evidence from SIPP. In *National Saving and Economic Policy*, ed. B. D. Bernheim and J. Shoven. Chicago: University of Chicago Press.
———. 1992. Government policy and personal retirement saving. In *Tax policy and the economy*, vol. 6, ed. J. Poterba, 1–41. Cambridge: MIT Press.

Comment   Jonathan Skinner

The paper by Poterba, Venti, and Wise has two parallel goals. The first is to present heretofore unknown facts about 401(k) programs. Given the growing importance of 401(k) programs for retirement saving, such facts are highly useful and sometimes quite surprising. I would have never expected that half

Jonathan Skinner is associate professor of economics at the University of Virginia and a research associate of the National Bureau of Economic Research.

of lower-income employees eligible for 401(k) would contribute. By contrast, enrollment rates among lower-income families for Individual Retirement Accounts (IRAs) were less than 10 percent (Venti and Wise 1990). These simple tabulations are key pieces of evidence in thinking about the equitable design or expansion of tax-preferred saving programs.

Another goal of this paper is to compare wealth accumulation among 401(k) contributors, IRA contributors, and the large fraction of the population who avail themselves of neither program. Such comparisons are important in judging the effect of 401(k)s on overall saving. Finding, for example, that contributors to 401(k) programs have less in taxable assets (holding income constant) might suggest "shuffling," in which the taxable assets are shifted into the 401(k)s with no effect on overall wealth accumulation. While the authors are careful not to make claims that 401(k)s "cause" saving, the tabulations clearly show that 401(k) participants are avid savers in other assets as well.

In my comments, I will stress two points. First, the authors seek to measure the interactive effects of both the IRA and the 401(k) programs. This interactive effect is important for the design of policy if, for example, 401(k) plans substitute for IRA programs. As the authors stress, expanding IRA limits or eligibility could have minimal effects if the target population of savers are non-limit contributors to 401(k) plans. However, I am not convinced that the data are strong enough to measure this type of "crowding out." That is, contributors to *either* a 401(k) or an IRA are a relatively select group of enthusiastic savers. Trying to distinguish between substitution effects of IRAs versus 401(k)s, and differences in individual tastes for saving, is likely to strain the data.

My second point is to suggest some additional tests from the authors' data that might shed light on the question of whether 401(k)s have any effect on saving behavior. The authors demonstrate that those who contribute to 401(k)s save more in other assets relative to those who do not. While such evidence is consistent with the view that 401(k)s encourage saving, it is by no means conclusive, since it may be the case that contributors are simply active savers among the employees that would have saved anyway in the absence of the tax-preferred saving plan. In this view, 401(k)s, like IRAs, do nothing for personal saving.

The advantage of studying 401(k)s relative to studying IRAs is that some firms offer 401(k)s to their employers and others do not. Hence one can potentially compare the saving behavior of those *eligible* to contribute to 401(k)s with those who are ineligible, as Poterba, Venti, and Wise do. The question I address in more detail is, Are average saving rates of those who are eligible higher or lower than saving rates of those who are ineligible?

This proposed test of whether 401(k)s stimulate saving can also be viewed as an instrumental variables (IV) estimator.[1] Suppose that total wealth holding

---

1. A good explanation of the IV approach is in Permutt and Hebel (1989). For a similar application, see McClellan and Newhouse (1992).

for family i, W_i, is a linear function of exogenous variables X_i, such as age, earnings, family size, the availability of a 401(k) program, and individual tastes toward saving v_i, then

$$W_i = X_i\beta + Z_iQ_i\delta + v_i,$$

where β is a vector of coefficients, Z_i is an indicator variable equal to 1 if the firm offers a 401(k) program, Q_i is equal to 1 if the individual contributes to a 401(k), and δ is the net effect of the 401(k) saving program on wealth accumulation.[2]

What does a comparison of contributors versus (eligible) noncontributors tell us? The average difference in wealth across groups can be written as

$$W_c - W_{nc} = (X_c - X_{nc})\beta + \delta + (v_c - v_{nc}),$$

where c and nc denote average for contributors and noncontributors, respectively. Ignoring observable differences in wealth owing to $(X_c - X_{nc})\beta$, the difference in average wealth can be attributed to $\delta + v_c - v_{nc}$, the sum of the true effect of 401(k)s on saving plus the difference in tastes. The sum of these terms is large and positive, as the authors show. But there are a priori grounds for believing that 401(k) contributors have a strong taste for saving, so one cannot separately determine the value of δ.

A different test separates the data into those who are eligible to contribute and those who are not;

$$W_e - W_{ne} = (X_e - X_{ne})\beta + p\delta + (v_e - v_{ne}),$$

where e and ne denote those eligible and not eligible for the 401(k) plans, respectively, and p is the average fraction of those eligible who contribute. Once again, the difference in wealth is the sum of the true effect of the 401(k) plan (times the percentage of people who enroll) plus the difference in average tastes toward saving. It is easier to argue that this latter difference should be zero, on average, unless there is strong self-selection among firms in choosing to institute a 401(k) plan. I will return to this issue below.

The Poterba, Venti, and Wise paper contains the basic numbers necessary to make this instrumental variables calculation, although I cannot control for differences in observable characteristics $(X_e - X_{ne})\beta$. Table 4C.1 shows median financial wealth by income (between \$10,000 and \$75,000) for those eligible and those not eligible for 401(k)s, taken from Poterba, Venti, and Wise's table 4.13. The difference in 1987 financial wealth between those eligible and those not eligible, shown in row 3, is equivalent to $p\delta + v_e - v_{ne}$. If there is no self-selection of employees with a strong preference for saving into firms that offer 401(k)s, so that $E\{v_e - v_{ne}\} = 0$, then the number reported in the third row of

---

2. In this simple example, δ is assumed constant. It might be expected to have a larger impact on wealth, the larger income and the more years of participation in the 401(k).

Table 4C.1   **Median Financial Wealth by 401(k) Status and Income, 1984 and 1987**

401(k) Status	Income (thousand $)				
	10–20	20–30	30–40	40–50	50–75
			1987		
Eligible	1,190	4,000	9,205	12,650	25,343
Not eligible	400	1,366	4,000	6,630	14,650
Difference	790	2,634	5,205	6,020	10,693
			1984		
Eligible	550	2,075	4,450	6,850	16,268
Not eligible	458	1,768	3,950	7,150	15,870
Difference	92	307	500	−300	398

Source: Poterba, Venti, and Wise (chap. 4 in this volume, table 4.13; unpublished data).
Note: Financial assets in 1984 do not include 401(k) assets.

table 4C.1 is an estimate of $p\delta$. For example, employees with income between $30,000 and $40,000 in firms that offered 401(k)s held $5,205 more in financial wealth than those in firms without 401(k)s. Dividing through by p, which for this group is equal to .618, yields an estimate of $\delta = 8422$. This simple calculation certainly suggests strong saving effects associated with 401(k)s.

One objection to this inference, as noted above, is that there could be systematic differences between employees of firms that go to the trouble of instituting 401(k)s and employees of those that do not. One way to test for this heterogeneity is to compare wealth of those eligible and those not eligible during 1984, a period when 401(k)s were still quite new and presumably had had little impact on overall wealth holdings. Median financial wealth comparisons, which unfortunately do not include 401(k) balances in 1984, are shown in table 4C.1, rows 4–6, and are taken from unpublished data kindly provided by Poterba, Venti, and Wise. There is little difference in median financial wealth between those eligible and those not eligible during 1984, providing at least some support for the notion that, at least in 1984, there were no systematic differences in tastes for saving across the two groups. On the whole, then, these preliminary calculations provide some evidence that 401(k)s exert a real influence over saving decisions of households.

This paper is the first of what I hope is a continued research program by the authors on the saving effects of 401(k)s. These retirement programs ultimately hold greater promise, I think, for two reasons. First, 401(k)s provide an excellent natural experiment to test the hypothesis that tax-sheltered saving incentives affect saving. And second, based on the statistics presented in the Poterba, Venti, and Wise paper, 401(k) programs hold out at least a promise for encouraging saving across a wide range of income groups.

References

McClellan, Mark, and Joseph Newhouse. 1992. Management of acute MI in the elderly: Practice patterns and treatment effectiveness. Cambridge, Mass.: National Bureau of Economic Research. Mimeograph.

Permutt, Thomas, and J. Richard Hebel. 1989. Simultaneous-equation estimation in a clinical trial of the effect of smoking on birth weight. *Biometrics* 45 (June): 619–22.

Venti, Steven, and David A. Wise. 1990. The saving effects of tax-deferred retirement accounts: Evidence from SIPP. In *National saving and economic policy,* ed. B. D. Bernheim and J. Shoven. Chicago: University of Chicago Press.

5 Some Thoughts on Savings

Edward P. Lazear

Concern over the poor savings performance of the United States has been growing. Many pointed out the "problem" early, and Feldstein made it a major theme of his time on the Reagan Council of Economic Advisors. Some have tried to explain the differences between savings rates in Japan and the United States, attributing the differences sometimes to measurement and sometimes to real factors.

This essay asks more fundamentally whether differences or inadequacies in savings behavior affect welfare, and if so, how. Essentially, it is an attempt to reconcile taste differences and to ask whether the differences have implications for government-sponsored saving. Further, it asks whether differences in savings behavior across countries or over time have any implications for welfare.

The discussion is divided into three parts. The paper begins with a brief review of the issues, focusing on low U.S. savings rates, the behavior of the rates over time, and the rates in comparison to those of other countries, primarily Japan. Second, implications of low-saving behavior for social welfare are examined. This section forms the heart of the paper because it discusses by which criterion savings rates are too low. Third, some conceptually different measurement issues are discussed. The key points are:

1. There is no apparent way to reconcile differences between the U.S. and Japanese savings rates without an appeal to tastes differences. Even within the United States, it is difficult to explain savings behavior over time in the frame-

Edward P. Lazear is a senior fellow of the Hoover Institution and professor of human resources management and economics at Stanford University. He is also editor of the *Journal of Labor Economics* and a research associate of the National Bureau of Economics Research.

This work was supported by the National Science Foundation and by the National Bureau of Economic Research Aging project. The author acknowledges helpful discussions with Gary Becker, Kenneth Judd, and Charles McLure. Mary Beth Wittekind provided able research assistance.

143

work of a population with a homogeneous utility function. Particularly, differences in demographics cannot go far enough to explain the dramatic fall in savings rates during the 1980s.

2. In a world without tax distortions and other externalities, any attempt to increase American savings rates would raise income for most of the individuals in society, but would lower social welfare.

3. The most obvious type of intergenerational externality, which takes the form of underinvestment in human capital, does nothing to reconcile differences in savings rates. Reducing the externality in the United States would, if anything, increase the divergence between American and Japanese measured savings rates.

4. When we argue that there is too little saving, it is important to specify how we establish the optimal level of saving from which the observed level deviates. Depending on the social welfare function, over- or undersavings can result. If the social planner cares only about efficiency, then private savings decisions are optimal even if they result in low savings rates. If the social planner has a utilitarian function, then saving is too high or too low depending on the amount that parents love their children relative to the amount that children love their parents. If love is symmetric, then private savings rates are optimal. When love goes primarily one way (from parent to the child), undersavings, possibly by a very large amount, by both generations results.

5. The ability of the older generation to free ride on their children results in less saving by both generations. The extent of the undersavings depends on the amount that children care for their parents and on the social welfare function.

6. If the worry over low savings is that one's child suffers for one's current consumption, the concern can be alleviated individually. Any one person can save and pass income to his child directly, without the acquiescence of fellow citizens. Collective action is necessary only when one American cares about another American's child but not about foreign children.

7. On-the-job saving is likely to make it more rather than less difficult to explain differences in saving between the United States and Japan. If anything, taking on-the-job saving and investment into account would make Japanese rates even higher relative to American ones.

The conclusion is that there may well be too little saving in the United States. Whether there is or not depends on the preferences of individuals in society and on the social welfare function. Indeed, some increases in saving may even be Pareto improving under specific assumptions about individual utility functions. Unfortunately, none of the evidence on cross-country comparisons nor on time-series changes in savings rates in the United States bears on the undersaving issue. The fact that the United States saves less than Japan indicates neither that we save too little nor that they save too much. Other evidence about preferences is necessary to determine whether our savings rates are too low.

5.1 Macroeconomic Issues

The thrust of the literature over the past few years is that the American savings rate is too low, particularly when compared to other countries (see Summers 1986; Summers and Carroll 1987; Munnell and Cook 1991; Kopcke, Munnell, and Cook 1991; Auerbach and Kotlikoff 1983; Christiano 1989). A number of researchers have tried to rationalize that fact, whereas others have tried to show that it is not a fact, i.e., that the data give a misleading picture, especially for international comparisons.

5.1.1 The Standard Model

Before considering these claims, let us specify the problem more clearly. The usual way to think about saving is in an overlapping generation context. Each individual lives two or three periods, and the first generation is old when the next generation is young or middle-aged. The model here uses a three-period lifetime. Think of the individual as living to age 90; period 1 corresponds to ages younger than 30, period 2 to ages 30–60, and period 3 to ages above 60. The individual is assumed to work in periods 1 and 2 and to retire during period 3. Retirement can be defined as that period when marginal productivity at work falls short of the value of leisure, so that retirement is endogenous rather than given.

No explicit bequest motive is incorporated into the analysis. Of course, one can think of the utility from consumption in period 3 as being partially the result of own consumption and partially the result of utility from bequests.

An individual of generation i has wages during period t of W_{it}. Individuals of generation i live during periods i, $i + 1$, and $i + 2$, so the first generation lives in periods 1, 2, and 3, whereas the second generation lives during periods 2, 3, and 4, and so forth. Consumption by i in t is denoted as C_{it}, and savings are similarly denoted S_{it}.

First, consider only the first generation's consumption program. Individuals of this generation earn wages during periods 1 and 2 but have no wages in period 3. Their problem is to save so as to maximize utility according to

$$(1) \quad \underset{S_1, S_2}{\text{Max}} \ U(W_1 - S_1) + \delta U(W_2 + S_1(1 + \rho) - S_2) + \delta^2 U(S_2(1 + \rho)),$$

assuming time-separable utility. The first-generation subscript is suppressed, δ is the discount factor, and ρ is the rate of return on capital.[1] The first-order conditions are

$$(2a) \qquad -U'(W_1 - S_1) + \delta U'(W_2 + S_1(1 + \rho) - S_2)(1 + \rho) = 0,$$

$$(2b) \qquad -U'(W_2 + S_1(1 + \rho)) + \delta U'(S_2(1 + \rho))(1 + \rho) = 0.$$

1. Under the standard assumptions, in equilibrium, the marginal rate of return to capital equals $(1 - \delta)/\delta$.

Comparative statics are generally ambiguous. They can more easily be illustrated by assuming log utility, as is common. Under these circumstances, equation (2) becomes

(3a)
$$\frac{-1}{W_1 - S_1} + \frac{\delta(1 + \rho)}{W_2 + S_1(1 + \rho) - S_2} = 0,$$

(3b)
$$\frac{-1}{W_2 + S_1(1 + \rho) - S_2} + \frac{\delta}{S_2} = 0.$$

A number of points can be illustrated using this basic model. First, rewrite equation (3a) as

(4)
$$S_2 = W_2 - W_1\delta(1 + \rho) + S_1(1 + \rho)(1 + \delta).$$

It is very likely that W_2 exceeds W_1, since the former is defined as earnings between ages 30 and 60 and the latter as earnings between ages 0 and 30. If so, then $S_2 > S_1$, because the usual equilibrium condition is that $(1 + \rho) = 1/\delta$.

This is the intuitive and empirically valid result that individuals save more when middle-aged than they do when they are young. Even without invoking the impetuousness of youth, it is natural to do more saving as a middle-aged individual because income is higher during the middle years.

The evidence from the United States is consistent with this basic result. Both Auerbach and Kotlikoff (1990) and Attanasio (1993) use the Consumer Expenditure Survey to estimate saving over the life cycle. Both sets of authors find that savings rates are relatively low before age 30, then peak and decline during the final years of life. Auerbach and Kotlikoff find that that consumption is less than earnings approximately between ages 20 and 60, but that consumption exceeds earnings at both ends of the life cycle.

Some of the results are consistent with observed international phenomena and some are not. Of particular interest is the comparison between the United States and Japan. Table 5.1 and figure 5.1 (a histogram) present information on the age distribution of the population in Japan and the United States in 1970. Table 5.2 presents a time series of savings rates.

The tables reveal not only that American rates are low but that Japanese rates are very high. When put in the context of the world economy, the U.S. rates do not appear to be low, except during the period of the 1980s. In some sense, the question is, Why are Japanese rates so high? not, Why are American rates so low? Still, the 1980s present a real discrepancy and one that has persistence without obvious explanation.

There is no particular trend in the difference between Japanese and American savings rates over the 1960–89 period. There has been some convergence since 1970, primarily because the Japanese savings rate, which was around 25 percent in 1970, has declined to more modest levels. But the fall in the American savings rate that occurred during the 1980s is reversing the convergence.

Demographics cannot explain all differences. The peak difference between

Table 5.1   Population Composition in Japan and the United States, 1970

Highest Age in Five-year Block	Japan	United States
Number (millions)		
4	8.7	16.8
9	8.1	19.8
14	7.8	20.5
19	9	18.8
24	10.6	16.1
29	9	13.2
34	8.3	11.2
39	8.2	10.9
44	7.3	11.8
49	5.8	11.9
54	4.8	10.9
59	4.4	9.8
64	3.7	8.4
69	2.9	6.8
74	2.1	5.2
79	1.2	3.6
84	0.6	2.1
85+	0.2	1.5
Proportion (%)		
30–59	37.7799	33.3668
20–49[a]	47.9065	37.6819
10–39[b]	51.5093	45.5093
40–69[c]	28.1402	29.9047

Sources: United Nations (1971, 1981); U.S. Bureau of the Census (1970, 1980).
[a]Relevant for 1980.
[b]Relevant for 1990.
[c]Relevant for 1960.

U.S. and Japanese savings rates was in 1970, when the difference was 19 percent. But the proportions of individuals 30–59 years old were more equal in 1970 than in 1980 (see table 5.1), even though savings rates were more equal in 1980. Indeed, middle-age population proportions were most equal in 1960, even though savings rate differences were about as large in 1960 as they were in 1980. While different ages can be defined as the high-saving years, it appears that a simple demographic explanation, based on the number of individuals in the high-saving cohort, does not explain the data. Japan always has a much higher savings rate than the United States, and the differences do not conform to differences in the age distribution of the population.

Perhaps a more sophisticated approach will reconcile some of the differences. One approach is to ask, How much higher would the U.S. savings rate be if the United States had the same age distribution as Japan? To do that, I have used the age distribution from table 5.1 and combined it with the earnings

Table 5.2   Savings Rates, 1960–89

Year	United States	Japan	Europe	Japan − United States	Europe − United States
1960	0.092	0.220	0.035	0.128	−0.057
1961	0.084	0.238	0.035	0.154	−0.049
1962	0.091	0.217	0.035	0.126	−0.056
1963	0.097	0.207	0.034	0.110	−0.063
1964	0.103	0.204	0.039	0.101	−0.064
1965	0.113	0.192	0.040	0.079	−0.073
1966	0.106	0.199	0.040	0.093	−0.066
1967	0.097	0.222	0.039	0.125	−0.058
1968	0.096	0.240	0.042	0.144	−0.054
1969	0.099	0.252	0.047	0.153	−0.052
1970	0.078	0.269	0.051	0.191	−0.027
1971	0.082	0.245	0.051	0.163	−0.031
1972	0.088	0.244	0.054	0.156	−0.034
1973	0.109	0.256	0.059	0.147	−0.050
1974	0.088	0.231	0.057	0.143	−0.031
1975	0.060	0.194	0.049	0.134	−0.011
1976	0.067	0.201	0.056	0.134	−0.011
1977	0.076	0.196	0.059	0.120	−0.017
1978	0.089	0.200	0.065	0.111	−0.024
1979	0.084	0.190	0.071	0.106	−0.013
1980	0.059	0.183	0.070	0.124	0.011
1981	0.064	0.179	0.062	0.115	−0.002
1982	0.027	0.170	0.064	0.143	0.037
1983	0.022	0.161	0.070	0.139	0.048
1984	0.044	0.170	0.081	0.126	0.037
1985	0.033	0.180	0.087	0.147	0.054
1986	0.022	0.180	0.098	0.158	0.076
1987	0.021	0.183	0.101	0.162	0.080
1988	0.031	0.192	0.119	0.161	0.088
1989	0.032	0.200	0.136	0.168	0.104

Source: National Accounts, 1960–89, Main Aggregates, vol. 1 (Paris: OECD, 1991).
Note: Savings is defined at net savings divided by GDP.

and consumption results from Auerbach and Kotlikoff (1990). I use the base year of 1980, when the difference in savings rates between the United States and Japan was 12 percent. The approach is to calculate weighted earnings and weighted consumption, where the weights are the population proportions. An "actual" number for the United States and a predicted number based on Japanese demographics are reported. They are calculated as

$$
(5) \qquad \text{Actual savings rate on earnings} = \frac{\sum_{j=1}^{N} \gamma_j^{\text{US}} (W_j^{\text{US}} - C_j^{\text{US}})}{\sum_{j=1}^{N} \gamma_j^{\text{US}} W_j^{\text{US}}},
$$

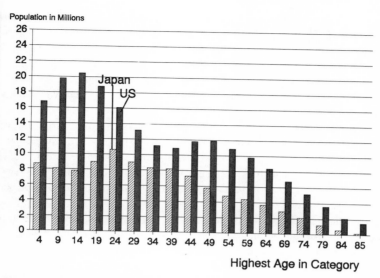

Fig. 5.1   Age distribution of population in Japan and the United States, 1970
Note: Horizontal axis reports highest age in five-year cell, except that "85" refers to individuals 85 or more years old.

where γ_j^{US} is the proportion of the population age group j in the United States in 1980, W_j^{US} is earnings, and C_j^{US} is consumption of group j in 1980. Correspondingly,

$$
(6) \qquad \text{Predicted savings rate on earnings} = \frac{\displaystyle\sum_{j=1}^{N} \gamma_j^{Japan} \left(W_j^{US} - C_j^{US}\right)}{\displaystyle\sum_{j=1}^{N} \gamma_j^{Japan} \, W_j^{US}}
$$

The results is that the U.S. savings rate would have been 8.4 percent higher in 1980 if the United States had Japan's demographics.[2] This goes much of the way toward explaining differences across countries. The rest, it might be argued, results from measurement error. But demographics and measurement error cannot explain everything. Specifically, the rapid fall off in U.S. savings in the 1980s and the widening gap between American and Japanese savings cannot be attributed to demographics, which change slowly.

The time-series puzzle has been observed for the United States by others. As a number of authors have pointed out, it is impossible to explain the U.S. time series of savings rates simply by resorting to demographics (see, e.g., Attanasio 1993; Auerbach and Kotlikoff 1990; Summers and Carroll 1987).

---

2. This savings rate is not the same as the one reported in official accounts. The rate calculated is personal savings and does not correct for differences in business savings.

Attanasio invokes cohort effects to explain the decline in savings rates during the 1980s. He argues that the cohorts born between 1925 and 1939 were responsible for the decline in U.S. savings in the 1980s, because they are a low-saving cohort. During the 1980s, they were in the part of the life cycle when saving is highest. Cohort effects are, in this context, synonymous with taste differences, so resorting to cohort effects is an admission that we have no explanation.

The 1980s were a period when real income declined for a large portion of the population (see, e.g., Murphy and Welch 1991; Katz and Murphy 1991). One additional possibility is that the decline in real income affected saving, either because it was seen as a transitory shock, in which case savings would fall, or because it had an adverse impact on that part of the population which should be saving.

A decline in the wages of middle-aged workers depresses the savings of middle-aged workers but increases the savings of young workers. Differentiating along the first-order conditions in equation (3), one obtains

(7a)
$$\left.\frac{\partial S_1}{\partial W_2}\right|_{(3)} = \frac{-1}{\delta(1 + 1/\delta)(1 + \rho)} < 0,$$

(7b)
$$\left.\frac{\partial S_2}{\partial W_2}\right|_{(3)} = \frac{1}{1 + 1/\delta} > 0,$$

(7c)
$$\left.\frac{\partial S_1}{\partial W_1}\right|_{(3)} = \frac{1}{1 + 1/\delta} > 0.$$

A fall in the wages of the middle-aged would increase savings of the young, who are not big savers, and decrease savings of the middle-aged group that does the most saving. Further, decreased income among the young would depress their savings as well.

Still, this can at best explain the decline in savings rates in the 1970s and 1980s. It cannot reconcile differences across countries, nor is it consistent with low rates of saving during the 1960s.

In some sense, the life-cycle model, or some variant of it, is the only real model to explain savings behavior. Unfortunately, the model in its purest form, where tastes are assumed to be stable across countries and over time, does not explain enough. Invoking cohort effects, as Attanasio does, is analogous to using taste differences across countries to explain differences in saving behavior. Differences in the utility function (rather than prices or income) are the most natural candidate to explain differences in savings by cohort. But this is little better than saying that the Japanese save more than Americans because the Japanese have longer horizons and Americans live for today.

5.1.2 Interest Rate Sensitivity

One possibility is that interest rate differences over time or across countries explain savings behavior. At least the time-series behavior of savings and interest rates can be easily examined. It is quite apparent that interest rates do not explain the U.S. time series of savings behavior.

Regressions of U.S. savings rates from table 5.2 on interest rates are presented in table 5.3. Three definitions of interest rates are used. In the first regression, nominal six-month T-bill rates are the independent variables. In the second and third regressions, real rates, either ex ante or ex post, are used. OLS regressions of savings on these rates do not support the view that savings responds positively to interest rates. Of course, there is a question of simultaneity here. Under the assumption that capital markets are global, American savers can be assumed to be price takers. If so, the elasticity of savings with respect to interest rates should be positive. But if individual countries face a given interest rate, then interest rates cannot possibly reconcile differences between U.S. and Japanese saving behavior. Both would face the same rates, and the United States saves at lower rates. Only if Japan were in one market and the United States in another could differences in interest rates reconcile international saving behavior.

A regression is not needed to point out the obvious. Table 5.4 presents data on interest rates and savings for the United States during the past 30 years. During the late 1960s, savings rates fell as interest rates rose. The relatively high savings period during the late 1970s had, on average, low interest rates. There is no clear pattern that emerges from looking at the data.

Table 5.3   **Regression of U.S. Savings Rates on Six-Month T-Bill Rates: Dependent Variable is U.S. Savings Rate**

Variable	DF	Parameter Estimate	Standard Error	T-Ratio	Prob $> |T|$
		1: Independent Variable Is the Nominal Rate			
INTERCEP	1	0.156995	0.03075496	5.105	0.0001
tbill	1	−2.000409	0.83798562	−2.387	0.0249
tbill×tbill	1	9.063007	5.10747294	1.774	0.0882
		$n = 28,\quad R^2 = .34$			
		2: Independent Variable Is the Ex Ante Real Rate[a]			
INTERCEP	1	0.085371	0.00657687	12.981	0.0001
Real	1	−0.199755	0.22157425	−0.902	0.3759
Real×Real	1	−10.476829	2.68034044	−3.909	0.0006
		$n = 28,\quad R^2 = .39$			
		3: Independent Variable Is the Ex Post Real Rate[b]			
INTERCEP	1	0.081496	0.00562217	14.496	0.0001
"Real"	1	−0.404860	0.18993127	−2.132	0.0430
"Real"×"Real"	1	−3.418567	3.34519428	−1.022	0.3166
		$n = 28,\quad R^2 = .33$			

[a]Calculated as the nominal rate minus the predicted rate of inflation, using a three-year moving average of CPI-based inflation figures.

[b]Calculated as the nominal rate minus actual inflation during the subsequent year, based on CPI figures.

Table 5.4   Savings and Interest Rates in the United States

Year	Savings	Six-Month T-Bill	Real Ex Ante	Real Ex Post
1962	0.091	0.030	0.018	0.018
1963	0.097	0.030	0.018	0.016
1964	0.103	0.037	0.024	0.013
1965	0.113	0.039	0.025	0.024
1966	0.106	0.047	0.031	0.020
1967	0.097	0.048	0.027	0.016
1968	0.096	0.054	0.025	0.011
1969	0.099	0.063	0.025	0.007
1970	0.078	0.079	0.030	0.001
1971	0.082	0.045	−0.009	0.026
1972	0.088	0.037	−0.012	0.013
1973	0.109	0.055	0.015	0.000
1974	0.088	0.076	0.021	−0.041
1975	0.060	0.065	−0.018	−0.041
1976	0.067	0.052	−0.041	−0.002
1977	0.076	0.048	−0.031	0.000
1978	0.089	0.067	0.005	−0.020
1979	0.084	0.095	0.024	−0.026
1980	0.059	0.119	0.019	−0.044
1981	0.064	0.139	0.022	0.001
1982	0.027	0.129	0.016	0.056
1983	0.022	0.079	−0.000	0.092
1984	0.044	0.091	0.036	0.036
1985	0.033	0.080	0.042	0.055
1986	0.022	0.071	0.032	0.041
1987	0.021	0.055	0.025	0.057
1988	0.031	0.063	0.032	0.014
1989	0.032	0.084	0.050	0.017

Either the assumption of exogeneity does not hold or the savings elasticity is negative, which seems difficult to accept. The naive analysis contradicts some earlier claims (see, e.g., Summers 1984), but is backed up by more recent sophisticated studies. Since the positive relation of saving to interest rates cannot be observed in simple correlations, it is necessary to argue that simple OLS is inappropriate. Standard simultaneity arguments provide one reason for doubt. One of the more compelling studies is Hall (1988). By estimating elasticities of intertemporal substitution, Hall finds that the interest elasticity of savings is very low, which implies that exogenous shifts in interest rates do little to explain the time series of saving behavior. The conclusion, applied to the cross section, is that neither interest rates nor demographics can by themselves explain differences between U.S. and Japanese saving behavior.

5.2   International Differences in Tastes

Apparently, savings rates in the 1980s are much lower in the United States than in other developed countries, particularly Japan. If demographic and interest rate differences do not account for this savings rate differential, then perhaps other measurement considerations do. These are discussed below, but suppose, as is likely, that the differences are real and not mere measurement. The obvious question to ask is, Why should we care?

The differences in savings rates that cannot be rationalized most likely reflect differences in tastes across countries rather than differences in income or prices. But economists rarely pass judgement on taste differences. Few would be willing to criticize an individual because he prefers chocolate to vanilla ice cream. What is different about time preference that makes economists so uncomfortable? The purpose of this section is to discuss systematically the arguments for and against saving stimulation.

First, let us return to the model in equation (1). Differentiating the first-order conditions with respect to δ yields

$$(8a) \quad \left.\frac{\partial S_1}{\partial \delta}\right|_{(2)} = \frac{-U'(W_2 + S_1(1 + \rho) - S_2)(1 + \rho)}{U''(W_1 - S_1) + \delta U''(W_2 + S_1(1 + \rho) - S_2)(1 + \rho)^2} > 0,$$

$$(8b) \quad \left.\frac{\partial S_2}{\partial \delta}\right|_{(2)} = \frac{-U'(S_2(1 + \rho))(1 + \rho)}{U''(W_2 + S_1(1 + \rho) - S_2) + \delta U''(S_2(1 + \rho))(1 + \rho)^2} > 0.$$

An increase in δ increases saving among both the young and middle-aged. One way to rationalize the differences between the Japanese and American saving rates is to argue that δ is higher in Japan than in the United States.

If this were true, then for a given wage structure, the typical middle-aged or elderly Japanese would be richer than the typical middle-aged or elderly American. But younger Americans would have higher consumption than younger Japanese. It also follows immediately from optimization that, if an American were somehow induced (say through a tax or subsidy policy) to adopt the Japanese savings schedule, he would have lower lifetime utility, even though his consumption throughout most of his lifetime would be higher. If differences in time preference account for the results of the cross-country comparison, they do not imply that America's situation would be improved by closing the gap.

5.2.1   Intergenerational Externalities in Investment

In order to justify a concern over low savings rates, the basic model must be embellished to take other effects into account. The most obvious candidate is that future generations suffer as a result of the current generation's actions in a way that is not internalized by the current generation.[3] One direct way in which

3. There is now a long literature on intergenerational considerations. Some early papers are by Becker (1974), Barro (1974), Bernheim and Bagwell (1988), and Bernheim, Shleifer and Summers (1985).

this can work is within the family. Suppose that there are actions that a father can take on behalf of his child which yield higher than the market rate of return.

For example, in an early study, I estimated that there was a high payoff to being born in the urban north over the rural south (see Lazear 1983). The payoff was sufficiently high that a child could pay his parent to move to the urban north and apparently make both parties better off. But two conditions are necessary. First, the unmeasured costs borne by the parent must not be so large as to swamp the benefits. Second, the parent must be able to extract payment from the child either directly or through altruistic utility considerations. A move would imply deferred consumption by the parent now, in return for higher consumption (observed or true) later.

In the same paper, I found that black children benefit when they come from an educated household.[4] It is impossible to say whether black parents internalize these effects or not, but the potential exists for large gains from additional saving and investment in parental human capital among this disadvantaged group.

While these examples are interesting, they do not address the issue of differences in observed savings rates across countries. Even if we were to argue that these effects were large, they would not imply that the measured savings rate would rise. Additional schooling by the first generation shows up not only as low consumption, but also as low income. If anything, the measured savings rate would probably fall if more internally financed human capital investment were undertaken, since people may borrow when in school. Similarly, geographic relocation would probably imply a reduction in current earnings and an increase in the observed consumption/earnings ratio among those who move. Nor do these externalities speak to the decline in the U.S. saving rate during the 1980s. What kind of intergenerational externality would result in too little physical savings as we currently measure it?

5.2.2 Individual Utility and Social Welfare Functions

Bequests and inter vivos transfers from parents to children, during middle and old age, have been ignored. But even if they are taken into account, the argument for increased saving is not an obvious one. Suppose, for example, that consumption by generation 1 during period 3 were really a bequest to generation 2, at that point middle-aged. The choice of S_2 determines the size of the bequest, and if S_2 were higher, the bequest would be higher. But inducing a higher bequest is not obviously social welfare increasing.

In fact, there is nothing necessarily intertemporal about the argument. A transfer from one individual in generation 1 to another individual in generation 1 could provide both with utility, if the donor has the recipient in his utility

---

4. More recently, Borjas (1992) has documented a similar, but more general phenomenon across a large number of ethnic groups.

function. But it does not follow that the amount of transfer undertaken privately is necessarily socially inefficient.

To determine whether intergenerational considerations imply too little saving, let us return to the model in equation (1). Recall that C_{it} is consumption of generation i in period t (and similarly for other variables). Let us simplify the problem by shortening each person's life to two periods.

First, it is necessary to specify a social welfare function. There are two obvious candidates: efficient and utilitarian. Attention is restricted to these two welfare functions not only because they are the most commonly used, but also because a sufficiently perverted social planner might well have preferences over intergenerational consumption that deviate from any privately optimal allocation.

If the social welfare function maximizes efficiency, then the private saving rule must be optimal. The parent maximizes

$$(9) \quad \text{Max}_{T_{12}, S_{12}} U(W_{11} - S_{11}) + \delta[U(W_{12} + S_{11}(1 + \rho) - T_{12}) + \lambda U(W_{22} + T_{12} - S_{22})] + \delta^2 \lambda U(W_{23} + S_{22}(1 + \rho)),$$

where T_{12} is the transfer in period 2 from generation 1 to generation 2 and where the parent takes into account the child's saving behavior. The parent's altruism is measured by λ, which is the weight of the child's utility in the parent's utility function.

The child in turn maximizes

$$(10) \quad \text{Max}_{S_{22}} U(W_{22} + T_{12} - S_{22}) + \delta U(W_{23} + S_{22}(1 + \rho)),$$

given the transfer T_{12} from his parent.

All choices of T_{12} are on the utility frontier and are efficient. Since saving choice is privately optimal, efficiency is always served. There are no externalities; there is no amount that the child could pay the parent to save more. The child can borrow or lend at the market rate, and there is no necessity to obtain the funds from or lend directly to his parent. Further, as long as T_{12} is positive, additional saving does not affect the child's income. If the criterion is efficiency, there is no deviation of the private savings path from the welfare-maximizing path.

The utilitarian criterion allows for the possibility of undersavings. One reasonable social welfare function is

$$\text{Welfare} = (\text{Discounted utility of generation 1})$$
$$+ \gamma (\text{Discounted utility of generation 2}),$$
$$(11) \quad \text{Welfare} = U(W_{11} - S_{11}) + \delta[U(W_{12} + S_{11}(1 + \rho) - T_{12}) + (\lambda + \gamma)U(T_{12} + W_{22} - S_{22})] + \delta^2(\lambda + \gamma)U(W_{23} + S_{22}(1 + \rho)),$$

where γ is the weighting that the social planner places on generation 2 relative to generation 1.

The social planner counts the utility of the second generation $\lambda + \gamma$ times. Generation 2's utility enters the social welfare function directly, with a scalar of γ, but also indirectly since it boosts the welfare of the altruistic parent.

The social planner's first-order conditions are

$$(12a) \quad \frac{\partial}{\partial S_{11}} = -U'(W_{11} - S_{11}) + \delta U'(W_{12} + S_{11}(1 + \rho) - T_{12})(1 + \rho) = 0,$$

$$(12b) \quad \frac{\partial}{\partial T_2} = -U'(W_{12} + S_{11}(1 + \rho) - T_{12}) +$$

$$(\lambda + \gamma)U'(T_{12} + W_{22} - S_{22}) = 0,$$

$$(12c) \quad \frac{\partial}{\partial S_{22}} = U'(T_{12} + W_{22} - S_{22}) + \delta U'(W_{23} + S_{22}(1 + \rho))(1 + \rho) = 0.$$

By contrast, the private maximization problem proceeds in two stages. The parent can choose the transfer that he makes to the child during period 2, and he takes into account that the transfer affects the child's saving behavior as the child maximizes equation (10). For any given transfer of T_{12}, the child chooses S_{22} to maximize equation (10). The child's first-order condition is

$$(13) \quad \frac{\partial}{\partial S_{22}} = -U'(T_{12} + W_{22} - S_{22}) +$$

$$\delta U'(W_{23} + S_{22}(1 + \rho))(1 + \rho) = 0.$$

The parent's problem is then to choose S_{11} and T_{12} so as to maximize equation (9), taking into account that the child behaves in accordance with equation (13). The parent's first-order conditions are

$$(14a) \quad \frac{\partial}{\partial S_{11}} = -U'(W_{11} - S_{11}) + \delta U'(W_{12} + S_{11}(1 + \rho) - T_{12})(1 + \rho),$$

$$\frac{\partial}{\partial T_2} = -U'(W_{12} + S_{11}(1 + \rho) - T_{12}) + \lambda U'(T_{12} + W_{22} - S_{22})$$

$$(14b) \quad -\lambda U'(T_{12} + W_{22} - S_{22}) \frac{\partial S_{22}}{\partial T_{12}}\bigg|_{(13)}$$

$$+ \delta\lambda U'(W_{23} + S_{22}(1 + \rho))(1 + \rho) \frac{\partial S_{22}}{\partial T_{12}}\bigg|_{(13)}.$$

Savings and transfers are determined by the solutions to equations (13), (14a), and (14b). The social planner would like the choices to solve equations (12a)–(12c), instead. The difference between the two systems is that equation (12b) differs from equation (14b). The parent takes into account the effect of his transfer on his offspring in a different way than does the social planner. Most important, the parent only counts the utility that the child receives by λ, whereas the social planner counts it $\gamma + \lambda$. For reasonable parameters, this generally leads to too small a private transfer from the parent to child, which in turn leads to undersavings by both the parent and child.

Since the parent does not transfer as much as is socially desirable, he is richer in period 2 than he otherwise would be. As a result, he saves less. Put alternatively, he saves less because he must finance a smaller transfer to his child in period 2. Also, since the child's income in period 2 is lower than it would be under the social optimum, he has less income to smooth into generation 2. So savings by generation 2 are lower in period 2 as well.

To get a sense of the importance of the effect, consider a frequently used utility function, $U = \ln(C_t) + \delta \ln(C_{t+1})$. Further, suppose that the parent cares for his child as much as he does for himself, so that $\lambda = 1$. Finally, suppose that the social planner treats all generations the same (except for discounting), so that $\gamma = 1$. Initially, let income be constant over time, so that all wages in the economy are 1 and let $\delta = .95$. Table 5.5 gives the solution to the social planner's problem in equation (12) and to the private optimization in equations (13) and (14). Panel A reveals that savings are eight to nine times higher when society's objective function is maximized than when private optimization is done. These large differences obtain even when parents are genuinely altruistic, treating children's utility as as valuable as their own.

Key here is the double counting of children's utility by the social planner. The social planner prefers larger transfers because a transfer to the child contributes not only to the child's utility, but also to the parent's utility. Taking a dollar from the parent and transferring it to the child has no effect on the parent's utility at the private optimum, but increases social welfare by the marginal value of a dollar.

Assumptions can be changed to alter the size of these effects. One alteration is to build technological change that shows up through wage growth into the model. Suppose that wages in period 1 are 1, but that they grow by 10 percent each period. Panel B of table 5.5 contains the results of the simulation. Now private savings and transfers are actually negative. Since children are going to be richer than their parents, parents would like to take money away from their

Table 5.5   **Optimal Savings and Transfers**

Variable	Social Optimum	Private Optimum
	A: All Wages = 1	
S_{11}	.3555	.0415
S_{22}	.3705	.0424
T_{12}	.7175	.0441
	B: Wages Grow at 10 Percent per Period	
S_{11}	.2926	−.0519
S_{22}	.3044	−.0557
T_{12}	.6827	−.0564

kids and do so by extracting income from generation 2 when parents are old and children are young. As a result, parents are richer in period 2 and consequently borrow in period 1. But the same is true for generation 2. Since children are poor in period 2 relative to period 3, not only because wages are growing, but also because parents extract transfers from them, they wish to borrow as well. While the socially optimal level of transfers and saving falls, the extent of the reductions are smaller and none of the variables becomes negative.

The conclusion is that there is potential for undersavings when the social welfare function takes into account intergenerational utility in what might be termed an egalitarian way. These effects can be quite large. This conclusion depends crucially on an asymmetry. The parent cares about the child, but the child does not care about his parent. If altruism goes in both directions to the same extent, the deviation between private and social savings rates disappears.

The child cannot affect the transfers from parent to child because the parent can always fail to consume and simply bequeath the residual.[5] Thus, the private solution remains unchanged. But now the social welfare function becomes

$$(15) \quad \max_{S_{11}, S_{22}, T_{12}} \quad (1 + \theta)U(W_{11} - S_{11}) + \delta[(1 + \theta)U(W_{12} + S_{11}(1 + \rho) - T_{12})$$
$$+ (\lambda + \gamma)U(T_{12} + W_{22} - S_{22})] +$$
$$\delta^2(\lambda + \gamma)U(W_{23} + S_{22}(1 + \rho)),$$

where θ is the relative weight that children give to their parent's utility. As before, let utility be logarithmic and suppose that $\theta = 1$, so that children love their parents as much as themselves. It can then be shown that the social optima that are the maximum of equation (15) are exactly the private optima given in table 5.5.

The intuition before was that undersavings occurred because parents overvalued their own consumption, not taking into account that their child's consumption produced utility twice—once directly for the child and once indirectly for the parent. But now, parental consumption also produces utility twice—once directly for the parent and once indirectly for the child. Thus, social savings are lower because savings and subsequent transfers to the children reduce the utility that the children would receive from seeing their parents happy.

If the argument for undersavings is that the parent's utility-maximizing behavior differs from social-welfare-maximizing behavior, it must rely on an asymmetry that has parents loving children more than children love their parents. While the asymmetry is hardly an unreasonable assumption, I doubt that it lies behind most fears that Americans undersave. Nor does it help reconcile the differences between U.S. and Japanese savings rates. What kind of argument would one need to make to claim that the difference between U.S. and

---

5. This ignores tax and timing issues.

Japanese savings behavior reflects suboptimal savings by Americans? Unreciprocated love of their children by Americans could result in substantial undersavings. But it is difficult to understand why the Japanese would save at the socially optimal rates, rather than the privately optimal ones. If Japanese children were more loving of their parents than American children, the socially optimal rate of savings in Japan would fall to the privately optimal one in the United States, not the reverse. Then it would be necessary to explain why Japanese saving is too high, not why American savings are too low.

Key here is the idea that saving can be too low only after some criterion has been specified. Selecting a social welfare function is equivalent to selecting an optimal saving path, but the choice of the appropriate social welfare function is far from obvious. A strong case that Americans undersave can be made, but neither the cross-country comparisons nor the time-series decline provides evidence for this kind of undersaving.

5.2.3   Free Riding by the Elderly

Now that altruism has been considered, it is straightforward to analyze another possible concern about undersavings, namely, free riding by the elderly. One possibility is that individuals will undersave when young, leaving themselves destitute when old. As long as the young generation cares about the utility of the older generation, they will transfer resources toward parents. But these ex post transfers may differ from those that would be chosen if parents did not have the ability to force their children to care for them.

Above, T_{12} was positive, so there was no way for the child to force the parent to consume. But if T_{12} is negative, so that the net transfer goes from child to parent, then the child can affect T_{12} directly through inter vivos transfers, which the child can be confident will be consumed by the parent.

Suppose that parameters are such that the parent's optimum implies a negative level of transfer. The parent may be able to extract payments from his child while the child is under his direct supervision. The more interesting case, which captures the spirit of free riding, is that the child cares about his parent. Knowing this, the parent overconsumes when young, inducing his offspring to support him through direct inter vivos transfers when he is old.[6] While this may result in low saving levels by the parent, the issue is whether the savings level is low relative to some benchmark. One benchmark is the social welfare function. As already shown, savings may be higher or lower than optimal, depending on the social welfare function. In this case, however, a more natural comparison is the consumption path that the child would choose if he could control his parent's consumption before his own birth. The essence of free riding is that the child's love for his parent creates an opportunity for the parent to overconsume, relative to what the child would like. Let us consider this formally.

6. The importance of inter vivos transfers has been examined empirically by Donald Cox (1987).

The child is going to support his parent on net, so it is natural to determine the levels of consumption and savings that the child would choose were he able to control parental choice. Suppose that the child values his parent's utility at θ relative to his own. Then if the child could choose all variables, his problem would be

(16) $\underset{S_{11}, S_{22}, T_{22}}{\text{Max}} \quad \theta U(W_{11} - S_{11}) + \theta \delta U(W_{12} + S_{11}(1 + \rho) + T_{22})$

$$+ \delta U(W_{22} - S_{22} - T_{22}) + \delta^2 U(W_{23} + S_{22}(1 + \rho)),$$

where $T_{22} \equiv -T_{12}$, i.e., the transfer from child to parent. The first-order conditions are

(17a) $\dfrac{\partial}{\partial S_{11}} = -U'(W_{11} - S_{11}) + \delta(1 + \rho)U'(W_{12} + S_{11}(1 + \rho) + T_{22}) = 0,$

(17b) $\dfrac{\partial}{\partial S_{22}} = -U'(W_{22} - S_{22} - T_{22}) + \delta(1 + \rho)U'(W_{23} + S_{22}(1 + \rho)) = 0,$

(17c) $\dfrac{\partial}{\partial T_{22}} = \theta U'(W_{12} + S_{11}(1 + \rho) + T_{22}) - U'(W_{22} - S_{22} - T_{22}) = 0.$

If the parent can lead, however, by choosing sufficiently high consumption in period 1, then he will be destitute in period 2, inducing the child to make larger transfers. The child then takes S_{11} as given and maximizes

(18) $\underset{S_{22}, T_{22}}{\text{Max}} \quad \theta U(W_{11} - S_{11}) + \delta \theta U(W_{12} + S_{11}(1 + \rho) + T_{22}) + \delta U(W_{22}$

$$- S_{22} - T_{22}) + \delta^2 U(W_{23} + S_{22}(1 + \rho)),$$

with first-order conditions

(19a) $\dfrac{\partial}{\partial S_{22}} = -U'(W_{22} - S_{22} - T_{22}) + \delta(1 + \rho)U'(W_{23} + S_{22}(1 + \rho)) = 0,$

(19b) $\dfrac{\partial}{\partial T_{12}} = \theta U'(W_{12} + S_{11}(1 + \rho) + T_{22}) - U'(W_{22} - S_{22} - T_{22}) = 0.$

The problem for the parent (who does not care about his child) is

(20) $\underset{S_{11}}{\text{Max}} \quad U(W_{11} - S_{11}) + \delta U(W_{12} + S_{11}(1 + \rho) + T_{22}),$

with first-order condition

(21) $\dfrac{\partial}{\partial S_{11}} = -U'(W_{11} - S_{11}) +$

$$\delta U'(W_{12} + S_{11}(1 + \rho) + T_{22})\left[1 + \rho + \dfrac{\partial T_{22}}{\partial S_{11}}\bigg|_{(19b)}\right],$$

where $\left.\dfrac{\partial T_{22}}{\partial S_{11}}\right|_{(19b)}$ reflects the parent's taking into account that his child's transfer responds to his (the parent's) consumption. Note that

(22)
$$\left.\frac{\partial T_{22}}{\partial S_{11}}\right|_{(19b)} = \frac{-\theta U''(W_{12} + S_{11}(1 + \rho) + T_{22})(1 + \rho)}{\theta U''(W_{12} + S_{11}(1 + \rho) + T_{22}) + U''(W_{22} - S_{22} - T_{22})} < 0.$$

A decrease in savings in period 1 by the parent causes the child to transfer more to him in period 2. If θ were zero, so that the child did not care about his parent, then the expression in equation (22) would be zero. The child's love is necessary for the parent to overconsume in period 1.

To get a sense of the effect and to see that it can result in undersaving, consider the log utility example above, but let all wages equal 1, except for the wage in period 3 which equals 10. The high last-period wages make optimal (in almost any sense) that transfers go from child to parent, because the child is relatively rich. Table 5.6 reports the results of solving system (17) as well as (19) and (21) for the case of log utility with $\theta = 1/2$ and wages equal to 1, except that the period-3 wage equals 10.

The transfer to the parent is higher when the parent can lead the child. The parent, whose income is only 1 in each period, impoverishes himself by borrowing 2.911 during the first period. He has only 1 in period 2 and without his child's help would be bankrupt. But the child loves his parent to the tune of 3.811, allowing the parent to repay the loan and still have more left than he would in the absence of a child. If the child could choose the parent's saving/consumption stream, he would still end up transferring money to his parent, again, because of the high income that he receives in period 3. But the transfer would be considerably lower at 2.104, which would induce the parent to borrow much less in period 1 (0.959 instead of 2.911). Thus, savings by the parent are lower when he can affect the transfer of the child. Further, the child saves less, as well, in the parent-controlled environment. When the parent "free rides," he makes the child relatively poor in period 2. As a result, the child borrows more than he would were he in direct control of parental savings decisions (6.032 instead of 5.200).[7]

While free riding may be a problem, there is nothing inherently intergenerational about it, nor is the phenomenon one that bears only, or even primarily, on savings. In an economy where individuals care about one another, there is always an incentive to induce someone else to pay for one's consumption. This

---

7. Some have extended consideration of intergenerational externalities to other individuals' children. This is undersaving because each parent who cares about the child of another saves insufficiently, in order to force the other parent to save for the next generation. All individuals would rather see the next generation richer, but they would prefer that others in this generation bear the cost. The equilibrium level of savings is too low as a result.

Table 5.6   Savings and Transfers with Free Riding by the Elderly

Variable	Child's choice (eq. [17])	Parent's Choice (eqs. [19] and [21])
S_{11}	−0.959	−2.911
S_{22}	−5.200	−6.032
T_{22}	2.104	3.811

would be true even if everyone lived only one period and at exactly the same time, where saving is precluded by definition.

Further, while free riding might result in lower savings, it results in higher utility for the parent and lower utility for the child. Whether society disdains this outcome depends directly on the social welfare function. Again, saving is low relative to what the child would have arranged for his parent (and himself), not necessarily relative to what the parent likes.

The cross-country comparisons are consistent with the view that parents are taking advantage of their children in the United States to a greater extent than in Japan. In order for the differences to go in the right direction, however, it would be necessary that American children care more for their parents than Japanese children do for theirs. Then American parents would be more likely to play on their children's love (see eq. [22]). This could be done privately, through individual consumption, or through the government, by running large deficits and Social Security debt.

While possible, the view that American children are more attached to their parents than their Japanese counterparts contradicts the view that the Japanese family is a closer-knit unit than the American family. Perhaps more likely is that Japanese parents love their children more than American parents love theirs and so are less likely to put themselves in the position of requiring support in old age.

5.2.4   Concern over Identity of Capital Owners

One argument that is often heard, usually in the context of trade deficits, is that our children are going to be forced to pay for our consumption today. The implication is again that we are doing a disservice to our children. There are two types of disservice that can be done. The first is that the capital stock in the future will be too low. The second is that, while the capital stock may be sufficiently high, the wrong people will own it.

The first argument pertains most directly to growth in capital and endogenous technical change: if the economy were to save and invest more, future productivity and corresponding wages would be higher. While true, these arguments depend more on the total amount of saving and investment in the world than on the amount of savings by Americans. As long as capital (or labor) is mobile, and over the period of a generation there is reason to believe that there is reasonable mobility of capital,[8] the location of savings may be unimportant. If true, concern should be focused on the total amount of savings globally, not on the differences between American and Japanese savings rates. While total savings may be too low by the criteria of the last section, international differences in savings rates provide no evidence on this point. Japan's high savings rate may mean that total savings are too high. America's low savings rate may mean that world savings are too low. Or neither may be true.

The second argument is that while aggregate worldwide savings may not be too low, the problem is that the Japanese rather than the Americans have claim to capital. There are two variants of this argument. One is that the Japanese will use their capital only to help the Japanese. The other is that even if the capital flows to the United States, the Japanese will receive the return on the capital, making Japanese children rich relative to American children.

The first worry, that the Japanese will use their savings to help Japan, is an issue of investment, not saving. If the Japanese save by buying U.S. corporate (or government) bonds and if most of that investment is then used to create capital in the United States, then the Japanese will affect the productivity of future American workers, not of Japanese. Thus, worry about low American saving is misdirected, if the concern is the location of capital. Indeed, if capital is country specific, then encouraging foreign investment rather than high U.S. saving may be the correct strategy.

Further, physical capital depreciates over time. It is quite possible to argue that the capital that is most important for economic growth and the prosperity of our children is human rather than physical. Investments in human capital, as measured by education and health investments, are high in the United States relative to Europe and comparable to levels in Japan (see Becker 1991).

If the second worry holds—namely that Japanese children, rather than American children, will receive the return to capital—no collective action need be taken. Even if all other Americans choose not to save, any given individual can bestow ownership of capital on his children by his own personal saving. Whether he decides to do so depends on utility considerations discussed above. But the capital ownership issue is more closely tied to transfer and bequest behavior than it is to national savings rates.

The conclusion is altered when Americans care about the welfare of other children as well as that of their own. Then collective action might be needed to avoid free-rider problems which arise when each individual wants others to save for the future generation. But if the care is for all children, not only American ones, the issue becomes one of global saving rates, not American saving rates, and there is little evidence that total savings are too low relative to some benchmark.

---

8. See Barro and Sala-i-Martin's (1992) work on convergence of income within the United States and across international borders.

5.2.5   Substitution of Government Savings for Private Savings

It is possible that U.S. saving rates are not as low as they appear, say, because U.S. government savings displaces private savings and because the government accounts do not properly reflect government savings.[9] If so, the question is not so much about savings, but about investment policy. Government saving, which yields government investment, may be put to poorer use than private saving, which finances primarily private investment. Little evidence is available on which to base any conclusions. Further, if this is the concern, the remedy is to revise government expenditure patterns, not to encourage more private saving.

5.2.6   Taxes

One reason to be concerned about the low U.S. savings rate is that the U.S. tax system may create distortions which induce too little saving. The most obvious candidate is the double taxation of income, which results because income is taxed when it is earned and interest on it is also taxed. Capital gains taxation, if not properly indexed, can also lead to saving distortions.[10] This essay is not the place to argue the validity or importance of tax-induced distortions. One point is clear, however. In order for the tax argument to be important, there must be a significant (positive) interest elasticity of savings. Obviously, if the supply of savings is relatively inelastic, then it is difficult to argue that there is substantial undersaving as a result of a distorted return. The evidence in this paper and elsewhere does not support a large saving elasticity. Although the question remains open, the current evidence does not persuade this author that the tax distortion is an important reason to worry about undersaving.

5.2.7   Growth

There is a general perception that links savings to growth. But the focus here really should be on investment, not saving. No theory argues that saving per se is important to growth. Empirically, saving and investment are likely to be highly correlated, but there is no necessity that they are. The Japanese could use their savings to build factories in the United States, hiring American workers and taking their profits in American-made goods. Right now, many developing countries, particularly those of Eastern Europe, look to other countries to inject capital into their struggling economies. While their attempts are likely to be frustrated, there is nothing at the theoretical level to suggest that their strategies are misguided.

Even if high levels of domestic saving were necessary for growth, it is not automatic that more saving and more growth is better. Indeed, the ρ term that

---

9. Hayashi (1986) has discussed differences in savings measurement between the United States and Japan. The discussion on whether government savings crowds out private savings is illustrated by the debate between Barro (1974) and Feldstein (1974).

10. There is a large literature on the effects of taxes on savings. See, e.g., Kotlikoff (1984), King (1980), Feldstein (1974), and Auerbach and Kotlikoff (1983).

reflects the rate of return on capital can be interpreted as the growth parameter. Without growth externalities (which are not incorporated into the models), everything said about the trade-offs between current and future consumption pertains to growth as well.

5.3 Measurement Issues

A number of authors have attempted to reconcile the low U.S. savings rate and some of the differences between American and Japanese saving behavior by appealing to measurement differences (see, e.g., Hayashi 1986). Rather than reiterate those arguments, a few different points are briefly discussed in this section.

The point that is emphasized here is not new, but its application to savings and earnings is.[11] When savings rates as low as 3–5 percent are observed in the United States, they may well be swamped by implicit savings and investment that occurs on the job.

To see the point, suppose that every individual in the economy produced output stream $A(t)f(k(t))$, with $f' > 0, f'' < 0$. Let the economy run for two periods (0 and 1) with initial capital stock being given as k_0 and investment in period 0 denoted Δk. There is no depreciation, and $A(t)$ reflects exogenous technical change. Capital stock in period 1 is therefore $k_0 + \Delta k$ so the investment decision is

(23) $$\underset{\Delta k}{\text{Max}}\ A(0)f(k_0) - \Delta k + \delta A(1)f(k_0 + \Delta k).$$

The first-order condition is

(24) $$A(1)f'(k_0 + \Delta k) = 1/\delta,$$

and there is a Δk^* that solves equation (24). Since $f'' < 0$, Δk is increasing in δ.

How would a change in δ affect measured saving? The answer depends on reporting. Lowering the discount rate, say, from infinity to zero (i.e., increasing δ from 0 to 1), would increase Δk, while leaving unchanged $f(k_0)$. If firms were owned by individuals other than their workers and workers were paid a piece rate instead of being self-employed, each would take home $f(k_0)$ and would save Δk^* explicitly, say, by putting that amount in the bank. Firms would then borrow Δk^* to undertake optimal investment as in equation (24). Thus, raising δ would raise measured saving and measured investment.

But if workers were self-employed, the increase in saving and investment would be more likely to get lost. For example, suppose that investment takes the form of using workers' time and perhaps some cannibalized parts from an existing machine to build an additional machine to be used in period 1. Mea-

---

11. Jorgenson and Pachon (1983) recalculated the capital stock with the inclusion of human capital.

sured output would be $f(k_0) - \Delta k$, rather than $f(k_0)$, and measured saving and investment would be zero, even though the situation is identical to the one where firms are owned by outsiders and all transactions occur through the market.

Human capital is the kind of saving and investment that is perhaps most likely to be lost (see Jorgenson and Pachon 1983). Some human capital investment is explicit and works through the market. Formal schooling and health care fit into this category. But on-the-job training is most likely to go unrecorded in the firm's books, even though workers who invest in on-the-job training are undertaking both savings and investment. Measured output of the firm is reduced because of time spent on training, and wages of the worker who receives the training are correspondingly lower. The worker's reported saving does not include the value of the on-the-job training. Indeed, reported saving may be lower since the worker substitutes higher-return on-the-job saving for lower market-observed saving.

While the on-the-job training story may be plausible, it probably does not help reconcile the disparity between American and Japanese saving rates. First, it has been observed that age-earning profiles are steeper in Japan than in the United States (see Hashimoto 1990; Mincer and Higuchi 1988). If the slope reflects higher investment in on-the-job training in Japan, then observed savings rates understate true saving by more in Japan than in the United States. Second, today's on-the-job training is tomorrow's output. If the on-the-job training story were important, labor productivity would be positively affected. Unless the increase in investment is a very recent phenomenon, early investments in on-the-job training should already be affecting productivity today. But except for the last few years, productivity growth has been higher in Japan than in the United States, contradicting the hypothesis that unreported saving and investment is higher in the United States.

Another type of on-the-job saving may differ across countries. Consider a worker who lives two periods and produces $100 in each. There are no on-the-job training or work-life productivity effects. In one country, say, the United States, the worker is paid $100. During the first period, he consumes $90, puts $10 in the bank, and has an observed personal savings rate of 10 percent. In the last period, he consumes $100 plus $10(1 + ρ).

In another country, say, Japan, the worker receives $90 during the first period. In the last period, the worker receives wages of $100 + $10(1 + ρ). The Japanese firm then uses the proceeds to invest in its own plant and equipment or to buy stocks and bonds of other corporations.

This story fits the stylized facts. Japanese use financial institutions and their firms to do much of their investment. Firms hold portfolios of stocks and bonds in other firms. The steeper age-earnings profile seen in Japan is perfectly consistent with this story, even if no on-the-job training occurs. There would be no need to observe higher labor productivity growth rates in the United States, because investment patterns could well be identical across countries. Unfortunately, since Japanese in-firm saving is more likely to get lost in official accounts than is U.S. market-transacted saving, true Japanese saving would be understated by a greater margin than true U.S. saving. Once again, differences in tastes must be invoked to explain international differences in consumption patterns.

5.4 Conclusion

There appear to be some differences in saving behavior, both over time and internationally, that can be explained by resorting to demography. But large disparities remained unexplained. The big question is, So what? While there may be reasons to be concerned about the low and declining American savings rates, the mere discrepancy between U.S. and Japanese savings rates does not speak to these concerns. In most cases, reasonable assumptions about differences between the United States and Japan do not imply that American saving is too low. Similarly, the decline in the U.S. savings rate in the 1980s may be cause for concern, but not for the reasons generally presented when arguing that the United States undersaves.

Only a few of the many potential reasons for believing that the United States undersaves have been presented. In some sense, I have presented too many. It is quite clear that under some not unreasonable assumptions, a case can be made that the United States undersaves. But the point made herein is that neither the time-series nor cross-country data provide evidence on the issue. The fact that Japan's savings rate is higher than that of the United States does not imply that we undersave nor that they oversave. The fact that our rate is low today relative to 15 years ago does not imply that the savings rate then was closer to the social optimum than is the savings rate now. This essay, in attempting to shed some light on the issue, has a much more agnostic tone than the earlier literature. In large part, it reverts to the position that economists are not good at comparing one set of tastes to another.

References

Attanasio, Orazio P. 1993. A cohort analysis of savings behavior by U.S. households. NBER Working Paper no. 4454. Cambridge, Mass.: National Bureau of Economic Research.
Auerbach, Alan J., and Laurence J. Kotlikoff. 1983. National savings, economic welfare, and the structure of taxation in behavioral simulation methods. In *Tax policy analysis,* ed. Martin Feldstein, 459–98. Chicago: University of Chicago Press.
———. 1990. Demographics, fiscal policy, and U.S. saving in the 1980s and beyond. *Tax Policy and the Economy* 4:73–101.
Barro, Robert J. 1974. Are government bonds net wealth? *Journal of Political Economy* 82 (November/December): 1095–1117.

Barro, Robert J., and Xavier Sala-i-Martin. 1992. Convergence. *Journal of Political Economy* 100 (April): 223–51.

Becker, Gary S. 1974. A theory of social interactions. *Journal of Political Economy* 82 (November/December): 1063–94.

———. 1991. *A treatise on the family,* enlarged ed. Cambridge: Harvard University Press.

Bernheim, B. Douglas, and Kyle Bagwell. 1988. Is everything neutral? *Journal of Political Economy* 96 (April): 308–38.

Bernheim, B. Douglas, Andrei Shleifer, and Lawrence H. Summers. 1985. The strategic bequest motive. *Journal of Political Economy* 93 (October): 1045–76.

Borjas, George. 1992. Ethnic capital and intergenerational mobility. *Quarterly Journal of Economics* 107 (February): 123–50.

Christiano, Lawrence J. 1989. Understanding Japan's saving rate: The reconstruction hypothesis. *Federal Reserve Bank of Minnesota Quarterly Review* (Spring): 10–25.

Cox, Donald. 1987. Motives for private income transfers. *Journal of Political Economy* 95 (June): 508–46.

Feldstein, Martin. 1974. Incidence of a capital income tax in a growing economy with variable savings rates. *Review of Economic Studies* 41 (October): 505–13.

Hall, Robert E. 1988. Intertemporal substitution in consumption. *Journal of Political Economy* 96 (April): 339–57.

Hashimoto, Masanori. 1990. *The Japanese labor market in a comparative perspective with the United States.* Kalamazoo, Mich.: Upjohn Institute.

Hayashi, Fumio. 1986. Why is Japan's saving rate so apparently high? *NBER Macroeconomics Annual* 1:147–210.

Jorgenson, Dale W., and Alvaro Pachon. 1983. The accumulation of human and non-human capital. In *The determinants of national saving and wealth,* ed. Franco Modigliani and Richard Hemming, 302–50. New York: St. Martin's.

Katz, Lawrence F., and Kevin M. Murphy. 1991. Changes in relative wages, 1963–87: Supply and demand factors. NBER Working Paper no. 3927. Cambridge, Mass.: National Bureau of Economic Research, December.

King, R. 1980. Savings and taxation. In *Essays in public policy,* ed. Gordon A. Hughes and Geoffrey M. Heal. London: Chapman and Hall.

Kopcke, Richard W., Alicia Munnell, and Leah M. Cook. 1991. The influence of housing and durables on personal saving. *New England Economic Review* (November–December): 3–16.

Kotlikoff, Laurence J. 1984. Taxation and savings: A neoclassical perspective. *Journal of Economic Literature* 22 (December): 1576–1629.

Lazear, Edward P. 1983. Intergenerational externalities. *Canadian Journal of Economics* 16 (May): 212–28.

Mincer, Jacob, and Yoshio Higuchi. 1988. Wage structures and labor turnover in the United States and Japan. *Journal of the Japanese and International Economies* 2:97–133.

Munnell, Alicia, and Leah M. Cook. 1991. Explaining the postwar pattern of personal saving. *New England Economic Review* (November–December): 17–28.

Murphy, Kevin M., and Finis Welch. 1991. Wage differentials in the 1980s: The role of international trade. In *Workers and their wages: Changing patterns in the United States,* ed. Marvin Kosters, 39–69. Washington, D.C.: American Enterprise Institute.

Summers, Lawrence. 1984. The after-tax rate of return affects private savings. *American Economic Review* 74 (May): 249–53.

———. 1986. Issues in national savings policy. In *Savings and capital formation,* ed. F. Gerard Adams and Susan M. Wachter, 65–88. Lexington, Mass.: Lexington Books.

Summers, Lawrence, and Carroll, Chris. 1987. Why is U.S. national saving so low? *Brookings Papers on Economic Activity* 2: 607–42.

United Nations. 1971. *Demographic yearbook, 1970.* New York: United Nations.
————. 1981. *Demographic yearbook, 1980.* New York: United Nations.
U.S. Bureau of the Census. 1970. *Statistical abstract of the United States, 1970.* Washington, D.C.: Government Printing Office.
————. 1980. *Statistical abstract of the United States, 1980.* Washington, D.C.: Government Printing Office.

Comment   Jonathan Skinner

Many economists and politicians have sounded the alarm about the low U.S. level of saving in the 1980s. If we cannot save more, the argument goes, investment will fall, the Germans and Japanese will buy up the United States, and we will enslave our children to economic dependency. Edward Lazear's response is, So what? This may appear to be a callous question to ask, but in fact it is a very good question—in fact the first question—that should be asked before the government tries to "cure" the "problem" with regulatory or tax schemes.

Lazear argues that the low saving rates are a consequence of different tastes for saving. If Americans prefer consuming more today relative to the future, then that is their choice, and they should not be required, or even encouraged, to save more. Lazear considers alternative explanations for why the United States saves so little, but ultimately concludes that the difference in saving is a matter of taste.

The U.S. national saving rate has been consistently below comparable saving rates of other countries since the 1960s. In 1962, national saving (as a percentage of GDP) in the United States was 9.1 percent. In the same year, national saving was 21.7 percent in Japan, 17.4 percent in the Netherlands, 17.3 percent in France, and 18.6 percent in Germany (U.S. Congress, Joint Committee on Taxation 1991).

It is likely that much of these differences can be attributed to tastes, as Lazear suggests. What has many policymakers worried, however, is the sharp decline in national saving, and in personal saving, during the 1980s. National saving in the United States fell from 8.9 percent in 1978 to 2.2 percent in 1986. A part of this decline was due to the increased deficit, but a substantial part was a consequence of reduced private saving as well.[1] To explain this decline as a reflection of "tastes," one must identify *changes* in individual preferences toward saving.

Alternatively, the decline in saving could be the consequence of a market or

Jonathan Skinner is associate professor of economics at the University of Virginia and a research associate of the National Bureau of Economic Research.

1. One could also interpret the increase in the deficit as a symptom of the taste shift away from saving and toward current consumption inclusive of government consumption.

government failure that got worse during the 1980s. If such a failure were the cause, the policy implication would be much different. In that case, either fixing the distortion or providing preferential treatment of saving to offset the inefficiency would be the appropriate course of action.

Was the decline in saving a consequence of tastes or of market (or government) failure? To shed light on this question, I will randomly pick five from the many explanations for why saving fell in the 1980s (also see Bosworth, Burtless, and Sabelhaus 1991). Which of these explanations are market failures that should be rectified, and which are a consequence of individual tastes?

1. Suppose that bequests are a function of the number of one's children and that bequests comprise a large fraction of the national capital stock (e.g., Kotlikoff and Summers 1981). Then the smaller size of families could have shifted the demand for bequests to the left and thereby reduced saving. This is certainly one explanation that relies solely on tastes; there is no rationale for government intervention to push saving rates back up.[2]

2. The saving rate in the national income accounts does not reflect capital gains, either in housing wealth or in the stock market. Rapid increases in stock market wealth during the mid-1980s, by stimulating consumption, could have pushed down conventionally measured saving rates. In fact, an alternative measure of the saving rate that includes such capital gains in housing and wealth (and adds these gains to national income) implies saving rates of over 15 percentage points during 1983–88, that is, saving rates roughly equal to those during 1974–79 (Skinner and Feenberg 1990; also see Hendershott and Peek 1989). Of course, this explanation denies the existence of a saving problem at all; instead, it attributes the entire fuss to confusion over the proper measurement of "saving."

3. An increased fear of nuclear war may have caused the sharp decline in saving rates during the 1980s (Slemrod 1986). That is, why save if one faces nuclear annihilation? Whether this is a change in tastes or a failure of the U.S. (or the former Soviet) government to reduce nuclear tension is not entirely clear, but I will call this a draw.

4. An alternative explanation is the higher rates of return accruing to defined-benefit pension funds. Because pensions face fixed liabilities, a higher rate of return on their investment allows firm-owned pension funds to reduce contributions or even revert pension assets to the firm (Bernheim and Shoven 1987). Because pension funds are quintessential "target" savers, the higher interest rates during the 1980s could have reduced saving. Again, it is not clear whether the reduction in pension fund saving reflects individual tastes or opportunistic pension fund managers.

5. A final explanation suggests that corporate buy-outs and capital gains realizations led to the influx of cash into the hands of investors (Hatsopoulos,

---

2. Whether this is a plausible explanation is another question, since the decline in saving rates seemed too rapid to be explained by gradual shifts in fertility rates.

Krugman, and Poterba 1989). With the cash hot in their pockets, the theory suggests, the lucky investors spent their wealth on cars and other consumption goods rather than reinvesting it. If true, this view of saving and consumption behavior would bode ill for any optimizing model of intertemporal consumption behavior. The presumption that individuals are doing what is "best" for them presupposes that cashing out stock should have little or no real effects on consumption.

Of the five explanations presented above for the decline in saving in the 1980s, only one is clearly a matter of changes in tastes. Other explanations are possible, but they are unlikely to be motivated entirely by changing tastes toward saving. To be on the safe side, one should therefore admit the possibility that the saving decline has been encouraged by government regulatory or tax policies. If so, an active role for the government in encouraging saving behavior would be appropriate.

References

Bernheim, B. Douglas, and John Shoven. 1987. Pension funds and saving. In *Pensions in the U.S. economy,* ed. A. Bodie, J. B. Shoven, and D. A. Wise. Chicago: University of Chicago Press.

Bosworth, Barry, Gary Burtless, and John Sabelhaus. 1991. The decline in saving: Evidence from household surveys. *Brookings Papers on Economic Activity* 1:183–256.

Hatsopoulos, George N., Paul R. Krugman, and James M. Poterba. 1989. Overconsumption: The challenge to U.S. economic policy. Working Paper. Washington, D.C.: American Business Council, March.

Hendershott, Patric, and Joe Peek. 1989. Aggregate U.S. private saving: Conceptual measures and empirical tests. In *The measurement of saving, investment, and wealth,* ed. R. E. Lipsey and H. S. Tice. Chicago: University of Chicago Press.

Kotlikoff, Laurence, and Lawrence Summers. 1981. The role of intergenerational transfers in aggregate capital accumulation. *Journal of Political Economy* 89 (August): 706–732.

Skinner, Jonathan, and Daniel Feenberg. 1990. The impact of the 1986 tax reform act on personal saving. In *Do taxes matter? The impact of the tax reform act of 1986,* ed. J. Slemrod. Cambridge: MIT Press.

Slemrod, Joel. 1986. Saving and the fear of nuclear war. *Journal of Conflict Resolution* 30:403–19.

U.S. Congress, Joint Committee on Taxation. 1991. *Tax policy and the macroeconomy: Stabilization, growth, and income distribution.* Washington, D.C.: Government Printing Office, December.

Comment on Chapters 4 and 5   B. Douglas Bernheim

The fact that the United States saves so little, both by historical standards and in comparison to other countries (particularly Japan), has puzzled economists for many years. The literature is littered with possible explanations for this phenomenon, none of which are completely satisfying. Lazear is inclined to attribute international differences to "tastes," and to some extent he also seems to endorse the view that differences in rates of saving over time probably reflect "cohort effects," which he equates with tastes. Since economists are not usually inclined to pass judgment on tastes, Lazear concludes that the welfare implications of low saving are ambiguous.

Although I am inclined to agree with Lazear about the importance of tastes, I would emphasize a somewhat different point: tastes apparently change quite a lot. Rates of saving in Japan have varied enormously over the last 50 years. During the interwar period, as well as in the years immediately following World War II, the Japanese saved less than Americans. Similarly, Korea, Taiwan, and Singapore saved very little as recently as 1960 and have only lately earned reputations as countries with high rates of saving. It certainly appears, if tastes are the chief determinants of saving, that tastes can change dramatically within a very short period of time. Moreover, at least in the case of Japan, there is reason to believe that the government actively and successfully intervened in a manner designed to shape tastes (see Central Council for Savings Promotion 1981). These observations suggest that we, as economists, should focus on the following kinds of questions: Why do tastes for saving change? Can (and should) public policy affect the evolution of tastes?

The need to think seriously about the evolution of tastes becomes particularly serious once one steps outside the narrow confines of the life-cycle hypothesis. Dissatisfaction with the performance of this theory has led a growing number of economists, myself included, to ponder "behavioral" alternatives (see, e.g., Shefrin and Thaler 1988). Some have argued for abandoning the view that individuals act as if they maximize an intertemporal utility function and have instead emphasized the importance of habit, mental accounting, self-discipline, and so forth. In many contexts, one can argue that, through trial and error, an individual eventually learns to behave in a way that is consistent with utility maximization. However, this argument is not applicable to life-cycle saving. Each individual accumulates resources for retirement only once; there is no opportunity to learn from one's mistakes. Moreover, the life-cycle saving decision is extraordinarily complex, in that it requires an individual to contemplate labor earnings, investment strategies, macroeconomic trends, and a vast assortment of risks, all over a very long time frame. It would be astonishing if the average individual, with no practice and little or no training, could on his first try act as if he was a perfectly rational, farsighted utility maximizer.

By studying behavioral theories of household saving, it may be possible to understand differences in rates of saving both across countries and over time (for a more detailed discussion, see Bernheim 1991). Japanese households may

B. Douglas Bernheim is the John L. Weinberg Professor of Economics and Business Policy at Princeton University and a research associate of the National Bureau of Economic Research.

have acquired frugal habits out of necessity during the process of postwar reconstruction, and these habits may have been cultivated and preserved through government intervention. Higher rates of saving among U.S. citizens who lived through the Great Depression may reflect the effects of experiencing deprivation first hand. Another factor contributing to the recent decline in U.S. saving could be the rise in the fraction of private income that is received in "spendable" forms (see Hatsopoulos, Krugman, and Poterba 1989). It is also possible that the longest peacetime expansion on record contributed to a false sense of economic prosperity and stability. Alternatively, Americans may simply have become accustomed to rising consumption profiles, which, out of habit and myopia, they attempted to maintain ever after the productivity slowdown.

Within the context of a behavioral theory, one can give content to statements about welfare, such as "Americans do not save enough." Individuals may well regret their bad habits and lack of foresight after the fact. Moreover, the behavioral framework suggests some well-defined roles for public policy. First, and perhaps foremost, the government may be in a position to provide information and training, thereby helping individuals to further their own objectives through the design of more coherent and effective long-range financial plans. During much of the postwar period, the Japanese government assumed precisely this role. Second, it may also be desirable to encourage the acquisition of beneficial habits by subsidizing saving. In much the same way, the government discourages the consumption of cigarettes through education and taxation.

Even if one insists on adhering to the life-cycle framework, I would not agree that the welfare effect of low saving is ambiguous. On the contrary, there are at least seven good neoclassical reasons to believe that saving is too low.

1. Capital income is taxed, both explicitly and implicitly (e.g., through college scholarships). Lazear dismisses this argument, on the grounds that the interest elasticity of saving is very low. Although this strikes me as a fair characterization of the evidence, it is at odds with more direct evidence on the effect of taxes (e.g., Venti and Wise 1990). To infer tax effects from estimates of the interest elasticity, one must subscribe to an important unstated assumption: the effect of a change in the after-tax rate of return induced by a movement of the before-tax rate of return is the same as the effect of a change in the after-tax rate of return attributable to a movement of the effective tax rate. In the context of investment, other authors (e.g., Hall and Jorgenson 1967) have been roundly criticized for making precisely this assumption. One can easily imagine a number of reasons for questioning its validity. For example, if the stochastic processes governing gross interest rates and taxes differ, one would hardly expect investors to respond similarly to changes in these variables. Another possibility is suggested by my work with John Shoven. Several years ago (Bernheim and Shoven 1987), we pointed out that the interest elasticity of contributions to pension funds is large and negative. This may dampen the response of aggregate saving to a change in the gross rate of interest. How-

ever, it does *not* dampen the response of saving to a change in the tax rate. Hence, a low estimate of the interest elasticity of saving is consistent with a high tax elasticity.

2. The nature of intergenerational equilibria can create a bias against saving. Lazear adopts the formulation of intergenerational preferences popularized by Becker (1974) and Barro (1974). In particular, the preferences of generation *t* are summarized by a utility index U_t, where

$$U_t = U(c_t, U_{t+1}) = v(c_t) + \beta U_{t+1}.$$

In this equation, c_t represents generations *t*'s consumption, and U_{t+1} denotes the utility index for generation *t*'s successor generation. Implicitly, each generation has only one successor and one predecessor. When this formulation of preferences is used, authors typically focus attention on a class of equilibria that correspond to the solution of a standard dynamic programming problem, where the objective function is the present discounted value (discounting at the rate β) of the stream $v(c_t)$. This approach to intergenerational equilibria is extremely special. There are many plausible ways to deviate from it.

First, one could adopt an alternative formulation of preferences. Suppose, for example, that parents care about the felicity ($v(c_{t+1})$) of their children, rather than utility (U_{t+1}). Mathematically,

$$U_t = v(c_t) + v(c_{t+1}).$$

This formulation has a straightforward economic interpretation: parents receive pleasure from their children's consumption, but regard bequests to later generations as wasteful. While somewhat extreme, it captures a plausible situation: generation $t + 1$ cares more about the consumption of generations after $t + 1$ (relative to the consumption of generation $t + 1$) than does generation t. A number of authors have studied intergenerational equilibria with preferences of this form. The problem is complex, since the preference of successive generations are not dynamically consistent, and game-theoretic tools must be employed. However, it is known that Markov-perfect equilibria are *never* Pareto optimal. Moreover, one Pareto improves the equilibrium allocation by *increasing* saving (see Bernheim and Ray 1987).

Second, one could relax the counterfactual assumption that each generation has only a single successor and predecessor. It is well-known that this assumption is pernicious (see Bernheim and Bagwell 1988). Its importance in the current context stems from the fact that children marry other children from different families, so that each married household has two distinct predecessors. From the point of view of these two parent households, the consumption of the common child household is a public good. As a result, it is usually possible to improve on equilibrium allocations by increasing the intergenerational transfer of resources. This entails greater saving.

Third, even within the Barro-Becker framework, there is a vast multiplicity of equilibria, and there is no particular reason to believe that the economy will settle on an efficient one (see Gale 1985).

3. The government operates a large number of social insurance programs, including Social Security, Medicare, Medicaid, unemployment insurance, and so forth. These programs reduce precautionary motives for saving. Indeed, the fact that, until recently, Japan's social insurance system was underdeveloped has often been offered as a partial explanation for differences between the saving rates of Japan and the United States. Indeed, as Japan has improved its social insurance system, its rate of saving has fallen.

When insurance is provided by an efficient market, any depressive effects on saving are first-best. However, social insurance programs generally arise in response to market failures. There is no particular reason to believe that current social insurance programs lead to a second-best level of saving.[1]

4. Lazear describes an intertemporal incentive problem commonly known as the "Samaritan's dilemma" (see, e.g., Buchanan 1975; Bernheim and Stark 1988). The general statement of this problem is as follows. There are two parties, A and B. A cares about B, but B does not care about A. These parties interact over time; for simplicity, we assume that there are two periods. B will tend to save less in the first period than he would if A were selfish, because he knows that, in the second period, an altruistic A will bail him out.

Lazear describes a particular version of this problem, in which A is a child and B is a parent. The story is also often told the other way around (with A as the parent and B as the child), in order to explain why the children of wealthy parents save so little. A similar problem can arise between spouses, or even between unrelated individuals. Lazear is therefore correct in asserting that this is not inherently an intergenerational issue. However, this should not obscure the fact that it is an intertemporal issue and that it inherently involves saving. Moreover, when Lazear asserts that B is better off with low saving, this is misleading—in the presence of the Samaritan's dilemma, one can always Pareto improve the equilibrium allocation, and this improvement is achieved (in part) by increasing saving.

5. In a closed economy, saving necessarily equals investment. Consequently, if there are important external economies associated with investment, the levels of both saving and investment will tend to be low relative to the optimum. Externalities of this sort have featured prominently in the recent literature on endogenous growth.

Of course, the U.S. economy is not closed. Nevertheless, there appears to be some long-run tendency toward balanced current and capital accounts. As a result, the level of saving probably does have a significant impact on investment; with external economies, households will save too little.

---

1. It is worth mentioning, however, that second-best social insurance might entail provisions to reduce the level of saving. See Diamond and Mirrlees (1978).

6. Lazear mentions the possibility that there may be positive externalities associated with investments in children, but does not present this theory in its most favorable light. I believe that there are important externalities of this sort, but they are local, rather than national, in scope. For a variety of reasons, it is more enjoyable to live in communities where other people's children are well-educated and well provided for. This is not the result of nationalistic sentiment (Lazear's characterization), but rather a consequence of pragmatism.

7. It is also arguable that saving is too low from the standpoint of equity. To illustrate, consider once again the Becker-Barro "dynastic" equilibrium discussed under point 2 above. This equilibrium maximizes the utility of the first generation. It corresponds to the Pareto optimum found by assigning a weight of unity to the utility of the first generation and a weight of zero to all subsequent generations. If the planner attaches any positive weight to any subsequent generation, equilibrium saving will be suboptimal. Lazear touches on this point; for a more detailed discussion, see Bernheim (1989).

Lazear tends to discount this argument, on the grounds that children may also care about their parents. If altruism toward parents is sufficiently strong, then the preferences of subsequent generations will coincide with those of the first generation, and the equilibrium allocation will be equally beneficial for everyone. Aside from being a knife-edge case, this suggestion is also empirically implausible. Because of economic growth, children tend to be lifetime wealthier than parents. Despite this, transfers mostly flow from parents to children, and not from children to parents. This strongly suggests that parents are generally more altruistic toward children than children are toward parents.

In summary, Lazear and I agree that we cannot yet adequately explain the decline of saving in the United States, or the differences in rates of saving between the United States and other countries. However, I do not agree that the welfare consequences of low saving are ambiguous. There are good theoretical and empirical reasons to believe that Americans save too little. Lazear's skepticism should not discourage us from vigorously pursuing policies designed to stimulate the rate of saving.

One such policy permits households to receive tax-favored treatment on resources contributed to 401(k) plans. The paper by Poterba, Venti, and Wise (chap. 4) provides some useful background information on 401(k)s, as well as a preliminary analysis of the effect of these plans on household saving. This analysis suggests that contributions to 401(k)s represent new saving. If this conclusion is correct, then 401(k)s provide an extremely powerful policy tool.

Unfortunately, it is very difficult to measure the impact of tax-favored accounts on household saving. Poterba, Venti, and Wise have adopted an empirical strategy similar in spirit to that used by Venti and Wise in a series of earlier papers on Individual Retirement Accounts (IRAs). Although this methodology goes some distance toward producing believable results, it falls short of providing a completely convincing solution to problems arising from population heterogeneity and sample selection.

The Poterba-Venti-Wise methodology represents an attempt to statistically mimic a controlled experiment in which households are randomly assigned to two groups, one of which is eligible for 401(k)s and one of which is not. A comparison of average saving across these groups would presumably provide us with an estimate of the effect of 401(k) eligibility on saving.

The simplest approach would be to ignore the endogeneity of the decision to contribute to a 401(k) and to compare average saving across contributors and noncontributors. Unfortunately, we are not likely to learn very much from this calculation. Some households save a lot, while some save a little. This is presumably attributable to differences in preferences. One should not be surprised to discover that those who contribute to 401(k) accounts also save more in other forms; through self-selection, this group probably consists of households with strong preferences for saving.

In their work on IRAs, Venti and Wise refine this simple comparison by controlling for initial wealth. This variable is intended to capture the effects of heterogeneity along the dimension of preferences toward saving—households with strong preferences for saving will also have higher initial wealth. Even so, one should not be too surprised to discover that, controlling for initial wealth, IRA (or 401(k)) contributors saved more in other forms. It would be extreme to suggest that the disposition to save remains constant over an individual's life. Many people may pass through periods when they save a lot, as well as periods when they save a little. This could arise quite naturally from a variety of considerations. For example, some people may start saving for retirement only after achieving some specific age or stage of life (e.g., completion of child rearing). Alternatively, individuals may experience shocks to income that persist for several years before dissipating. When passing through a period of temporarily high income, such an individual will tend to save more.

It seems to me that these forms of population heterogeneity are not only plausible, but that they could well account for a positive correlation between contributions to tax-favored accounts and other forms of saving, even controlling for initial wealth. To emphasize this point, I will suggest a hypothetical calculation (which one could, in principle, perform): compute the correlation between wealth accumulation in the form of stocks and wealth accumulation in the form of bonds, controlling for initial wealth. My guess is that one would find a significant positive correlation. This would not prove that the availability of stocks causes people to save in the form of bonds. Rather, it would simply show that those who decide to save during any given period allocate their resources across a variety of asset classes.

The current paper improves on previous efforts to measure the effect of tax-favored accounts on saving by performing two additional calculations. First, it compares the assets of a group of households in 1984 with the assets of another group of households in 1987. These groups are selected to be as similar as possible. According to Poterba, Venti, and Wise, the important difference between these groups is that the 1987 sample had three more years of 401(k) eligibility than the 1984 sample. As it turns out, the 1987 sample had accumulated more assets.

I am not convinced that this procedure eliminates the problem of sample selection. The 1984 and 1987 samples only include 401(k) *contributors*. Thus, the sample selection criteria are different: in 1984, the authors study a group of households that still contributed to 401(k)s after (typically) not more than three years of eligibility; in 1987, they study a group that still contributed to 401(k)s after (typically) not more than six years of eligibility. What happens when one conditions sample selection on the continuation of contributions after N years of eligibility? Presumably, as N rises, one isolates the "die hard" households that are completely dedicated to saving. (Analogously, lapse rates for life insurance are highest during the first few years of a policy.) Consequently, one should not be surprised if total assets rise when the selection criteria is based on a larger value of N.

Poterba, Venti, and Wise also implement a second methodological innovation: they compare the assets of households that are eligible to make 401(k) contributions with the assets of ineligible households (controlling for income class). Since eligibility is determined by employers, the authors believe that cross-sectional variation in eligibility status provides an exogenous natural experiment. In effect, 401(k) eligibility is used as an instrument.

Unfortunately, there is probably a systematic relationship between 401(k) eligibility and other factors that influence saving. In many companies, benefits are influenced by the opinions of workers and, in some cases, are based on surveys of worker preferences. To some extent, workers self-select over jobs; those who care more about saving for retirement may be more likely to accept positions with firms that offer 401(k)s. Finally, eligibility for a 401(k) is correlated with other job characteristics (better jobs are more likely to provide 401(k) options).

The paper itself convincingly documents the endogeneity of 401(k)s. Refer in particular in table 4.13. For the moment, focus on the summary statistics provided for households with incomes between $50,000 and $75,000 in 1987. The median assets of households eligible for 401(k)s exceeded the median assets of ineligible households by $9,693 ($25,343 − $14,650). And yet median 401(k) balances for the eligible group were only $1,500. I doubt very much whether the authors would claim that 401(k)s crowd in other saving by a factor of six. Rather, something else is creating a correlation between assets and 401(k) eligibility. A similar conclusion follows for every other income class.

Overall, I found the authors' analysis interesting, and I am sympathetic to their conclusions. Their work continues to move my posterior beliefs in the direction suggested by their conclusions. However, the jury is still out, and further work is clearly warranted.

References

Barro, Robert J. 1974. Are government bonds net wealth? *Journal of Political Economy* 82 (November/December): 1095–1117.

Becker, Gary S. 1974. A theory of social interactions. *Journal of Political Economy* 82 (November/December): 1061–93.

Bernheim, B. Douglas. 1989. Intergenerational altruism, dynastic equilibria and social welfare. *Review of Economic Studies* 56 (January): 119–28.

———. 1991. *The vanishing nest egg: Reflections on saving in America.* New York: Priority Press.

Bernheim, B. Douglas, and Kyle Bagwell. 1988. Is everything neutral? *Journal of Political Economy* 96, no. 2 (April): 308–38.

Bernheim, B. Douglas, and Debraj Ray. 1987. Economic growth with intergenerational altruism. *Review of Economic Studies* 54, no. 2 (April): 227–42.

Bernheim, B. Douglas, and John B. Shoven. 1987. Pension funding and saving. In *Pensions in the U.S. economy,* ed. S. Bodie, J. Shoven, and D. Wise, 85–111. Chicago: University of Chicago Press.

Bernheim, B. Douglas, and Oded Stark. 1988. Altruism within the family reconsidered: Do nice guys finish last? *American Economic Review* 78, no. 5 (December): 1034–45.

Buchanan, James M. 1975. The Samaritan's dilemma. In *Altruism, morality and economic theory,* ed. Edmund S. Phelps, 71–85. New York: Russell Sage Foundation.

Central Council for Savings Promotion. 1981. *Savings and savings promotion movement in Japan.* Tokyo: Toppan Printing.

Diamond, P. A., and J. A. Mirrlees. 1978. A model of social insurance with variable retirement. *Journal of Public Economics* 10:295–336.

Gale, Douglas. 1985. The strategic analysis of bequest behavior: A critique of the Ricardian equivalence theorem. Center for Analytical Research in Economics and the Social Sciences, Department of Economics, University of Pennsylvania. Mimeograph.

Hall, Robert E., and Dale W. Jorgenson. 1967. Tax policy and investment behavior. *American Economic Review* 57:391–414.

Hatsopoulos, George N., Paul R. Krugman, and James M. Poterba. 1989. Overconsumption: The challenge to U.S. policy. Paper prepared for the American Business Conference. Washington, D.C.: American Business Council.

Shefrin, Hersh M., and Richard H. Thaler. 1988. The behavioral life-cycle hypothesis. *Economic Inquiry* 24 (October): 609–43.

Venti, Steven F., and David A. Wise. 1990. Have IRAs increased U.S. saving? Evidence from consumer expenditure surveys. *Quarterly Journal of Economics* 105 (August): 661–98.

IV Retirement Behavior

6 Pension Plan Provisions and Retirement: Men and Women, Medicare, and Models

Robin L. Lumsdaine, James H. Stock, and David A. Wise

Our ongoing analysis of the effects of pension plan provisions on retirement is pursued in this paper. The work to date has emphasized the dramatic effect of employer-provided pension plan provisions on age of retirement and the enormous effects of changing the provisions. The work has also highlighted the important limitations of using Social Security provisions to predict retirement behavior, without accounting for the effect of employer pension plan provisions, which, for employees who have such plans, is typically much more powerful than the effect of Social Security provisions.

Two aspects of our work have guided the analysis as the research progressed. The first is that a new method has been used to model retirement decisions. The second is that the empirical analysis has been based on data from individual firms. Thus we have been led to consider whether the model provided accurate predictions of the effects of plan provisions on retirement and whether the behavioral implications of analysis based on data from one firm could be generalized to other firms with different plan provisions.

In two initial papers, Stock and Wise (1990a, 1990b) developed an "option value" model of retirement. The central feature of this model is that in deciding whether to retire employees are assumed to compare the "value" of retiring now to the *maximum of the expected values* of retiring at all future retirement ages. If the maximum of the future values is greater than the value of retirement

Robin L. Lumsdaine is assistant professor of economics at Princeton University and a faculty research fellow of the National Bureau of Economic Research. James H. Stock is professor of political economy at the John F. Kennedy School of Government, Harvard University, and a research associate of the National Bureau of Economic Research. David A. Wise is the John F. Stambaugh Professor of Political Economy at the John F. Kennedy School of Government, Harvard University, and the area director for Health and Retirement Programs at the National Bureau of Economic Research.

Financial support from the National Institute on Aging and the Hoover Institution (Wise) is gratefully acknowledged. The authors also thank Jim Smith and John Rust for helpful comments.

183

now, the employee continues to work. We tested the predictive validity of this model in two ways: first, we considered the "within-sample fit" of the model, by comparing the actual pattern of retirement by age to the pattern predicted by the model, based on the data used for estimation. Second, in papers by Lumsdaine, Stock, and Wise (1990, 1991) we emphasized an external "out-of-sample" check of predictive validity, by considering how well the model predicted the effect on retirement of an unanticipated and temporary change in the pension plan provisions, occasioned by an early retirement window plan. In a subsequent paper, Lumsdaine, Stock, and Wise (1992) compared the predictive validity of the option value model with that of two versions of stochastic dynamic programming models. The stochastic dynamic programming model is close in spirit to the option value model, but the prediction of retirement is based on the comparison of the value of retirement now to the *expected value of the maximum* of the values of future retirement ages. The evidence was that the option value model predicted just as well as the stochastic dynamic programming models, but had the advantage of being much less complex numerically. Ausink (1991) pursued a similar comparison based on retirement from the military and found that the option value version was noticeably better than the stochastic dynamic programming versions.

All of these papers, with the exception of the work by Ausink, are based on data from a single firm. The use of firm data was motivated by the absence of information on pension plan provisions in standard data sources, such as the Retirement History Survey, and by the realization that the incentives inherent in such plans could be very substantial and varied widely among firms, as shown in papers by Bulow (1981), Lazear (1983), and Kotlikoff and Wise (1985, 1987, 1988). In principle, the ideal data source would provide retirement information and pension plan information for a random sample of employees, from a wide range of firms. Such information has not been available. The alternative we followed was to obtain data from several different firms. The hope was that similar results from different firms would tend to confirm the validity of the model, even though the firms themselves could not be considered a random sample of all firms. Thus there is a need to determine whether the results for the single firm are confirmed based on data from other firms.

Therefore, the first goal of this paper is to use data from a new firm to confirm that the age pattern of retirement corresponds to the pension plan provisions. Descriptive analysis confirms that this is the case.

A second emphasis in this paper is the comparison of the retirement behavior of men and women. It is sometimes proposed that women may tend to retire earlier than men because they are typically younger than their husbands and they may tend to retire when their husbands do. From descriptive analysis, it is clear that the retirement patterns of men and women are not appreciably different.

A third goal is to add another observation to the list of comparisons of the predictive validity of the option value versus that of the stochastic dynamic programming model. Predictive validity in this paper is judged by the model predictions of retirement under a special 1983 early retirement incentive plan. The models are estimated based on retirement decisions in 1982. The goal of the comparisons is to accumulate data on the extent to which the different models predict actual retirement choices and thus to determine which specification best approximates the considerations that determine actual retirement decisions. The emphasis is not on which model best approximates the economists' view of the "right" calculation, but rather which best approximates the calculations that the typical person makes. Or, better still, which predicts best the retirement decisions of the typical employee.

A fourth goal is to make limited inferences about the potential effect of Medicare availability on retirement, especially at age 65. We have found in our previous work that model predictions of the age-65 retirement rate are typically much lower than the actual rate. We have attributed the high actual rate to an "age-65 retirement effect." But our work, and we believe the work of others, has ignored the potential effect of Medicare insurance that becomes available at age 65. The approach used here is to consider how retirement rates—especially at age 65—would be affected were Medicare valued according to the average payments to the covered population. The final goal is to compare parameter estimates based on data from two firms with different pension plans.[1]

6.1 Background

6.1.1 The Firm III Plan

Employees are covered by a defined-benefit pension plan with normal retirement at age 65 and early retirement at age 55. Cliff vesting occurs at 10 years of service (YOS) or at age 65, whichever comes first. The normal retirement benefit at 65 depends on earnings, age, and years of service at retirement (that is, at the time of departure from the firm). A person can retire and elect to start receiving benefits before age 65, but the normal benefit will be reduced by 5 percent for each year that receipt of benefits precedes age 65, as shown in figure 6.1. A person who retired at age 55, for example, would receive 50 percent of the normal retirement benefit of a person who left the firm at age 65. (The normal benefit also depends on years of service at the time of retirement.)

However, if a person has 30 years of service at retirement and if the person is age 60 or older, the person is eligible for 100 percent of the normal benefit. Benefits are reduced 5 percent for each year that retirement precedes age 60,

---

1. In order to maintain numerical consistency throughout our work, we refer to the firm used in this analysis as "firm III." The comparison firm, used in Stock and Wise (1990a, 1990b) and Lumsdaine, et al. (1990, 1991, 1992), is "firm I."

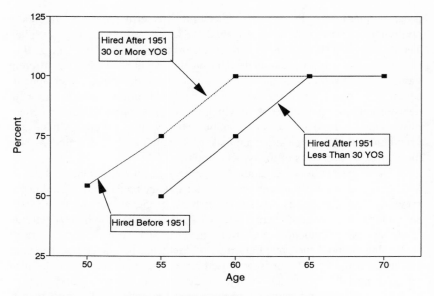

Fig. 6.1   Early retirement benefit (% of normal age-65 benefit)

if the person has 30 years of service. For example, a person who retired at age 55 with 30 years of service would receive 75 percent of the normal benefit.

Even a person who retires before age 55 and is vested can elect to receive benefits from the pension plan as early as age 55, but like the post-55 retiree, benefits are reduced 5 percent for each year that receipt of the benefits precedes age 65. Of course, this person's benefits would be based on earnings, age, and years of service at the time of retirement, unadjusted for earnings inflation, and would thus be lower than the benefits of a person who retired later.

Employees who joined the firm before 1951 can retire as early as age 50 and begin to receive benefits immediately, but at a reduced rate. An employee hired before 1951 had at least 31 years of service in 1982. The reduction for this group is indicated by the extended line that indicates benefits at age 50 to be 54.3 percent of the age-60 benefits for an employee who has 30 or more years of service at retirement.

To understand the effect of the pension plan provisions, figure 6.2A shows the expected future compensation of a person from our sample who is 51 years old and has been employed by the firm for 23 years. To compute the data graphed in figures 6.2A–6.2D, a 5 percent real discount rate and a 6 percent inflation rate are assumed. The discount rate is estimated in the empirical analysis, and the inflation rate is assumed to be 6 percent. Total compensation from the firm can be viewed as the sum of wage earnings, the accrual of pension benefits, and the accrual of Social Security benefits. (This omits medical and other unobserved benefits that should be included as compensation, but for which we have no data.) As compensation for working another year, the em-

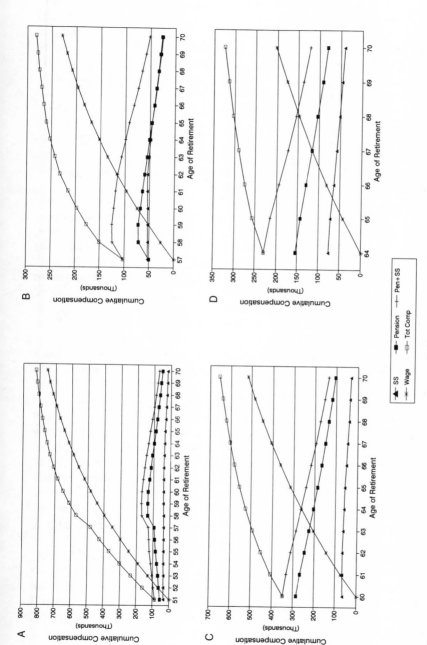

Fig. 6.2 Future compensation: persons (*A*) age 51 with 23 YOS, (*B*) age 57 with 29 YOS, (*C*) age 60 with 38 YOS, and (*D*) age 64 with 45 YOS

ployee receives salary earnings. Compensation is also received in the form of future pension benefits. The annual compensation in this form is the change in the present value of the future pension benefits entitlement, due to working an additional year. This accrual is comparable to wage earnings. The accrual of Social Security benefits may be calculated in a similar manner, and is also comparable to wage earnings. Figure 6.2A shows the present value at age 51 of expected future compensation in all three forms. Wage earnings represents cumulated earnings, by age of retirement from the firm (more precisely, by age of departure from the firm, since some workers might continue to work in another job). For example, the cumulated wage earnings of this employee between age 51 and age 60, were he to retire at age 60, would be about $482,000, discounted to age-51 dollars. The slope of the wage earnings line represents annual earnings discounted to age-51 dollars.

The pension line shows the accrual of firm pension benefits, again discounted to age-51 dollars. The shape of this profile is determined by the pension plan provisions. The present value of accrued pension benefit entitlements at age 51 is about $54,000. The present value of retirement benefits increases between ages 51 and 57 because years of service and nominal earnings increase. An employee could leave the firm at age 53, for example. If he were to do that and if he were vested in the firm's pension plan, he would be entitled to normal retirement pension benefits at age 65, based on his years of service and nominal dollar earnings at age 53. He could choose to start receiving benefits as early as age 55, the pension early retirement age, but the benefit amount would be reduced 5 percent for each year that the receipt of benefits preceded age 65. Because 5 percent is less than the actuarially fair discount rate, the present value of benefits of a person who leaves the firm before age 55 are always greatest if receipt of benefits begins at 55.

Recall that a person who has accumulated 30 years of service and is 55 or older is entitled to increased retirement benefits that would reach 100 percent of normal retirement benefits at age 60. No early retirement reduction is applied to benefits if they are taken then. So a person at age 60 with 30 years of service who continues to work will no longer gain 5 percent a year from fewer years of early retirement reduction, as occurs before age 60. There is a jump in the benefits of a person younger than 60 who attains 30 years of service. That accounts for the jump in the benefits of the person depicted in the figure 6.2A, when he attains 30 years of service at age 58.

The Social Security (SS) accrual profile is determined by the Social Security benefit provisions. The present value of accrued Social Security benefit entitlements at age 51 is about $33,000. Social Security benefits cannot begin until age 62. If real earnings do not change much between ages 51 and 62, then real Social Security benefits at age 62 will not change much either. After age 62, the actuarial adjustment is such that the present value of benefits, evaluated at the age of retirement, does not depend on the retirement age. But the present value of the benefits discounted to the same age (51 in this case) declines.

There is a further drop after age 65, because the actuarial adjustment is reduced from 7 percent to 3 percent.

The top line (Tot comp) shows total compensation. For example, the wage earnings of an employee who left the firm at age 60 would increase $482,000 between ages 51 and 60, shown by the wage earnings line. Thereafter, the employee would receive firm pension plan and Social Security retirement benefits with a present value—at age 51—of about $170,000. The sum of the two is about $652,000, shown by the top line. Compared to total compensation of $575,000 between ages 51 and 60, an average of $63,000 per year, total compensation between ages 60 and 65 would be only $100,000, or $23,000 per year. Thus the monetary reward for continued work declines dramatically with age.

Figures 6.2B–6.2D show comparable compensation profiles for employees who are ages 57, 60, and 64, respectively, in 1982; they have 29, 38, and 45 years of service, respectively. The person depicted in figure 6.2B attains 30 years of service at age 58; thus the jump in pension benefits at that age. The present value of pension plus Social Security compensation (Pen + SS) reaches a maximum at age 59 and declines thereafter. Were this employee to continue to work after age 59, until 65, the present value of total retirement benefits would fall by $33,000, offsetting about 28 percent of the present value of wage earnings over this period ($117,000). A similar prospect faces the employee depicted in figure 6.2C, but this employee is already entitled to 100 percent of normal retirement benefits and loses benefits for each year that he continues to work.

The employee who faces the figure 6.2D compensation profile is 64 years old and loses both pension and Social Security benefits for each year that retirement is postponed. At age 65, for example, about 54 percent of expected wage earnings would be offset by a reduction in retirement benefits, if retirement were postponed.

6.1.2   The 1983 Window

Under the window plan, which was in effect from January 1 to February 28, 1983, all employees were eligible for a separation bonus, but the most generous payments were available to persons age 55 and older who had at least 21 years of service. Retirement benefits for this group were increased depending on age and years of service. For example, a person age 59 with 28 years of service could receive 100 percent of normal retirement benefits, instead of 70 percent under the regular plan. That is, this person's retirement benefit would be increased by 43 percent. A person who was age 55 with 21 years of service could receive 55 percent of the normal benefits, instead of 50 percent. Persons age 60 or older with 30 years of service were eligible for 100 percent of normal benefits under the regular plan.

In addition, all employees were eligible for a separation bonus equal to one week's pay for every year of service, with a minimum of 2 weeks and a maximum of 26 weeks of pay. Thus even persons who were under 55 and those who were eligible for 100 percent of normal retirement benefits faced an added inducement to retire.

6.1.3   The Data

The data used in the analysis are drawn from the personnel records of all persons employed by the firm at any time between 1979 and 1988. A year-end file is available for each year. Earnings records back to 1979 (or to the date of hire, if after 1979) are available for each employee. In addition, the data contain some demographic information, such as date of birth, gender, marital status, and occupational group. The retirement date of employees who retire is also known. (More generally, the date of any departure is known, and the reason for the departure is recorded.) Thus we are able to determine whether a person who was employed at age a was also employed at age $a + 1$, and if not, the exact age at which the employee left the firm.

The estimation of the retirement model in this paper is based on 1982 data, whether or not an employee left the firm in 1982. (To simplify the determination of age of retirement, only employees born in January and February and who had not retired before March 1, 1982, are used in this analysis.) The primary test of the predictive validity of the model is based on how well the model, estimated on 1982 data, predicts retirement under the 1983 window plan that substantially increased standard retirement benefits.

6.2   Departure Rates for Men versus Women

6.2.1   Life-Cycle Departure Rates

Firm departure rates for employees aged 20–70 are shown in figure 6.3. The graph reflects average departure rates over the years 1979–82. After substantial turnover at younger ages, annual departure rates fall continuously to 1–2 percent at ages 45–54. Employees start to leave the firm in larger numbers at age 55, the early retirement age.

Figures 6.4A–6.4C compare the departure rates for men and women. Figure 6.4A pertains to employees with less than 10 years of service, who are not vested in the firm's pension plan. Figure 6.4B pertains to employees with 10–29 years of service, and figure 6.4C to those with 30 or more years of service. The striking aspect of the graphs is that there is virtually no difference between the departure rates of men and women, except at the principle child-bearing ages—say, 23 to 37. For example, between ages 37 and 54 the turnover rates of men and women with 10–29 years of service are almost identical. Among employees with less than 10 years of service, there is little difference in the departure rates of men and women between ages 37 and 65. Men and women with 30 or more years of service have almost identical departure rates at all ages.

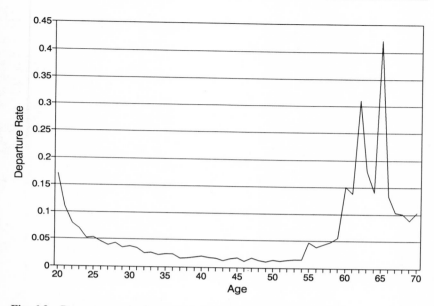

Fig. 6.3   Departure rates by age: men and women together

6.2.2   Retirement-Age Departure Rates

The departure rates for persons aged 50 and above are shown in figure 6.5 for men and women. These rates are based on 1982 data only. There is a noticeable increase in departure rates at age 55, from less than 1 percent for persons 50–54 years old to 3 or 4 percent for employees 55–59 years old. Although the increase in the annual departure may seem small, the cumulative effect of the increase is substantial. For example, with a 4 percent annual departure rate, 19 percent of persons in the firm at age 54 will leave before age 60. At a 1 percent annual rate, only 5 percent will leave.

There is also a sharp increase at age 60, the age at which persons with 30 years of service are entitled to 100 percent of normal (age-65) benefits. The sharp increases at ages 62 and 65 correspond to the Social Security early and normal retirement ages.

The plan provisions suggest that for employees age 55–64, and especially those 55–60 or 61, the departure rate for persons with 30 or more years of service should be higher than the rate for persons with less than 30 years of service. The descriptive data are shown in figure 6.6. The departure rates for men with 30 or more years of service are higher in the 55–61 age range. They are also higher for women at age 60, but the differences at other ages are small. Women with less than 30 years of service appear more likely than men to take early retirement between the ages of 55 and 61.

These data also reveal what may be an individual-specific work effect. Employees with 30 or more years of service who have not retired before age 65 are

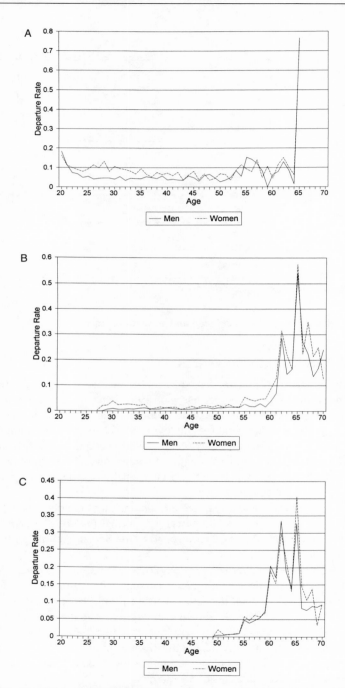

Fig. 6.4 Departure rates by age: men and women (*A*) with less that 10 YOS, (*B*) with 10–29 YOS, and (*C*) with 30 or more YOS

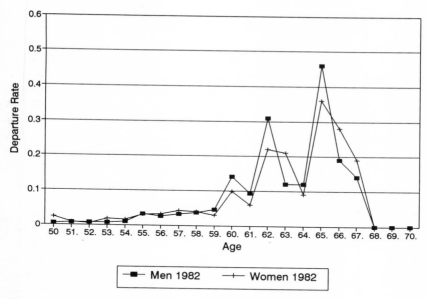

Fig. 6.5   **Departure rates: men and women compared, 1982**

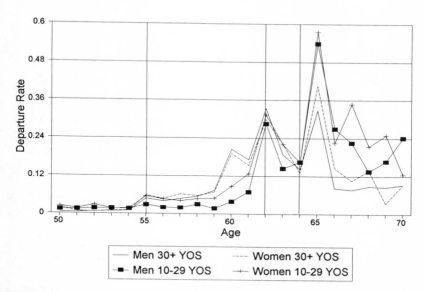

Fig. 6.6   **Departure rates by age and YOS: men and women aged 50–70**

thereafter less likely to retire than employees with less than 30 years of service.

In summary: even without formal analysis, the graphs make it clear that the pattern of departures reflects the provisions of the pension plan. The pattern is also consistent with Social Security provisions, but the magnitude of the age-65 departure rate seems much more abrupt than the reduction in Social Security benefits at age 65 would suggest. These graphs also make it clear that there is little appreciable difference between the retirement patterns of men and women, with the possible exception of a greater likelihood of early retirement for women with less than 30 years of service. But in general, there is no evidence of a substantial difference in the retirement patterns of men and women.

6.2.3   Window-Plan Retirement Rates

Departure rates under the 1983 window plan are shown for men in figure 6.7A and for women in figure 6.7B. These rates are contrasted with the average 1982 rates, shown on the same graph. Departure rates under the window plan were typically three to five times as large as the 1982 rates. Like 1982 departures, there was little difference in the departure rates of men and women under the window plan, as shown in figure 6.8. There is, however, some indication that women under age 55 may have been more likely than men to accept the separation bonus.

6.3   Formal Models and Prediction of Retirement

6.3.1   Models

Two models are compared during the course of the analysis: the "option value" model and a stochastic dynamic programming model. Both are described in Lumsdaine et al. (1992), and excerpts from that paper are included as an appendix to this chapter. The models are explained only briefly here.

The Option Value Model

At any given age, based on information available at that age, it is assumed that an employee compares the expected present value of retiring at that age with the value of retiring at each age in the future through age 74. The maximum of the expected present values of retiring at each future age, minus the expected present value of immediate retirement, is called the option value of postponing retirement. A person who does not retire this year maintains the option of retiring at a more advantageous age later on. If the option value is positive, the person continues to work; otherwise she retires. With reference to figure 6.1, for example, at age 51 the employee would compare the value of the retirement benefits that she would receive were she to retire then—approximately $87,000—with the value of wage earnings and retirement benefits in

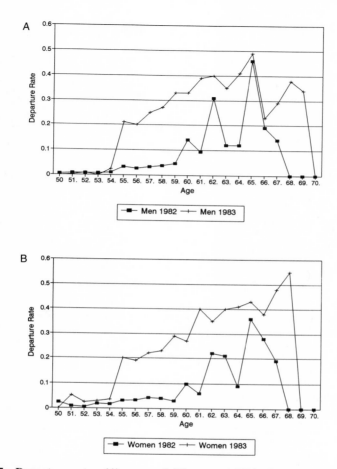

Fig. 6.7   Departure rates: (A) men and (B) women, 1982 window vs. 1983 window

each future year. The expected present value of retiring at age 60 (discounted to age 51), for example, is about $652,000. Future earnings forecasts are based on the individual's past earnings, as well as on the earnings of other persons in the firm. The precise model specification follows.

A person at age t who continues to work will earn Y_s at subsequent ages s. If the person retires at age r, subsequent retirement benefits will be $B_s(r)$. These benefits will depend on the person's age and years of service at retirement and on his earnings history; thus they are a function of the retirement age. We suppose that in deciding whether to retire the person weighs the indirect utility that will be received from future income. Discounted to age t at the rate β, the value of this future stream of income, if retirement is at age r, is given by

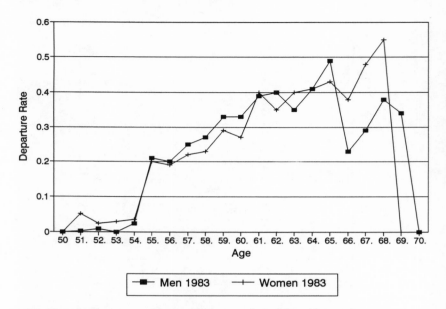

Fig. 6.8   Departure rates: men and women compared, 1983 window

$$(1) \qquad V_t(r) = \sum_{s=t}^{r-1}\beta^{s-t}U_w(Y_s) + \sum_{s=r}^{S}\beta^{s-t}U_r(B_s(r)),$$

where $U_w(Y_s)$ is the indirect utility of future wage income and $U_r(B_s(r))$ is the indirect utility of future retirement benefits. It is assumed that the employee will not live past age S. The expected gain, evaluated at age t, from postponing retirement until age r is given by

$$(2) \qquad G_t(r) = E_tV_t(r) - E_tV_t(t).$$

If r^* is the age that gives the maximum expected gain, the person will postpone retirement if the option value, $G_t(r^*)$, is positive:

$$(3) \qquad G_t(r^*) = E_tV_t(r^*) - E_tV_t(t) > 0.$$

The utilities of future wage and retirement income are parameterized as

$$(4a) \qquad U_w(Y_s) = Y_s^\gamma + \omega_s ,$$

$$(4b) \qquad U_r(B_s) = [kB_s(r)]^\gamma + \xi_s ,$$

where ω_s and ξ_s are individual-specific random effects, assumed to follow a Markovian (first-order autoregressive) process:

$$(5a) \qquad \omega_s = \rho\omega_{s-1} + \varepsilon_{\omega s}, \quad E_{s-1}(\varepsilon_{\omega s}) = 0 ,$$

$$(5b) \qquad \xi_s = \rho\xi_{s-1} + \varepsilon_{\xi s}, \quad E_{s-1}(\varepsilon_{\xi s}) = 0 .$$

The parameter k reflects that, in considering whether to retire, the employee's utility *associated* with a dollar of income while retired may be different from her utility associated with a dollar of income accompanied by work. Abstracting from the random terms, at any given age s, the ratio of the utility of retirement to the utility of employment is $[k(B_s/Y_s)]^\gamma$.

The Stochastic Dynamic Programming Model

The key simplifying assumption in the Stock-Wise option value model is that the retirement decision is based on the maximum of the expected present values of future utilities if retirement occurs now versus at each of the potential future ages. The stochastic dynamic programming rule considers instead the expected value of the maximum of current versus future options. The expected value of the maximum of a series of random variables will be greater than the maximum of the expected values. Thus, to the extent that this difference is large, the Stock-Wise option value rule underestimates the value of postponing retirement. And, to the extent that the dynamic programming rule is more consistent with individual decisions than the option value rule, the Stock-Wise rule may undervalue individual assessment of future retirement options. Thus we consider a model that rests on the dynamic programming rule.

It is important to understand that there is no single dynamic programming model. Because the dynamic programming decision rule evaluates the maximum of future disturbance terms, its implementation depends importantly on the error structure that is assumed. Like other users of this type of model, we assume an error structure—and thus a behavioral rule—that simplifies the dynamic programming calculation.[2] In particular, although the option value model allows correlated disturbances, the random disturbances in the dynamic programming model are assumed to be uncorrelated. Thus the two models are not exactly comparable. Whether one rule is a better approximation to reality than the other may depend not only on the basic idea, but on its precise implementation. In the version of the dynamic programming model that we implement here, the disturbances are assumed to follow an extreme value distribution.

In most respects, our dynamic programming model is analogous to the option value model. As in that model, at age t an individual is assumed to derive utility $U_w(Y_t) + \varepsilon_{1t}$ from earned income or $U_r(B_t(s)) + \varepsilon_{2t}$ from retirement benefits, where s is the retirement age. The disturbances ε_{1t} and ε_{2t} are random perturbations to these age-specific utilities. Unlike the additive disturbances in the option value model, these additive disturbances in the dynamic programming model are assumed to be independent. Future income and retirement benefits are assumed to be nonrandom; there are no errors in forecasting future wage earnings or retirement benefits.

---

2. See the Appendix for a more complete description of the error structure.

6.3.2   Results

Parameter estimates are shown in table 6.1. The effect of the special plan provisions for the pre-1951 hires is considered first (cols. [1] and [2]). Estimates for men versus women and stochastic dynamic programming (SDP) versus option value (OV) estimates are then considered (cols. [3]–[8]). Estimates with the "value" of Medicare and firm retiree health insurance benefits counted as equivalent to Social Security benefits, and with firm current employee health insurance benefits counted as equivalent to wage earnings, are also presented (col. [9]). Finally, results imposing firm I parameter estimates (taken from Lumsdaine et al. 1992) on the firm III data are reported (col. [10]).

Pre-1951 Pension Plan Provisions

The estimates in column (1) are based on the assumption that the pre-1951 hires face the same pension plan provisions as later hires. These estimates, as well as those in column (2), are based on a sample of 400 employees. Taken literally, the estimated value of γ (1.045) suggests that with respect to retirement income employees are essentially risk neutral. The estimated value of k is 1.605, implying that a dollar of retirement benefit income—unaccompanied by work—is valued at 60 percent more than a dollar of income accompanied by work. These estimates are very similar to those obtained in our previous work. The estimated value of β, however, is extremely small. If taken literally, it would suggest that in making retirement decisions, future income is given very little weight, compared to income in the current year. Indeed, a value of zero would imply that the decision to retire is based only on the comparison of wage income versus retirement benefits—the replacement ratio—without concern for future possibilities. When the immediate ratio is large enough, the person retires. (Based on our experience elsewhere, we are not inclined to believe this estimate.)

The model fits the data rather well, however, as shown in figures 6.9A and 6.9B. The principal discrepancy between actual and predicted rates occurs at age 55, where the jump in the predicted rates is noticeably less than the jump in the sample rates. The sample data show a 10 percent departure rate at age 55, which is twice as large as the rates shown in the graphs above, based on larger sample sizes. The predicted and actual cumulative departure rates are very close. Based on the likelihood values, the model fits the data better than a model with dummy variables for each age—that is, better than predictions based on average retirement rates by age. The model does not allow directly for an effect of age on retirement.

The primary test of the predictive validity of the model is how well it predicts retirement rates under the 1983 window plan. The model predictions capture the general pattern of retirement under the window, but substantially overpredict retirement rates between ages 55 and 60, as shown in figure 6.9C. The model also predicts some retirements among employees aged 52–54, whereas the actual data show essentially no retirements in this age group.

Table 6.1   **Parameter Estimates by Method and Sample**

| | Pre-1951 Provisions | | Option Value versus SDP Model and Men versus Women | | | | | | | |
| | | | OV Model | | | SDP Model | | | | |
Parameter	SDP Model Pre-51 Ignore (1)	SDP Model Pre-51 Correct (2)	Men (3)	Women (4)	Men and Women (5)	Men (6)	Women (7)	Men and Women (8)	Medicare SDP Model Men and Women (9)	Firm I Comparison SDP Model Men (10)
γ	1.045	0.793	0.599	0.842	0.656	0.898	0.866	0.839	0.789	1.018[a]
	(0.245)	(0.273)	(0.155)	(0.134)	(0.080)	(0.134)	(0.245)	(0.098)	(0.127)	
k	1.605	1.606	2.516	1.628	2.408	1.858	1.446	1.877	1.892	1.881[a]
	(0.147)	(0.052)	(0.722)	(0.360)	(0.272)	(0.250)	(0.362)	(0.035)	(0.073)	
β	0.185	0.185[a]	0.973	0.847	0.963	0.549	0.301	0.564	0.630	0.620[a]
	(0.337)		(0.053)	(0.123)	(0.020)	(0.135)	(0.398)	(0.032)	(0.032)	
σ	0.224	0.152	0.114	0.092	0.120	0.252	0.224	0.229	0.203	0.303
	(0.054)	(0.057)	(0.031)	(0.027)	(0.027)	(0.031)	(0.045)	(0.024)	(0.034)	(0.024)
Log likelihood										
At maximum	122.839	121.768	380.59	100.52	485.64	385.86	101.84	489.69	489.34	387.00
Age	127.051	127.051	362.55	91.26	461.30	362.55	91.26	461.30	461.30	362.55
χ^2										
Fitted data	13.059	12.433	28.24	14.39	30.92	64.30	17.12	59.17	61.78	78.89
Window	78.997	37.782	74.04	44.50	86.52	49.59	15.60	68.69	86.79	89.87
Figure	9A–9C	10A–10C	11A–11C	–	–	12A–12C	–	–	13A–13C	–

Note: Numbers in parentheses are standard errors.

[a]Parameters were fixed at these values.

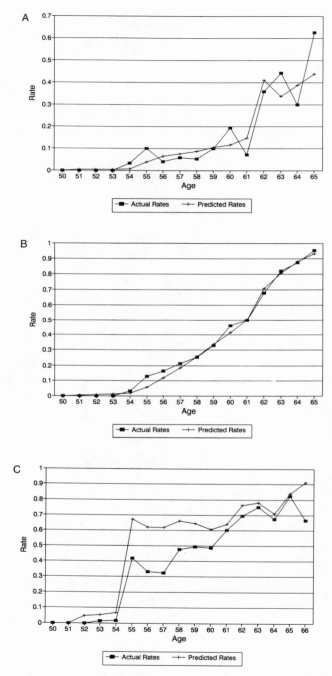

Fig. 6.9 Predicted vs. actual (*A*) annual departure rates, (*B*) cumulative departure rates, and (*C*) window departure rates: men, ignoring pre-1951 provisions

The estimates in column (2) of table 6.1 are obtained if the special pension plan provisions that pertain to employees hired before 1951 are used to determine their options. (Because there are so few retirements among employees younger than 55, we have questioned whether these provisions translate into visible alternatives that are actively considered by older employees, or whether in practice these older employees consider their options to be the same as employees of the same age who are covered by the current plan provisions. Thus we have obtained the two sets of estimates.) The estimated parameter values are very similar to those reported in column (1), although to hasten convergence the discount factor is set in this case. Predicted versus actual rates are shown in figures 6.10A–6.10C. In general, the fit to actual values is close. The major exception is at age 55, and in this case the actual sample rate is abnormally high; the predicted rate is more in line with typical retirement rates at this age. The difference in the age-55 retirement rate is reflected in the difference between the actual and predicted cumulative rates through age 60. The model predictions of the effects of the 1983 window are very accurate, with the exception of predictions for employees aged 53–54 and 56–57. The actual sample rates for the 56–57 ages are abnormally low; the typical rates are more like the model predictions. Thus for these ages at least, the model predictions give a more accurate indication of actual behavior than the actual sample values.

Stochastic Dynamic Programming versus "Option Value" Estimates

The two sets of parameter values are shown for men (cols. [3] and [6]), for women (cols. [4] and [7]), and for men and women combined (cols. [5] and [8]). In general, the estimated parameters are similar. The most noticeable difference is that the SDP estimated values of β are lower than the OV estimates. For men and women combined, for example, the SDP estimate is 0.564 and the OV estimate is 0.963. The estimated value of k based on the OV model is somewhat larger than the SDP estimate (2.408 vs. 1.877), and the estimated value of γ is somewhat smaller (0.656 vs. 0.839).

The OV model fits the sample data considerably better than the SDP model, based on the likelihood and χ^2 values pertaining to the fitted data. This is revealed graphically for men in figures 6.11A and 6.11B versus figures 6.12A and 6.12B. On the other hand, the SDP model predictions of retirement under the 1983 window fit actual retirement rates better than do those of the OV model. This can be seen by comparing figures 6.11C and 6.12C and in the χ^2 values pertaining to the window. Thus, in general, there is no reason to prefer one model over the other.

Separate Estimates for Men and Women

The estimates for men and women are not statistically different, judged by likelihood ratio tests. The OV model χ^2 statistic is 9.06 (and with four degrees of freedom, the .05 significance level is 9.49), and the SDP model χ^2 statistic

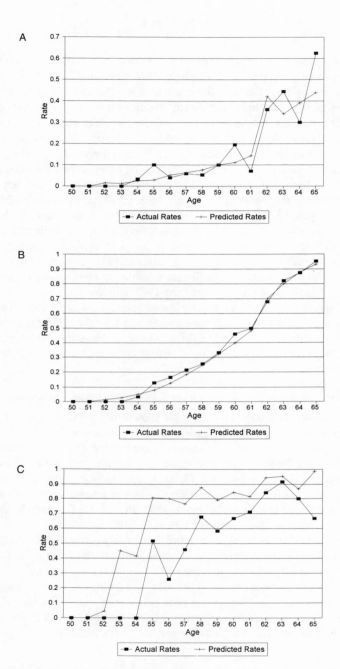

Fig. 6.10   Predicted vs. actual (*A*) annual departure rates, (*B*) cumulative departure rates, and (*C*) window departure rates: men, including pre-1951 provisions

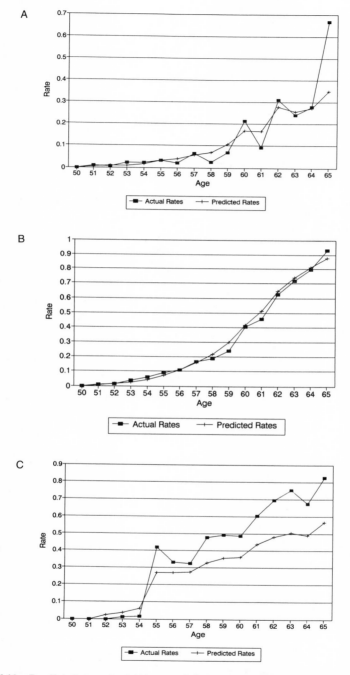

Fig. 6.11   Predicted vs. actual (*A*) annual departure rates, (*B*) cumulative
departure rates, and (*C*) window departure rates: men, OV

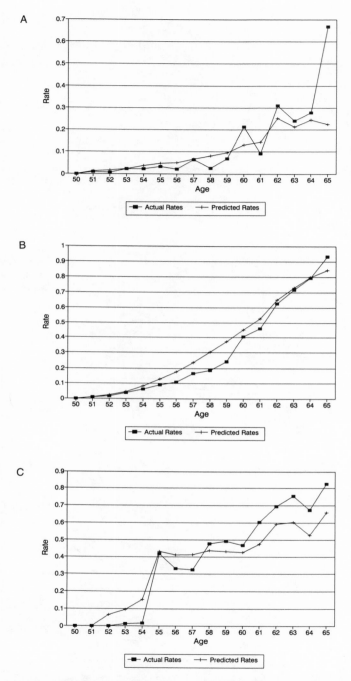

Fig. 6.12 Predicted vs. actual (*A*) annual departure rates, (*B*) cumulative departure rates, and (*C*) window departure rates: men, SDP

is only 3.98, neither of which is statistically significant. The *t*-statistics for the individual parameters also suggest that the estimates for men and women are not statistically different. Thus the formal estimates appear to be consistent with the graphical evidence in figures 6.4, 6.5, 6.6, and 6.8 showing that departure rates for men and women are virtually indistinguishable after age 40.

Valuing Medicare

The OV and the SDP models underpredict retirement at age 65 for both men and women. A possible reason for the underprediction is that Medicare insurance becomes available at age 65 and provides an inducement to retire similar to the Social Security inducement. But employees at this firm have health insurance while working, and after retirement the same coverage is provided, at no cost to the retiree. For example, a person who retired at age 60 would be covered by retiree health insurance until age 65. After age 65, medical costs up to the Medicare limit would be paid by Medicare, and any additional costs—that are covered by the firm plan—would be paid by the firm retiree insurance. A simple assumption, albeit one that is unlikely to be precisely true, is that medical insurance is valued at its cost, which is treated by employees as comparable to wage or pension benefit compensation. Following this rule, there are three parts to medical coverage: First, while employed at the firm, health benefits are valued at the cost of insurance to the firm.[3] Second, if the person retires before age 65, firm pension benefits are increased by the cost of insurance with coverage comparable to the retiree health insurance.[4] After age 65, Social Security benefits are increased according to the average payment to persons covered by Medicare.[5] Estimates incorporating these assumptions and based on the SDP model for men and women are reported in column (9) of table 6.1.

The parameter estimates are affected very little, relative to comparable estimates without these adjustments, shown in column (8). The likelihood value and the fitted-data χ^2 statistic are almost the same as in the comparable column (8) estimates, that do not account for the value of medical insurance. In particular, the addition of these measures of the value of medical insurance does nothing to explain the departure rate at age 65, as can be seen in figure 6.13A. The

3. This cost was estimated by the average cost at large firms for group insurance with coverage like the plan offered by our firm—$105 and $247 for individual and family coverage, respectively, in 1989 dollars. These costs were deflated to 1982 dollars based on a constructed index of Blue-Cross–Blue-Shield premiums per insured person, obtained from the U.S. Health Insurance Institute (1991). We are grateful to Jonathan Gruber for assistance in developing these numbers.
4. The value of this insurance was estimated by increasing the basic group insurance premium according to age, by 5.4 percent per year for each year after age 50. This rate is based on the annual premium costs by age reported by the Congressional Research Service (1988).
5. The costs were estimated based on the average 1986 Medicare payments by age to married and single persons, reported in Shoven, Topper, and Wise (chap. 1 in this volume). The 1986 values were deflated to 1982 dollars based on the Blue-Cross–Blue-Shield index described in n. 3, above. Linear interpolation was used to convert the payments by age interval, reported by Shoven, Topper, and Wise, to payments for each age.

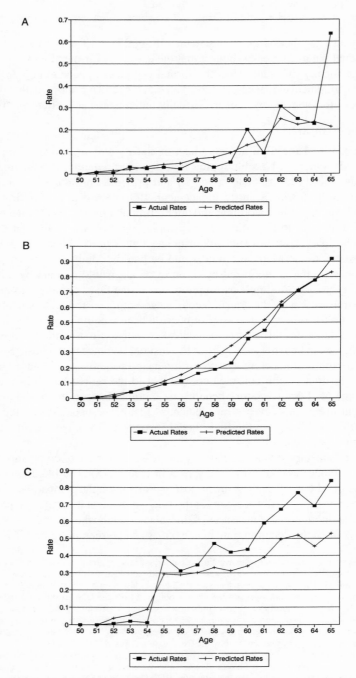

Fig. 6.13 Predicted vs. actual (*A*) annual departure rates, (*B*) cumulative departure rates, and (*C*) window departure rates: men and women, SDP, Medicare

actual rate is .636, but the predicted rate is only .215, somewhat *lower* than the predicted rate without accounting for medical insurance (.277, based on col. [8] estimates). In addition, the model yields worse predictions of retirement under the window plan, judging by the window χ^2 statistic. Thus these results lend no support to the conjecture that retirement at age 65 is strongly affected by the availability of Medicare at that age. However, these exploratory results should not be interpreted to mean that Medicare does not matter. It may well be that the rough specification that we experimented with does not capture the effect of Medicare but that a more careful treatment of the value of medical coverage would show an effect. For example, the assumption that medical insurance is valued at its cost may be incorrect.

Estimates from Firms I and III Compared

The parameter estimates based on firm III data are surprisingly close to those based on firm I data. Results, for firm III, with parameter estimates set to those that we obtained for firm I (Lumsdaine et al. 1992) are shown in column (10) of table 6.1.[6] By comparing the estimates in columns (6) and (10), it can be seen that the firm I estimates for men are very close to the estimates for firm III, based on the SDP specification. The hypothesis that the parameters are the same cannot be rejected, based on a likelihood ratio test. From the χ^2 statistics, however, it is clear that the firm I parameter estimates do not fit the data or predict departure rates under the window plan quite as well as the firm III estimates. Option value model estimates for the two firms (not shown) are also similar but not as close as the SDP estimates, and the hypothesis that the estimates are the same is rejected at the 5 percent level. Again, based on χ^2 statistics, the firm I estimates do not fit the data or predict window departure rates as well as the firm III parameter estimates. On balance, however, the results provide strong confirmation that employees in these two firms react similarly to the incentives inherent in pension plan provisions.

6.4   Summary and Conclusions

The data for firm III confirm a principal conclusion based on firm I data. It is clear that the changes in retirement rates by age correspond closely to provisions of the pension plan. And, as for the results based on firm I, we find that the OV and the SDP models yield similar results. There is no apparent reason to choose one over the other, except based on numerical simplicity. In this case, the OV model fits the sample data better than the SDP model, but the SDP model predicts the window plan retirement rates better than the OV model. We also find that there is essentially no difference between the retirement behavior of men and women. There is some indication that women may be slightly more

---

6. The scale parameter σ was estimated; this normalization enables comparison of the results from the two firms.

likely than men to take early retirement between ages 55 and 60. But at most ages, the annual retirement rates of men and women are very close. In addition, we explored the possibility that retirement at age 65 is induced by Medicare benefits that become available at that age. Our method of incorporating medical insurance, however, did little to explain the large retirement rates at age 65. Thus we are still left with an "age-65 retirement effect" that is not explained by monetary gain.

Appendix

The "option value" and stochastic dynamic programming models used in the analysis are described.

The Option Value Model

Given the specification as described via equations (1)–(5) in the text, the function $G_t(r)$ can be decomposed into two components,

$$(A1) \qquad G_t(r) = g_t(r) + \phi_t(r) ,$$

where $g_t(r)$ and $\phi_t(r)$ distinguish the terms in $G_t(r)$ containing the random effects, ω and ξ, from the other terms. If whether the person is alive in future years is statistically independent of his earnings stream and of the individual effects ω_s and ξ_s, $g_t(r)$ and $\phi_t(r)$ are given by

$$(A2a) \qquad g_t(r) = \sum_{s=t}^{r-1}\beta^{s-t}\pi(s|t)E_t(Y_s^\gamma) + \sum_{s=r}^{S}\beta^{s-t}\pi(s|t)[E_t(kB_s(r))^\gamma] - \sum_{s=t}^{S}\beta^{s-t}\pi(s|t)[E_t(kB_s(t))^\gamma],$$

$$(A2b) \qquad \phi_t(r) = \sum_{s=t}^{r-1}\beta^{s-t}\pi(s|t)E_t(\omega_s - \xi_s),$$

where $\pi(s|t)$ denotes the probability that the person will be alive in year s, given that he is alive in year t. Given the random Markov assumption, $\phi_t(r)$ can be written as

$$(A3) \qquad \phi_t(r) = \sum_{s=t}^{r-1}\beta^{s-t}\pi(s|t)\rho^{s-t}(\omega_t - \xi_t) = K_t(r)\upsilon_t ,$$

where $K_t(r) = \sum_{s=t}^{r-1}(\beta\rho)^{s-t}\pi(s|t)$ and $\upsilon_t = \omega_t - \xi_t$. The simplification results from the fact that at time t the expected value of $\upsilon_s = \omega_s - \xi_s$ is $\rho^{s-t}\upsilon_t$, for all future years s. (The term $K_t(r)$ cumulates the deflators that yield the present value in year t of the future expected values of the random components of utility. The further r is in the future, the larger is $K_t(r)$. That is, the more distant the potential retirement age, the greater the uncertainty about it, yielding a heteroskedastic disturbance term.) Thus, $G_t(r)$ may be written simply as

(A4) $G_t(r) = g_t(r) + K_t(r)v_t$.

If the employee is to retire in year t, $G_t(r)$ must be less than zero for every potential retirement age r in the future. If r_t^+ is the r that yields the maximum value of $g_t(r)/K_t(r)$, the probability of retirement becomes

(A5) $Pr[\text{Retire in year } t] = Pr[g_t(r_t^+)/K_t(r_t^+) < -v_t]$.

If retirement in only one year is considered, this expression is all that is needed.

More generally, retirement decisions may be considered over two or more consecutive years. In this case, the retirement probabilities are simply an extension of equation (10). The probability that a person who is employed at age t will retire at age $\tau > t$ is given by

(A6) $Pr[R = \tau] = Pr[g_t(r_t^+)/K_t(r_t^+) > -v_t, \ldots,$
$g_{\tau-1}(r_{\tau-1}^+)/K_{\tau-1}(r_{\tau-1}^+) > -v_{\tau-1}, g_\tau(r_\tau^+)/K_\tau(r_\tau^+) < -v_\tau]$.

The probability that the person does not retire during the period of the data is given by

(A7) $Pr[R > T] = Pr[g_t(r_t^+)/K_t(r_t^+) > -v_t, \ldots,$
$g_{T-1}(r_{T-1}^+)/K_{T-1}(r_{T-1}^+) > -v_{T-1}, g_T(r_T^+)/K_T(r_T^+) > -v_T]$.

This is a multinomial discrete choice probability with dependent error terms v_s.

Finally, we assume that v_s follows a Gaussian Markov process, with

(A8) $v_s = \rho v_{s-1} + \varepsilon_s$,   with ε_s i.i.d. $N(0, \sigma_\varepsilon^2)$,

where the initial value, v_t, is i.i.d. $N(0,\sigma^2)$ and is independent of ε_s. The covariance between v_τ and $v_{\tau+1}$ is $\rho \text{Var}(v_\tau)$, and the variance of v_τ, for $\tau > t$, is $(\rho^{2(\tau-t)})\sigma^2 + (\sum_{j=0}^{\tau-t-1} \rho^{2j})\sigma_\varepsilon^2$.

The estimates in this paper are based on retirement decisions in only one year, and the random terms in equation (5) are assumed to follow a random walk, with $\rho = 1$. In this case, the covariance between v_τ and $v_{\tau+1}$ is $\text{Var}(v_\tau)$, and the variance of v_τ, for $\tau \geq t$, is $\sigma^2 + (\tau - t)\sigma_\varepsilon^2$. Prior estimates show that one- and multiple-year estimates are very similar. (Estimates based on several consecutive years and with ρ estimated are shown in Stock and Wise 1990b. These generalizations have little effect on the estimates.)

The Stochastic Dynamic Programming Model

The dynamic programming model is based on the recursive representation of the value function. At the beginning of year t, the individual has two choices: retire now and derive utility from future retirement benefits, or work for the year and derive utility from income while working during the year and retaining the option to choose the best of retirement or work in the next year. Thus the value function W_t at time t is defined as

$$W_t = \max\{E_t[U_w(Y_t) + \varepsilon_{1t} + \beta W_{t+1}], E_t[\sum_{\tau=t}^{S}\beta^{\tau-t}(U_r(B_\tau(t)) + \varepsilon_{2\tau})]\},$$

(A9)   with $W_{t+1} = \max\{E_{t+1}[U_w(Y_{t+1}) + \varepsilon_{1t+1} + \beta W_{t+2}],$

$$E_{t+1}[\sum_{\tau=t+1}^{S}\beta^{\tau-t-1}(U_r(B_\tau(t+1)) + \varepsilon_{2\tau})]\},$$

etc., where β is the discount factor and, as in the option value model, S is the year beyond which the person will not live.

Because the errors ε_{it} are assumed to be i.i.d., $E_t\varepsilon_{it+\tau} = 0$, for $\tau > 0$. In addition, in computing expected values, each future utility must be discounted by the probability of realizing it, i.e., by the probability of surviving to year τ given that the worker is alive in year t, $\pi(\tau|t)$. With these considerations, the expression (A9) can be written as

$$W_t = \max\{\bar{W}_{1t} + \varepsilon_{1t}, \bar{W}_{2t} + \varepsilon_{2t}\}, \quad \text{where}$$

(A10) $$\bar{W}_{1t} = U_w(Y_t) + \beta\pi(t+1\mid t)E_t W_{t+1} \quad \text{and}$$

$$\bar{W}_{2t} = \sum_{\tau=t}^{S}\beta^{\tau-t}\pi(\tau\mid t)U_r(B_\tau(t)).$$

The worker chooses to retire in year t if $\bar{W}_{1t} + \varepsilon_{1t} < \bar{W}_{2t} + \varepsilon_{2t}$; otherwise he continues working. The probability that the individual retires is $Pr[\bar{W}_{1t} + \varepsilon_{1t} < \bar{W}_{2t} + \varepsilon_{2t}]$. If a person works until the mandatory retirement age (74), he retires and receives expected utility $\bar{W}_{2t_{74}}$.

Recursions and Computation

With a suitable assumption on the distribution of the errors ε_{it}, the expression (A10) provides the basis for a computable recursion for the nonstochastic terms $\bar{W}_{it}$ in the value function. The extreme value and normal distribution versions of the model are considered in turn.

Extreme value errors. Following Berkovec and Stern (1988), the ε_{it} are assumed to be i.i.d. draws from an extreme value distribution with scale parameter σ. Then, for the years preceding mandatory retirement, these assumptions together with equation (16) imply that

$$E_t W_{t+1}/\sigma \equiv \mu_{t+1}$$

(A11) $$= \gamma_e + \ln[\exp(\bar{W}_{1t+1}/\sigma) + \exp(\bar{W}_{2t+1}/\sigma)]$$

$$= \gamma_e + \ln[\exp(U_w(Y_{t+1})/\sigma)\exp(\beta\pi(t+2\mid t+1)\mu_{t+2}) + \exp(\bar{W}_{2t+1}/\sigma)],$$

where γ_e is Euler's constant. Thus equation (A11) can be solved by backward recursion, with the terminal value coming from the terminal condition that $\mu_{t_{74}} = \bar{W}_{2t_{74}}$.

The extreme value distributional assumption provides a closed form expression for the probability of retirement in year t:

(A12) $Pr[\text{Retire in year } t] = Pr[\bar{W}_{1t} + \varepsilon_{1t} < \bar{W}_{2t} + \varepsilon_{2t}]$

$$= \exp(\bar{W}_{2t}/\sigma)/[\exp(\bar{W}_{1t}/\sigma) + \exp(\bar{W}_{2t}/\sigma)].$$

Gaussian errors. Following Daula and Moffitt (1989), the ε_{it} are assumed to be independent draws from an $N(0,\sigma^2)$ distribution. The Gaussian assumption provides a simple expression for the probability of retiring:

(A13)
$$Pr[\text{Retire in year } t]$$
$$= Pr[(\varepsilon_{1t} - \varepsilon_{2t})/\sqrt{2}\sigma < (\bar{W}_{2t} - \bar{W}_{1t})/\sqrt{2}\sigma] = \Phi(a_t),$$

where $a_t = (\bar{W}_{2t} - \bar{W}_{1t})/\sqrt{2}\sigma$. Then the recursion (A10) becomes

(A14)
$$E_t W_{t+1}/\sigma \equiv \mu_{t+1}$$
$$= (\bar{W}_{1t+1}/\sigma)[1 - \Phi(a_{t+1})] + (\bar{W}_{2t+1}/\sigma)\Phi(a_{t+1}) + \sqrt{2}\phi(a_{t+1})$$

where $\phi(\cdot)$ denotes the standard normal density and $\Phi(\cdot)$ denotes the cumulative normal distribution function. As in equation (A13), $\Phi(a_t)$ is the probability that the person retires in year t and receives utility $\bar{W}_{2t}$, plus utility from $E(\varepsilon_{2t} \mid \varepsilon_{1t} - \varepsilon_{2t} < \bar{W}_{2t} - \bar{W}_{1t})$. The latter term, plus a comparable term when the person continues to work, yields the last term in equation (A14).

Individual-specific Effects

Individual-specific terms are modeled as random effects but are assumed to be fixed over time for a given individual. They enter the two versions of the dynamic programming models in different ways. Each is discussed in turn.

Extreme value errors. Single-year utilities are

(A15a)
$$U_w(Y_t) = Y_t^\gamma,$$

(A15b)
$$U_r(B_t(s)) = [\eta k B_t(s)]^\gamma,$$

where ηk is constant over time for the same person, but random across individuals. Specifically, it is assumed that η is a lognormal random variable with mean one and scale parameter λ: $\eta = \exp(\lambda z + 1/2\,\lambda^2)$, where z is i.i.d. $N(0,1)$. A larger λ implies greater variability among employee tastes for retirement versus work; when $\lambda = 0$ there is no variation and all employees have the same taste.

Normal errors. In this case, the unobserved individual components are assumed to enter additively, with

(A16a)
$$U_w(Y_t) = Y_t^\gamma + \zeta,$$

(A16b)
$$U_r(B_t(s)) = [k B_t(s)]^\gamma,$$

where γ and k are nonrandom parameters, as above, but ζ is a random additive taste for work, assumed to distributed $N(0,\lambda^2)$. When $\lambda = 0$, there is no taste variation.

In summary, the dynamic programming models are given by the general recursion equation (A9). It is implemented as shown in equation (A11) under the assumption that the ε_{it} are i.i.d. extreme value, and as shown in equation (A14) under the assumption that ε_{it} are i.i.d. normal. The retirement probabilities are computed according to equations (A12) and (A13) respectively. The fixed effects specifications are given by equations (A15) and (A16). The unknown parameters to be estimated are γ, k, β, σ, and λ. Because of the different distributional assumptions, *the scale parameter σ is not comparable across option value or dynamic programming models, and λ is not comparable across the two dynamic programming models.*

References

Ausink, John A. 1991. The effect of changes in compensation on a pilot's decision to leave the air force. Ph.D. dissertation, Harvard University.
Berkovec, James, and Steven Stern. 1991. Job exit behavior of older men. *Econometrica* 59(1): 189–210.
Bulow, J. 1981. Early retirement pension benefits. NBER Working Paper no. 654. Cambridge, Mass.: National Bureau of Economic Research.
Congressional Research Service. 1988. Costs and effects of extending health insurance coverage. Washington, D.C.: Library of Congress.
Daula, Thomas V., and Robert A. Moffitt. 1991. Estimating a dynamic programming model of army reenlistment behavior. In *Military compensation and personnel retention: Models and evidence,* ed. C. L. Gilray, D. K. Horne, and D. Alton Smith. Alexandria, Va.: U.S. Army Research Institute for the Behavioral and Social Sciences.
Kotlikoff, Laurence J., and David A. Wise. 1985. Labor compensation and the structure of private pension plans: Evidence for contractual versus spot labor markets. In *Pensions, labor, and individual choice,* ed. D. Wise, 55–85. Chicago: University of Chicago Press.
———. 1987. The incentive effects of private pension plans. In *Issues in pension economics,* ed. Z. Bodie, J. Shoven, and D. Wise, 283–339. Chicago: University of Chicago Press.
———. 1988. Pension backloading, wage taxes, and work disincentives. In *Tax policy and the economy,* vol. 2, ed. L. Summers, 161–96. Cambridge: MIT Press.
Lazear, Edward P. 1983. Pensions as severance pay. In *Financial aspects of the United States pension system,* ed. Z. Bodie and J. Shoven, 57–85. Chicago: University of Chicago Press.
Lumsdaine, Robin L., James H. Stock, and David A. Wise. 1990. Efficient windows and labor force reduction. *Journal of Public Economics* 43:131–59.
———. 1991. Windows and retirement. *Annales d'Economie et de Statistique* 20/21:219–42.
———. 1992. Three models of retirement: Computational complexity versus predictive validity. In *Topics in the economics of aging,* ed. D. Wise, 19–57. Chicago: University of Chicago Press.
Stock, James H., and David A. Wise. 1990a. Pensions, the option value of work, and retirement. *Econometrica* 58, no. 5 (September): 1151–80.
———. 1990b. The pension inducement to retire: An option value analysis. In *Issues in the economics of aging,* ed. D. Wise, 205–24. Chicago: University of Chicago Press.
U.S. Health Insurance Institute. 1991. *Sourcebook of health insurance data, 1990.* New York: U.S. Health Insurance Institute.

Comment   John Rust

This paper continues and extends earlier research by the authors (Lumsdaine, Stock, and Wise 1991) that compares two different dynamic structural models—the Stock-Wise (1990) "option-value" (OV) model and a dynamic programming (DP) model—on the basis of their ability to make accurate out-of-sample predictions of the effect of "window plans," which provide special pension incentives to retire from a firm. I like this research very much, especially for its clever use of the window plans as "natural experiments" to evaluate predictive validity of structural econometric models. In my survey of the literature (Rust, in press), I cite the authors' results as one of the clearest demonstrations of the potential payoffs to dynamic structural modeling: both the OV and DP models do a much better job of predicting the large increase in firm departure rates than any of the traditional "reduced-form" econometric specifications. These are the kind of results that Marschak (1953) and Lucas (1976) must have had in mind when they wrote their critiques of the traditional reduced-form econometric approaches to policy evaluation. However, for reasons I discuss below, the structural forecasts from these models are still a long way from being definitive. I think the most important contribution of this paper is that it provides an excellent example of the kinds of discriminating out-of-sample predictive tests we ought to be subjecting our econometric models to. Unfortunately, too many structural estimation exercises are little more than displays of technique that do not seriously attempt to evaluate model performance. I believe that this research will set a new standard for demonstrating the credibility of structural econometric models.

Although there are some differences in the predictions of the two models (with the OV model fitting better in-sample and the DP model fitting better out-of-sample), as well as significant differences in the parameter estimates (with the OV model yielding a significantly higher estimate of the postretirement "leisure value" of income K, and the DP model yielding a significantly lower estimate of the discount factor β), I am more struck by the overall similarity of the predictions of the two models rather than their differences. The similarity is striking in view of the large conceptual differences in the two approaches and is suggestive of an identification problem I have discussed elsewhere (Rust, in press). Even within the class of DP models, there are different parameter combinations that generate similar retirement behavior: for example, the predictions of DP models with a low value of β, a high value of K, and a high value of γ (the coefficient of relative risk aversion, with $\gamma = 1$ corresponding to risk neutrality) look very similar to models with a high value for β and lower values for K and γ. We can also see this effect in comparing the estimated parameters of the OV and DP models in columns (3) and (6) of

John Rust is professor of economics at the University of Wisconsin and a research associate of the National Bureau of Economic Research.

table 6.1. The fact that very different parameter estimates yield similar behavioral predictions is a bit disturbing. The problem is even more pronounced in the authors' earlier paper, in which a DP model with normally distributed unobservables has $\hat{\beta} = .916$ and $\hat{K} = 2.975$, whereas a comparably fitting extreme value specification has $\hat{\beta} = .62$ and $\hat{K} = 1.88$. Despite the fact that the normal specification seems to put much more weight on the future than the extreme value specification, the fit and predictions of the two models is very similar. Undoubtedly, the reason for this similarity can be traced to important differences in the variance of the error terms and the specification of unobserved heterogeneity. However, for prediction purposes, this raises some difficult issues: which is the "right" behavioral model, OV or DP? Even if we limit ourselves, a priori, to the narrower class of DP models, it is not difficult to show that there are equivalence classes of distinct error distributions and parameter values that yield similar behavioral predictions. We might be tempted to believe that as long as the predictions of these different models are similar, the question of deciding which is the "right" model is moot. For reasons I discuss below, I think it is likely that there are many hypothetical pension policies for which the predictions of these models will be significantly different, such as pension plans where there is nonnegligible uncertainty regarding future payoffs (as in defined contribution plans). I would like to see more work in delineating the conditions under which the predictions of their various models diverge—this might suggest new experiments that might help us discriminate between the various models.

Another problem is that the structural coefficient estimates vary substantially from data set to data set. For example the OV model estimated in the previous paper had $\hat{\beta} = .895$, which is significantly lower than the .962 value reported here, and the estimated value of K is 2.42 in this data set, versus 1.47 in the earlier paper. How are we to interpret this parameter variability? If people really are this heterogeneous, will we have to gather separate data to forecast the retirement behavior at each different firm? One way to get a handle on this issue is to see how well out-of-sample forecasts using the parameters from their previous data set perform on the current data, and vice versa.

The remainder of my comments focus on identifying the situations where the predictions of the OV and DP models will be similar and the situations where their predictions will diverge. As the authors have noted in their paper, the OV and DP models differ primarily in the interchange of the orders in which the maximization and expectation operators are taken. In the OV model, at each time t the worker calculates the maximum of the expected discounted utility of retiring at different future dates, whereas in the DP model the worker compares the value of retiring now with the value of continuing to work at least one more period, where the value function (or "shadow price") is calculated as the expectation of the maximum of the discounted utility retiring next period versus continuing to work in period $t + 1$. In the OV model, a worker retires in the first period t in which the expected utility of immediate retirement exceeds the expected utility of retiring at any future date $t + r$, whereas in the DP model, the worker retires in the first period t where the value of retiring at time t exceeds the value of continuing to work until date $t + 1$. In a certain sense, the OV model seems to take a longer view of the future, since it calculates the value of retiring at all future dates $t + r$, whereas the DP model appears to look only one period ahead at the value function V_{t+1}. However, since V_{t+1} is calculated by backward induction, it provides the correct valuation of discounted expected utility, recursively generating the optimal retirement policy. The OV calculations are not based on a correct evaluation of expected discounted utility and, hence, will generally not yield an optimal decision rule. Indeed, the very terminology "option value model" is actually a misnomer since the Stock-Wise model ignores the option value of staying on the job to take advantage of a possible increase in future salary, an option that is lost if one retires (since retirement is treated as an absorbing state in this model). By evaluating future utility as the expected value of the maximum of the options of staying with the firm at least one more period versus retiring now, the DP model assigns the correct value to this option. Given that an OV decisionmaker is in a sense myopic, or "time inconsistent," why is it that the predictions of the DP and OV models are so similar?

The answer is that the predictions of the two models will coincide provided that the level of future uncertainty is sufficiently small: in that case the maximum of the expected values is close to the expected value of maximum. In particular, if there is little uncertainty about future wages, then the option value of possible future wage increases is negligible, so the predictions of the OV model, which ignores this option, will be very similar to the DP model, which explicitly accounts for it. However in models where there are significant future uncertainties, we can expect that the predictions of the models will be very different. Steven Stern (1994) was one of the first to make this point, and his paper provides numerical examples showing conditions under which the OV and DP decision rules diverge. His Monte Carlo experiments show that if agents are really behaving according to a DP model and one tries to approximate this behavior using an OV model, the parameter estimates and predictions of the OV model can be significantly biased "because . . . the option value of working is significant relative to the option value of retiring" (p. 6). On the other hand, Stern found that biases resulting from incorrect specification of the particular distribution of the error term were insignificant, provided one stays within the basic DP framework.

It is easiest to illustrate the conditions under which the DP and OV solutions differ in a simple two-period model, but the logic extends to any number of periods. Consider the model with no uncertainty, first. Suppose the worker is risk neutral and earns wage $W_1 = W_2$ if working in periods 1 and 2, and retirement benefit rW_1 if retired, where r is the replacement rate (if the worker retires at the beginning of period 2, he also receives retirement benefits rW_1). Thus, at time t the utility of working is W_1 and the utility of retiring is KrW_1, where

K is the parameter reflecting the additional value of leisure in retirement. For concreteness assume that $r = 3/4$ and $K = 8/5$, so the utility of retiring equals $(6/5)W_1$. Now consider the worker's decision problem at time 1 under the OV model: the worker compares the utility of retiring immediately, $(6/5)W_1 + (6/5)W_1 = (12/5)W_1$, with the utility of retiring at time 2, $W_1 + (6/5)W_1 = (11/5)W_1$, or of not retiring at all, $W_1 + W_2 = (10/5)W_1$. The optimal decision is clearly to retire at time 1. Now consider solving the problem by DP. We start in the last period and note that if the worker is already retired his value function is $V_2 = (6/5)W_2 = (6/5)W_1$, whereas if the worker has not yet retired his value function $V_2 = \max[W_2, (6/5)W_1]$, which also equals $(6/5)W_1$. Then in period 1 an unretired worker compares the value $W_1 + V_2 = (11/5)W_1$ of continuing to work with the value $(6/5)W_1 + V_2 = (12/5)W_1$ of retiring immediately, and we see that the DP and OV decision rules coincide with the recommendation to retire in period 1.

Now suppose that period 2 wages are uncertain but are not expected to increase: $E\{\tilde{W}_2|W_1\} = W_1$. It is easy to see that the OV model predicts that retirement in period 1 is still optimal: since $\tilde{W}_2$ has conditional expectation W_1, the earlier calculations are unchanged. The presence of uncertainty does change the DP decision rule, which differs from the OV decision rule when the variance in $\tilde{W}_2$ is sufficiently large. In period 2, we have $V_2 = (6/5)W_1$ if the worker is already retired, and $V_2 = \max[\tilde{W}_2, (6/5)W_1]$ if the worker is not yet retired. The optimal decision rule is to continue working in period 2 provided $\tilde{W}_2 > (6/5)W_1$. In period 1, an unretired worker compares the expected value of retiring immediately, $(12/5)W_1$, with the expected value of continuing to work one more period, $W_1 + E\{V_2|W_1\}$. If $E\{V_2|W_1\} > (7/5)W_1$, then the worker will decide to continue to work rather than retire in period 1, and the difference in these terms gives the loss in utility of following the OV decision rule. This difference is positive provided that the variance in $\tilde{W}_2$ is sufficiently large. In such a situation a worker would want to use DP to calculate the optimal retirement policy, since it correctly accounts for the option value of continued employment, yielding higher utility than the OV decision rule.

In the specifications estimated in this paper, the major computational simplification is the assumption that there is no future uncertainty about wages: workers have perfectly certain point predictions about their future wage profiles at the firm (computed from regressions on individuals' wage histories). The only uncertainty in the OV model comes via two error terms corresponding to unobservable factors affecting the utility of work and retirement. Although these error terms are treated as random walk processes, the estimated standard deviation of the innovation of the random walk is relatively small (.11), so the error components are not a major source of future uncertainty. In the DP model, the error terms entering the period utility functions are assumed to be i.i.d., and the estimated standard deviation of these error terms is also small (.22). Thus, there are two factors responsible for the similarity in the predictions of the OV and DP models: (1) the authors do not allow for uncertainty in future wage profiles, and (2) the estimated variances of random utility components are small.

My guess is that we would see much more significant differences between the DP and OV models once we allow for future wage uncertainty. It is not clear how uncertain workers are about their future wages, but this is clearly an empirical matter that needs to be addressed. At a minimum, it would be interesting to see the R^2 values from the wage regressions (which are not reported). I have estimated DP models that allow for wage uncertainty (Phelan and Rust 1991; Rust and Phelan 1993), predicting the entire distribution of future wages, not just the mean. I find substantial variation in future wage earnings even conditional on the worker's past wage history, in real terms. Part of this uncertainty is undoubtedly an artifact of aggregation of planned hours of work, since my model forecasts future earnings over an entire year, conditional on next year's employment being in one of two categories, full- or part-time. It is plausible that many workers have a fairly good idea of their future wages on a week-by-week or month-by-month basis. Thus, to some extent, the appropriate level of variance in future wages depends on the fineness of the time grain of the decision problem. However, many workers do face significant uncertainties regarding the level of future bonuses (including the window plan itself). These uncertainties may induce a significant option value for remaining with the firm. I would have liked to have seen a fuller discussion of this issue, since it seems to be the most important factor underlying the similarities in the predictions of these two very different models.

Beyond wage earnings, the major source of uncertainty neglected by the models in this paper is health-care costs. All of the models estimated in this paper and in the authors' earlier work miss the big peak in retirements at age 65. Although one might argue that the age-65 peak reflects a sociological effect, I think a much more compelling economic story is that the peak reflects an interaction effect between private health insurance and the "Medicare option": unhealthy workers choose to remain under the firm's more generous group health plan until they are able to supplement their pension health-care coverage with Medicare insurance at age 65, whereas relatively healthy workers take advantage of the window plan, since they are able to purchase supplemental private medical insurance at attractive rates. The authors include Medicare by adding the average value of Medicare payments to the retirement benefit calculated without Medicare and find "little support for the value of Medicare that we have used here." I do not think that this is the proper way to treat Medicare: risk-averse workers are concerned about the small chance of uninsured catastrophic health-care costs, so the certainty equivalent value of Medicare is much higher than the expected value of benefits paid. It seems likely that many of the workers in the age-65 peak could have health problems that would make it prohibitively costly for them to purchase supplemental private health insurance if they retire before age 65. Many of these workers will prefer to remain with the firm to take advantage of the group health-care benefits until Medicare kicks in at age 65, removing a substantial share of the risks of catastrophic health-care costs. Indeed, this is what I have found after explicitly incorporating the uncertainties surrounding health-care costs into my DP model (with health-care expenditures turning out to be almost perfectly approximated by the Pareto distribution). Our recent paper (Rust and Phelan 1993) shows that by explicitly modeling the distribution of health-care costs (as opposed to treating it as an expected value), we obtain DP models that are able to capture the peak in retirement at age 65 that the Lumsdaine, Stock, and Wise approach misses.

There is a final option that the models in this paper ignore: the option of returning to work after retirement. The authors' models rule out this option by assumption: retirement is treated as an absorbing state. One might argue that future re-employment opportunities are implicitly captured in the error terms. However, the fact that the error terms are i.i.d. in the DP model makes this interpretation less plausible: the calculation of the value of retiring does not properly value the option of finding an attractive new job after retiring from the current job. In reality, some workers know that their employment record is sufficiently good that they will always have the option of returning to their career job or a similar job if they find that retirement does not suit them, experience unexpected financial problems, or encounter an unexpected, attractive job offer. The possibility of the re-employment option may be a crucial element of a risk-averse worker's decision to take advantage of an early retirement plan. In Rust (1990) and Rust and Phelan (1993), I show that in the Retirement History Survey, less than half of all work histories involve the discontinuous employed/retired trajectory implicit in the authors' model. Indeed, at least one-third of all work histories involve multiple transitions in and out of the labor force, suggesting that postretirement work in a noncareer job is a fairly common phenomenon (similar results can be found in Berkovec and Stern 1991, using the National Longitudinal Survey). It is not clear what kinds of specification errors are generated by ruling out the possibility of postretirement work. For the fraction of the sample who follow the "traditional" retirement profile, preferring to remain permanently out of work, the error may not be substantial. However for risk-averse workers who face substantial financial uncertainties at the brink of retirement, ruling out the re-employment option substantially increases the riskiness of the retirement decision. The model may be able to generate a good overall fit to the data by underestimating β and overestimating the value of leisure, K, but it is not clear whether the resulting model will do a good job of tracking the behavior of various subgroups of employees with differing views of their re-employment prospects.

From a larger perspective, we are not only concerned about departure rates from particular firms, but the overall dynamics of employment at the end of the life cycle. The simple models estimated here are unable to address this larger question. Although the DP model is sufficiently flexible that it can be generalized to address a broad variety of issues, including uncertain future health, earnings, and re-employment prospects (see Rust 1989; Berkovec and

Stern 1991; Rust and Phelan 1993), it is unclear whether the OV model can be generalized to encompass these features. In their earlier paper, the authors stressed the point of computational complexity, arguing that the OV calculations are simpler to implement than the DP calculations. However I have seen no clear-cut evidence that this is so: both the OV and DP models can be solved very quickly on a 386 computer, and if there is any speed advantage to the OV model, it does not seem to be substantial. Viewing the brain as a massive parallel processor, I think few would disagree that people have far greater reasoning abilities than a 386 computer. Therefore I find it hard to buy the story that humans adopt the OV decision rule because it is simpler to implement than a DP decision rule.

Once we allow for the possibility of re-employment after retirement, there is no obvious way to calculate the value of retirement other than the backward induction process of DP. While I view the OV model as a very useful point of departure for addressing the specific question of modeling the effect of firm pension plan provisions on exit rates, I think it has real limitations in its ability to properly account for the options arising from uncertainty about future earnings and employment possibilities. However at the same time, I must stress that there is nothing sacred about DP models: which type of model best describes people's behavior is ultimately an empirical issue. Even though all of these models will probably ultimately be regarded as stepping stones toward more realistic behavioral models, it is clear that the authors' careful attempts to discriminate between their simple OV and DP specifications have contributed a great deal to our understanding of retirement behavior.

References

Berkovec, J., and S. Stern. 1991. Job exit behavior of older men. *Econometrica* 59(1): 189–210.

Lucas, R. E., Jr. 1976. Econometric policy evaluation: A critique. In *The Phillips curve and labour markets,* ed. K. Brunner and A. K. Meltzer. Amsterdam: North-Holland.

Lumsdaine, R., J. Stock, and D. Wise. 1991. Three models of retirement: Computational complexity vs. predictive validity. In *Topics in the economics of aging,* ed. D. A. Wise, 19–57. Chicago: University of Chicago Press.

Marschak, T. 1953. Economic measurements for policy and prediction. In *Studies in econometric method,* ed. W. C. Hood and T. J. Koopmans. New York: Wiley.

Phelan, C., and J. Rust. 1991. U.S. Social security policy: A dynamic analysis of incentives and self-selection. Department of Economics, University of Wisconsin—Madison. Manuscript.

Rust, J. 1989. A dynamic programming model of retirement behavior. In *The economics of aging,* ed. D. A. Wise, 359–98. Chicago: University of Chicago Press.

———. 1990. Behavior of male workers at the end of the life-cycle: An empirical analysis of states and controls. In *Issues in the economics of aging,* ed. D. A. Wise. Chicago: University of Chicago Press.

———. 1992a. Do people behave according to Bellman's principle of optimality? Hoover Institution Working Paper no. E-92-10. Stanford, Calif.: Hoover Institution.

———. 1992b. A dynamic programming model of retirement behavior. In *Computer assisted analysis and modelling on the IBM 3090*, ed. K. R. Billingsley, H. U. Brown III, and E. Derohanes, vol. 2, 887–912. Athens: Baldwin Press, University of Georgia.

————. In press. Structural estimation of Markov decision processes. In *Handbook of econometrics*, ed. R. Engle and D. McFadden, vol. 4.

Rust, J., and C. Phelan. 1993. How Social Security and Medicare affect retirement behavior in a world of incomplete markets. Department of Economics, University of Wisconsin—Madison. Manuscript.

Stern, S. 1994. Approximate solutions to stochastic dynamic programs. *Econometric Theory.* Forthcoming.

Stock, J., and D. Wise. 1990. Pensions, the option value of work and retirement. *Econometrica* 58(5): 1151–80.

Comment   James P. Smith

In the first-generation economic research on retirement, the emphasis was on learning about the role of Social Security. In that work, private pensions were assigned a largely secondary role, partly because the data on private pensions were so limited. Largely due to the impetus of the NBER's program project on the economics of aging, the best of the second-generation studies demonstrated how critical the provisions of private pension plans were for retirement. Lumsdaine, Stock, and Wise have been the major contributors to that literature, and in this paper, they offer us another impressive addition to their body of work. In my view, this trio of authors is largely responsible for convincing the economics and policy community about the importance of private pensions. Their earlier work was based on data from a single firm. This paper generalizes that work in an important and necessary direction by using data from another large private-sector firm.

This paper sets out four principal goals: (1) to compare the predictive value of options value and dynamic programming models, (2) to evaluate how well pension plan provisions predict retirement behavior, (3) to compare how well these models predict retirement behavior of men and women, and (4) to evaluate the effect of Medicare on retirement. Much of the emphasis is devoted to the first two aims, with considerably less attention paid to the last two. My main suggestion, in fact, is that the value added of their work could be higher if that emphasis were reversed.

I found the battle between the two dominant theoretical models the least interesting part of the paper. This battle is part of a war no one can win. Indeed, winning or losing the battle as described here has little to do with the war. As the authors recognized, their dynamic programming model is a very specialized and quite restrictive case of an infinite variety of equally plausible alterna-

James P. Smith is RAND Chair Economist in Labor Markets and Demographic Studies and director of Rand's Labor and Population Program.

tives. They are able to test particular variants of two theoretical frameworks, but this is certainly not a test of the relative usefulness of the option value and the dynamic programming approaches. Their work here, and similar tests contained in their earlier papers, demonstrate that both theoretical approaches are useful and give reasonable results. Perhaps we should leave it at that and, within either model, get on to the more substantive issues that occupy the rest of their paper.

To obtain out-of-sample tests of their model, Lumsdaine et al. predict departure rates during years when the firm instituted a window plan. This use of window plans to test retirement models is growing in popularity, but I want to sound some cautionary notes because it makes me uneasy. In a nutshell, my problem is that, when firms introduce these windows, many other fundamental changes are taking place in the work environment. These other, coincident changes may also affect departure rates so that the experiment may be contaminated.

Windows are typically used, as appears to be the case here, to achieve a large-scale downsizing of the work force. My concern stems from my work with another large Fortune 500 firm which also introduced pension plans. I am familiar with this firm because they were involved in litigation about their pension plan, including its window provisions.

In my case, when the window plan was introduced, the very viability of the firm was at stake. In fact, the smart bet, as confirmed by its low single-digit stock price, was that the firm would not make it. The prospect for the employees of that firm were dim indeed. They were understandably worried about whether they would even have their current salaries or jobs in a few years. There were allegations that employees were told that they would be fired if they did not participate in the pension plan. Most instances when firms use window plans are not so severe as this one, but the more general principle applies. When window plans are used, firms are trying to seriously restructure the size and composition of their work force. They may be dropping entire lines in which older workers' skills are specialized, and they have little incentive to invest in new skills for these older employees. At best, prospects for salary increases and promotions for these workers become much worse than they were. If this is a reasonably accurate characterization of the time period when window plans are used, it may be problematic to use the window period as a test of the parameters of the pension plan.

An alternative way of providing out-of-sample tests is available, which at the very least is complementary to the use of windows. Lumsdaine et al. have previously estimated the parameters of this model with data from another private-sector firm. Using the parameters estimated in the previous firm, the model can be used to predict retirement behavior in this new firm. One objection is that the worker or the nature of the firm are too different to provide a meaningful test. But at some level that objection has to fail. If firms are so heterogeneous that they have little in common, we may not be learning much from data on individual firms.

In future work, I hope that the emphasis of the authors' research shifts to looking at the second two goals of the paper—predicting women's retirement rates and incorporating other components of the fringe package into their model, particularly those involving health benefits. Almost all existing research examines male retirement decisions. The eye-catching result here is that women's hazard rates of leaving the firm are little different from those of men. The reason this seems surprising at first blush is that it runs against the grain of most of the labor supply literature. Female labor-force participation begins to decline at a younger age and more rapidly than men's. In addition, female labor supply appears to be sensitive to male characteristics such as husband's wages. In contrast, Lumsdaine et al. are able to predict similar female exit rates without knowing anything about husbands, including whether they have retired.

The patterns of these female departure rates are fascinating, and Lumsdaine et al. are on the brink of an important contribution. The differences with the age pattern of female labor-force participation rates may be reconciled, in part, because their data actually measure departure rates from the firm. Any departures from the firm for women are more likely to be out of the labor force than to another job. In a similar vein, the departure rates in their paper are conditional on years of service. Most of the male-female difference may come in the distribution of years of service rather than in these conditional departure rates.

But even this reconciliation fails to address the question of why they are so successful in predicting female departure rates without any knowledge about the current situation of the husbands of these women. Since the husbands are typically older, does this mean that the family waits until both members retire optimally (based on their own financial incentives) before entering retirement life (including migrating to more amenable areas)? Current sex discrimination laws have had the bizarre interpretation of not permitting the longer life expectancies of women to affect the yearly flows of benefits. What is the impact of that sex bias in favor of women in their retirement behavior? The Lumsdaine et al. paper is breaking new ground in which we will be able for the first time to explore these fascinating questions.

V   Demographic Transition and Housing Values

7   Demographics, the Housing Market, and the Welfare of the Elderly

Daniel McFadden

7.1   Introduction

The birthrate in the United States has fluctuated sharply in the past century, as shown in figure 7.1, with "baby booms" in 1900–25 and 1947–62 and "baby busts" in 1930–46 and after 1962; Census Bureau "low" and "mid" projections are that the current bust will continue into the next century. The age composition of the population has varied in proportions reflecting the lagged birthrate, with smoothing and stretching due to immigration and changing life expectancy, as shown in figure 7.2. If fertility rates remain at current below-replacement levels over the coming century, as projected by many demographers, then the U.S. population will peak between 2030 and 2050. After this, it will under "low" projections decline by 2100 to approximately 1990 levels, or under "mid" projections remain almost stationary. The elderly population will peak around 2035, as the 1947–62 baby-boom cohorts pass age 65, but increasing longevity will keep the *elderly dependency ratio*[1] high through the end of the next century. The *total dependency ratio* will rise sharply after 2010, and although it will not reach the historic highs attained at the end of past baby booms, the relative shift in dependency toward the elderly will be drastic. If

Daniel McFadden is professor of economics at the University of California, Berkeley, and a research associate of the National Bureau of Economic Research.

This research was sponsored by the Institute on Aging, through a program project at the National Bureau of Economic Research, with additional funding from the C. Morris Cox Endowment at the University of California, Berkeley. Research assistance has been provided by Padmini Narayan, Chris Dowling, and Pinghua Young. The author has benefited from comments by Greg Mankiw, Linda Martin, Jonathan Skinner, and Jim Stock.

1. The elderly [resp. youth] dependency ratio equals the population age 65 and over [resp. the population age 0–19] divided by the population age 20–64. The total dependency ratio is the sum of the elderly and youth dependency ratios.

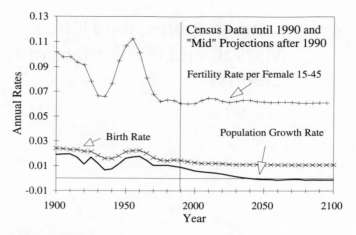

Fig. 7.1   U.S. population growth

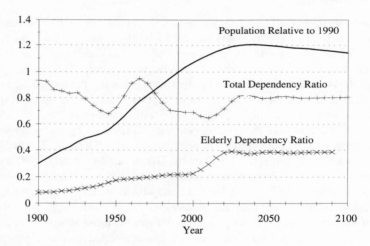

Fig. 7.2   Dependency ratios

these demographic projections are correct, then the United States faces a "regime shift" that will substantially change the characteristics of institutions influenced by demographic factors. These changes will in turn have some significant impacts on the welfare of elderly cohorts, particularly those that span the regime shift.

The institution that has perhaps the greatest impact on the welfare of the elderly is the Social Security/Medicare system. The implications of demographics for this program have been investigated in detail, for example, by Boskin and Shoven (1987), the Consulting Panel on Society Security (1976),

Darby (1979), Diamond and Hausman (1984), Hurd (1991), Hurd and Shoven (1982), Kotlikoff and Smith (1983), and Poterba and Summers (1987).

Markets such as health services and housing are also likely to see substantial impacts. Recently, several economists have examined the impact of demographics on the housing market. In a seminal paper, Mankiw and Weil (1989) show that a simple age-specific housing demand function, combined with demographic profiles, generates aggregate *potential* housing demand with substantial intertemporal variation. Related studies have been done by Rosen (1984) and Russell (1982). Mankiw and Weil argue that real housing stocks are not very responsive to housing prices and that the price elasticity of demand is low. They conclude that the demographic swings will be converted in this relatively rigid market into large swings in housing prices and that the past pattern of housing wealth generated by real capital gains will be largely reversed in coming decades. Figures 7.3–7.5 give time series for real housing stock, the demographic component of potential housing demand as defined by Mankiw and Weil, and real housing prices. The construction of these series is detailed in section 7.3. The high correlations among these three series (.9668 between stock and the demographic factor, .8875 between stock and price, and .9423 between price and the demographic factor) are consistent with the economic hypothesis that demographics are causal to housing stock and price.

Housing equity is the most important asset of most elderly households, and for many is the *only* significant asset; see McFadden (1994). The 1983 Survey of Consumer Finances finds that in the population over age 65, 69 percent of net worth is in house equity. The 1984 Survey of Income and Program Participation finds that 73 percent of households over age 65 have equity in a home and that the median equity among holders was $46,192. The only other assets

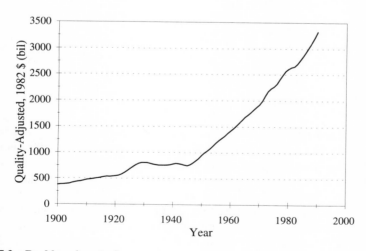

Fig. 7.3   Real housing stock

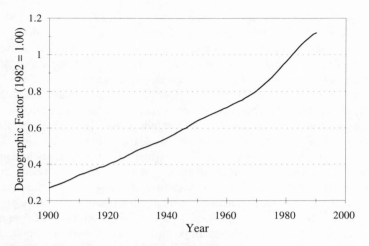

Fig. 7.4   Demographic factor in housing demand

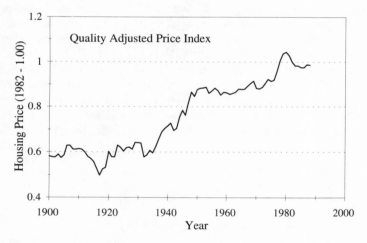

Fig. 7.5   Real housing price

held by a majority of households are bank accounts and equity in automobiles, and the medians among holders of these assets total less than $17,000. Further, a substantial fraction of home equity held by current elderly cohorts comes from capital gains. For example, from figure 7.5, real capital gains created more than a third of the equity of a household that purchased a house in 1945 at age 30 and that sold it in 1980 to finance retirement. Then, variations in real housing prices that affect net equity can have a significant impact on the wealth of the elderly and on intergenerational distribution of welfare. The increasing importance of housing equity as an asset in recent decades—from 22 percent of holdings in 1965, to a high of 34 percent in 1979, and to 31 percent in 1988, according to Federal Reserve Board balance sheets (C-9)—combined with the high volatility of housing prices, has increased the riskiness of consumers' asset portfolios. The potential welfare effects are particularly large if the price changes are unanticipated, so that households have a significant fraction of their assets at risk and are unable to adjust savings and bequest behavior in anticipation of market variations. It remains true if the price changes are predictable, but myopia or credit constraints prevent households from forming intertemporally consistent life-cycle savings plans.

This paper examines the long-run behavior of the housing market in response to demographic swings and the consequences of market characteristics for the welfare of current and future cohorts of the elderly. Section 7.2 uses a simple demographic model, along with U.S. Department of Commerce middle-range assumptions, to project population by age over the next century. Section 7.3 assembles measures of per capita income, quality-adjusted housing stock, real housing price, and the real user cost of owner-occupied housing. Section 7.4 examines the age distribution of housing consumption and income and its stability over time. Section 7.5 obtains estimates of demand and supply elasticities, using aggregate data and information from various censuses. Section 7.6 assembles these components and forecasts market-clearing housing prices and stocks. Section 7.7 analyzes the welfare impacts on successive elderly cohorts of these housing market variations.

7.2 Demographics

Estimates and "mid-range" forecasts of the U.S. population by age and sex, from the U.S. Census, are given in tables 7.1–7.3 for the years 1900–2100. Historical estimates are from *Historical Statistics of the United States* (U.S. Department of Commerce, 1975), and *Statistical Abstract* (U.S. Department of Commerce, various years). Projections are from Spencer (1989). For intercensus years after 2050, and all years after 2080, I complete the table using a cohort-component projection procedure plus the fertility rate lagged one period; see Haub (1987) for an explanation of this methodology. For years prior to 1940, it was necessary to disaggregate census tables for persons over age 65. This was done using contemporaneous life tables, as described below.

A critical component of projections of the elderly population is an assumption about mortality trends. I followed the actuarial approach used by Spencer (1989) and Palmer (1989), fitting Gompertz curves in each census year to age-specific death rates after age 55. The death rate H per 1,000 persons of age A and sex i in year t is approximated by the function

$$(1) \qquad H = \exp(\alpha_{it} + \beta_{it}A).$$

The estimates for the Gompertz coefficients, along with projections past 1990, are given in table 7.4.

Table 7.1   U.S. Census Estimates and Projections of Male Population by Age, Middle Series P-25, 1989 (thousands)

Year	\multicolumn{10}{c}{Age Group}
	0–4	5–9	10–14	15–19	20–24	25–29	30–34	35–39	40–44	45–49
1900	4,655	4,500	4,102	3,767	3,642	3,339	2,914	2,629	2,266	1,846
1905	5,047	4,638	4,522	4,351	4,014	3,657	3,360	2,854	2,509	2,192
1910	5,420	4,959	4,635	4,560	4,613	4,275	3,683	3,391	2,803	2,396
1915	5,881	5,504	4,914	4,674	4,642	4,460	4,259	3,555	3,321	2,724
1920	5,910	5,805	5,417	4,716	4,568	4,579	4,168	4,111	3,315	3,146
1925	6,325	6,051	5,841	5,432	4,838	4,612	4,677	4,195	3,930	3,257
1930	5,826	6,403	6,090	5,778	5,355	4,877	4,578	4,696	4,150	3,685
1935	5,188	5,916	6,315	5,913	5,635	5,232	4,829	4,515	4,469	3,966
1940	5,378	5,442	5,987	6,206	5,716	5,474	5,092	4,766	4,438	4,227
1945	6,513	5,542	5,411	5,890	6,138	5,724	5,529	5,106	4,665	4,292
1950	8,314	6,778	5,713	5,361	5,659	6,028	5,678	5,570	5,118	4,569
1955	9,411	8,495	6,916	5,536	5,329	5,833	6,085	5,810	5,437	5,008
1960	10,337	9,563	8,600	6,802	5,568	5,422	5,903	6,139	5,731	5,396
1965	10,070	10,367	9,696	8,633	6,903	5,607	5,519	5,893	6,068	5,552
1970	8,869	10,312	10,741	9,771	8,029	6,715	5,675	5,489	5,902	5,934
1975	8,240	8,972	10,534	10,817	9,839	8,617	7,018	5,702	5,497	5,712
1980	8,423	8,601	9,384	10,833	10,711	9,776	8,740	6,912	5,750	5,427
1985	9,213	8,610	8,763	9,479	10,708	11,007	10,167	8,794	6,910	5,684
1990	9,426	9,408	8,858	8,900	9,427	10,818	11,260	10,072	8,713	6,815
1995	9,118	9,609	9,660	8,979	8,830	9,526	11,053	11,138	9,966	8,586
2000	8,661	9,683	10,073	9,765	8,799	8,881	9,664	11,020	11,036	9,824
2005	8,517	9,165	9,766	10,143	9,807	8,875	8,947	9,669	10,952	10,886
2010	8,668	9,062	9,247	9,834	10,178	9,871	8,941	8,957	9,616	10,802
2015	8,829	9,305	9,131	9,303	9,857	10,223	9,911	8,937	8,898	9,477
2020	8,768	9,546	9,401	9,211	9,350	9,928	10,293	9,934	8,902	8,793
2025	8,544	9,495	9,639	9,477	9,251	9,411	9,989	10,310	9,890	8,792
2030	8,357	9,283	9,589	9,719	9,521	9,314	9,471	10,008	10,266	9,769
2035	8,300	9,125	9,567	9,652	9,747	9,568	9,356	9,472	9,947	10,123
2040	8,308	9,123	9,399	9,624	9,675	9,790	9,607	9,353	9,410	9,803
2045	8,267	9,165	9,392	9,450	9,641	9,712	9,824	9,598	9,286	9,269
2050	8,143	9,122	9,431	9,439	9,463	9,675	9,742	9,811	9,526	9,143
2055	8,136	8,985	9,386	9,479	9,452	9,496	9,704	9,728	9,737	9,379
2060	7,916	8,853	9,246	9,434	9,492	9,485	9,526	9,692	9,656	9,587
2065	7,864	8,613	9,109	9,293	9,448	9,525	9,515	9,513	9,619	9,507
2070	7,823	8,777	9,059	9,171	9,320	9,496	9,570	9,517	9,457	9,486
2075	7,803	8,731	9,231	9,120	9,198	9,368	9,540	9,572	9,461	9,326
2080	7,661	8,679	9,012	9,101	9,141	9,239	9,406	9,537	9,510	9,324
2085	7,626	8,522	8,959	8,885	9,122	9,182	9,277	9,402	9,474	9,372
2090	7,586	8,483	8,797	8,833	8,905	9,162	9,219	9,273	9,341	9,338
2095	7,552	8,438	8,756	8,672	8,853	8,945	9,200	9,216	9,213	9,206
2100	7,525	8,401	8,710	8,633	8,692	8,893	8,982	9,197	9,156	9,080

Table 7.1 (continued)

					Age Group						
50–54	55–59	60–64	65–69	70–74	75–79	80–84	85–89	90–94	95+	Total	Year
1,572	1,150	921	724	446	240	106	36	8	1	38,867	1900
1,670	1,382	990	753	508	300	147	54	13	2	42,965	1905
2,125	1,499	1,195	834	569	341	170	65	17	3	47,554	1910
2,181	1,890	1,252	953	657	399	203	80	22	3	51,573	1915
2,559	1,897	1,596	967	707	456	244	100	27	4	54,291	1920
2,813	2,272	1,612	1,213	845	517	259	96	23	3	58,813	1925
3,142	2,434	1,949	1,300	936	598	321	134	39	7	62,297	1930
3,360	2,780	2,060	1,486	1,098	720	397	171	51	9	64,110	1935
3,769	3,024	2,408	1,680	1,241	811	443	187	53	9	66,352	1940
3,941	3,413	2,734	1,930	1,419	935	526	236	76	15	70,035	1945
4,168	3,664	3,067	2,446	1,645	1,001	470	209	67	14	75,539	1950
4,317	3,825	3,317	2,711	1,914	1,166	550	258	91	21	82,030	1955
4,762	4,144	3,413	2,939	2,193	1,369	639	288	94	19	89,320	1960
5,087	4,578	3,639	2,934	2,342	1,514	734	336	112	24	95,609	1965
5,424	4,834	4,084	3,166	2,342	1,586	801	398	152	40	100,266	1970
5,737	5,048	4,368	3,596	2,441	1,653	904	455	173	44	105,366	1975
5,662	5,522	4,704	3,948	2,894	1,875	989	502	189	46	110,888	1980
5,284	5,383	5,118	4,254	3,213	2,135	1,086	566	220	55	116,648	1985
5,591	5,071	5,032	4,655	3,516	2,413	1,350	627	222	70	122,243	1990
6,705	6,386	4,763	4,603	3,873	2,668	1,548	752	275	84	127,123	1995
8,531	6,419	4,952	4,144	3,697	2,894	1,786	915	338	109	131,191	2000
9,580	8,169	6,000	4,444	3,498	2,879	1,988	1,016	411	145	134,858	2005
10,617	9,180	7,648	5,400	3,771	2,741	1,996	1,147	469	186	138,333	2010
10,520	10,158	8,583	6,881	4,586	2,965	1,908	1,161	538	223	141,393	2015
9,254	10,092	9,523	7,742	5,860	3,615	1,908	1,113	546	256	144,035	2020
8,581	8,872	9,455	8,585	6,590	4,616	2,325	1,112	523	260	145,717	2025
8,581	8,229	8,314	8,526	7,309	5,192	2,969	1,356	523	249	146,543	2030
9,518	8,215	7,697	7,483	7,245	5,748	3,333	1,728	636	248	146,711	2035
9,858	9,107	7,680	6,925	6,356	5,696	3,689	1,939	810	302	146,454	2040
9,541	9,426	8,509	6,906	5,878	4,994	3,653	2,145	909	385	145,950	2045
9,017	9,120	8,804	7,648	5,860	4,616	3,201	2,123	1,005	431	145,320	2050
8,895	8,619	8,518	7,913	6,490	4,602	2,959	1,861	994	490	144,824	2055
9,125	8,502	8,051	7,656	6,715	5,097	2,950	1,720	872	472	144,046	2060
9,327	8,722	7,942	7,236	6,497	5,274	3,268	1,715	806	430	143,224	2065
9,264	8,930	8,160	7,149	6,150	5,111	3,386	1,902	804	383	142,915	2070
9,244	8,869	8,354	7,346	6,076	4,838	3,282	1,971	892	401	142,621	2075
9,082	8,844	8,293	7,516	6,239	4,777	3,104	1,909	924	424	141,722	2080
9,080	8,690	8,269	7,461	6,384	4,905	3,065	1,806	895	470	140,847	2085
9,127	8,688	8,125	7,439	6,337	5,019	3,148	1,783	847	458	139,909	2090
9,094	8,733	8,123	7,309	6,319	4,982	3,221	1,831	836	437	138,937	2095
8,966	8,701	8,165	7,308	6,209	4,968	3,197	1,874	859	434	137,947	2100

Table 7.2   U.S. Census Estimates and Projections of Female Population by Age,
                              Middle Series P-25, 1989 (thousands)

					Age Group					
Year	0–4	5–9	10–14	15–19	20–24	25–29	30–34	35–39	40–44	45–49
1900	4,594	4,450	4,047	3,854	3,757	3,246	2,688	2,378	2,016	1,637
1905	4,942	4,542	4,487	4,257	3,889	3,529	3,132	2,577	2,229	1,900
1910	5,283	4,866	4,532	4,563	4,504	3,960	3,335	3,047	2,490	2,103
1915	5,712	5,363	4,889	4,717	4,630	4,290	3,893	3,249	2,893	2,382
1920	5,762	5,690	5,314	4,795	4,788	4,585	3,972	3,731	3,085	2,667
1925	6,168	5,908	5,800	5,479	4,933	4,720	4,603	3,952	3,586	2,993
1930	5,655	6,246	5,954	5,811	5,551	4,988	4,573	4,543	3,866	3,380
1935	5,044	5,755	6,232	5,956	5,759	5,389	4,920	4,494	4,317	3,704
1940	5,200	5,279	5,808	6,168	5,910	5,660	5,185	4,812	4,380	4,056
1945	6,285	5,336	5,270	5,828	6,210	5,907	5,693	5,156	4,679	4,258
1950	7,955	6,508	5,478	5,324	5,897	6,292	5,913	5,749	5,152	4,570
1955	9,082	8,188	6,668	5,461	5,342	5,954	6,313	6,000	5,575	5,111
1960	10,002	9,245	8,323	6,640	5,566	5,512	6,079	6,403	5,946	5,535
1965	9,715	10,011	9,360	8,380	6,852	5,723	5,609	6,115	6,380	5,828
1970	8,415	9,768	10,230	9,517	8,547	6,915	5,872	5,680	6,148	6,277
1975	7,881	8,623	10,112	10,468	9,688	8,663	7,173	5,931	5,700	6,072
1980	8,005	8,181	8,948	10,438	10,681	9,840	8,906	7,121	5,975	5,716
1985	8,792	8,214	8,339	9,109	10,507	10,886	10,179	8,969	7,167	5,968
1990	8,982	8,971	8,427	8,518	9,262	10,694	11,154	10,148	8,964	7,132
1995	8,681	9,151	9,187	8,588	8,652	9,440	10,944	11,107	10,126	8,903
2000	8,604	9,131	9,503	9,234	8,397	8,566	9,411	10,795	11,016	9,994
2005	8,518	8,637	9,206	9,578	9,338	8,555	8,687	9,459	10,786	10,945
2010	8,774	8,541	8,716	9,287	9,715	9,497	8,681	8,744	9,465	10,725
2015	9,003	8,775	8,394	8,789	9,385	9,833	9,608	8,730	8,746	9,410
2020	8,960	8,990	8,630	8,470	8,888	9,506	9,956	9,669	8,738	8,701
2025	8,765	8,939	8,847	8,713	8,571	9,008	9,630	10,025	9,684	8,699
2030	8,637	8,740	8,800	8,936	8,821	8,690	9,129	9,701	10,045	9,645
2035	8,660	8,607	8,604	8,888	9,046	8,943	8,807	9,196	9,720	10,003
2040	8,729	8,629	8,476	8,693	9,001	9,174	9,067	8,875	9,218	9,683
2045	8,720	8,703	8,504	8,571	8,810	9,136	9,309	9,144	8,902	9,190
2050	8,621	8,704	8,582	8,604	8,692	8,948	9,275	9,393	9,177	8,881
2055	8,527	8,605	8,583	8,683	8,725	8,827	9,084	9,359	9,428	9,155
2060	8,498	8,513	8,478	8,666	8,786	8,842	8,943	9,147	9,374	9,385
2065	8,504	8,484	8,387	8,559	8,769	8,905	8,958	9,005	9,161	9,332
2070	8,496	8,479	8,346	8,464	8,667	8,893	9,027	9,026	9,025	9,126
2075	8,452	8,471	8,342	8,423	8,570	8,789	9,015	9,095	9,046	8,990
2080	8,395	8,422	8,339	8,435	8,538	8,690	8,909	9,083	9,115	9,011
2085	8,341	8,365	8,291	8,433	8,551	8,658	8,809	8,977	9,103	9,080
2090	8,310	8,312	8,235	8,384	8,548	8,671	8,777	8,876	8,996	9,067
2095	8,292	8,282	8,182	8,327	8,498	8,668	8,790	8,843	8,895	8,961
2100	8,267	8,263	8,152	8,274	8,441	8,618	8,787	8,856	8,862	8,861

Table 7.2 (continued)

			Age Group								
50–54	55–59	60–64	65–69	70–74	75–79	80–84	85–89	90–94	95+	Total	Year
1,395	1,079	885	539	340	190	89	31	8	1	37,227	1990
1,465	1,236	929	709	494	304	157	61	16	2	40,857	1905
1,801	1,307	1,088	788	558	350	183	73	20	3	44,853	1910
1,916	1,627	1,131	899	641	406	216	89	25	4	48,973	1915
2,217	1,682	1,412	927	692	457	252	107	30	5	52,170	1920
2,467	2,033	1,461	1,147	826	525	276	108	27	3	57,016	1925
2,853	2,227	1,815	1,217	915	616	353	159	50	9	60,780	1930
3,123	2,605	1,923	1,372	1,067	746	444	208	68	13	63,140	1935
3,513	2,840	2,336	1,603	1,262	890	532	247	77	13	65,770	1940
3,834	3,269	2,812	1,821	1,433	1,024	633	312	110	23	69,893	1945
4,159	3,618	3,033	2,700	1,738	1,109	552	277	99	21	76,146	1950
4,373	3,932	3,491	2,947	2,196	1,407	678	358	138	33	83,246	1955
4,901	4,326	3,741	3,347	2,574	1,712	859	444	163	35	91,352	1960
5,343	4,916	4,053	3,532	2,981	2,057	1,039	549	206	45	98,694	1966
5,786	5,225	4,624	3,858	3,121	2,281	1,224	714	317	92	104,613	1970
6,235	5,598	5,031	4,536	3,344	2,593	1,506	905	419	128	110,606	1975
6,104	6,148	5,431	4,903	3,978	2,973	1,753	1,081	518	166	116,866	1980
5,661	5,960	5,877	5,176	4,352	3,360	2,017	1,265	623	209	122,631	1985
5,949	5,552	5,708	5,596	4,605	3,691	2,478	1,438	652	247	128,167	1990
7,102	5,842	5,333	5,453	5,001	3,939	2,766	1,682	799	321	133,016	1995
8,872	6,896	5,561	4,974	4,901	4,413	3,242	2,112	1,017	437	137,076	2000
9,864	8,671	6,655	5,255	4,561	4,312	3,595	2,311	1,229	583	140,746	2005
10,810	9,646	8,373	6,300	4,658	4,035	3,541	2,600	1,382	750	144,241	2010
10,582	10,559	9,306	7,921	5,803	4,286	3,322	2,579	1,576	896	147,504	2015
9,291	10,344	10,194	8,809	7,301	5,344	3,532	2,421	1,564	1,022	150,329	2020
8,597	9,088	9,993	9,656	8,125	6,728	4,406	2,576	1,469	1,015	152,535	2025
8,597	8,412	8,782	9,469	8,910	7,490	5,550	3,215	1,564	954	154,086	2030
9,532	8,412	8,129	8,322	8,737	8,213	6,178	4,049	1,951	1,015	155,014	2035
9,890	9,330	8,132	7,706	7,681	8,057	6,777	4,509	2,459	1,268	155,353	2040
9,581	9,689	9,027	7,715	7,118	7,089	6,653	4,950	2,740	1,598	155,150	2045
9,099	9,391	9,379	8,569	7,131	6,573	5,857	4,862	3,010	1,782	154,529	2050
8,792	8,918	9,091	8,903	7,920	6,584	5,431	4,280	2,957	2,041	153,893	2055
9,045	8,600	8,615	8,611	8,211	7,297	5,429	3,961	2,598	1,919	152,917	2060
9,272	8,847	8,308	8,160	7,942	7,566	6,017	3,959	2,403	1,780	152,318	2065
9,225	9,075	8,552	7,874	7,531	7,323	6,243	4,391	2,404	1,561	151,727	2070
9,022	9,029	8,772	8,106	7,267	6,944	6,042	4,555	2,666	1,666	151,262	2075
8,887	8,830	8,727	8,314	7,480	6,700	5,729	4,409	2,766	1,732	150,513	2080
8,908	8,698	8,535	8,272	7,673	6,897	5,528	4,181	2,677	1,902	149,877	2085
8,976	8,718	8,407	8,089	7,634	7,075	5,690	4,034	2,538	1,852	149,190	2090
8,963	8,784	8,427	7,968	7,465	7,038	5,837	4,152	2,449	1,767	148,592	2095
8,859	8,772	8,491	7,987	7,354	6,883	5,807	4,259	2,521	1,716	148,031	2100

Table 7.3   **U.S. Census Estimates and Projections of Total Population by Age, Middle Series P-25, 1989 (thousands)**

Year	0–4	5–9	10–14	15–19	20–24	25–29	30–34	35–39	40–44	45–49
					Age Group					
1900	9,249	8,950	8,149	7,621	7,398	6,586	5,603	5,007	4,282	3,484
1905	9,988	9,180	9,009	8,607	7,903	7,186	6,493	5,431	4,738	4,092
1910	10,702	9,826	9,167	9,123	9,117	8,234	7,018	6,439	5,293	4,499
1915	11,593	10,867	9,803	9,391	9,271	8,750	8,151	6,805	6,213	5,106
1920	11,672	11,495	10,732	9,511	9,356	9,163	8,140	7,841	6,400	5,813
1925	12,494	11,959	11,641	10,911	9,771	9,333	9,280	8,147	7,516	6,250
1930	11,481	12,649	12,044	11,589	10,906	9,865	9,150	9,239	8,016	7,065
1935	10,232	11,670	12,547	11,869	11,394	10,621	9,749	9,009	8,786	7,670
1940	10,578	10,721	11,796	12,374	11,626	11,134	10,276	9,578	8,818	8,283
1945	12,797	10,878	10,680	11,718	12,348	11,632	11,222	10,262	9,344	8,550
1950	16,269	13,287	11,192	10,685	11,556	12,321	11,591	11,320	10,270	9,139
1955	18,493	16,683	13,584	10,996	10,672	11,787	12,398	11,810	11,011	10,119
1960	20,339	18,808	16,923	13,442	11,134	10,934	11,982	12,542	11,677	10,931
1965	19,785	20,378	19,056	17,013	13,755	11,330	11,128	12,008	12,448	11,380
1970	17,285	20,081	20,972	19,288	16,577	13,630	11,548	11,169	12,050	12,211
1975	16,121	17,595	20,646	21,285	19,527	17,280	14,191	11,633	11,197	11,784
1980	16,428	16,782	18,332	21,272	21,391	19,616	17,646	14,033	11,725	11,143
1985	18,005	16,824	17,102	18,588	21,215	21,893	20,346	17,763	14,077	11,652
1990	18,408	18,379	17,285	17,418	18,689	21,512	22,414	20,220	17,677	13,947
1995	17,799	18,760	18,847	17,567	17,482	18,966	21,997	22,245	20,092	17,489
2000	17,265	18,814	19,576	19,000	17,196	17,447	19,074	21,816	22,052	19,818
2005	17,035	17,802	18,973	19,722	19,144	17,431	17,634	19,128	21,737	21,831
2010	17,442	17,604	17,964	19,121	19,894	19,368	17,621	17,701	19,081	21,528
2015	17,832	18,080	17,525	18,092	19,242	20,057	19,520	17,666	17,644	18,887
2020	17,728	18,536	18,031	17,681	18,238	19,433	20,248	19,603	17,640	17,494
2025	17,309	18,434	18,486	18,191	17,822	18,419	19,619	20,335	19,574	17,491
2030	16,994	18,023	18,389	18,655	18,342	18,004	18,600	19,709	20,311	19,414
2035	16,960	17,733	18,170	18,540	18,793	18,511	18,163	18,669	19,667	20,126
2040	17,037	17,752	17,875	18,318	18,675	18,964	18,674	18,227	18,628	19,487
2045	16,987	17,867	17,896	18,022	18,452	18,848	19,133	18,742	18,188	18,459
2050	16,764	17,825	18,013	18,043	18,155	18,622	19,017	19,204	18,703	18,024
2055	16,663	17,590	17,969	18,161	18,177	18,323	18,788	19,088	19,164	18,534
2060	16,414	17,365	17,723	18,100	18,278	18,328	18,468	18,838	19,029	18,972
2065	16,368	17,097	17,496	17,852	18,217	18,430	18,473	18,518	18,780	18,839
2070	16,319	17,256	17,405	17,634	17,987	18,388	18,597	18,543	18,481	18,612
2075	16,255	17,202	17,573	17,542	17,768	18,157	18,555	18,667	18,507	18,316
2080	16,056	17,102	17,351	17,536	17,679	17,929	18,315	18,620	18,625	18,335
2085	15,968	16,887	17,250	17,317	17,673	17,840	18,086	18,379	18,577	18,452
2090	15,897	16,795	17,031	17,216	17,453	17,834	17,996	18,149	18,337	18,405
2095	15,845	16,720	16,939	17,000	17,352	17,614	17,990	18,059	18,108	18,168
2100	15,793	16,664	16,862	16,907	17,134	17,511	17,769	18,053	18,018	17,940

Table 7.3   (continued)

				Age Group							
50–54	55–59	60–64	65–69	70–74	75–79	80–84	85–89	90–94	95+	Total	Year
2,968	2,230	1,806	1,264	786	430	195	68	16	2	76,094	1900
3,135	2,618	1,920	1,463	1,002	605	303	116	29	4	83,822	1905
3,926	2,806	2,282	1,622	1,127	691	353	139	37	6	92,407	1910
4,097	3,517	2,384	1,852	1,298	805	419	169	47	7	100,546	1915
4,775	3,579	3,008	1,894	1,399	913	496	207	57	9	106,461	1920
5,280	4,305	3,073	2,360	1,672	1,042	535	205	51	6	115,829	1925
5,994	4,661	3,764	2,516	1,851	1,214	674	294	89	16	123,077	1930
6,483	5,384	3,983	2,858	2,165	1,466	841	379	120	22	127,250	1935
7,282	5,864	4,744	3,283	2,503	1,702	975	433	130	22	132,122	1940
7,775	6,681	5,547	3,751	2,852	1,959	1,159	549	186	38	139,928	1945
8,327	7,282	6,099	5,146	3,383	2,111	1,022	485	166	35	151,685	1950
8,691	7,757	6,807	5,658	4,110	2,573	1,228	616	229	54	165,276	1955
9,663	8,470	7,154	6,285	4,767	3,081	1,498	732	257	54	180,672	1960
10,430	9,494	7,692	6,466	5,323	3,571	1,773	885	318	69	194,303	1965
11,210	10,059	8,708	7,023	5,463	3,867	2,024	1,112	469	133	204,879	1970
11,972	10,646	9,399	8,132	5,785	4,246	2,410	1,360	592	172	215,972	1975
11,766	11,670	10,135	8,850	6,872	4,848	2,742	1,582	708	213	227,754	1980
10,945	11,343	10,995	9,430	7,565	5,495	3,103	1,831	843	264	239,279	1985
11,540	10,623	10,740	10,251	8,121	6,104	3,828	2,065	874	317	250,410	1990
13,807	12,228	10,096	10,056	8,874	6,607	4,314	2,434	1,074	405	260,139	1995
17,403	13,315	10,513	9,118	8,598	7,307	5,029	3,027	1,355	546	268,267	2000
19,444	16,840	12,656	9,699	8,059	7,192	5,583	3,327	1,640	728	275,604	2005
21,427	18,826	16,022	11,700	8,429	6,775	5,536	3,748	1,851	937	282,574	2010
21,102	20,718	17,888	14,802	10,389	7,251	5,230	3,740	2,114	1,118	288,897	2015
18,544	20,436	19,717	16,551	13,161	8,959	5,440	3,534	2,110	1,278	294,364	2020
17,178	17,960	19,448	18,242	14,715	11,344	6,731	3,688	1,992	1,275	298,252	2025
17,179	16,641	17,096	17,995	16,218	12,682	8,519	4,570	2,086	1,203	300,629	2030
19,050	16,627	15,826	15,805	15,982	13,961	9,512	5,777	2,587	1,264	301,725	2035
19,748	18,437	15,813	14,631	14,037	13,752	10,466	6,448	3,269	1,570	301,807	2040
19,123	19,115	17,537	14,621	12,997	12,083	10,306	7,095	3,649	1,983	301,100	2045
18,116	18,511	18,183	16,217	12,990	11,189	9,059	6,985	4,015	2,213	299,849	2050
17,687	17,537	17,609	16,816	14,409	11,186	8,391	6,141	3,951	2,532	298,717	2055
18,170	17,102	16,666	16,268	14,926	12,394	8,379	5,681	3,469	2,391	296,963	2060
18,600	17,569	16,249	15,397	14,439	12,840	9,285	5,674	3,209	2,210	295,542	2065
18,489	18,005	16,712	15,024	13,681	12,434	9,629	6,293	3,209	1,944	294,642	2070
18,265	17,898	17,126	15,451	13,343	11,782	9,324	6,527	3,559	2,066	293,883	2075
17,969	17,674	17,020	15,830	13,720	11,477	8,834	6,318	3,690	2,155	292,235	2080
17,988	17,387	16,804	15,732	14,057	11,802	8,593	5,987	3,572	2,372	290,724	2085
18,103	17,406	16,532	15,529	13,971	12,093	8,838	5,817	3,385	2,311	289,098	2090
18,057	17,518	16,550	15,278	13,784	12,020	9,057	5,983	3,286	2,204	287,529	2095
17,824	17,473	16,656	15,295	13,562	11,851	9,004	6,133	3,380	2,150	285,978	2100

Table 7.4   **Gompertz Approximation to Death Rate per 1,000 Population, exp(α + β Age), with Linear Spline Extrapolation**

Year	Male α	Male β	Female α	Female β
1900	−1.010	0.073	−1.323	0.076
1905	−1.091	0.074	−1.411	0.077
1910	−1.171	0.075	−1.498	0.078
1915	−1.251	0.076	−1.586	0.079
1920	−1.332	0.077	−1.674	0.080
1925	−1.304	0.076	−1.777	0.081
1930	−1.277	0.075	−1.881	0.082
1935	−1.249	0.075	−1.985	0.082
1940	−1.222	0.074	−2.089	0.083
1945	−1.189	0.074	−2.339	0.085
1950	−1.156	0.073	−2.589	0.088
1955	−1.122	0.072	−2.839	0.090
1960	−1.089	0.071	−3.090	0.092
1965	−1.227	0.072	−3.130	0.092
1970	−1.365	0.074	−3.170	0.092
1975	−1.503	0.075	−3.210	0.092
1980	−1.641	0.076	−3.250	0.091
1985	−1.779	0.078	−3.290	0.091
1990	−2.007	0.080	−3.343	0.092
1995	−2.078	0.081	−3.364	0.092
2000	−2.149	0.082	−3.386	0.091
2005	−2.220	0.082	−3.407	0.091
2010	−2.291	0.083	−3.428	0.091
2015	−2.362	0.084	−3.449	0.091
2020	−2.433	0.084	−3.471	0.091
2025	−2.504	0.085	−3.492	0.091
2030	−2.576	0.086	−3.513	0.091
2035	−2.647	0.086	−3.535	0.091
2040	−2.718	0.087	−3.556	0.091
2045	−2.789	0.088	−3.577	0.091
2050	−2.860	0.088	−3.598	0.091
2055	−2.931	0.089	−3.620	0.091
2060	−3.002	0.090	−3.641	0.091
2065	−3.073	0.090	−3.662	0.091
2070	−3.144	0.091	−3.683	0.091
2075	−3.215	0.092	−3.705	0.091
2080	−3.286	0.092	−3.726	0.091
2085	−3.357	0.093	−3.747	0.091
2090	−3.428	0.094	−3.769	0.091
2095	−3.499	0.094	−3.790	0.091
2100	−3.570	0.095	−3.811	0.091

For interpolation or extrapolation of population by the cohort-component method, the survivor rates implied by the Gompertz model can be used directly. Reconstruction of the elderly age distribution requires further assumptions. Suppose one starts with a population with a stationary age distribution growing at rate g; this ignores the drift in the life tables, the age distribution of immigrants, and variations in birth and immigration rates. Then, the population $N(i, A, t)$ of sex i and age A at date t satisfies

(2) $$\partial \log N(i, A, t)/\partial A = -g - \exp(\alpha_i + \beta_i A)/1000,$$

implying that the age distribution past age A_0 satisfies

(3) $$N(i, A, t_0)/N(i, A_0, t_0) = \exp\left[-g(A - A_0) + \left(e^{\alpha_i + \beta_i A_0} - e^{\alpha_i + \beta_i A}\right)\Big/1000\beta_i\right].$$

This formula with g equal to the average population growth rate over the past 30 years and the contemporary Gompertz coefficients was used to estimate the age distribution past age 65 from 1900 to 1940. There are two potential biases in these estimates. Increasing life expectancy over time leads one to overestimate the number of very old, while the effect of immigration at mostly younger ages leads one to underestimate the number of very old.

Figures 7.6 and 7.7 show survivor curves at various dates, obtained using equation (3) with Gompertz distribution parameters projected by fitting a linear spline to the coefficients in table 7.4. Table 7.5 compares the survivor rates implied by the Gompertz trend fits with the Census Bureau "mid" mortality assumptions. The Gompertz curves give slightly lower survivor rates for males and substantially lower rates for females, in comparison to the Census Bureau projections. Manton, Stallard, and Singer (chap. 2 in this volume) emphasize that there is considerable uncertainty in these actuarial trend approaches that do not take into account the structural impacts on mortality of shifts in environmental hazards or in disease-specific treatments.

Adopting low rather than mid projections would increase the cohort welfare shifts found in the final section of this paper. However, the pressures for immigration of workers created by high dependency ratios in the next century are likely to push population closer to the mid projections.

7.3   Economic Data

The economic data for this study are drawn from standard sources, mostly *Historical Statistics of the United States* (U.S. Department of Commerce, 1975), and *Statistical Abstract* (U.S. Department of Commerce, various years). Where necessary, I have spliced and interpolated to construct complete series from 1869 through 1989. Table 7.6 gives GNP per capita, and the GNP implicit price deflator. These are given by historical series F4 and F5, with the Burgess

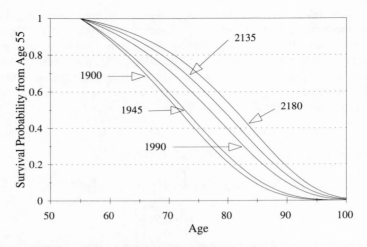

Fig. 7.6   Male survivor rates (Gompertz approximations)

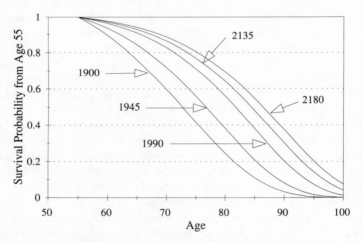

Fig. 7.7   Female survivor rates (Gompertz approximations)

cost-of-living index (Historical Series E184) used to interpolate within each decade from 1869 to 1888.

Table 7.7 gives, in successive columns, the residential investment component of the GNP implicit price deflator, a construction cost index (in current dollars), a constant-quality construction cost index (in current dollars), a quality-adjusted housing price index (in 1982 dollars), real housing investment (in 1982 dollars), and real housing stock (in 1982 dollars). The construction cost index is the Boeckh construction cost index (Historical Series N121) for small residential buildings after 1914. From 1889 through 1914, the Blank

Table 7.5   **Survivor Rates**

		1990		2020	
Start Age	End Age	Census[a]	Gompertz[b]	Census[a]	Gompertz[b]
		Males			
65–69	70–74	0.826	0.794	0.853	0.836
75–79	80–84	0.659	0.640	0.703	0.685
85–89	90–94	0.400	0.396	0.480	0.431
		Females			
65–69	70–74	0.907	0.851	0.923	0.892
75–79	80–84	0.784	0.725	0.829	0.783
85–89	90–94	0.518	0.484	0.616	0.567

[a]Share of individuals in one cohort who survive in the following cohort, Census P-25 assumptions, 1988.
[b]Projections from Gompertz distribution trends.

Table 7.6   **Population and GNP**

Year	GNP Price Deflator	GNP per Capita (1982 dollars)	Population (thousands)	Year	GNP Price Deflator	GNP per Capita (1982 dollars)	Population (thousands)
69	10.68	1060	37,779	1896	6.74	2787	70,388
70	10.10	1197	38,558	1897	6.77	2996	71,773
71	9.49	1333	39,585	1898	6.95	3006	73,186
72	10.52	1470	40,640	1899	7.20	3222	74,626
73	9.25	1606	41,723	1900	7.54	3257	75,995
74	9.08	1743	42,835	1901	7.48	3560	76,094
75	8.87	1880	43,976	1902	7.73	3521	77,580
76	8.52	2016	45,148	1903	7.82	3628	79,096
77	8.43	2153	46,351	1904	7.92	3518	80,641
78	7.60	2289	47,586	1905	8.10	3702	82,216
79	7.51	2426	48,854	1906	8.29	4053	83,822
80	7.79	2439	50,156	1907	8.63	4043	85,473
81	8.06	2453	51,282	1908	8.57	3641	87,156
82	8.31	2467	52,433	1909	8.88	4156	88,872
83	7.83	2480	53,610	1910	9.13	4185	90,622
84	7.25	2494	54,813	1911	9.03	4230	92,407
85	7.06	2507	56,043	1912	9.41	4401	93,980
86	7.13	2521	57,301	1913	9.34	4353	95,580
87	7.14	2534	58,588	1914	9.53	4082	97,208
88	7.37	2548	59,903	1915	9.96	3988	98,863
89	7.88	2561	61,247	1916	11.17	4243	100,546
90	7.73	2693	62,622	1917	13.87	4220	101,702
91	7.64	2758	63,854	1918	15.61	4739	102,872
92	7.33	2964	65,111	1919	17.82	4514	104,054
93	7.48	2767	66,392	1920	20.30	4237	105,251
94	7.01	2639	67,698	1921	16.92	3792	106,461
95	6.92	2900	69,030	1922	15.55	4333	108,272

ntinued)

Table 7.6 (continued)

Year	GNP Price Deflator	GNP per Capita (1982 dollars)	Population (thousands)	Year	GNP Price Deflator	GNP per Capita (1982 dollars)	Population (thousands)
1923	15.92	4775	110,114	1958	31.04	8277	171,984
1924	15.89	4671	111,987	1959	31.54	8660	174,882
1925	16.11	4990	113,892	1960	32.06	8695	177,830
1926	15.86	5216	115,829	1961	32.47	8718	180,671
1927	15.52	5135	117,244	1962	32.84	9150	183,691
1928	15.77	5103	118,676	1963	33.27	9382	186,538
1929	15.71	5383	120,125	1964	33.77	9755	189,242
1930	15.30	4800	121,592	1965	34.42	10245	191,889
1931	13.91	4394	123,077	1966	35.35	10786	194,303
1932	12.48	3718	123,901	1967	36.50	10947	196,560
1933	12.20	3628	124,730	1968	37.96	11344	198,712
1934	13.10	3930	125,564	1969	39.79	11534	200,706
1935	13.22	4288	126,404	1970	41.97	11453	202,677
1936	13.25	4852	127,250	1971	44.36	11993	204,879
1937	13.81	5077	128,210	1972	46.44	12460	207,661
1938	13.63	4781	129,177	1973	49.46	12972	209,896
1939	13.41	5148	130,151	1974	53.96	12769	211,909
1940	13.63	5541	131,133	1975	59.25	12478	213,854
1941	14.65	6369	132,122	1976	63.04	12950	215,972
1942	16.45	7113	133,648	1977	67.27	13411	218,035
1943	17.63	7941	135,191	1978	72,18	13972	220,239
1944	18.07	8412	136,752	1979	78.60	14166	222,585
1945	18.53	8177	138,331	1980	85.67	13993	225,055
1946	20.70	7123	139,928	1981	93.98	14117	227,754
1947	23.16	6927	142,204	1982	100.00	13616	229,945
1948	24.71	7113	144,517	1983	103.90	13966	232,171
1949	24.55	6998	166,868	1984	107.74	14774	234,296
1950	24.89	7545	149,257	1985	110.98	15123	236,343
1951	26.57	8006	151,685	1986	113.86	15387	239,279
1952	27.16	8109	154,878	1987	117.51	15798	204,658
1953	27.41	8335	157,553	1988	121.38	16337	242,820
1954	27.81	8074	160,184	1989	126.09	16612	245,051
1955	28.22	8537	163,026	1990	130.33	16937	247,350
1956	29.18	8544	165,276				
1957	30.26	8512	168,903				

residential construction cost index (Historical Series N139) is spliced in, and from 1869 through 1888, the Riggleman building cost index (Historical Series N138) is spliced in. Taking the quality adjustment in the GNP implicit price component for housing as correct, the ratio of the construction cost index to the GNP residential investment deflator gives an index of housing quality for the years 1929–88. The annual growth rate of housing quality over this period, 0.26 percent, is assumed to have prevailed over the period 1869–1928. Then,

Table 7.7   **Housing Price, Investment, and Stock**

Year	Residential Investment Component of GNP Implicit Price Deflator	Construction Cost Index	Constant-Quality Construction Cost Index	House Price Index (1982 = 1)	Real Housing Investment (1982 $)	Real Housing Stock (1982 $)
1869	4.99	0.0642		0.6006	6,771	107.7
1870	4.52	0.0579		0.5727	7,508	112.3
1871	4.71	0.0602		0.6342	7,217	116.5
1872	4.70	0.0599		0.5696	7,251	120.6
1873	4.60	0.0584		0.6317	7,435	124.8
1874	4.27	0.0542		0.5971	8,344	129.8
1875	3.89	0.0491		0.5541	9,564	135.9
1876	3.74	0.0472		0.5543	10,329	142.6
1877	3.49	0.0439		0.5204	11,520	150.3
1878	3.30	0.0414		0.5452	12,625	158.8
1879	3.19	0.0399		0.5312	14,098	168.7
1880	3.47	0.0433		0.5560	13,906	178.1
1881	3.68	0.0458		0.5680	14,013	187.3
1882	3.86	0.0480		0.5770	14,199	196.4
1883	3.88	0.0481		0.6139	14,987	206.2
1884	3.47	0.0429		0.5917	18,213	218.8
1885	3.46	0.0427		0.6050	19,742	232.7
1886	3.70	0.0455		0.6377	19,869	246.3
1887	3.69	0.0452		0.6327	21,350	261.0
1888	3.56	0.0436		0.5910	23,548	277.6
1889	3.56	0.0434		0.5504	20,532	290.6
1890	3.58	0.0435		0.5629	20,112	302.9
1891	3.46	0.0420		0.5494	16,542	311.4
1892	3.36	0.0406		0.5547	20,748	323.7
1893	3.35	0.0404		0.5403	16,380	331.4
1894	3.23	0.0389		0.5543	17,283	339.8
1895	3.18	0.0382		0.5524	19,773	350.4
1896	3.20	0.0384		0.5694	17,809	358.8
1897	3.14	0.0375		0.5540	19,178	368.4
1898	3.28	0.0390		0.5613	16,554	375.0
1899	3.51	0.0417		0.5796	16,267	381.2
1900	3.70	0.0439		0.5821	11,457	382.4
1901	3.66	0.0432		0.5782	15,792	387.9
1902	3.79	0.0446		0.5776	14,515	392.0
1903	3.92	0.0461		0.5898	14,977	396.5
1904	3.88	0.0455		0.5746	17,325	403.1
1905	4.06	0.0475		0.5863	26,611	418.9
1906	4.46	0.0521		0.6282	24,606	432.3
1907	4.66	0.0543		0.6288	21,157	441.8
1908	4.52	0.0524		0.6119	21,898	451.8
1909	4.69	0.0543		0.6116	25,600	465.3
1910	4.85	0.0561		0.6142	25,691	478.5
1911	4.79	0.0552		0.6108	20,101	485.7
1912	4.91	0.0564		0.5996	21,653	494.3
1913	4.74	0.0543		0.5807	22,375	503.4

(continued)

Table 7.7   (continued)

Year	Residential Investment Component of GNP Implicit Price Deflator	Construction Cost Index	Constant-Quality Construction Cost Index	House Price Index (1982 = 1)	Real Housing Investment (1982 $)	Real Housing Stock (1982 $)
1914		4.76	0.0544	0.5712	21,808	511.7
1915		4.88	0.0556	0.5584	23,886	521.8
1916		5.19	0.0591	0.5285	25,892	533.7
1917		6.10	0.0692	0.4987	20,075	539.5
1918		7.26	0.0821	0.5259	13,617	538.6
1919		8.42	0.0950	0.5329	22,359	546.5
1920		10.86	0.1222	0.6018	18,672	550.4
1921		8.73	0.0980	0.5791	22,487	558.1
1922		8.04	0.0900	0.5788	38,651	581.8
1923		8.98	0.1003	0.6296	45,304	611.5
1924		8.86	0.0986	0.6204	52,666	647.7
1925		8.76	0.0973	0.6040	58,128	688.4
1926		8.86	0.0981	0.6184	58,487	728.4
1927		8.73	0.0965	0.6215	55,157	764.0
1928		8.76	0.0965	0.6123	51,022	794.5
1929	38.1	9.17	0.1008	0.6416	37,433	810.6
1930	37.1	8.92	0.0981	0.6412	22,237	811.0
1931	33.6	8.23	0.0889	0.6391	18,275	807.5
1932	27.3	6.95	0.0722	0.5786	9,058	794.9
1933	27.1	6.95	0.0717	0.5876	6,962	780.5
1934	30.1	7.57	0.0796	0.6078	8,303	767.8
1935	29.8	7.38	0.0788	0.5961	13,589	760.8
1936	31.3	7.63	0.0828	0.6246	19,823	760.2
1937	34.3	8.54	0.0907	0.6568	21,771	761.5
1938	35.5	8.79	0.0939	0.6890	22,036	763.1
1939	35.7	8.95	0.0944	0.7041	29,507	772.1
1940	36.9	9.26	0.0976	0.7162	32,072	783.4
1941	40.3	9.98	0.1066	0.7275	34,639	797.0
1942	43.3	10.58	0.1145	0.6961	16,154	791.7
1943	47.0	11.01	0.1243	0.7051	8,093	778.5
1944	51.6	11.98	0.1365	0.7554	6,763	764.4
1945	54.9	12.86	0.1452	0.7836	9,477	753.2
1946	59.7	14.11	0.1579	0.7627	42,155	775.2
1947	71.7	17.08	0.1896	0.8190	54,864	809.3
1948	80.8	19.21	0.2137	0.8649	64,717	852.2
1949	78.5	18.71	0.2076	0.8456	63,150	892.5
1950	82.5	19.71	0.2182	0.8765	86,014	954.5
1951	88.6	21.28	0.2343	0.8819	70,610	999.5
1952	90.8	21.81	0.2401	0.8842	68,574	1041.2
1953	91.9	22.22	0.2431	0.8868	70,818	1084.0
1954	90.4	22.03	0.2391	0.8597	78,460	1133.4
1955	92.9	22.69	0.2457	0.8708	91,204	1194.1
1956	97.4	23.69	0.2576	0.8829	80,383	1242.4
1957	99.8	24.16	0.2640	0.8722	74,040	1283.1
1958	100.0	24.38	0.2645	0.8521	74,822	1323.4

Table 7.7   (continued)

Year	Residential Investment Component of GNP Implicit Price Deflator	Construction Cost Index	Constant-Quality Construction Cost Index	House Price Index (1982 = 1)	Real Housing Investment (1982 $)	Real Housing Stock (1982 $)
1959	103.1	25.19	0.2727	0.8647	88,936	1376.8
1960	104.5	25.60	0.2764	0.8620	83,127	1422.9
1961	105.0	25.69	0.2777	0.8553	83,207	1467.9
1962	106.7	26.10	0.2822	0.8593	89,121	1517.6
1963	108.9	26.66	0.2880	0.8656	96,778	1573.6
1964	112.3	27.44	0.2970	0.8795	94,306	1625.6
1965	114.2	28.29	0.3020	0.8774	100,103	1682.0
1966	117.4	29.51	0.3105	0.8783	92,145	1729.0
1967	123.1	31.29	0.3256	0.8919	91,336	1773.9
1968	129.7	33.58	0.3430	0.9036	99,617	1825.8
1969	137.7	36.36	0.3642	0.9152	102,183	1878.9
1970	140.0	38.30	0.3703	0.8823	96,855	1925.3
1971	147.6	41.55	0.3903	0.8798	124,309	1997.9
1972	155.8	45.62	0.4121	0.8874	147,269	2091.5
1973	169.4	49.82	0.4480	0.9057	145,286	2180.6
1974	188.4	53.82	0.4982	0.9232	112,349	2234.3
1975	204.9	57.42	0.5420	0.9147	95,170	2269.4
1976	219.3	62.02	0.5799	0.9199	117,727	2326.2
1977	244.3	67.79	0.6460	0.9604	142,412	2406.1
1978	274.6	73.89	0.7261	1.0061	151,261	2492.7
1979	307.8	80.70	0.8140	1.0356	143,049	2568.8
1980	337.9	87.40	0.8938	1.0432	112,310	2612.1
1981	365.3	92.20	0.9662	1.0280	102,714	2644.6
1982	378.1	100.00	1.0000	1.0000	84,676	2658.2
1983	386.4	105.90	1.0220	0.9836	122,819	2709.6
1984	400.7	111.90	1.0598	0.9836	145,166	2782.0
1985	409.5	115.10	1.0831	0.9760	146,311	2853.5
1986	420.2	117.30	1.1113	0.9760	168,406	2945.3
1987	439.5	119.70	1.1624	0.9892	167,459	3033.6
1988	452.7	122.70	1.1973	0.9864	165,459	3117.5

deflating the construction cost index by the quality index gives the constant-quality construction cost index. This is divided by the GNP total implicit price deflator to give the housing price index. Note that for the period 1929–88, the housing price index coincides with the ratio of the GNP residential investment implicit price index to the GNP total implicit price index. This housing price index does *not* include land cost and hence probably systematically understates the growth in real housing prices. If prices of existing dwellings were determined by the cost of new dwellings at the margin, this index would be reasonably accurate for all housing. However, the substantial urbanization and growth of cities over the last century, with increased transportation cost from the periphery to the center, has probably increased the value of sites near the center of cities relative to sites at the edge and hence increased the gap between average prices of existing dwellings and of new dwellings, adjusting for quality. In addition, population migration between regions creates a gap between sales-weighted prices of existing dwellings and prices of new dwellings. Taken together, these reservations suggest that the housing price index be treated with caution.

Real housing investment in table 7.5 is obtained by first splicing expenditures for new residential construction (Historical Series N72, 1869–1914) to value of new residential construction put in place (Historical Series N32, 1915–1988), and then deflating these by the constant-quality construction cost index. This is then a constant-quality real residential investment series. This series is then accumulated to obtain a constant-quality residential real capital stock. For this accumulation, a depreciation rate of 2.687 percent and a growth rate of real investment prior to 1869 of 3.6 percent were assumed. These rates were chosen so that the stock series is commensurate with the Department of Commerce's value of net stocks of residential structures (Historical Series N208) between 1925 and 1970. With this construction, the two series have the same mean (in 1982 dollars) and a correlation of 0.99964 over this period.

In the absence of capital market imperfections and transactions costs, there is a simple relationship between housing prices and the user cost, or implicit rent, for housing. Let P_t denote nominal housing price in year t, π_t denote the GNP implicit price deflator, r_t denote the nominal interest rate, m_t denote the marginal income tax rate, δ denote the depreciation/maintenance rate, τ denote the property tax rate, θ denote the proportion of property mortgaged, and g denote the rate of nominal capital gains, $g_t = (P_{t+1} - P_t)/P_t$. Then, the nominal present value of the outlay from a purchase followed by a sale one year later is

$$(4) \qquad C_t = (1 - \theta)P_t + r_t\theta P_t + \delta P_t + \tau_t P_t - m_t(r_t\theta + \tau_t)P_t \\ + (1 - r_t)(\theta P_t - P_{t+1}).$$

The first term in this expression is the down payment, the second is the mortgage interest payment, the third is the maintenance (to offset depreciation), the fourth is the property tax payment, the fifth is the income tax offset from the deductability of mortgage interest and property taxes, and the sixth is the net outlay from selling the dwelling and repaying the mortgage, discounted to period t. Neglecting products of small rates and converting to real user cost, equation (4) simplifies to

$$(5) \qquad C_t = (P_t/\pi_t)[r_t(1 - \theta m_t) + \tau_t(1 - m_t) + \delta - g_t].$$

Ex ante, the consumer must form expectations regarding the nominal capital gains rate g_t. I consider four simplistic models of expectations: (1) naive expectations that last year's rate will continue (LAG1), (2) naive expectations that the average rate over the past three years will prevail (LAG3), (3) perfect foresight regarding the rate over the next year (LEAD1), and (4) perfect foresight regarding the rate over the next three years (LEAD3). The perfect foresight models should capture some of the behavioral response one would expect if consumers have forward-looking rational expectations, although of course they neglect the statistical properties of rational expectations.

Table 7.8 gives the real user cost of housing under each of the expectations models. The home mortgage interest rate in this table is the Federal Home Loan Bank Board new home mortgage rate after 1962. From 1919 to 1962, it is approximated by the Moody's Aaa corporate Bond Rate (Historical Series X447), plus the net risk premium that prevailed between these rates in 1963–88. From 1869 to 1918, it is approximated by the unadjusted index of yields on American railroad bonds (Historical Series 476), plus the sum of the previous net risk premium and the net risk premium between corporate and railroad bonds that prevailed in 1919–36. This construction has some obvious flaws. The protected status of the home mortgage rate from the 1930s through the late 1970s produced lower net risk premiums in this era than presumably prevailed at other times. Then, the splicing used probably overstates home mortgage rates from 1936 to 1962 and understates them earlier than 1936.

The marginal income tax rate in table 7.8 was calculated by computing in each year average nominal family income for a married couple with two dependents and, for this income level, taking the marginal tax rate from U.S. Treasury data (U.S. Department of Commerce, *Statistical Abstract* 1989, table 511). Prior to 1954, the effective (average) tax rate (Historical Series Y426–439) was used, scaled by the ratio of marginal to average rates in 1954–70. This construction is biased because adjusted gross income of families is somewhat overstated and the progressivity of the tax has changed over time, in addition to the obvious bias in using a "representative" family size and income level for a rate that is nonlinear over sizes and incomes.

The nominal annual capital gains rates in table 7.8 are computed from the real housing price index in table 7.7 and the GNP implicit price deflator in table 7.6, for each of the expectations models described earlier. The real user costs are then calculated for each expectations model using equation (5) and assuming that 70 percent of home purchases are mortgage financed, that the depreciation rate is 2.687 percent, and that the property tax rate is 2 percent.[2] The real user costs are denominated in 1982 dollars, with the price of housing indexed to one in this year.

7.4. The Age Distribution of Income and Housing Assets

Mankiw and Weil (1989) have used the 1970 1-in-1,000 Public Use Sample from the U.S. Census, containing 203,190 individuals grouped into 74,565 households, to run the regression

---

2. The property tax rate varies widely across states, and its national average has fallen from 2.02 in 1974 to 1.36 in 1984, a period of extraordinary increases in real housing prices.

Table 7.8   User Cost of Housing

Year	Home Mortgage Interest Rate	Marginal Income Tax Rate	Nominal Annual Capital Gains Rate				Real User Cost of Housing			
			LAG1	LAG3	LEAD1	LEAD3	LAG1	LAG3	LEAD1	LEAD3
1869	8.093	0.000			−9.817	−2.279			0.136	
1870	7.883	0.000	−10.333		4.031	0.329			0.049	
1871	7.743	0.000	3.952		−0.460	−3.494			0.082	
1872	7.563	0.000	−0.461	−2.279	−2.472	−6.601	0.072	0.083	0.084	0.107
1873	7.723	0.000	−2.503	0.329	−7.252	−7.095	0.094	0.076	0.124	0.123
1874	7.493	0.000	−7.528	−3.494	−9.327	−7.032	0.118	0.094	0.128	0.115
1875	7.023	0.000	−9.791	−6.601	−3.909	−5.672	0.119	0.101	0.087	0.096
1876	6.643	0.000	−3.987	−7.095	−7.077	−5.597	0.085	0.102	0.102	0.094
1877	6.583	0.000	−7.340	−7.032	−5.545	−0.441	0.097	0.095	0.088	0.061
1878	6.413	0.000	−5.704	−5.672	−3.694	3.316	0.092	0.091	0.081	0.042
1879	5.943	0.000	−3.764	−5.597	8.484	6.115	0.076	0.086	0.011	0.024
1880	5.563	0.000	8.144	−0.441	5.736	3.480	0.012	0.059	0.025	0.038
1881	5.153	0.000	5.577	3.316	4.753	−2.158	0.024	0.037	0.029	0.068
1882	5.203	0.000	4.644	6.115	0.230	−3.882	0.030	0.022	0.056	0.079
1883	5.193	0.000	0.230	3.480	−10.733	−1.842	0.059	0.039	0.127	0.072
1884	5.113	0.000	−11.354	−2.158	−0.532	1.724	0.125	0.071	0.061	0.048
1885	4.853	0.000	−0.533	−3.882	6.563	0.683	0.061	0.081	0.018	0.054
1886	4.513	0.000	6.356	−1.842	−0.643	−1.562	0.018	0.070	0.063	0.069
1887	4.613	0.000	−0.645	1.724	−3.593	−1.264	0.063	0.048	0.082	0.067
1888	4.553	0.000	−3.659	0.683	−0.387	−1.255	0.076	0.051	0.057	0.062
1889	4.393	0.000	−0.388	−1.562	0.252	−2.193	0.052	0.059	0.049	0.062
1890	4.513	0.000	0.252	−1.264	−3.567	−2.454	0.050	0.059	0.072	0.066
1891	4.673	0.000	−3.633	−1.255	−3.155	−2.532	0.071	0.058	0.069	0.065

Year										
1892	4.493	0.000	−3.205	−2.193	−0.531	−2.025	0.069	0.063	0.054	0.062
1893	4.613	0.000	−0.532	−2.454	−3.793	−1.744	0.053	0.064	0.071	0.060
1894	4.373	0.000	−3.866	−2.532	−1.668	−1.214	0.072	0.064	0.059	0.057
1895	4.233	0.000	−1.682	−2.025	0.312	0.681	0.059	0.060	0.048	0.046
1896	4.303	0.000	0.311	−1.744	−2.249	2.819	0.049	0.061	0.064	0.035
1897	4.073	0.000	−2.274	−1.214	4.089	5.258	0.061	0.055	0.026	0.019
1898	3.993	0.000	4.008	0.681	6.964	3.425	0.026	0.045	0.010	0.029
1899	3.813	0.000	6.732	2.819	5.181	2.239	0.010	0.033	0.109	0.036
1900	3.853	0.000	5.051	5.258	−1.488	1.653	0.020	0.019	0.058	0.040
1901	3.793	0.000	−1.499	3.425	3.223	1.676	0.058	0.029	0.030	0.039
1902	3.803	0.000	3.172	2.239	3.345	2.064	0.031	0.036	0.030	0.037
1903	3.993	0.000	3.291	1.653	−1.419	4.022	0.032	0.041	0.060	0.027
1904	3.943	0.000	−1.430	1.676	4.434	5.877	0.058	0.040	0.024	0.016
1905	3.853	0.000	4.339	2.064	9.602	3.286	0.025	0.038	−0.006	0.031
1906	3.963	0.000	9.169	4.022	4.228	1.401	−0.003	0.029	0.028	0.046
1907	4.233	0.000	4.141	5.877	−3.383	1.081	0.030	0.019	0.077	0.049
1908	4.183	0.000	−3.441	3.286	3.569	1.700	0.075	0.034	0.032	0.044
1909	4.033	0.000	3.507	1.401	3.233	1.260	0.032	0.045	0.034	0.046
1910	4.143	0.000	3.182	1.081	−1.572	−1.084	0.035	0.048	0.064	0.061
1911	4.153	0.000	−1.585	1.700	2.210	−0.451	0.064	0.044	0.040	0.057
1912	4.193	0.000	2.186	1.260	−3.782	−0.446	0.040	0.046	0.076	0.056
1913	4.403	0.000	−3.855	−1.084	0.317	2.820	0.075	0.059	0.051	0.036
1914	4.403	0.000	0.316	−0.451	2.224	7.990	0.050	0.054	0.039	0.006
1915	4.583	0.000	2.200	−0.446	6.134	12.956	0.039	0.054	0.018	−0.021
1916	4.453	0.000	5.953	2.820	17.165	15.815	0.017	0.033	−0.042	−0.035
1917	4.753	0.000	15.841	7.990	18.665	18.932	−0.032	0.007	−0.046	−0.047
1918	5.193	0.000	17.114	12.956	15.647	5.883	−0.038	−0.016	−0.030	0.021
1919	6.277	0.000	14.537	15.815	28.661	−1.779	−0.019	−0.026	−0.094	0.068
1920	6.907	0.000	25.201	18.932	−19.805	−6.581	−0.082	−0.044	0.189	0.109
1921	6.757	0.000	−22.071	5.883	−8.124	0.214	0.194	0.032	0.113	0.065
1922	5.887	0.000	−8.474	−1.779	11.383	2.595	0.110	0.072	−0.005	0.046
1923	5.907	0.000	10.781	−6.581	−1.650	−0.727	−0.001	0.108	0.077	0.071

(*continued*)

Table 7.8   (continued)

Year	Home Mortgage Interest Rate	Marginal Income Tax Rate	Nominal Annual Capital Gains Rate				Real User Cost of Housing			
			LAG1	LAG3	LEAD1	LEAD3	LAG1	LAG3	LEAD1	LEAD3
1924	5.787	0.000	-1.664	0.214	-1.317	-0.734	0.075	0.064	0.073	0.070
1925	5.667	0.000	-1.326	2.595	0.809	-0.260	0.071	0.047	0.058	0.064
1926	5.517	0.000	0.806	-0.727	-1.669	0.897	0.058	0.068	0.073	0.058
1927	5.357	0.000	-1.684	-0.734	0.098	0.572	0.073	0.067	0.062	0.059
1928	5.337	0.000	0.098	-0.260	4.371	-2.761	0.061	0.063	0.035	0.078
1929	5.517	0.000	4.278	0.897	-2.625	-11.100	0.038	0.060	0.082	0.137
1930	5.337	0.000	-2.660	0.572	-9.434	-10.459	0.081	0.061	0.125	0.131
1931	5.367	0.000	-9.909	-2.761	-18.750	-3.663	0.128	0.082	0.184	0.088
1932	5.797	0.000	-20.764	-11.100	-0.733	2.918	0.181	0.125	0.065	0.044
1933	5.277	0.000	-0.735	-10.459	11.070	4.798	0.063	0.120	-0.006	0.030
1934	4.787	0.000	10.499	-3.663	-0.997	4.350	-0.006	0.080	0.064	0.031
1935	4.387	0.000	-1.002	2.918	5.034	5.828	0.060	0.037	0.024	0.019
1936	4.027	0.000	4.911	4.798	9.585	4.380	0.024	0.024	-0.005	0.027
1937	4.047	0.000	9.153	4.350	3.499	2.433	-0.003	0.029	0.034	0.041
1938	3.977	0.000	3.439	5.828	0.563	4.223	0.036	0.020	0.056	0.031
1939	3.797	0.000	0.562	4.380	3.361	6.427	0.056	0.029	0.036	0.014
1940	3.627	0.000	3.306	2.433	9.214	8.056	0.036	0.042	-0.006	0.002
1941	3.557	3.393	8.814	4.223	7.444	8.231	-0.005	0.028	0.005	-0.001
1942	3.617	13.672	7.180	6.427	8.545	7.904	0.004	0.009	-0.006	-0.002
1943	3.517	16.840	8.199	8.056	9.787	7.965	-0.005	-0.004	-0.016	-0.004
1944	3.507	19.231	9.337	8.231	6.395	10.955	-0.015	-0.007	0.007	-0.027
1945	3.407	19.224	6.199	7.904	8.743	12.869	0.008	-0.005	-0.012	-0.044
1946	3.317	15.660	8.382	7.965	20.101	9.116	-0.008	-0.005	-0.097	-0.014

1947	3.397	15.866	18.316	10.955	12.692	4.672	-0.089	-0.029	-0.043	0.022
1948	3.607	12.812	11.949	12.869	-2.847	3.069	-0.037	-0.045	0.091	0.040
1949	3.447	12.749	-2.888	9.116	5.096	4.847	0.088	-0.013	0.021	0.023
1950	3.407	13.405	4.970	4.672	7.394	3.593	0.022	0.025	0.001	0.034
1951	3.647	18.103	7.133	3.069	2.483	0.670	0.003	0.039	0.044	0.060
1952	3.747	19.524	2.453	4.847	1.211	0.761	0.045	0.024	0.056	0.060
1953	3.987	19.655	1.204	3.593	-1.632	1.936	0.058	0.037	0.083	0.051
1954	3.687	17.993	-1.646	0.670	2.765	3.294	0.079	0.059	0.041	0.037
1955	3.847	19.754	2.728	0.761	4.844	2.452	0.042	0.060	0.024	0.045
1956	4.147	19.889	4.730	1.936	2.464	1.894	0.028	0.052	0.048	0.053
1957	4.677	20.022	2.434	3.294	0.200	1.532	0.051	0.044	0.071	0.059
1958	4.577	22.000	0.200	2.452	3.100	1.625	0.067	0.048	0.043	0.055
1959	5.167	22.000	3.053	1.894	1.358	1.143	0.048	0.058	0.063	0.065
1960	5.197	22.000	1.349	1.532	0.478	1.373	0.063	0.061	0.070	0.063
1961	5.137	22.000	0.477	1.625	1.619	2.238	0.069	0.060	0.060	0.054
1962	5.117	22.000	1.606	1.143	2.062	2.262	0.060	0.064	0.056	0.054
1963	5.890	22.000	2.041	1.373	3.122	2.503	0.062	0.068	0.053	0.058
1964	5.820	22.000	3.074	2.238	1.692	3.058	0.054	0.061	0.066	0.054
1965	5.810	22.000	1.678	2.262	2.802	4.238	0.066	0.061	0.056	0.043
1966	6.250	22.201	2.764	2.503	4.855	5.311	0.059	0.062	0.041	0.037
1967	6.460	22.494	4.741	3.058	5.361	4.284	0.044	0.059	0.039	0.048
1968	6.970	24.190	5.223	4.238	6.168	4.296	0.043	0.052	0.035	0.051
1969	7.800	25.043	5.985	5.311	1.670	4.117	0.042	0.049	0.082	0.060
1970	8.450	25.600	1.657	4.284	5.400	6.344	0.083	0.060	0.050	0.042
1971	7.740	27.267	5.259	4.296	5.600	8.128	0.045	0.054	0.042	0.020

(continued)

Table 7.8 (continued)

Year	Home Mortgage Interest Rate	Marginal Income Tax Rate	Nominal Annual Capital Gains Rate				Real User Cost of Housing			
			LAG1	LAG3	LEAD1	LEAD3	LAG1	LAG3	LEAD1	LEAD3
1972	7.600	28.783	5.449	4.117	8.700	9.122	0.042	0.054	0.013	0.009
1973	7.960	30.827	8.342	6.344	11.200	8.597	0.018	0.036	-0.008	0.016
1974	8.920	32.367	10.616	8.128	8.800	8.657	0.003	0.026	0.020	0.021
1975	9.000	34.000	8.434	9.122	7.000	9.741	0.022	0.016	0.035	0.010
1976	9.000	35.441	6.766	8.597	11.400	11.291	0.037	0.020	-0.006	-0.005
1977	9.020	37.045	10.796	8.657	12.400	10.809	-0.002	0.019	-0.017	-0.002
1978	9.560	39.034	11.689	9.741	12.100	9.510	-0.008	0.011	-0.013	0.014
1979	10.780	41.000	11.422	11.291	9.800	6.852	0.001	0.003	0.018	0.049
1980	12.660	42.000	9.349	10.809	8.100	4.464	0.036	0.021	0.049	0.087
1981	14.700	42.000	7.789	9.510	3.500	3.080	0.066	0.048	0.110	0.115
1982	15.140	42.000	3.440	6.852	2.200	2.659	0.111	0.077	0.123	0.119
1983	12.570	42.000	2.176	4.464	3.700	2.789	0.104	0.081	0.089	0.098
1984	12.380	38.000	3.633	3.080	2.200	3.077	0.092	0.098	0.106	0.098
1985	11.550	38.000	2.176	2.659	2.600	3.337	0.100	0.095	0.096	0.089
1986	10.170	30.000	2.567	2.789	4.600		0.093	0.091	0.073	
1987	9.310	30.000	4.497	3.077	3.000		0.069	0.083	0.084	
1988	9.190	30.000	2.956	3.337			0.083	0.079		

(6)
$$v_{ht} = \sum_{a=0}^{99} \alpha_{at} n_{aht} + \varepsilon_{ht},$$

where h indexes households, t indexes census years, v is the (self-reported) value of the residence, with the value of rental property imputed to be 100 times gross monthly rent, and n_{aht} is the number of persons of age a in household h. Then, the α_{at} estimate the consumption of housing by age in census year t. This formulation does not adjust for economies of scale in household formation and thus is likely to overpredict the demand of large households and underpredict the demand of small ones; on household formation and housing consumption, see Börsch-Supan (1989).

I extend this approach to the allocation of income, as well as the allocation of housing consumption, and address the econometric problem of endogenous selection of tenure status. Analogously to equation (6), consider the regression

(7)
$$y_{ht} = \sum_{i=1}^{20} \psi_{it} K_{hit} + \eta_{ht},$$

where y_{ht} is the income of household h in census year t, and K_{hit} is the number of household members in cohort i. Cohort i contains ages a satisfying the inequalities $5(i - 1) \leq a < 5i$, for $i = 1, \ldots, 19$, or the inequality $a \geq 95$ when $i = 20$. The coefficient ψ_{it} can be interpreted as the marginal contribution to household income from an individual in cohort i in census year t. Determining age-specific income by this imputation method has several advantages. First, it avoids the misspecification that occurs when household income is associated with the age of the head of the household, since household size, income contributions from other household members, and the age distribution of household members are all likely to be correlated with the age of the head. Second, it avoids the selection bias that occurs because income of an individual may endogenously enter the determination of whether the individual lives alone or as a member of a larger household, say, with children.

In setting up a model of housing demand, we will start from an age-specific individual indirect utility function and explicitly aggregate to obtain market demand. Then, aggregate demand will depend not only on aggregate income but also on the age distribution of this income. Let N_{it} denote the population in cohort i in year t, and let N_t denote the total population. Then average real income per capita satisfies $Y_t = \sum_i N_{it} \psi_{it}/N_t$. Define an aggregation factor relative to a base census year 0,

(8)
$$\psi_t = \left[\sum_i \psi_{i0} N_{it}/N_t \right] / \left[\sum_i \psi_{i0} N_{i0}/N_0 \right].$$

If the age distribution of relative income is stationary, so that an increase in aggregate income "raises all boats," then age-specific relative income satisfies

(9)
$$\psi_{it}/\psi_{i0} = (Y_t/Y_0)/\psi_t;$$

the deflator ψ_t adjusts for changes in the population age distribution so that aggregation is consistent.

To examine the assumption that the age distribution of relative income is stationary, I run the regression (7) on the U.S. Census Public Use Samples for 1940, 1960, 1970, and 1980.[3] The estimation results are given in table 7.9. Figure 7.8 shows the age distributions of income, and figure 7.9 shows these distributions normalized by income in the 40–44 age bracket, for each census year. There is stability in the relative income distributions between 1960 and 1980. However, the elderly are substantially poorer in the 1940 relative income profile. This is due in part to the lingering effects of a decade of depression but shows primarily the contrast of the status of the elderly before and after full implementation of the Social Security system. Figure 7.10 shows the 1970 income distribution with 95 percent confidence bounds. One sees that the distribution is tightly determined up to age 75, but that the confidence bounds are larger for older individuals, so that trends are less reliably determined for the very old.

I conclude from this analysis that the age distribution of income is indeed stable after World War II. Provided there are no major changes in the Social Security system over the next century, it is not unreasonable to assume that the age distribution of income will remain stable. Factors that could alter this conclusion would be (1) high immigration rates of relatively unskilled workers, which would tend to flatten the income distribution at younger ages, (2) a declining share of manufacturing and unskilled jobs, which would tend to postpone the peak, and (3) delays in retirement, which would postpone the decline after the peak.[4]

I next examine the age distribution of housing consumption in the 1940, 1960, 1970, and 1980 Census Public Use Samples, using the Mankiw-Weil model (6) adapted to five-year cohorts,

$$(10) \qquad v_{ht} = \sum_{i=0}^{20} \alpha_{it} K_{iht} + \varepsilon_{ht}.$$

Rather than impute a value to rental property, I run these regressions only on home owners. To correct for selection bias caused by endogenous choice of tenure, I estimate probit models of tenure choice, of the form

$$(11) \qquad Prob(\text{owner}) = \Phi(\gamma_0 + \gamma_1 y_{ht} + \gamma_2 (y_{ht})^2/1000 + \sum_{i=0}^{20} \beta_{it} K_{iht}).$$

Then, an inverse Mills ratio calculated from this probit equation is added to equation (10) to absorb the nonzero conditional expectation of ε_{ht} in the presence of selection; see Henderson and Ioannides (1983) for a discussion of selection due to tenure choice.

Table 7.10 gives the probit model estimates. In specification (11), the proba-

3. Income and house value were not collected in the 1950 Public Use Sample.
4. Note that under retirement policies prevailing over the past several decades, average retirement age is falling and length of life in retirement is rising sharply. It is possible that policy changes in the next several decades to reduce the burden of the Social Security system will reverse these trends.

Table 7.9   Individual Income by Age (thousand 1982 $)

Age	1940		1960		1970		1980	
	Coefficient	Standard Deviation	Coefficient	Standard Deviation	Coefficient	Standard Deviation	Coefficient	Standard Deviation
0–4	−0.877	0.061	−0.619	0.086	−0.651	0.171	−1.285	0.124
5–9	−0.924	0.060	−0.753	0.092	−1.013	0.110	−1.477	0.124
10–14	−0.730	0.059	−0.657	0.097	−0.380	0.110	−1.071	0.117
15–19	−0.049	0.058	0.786	0.110	1.511	0.119	0.735	0.111
20–24	2.683	0.058	6.076	0.117	7.640	0.121	7.393	0.115
25–29	3.990	0.060	9.117	0.121	12.460	0.138	11.775	0.120
30–34	4.609	0.063	10.478	0.117	13.940	0.155	14.626	0.127
35–39	4.764	0.065	11.464	0.113	14.702	0.157	16.052	0.143
40–44	4.642	0.068	11.281	0.116	15.200	0.148	16.213	0.151
45–49	4.265	0.071	10.712	0.116	14.875	0.139	15.704	0.150
50–54	3.651	0.074	10.226	0.119	13.638	0.143	14.679	0.139
55–59	2.785	0.084	8.932	0.126	12.371	0.149	13.746	0.139
60–64	2.098	0.092	7.816	0.141	10.596	0.160	11.630	0.155
65–69	0.806	0.103	5.509	0.152	7.396	0.179	8.027	0.175
70–74	0.368	0.125	3.932	0.176	5.971	0.205	7.390	0.207
75–79	0.246	0.168	3.198	0.225	5.727	0.252	6.156	0.269
80–84	0.321	0.238	3.097	0.336	4.667	0.342	6.484	0.389
85–89	0.437	0.408	3.235	0.536	4.411	0.553	4.789	0.582
90–94	−0.586	0.787	0.500	1.109	5.180	1.059	3.862	0.888
95+	−1.735	1.440	0.523	2.225	5.043	2.125		
Observations	51,159		52,982		63,408		58,706	
Standard Error	8.016		12.775		16.316		15.869	
Mean Income	7.748		18.013		22.754		26.225	

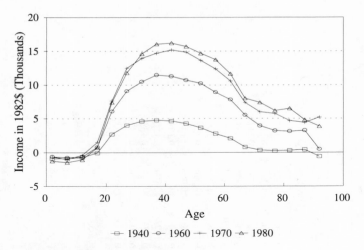

Fig. 7.8   Age distribution of income

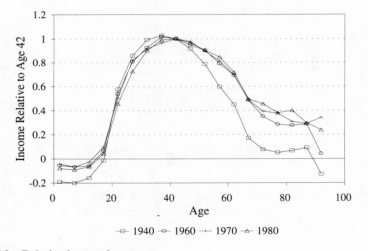

Fig. 7.9   Relative income by age

bility of ownership is related to income and, via the terms K_{iht}, to the size and age composition of the household. The estimates for 1960, 1970, and 1980 are qualitatively similar. Small children living at home have a small positive impact on ownership. Individuals between the ages of 20 and 30 have a negative impact, obviously because they are forming new households without the wealth required for home purchase. This effect became significantly stronger in 1980, compared with the earlier census years. There is a sharply increasing positive impact beginning at age 30 and peaking around age 70. The model

Table 7.10 Probability of Home Ownership (binomial probit)

Variables	1940 Coefficient	1940 Standard Deviation	1960 Coefficient	1960 Standard Deviation	1970 Coefficient	1970 Standard Deviation	1980 Coefficient	1980 Standard Deviation
Number aged 0–4	−0.043	0.010	0.081	0.009	0.105	0.010	0.060	0.011
Number aged 5–9	−0.015	0.010	0.086	0.010	0.097	0.009	0.044	0.011
Number aged 10–14	0.008	0.009	0.088	0.011	0.071	0.010	0.004	0.011
Number aged 15–19	0.017	0.009	0.016	0.012	0.048	0.011	−0.020	0.011
Number aged 20–24	−0.057	0.010	−0.201	0.015	−0.159	0.013	−0.166	0.013
Number aged 25–29	−0.044	0.011	0.042	0.016	0.080	0.014	−0.247	0.015
Number aged 30–34	0.049	0.012	0.205	0.016	0.265	0.016	0.210	0.016
Number aged 35–39	0.138	0.013	0.306	0.016	0.360	0.017	0.331	0.018
Number aged 40–44	0.242	0.013	0.351	0.016	0.462	0.016	0.393	0.019
Number aged 45–49	0.317	0.013	0.414	0.016	0.509	0.015	0.440	0.019
Number aged 50–54	0.395	0.013	0.453	0.016	0.554	0.016	0.475	0.018
Number aged 55–59	0.446	0.015	0.452	0.017	0.576	0.016	0.516	0.018
Number aged 60–64	0.519	0.016	0.518	0.018	0.626	0.017	0.543	0.020
Number aged 65–69	0.518	0.018	0.587	0.020	0.644	0.018	0.601	0.021
Number aged 70–74	0.521	0.021	0.618	0.021	0.671	0.020	0.522	0.023
Number aged 75–79	0.525	0.028	0.597	0.027	0.630	0.024	0.529	0.027
Number aged 80–84	0.487	0.039	0.610	0.040	0.602	0.031	0.555	0.041
Number aged 85–89	0.529	0.068	0.574	0.064	0.709	0.050	0.430	0.058
Number aged 90–94	0.477	0.133	0.386	0.128	0.495	0.092	0.361	0.090
Number aged 95+	0.417	0.231	0.011	0.234	0.962	0.236	NA	NA
Constant	−0.618	0.017	−0.685	0.020	−0.829	0.018	−0.818	0.026
HH income	−0.014	0.002	0.024	0.001	0.024	0.001	0.052	0.001
HH income SQ/1000	0.529	0.048	−0.148	0.019	−0.131	0.001	−0.248	0.016
Observations	51,159		50,795		61,534		57,549	
Share owners	0.564		0.645		0.648		0.751	
Percent correct	0.640		0.704		0.719		0.796	

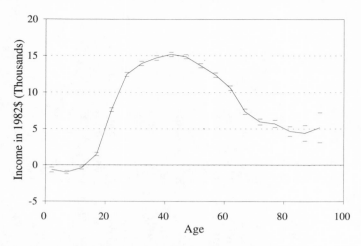

Fig. 7.10   1970 Income by age (with 95% confidence bounds)

implies that the impact of household size is the sum of the impacts of its members of various ages. This specification is likely to miss scale effects with family size and thus to overpredict ownership for large families and underpredict ownership for small ones. In the range of the data, the marginal effect of income on ownership is positive but decreasing and is near zero over age 80. In part, the last phenomenon may be due to the fact that ownership is closely tied to permanent income, and current income for the elderly is not necessarily a good proxy for permanent income. The 1940 estimates show a somewhat different pattern, with the number of individuals between ages 30 and 39 having a small impact on ownership, presumably because these individuals did not have the assets required to form households or purchase property during the depression, in what would otherwise have been a prime decade for house purchase. The marginal effect of income is positive and increasing.

Table 7.11 reports the house value regression (10) for owners, with and without the inverse Mills ratio correction for selection bias. I have not corrected the standard errors of the coefficients to account for the fact that the inverse Mills ratio is estimated, but the probit model coefficients are so precisely determined in samples of this size that the corrections would be negligible. Table 7.12 gives the housing regression estimates, relative to age 40–44, for 1970, unadjusted and adjusted for selection. The table includes cohort averages of the estimates obtained by Mankiw and Weil. These profiles are plotted in figure 7.11. I find that the regressions in table 7.12 give a sharper peak than do the Mankiw-Weil estimates. One possible explanation for this is that the procedure that Mankiw and Weil use to impute value to rental units overstates the value of these units for the very young or for the elderly, relative to middle-aged individuals. Another is that the inverse Mills ratio, which depends on household income, is correlated with an omitted income effect on housing consumption in equation (10), so that the adjusted regression overcorrects for selection. Investigation of these alternatives is left for future research.

One would expect that individuals with relatively high demand for housing services are more likely to select ownership, so that selection would lead a regression on owners to overstate population mean housing consumption. Further, the selection correction should be weakest for population cohorts where ownership rates are very high, and strongest for cohorts where rates are near one-half. I find a relatively small correction for selection, which goes in the expected direction, reducing the consumption levels of the young and the old relative to the middle-aged.

In analysis of housing demand, I use the 1970 housing consumption relatives, obtained from the regression adjusted for selection. Figure 7.12 shows 95 percent confidence bounds for this profile. The curve is precisely determined for individuals up to age 85, but is less accurate for the very old. Following Mankiw and Weil, I will make the assumption that the profile in figure 7.12 is stationary through time, with aggregate income and price affecting aggregate housing demand but not age-specific relative demand. Microeconomic considerations suggest that this assumption cannot be correct, as housing markets embody substantial transactions costs that will to some degree "lock in" individuals to historical housing units and induce a profile of consumption that is sensitive to history. In particular, periods of high income growth, not fully anticipated, will in the presence of transactions costs lead the elderly to lag further behind in relative housing consumption, while periods of unanticipated capital gains will tend to raise the consumption of individuals holding housing assets at the start of the period relative to individuals who enter the market later.

An empirical assessment of the importance of transaction cost effects, and the consequent instability in the profile of relative housing consumption, can be made by comparing profiles estimated for different census years. Figure 7.13 shows housing consumption profiles, in real dollars, obtained from the adjusted regressions in table 7.11. These profiles show an upward drift over time, as expected given real per capita income growth over this period. It is perhaps noteworthy that there is no systematic increase for the very young or very old, but the statistics for the latter group are not determined very precisely. Recall from figure 7.8 that real income increased substantially from 1960 to 1970, across all cohorts, but increased very little from 1970 to 1980. On the other hand, real housing consumption increased substantially in both decades. This suggests either that user cost of housing was lower in the decade of the 1970s, and demand was sensitive to user cost, or else that transactions costs were sufficient to "lock in" consumers to unintended housing consumption at the end of the 1970s.

Figure 7.14 shows the housing consumption profiles for 1940, 1960, 1970, and 1980 relative to consumption at ages 40–44. These profiles are remarkably stable between 1960 and 1980. The profile for 1940 shows less relative housing

Table 7.11   **Housing Consumption by Age**

Variable: Age Cohort	1940				1960			
	Unadjusted Coefficient	Standard Deviation	Adjusted Coefficient	Standard Deviation	Unadjusted Coefficient	Standard Deviation	Adjusted Coefficient	Standard Deviation
0–4	−0.583	0.435	−2.717	0.437	3.034	0.309	2.430	0.308
5–9	−2.497	0.404	−3.378	0.400	0.733	0.307	0.841	0.304
10–14	−2.149	0.365	−2.525	0.360	−0.324	0.311	−0.188	0.309
15–19	−2.030	0.346	−2.479	0.342	−1.295	0.364	−1.575	0.362
20–24	2.754	0.376	0.893	0.377	4.792	0.484	0.745	0.513
25–29	6.859	0.419	3.129	0.438	14.354	0.445	10.335	0.476
30–34	12.012	0.429	7.319	0.461	18.321	0.396	15.229	0.417
35–39	15.170	0.414	10.699	0.444	20.593	0.366	18.015	0.381
40–44	17.156	0.407	13.081	0.432	20.598	0.367	18.222	0.379
45–49	17.478	0.405	14.022	0.421	18.583	0.362	16.550	0.370
50–54	15.994	0.408	13.222	0.416	17.376	0.367	15.499	0.374
55–59	12.877	0.443	10.475	0.447	15.612	0.394	13.377	0.404
60–64	12.863	0.469	11.010	0.468	15.441	0.432	13.226	0.440
65–69	11.536	0.524	9.522	0.522	13.016	0.467	10.847	0.473
70–74	10.601	0.629	8.718	0.625	12.145	0.538	9.918	0.543
75–79	11.408	0.840	9.265	0.831	9.342	0.690	7.152	0.692
80–84	9.093	1.190	7.430	1.175	10.973	1.029	9.244	1.024
85–89	12.170	2.020	11.652	1.991	8.656	1.659	7.244	1.648
90–94	7.040	3.842	6.109	3.787	6.946	3.514	5.360	3.488
95+	−1.875	7.279	−3.857	7.175	5.985	7.140	3.073	7.087
Mills	NA	NA	13.029	0.509	NA	NA	13.113	0.584
Observations	22,310		22,310		32,772		32,772	
Standard error	32.538		32.071		33.468		33.214	

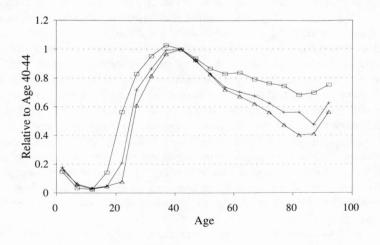

‑□‑ Mankiw-Weil   ‑+‑ Unadjusted Reg.   ‑△‑ Adjusted Reg.

Fig. 7.11   1970 housing consumption

1970				1980				Variable: Age Cohort
Unadjusted Coefficient	Standard Deviation	Adjusted Coefficient	Standard Deviation	Unadjusted Coefficient	Standard Deviation	Adjusted Coefficient	Standard Deviation	
4.350	0.384	3.751	0.386	2.708	0.473	4.074	0.493	0–4
1.344	0.314	1.418	0.312	−0.069	0.444	0.917	0.459	5–9
0.665	0.297	0.707	0.296	0.941	0.404	1.701	0.418	10–14
1.064	0.325	1.052	0.324	−1.033	0.377	−0.315	0.389	15–19
5.098	0.433	1.764	0.463	5.300	0.433	6.341	0.493	20–24
17.393	0.435	13.849	0.469	19.507	0.435	20.237	0.513	25–29
20.983	0.439	18.552	0.454	27.391	0.432	27.338	0.470	30–34
24.092	0.274	21.990	0.438	30.287	0.473	30.159	0.500	35–39
24.267	0.391	22.754	0.410	29.293	0.491	29.068	0.515	40–44
22.339	0.362	21.066	0.366	26.156	0.477	26.068	0.498	45–49
20.159	0.369	18.796	0.373	23.423	0.432	23.578	0.454	50–54
17.860	0.385	16.357	0.390	22.585	0.423	22.464	0.449	55–59
17.050	0.414	15.291	0.421	20.601	0.462	20.543	0.502	60–64
16.396	0.473	14.123	0.483	19.124	0.510	18.553	0.575	65–69
15.143	0.544	12.746	0.555	18.461	0.598	17.466	0.700	70–74
13.570	0.681	10.734	0.692	16.785	0.749	14.208	0.900	75–79
13.630	0.940	9.143	0.301	17.202	1.050	14.651	1.277	80–84
11.520	1.486	9.326	1.482	14.009	1.535	10.304	1.917	85–89
15.215	2.912	12.787	2.901	11.855	2.427	8.033	2.935	90–94
15.134	5.240	15.251	5.214	NA	NA	NA	NA	95+
NA	NA	11.122	0.552	NA	NA	−6.746	0.935	Mills
39,851		39,851		52,280		47,745		Observations
36.670		36.479		48.148		48.003		Standard error

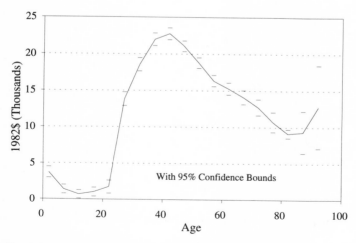

Fig. 7.12   1970 housing consumption (adjusted for selection)

Table 7.12   **1970 Housing Consumption Relative to Age 40–44**

Age cohort	Mankiw-Weil	Unadjusted Regression	Adjusted Regression
0–4	0.147	0.179	0.165
5–9	0.034	0.055	0.062
10–14	0.024	0.027	0.031
15–19	0.143	0.044	0.046
20–24	0.563	0.210	0.078
25–29	0.829	0.717	0.609
30–34	0.952	0.865	0.815
35–39	1.028	0.993	0.966
40–44	1.000	1.000	1.000
45–49	0.938	0.921	0.926
50–54	0.867	0.831	0.826
55–59	0.829	0.736	0.719
60–64	0.838	0.703	0.672
65–69	0.792	0.676	0.621
70–74	0.762	0.624	0.560
75–79	0.743	0.559	0.472
80–84	0.681	0.562	0.402
85–89	0.697	0.475	0.410
90–94	0.752	0.627	0.562
95+	0.459	0.624	0.670

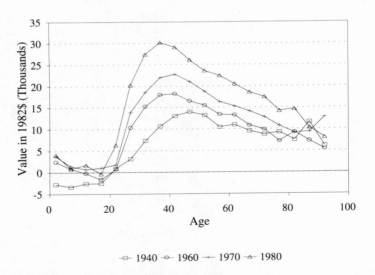

−□− 1940 −○− 1960 −+− 1970 −△− 1980

Fig. 7.13   Housing consumption by census year

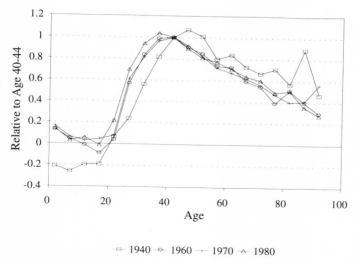

—□— 1940   —○— 1960   —+— 1970   —△— 1980

Fig. 7.14   Relative housing consumption

consumption for the cohorts between ages 25 and 39 than is observed in the later censuses. This is almost certainly attributable to the lack of consumer confidence and shortage of liquidity during the depression, when these cohorts might normally have been rapidly increasing their housing consumption. From this figure, I conclude that there is empirical justification for an assumption that the relative housing consumption profile is stable over time.

I use the 1970 adjusted regression coefficients, relative to the age 40–44 cohort, multiplied by the U.S. population from tables 7.1–7.3, to form estimates of housing demand at 1970 income and prices. Table 7.13 gives this demographic factor, normalized to one in 1982. Also calculated in this table is the aggregation factor ψ_t that will appear when individual income effects are aggregated. Figure 7.15 plots the demographic factor.

7.5   Supply and Demand for Housing

Supply of new housing per capita is modeled as a log linear function of current housing price, GNP per capita, and the mortgage interest rate,

$$(12) \qquad \log\left[\frac{\text{Invest}_t}{\text{Pop}_t}\right] = \theta_1 + \theta_2 \log\left[\text{Housing price}_t\right]$$
$$+ \theta_3 \log\left[\text{GNP per capita}_t\right] + \theta_4 \, \text{Intr}_t,$$

where the variables

Table 7.13   Income Aggregation Factor and Demographic Demand Factor

Year	Income Aggregation	Demographic Demand	Year	Income Aggregation	Demographic Demand	Year	Income Aggregation	Demographic Demand	Year	Income Aggregation	Demographic Demand
1900	0.926	0.277	1950	1.099	0.668	2000	1.183	1.283	2050	1.161	1.437
1901	0.929	0.283	1951	1.091	0.677	2001	1.185	1.290	2051	1.161	1.436
1902	0.931	0.289	1952	1.082	0.687	2002	1.187	1.298	2052	1.161	1.436
1903	0.934	0.296	1953	1.074	0.696	2003	1.190	1.305	2053	1.161	1.435
1904	0.937	0.302	1954	1.065	0.706	2004	1.192	1.313	2054	1.161	1.435
1905	0.939	0.309	1955	1.057	0.716	2005	1.194	1.320	2055	1.161	1.434
1906	0.945	0.317	1956	1.048	0.724	2006	1.195	1.327	2056	1.161	1.432
1907	0.951	0.325	1957	1.038	0.732	2007	1.196	1.334	2057	1.161	1.431
1908	0.958	0.333	1958	1.029	0.740	2008	1.197	1.341	2058	1.161	1.429
1909	0.964	0.341	1959	1.020	0.749	2009	1.198	1.348	2059	1.162	1.427
1910	0.970	0.350	1960	1.012	0.757	2010	1.198	1.355	2060	1.162	1.426
1911	0.973	0.357	1961	1.007	0.763	2011	1.197	1.361	2061	1.162	1.424
1912	0.975	0.365	1962	1.002	0.769	2012	1.196	1.368	2062	1.163	1.423
1913	0.978	0.373	1963	0.997	0.775	2013	1.195	1.375	2063	1.163	1.421
1914	0.981	0.381	1964	0.992	0.780	2014	1.194	1.382	2064	1.163	1.420
1915	0.984	0.389	1965	0.988	0.786	2015	1.193	1.388	2065	1.163	1.418
1916	0.986	0.395	1966	0.990	0.793	2016	1.191	1.394	2066	1.163	1.417
1917	0.989	0.401	1967	0.993	0.800	2017	1.188	1.400	2067	1.163	1.416
1918	0.992	0.407	1968	0.995	0.807	2018	1.186	1.405	2068	1.163	1.415
1919	0.995	0.413	1969	0.998	0.814	2019	1.184	1.411	2069	1.163	1.413
1920	0.997	0.419	1970	1.000	0.821	2020	1.181	1.417	2070	1.163	1.412
1921	0.999	0.427	1971	1.008	0.832	2021	1.179	1.420	2071	1.163	1.412
1922	1.000	0.435	1972	1.015	0.843	2022	1.176	1.423	2072	1.163	1.411
1923	1.001	0.443	1973	1.023	0.855	2023	1.173	1.427	2073	1.163	1.410

Year			Year			Year			Year		
1924	1.002	0.452	1974	1.031	0.867	2024	1.171	1.430	2074	1.162	1.410
1925	1.004	0.460	1975	1.039	0.878	2025	1.168	1.433	2075	1.162	1.409
1926	1.009	0.468	1976	1.048	0.894	2026	1.167	1.435	2076	1.162	1.408
1927	1.014	0.475	1977	1.057	0.911	2027	1.165	1.436	2077	1.162	1.407
1928	1.020	0.483	1978	1.066	0.927	2028	1.163	1.437	2078	1.162	1.406
1929	1.025	0.490	1979	1.076	0.944	2029	1.162	1.438	2079	1.163	1.405
1930	1.031	0.498	1980	1.085	0.961	2030	1.160	1.440	2080	1.163	1.403
1931	1.038	0.504	1981	1.094	0.980	2031	1.160	1.440	2081	1.163	1.402
1932	1.046	0.511	1982	1.103	1.000	2032	1.159	1.440	2082	1.163	1.401
1933	1.054	0.517	1983	1.112	1.020	2033	1.159	1.440	2083	1.163	1.400
1934	1.061	0.523	1984	1.121	1.040	2034	1.159	1.440	2084	1.163	1.399
1935	1.069	0.530	1985	1.130	1.061	2035	1.158	1.440	2085	1.163	1.398
1936	1.076	0.537	1986	1.136	1.080	2036	1.159	1.440	2086	1.163	1.396
1937	1.082	0.544	1987	1.142	1.099	2037	1.159	1.440	2087	1.164	1.395
1938	1.088	0.551	1988	1.147	1.118	2038	1.159	1.440	2088	1.164	1.393
1939	1.095	0.559	1989	1.153	1.138	2039	1.159	1.440	2089	1.164	1.392
1940	1.101	0.566	1990	1.158	1.158	2040	1.160	1.439	2090	1.164	1.391
1941	1.104	0.575	1991	1.163	1.174	2041	1.160	1.439	2091	1.164	1.389
1942	1.108	0.584	1992	1.168	1.190	2042	1.160	1.439	2092	1.164	1.388
1943	1.111	0.594	1993	1.173	1.207	2043	1.160	1.439	2093	1.164	1.386
1944	1.115	0.603	1994	1.178	1.223	2044	1.161	1.439	2094	1.164	1.385
1945	1.118	0.613	1995	1.183	1.241	2045	1.161	1.439	2095	1.164	1.383
1946	1.114	0.623	1996	1.183	1.249	2046	1.161	1.438	2096	1.164	1.382
1947	1.111	0.634	1997	1.183	1.257	2047	1.161	1.438	2097	1.164	1.380
1948	1.107	0.645	1998	1.183	1.266	2048	1.161	1.438	2098	1.164	1.379
1949	1.103	0.657	1999	1.183	1.275	2049	1.161	1.437	2099	1.164	1.378
									2100	1.163	1.376

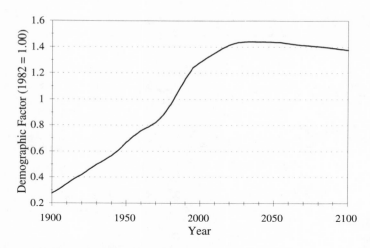

Fig. 7.15   Housing demand demographic factor

Invest =   real constant-quality housing investment (in 1982 dollars),

Pop =   U.S. population (in thousands),

Housing price =   real quality-adjusted price (in 1982 dollars), and

Intr =   home mortgage interest rate,

are taken from tables 7.1–7.3, 7.7, and 7.8. This model is loosely justified by an argument that the economy has a production frontier for housing and other goods, and competition will result in observations on this frontier where marginal revenue equals price. A C.E.S. frontier, for example, will yield a relationship like equation (12).[5]

Equation (12) was estimated by generalized least squares (GLS), with a correction for first-order serial correlation, using data for the years 1947–88. To handle endogeneity of housing price, the model was also estimated by GLS after replacing log housing price with a fitted value from a regression on a constant, the home mortgage interest rate, the rate of inflation, log GNP per capita, log population, log demographic demand factor, and log real housing stock. The standard errors in the two-stage procedure are not corrected for the first-stage estimation. The model was also estimated by an instrumental variables (IV) procedure, ignoring serial correlation. The estimates for these models are given in table 7.14. This table also gives estimates for the observation

---

5. Suppose housing H and nonhousing goods N are produced subject to a C.E.S. frontier $Z = [H^{1+\sigma} + AN^{1+\sigma}]^{1/(1+\sigma)}$, where Z is the primary input. Assume competitive industries maximize revenue $G = pH + N$, where p is the real price of housing. Then $G = Z\pi(p)$, where $\pi(\cdot)$ is a revenue function, and one has $H = G\pi_p(p)/\pi(p)$ is linear in G and increasing in p. Equation (14) is of this form, with an added parameter to allow for nonconstant returns to scale.

Table 7.14   **Housing Supply Regressions—Dependent Variable: Log Real Housing Investment per Capita (Standard errors in parentheses)**

	Model					
	(1)	(2)	(3)	(4)	(5)	(6)
Observation period	1947–88	1947–88	1947–88	1900–88	1900–88	1900–88
Estimator	GLS	2SGLS	IV	GLS	2SGLS	IV
Variables						
Constant	−10.120	−8.783	−8.759	−17.240	−2.236	−3.323
	(2.833)	(2.274)	(1.548)	(3.941)	(74.03)	(5.870)
Log GNP per capita	1.085	0.977	0.959	1.899	0.299	0.332
	(0.303)	(0.286)	(0.165)	(0.425)	(7.854)	(0.632)
Log real housing price	1.200	2.510	1.982	−0.486	2.997	1.678
	(1.001)	(1.340)	(0.780)	(0.904)	(15.028)	(1.178)
Nominal interest rate	−0.079	−0.094	−0.082	−0.125	−0.101	−0.034
	(0.020)	(0.024)	(0.014)	(0.040)	(0.120)	(0.024)
Rate of inflation	−0.008	−0.007	−0.006	−0.008	−0.004	−0.002
	(0.007)	(0.007)	(0.005)	(0.006)	(0.023)	(0.011)
Rho	0.405	0.379	NA	0.887	0.883	NA
Observations	42.000	42.000	42.000	81.000	81.000	81.000
Standard error	0.088	0.084	0.102	0.232	0.236	0.263

period 1900–88, excluding the war years 1917–18 and 1941–46 when supply restrictions were in place.

The estimates for 1947–88 imply that new housing investment is approximately homogeneous in GNP and responds negatively to the mortgage interest rate, reflecting the impact of the cost of working capital. Supply is found to be quite price elastic, with an elasticity value of 1.98 in the IV regression. This is in the range found by other authors using different data constructions and time periods (see Poterba 1984; Topel and Rosen 1988). The estimates for the longer observation period are less well determined. The IV regression gives a comparable price elasticity of supply but shows a much weaker elasticity with respect to GNP. These results provide mixed support for the stability of the supply relationship. In further analysis, I use the IV estimates of equation (12) based on post–World War II data (model [3]). An important feature of this model, which plays a critical role in the final results in this paper, is that at fixed real housing prices, housing investment expands nearly in proportion to GNP. This implies that if housing demand at fixed real prices grows less than linearly in GNP, due to demographic factors or a low income elasticity, then there will necessarily be downward movement of prices, even with growing demand for housing.

The specification of demand starts from a simple age-specific individual demand function. Consider an individual in cohort i in year t, and assume that his or her real housing demand, denoted D_{it}, differs from the demand of a person of the same cohort in base year 0 only because of differences in real income or real user cost of housing, with the functional form

(13) $$D_{it} = \alpha_{i0}(\psi_{it}/\psi_{i0})^\gamma \exp(\lambda(u_t - u_0)),$$

where ψ_{it} is real income, u_t is real user cost, and the α_{i0} are the age-specific selection-adjusted housing demand coefficients obtained using the 1970 census and given in table 7.12. This equation can be derived from the indirect utility function

(14) $$V_{it} = \psi_{it}^{1-\gamma}/(1 - \gamma) - \lambda^{-1}\alpha_{i0}\exp(C + \lambda u_t),$$

where C is a constant that collects the base-year variable values.

Recall from equation (8) that $\psi_{it}/\psi_{i0} = (Y_t/Y_0)/\psi_t$. The demographic factor constructed in table 7.13 can be defined, except for normalization, as

(15) $$F_t = \sum_{i=1}^{20} N_{it}\alpha_{i0} \bigg/ \sum_{i=1}^{20} N_{i0}\alpha_{i0}.$$

The individual demand functions can then be aggregated across cohorts, given the population profile, to obtain aggregate housing demand,

(16) $$D_t = A\, F_t\, Y_t^\gamma \exp(\lambda u_t)\, \psi_t^{-\gamma},$$

where A is a constant. For econometric analysis, I work with the model

(17) $$\log(D_t/F_t) = \log(A) + \lambda u_t + \gamma\log(Y_t/\psi_t) + v_t.$$

Because of transactions costs, consumers are likely to adjust slowly toward desired housing consumption levels. To incorporate this effect, I consider a partial adjustment version of model (17),

(18) $$\begin{aligned}\log(D_t/F_t) = {} & \theta\log(D_{t-1}/F_{t-1}) + (1 - \theta)\log(A) \\ & + (1-\theta)\lambda u_t + (1 - \theta)\gamma\log(Y_t),\end{aligned}$$

where $1 - \theta$ is the adjustment rate.

I estimate equations (17) and (18) using data from tables 7.7 and 7.8, with demand defined as the real constant-quality housing stock. The fitted demand equations for the four models of expectations described earlier (denoted LAG1, LAG3, LEAD1, and LEAD3) and the corresponding user cost measures are given in tables 7.15–7.18. Each equation is estimated for the period 1900–88, excluding the war years, and also for the period 1947–88.

Let $y = X\beta + \varepsilon$ denote equation (17), with ε assumed to follow an autoregressive process of order one (AR1), process with serial correlation ρ. First, I estimate this equation by GLS. Next, to accommodate possible endogeneity of the price of housing that enters user cost, I apply Durbin's transformation,

(19) $$y = \rho y_{-1} + X\beta - X_{-1}(\rho\beta) + v,$$

and estimate this equation by instrumental variables (IV), without imposing the nonlinear constraint on parameters, and use this equation to estimate ρ. The instruments used are a constant, log population, the home mortgage interest rate, the inflation rate, the log of aggregation-adjusted GNP per capita and its lagged value, and one and two period lags of the dependent variable. This method is consistent even if user cost and the lagged dependent variable are correlated with the disturbance. Finally, I do IV estimation of the ρth difference equation

(20) $$y - \rho y_{-1} = (X - \rho X_{-1})\beta + v,$$

using the estimate of ρ from the preceeding IV regression.

A potential problem with these demand estimates is that some of the instruments, such as GNP per capita and the mortgage rate, are in fact jointly determined along with housing prices by macroeconomic equilibrium and thus may themselves be correlated with the disturbances in these regressions.

I first summarize the results in tables 7.15 and 7.16 for the demand equation (17) without partial adjustment. The income elasticities, as measured by the endogenity-corrected ρth difference estimates, are relatively insensitive to the definition of user cost or to the observation period, with values between 0.2 and 0.5. There is no consistent pattern to the coefficients of user cost, with the regressions for the full period giving responses that are insignificant or of unexpected sign, and the regressions for 1950–88 giving responses that are mostly of expected sign, but not consistently significant.

If the partial adjustment effect θ introduced in equation (18) is significant, then equation (17) is misspecified, and its estimated coefficients are biased.[6] Equation (18) has the form

$$y = \theta y_{-1} + X\beta + \varepsilon,$$

and Durbin's transformation yields

$$y = (\theta + \rho)y_{-1} - \theta\rho y_{-2} + X\beta - X_{-1}(\rho\beta) + v.$$

I report the GLS results, but they are biased due to the lagged dependent variable. To obtain consistent estimates, I apply IV to Durbin's transformation of equation (18), using the same instruments as for equation (17), without imposing nonlinear parameter restrictions. The coefficients of y_{-1} and y_{-2} define a quadratic whose roots are estimates of θ and ρ; I use these, with the relative coefficients of X and X_{-1} used to identify which root estimates ρ. I then use this estimate to form the ρth difference equation,

---

6. The bias in IV estimates of model (17) when the specification (18) is true can be worked out by rewriting equation (17) as

$$y = [y_{-1}|X|X_{-1}]\left\{\begin{bmatrix}\theta + \rho \\ \beta \\ \beta\rho\end{bmatrix} - \rho\theta\begin{bmatrix}y'_{-1}y_{-1} & y'_{-1}X & y'_{-1}X_{-1} \\ X'y_{-1} & X'X & X'X_{-1} \\ X'_{-1}y_{-1} & X'_{-1}X & X'_{-1}X_{-1}\end{bmatrix}^{-1}\begin{bmatrix}y'_{-1}y_{-2} \\ X'y_{-2} \\ X'_{-1}y_{-2}\end{bmatrix}\right\} + \eta,$$

where lags are denoted by subscripts and the disturbance η is orthogonal to the right-hand-side variables.

Table 7.15 Demand Functions for Model (17): Observations 1900–88, except 1917–18 and 1941–46 (standard errors below coefficient estimates)

	Regression											
	(1)	(2)	(3)	(4)	(5)	(6)	(7)	(8)	(9)	(10)	(11)	(12)
Expectations model	LAG1	LAG1	LAG1	LAG3	LAG3	LAG3	LEAD1	LEAD1	LEAD1	LEAD3	LEAD3	LEAD3
Estimation method	GLS	IV	IV on ρ-Diff	GLS	IV	IV on ρ-Diff	GLS	IV	IV on ρ-Diff	GLS	IV	IV on ρ-Diff
Constant	4.880	0.367	0.550	5.212	0.358	0.597	5.233	0.213	0.487	5.329	0.205	0.494
	1.276	0.127	0.051	1.269	0.070	0.043	1.184	0.070	0.038	1.268	0.054	0.033
User cost	0.219	−0.094	0.457	0.492	0.167	0.451	0.038	0.310	0.097	−0.173	0.229	0.068
	0.208	0.130	0.164	0.482	0.111	0.222	0.206	0.152	0.119	0.508	0.147	0.218
Adjusted income	0.295	−0.022	0.495	0.256	0.079	0.446	0.225	0.170	0.362	0.245	0.136	0.348
	0.143	0.107	0.032	0.143	0.030	0.029	0.134	0.045	0.037	0.144	0.032	0.034
User cost, LAG1		0.156			0.234			−0.046			0.010	
		0.304			0.139			0.080			0.133	
Adjusted income, LAG1		0.130			0.023			−0.099			−0.066	
		0.128			0.036			0.047			0.033	
Dependent variable, LAG1		0.822			0.831			0.887			0.889	
		0.047			0.023			0.021			0.016	
Observations	81	79	79	81	79	79	80	78	78	78	76	76
R^2	0.899	0.995	0.728	0.890	0.998	0.736	0.886	0.996	0.571	0.878	0.997	0.575
Standard error	0.087	0.019	0.028	0.091	0.013	0.026	0.091	0.018	0.024	0.092	0.014	0.023
Rho	0.928	0.822	NC	0.932	0.831	NC	0.917	0.887	0.571	0.924	0.889	0.889

Table 7.16   Demand Functions for Model (17): Observations 1947–88 (standard errors below coefficient estimates)

Regression

	(13)	(14)	(15)	(16)	(17)	(18)	(19)	(20)	(21)	(22)	(23)	(24)
Expectations model	LAG1	LAG1	LAG1	LAG3	LAG3	LAG3	LEAD1	LEAD1	LEAD1	LEAD3	LEAD3	LEAD3
Estimation method	GLS	IV	IV on ρ-Diff	GLS	IV	IV on ρ-Diff	GLS	IV	IV on ρ-Diff	GLS	IV	IV on ρ-Diff
Constant	-0.460	0.191	0.367	-0.571	0.290	0.349	-0.834	0.189	0.420	-0.906	0.228	0.376
	0.459	0.066	0.046	0.460	0.079	0.027	0.414	0.059	0.040	0.413	0.063	0.022
User cost	0.337	-0.015	0.117	0.212	-0.222	-0.236	-0.009	-0.182	-0.152	0.000	-0.269	-0.217
	0.120	0.058	0.074	0.264	0.109	0.105	0.128	0.053	0.083	0.256	0.085	0.127
Adjusted income	0.887	0.203	0.411	0.890	0.172	0.247	0.920	0.206	0.353	0.928	0.189	0.248
	0.050	0.062	0.052	0.050	0.046	0.044	0.045	0.035	0.046	0.045	0.035	0.035
User cost, LAG1		0.019			0.303			0.098			0.136	
		0.091			0.120			0.039			0.080	
Adjusted income, LAG1		-0.145			-0.151			-0.147			-0.156	
		0.063			0.049			0.038			0.037	
Dependent variable LAG1		0.908			0.938			9.907			0.933	
		0.035			0.040			0.033			0.033	
Observations	42	42	42	42	42	42	41	41	41	39	39	39
R^2	0.990	0.999	0.553	0.989	0.999	0.517	0.990	0.999	0.606	0.989	1.000	0.511
Standard error	0.025	0.006	0.011	0.026	0.007	0.007	0.025	0.006	0.010	0.025	0.006	0.008
Rho	0.764	0.908		0.725	0.938		0.703	0.907		0.686	0.933	

$$y - \rho y_{-1} = \theta(y_{-1} - \rho y_{-2}) + (X - \rho X_{-1})\beta + \nu,$$

which I estimate by IV.

Summarizing the estimates of the partial adjustment model (18) in tables 7.17 and 7.18, there are again substantial differences between the coefficients from regressions run on the full period 1900–88 and on the truncated period 1947–88. This may reflect a regime change in macroeconomic structure or housing finance after World War II, special problems of disequilibrium in the 1930s, or problems in consistent measurement of variables early in the century. Another factor that may be important is the fairly rapid decrease in household size over the 1960–88 period, due to reduced number of children and to increased household formation from delayed marriage, increased divorce rates, and increased rates of elderly living alone. In several cases, the estimation method applied to the 1900–88 observation period does not yield a real estimate for the serial correlation coefficient, and the ρth difference regression cannot be run. Whenever these regressions are available, in either the full or post–World War II data, they give income elasticities near 0.2, no matter what the expectations model. Estimates of the partial adjustment parameter θ vary from 0.3 to 0.6 in the 1947–88 data, depending on the expectations model. The one consistent estimate for the full data is 0.8. The postwar data estimates then imply long-run income elasticities between 0.2 and 0.6. The coefficients of user cost vary with both the expectations model and the observation period but are generally insignificant for the longer period. Concentrating on the regressions from the 1947–88 period, the long-run response to a unit increase in user cost ranges from -0.2 to -0.3. These values imply very small elasticities with respect to housing price: In the LEAD3 expectations model, a uniform 100 percent increase in housing price yields, on average over 1947–88, a long-run decrease of 1.4 percent in housing demand.

There are insufficient differences in overall fit to sharply discriminate between the different expectations models. The lack of strong evidence supporting forward-looking rather than naive expectations is consistent with the findings of Ai et al. (1990) from panel data that households are relatively insensitive to user costs, particularly the capital gains component. Skinner (1989) also finds myopic behavior. The possibility that households make substantial intergenerational gifts or bequests, mitigating the cross-cohort effects of housing price variations, has been examined by Skinner (1989) and M. Hurd (personal communication). They find dissaving among the elderly too low to be easily explained by one-generation life-cycle behavior unless risk aversion is very strong. On the other hand, this behavior does not appear to be systematically related to bequest motives, as it does not depend on number of children or children's economic status.

On the basis of the results in tables 7.15–7.18, I selected the LEAD3 model, fitted to post–World War II data, for further analysis. It appears unlikely that the choice of expectations model would have much impact on the long-run

Table 7.17 Demand Functions for Model (18): Observations 1900–88, except 1917–18 and 1941–46 (standard errors below coefficient estimates)

						Regression						
	(25)	(26)	(27)	(28)	(29)	(30)	(31)	(32)	(33)	(34)	(35)	(36)
Expectations model	LAG1	LAG1	LAG1	LAG3	LAG3	LAG3	LEAD1	LEAD1	LEAD1	LEAD3	LEAD3	LEAD3
Estimation method	GLS	IV	IV on ρ-Diff	GLS	IV	IV on ρ-Diff	GLS	IV	IV on ρ-Diff	GLS	IV	IV on ρ-Diff
Constant	0.230	0.071	0.088	0.273	0.099		0.185	0.117		0.204	0.114	
	0.112	0.070	0.048	0.114	0.047		0.127	0.034		0.124	0.032	
User cost	0.017	0.087	0.202	0.109	0.121		-0.039	0.067		-0.132	-0.015	
	0.023	0.065	0.091	0.049	0.059		0.021	0.075		0.050	0.085	
Adjusted income	0.080	0.124	0.243	0.085	0.084		0.072	0.100		0.081	0.096	
	0.014	0.053	0.028	0.013	0.016		0.014	0.022		0.013	0.018	
User cost, LAG1		-0.115			-0.106			0.020			0.018	
		0.159			0.083			0.037			0.098	
Adjusted income, LAG1		-0.107			-0.059			-0.071			0.074	
		0.067			0.021			0.022			-0.068	
Dependent variable, LAG1	0.876	1.652	0.641	0.864	1.625		0.891	1.578		0.879	1.603	
	0.026	0.108	0.064	0.025	0.091		0.026	0.085		0.025	0.077	
Dependent variable, LAG2		-0.682			-0.668			-0.629			-0.652	
		0.087			0.076			0.077			0.070	
Observations	80	79	79	80	79		79	78		77	76	
R^2	0.999	0.999	0.894	0.999	0.999		0.999	0.999		0.999	0.999	
Standard error	0.009	0.009	0.015	0.008	0.007		0.009	0.008		0.009	0.008	
Rho	0.776	0.848	0.848	0.783	NC		0.801	NC		0.790	NC	
Theta	0.876	0.804	0.641	0.864	NC		0.891	NC		0.879	NC	

Table 7.18   Demand Functions for Model (18): Observations 1947–88 (standard errors below coefficient estimates)

	(37)	(38)	(39)	(40)	(41)	(42)	(43)	(44)	(45)	(46)	(47)	(48)
Expectations model	LAG1	LAG1	LAG1	LAG3	LAG3	LAG3	LEAD1	LEAD1	LEAD1	LEAD3	LEAD3	LEAD3
Estimation method	GLS	IV	IV on ρ-Diff	GLS	IV	IV on ρ-Diff	GLS	IV	IV on ρ-Diff	GLS	IV	IV on ρ-Diff
Constant	0.023	0.175	0.240	0.058	0.219	0.261	-0.003	0.141	0.259	0.020	0.172	0.268
	0.101	0.078	0.033	0.102	0.072	0.040	0.102	0.051	0.031	0.097	0.058	0.034
User cost	0.006	-0.135	-0.020	0.062	-0.166	-0.228	-0.052	-0.142	-0.105	-0.119	-0.241	-0.196
	0.037	0.078	0.046	0.062	0.096	0.099	0.035	0.046	0.042	0.058	0.075	0.081
Adjusted income	0.162	0.025	0.196	0.157	0.147	0.200	0.160	0.176	0.200	0.149	0.163	0.194
	0.046	0.091	0.038	0.040	0.041	0.041	0.042	0.031	0.031	0.041	0.032	0.033
User cost, LAG1		0.240			0.230			0.083			0.147	
		0.126			0.107			0.033			0.070	
Adjusted income, LAG1		-0.001			-0.136			-0.133			-0.139	
		0.086			0.043			0.032			0.033	
Dependent variable, LAG1	0.804	1.463	0.526	0.805	1.261	0.234	0.810	1.219	0.444	0.820	1.244	0.307
	0.048	0.171	0.041	0.041	0.121	0.079	0.043	0.100	0.045	0.041	0.104	0.066
Dependent variable, LAG2		-0.514			-0.302			-0.287			-0.293	
		0.154			0.109			0.089			0.093	
Observations	42	42	42	42	42	42	41	41	41	39	39	39
R^2	0.999	0.999	0.931	0.999	0.999	0.628	0.999	1.000	0.894	0.999	1.000	0.709
Standard error	0.007	0.008	0.006	0.007	0.006	0.006	0.007	0.005	0.006	0.006	0.005	0.007
Rho	0.610	0.877		0.600	0.939		0.582	0.899	0.899	0.544	0.928	0.928
Theta	0.804	0.586		0.805	0.322		0.810	0.319	0.444	0.820	0.316	0.307

conclusions of the study, although short-run dynamics will obviously depend on this choice. It is also unlikely that the analysis would be much affected by using rational expectations rather than the LEAD3 perfect foresight expectations. In the equilibrium I obtain, the LEAD3 expectations are highly predictable from the information set at each time period, and the equilibrium does not have change points or sharp breaks where rational expectations might differ significantly from the LEAD3 expectations.

For projections, I need auxiliary forecasts of the inflation rate, real GNP per capita, the home mortgage rate, the property tax rate, and the marginal income tax rate. The following regressions are used; t-Statistics are given in parentheses. Log price index for GNP (LPGNP):

$$(21) \quad \text{LPGNP} = 0.2516 + 0.0023(\text{year} - 1990) + 1.77049 \text{ LPGNP}_{-1}$$
$$\qquad (2.86) \qquad (2.77) \qquad\qquad\qquad (12.05)$$
$$\qquad - 1.1747 \text{ LPGNP}_{-2} + 0.70223 \text{ LPGNP}_{-3} - 0.2591 \text{ LPGNP}_{-4}$$
$$\qquad (-3.96) \qquad\qquad (2.14) \qquad\qquad\qquad (-0.92)$$
$$\qquad -0.0909 \text{ LPGNP}_{-5},$$
$$\qquad (-0.71)$$

1950–88 sample, $R^2 = 0.9995$.

Log GNP per capita (LGNPC):

$$(22) \quad \text{LGNPC} = 2.5513 + 0.00516 \,(\text{year} - 1990) + 0.73946 \text{ LGNPC}_{-1},$$
$$\qquad\qquad (2.49) \qquad (2.34) \qquad\qquad\qquad\qquad (7.02)$$

$$1950\text{–}88 \text{ sample,} \quad R^2 = 0.9893.$$

Nominal mortgage interest rate (MORTR):

$$(23) \quad \text{MORTR} = 0.\qquad 25365 + 0.2151 \,(\text{inflation rate, GNP index})$$
$$\qquad\qquad\qquad (0.96) \qquad\quad (4.58)$$
$$\qquad\qquad + 0.8718 \text{ MORTR}_{-1},$$
$$\qquad\qquad (23.66)$$

$$1950\text{–}88 \text{ sample,} \quad R^2 = 0.9617.$$

I assume the property tax rate and marginal income tax rate remain at 1989 levels. The annual *growth rates* of the auxiliary variables follow:

Variable	Growth Rate 1950–89	Growth Rate 1990–2100
GNP price deflator (PGNP)	4.06	4.37
Real GNP per capita (GNPC)	1.97	1.98
Nominal mortgage interest rate (MORTR)	2.76	0.00
Demographic factor in housing demand	1.41	0.02

A potential problem with the preceding analysis of the market for housing is that the estimated serial correlation coefficients in the demand and supply functions are near one, suggesting that these variables may have unit roots and cointegrating relationships. I have tested log real GNP per capita, log housing investment, log housing stock, the GNP implicit price deflator, and the home mortgage interest rate for unit roots, using augmented Dickey-Fuller tests on annual observations from 1869 through 1989. I do the tests with and without the maintained hypothesis of a deterministic trend. To take partial account of moving-average effects introduced by demographic factors, I include five years of lagged first differences in the variable being tested. I reject the hypothesis of a unit root for the GNP price deflator with a deterministic trend and otherwise accept the unit root hypothesis, at the 5 percent significance level. For forecasting, I use the previous point estimates of autoregression coefficients but note, in light of the unit root tests, that the standard errors for regression coefficients, and confidence bounds for forecasts, may be severely underestimated.

7.6   Housing Market Projections

The estimated supply and demand models for the housing market, combined with auxiliary forecasts, define a system that can be solved for market-clearing housing prices, user costs, investment, and stocks. I use supply model (3) from table 7.14, demand model (48) from table 7.18, and the LEAD3 expectations model. The following method is used to determine equilibrium in the model: Starting from a trial real housing price sequence from 1989 to 2100, I calculate nominal capital gain rates, imposing a transversality condition that real capital gains rates in 2098–2100 are zero. For these fixed capital gains rates, I solve the model by forward recursion, obtaining a modified price sequence. I then adjust nominal capital gains rates partially to the new price sequence and repeat the process. The method converges in a few-score iterations and takes about 10 seconds on a fast workstation.

The results of the forecasting exercise are given in table 7.19. It should be noted that the price forecast is much smoother than the historical series, which is highly volatile. The forecast is for continued growth in housing demand, fueled by rising income, which offsets the slow decline in the demographic factor. However, rising income also increases supply of new housing investment, leading to steadily declining real housing prices. The model does not predict a precipitous decline, although it does suggest a substantial fall through the 1990s. It is likely that a rational expectations model with more forward-looking consumers would react more quickly to pending declines and accelerate their onset.

The results of the projections are summarized in figures 7.16–7.18. Figure 7.16 shows that real housing prices fell about 7 percent from a peak in 1980 until 1988, with a small rebound after 1986. The projections show a brief increase in 1989 and 1990, followed by a decline that is relatively sharp in the late 1990s, shallow in the 2010s, and sharper again after 2020. Figure 7.17

Table 7.19   Forecasts of Housing Market Real Stocks and Real Prices

Year	Price	Stock	Year	Price	Stock
1869	0.601	107.7	1910	0.614	478.5
1870	0.573	112.3	1911	0.611	485.7
1871	0.634	116.5	1912	0.600	494.3
1872	0.570	120.6	1913	0.581	503.4
1873	0.632	124.8	1914	0.571	511.7
1874	0.597	129.8	1915	0.558	521.8
1875	0.554	135.9	1916	0.528	533.7
1876	0.554	142.6	1917	0.499	539.5
1877	0.520	150.3	1918	0.526	538.6
1878	0.545	158.9	1919	0.533	546.5
1879	0.531	168.7	1920	0.602	550.5
1880	0.556	178.1	1921	0.579	558.1
1881	0.568	187.3	1922	0.579	581.8
1882	0.577	196.5	1923	0.630	611.5
1883	0.614	206.2	1924	0.620	647.7
1884	0.592	218.8	1925	0.604	688.4
1885	0.605	232.7	1926	0.618	728.4
1886	0.638	246.3	1927	0.621	764.0
1887	0.633	261.0	1928	0.612	794.5
1888	0.591	277.6	1929	0.642	810.6
1889	0.550	290.6	1930	0.641	811.0
1890	0.563	303.0	1931	0.639	807.5
1891	0.549	311.4	1932	0.579	794.9
1892	0.555	323.7	1933	0.588	780.5
1893	0.540	331.4	1934	0.608	767.8
1894	0.554	339.8	1935	0.596	760.8
1895	0.552	350.4	1936	0.625	760.2
1896	0.569	358.8	1937	0.657	761.5
1897	0.554	368.4	1938	0.689	763.1
1898	0.561	375.0	1939	0.704	772.1
1899	0.580	381.2	1940	0.716	783.4
1900	0.582	382.4	1941	0.728	797.0
1901	0.578	387.9	1942	0.696	791.7
1902	0.578	392.0	1943	0.705	778.5
1903	0.590	396.5	1944	0.755	764.4
1904	0.575	403.1	1945	0.784	753.3
1905	0.586	418.9	1946	0.763	775.2
1906	0.628	432.3	1947	0.819	809.3
1907	0.629	441.8	1948	0.865	852.3
1908	0.612	451.8	1949	0.846	892.5
1909	0.612	465.3	1950	0.877	954.5

(*continued*)

Table 7.19   (continued)

Year	Price	Stock	Year	Price	Stock
1951	0.882	999.5	1992	0.985	3,547.9
1952	0.884	1,041.2	1993	0.965	3,665.5
1953	0.887	1,084.0	1994	0.952	3,784.2
1954	0.860	1,133.4	1995	0.943	3,904.5
1955	0.871	1,194.1	1996	0.907	4,012.5
1956	0.883	1,242.4	1997	0.883	4,113.2
1957	0.872	1,283.1	1998	0.865	4,208.4
1958	0.852	1,323.4	1999	0.854	4,300.6
1959	0.865	1,376.8	2000	0.846	4,391.1
1960	0.862	1,422.9	2001	0.834	4,476.8
1961	0.855	1,467.9	2002	0.827	4,559.6
1962	0.859	1,517.6	2003	0.822	4,640.3
1963	0.866	1,573.6	2004	0.819	4,719.6
1964	0.879	1,625.6	2005	0.817	4,798.2
1965	0.877	1,682.0	2006	0.815	4,875.6
1966	0.878	1,729.0	2007	0.813	4,952.3
1967	0.892	1,773.9	2008	0.812	5,028.7
1968	0.904	1,825.8	2009	0.811	5,105.1
1969	0.915	1,878.9	2010	0.810	5,181.4
1970	0.882	1,925.3	2011	0.809	5,258.1
1971	0.880	1,997.9	2012	0.807	5,335.1
1972	0.887	2,091.5	2013	0.804	5,412.3
1973	0.906	2,180.6	2014	0.801	5,490.0
1974	0.923	2,234.3	2015	0.797	5,568.2
1975	0.915	2,269.4	2016	0.790	5,645.3
1976	0.920	2,326.2	2017	0.784	5,722.2
1977	0.960	2,406.1	2018	0.775	5,797.9
1978	1.006	2,492.7	2019	0.769	5,873.7
1979	1.036	2,568.8	2020	0.762	5,949.8
1980	1.043	2,612.1	2021	0.748	6,021.8
1981	1.028	2,644.6	2022	0.737	6,091.4
1982	1.000	2,658.2	2023	0.725	6,158.3
1983	0.984	2,709.6	2024	0.716	6,224.3
1984	0.984	2,782.0	2025	0.708	6,290.0
1985	0.976	2,853.5	2026	0.693	6,350.3
1986	0.976	2,945.3	2027	0.681	6,407.5
1987	0.989	3,033.6	2028	0.671	6,461.9
1988	0.986	3,119.7	2029	0.662	6,514.9
1989	0.991	3,204.8	2030	0.655	6,567.3
1990	1.008	3,313.3	2031	0.644	6,616.1
1991	0.997	3,428.6	2032	0.636	6,662.5

Table 7.19   (continued)

Year	Price	Stock	Year	Price	Stock
2033	0.629	6,707.3	2074	0.469	8,250.5
2034	0.623	6,751.2	2075	0.467	8,291.3
2035	0.618	6,794.5	2076	0.462	8,330.8
2036	0.612	6,836.4	2077	0.459	8,369.6
2037	0.607	6,877.3	2078	0.455	8,407.9
2038	0.602	6,917.7	2079	0.452	8,446.1
2039	0.598	6,957.8	2080	0.449	8,484.3
2040	0.595	6,997.7	2081	0.446	8,522.4
2041	0.591	7,037.4	2082	0.443	8,560.6
2042	0.588	7,077.1	2083	0.440	8,598.6
2043	0.585	7,116.7	2084	0.437	8,636.6
2044	0.582	7,156.3	2085	0.434	8,674.9
2045	0.579	7,196.0	2086	0.430	8,712.3
2046	0.575	7,235.5	2087	0.427	8,749.1
2047	0.572	7,274.8	2088	0.424	8,785.7
2048	0.568	7,314.0	2089	0.421	8,822.5
2049	0.565	7,353.3	2090	0.417	8,859.2
2050	0.561	7,392.5	2091	0.414	8,895.6
2051	0.557	7,431.3	2092	0.412	8,932.7
2052	0.553	7,470.2	2093	0.408	8,969.4
2053	0.548	7,508.0	2094	0.405	9,005.7
2054	0.544	7,545.8	2095	0.404	9,044.3
2055	0.541	7,583.9	2096	0.400	9,082.1
2056	0.533	7,618.8	2097	0.396	9,118.3
2057	0.527	7,651.9	2098	0.398	9,161.8
2058	0.522	7,684.2	2099	0.393	9,202.5
2059	0.517	7,716.1	2100	0.385	9,243.3
2060	0.513	7,747.7			
2061	0.509	7,779.8			
2062	0.505	7,812.1			
2063	0.502	7,845.1			
2064	0.498	7,878.2			
2065	0.495	7,911.6			
2066	0.492	7,946.2			
2067	0.489	7,981.6			
2068	0.486	8,017.9			
2069	0.483	8,054.7			
2070	0.479	8,091.5			
2071	0.478	8,130.1			
2072	0.475	8,169.9			
2073	0.472	8,210.0			

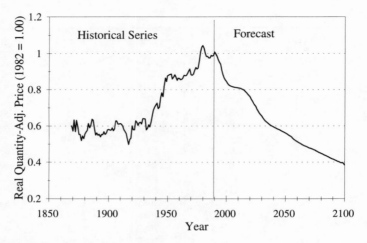

Fig. 7.16   Housing price forecast

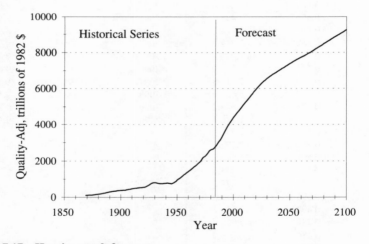

Fig. 7.17   Housing stock forecast

shows the real, constant-quality housing stock continuing a trend that began in 1950, with some slowing between 2020 and 2040 as the baby-boom cohorts disappear.

The patterns in these figures suggest that demographic factors will slow housing market growth over the next 60 years. The offsetting effect of rising income will be to increase housing demand, but not rapidly enough to keep pace with increasing supply of new housing at constant price, leading to steady price erosion. Under these projections, there will be no periods of rapid capital gains matching the sharp increases of 1938–55 or 1974–80. On the other hand, there will be no periods of precipitous capital losses that could impose an un-anticipated heavy burden on some elderly cohorts, except for a few years around the present.

Figure 7.18 gives a more detailed picture of housing price behavior in the near term, as projected by the model. The feature of a small upturn in the first two forecast years is certainly related to the persistence in demand shocks and the use of the LEAD3 expectation model and makes no allowance for macro-economic cyclic conditions. More important are the market fundamentals driv-ing the longer-run forecast, particularly the declines after 1995.

7.7   Welfare Implications for the Elderly

Population cohorts that are able to "buy low and sell high" in the housing market gain relative to cohorts in the opposite circumstance. I examine the implications of housing market changes on intergenerational distribution by comparing rates of real capital gains, proportion of income spent on shelter, and the income adjustments (compensating variations) necessary to equate utilities of different cohorts. This analysis gives a picture of the effects of the housing market on individuals who anticipate the housing price changes and adjust savings behavior to achieve desired life-cycle consumption and be-quests.

There are further, and perhaps more significant, welfare implications of housing price changes for consumption and welfare in old age. Unanticipated price changes can cause consumption squeezes or unintended bequests; the risk penalty, and cost of carrying precautionary assets, may be an important welfare effect. A significant source of financing of consumption among the very old is extraction of housing equity. Although several authors (Feinstein and McFadden 1989; Venti and Wise 1990) have noted that housing transac-tions prior to age 70 on average do not result in extraction of equity, Ai et al. (1990) find that equity extraction is substantial in transactions after age 75. This is particularly important as an income source for surviving spouses. Hous-ing price volatility that translates into a volatility of 1–3 percent in lifetime income, if concentrated into the last decade of life without compensating ad-justments in savings or steps to reduce risk, will lead to volatility of about 12 percent in final decade consumption.

To calculate the rate of real capital gains for a cohort, I assume that the individual purchases housing at age 30, levering the purchase with a 30 percent equity investment and 70 percent mortgage, and resells this housing at age 70. The formula

(24) $RCG_t = [(P_{t+40}/P_t)^{1/40} - 1]/0.3,$

where P_t is real housing price, is used to calculate the rate of real capital gains. Figure 7.19 shows this rate for population cohorts with birth years between 1840 and 2030. For birth years past 1918, these calculations use the projected

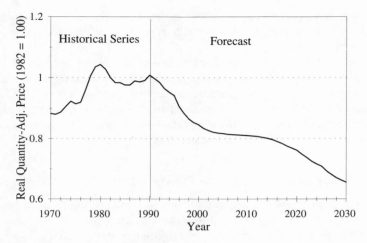

Fig. 7.18   Near-term housing prices

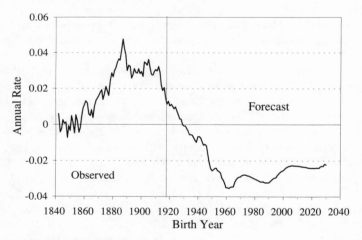

Fig. 7.19   Real rate of capital gains

prices from figure 7.16. Cohorts born in 1880–1910, who purchased housing in 1910–40, and sold it in 1950–80, achieved real returns around 3 percent per year. For cohorts born between 1915 and 1945, real capital gain rates decline steadily from +1 percent to −1 percent. There is then a sharp drop to a minimum annual rate near −3 percent for the 1960 cohort. Thereafter, the rate remains low for cohorts born through 1990 and then rises slightly to the range of −2 percent for cohorts born thereafter. The most disadvantaged cohorts by this measure will then be the baby boomers that become elderly in the years 2005–2020, and their children born between 1980 and 1990. This suggests the possible policy inference that substantial intergenerational redistribution to offset housing market effects is not needed but that it may be useful to dampen expectations of positive future housing capital gains that could distort life-cycle savings for consumption in old age.

A high share of income spent on shelter tends to reduce welfare, as it lowers consumption of other goods, and reflects mostly higher housing cost rather than increased housing consumption. I have calculated a measure of shelter share of income for each cohort by the following method. Equation (13) gives age-specific housing demand, which when combined with the assumption from equation (9) on the stability of the age distribution of income, implies

$$(25) \qquad D_{it} = \alpha_{i0}(Y_t/\psi_t Y_0)^\gamma \exp(\lambda(u_t - u_0)),$$

where Y_t is per capita income in period t and i is the cohort. Then, the present value of the stream of service costs (PVSC) incurred by an individual born in year v is

$$(26) \qquad \text{PVSC}_v = \sum_{t=v}^{v+L} \delta^{t-v} u_t D_{i(t-v),t},$$

where $i(t - v)$ is the five-year cohort into which an individual of age $t - v$ falls and δ is a discount factor. For this calculation, I use a constant discount rate of 2.16 percent, equal to the growth rate of real GNP per capita estimated and projected over the period 1869–2100. Corresponding to equation (26), the present value of the individual income stream is

$$(27) \qquad \text{PVINC}_v = \sum_{t=v}^{v+L} \delta^{t-v} \psi_{i(t-v),0}(Y_t/\psi_t Y_0),$$

where ψ_{i0} is the income of cohort i in the base year of 1970. In principle, L should be taken to be length of life, but I truncate the present value calculations at $L = 70$ to facilitate computation; the discount rate is sufficient to make the error in this approximation small. I then take the ratio of (26) to (27), normalized in 1989 to equal the share of housing in personal consumption expenditures from the *Survey of Current Business* (U.S. Department of Commerce, 1990). The lifetime share of income spent on housing, by birth cohort, is graphed in figure 7.20. The share was high for cohorts born before 1890, then dropped sharply, reaching a minimum around 1910, rose to 0.3 in 1925, and then remained between 0.2 and 0.3 until the end of the baby-boom cohorts. The share then falls steadily for cohorts after 1960. This shape can be explained by the relatively low income elasticity of demand for housing, near 0.3, and the additional effect of falling housing prices.

The housing demand equation I have estimated integrates to an explicit utility function (14), within which the utility impacts of changing income or user cost of housing can be calculated (see also Smeeding 1989). Then, the following question can be addressed: If an individual born in year t faced, instead of his or her actual stream of housing user costs, the stream of user costs that

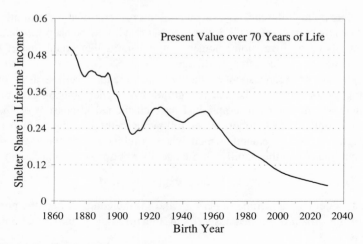

Fig. 7.20   Shelter share of income

individuals born in 1950 faced, by what percentage would income have to be adjusted (compensated) to keep the cohort-t individual as well off as before?

To answer this question, I calculate the change in income in each year necessary to compensate for the change in service cost and then take the present value of these compensating changes. For small changes, the compensation can be calculated from the total differential, yielding the crude consumer surplus formula

(28) $$\Delta\psi_{it} = \alpha_{i0}\psi_{it}^{\gamma}\exp(C + \lambda u_t)\,\Delta u_t = D_{it}\Delta u_t.$$

Substituting the expression (9) for age-specific income into the age-specific demand equation (14) and forming the present value of the compensating changes in income yields the present value of the compensation,

(29) $$\text{PVCOMP} = \sum_{t=v}^{v+L} \delta^{t-v}\Delta\psi_{it} = \sum_{t=v}^{v+L} \delta^{t-v}\alpha_i\left(\frac{Y_t}{\psi_t Y_0}\right)e_{\lambda(u_t-u_0)}\Delta u_t.$$

Figure 7.21 plots the present value of the compensation, expressed as a percentage of the present value of income, for cohorts born between 1869 and 2030. Cohorts born between 1869 and 1915 would have required a lifetime income reduction of about 0.7 percent to offset the more favorable housing user costs they faced than were faced by the 1950 cohort. Beginning in 1910, the magnitude of the compensating variation is reduced sharply, remaining at around a 0.2 percent income reduction for the 1920–40 cohorts. There are no current or future cohorts that are worse off than the baby-boom cohorts, and only minor compensating variations are required for cohorts after 1980.

To provide some perspective on the calculations of compensating variations for housing cost differences, I have also calculated the percentage adjustments

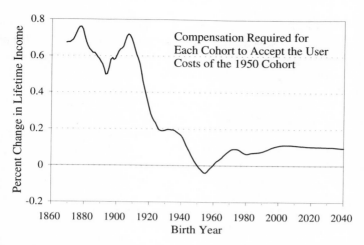

Fig. 7.21   Compensating variations

in income necessary to equate the present value of utility for different cohorts, under the assumption that all cohorts face the housing user cost series starting in 1950. The results suggest that intercohort inequality generated by real income growth dwarfs the effects of housing market variations. Thus, these calculations suggest that the policy issues arising from housing market volatility are primarily the risk exposure and ex post mistakes in life-cycle savings behavior of individuals that such volatility may cause, and insurance or other correctives for these mistakes, rather than large-scale distributional inequities between cohorts.

The compensating variation calculations could be refined further. Obvious corrections are to eliminate the truncation of the utility calculation at age 70 and to take account of individual mortality rates in forming discounted utility. Deeper issues are the treatment of bequest motives and the adequacy of the additively separable model of intertemporal utility. In fact, a strongly concave transformation of the utility function (14) prior to formation of the present value of utility is probably justified, to reflect what are likely to be relatively low elasticities of intertemporal substitution of consumption. If, in addition, the utility function is given a von Neumann–Morgenstern interpretation to assess the welfare effects of risk, then these transformations should reflect the degree of risk aversion. (As is well known, it is unlikely that intertemporal substitution and risk aversion can both be described satisfactorily by an additively separable utility function.)

7.8 Summary

This paper has developed a framework for projecting housing market prices and stocks in response to demographics and income and, from these projections, calculated the welfare effects of housing market volatility. The results suggest that cohorts born in the last baby boom and after, from 1950 on, are all in roughly the same boat, without major cohort inequities arising from housing opportunities. However, these cohorts are slightly worse off than cohorts born in 1920–40. The only cohorts that were substantially better off than the post-1950 cohorts in terms of housing were those born before 1920.

The relatively modest compensating variations for housing cost differences across cohorts may mask more serious problems caused by the effects of housing price risk on life-cycle saving and consumption levels of the elderly. Quantification of these effects will have to await further research.

Topics for further research include construction of a demographic model of household formation and control for the effects of household size on housing demand. Further work is needed on savings behavior and expectations. A promising approach is to combine macroeconomic and demographic data with the 1989 wave of the Panel Study for Income Dynamics, which contains wealth inventories in 1984 and 1989 for about 2,000 elderly households. This should permit assessment of some major open questions about behavioral response to housing variables, particularly evidence about the degree of myopia in housing decisions, about adjustments in savings in response to anticipated capital gains, and about intergenerational transfers.

References

Ai, C., J. Feinstein, D. McFadden, and H. Pollakowski. 1990. The dynamics of housing demand by the elderly: User cost effects. In *The economics of the elderly,* ed. D. Wise. Chicago: University of Chicago Press.

Börsch-Supan, A. 1989. Household dissolution and the choice of alternative living arrangements among elderly Americans. In *The economics of aging,* ed. David Wise. Chicago: University of Chicago Press.

Boskin, M., and J. Shoven. 1987. Concepts and measures of earnings replacement during retirement. In *Issues in pension economics,* ed. Z. Bodie, J. Shoven, and D. Wise. Chicago: University of Chicago Press.

Consulting Panel on Social Security. 1976. Report, Committee on Ways and Means, U.S. House of Representatives.

Darby, M. 1979. *Effects of Social Security on income and the capital stock.* Washington, D.C.: American Enterprise Institute.

Diamond, P., and J. Hausman. 1984. Individual retirement and savings behavior. *Journal of Public Economics:*

Feinstein, J., and D. McFadden. 1989. The dynamics of housing demand by the elderly I: Wealth, cash-flow, and demographic effects. In *The economics of aging,* ed. David Wise. Chicago: University of Chicago Press.

Haub, C. 1987. Understanding population projections. *Population Bulletin* 42, No. 4: 3–41.

Henderson, J., and Y. Ioannides. 1983. A model of housing tenure choice. *American Economic Review* 73:98–113.

Hurd, M. 1991. Research on the elderly: Economic status, retirement, and consumption and saving. *Journal of Economic Literature* 23:565–637.

Hurd, M., and J. Shoven. 1982. The economic status of the elderly. In *Financial aspects of the United States pension system,* ed. Z. Bodie and J. Shoven. Chicago: University of Chicago Press.

Kotlikoff, L., and D. Smith. 1983. *Pensions in the American economy,* Chicago: University of Chicago Press.

McFadden, D. 1994. Problems of housing the elderly in the United States. In *Aging in the United States and Japan: Economic trends,* eds. Y. Noguchi and D. A. Wise. Chicago: University of Chicago Press.

Mankiw, G., and D. Weil. 1989. The baby boom, the baby bust, and the housing market. *Regional Science and Urban Economics* 19:235–58.

Palmer, Brian. 1989. Implications of the changing elderly male mortality. Ph.D. thesis, Massachusetts Institute of Technology.

Poterba, J. 1984. Tax subsidies to owner-occupied housing: An asset market approach. *Quarterly Journal of Economics* 99:729–52.

Poterba, J., and L. Summers. 1987. *Public policy implications of declining old-age mortality.* In *Work health and income among the elderly,* ed. G. Burtless. Washington, D.C.: Brookings Institution.

Rosen, K. 1984. *Affordable housing: New policies and the housing and mortgage markets.* Cambridge, Mass.: Ballinger.

Russell, L. 1982. *The baby boom generation and the economy.* Washington, D.C.: Brookings Institution.

Skinner, J. 1989. Housing wealth and nonresidential savings. NBER Working Paper. Cambridge, Mass.: National Bureau of Economic Research.

Smeeding, T. 1989. Full income estimates of the relative well-being of the elderly and the nonelderly. In *Research in Income Inequality,* ed. D. Bloom and D. Slottje. Greenwich, Conn.: JAI.

Spencer, G. 1989. *Projections of the population of the United States, by age, sex, and race.* U.S. Department of Commerce, Bureau of the Census, Series P-25.

Topel, R., and S. Rosen. 1988. Housing investment in the United States. *Journal of Political Economy* 96:718–40.

U.S. Congress, Joint Economic Committee. 1986. *Demographic changes in the United States: The economic and social consequences into the 21st Century,* 99–1088. Washington: U.S. Government Printing Office.

U.S. Department of Commerce. 1975. *Historical statistics of the United States: Colonial times to 1970.* Bureau of the Census. Washington: U.S. Government Printing Office.

U.S. Department of Commerce. Yearly. *Statistical abstract of the United States.* Bureau of the Census. Washington: U.S. Government Printing Office.

U.S. Department of Commerce. Monthly. *Survey of current business.* Bureau of Economic Analysis. Washington: U.S. Government Printing Office.

Venti, S., and D. Wise. 1990. But they don't want to reduce housing equity. In *Issues in the economics of aging,* ed. D. Wise. Chicago: The University of Chicago Press.

Comment   N. Gregory Mankiw

In this paper Daniel McFadden offers a grand theory—or, more precisely, a grand prediction. He presents and estimates an econometric model of the housing market, and he then simulates the model into the future, given the dramatic (and largely uncontroversial) changes that are occurring in U.S. demography. McFadden predicts that real housing prices will fall about 2 or 3 percent per year for the next 112 years. When David Weil and I made a similar prediction in a paper several years ago, we were bold enough to forecast out only 20 years (Mankiw and Weil 1989). McFadden has outdone us by 92 years.

The Coming Real Estate Bust

The prediction that housing prices are going to fall over the next couple of decades is based on a simple story about supply and demand. Cross-sectional data tell us that the demand for housing is closely related to the number of adults in a household: as McFadden's figure 7.11 shows, children do not generate much housing demand. This finding implies, at the aggregate level, that the demand for housing is roughly proportional to the adult population. There is little doubt that, because of low birthrates in the 1970s, the adult population will grow more slowly in the future than it has in the past. Hence, housing demand will grow more slowly as well.

The impact of demand on prices depends, of course, on the elasticity of supply. If the supply elasticity were very large, then fluctuations in demand would not influence prices much. Yet experience suggests that this is not the case. In the 1970s, when the baby-boom generation of the 1950s was reaching adulthood, housing prices rose substantially. This experience suggests that the elasticity of supply is not very large, and that housing prices will fall when the baby-bust generation reaches adulthood.

This is the essence of my paper with David Weil. It is also, I believe, the essence of this paper by Dan McFadden. These two papers are similar in the "big pictures" they present. Yet, in their methodologies, the papers are quite different. In the most general terms, the difference between the two papers is that between structural and reduced-form estimation.

Two Approaches

The approach that McFadden takes is to estimate a structural model of the housing market. That is, he estimates the demand for the stock of housing and the supply of residential investment. He then simulates this model into the future under standard demographic assumptions. By contrast, although David

N. Gregory Mankiw is professor of economics at Harvard University and a research associate of the National Bureau of Economic Research.

Weil and I presented and were guided by a theoretical model similar to McFadden's, we did not try to estimate it. In our empirical analysis, we relied more on the estimation of simple reduced-form regressions.

As we all learned in basic econometrics, structural and reduced-form estimation each has its own advantages. Structural estimation links empirical analysis closer to a particular economic theory, which is an advantage if one believes the theory. Yet structural estimation imposes more restrictions on the data than does reduced-form estimation; any forecast from a structural model is based on those restrictions as well as on past experience. For the purpose of forecasting, one might want to avoid imposing any prior theoretical restrictions, since those restrictions are open to dispute. Thus one might prefer reduced-form estimation.[1]

In the case at hand, however, the situation is not this simple. Since McFadden's model is dynamic, forward-looking, and nonlinear, its reduced-form is complicated. It is far easier to estimate the structural model, as McFadden does, than to solve for and estimate the model's reduced form. For forecasting, therefore, it is not clear which method to prefer. One way to view the regressions that Weil and I ran is that they are approximations to the reduced-form of a structural model such as McFadden's; whether they are good approximations is hard to tell.

One might be tempted to conclude that McFadden's structural model is picking up the same phenomenon that Weil and I emphasized in our paper, since the predictions are so similar. Yet I am reticent to endorse McFadden's model as confirmation for our view, for the paper presents few model diagnostics. In particular, I would like to see how well McFadden's model explains housing prices in sample. As a crude specification test, one could examine whether this structural model does better at explaining history than do much simpler reduced-form equations. If it does better fitting the data in sample, that would provide a compelling case for the structural model; if it does worse, that would constitute a rejection.

I also think McFadden could do more with his model. For example, he could use it to explain historical fluctuations in the housing market, such as the large increase in prices in the 1970s. David Weil and I argued that this increase was driven largely by demographic changes, whereas Jim Poterba (1984) has argued that it was driven largely by changes in the user cost due to rising inflation and the nonindexed tax system. One could consider several historical counterfactuals. What would have happened to housing prices if there had been no postwar baby boom? Or what would have happened if inflation had not risen in the 1970s? One advantage of estimating a structural model of the housing market is that it can be used to answer these questions.

---

1. This is similar to the argument that Sims (1980) makes for the use of vector autoregressions rather than structural macroeconomic models.

The Generational Distribution

McFadden does use his model to gauge the intergenerational impact of changes in housing prices. I am somewhat skeptical about his conclusion. Comparing the lucky and unlucky generations, McFadden finds a small compensating variation: less than 1 percent of lifetime income.

A back-of-the-envelope calculation, however, suggests a much larger impact. Consider McFadden's figure 7.19. According to this figure, someone born in 1958 (like me) can expect a real capital loss of about 3 percent per year over his life. His grandfather, born in 1900, received a real capital gain of 3 percent per year. Therefore, the increase in user cost of housing (from this change alone) is about 6 percent per year. Using the conservative estimate that house value is about one year's income, one reaches a compensating variation of 6 percent of income, almost 10 times McFadden's estimate. McFadden's estimate differs from mine in part because it incorporates various macroeconomic factors that influence the user cost of housing, such as changes over time in tax rates and interest rates. It seems more natural, however, to separate the impact of housing prices from that of these other factors.

A more difficult question is what policymakers should make of all this. Here I agree with McFadden: probably nothing. Many things influence the relative income of different generations; the price of housing is only one of them. Moreover, given the importance of bequests in wealth accumulation, it is not clear how to interpret these intergenerational redistributions. It is noteworthy, however, that the generations that are hurt by the trends in housing prices are, coincidentally, also those that are hurt by the increases in Social Security in the 1970s and the large budget deficits of the 1980s. Nineteen fifty-eight was not a good year to be born.

References

Mankiw, N. Gregory, and David N. Weil. 1989. The baby boom, the baby bust, and the housing market. *Regional Science and Urban Economics* 19 (May): 235–58.

Poterba, James. 1984. Tax subsidies to owner-occupied housing: An asset market approach. *Quarterly Journal of Economics* 99:729–52.

Sims, Christopher. 1980. Macroeconomics and reality. *Econometrica* January: 1–48.

VI International Comparisons

8 Aging in Germany and the United States: International Comparisons

Axel Börsch-Supan

8.1 Introduction

This paper reports on a set of international comparisons of how the German and the U.S. economies are affected by population aging. The purpose of the paper is to employ cross-national comparisons to learn about the microeconomic mechanisms in labor, financial, and housing markets that are most important for an analysis of how population aging affects our economies and, from an understanding of these mechanisms, to discuss policy options that may moderate the implications of population aging. The paper concentrates on three microeconomic decisions: when to retire, how much to save, and where to live. The paper is a continuation of Börsch-Supan (1991b). For a more macroeconomic view, the reader is referred to the many comparative studies that describe cross-national differences in the aging process and analyze aggregate economic implications (e.g., Organisation for Economic Cooperation and Development [OECD] 1988; Hagemann and Nicoletti 1989; Auerbach et al. 1990).

In order to discuss our policy options to alleviate negative implications of population aging on labor, financial, and housing markets, we must elucidate the economic mechanisms underlying retirement, savings, and housing choices by the elderly. In particular, we must understand how strongly they are affected by public policy, such as institutional arrangements, government regulations,

Axel Börsch-Supan is professor of economics at the University of Mannheim and a research associate of the National Bureau of Economic Research.

Research in this paper was supported by National Institute of Aging grant 5 PO1 AG05842. The author is indebted to Anette Reil-Held, Hermann Buslei, Ernst Seiler, Gerald Schehl, Peter Schmidt, and Johannes Velling, who provided valuable research assistance at various stages of this project. Earlier versions of parts of this paper have appeared in *Economic Policy* 12. The author wishes to thank Charles Wyplosz for his comments, many of which have led to work which is now included in this paper.

and laws. The main idea of this paper is to exploit international differences in public policy in order to learn about the responses by the elderly to these policies.

The power of an international comparison comes from the fact that different countries have different institutional arrangements, government regulations, subsidies, and laws. In a study of only one country, it is often impossible to separate preferences from the impact of institutions and regulations, because there are commonly too few changes of institutions and regulations in one country to properly identify their impacts. Germany and the United States are particularly well suited for comparison. While they are sufficiently similar in mentality and social customs to make a comparison meaningful, they also feature important differences in institutions and public policy.[1] Moreover, Germany is one of the countries in which population aging is most advanced, leading the aging process in the United States by about 20 years. In this respect, changes that are occurring in Germany now may be indicative of changes to come in the United States. Indeed, retirement, savings, and housing behavior differ quite markedly between Germany and the United States, and I will show that most of these differences are consistent with the incentives applicable to each country.

The paper proceeds as follows. Section 8.2 summarizes the basic demographic trends in Germany, contrasting it to the United States. Section 8.3 reports on retirement decisions, particularly early retirement and its causes. Section 8.4 is devoted to a descriptive analysis of the strikingly different savings patterns among the aged in the two countries. Housing markets are examined in section 8.5 with particular attention to the elderlys' choice of living arrangements. Each of these sections provides a sketch of the relevant government regulations, evidence of how these square with actual behavior, and implications for public policy. The paper concludes with a brief general summary.

8.2 Basic Demographic Facts

The expected change in the age structure of the industrialized countries is dramatic and will lead to a substantially higher proportion of older people. Population aging is particularly pronounced in Germany; see table 8.1.[2] Among the seven large OECD countries, the aging process is least marked but

1. On a more mundane yet important level, West Germany and the United States have rich and comparable longitudinal micro data sets that shed light on the economic situation of the elderly: the Panel Study of Income Dynamics (PSID) and its German counterpart, the Socio-Economic Panel (SOEP).

2. The numbers in this section are from OECD (1988) and refer to the former West Germany. Because East and West Germany have approximately the same age distributions, German unification does not affect the aging of the German population in any substantial way. East Germany features a higher mortality rate and had a decade of higher fertility between the mid-seventies and reunification. Higher mortality is commonly attributed to environmental problems and insufficient health services in the former East Germany. It is likely to adjust quickly to West German mortality rates. The period of high fertility appears to have been caused by the omnipresent East German

Table 8.1   **Elderly Population in Seven OECD Countries**

	Population Aged 65 and Over (%)			Population Aged 80 and Over (millions)	
	1950	1990	2030	1980	2030
Canada	7.7	11.4	22.4	0.44	1.89
France	11.4	13.8	21.8	1.53	3.40
Germany	9.4	15.5	25.8	1.60	2.65
Italy	8.0	13.8	21.9	1.28	2.56
Japan	5.2	11.4	20.0	1.63	6.64
United Kingdom	10.7	15.1	19.2	1.48	2.60
United States	8.1	12.2	19.5	5.22	12.43

Source: OECD (1988).

still dramatic in the United Kingdom and the United States. Within the next 40 years, the proportion of elderly in Germany will increase to more than a quarter of the population. Even more accentuated is the aging of households. The proportion of elderly households (headed by persons over age 60) in the German population is projected to increase from 21 percent in 1980 to 37 percent in 2030. Most marked is the increase among the oldest old: in the year 2030, Germany will have twice as many elderly over age 85 as now.

Two distinct processes are causing these dramatic changes. From 1950 to 1980, life expectancy at birth increased by about 7.2 percent on average in the OECD, while fertility in the industrialized countries declined to below replacement level; see table 8.2. From 1950 to 1980, German life expectancy increased by almost 7 years, from 66.4 to 73.3 years,[3] while at the same time the fertility rate in West Germany decreased from 2.1 to 1.4, considerably below the reproduction rate necessary for a stable population. The effects of both processes sum to what is commonly termed "double aging" of the industrialized countries.

The effects of double aging on an economy are best captured by the old-age dependency ratio depicted in table 8.3. Again, the numbers for Germany are particularly dramatic. Its old-age dependency ratio will increase from 0.22 currently to almost 0.44 in the year 2030. Therefore, in 2030, twice as many elderly aged 65 and above will have to be supported by the same number of persons aged 15–64 as today. The projected German dependency ratio is the highest among all OECD countries except Switzerland.[4] The dependency ratio will fall again after 2030, when the bulge of the baby boom works its way

---

child-care system, which used to support labor-force participation during the childbearing years of young women (Chesnais 1987). This system was dismantled after unification, and the East German fertility rate has dropped below the West German level.

3. In 1985, life expectancy at birth was 71.5 years for German males, 78.1 years for German females.

4. The projected old-age dependency ratio for Switzerland in 2030 is 0.47.

Table 8.2   Life Expectancy and Fertility Rates in Seven OECD Countries

	Life Expectancy[a]			Fertility Rate[b]		
	1950	1980	Increase (%)	1950	1980	1980/1950 (%)
Canada	68.4	75.0	9.6	3.4	1.8	52.9
France	66.8	74.3	11.2	2.9	1.9	65.5
Germany	66.4	73.3	10.4	2.1	1.4	66.7
Italy	66.1	74.4	12.6	2.6	1.7	65.4
Japan	59.2	76.4	29.1	2.4	1.8	75.0
United Kingdom	68.9	73.8	7.1	3.0	1.8	60.0
United States	68.4	73.5	7.5	2.2	1.8	81.8

Source: OECD (1988).
[a]Average life expectancy at birth in years.
[b]Age-specific fertility rates summed across all child-bearing ages.

Table 8.3   Old-Age Dependency Ratios for Seven OECD Countries

	Population Aged 65+/Population Aged 15–64					
	1980	1990	2000	2010	2020	2030
Canada	14.1	16.8	19.0	21.4	28.9	37.3
France	21.9	20.9	23.3	24.5	30.6	35.8
Germany	23.4	22.3	25.4	30.6	33.5	43.6
Italy	20.8	20.1	22.6	25.7	29.3	35.3
Japan	13.5	16.2	22.6	29.5	33.6	31.9
United Kingdom	23.2	23.0	22.3	22.3	25.5	31.1
United States	17.1	18.5	18.2	18.8	25.0	31.7

Source: OECD (1988).

through the age distribution. However, it is likely to remain substantially higher than now: the OECD estimate for 2050 is 41.6 percent.

The increase in the ratio of retirees to workers is even more accentuated than that in the demographic old-age dependency ratio. The retiree/worker ratio is closer to the economic meaning of an old-age dependency ratio but more difficult to project because of potential changes in labor supply behavior. The German ministry of labor affairs projects that this ratio will climb from 0.48 currently to about 0.91 retirees per worker in the year 2030.

The dependency ratios in table 8.3 show quite clearly how the double aging process will strain the pay-as-you-go social security systems of our countries simply because fewer contributors will have to support more retirees. However, this is not the only policy problem facing the industrialized countries. Because the average age of the work force will increase, aggregate productivity will decline, unless the hump-shaped age-productivity profile also shifts. Increasing the contribution rates to public pension systems will create work disincentives, exacerbating the potential productivity decline and partly offsetting the contribution increases. The double aging process will also change the accumulation of aggregate wealth and skew its intergenerational distribution in a complicated fashion, because older people save differently than younger people. It will assign a growing burden of family support to the young generation, when the elderly become frail and unable to live independently. These issues are taken up in the following sections.

8.3   Retirement Decisions

8.3.1   Institutional Background

Germany and the United States have pay-as-you-go public pension systems, with the resulting sensitivity to shifts in the age distribution that is the focus of most debates about population aging. Both countries supply, in effect, a minimum level of retirement income to workers with little labor income. And both countries feature fairly broad coverage of workers by social security: in the United States, about 95 percent of all workers are insured by Social Security, including the self-employed, while in Germany only the self-employed (8.9 percent of the labor force in 1988) and workers with very small incomes (5.6 percent) are not covered (Casmir 1989).

Apart from these similarities, Germany and the United States differ substantially in their retirement incentives. First, about a quarter of the German labor force is subject to mandatory retirement. This includes the entire public sector and some private sectors. In most cases, the mandatory retirement age is 65 years. In the United States, age discrimination laws prohibit mandatory retirement. Part-time work is also very restricted in Germany, because of inflexible work regulations and high fringe benefits, independent of hours worked, sustained by an insider coalition of unions and employers.

Second, although in both countries the public retirement system is augmented by private pensions, they play only a minor role in Germany, while they are a significant source of retirement income in the United States. About half of the American elderly aged 60 and above are covered by pension plans. For 13 percent of these, pensions contribute more than 20 percent of their incomes, for 2 percent, more than half their retirement incomes (Hurd 1989, table II 6). This is in striking contrast to Germany. In 1984, 82 percent of all elderly in West Germany received only social security income. Another 8.5 percent have additional private pension income (mainly annuities from life insurance), and only 7.6 percent have both social security and firm pension income.[5] The difference in the importance of private pension plans is most striking when the average contribution of firm pensions to retirement income is

---

5. According to the 1984 wave of the German SOEP.

considered: Private pensions contribute about 15 percent of the income of the American elderly, but only slightly more than 3 percent for the German elderly.

Not only the significance but also the pattern of private pension plans is different. The United States features a broad range of pension provisions among firms even within the same industry (Kotlikoff and Wise 1987), while pension plans are rather homogeneous in Germany (Jacobs, Kohli, and Rein 1987). The main reason for the homogeneity in Germany is the centralization of union activities: all unionized employees in a German industry are members of the same union, and labor contracts also apply for nonunion members of the same industry.

A third difference between the social security systems in the United States and Germany is the general level of public retirement income. In the United States, Social Security is tailored to prevent poverty among the elderly and to secure a minimum reasonable standard of living. In Germany, public pensions are essentially proportional to lifetime earnings, because they are intended to ensure approximately the same living standard before and after retirement. Hence, German public pensions provide for substantially higher replacement rates than their U.S. counterparts, particularly for higher income levels. As a matter of fact, the stated rationale for not having complete replacement in Germany is not the added utility of leisure but the cessation of work-related expenses after retirement. Only very high incomes are not subject to the proportionality rule, because the income subject to social security contributions is capped. Table 8.4 presents net replacement ratios by income class, i.e., average after-tax retirement incomes as percentages of average after-tax labor incomes. On average, German social security income is about 33 percent higher than American, resulting in an average net replacement ratio of more than 70 percent. This also implies that unbequeathable and intangible social security wealth is considerably higher in Germany than in the United States. This is, on average, only partially compensated by higher private pension wealth in the United States.

Incentives with respect to retirement timing also differ between the United States and Germany. While the social security provisions in both countries offer the opportunity to retire at different ages (the so-called "window of retirement"), they differ considerably in how benefit levels are adjusted for retirement at different ages. Table 8.5 displays these adjustments. They relate retirement income for retirement at age 65 (normalized to 100 percent) to retirement income at earlier or later retirement ages and combine the reduction factors for early retirement with the delayed retirement credit for retirement after full-benefit retirement age. Currently, full-benefit retirement age is 65 in both countries. It will remain so in Germany, while in the United States it will gradually increase to age 66 in the year 2005 and to age 67 in 2022.

The first column in table 8.5 displays nondistortionary adjustment factors

Table 8.4   **Replacement Ratios of Social Security Old Age Pensions**

	Net Replacement Ratio[b] (%)	
Relative Income[a] (%)	United States	Germany
50	61	67
75	55	66
100	53	71
150	45	77
200	41	75
300	30	53

Source: Casmir (1989).

[a]As a percentage of the wages of an average production worker.

[b]Average after-tax pension divided by average after-tax labor income; 40 years of services assumed; married couple supplement not included.

Table 8.5   **Adjustment of Public Pensions by Retirement Age: Pension as a Percentage of Pension One Would Obtain by Retiring at Age 65**

	"Fair"	Germany		United States	
Retirement Age	System[a]	Before Reform[b]	After Reform[c]	Before Reform[d]	After Reform[e]
60	64.6	87.5[f]	69.5[g]	[h]	[h]
61	70.4	90.0[f]	75.6[g]	[h]	[h]
62	76.7	92.5[f]	81.7[g]	80.0	77.8
63	83.7	95.0[i]	87.8[g]	86.7	85.2
64	91.4	97.5[i]	93.9[g]	94.4	92.6
65	100.0	100.0	100.0	100.0	100.0
66	109.6	109.9	108.5	103.0	105.6
67	120.4	120.1	117.0	106.0	111.1
68	132.5	123.0	125.5	109.0	120.0
69	146.2	125.8	134.0	112.0	128.9
70	161.9	128.7	142.5	115.0	137.8

Sources: Frerich (1987); Casmir (1989); *Social Security Bulletin* 46, no. 7 (July 1983).

[a]Hypothetical adjustments that keep the present discounted value of retirement benefits minus contributions constant across all retirement ages between 60–70 at a 3.3 percent discount rate.

[b]Gesetzliche Rentenversicherung until 1992.

[c]Gesetzliche Rentenversicherung after 1992 reform has been fully phased in.

[d]Old Age Social Security (OASDI) until 1983.

[e]Old Age Social Security (OASDI) after 1983 reform has been fully phased in.

[f]Applicable only to women and workers who cannot be appropriately employed due to health or mismatch reasons (*berufs- oder erwerbsunfähig*).

[g]Applicable only to workers who cannot be appropriately employed due to health or mismatch reasons (*berufs- oder erwerbsunfähig*).

[h]Not yet eligible for Social Security benefits.

[i]Requires 35 years of service.

which I dub "fair."[6] These adjustment factors keep the present discounted value of retirement benefits minus contributions constant across all retirement ages between 60 and 70 and therefore do not distort the choice of retirement age, conditional on the fact that the worker has worked at least until age 59. I will use these adjustment factors as a yardstick for the current and the reformed relative pension benefits in the United States and Germany.

In the United States, benefits increase during the window of early retirement—ages 62–65—in a way that is reasonably close to actuarially fair. For retirement ages past 65, benefits increase less than actuarially fairly. The latest age to apply for an old-age pension is 70.

In Germany, until 1992, benefits were proportional to years of service, with no further adjustment applied, resulting in a very small percentage increase in retirement benefits for postponing retirement once a large number of years in service is reached. The window period—effectively ages 60–65—is characterized by three regulations. First, everybody can retire at age 65. Second, in order to receive retirement benefits at age 63, 35 years of service are necessary.[7] Third, retirement at age 60 is possible for all women and for those male workers who cannot be appropriately employed (*berufs- oder erwerbsunfähig*) for health- or job-related reasons. The latter rule has been interpreted very broadly, and its application—loosely speaking—required only the help of the family doctor. Its application was traditionally encouraged by employers who wanted to thin out their work forces. The rule also applies when there are no vacancies for the worker's specific job description available, thereby fudging the distinction between unemployment and retirement.[8]

In both countries, social security was reformed to steepen the adjustment rate profiles. In the United States, the reduction factors for retirement before age 65 are now very close to actuarially fair. For retirement past age 65, benefits increase faster than under the old law, but the increase remains less than actuarially fair. The reformed German system provides substantially more incentives for later retirement than does the American one. However, the reduced benefits for retirement before age 65 are still substantially higher than the nondistortionary ones in the first column of table 8.5.

Although not completely free of distortive incentives, the American public retirement system is more age neutral during the window period than the German system. Particularly in the reformed U.S. system, there is little economic

6. This term is somewhat misleading because the system as a whole is not actuarially fair. The present discounted values were computed for a discount rate of 3.3 percent, the value which would equalize lifetime discounted benefits and contributions for the historical contribution rates and current life expectancy.

7. This includes time spent in military service, on education, for childbearing (about one year), etc.

8. In the years between 1984 and 1989, Germany reduced the retirement age de facto to age 58 (Vorruhestandsregelung) because workers could apply for the status *berufsunfähig* at that age. They received unemployment compensation at ages 58 and 59 and then a social security pension as if they had retired at age 60.

incentive for Americans to retire at any particular age in the window of early retirement and only a small disincentive to retire later than at age 65, while the German social security system tilts the retirement decision heavily toward the applicable early retirement date. Strangely enough, the old German system provided a large increase in retirement benefits for work at ages 66 and 67. However, this reward was too small to offset the early retirement incentives (see below).

The tax treatment of labor earnings while receiving public pensions also differs strongly between the two countries. In the United States, receiving a public pension does not preclude working, although additional labor income during the entire window period of ages 60–70 is taxed at 50 percent if it exceeds certain limits. In Germany, labor income, additional to a public pension, which exceeds a very small allowance is taxed at 100 percent during the early retirement period. However, there is no penalty at all for working after age 65.

All differences between the public and private pension systems in the two countries—mandatory retirement age, the role of private pensions, replacement levels, adjustment factors of public pensions, and taxation of labor income while receiving public pensions—are likely to generate similar implications for retirement choices. If retirement choices respond at all to the economic incentives provided by public and private pension plans, they are likely to be more uniform in Germany, while they should be more diverse in the United States, i.e., more individual specific and more firm specific. Moreover, because retirement income in Germany is on average higher than in the United States and because the German system is less than actuarially fair for late retirees, we should observe a lower supply of labor in old age in Germany than in the United States—provided that the preference for leisure is roughly comparable in the two countries.

8.3.2   Descriptive Evidence: Old-Age Labor Supply

Indeed, this is what we find in a first glance at the data. Table 8.6 presents labor-force participation trends in seven OECD countries. The differences between Germany and the United States are striking. Although both countries have experienced a declining trend in retirement age (similar to that in the other OECD countries), labor-force participation of the elderly is substantially lower in West Germany than in the United States.[9] In the United States, labor-force participation among persons aged 65 and over has fallen from 26.6 percent in 1965 to 10.3 percent in 1985. While in West Germany 24 percent of the elderly still had a job in 1965, this percentage has fallen to a mere 5.2 percent in 1985. This participation rate is the lowest in the seven major OECD countries.

The trend visible in table 8.6 is approximately in line with changes in the

9. Since I use pre-1990 data, I refer to West Germany only.

Table 8.6   Labor-Force Participation Rates among Persons Aged 65 and Over
                   (%)

	1965	1975	1985
Canada	26.3	18.5	12.3
France	28.3	13.9	5.3
Germany	24.0	10.8	5.2
Italy	18.4	10.4	8.9
Japan	56.3	44.4	37.0
United Kingdom	23.7	15.8	7.6
United States	26.6	20.7	10.3

Source: OECD (1988).

ratio of retirement to labor income. In the United States as well as in West Germany, social security retirement income has increased relative to labor income. While nominal wages have increased 3.7-fold in the United States and 4.1-fold in West Germany, the average old-age social security benefits have increased 4.6-fold in the United States and 4.3-fold in West Germany.[10] This increase of pension income relative to labor income is due to the effective indexation of social security benefits in both countries. In West Germany, for example, pension benefits have been linked to gross average labor income.[11] Retirement income is taxed at a much lower rate than labor income because of the generous exemptions. Hence, the progressivity of the income tax schedule has produced a more than proportional increase of net retirement income relative to the increase of net labor income.

Cross-national survey data provide additional evidence that economic factors have strongly influenced old-age labor supply behavior. Table 8.7 presents a closer look at retirement rates for male workers in West Germany and the United States, based on the 1984 wave of the Panel Study of Income Dynamics (PSID) and its German counterpart, the 1984 wave of the Socio-Economic Panel (SOEP). Because incentives for part-time work are rather different in the two countries, it is important to define retirement consistently and to distinguish full retirement from partial and no retirement. We define retirement by hours worked and use three states of labor-force participation. Full-time work is 35 hours or more per week, part-time work is between 15 and 34 weekly hours, and full retirement is less than 15 hours of work per week.

The range of retirement ages is much wider in the United States than in West Germany. While the United States features a smooth transition between work and retirement, with a large percentage of part-time work, the West German

10. The numbers are obtained from *Statistical Abstracts of the United States* (*Statistical Abstract,* various issues) and the *Statistisches Jahrbücher für die Bundesrepublik Deutschland* (Statistisches Jahrbuch, various issues).

11. The 1992 social security reform has changed this to an indexation with respect to net income.

Table 8.7   **Male Retirement and Labor-Force Participation Rates (%)**

Age	United States			West Germany		
	Full-Time	Part-Time	Retired	Full-Time	Part-Time	Retired
50–54	76.6	11.0	12.4	91.5	0.6	7.8
55–59	65.9	17.4	16.7	79.1	1.5	19.4
60–64	38.8	16.9	44.3	37.7	1.6	60.8
65–69	12.2	22.3	65.4	4.1	7.5	88.4
70–74	7.2	13.7	79.1	1.7	3.2	95.3
75–79	2.5	12.7	84.8	2.5	1.7	95.7
80+	1.6	4.8	93.5	1.2	0.0	98.8

Sources: 1984 PSID; 1984 SOEP.

Notes: Full-time: More than 35 weekly work hours. Part-time: Between 15 and 35 weekly work hours. Retired: Less than 15 weekly work hours.

age-retirement profile is characterized by a sudden jump from full-time work to full-time retirement in the age range 60–64, accompanied by a rather low percentage of part-time occupation. More detailed analysis shows that in the United States retirement ages are more evenly distributed, with a peak at age 62. This is consistent with the fact that the adjustment of benefits in the United States is approximately actuarially fair. We observe that in the United States people retire at all ages, most notably also at ages 63 and 64 in the interior of the window period. This is quite different from Germany. Here, retirement is very much concentrated at ages 60, 63, and 65, at exactly the first years when each of the three retirement regulations mentioned in subsection 8.3.2 apply, and very few people retire at ages between these.

In order to turn these pieces of suggestive evidence into numbers which can be employed for policy analysis, I employ a simplified version of the option value model developed by Stock and Wise (1990). It relates applicable economic incentives—mainly the replacement rate and the retirement-age-dependent adjustment factors—to observed retirement age, conditional on other determinants of retirement behavior, such as sociodemographics and health. Its key variable capturing economic incentives is the value of the option to postpone retirement at a given age. It is defined as the maximum attainable expected discounted utility from consumption if the worker were to retire at some later age minus the expected discounted utility if the worker were to retire now (Lazear and Moore 1988).

The consumption possibilities entering the option value are computed using the applicable pension rules. In Germany, the public pension system dominates retirement income. Therefore, economic retirement incentives are rather well captured by the replacement rates of the public pension system from table 8.4 together with the retirement-age-dependent adjustment factors from table 8.5. In the United States, private pension plans may dominate the importance of the public pension system for an individual worker. However, survey data in the United States give little information on the structure of each private pension plan that may be applicable to each individual worker. I will therefore not attempt to make parallel analyses for the United States and Germany.

The detailed construction of the model and estimation results are presented in Börsch-Supan (1992a). In essence, I estimate a logit model, regressing the probability of being retired on the option value, the sociodemographic variables, the health variables, and a set of age-specific constants for each age in the window period. The main results can be summarized as follows: the model fits the data rather well, the option value is statistically highly significant, and the age-specific constants remain insignificant. These are strong findings because they imply that, during the main window of retirement, actual behavior is well described by the option value, the main economic incentive for retirement.

These estimation results can be used in a microsimulation model to predict retirement ages under alternative social security rules. Specifically, I replace each person's actual option value by the option value computed with alternative retirement-age-dependent adjustment factors. The baseline retirement probabilities are fitted to replicate the population retirement probabilities. I therefore project all other determinants of retirement timing not included in the explanatory variables into the future, particularly preferences and social customs. In this respect, I am likely to underestimate the total effects of the simulated social security changes.

Table 8.8 summarizes the microsimulation results in form of the average retirement age and required contribution rates. From the number of pensioners implied by the simulation results, I compute the average retirement age and the ratio of pensioners to employed persons. Using the pay-as-you-go budget equation of the social security system, I then calculate the social security contribution rates necessary to balance contributions and payments for the years 1990 and 2000. The first row of table 8.8 relates to the old German social security system, as it was in place until 1992. The second row presents simulation results for the German social security system, employing the adjustment factors of the 1992 reform. Finally, the third row displays results for a "fair" system using the nondistortionary adjustment factors of column 1 in table 8.5.

Taking the 1992 social security reform into account removes some but by no means all of the distortion toward early retirement in Germany. The proportion of the population retiring before age 60 drops from 32.2 percent to 28.4 percent, in 1990, and the average retirement age increases by about half a year. As a consequence, the contribution rates necessary for a balanced budget are 18.1 percent rather than 18.7 percent, in 1990, and are 19.5 percent rather than 20.1 percent, in 2000.

However, a system with nondistortionary adjustment factors, as defined above, has a much stronger effect on retirement age and also therefore on the contribution rate necessary to balance the public pension system's budget. It increases the average retirement age by about two years and results in contribution rates that are substantially lower (by more than two percent) than the ones under the old and under the reformed German social security systems.

Table 8.8   **Simulated Average Retirement Age and Contribution Rates**

	Mean Retirement Age	Contribution Rate (%)	
		1990	2000
System before 1992 reform	58.5	18.7	20.1
System after 1992 reform	59.0	18.1	19.5
Nondistortionary ("fair") system	60.7	16.2	17.4

Source: Author's calculations.

8.3.3   Policy Implications

The main conclusion from the evidence presented is the strong and consistent response of retirement behavior to public policy. The differences in retirement behavior between Germany and the United States are clearly in line with economic incentives to retirement in each country and with the institutional differences between them. The fine tuning by retirement-age-dependent benefit adjustments appears to be well reflected in observed choices of retirement ages. We learned that our pension systems indeed powerfully influence retirement decisions.

In principle, an individual should be able to choose his retirement date. However, changes in the average retirement age have side effects on the soundness of the social security system, on average wages, on aggregate productivity, on tax revenues, and on aggregate savings. Advancing retirement ages amplify the effects of a rising old-age dependency ratio, potentially above the economic potential and the will of a generation of workers to come. While this affects mainly the public pension system, private pension funds and health insurance systems are also affected because health insurance for retirees is heavily subsidized in Germany and in the United States. The increase in the general support ratio will lead to a level of social security and general taxes that will create strong work disincentives. In West Germany, Schmähl (1989) projected social security contribution rates exceeding 40 percent of gross labor income, not including rising general taxes to finance added health expenditures. Such high tax rates are simply not sustainable. Although this effect has been the focus of most debates about population aging and has led to the above-mentioned social security reforms in Germany and in the United States, our simulation shows that this lesson has not yet been learned in Germany because the 1992 social security reform has not really removed early retirement incentives.

Replacing the strong incentives for German workers to retire early by a more age-neutral system appears likely to generate more evenly distributed retirement ages than those depicted in table 8.7. As a way to induce later retirement, a gradual adjustment of replacement rates may be not only more subtle but also more efficient than the shift of eligibility ages that was enacted in the German social security reform act of 1992. It is likely to be more efficient, because it avoids the bunching that is a current characteristic of German retirement behavior and that appears to be an expression of constraints imposed on retirement choices.

Changing the retirement system too late will be complicated by the change in the politics of the social security system. Political power will shift from the working population, where it now resides, to the older generation, along with the surge in the dependency ratio. In West Germany, for example, from about 2020 onward, the majority of the voters will be pensioners and workers who will retire within the next 10 years. We then obtain a typical free-rider situation because the older generation can outvote the younger generation in determining their retirement income as well as the rate of social security taxes the younger generation has to pay.

8.4   Savings Behavior

8.4.1   Historical and Institutional Background

American and German attitudes toward saving are very different. Germans have traditionally valued saving per se and were reluctant to follow American consumerism, despite the strong American influence on German postwar development. Although this attitude appears to be changing with each new generation, it changes surprisingly slowly. Table 8.9 presents comparable personal savings rates for the two countries. Savings rates have always been higher in Germany than in the United States, but the discrepancy has been particularly large in recent years. Although both countries have experienced declining savings rates since 1975, the relative decline is much larger in the United States.

The different historical experiences of Germans and Americans may help explain the higher aggregate savings rates that emerged in Germany as soon as a moderate standard of living was achieved in the 1960s. The elderly in this decade all experienced World War II. This catastrophe, however, has affected Americans and Germans very differently. During the war and until the Germany currency reform in 1948, most Germans could not even satisfy their basic need for food and clothing. This experience was not shared by their American contemporaries. In addition, during the so-called economic miracle in the 1950s in Germany, saving was heavily promoted in large-scale public campaigns.

The attitude that saving is good per se (and that personal loans are something to be avoided) is reflected in the German tax treatment of savings and loans. There are several schemes subsidizing savings in Germany, many of them heavily advertised. And taxation of interest income is only half-heartedly enforced.

On paper, asset income, including capital gains, is taxed as ordinary income. Income from stocks and bonds is subject to automatic 25 percent withholding, which is then credited against the actual income tax burden. Although divi-

Table 8.9   **Aggregate Savings Rates (%)**

Year	West Germany	United States
1960	8.6	5.7
1965	12.2	7.0
1970	13.8	8.0
1975	16.2	8.7
1980	14.2	7.9
1985	13.0	6.4
1990	14.8	5.1

Sources: Monatsberichte der Deutschen Bundesbank (Frankfurt am Main: Deutsche Bundesbank, various issues); *Economic Report of the President,* Statistical Appendix (Washington, D.C.: Government Printing Office, 1992).

Note: Table reports personal saving as percentage of personal disposable income.

dends are subject to corporate income tax, this tax is credited against personal income taxes. Hence, Germany has no double taxation of dividend income as in the United States. Interest income from passbook savings and similar liquid capital is not currently subject to automatic withholding. Moreover, direct notification of the internal revenue service by the bank (as routinely done in the United States on form 1099) would be a violation of German privacy laws. Although the government has stepped up its public relations effort to stimulate compliance with the tax code, interest income remains routinely undeclared. Finally, capital gains are only taxable when earned by "speculation." The law considers the holding of financial assets to be speculative if the assets are sold within six months of purchase. For land, holding periods are speculative if they are shorter than two years. Long-run capital gains therefore escape taxation in Germany.

The German government has several special incentive programs to subsidize savings. A general program is designed to foster capital accumulation among the lower-income groups (Vermögensbildungsgesetz). This program has been in place since 1961 and was substantially extended in the 1970s. Employees or pensioners deduct a certain amount from their incomes and direct deposit it in long-term savings accounts. The government then supplements the contributions of eligible savers by a fixed-percentage savings premium capped by an upper limit. In the seventies, these premia were as high as 40 percent and the income limit for eligibility was high enough to cover incomes far into the middle class. Currently, savings in productive capital are subsidized by a 20 percent savings premium, savings in real estate by 10 percent, and the income limit is DM 54,000 per year for married couples, a lower middle-class income of about $33,000.

Capital market institutions do not differ greatly between the United States and Germany. In both countries, financial markets are only mildly regulated, and portfolio options are quite comparable. If they differ at all, it is because the well-to-do in the United States face more portfolio options than their German counterparts, because of a somewhat more dynamic U.S. market for financial instruments. Differences in savings options between Germany and the United States mainly include different dedicated savings programs. In the United States, IRAs and Keoghs are subsidized savings dedicated to retirement income (Venti and Wise 1987); such programs do not exist in Germany. However, bequeathable savings dedicated to housing investments are substantially subsidized and play a major role in German private capital accumulation (Börsch-Supan and Stahl 1991a).

An important difference in the institutional background for savings decisions in the two countries is the extent of income maintenance by compulsory social security programs. This brings up the question of whether social security and private savings are substitutes, a topic of great interest and the subject of controversial discussions (Barro 1974; Feldstein 1974). Because one needs to observe differences in the extent of social security programs in order to measure these potential substitution effects, an international perspective is helpful. As we have seen in table 8.4, social security income differs dramatically between Germany and the United States. The German old-age social security system replaces net income across all income ranges much more generously than the U.S. social security system. The high average net replacement ratio of more than 70 percent may provide a sufficient level of retirement income for the elderly and hence reduce the incentive for life-cycle savings in order to finance consumption in retirement.

In addition, there are pronounced differences in the health insurance systems between the two countries. In Germany, all retirees are enrolled in the mandatory health insurance system which covers all health expenditures, with the exception of long-term institutionalized care not related to acute illness. This coverage is far more comprehensive than that of Medicaid and Medicare in the United States. Therefore, the precautionary savings motive to safeguard against unexpected expenditures, particularly health-care-related expenditures, should be less pronounced in Germany.

In summary, we receive a mixed message about the impact of institutions on savings. On one hand, tax treatment of savings is more favorable in Germany than in the United States, which should, ceteris paribus, induce relatively higher savings rates in Germany. On the other hand, two of the main economic rationales for saving—assuring a comfortable retirement income and taking precautions against high health expenses—are less important in Germany than they are in the United States, because the safety net is tighter in Germany. This should, ceteris paribus, reduce savings among households younger than retirement age. Among the older elderly, however, the tighter safety net in Germany might actually increase net savings, since the generous retirement income might not only prevent the German elderly from depleting their assets but even provide income levels sufficiently large to induce savings in old age. We will take up this point when we look at the evidence on savings behavior among the aged.

8.4.2   Evidence on Savings Behavior among the Aged

It is not straightforward to compare wealth data between the two countries. In both, the wealth distribution is very skewed. Average wealth is therefore sensitive to a few very wealthy persons, while median wealth is zero for most asset categories. I employ wealth data from the PSID and SOEP wealth supplements in 1984 and 1988. Response rates to these supplements were lower than to the core questionnaire (particularly in Germany), and the quality of the wealth data is likely to be less reliable than other PSID and SOEP data, mainly because the wealth data is self-reported and subject to severe underreporting. However, the wealth data presented is roughly comparable between the two countries, because the PSID and SOEP wealth supplements are based on the same design principles. Valuation is complicated by the large discrepancy between exchange rate and purchasing power in the mid-1980s. The average exchange rate between the deutsche mark and the U.S. dollar was about $1 to DM 2.70, substantially higher than the average purchasing power parity, which was about $1 to DM 1.70, according to OECD figures. Because I am interested in real wealth, I use purchasing power parity.

Table 8.10 displays tangible wealth by household, stratified by age categories. The reported values for the United States are in line with data from the American Retirement History Survey reported by Hurd (1989), which gives us some confidence in the data.[12] Total tangible household wealth is the sum of several asset categories reported in the two surveys. Financial wealth includes liquid wealth, such as passbook savings and money market mutual funds, dedicated savings, such as the above-mentioned IRA and Keogh accounts in the United States and *Bausparkassen* (building societies) savings in West Germany, and stocks and bonds. Nonhousing wealth is defined as the sum of financial wealth plus farm and business property plus real estate not including an owner-occupied home. The self-reported estimated sales value of an owner-occupied home is then added, to yield total tangible household wealth.

In addition to the tangible wealth reported in table 8.10, almost all elderly persons have intangible and unbequeathable wealth, mainly social security and pension wealth. Total intangible wealth in the United States is estimated to be almost as large as the tangible wealth reported in table 8.10 (Hurd 1989), and it is even more in Germany.

According to the PSID and SOEP data, total tangible household wealth is, on average across ages 50 and above, lower in West Germany than in the United States. Valued by purchasing power, West German elderly households hold roughly 20 percent less tangible wealth than American elderly households. However, this 20 percent lower level of tangible wealth in West Germany corresponds to a 33 percent higher level of intangible social security wealth (according to the replacement ratios in table 8.5). The higher sum of tangible and intangible wealth in West Germany is a reflection of the higher

---

12. However, the Retirement History Survey data are subject to measurement problems similar to those for PSID data.

Table 8.10   **Household Wealth by Age and Asset Category**
                        (averages across households; thousand $)

Age	United States			West Germany		
	Nonhousing	Own Housing	Total	Nonhousing	Own Housing	Total
50–54	40.2	51.9	92.1	19.8	54.2	73.9
55–59	47.1	48.2	95.3	29.8	43.4	73.2
60–64	45.1	41.6	86.7	41.9	54.5	96.4
65–69	37.8	38.8	76.6	35.0	36.8	71.8
70–74	38.0	31.5	69.5	22.4	45.7	68.1
75–79	41.3	34.3	75.6	31.4	28.7	60.1
80+	37.2	30.5	67.7	31.0	29.8	60.8

Sources: 1984 PSID; 1988 SOEP at 1984 prices, valued at purchasing power parity ($1 = DM 1.70).

Notes: Financial wealth includes passbook savings, money market mutual funds, dedicated savings (IRA, Keogh, *Bausparkassen*, etc.), stocks and bonds. Nonhousing wealth is financial wealth plus real estate (except an owner-occupied home), farm, and business property. Housing wealth is the estimated sales value of an owner-occupied home. All values are self-reported.

aggregate savings rate depicted in table 8.9. The difference in wealth levels between the two countries is therefore consistent with Feldstein's (1974) view that private wealth has, at least in part, been substituted for by social security wealth in West Germany.

Another, although more indirect, piece of evidence in favor of the Feldstein view can be drawn from data on income sources displayed in table 8.11. In West Germany, annuity income (almost exclusively social security income, as I noted in the discussion about the role of private pensions, in section 8.3) is the most important income source for all households aged 60 and above. In turn, asset and labor income play a more important role in the United States. For very old Americans (aged 75 and above), income from assets contributes about one-quarter of total income. Hurd obtains similar results based on a much larger sample from the American Current Population Survey (Hurd 1989, table I 5).

Not only the levels of tangible and intangible wealth but also the age-wealth profiles are different between the two countries, as revealed by table 8.10. While American elderly have nonhousing wealth levels that only slowly decline after age 55, the German age-wealth profile is irregularly shaped with a pronounced peak at ages 60–64 and a remarkable increase in financial wealth at very old ages. These observations are not in line with pure life-cycle theory predictions and deserve a more careful analysis than the PSID and SOEP data can provide.

Wolff (1990) analyzes American wealth data, using the Survey of Consumer Finances and the Consumer Expenditure Survey. His results show a similarly slow decline in wealth levels. Also, the German age-wealth profiles are not specific to the relatively small SOEP sample on which table 8.10 is based. The

Table 8.11   **Sources of Income (% of total income)**

	United States			West Germany		
Age	Labor	Annuities	Assets	Labor	Annuities	Assets
50–54	75.6	18.7	5.6	85.4	7.3	7.3
55–59	66.1	26.0	7.8	76.5	14.4	9.0
60–64	43.2	47.4	9.3	37.0	51.9	11.1
65–69	14.5	70.1	14.8	4.1	87.0	8.9
70–74	6.4	79.9	13.7	2.7	82.0	15.3
75–79	2.6	74.1	23.2	0.6	81.8	17.6
80+	1.8	72.9	25.3	0.7	86.3	12.9

Sources: 1984 PSID; 1984 SOEP.
Notes: Labor includes full-time and part-time wages. Annuity income includes social security, pensions, and other transfers. Asset income includes interests, dividends, rents, and profits.

same pattern is also evident in the much larger sample of the German 1978 and 1983 consumer expenditure surveys.[13]

Tables 8.12 through 8.14 display results from these two surveys. Table 8.12 reports on net household savings, defined as the sum of all purchases of assets minus the sum of all sales of assets. These assets include financial assets and real estate, including owner-occupied housing. Changes in financial assets are deposits and withdrawals to and from all kinds of savings accounts and purchases and sales of stocks and bonds, partnerships, and dedicated savings programs (particularly to building societies). New loans are subtracted and repayments added to net savings. Not included in savings are durables (other than housing), cash, and unrealized capital gains.

Savings rates in table 8.13 are computed by dividing the above net household savings by household income net of taxes and social security contributions, if applicable. Finally, table 8.14 reports on financial wealth, defined as in table 8.10.[14] All three tables are stratified by survey year, age, and birth cohort. Cell sizes range from 776 to 4,343 observations, resulting in precise averages. The upper number refers to the 1978 German income and expenditure survey, the lower number to the survey conducted in 1983.

Although it would be desirable to consider more than just two periods, the data permit a rough distinction between age and cohort effects. In particular, table 8.12 reveals that savings among the very old in Germany are not only positive, but actually increase with age, holding birth cohort constant. This increase is even more pronounced in the savings rates (table 8.13) and generates levels of financial wealth that are increasing with age (table 8.14). Since housing wealth stays virtually unchanged as households age (see section 8.5

13. Einkommens- und Verbrauchstichproben; see Börsch-Supan and Stahl (1991b) and Börsch-Supan (1992b).
14. It excludes business and farm property included in table 8.10.

Table 8.12   **Household Savings by Age and Cohort, 1978 and 1983 (DM per year, in 1983 DM)**

	Birth Cohort					
Age	1928–24	1923–19	1918–13	1912–09	1908–04	<1904
50–54	5,136					
55–59	3,771	4,477				
60–64		2,468	2,830			
65–69			1,459	2,450		
70–74				2,016	2,368	
75–79					2,501	3,717
80+						4,015

Source: Einkommens- und Verbrauchstichproben (EVS) tapes (Stuttgart: Statistisches Bundesamt, 1978, 1983).

Table 8.13   **Saving Rates by Age and Cohort, 1978 and 1983 (net household savings/net household income)**

	Birth Cohort					
Age	1928–24	1923–19	1918–13	1912–09	1908–04	<1904
50–54	7.3					
55–59	5.3	7.0				
60–64		3.5	3.8			
65–69			2.4	3.9		
70–74				4.1	4.8	
75–79					5.8	8.8
80+						9.7

Source: EVS tapes (Stuttgart: Statistisches Bundesamt, 1978, 1983).
Notes: Age is age of household head. In each column, the upper number refers to 1978, the lower number to 1983.

Table 8.14   **Financial Wealth by Age and Cohort, 1978 and 1983 (thousand DM, in 1983 DM)**

	Birth Cohort					
Age	1928–24	1923–19	1918–13	1912–09	1908–04	<1904
50–54	26.5					
55–59	27.1	28.3				
60–64		28.9	27.5			
65–69			27.5	25.8		
70–74				28.7	26.5	
75–79					28.7	30.3
80+						31.9

Source: EVS tapes (Stuttgart: Statistisches Bundesamt, 1978, 1983).
Notes: Age is age of household head. In each column, the upper number refers to 1978, the lower number to 1983.

on housing), the German data feature a flat, if not increasing, age profile of total wealth. Börsch-Supan (1992) shows that qualitatively similar profiles are obtained by analyzing mean and median savings, savings per household and per capita, and savings by pensioners and savings averaged across all households.

The American and the German age-wealth profiles are not consistent with the ones predicted by the pure life-cycle hypothesis. The upward swing in the German age profile of savings rates is in straight contradiction to the predictions of the life-cycle hypothesis. In the United States, according to the PSID wealth data (table 8.10), the elderly aged 80 and above still hold more than two-thirds of the maximum wealth attained immediately before retirement.

Why do the elderly draw down so little of their financial assets at old ages, particularly in West Germany? One reason would be to leave bequests. If that were the case, the elderly with children should, on average, arrive at higher wealth levels than the elderly without children—otherwise, there would be little reason to bequeath.[15] However, regressions of nonhousing wealth on the number of children born, holding age and income constant, produce positive coefficients neither in Germany nor in the United States.[16] While the estimated negative coefficients are only weakly significant, they rule out the idea that a bequest motive has created the flat or increasing asset profiles in Germany.[17]

There is also little reason to suspect that precautionary savings generate the observed savings pattern in Germany. As I mentioned in the previous subsection, the comprehensive coverage of German health insurance should permit the German elderly to draw down their assets, disregarding potential health expenditures, while the American elderly, on average much less covered, should have a stock of precautionary liquid wealth. However, the opposite is the case: nonhousing assets increase with old age in West Germany, while they slightly decrease in the United States. Hence, it is unlikely that precautionary savings drive the pattern of age-asset profiles in the two countries.

Concerning the German sample, it also appears unlikely that mortality differences between the rich and the poor are behind the U-shaped age-savings profile. If the rich survive the poor and if saving is positively correlated with income, sample selection generates higher savings in the sample of older people, unless income had concurrently fallen, which was not the case between 1978 and 1983. Savings rates, however, should stay approximately constant, because they hold income constant and therefore roughly correct for the sample selection by differential mortality. However, savings rates rise even faster

15. One might also wish to leave bequests to persons or institutions other than one's children, but the bequest motive appears strongest with respect to children.
16. See Börsch-Supan (1991b). I intentionally excluded housing wealth, because larger families have larger houses that have, on average, higher sales prices. Because mobility is low among homeowners, many elderly who had large families are still living in their large houses, with or without a bequest motive.
17. To get the semantics straight: the point is not to test for the presence of a bequest motive per se, but to test whether a bequest motive is the source of the asset and savings profiles observed as people age.

than absolute savings (see tables 8.12 and 8.13). It is therefore unlikely that the observed patterns have been created by differential mortality between rich and poor elderly.

I favor a different interpretation of the data, one supported by table 8.15. This table displays the relative frequency of elderly households with an excess of annuity income over consumption expenditures. This table points out that it is more helpful to investigate why the German elderly consume so little than to wonder why the German elderly save so much. Annuity income exceeds consumption expenditures, and this happens increasingly with age. The decline in consumption expenditures is too large to be attributed merely to underreporting: for about a quarter of the elderly aged 75 and above, annuity income is more than 50 percent higher than consumption expenditures. In fact, almost all of this decline can be attributed to a reduction in food, travel, and transportation consumption, categories in which the marginal utility from consumption is very likely to decline in old age because of deteriorating health or increasing loneliness. It is important to note that in Germany the decline in food, travel, and transportation expenditures is not offset by larger health expenditures since almost all of the (indeed increasing) health bills are covered by compulsory health insurance, unlike in the United States.

The wealth pattern observed in table 8.10 is therefore consistent with the view that the elderly in Germany find themselves saving out of generous annuity income and not drawing down their existing wealth, as they might have planned before realizing their declining marginal utility from certain kinds of consumption. Moreover, since borrowing against social security wealth is impossible, anticipation of declining expenditures may generate low levels of tangible wealth immediately before retirement but could not prevent asset accumulation once expenditures fall short of retirement income.

8.4.3 Policy Implications

A first, though tentative, conclusion can be drawn about future aggregate savings as the German and the American population ages. It appears counterfactual to employ asset profiles drawn from a textbook version of the life-cycle hypothesis in order to forecast lower future wealth levels in Germany and, to a lesser degree, in the United States. Decreases in savings in the United States and Germany may be less dramatic than projected by Auerbach et al. (1990) or may not occur at all. The high savings rates and the associated large asset holdings among the elderly in Germany are more likely to lead to an increase in aggregate savings, at least during the medium-run transition period in the next 30 years when the baby-boom generation becomes aged. One should be careful not to exaggerate the dread of lower capital intensity due to population aging and a need to borrow at the expense of worsening the terms of trade. Whether aggregate savings will be lower or higher in the long-run, when the bulge of the baby-boom generation has disappeared and new cohorts with potentially very different savings attitudes are present, is impossible to tell.

Table 8.15   **Elderly with Expenditures Lower than Annuity Income (% of elderly in age group)**

Age Group	Ratio of Annuity Income to Consumption Expenditures			
	<1.0	1.0–1.2	1.2–1.5	>1.5
50–54	97.7	1.5	0.5	0.3
55–59	92.0	3.9	2.9	1.2
60–64	69.3	13.4	11.4	5.9
65–69	47.3	23.5	18.0	11.2
70–74	42.9	22.7	20.6	13.8
75–79	38.1	19.2	21.6	21.1
80+	30.5	17.3	23.2	29.0

Source: EVS tapes (Stuttgart: Statistisches Bundesamt, 1983), based on 18,259 elderly age 50 and above.

Notes: Annuity income includes public and private pensions, payments from life insurance, and private transfers.

Second, the cross-sectional evidence is consistent with the so-called Feldstein view that social security wealth replaces private savings. Although aggregate savings are higher in West Germany, this is due to higher annuity wealth, while the average tangible wealth held by elderly German households is actually lower than in the United States.

Moreover, the evidence is consistent with the view that the elderly reduce their consumption because of declining health and that the German elderly, endowed with generous social security benefits, even realize savings which may have been unintended when they were younger and against which they cannot borrow.

This raises several welfare issues. There is the question of whether the elderly are "overannuitized," specifically in Germany. Evidence that the level of annuity income for the oldest old is, on average, considerably larger than their expenditures has strong implications for social security reform. Notwithstanding the need to prevent poverty among some of the elderly, it may be reasonable to tax wealth more heavily or to adjust annuity incomes more than the recent social security reforms did. Such an argument must be judged in light of the above-mentioned projections that social security contribution rates will exceed an unsustainable 40 percent in Germany when the dependency ratio peaks.

Finally, there is little evidence for a bequest-motive-driven increase in savings during old age. Although bequest volumes are relatively large—about 1.8 percent of GDP in the United States (Kotlikoff and Summers 1981) and 3 percent of GDP in France (Kessler 1990)—the bulk of this appears to be unintended bequests. The efficiency arguments against taxing bequests—distorting efficient intergenerational transfers—are therefore not really applicable.

8.5   Housing and Living Arrangement Choices

8.5.1   Institutional Background

Policy intervention in housing markets is intense both in Germany and in the United States. Subsidies and regulations strongly distort tenure choice, mobility, and living arrangement decisions in the two countries. However, the actual subsidies and regulations are quite different. Once again, an international perspective illuminates how public policy influences actual behavior.

In the United States, most housing subsidies are directed to home ownership, while subsidies in Germany are directed toward rental housing (Mayo and Barnbrock 1985). Both countries subsidize homeownership by deductions from income taxes. In the United States, mortgage interest for the purchase of a home and land can be deducted without any upper limit, thereby changing the marginal price of housing and inducing more housing consumption in terms of land, dwelling space, and housing quality. In Germany, mortgage interest is not deductible for owner-occupied homes. Rather, depreciation of the dwelling can be deducted as a fixed percentage of dwelling value, up to a limit which is slightly lower than the average dwelling value in Germany. Hence, the marginal price of housing is lowered only for relatively small houses. Land, which is a much larger percentage of total purchase price in Germany than in the United States, is not subsidized at all. For middle-class households and a typical home in 1985, homeownership subsidies were approximately 2.5 to 3 times higher in the United States than in Germany (Börsch-Supan 1985, tables 3–6).

Rental housing subsidies in the United States are typically directed to low-income families, while the rental allowances in Germany are administered as entitlements. Traditionally, most older people were eligible for housing assistance, which covered, on average, 23 percent of rent in 1985 (Mayo and Barnbrock 1985). Since mobility in rental housing is much higher than in owner-occupied housing, largely because of much higher transaction costs, the subsidies in the United States not only distort tenure choice but indirectly reduce mobility and may therefore create lock-in effects for the elderly.

Differences in rental housing regulations between the two countries are also important. Germany has very stringent tenant protection laws. While initial rents are essentially unrestricted, later rent increases are bound by an index that considerably lags the spot-market level, preventing fast rent increases when land and house values appreciate quickly. Eviction is generally not permitted. In the United States, only very few cities have rental housing regulations; the most notable is New York. These rules make rental housing relatively more attractive in Germany than in the United States, and they are likely to discourage housing mobility, particular for the elderly who typically have particularly long tenure and therefore high tenure discounts.

The financial and regulatory incentives which reduce mobility in West Germany may also induce the elderly to live in housing units larger (and possibly more expensive) than those the elderly would choose in an undistorted housing market. At the same time, the housing market distortions in Germany make it more difficult for younger households to buy larger housing units (Behring, Börsch-Supan, and Goldrian 1988).

Another major institutional difference between Germany and the United States that is likely to distort housing and living arrangement choices is the already-mentioned extent of compulsory health insurance. In Germany, compulsory health insurance includes coverage for long-term hospital care, while there is virtually no compensation for in-home care of elderly parents.[18] Until recently, hospitals had an excess supply of beds, and the elderly used to stay for extended periods in hospitals. Public health insurance has no preset limit on the length of hospital stays to be covered, as long as a hospital doctor approves the stay. In the United States, hospital and nursing home bills not covered by health insurance may force the elderly to leave hospitals and nursing homes early and to stay with their children.

Health-care coverage, public subsidies which reduce rental housing costs for the elderly, and the generally tighter social safety net for the elderly in West Germany represent economic disincentives for family support and shared living arrangements as compared to the United States.

8.5.2 Evidence on Housing and Living Arrangement Choices

The institutional differences between Germany and the United States are indeed reflected in the differences in housing and living arrangement choices. Consider first the choice of tenure. Table 8.16 presents ownership rates and average relative shares of housing and nonhousing assets for the elderly in the two countries. The elderly in West Germany are much more likely to live in rental housing than the elderly in the United States. While in the United States roughly 70 percent of the elderly own their own homes, less than half the elderly do so in West Germany. In both countries, ownership rates peak at ages 55–59 and decline thereafter. The decline of homeownership is, of course, reflected in the increasing share of nonhousing assets in total wealth among the elderly. In spite of lower ownership rates, the average share of housing assets is quite high in Germany, because the relative price of housing and land is substantially higher in Germany than in the United States.

Another important housing policy difference mentioned above is the tenant protection regulations in West Germany, which are much tighter than in the United States. They are indeed mobility deterring, as can be seen from table 8.17, which presents mobility rates in the two countries. Mobility is much higher in the United States for all age groups, but particularly for the elderly aged 70 and above, who have mobility rates about five times higher than their German counterparts. The very large number of moves among the elderly aged

---

18. German income tax provides a tax deduction of just DM 1,800 (roughly $1,100) in this case.

Table 8.16   Ownership Rates and Shares of Housing and Nonhousing Assets

	United States		West Germany	
Age	Ownership Rate (%)	Housing Wealth Share (%)	Ownership Rate (%)	Housing Wealth Share (%)
50–54	75.8	63.4	56.3	73.3
55–59	76.0	61.2	60.8	59.3
60–64	73.5	58.4	53.7	56.5
65–69	69.2	55.5	49.2	51.3
70–74	64.8	50.1	41.7	67.1
75–79	68.4	53.1	46.7	48.3
80+	62.4	46.2	40.8	49.0

Sources: 1984 PSID; 1984 and 1988 SOEP.
Note: Housing wealth is a self-reported estimate of the sales price of an owner-occupied home.

Table 8.17   Mobility Rates and Housing Consumption Adjustments

	United States			West Germany		
	Mobility Rate (%)	Dwelling Size		Mobility Rate (%)	Dwelling Size	
Age		Mover	Nonmover		Mover	Nonmover
50–54	10.6	3.8	5.0	2.6		
55–59	10.2	3.2	4.8	2.0		
60–64	9.4	2.7	4.5	2.5		
65–69	6.9	3.3	4.2	2.8	2.8	3.7
70–74	9.1	3.0	4.1	1.8		
75–79	4.8	3.3	3.9	1.1		
80+	15.4	2.7	4.0	1.3		

Sources: 1984 PSID; 1984 SOEP.
Note: Mobility rate is the percentage of movers, i.e., households who moved within the last 12 months since being interviewed. Dwelling size is number of rooms excluding kitchen, bathrooms, and rooms smaller than 6 square meters (about 60 square feet).

80 and above in the United States are moves to family members, particularly to their own adult children.

Moves among the elderly, when they occur, release housing for the younger generation, as can be seen in the other columns of table 8.17. On average, in both countries, recent movers have about one room less than nonmovers.[19] This result is in line with panel data observations (Venti and Wise 1990; Feldstein and McFadden 1988).

However, though movers reduce dwelling size in both countries, there are just too few moves in Germany to have an impact on dwelling size consump-

19. It should be noted that the observed reduction in dwelling size does not, at least on average, imply a reduction in housing equity among elderly American homeowners when they move (Venti and Wise 1990).

tion. This is in line with the speculation that the mobility-reducing regulations in Germany have, in effect, reduced dwelling size adjustments among the aged. Indeed, table 8.18 shows that, although Germans have smaller houses than Americans when they are aged 50 and younger, this difference levels out when they become aged.

The decline in housing consumption with age is much more pronounced in the United States than in West Germany. In particular, there is little if any reduction of dwelling size among German homeowners as they age.

Per capita housing consumption increases in both countries, a consequence of the decreasing average household size. In the United States, this increase is partially offset by moves to smaller dwellings, in contrast to Germany where low mobility implies a much steeper increase of per capita dwelling size consumption.

So far we have relied on cross-sectional evidence. In both countries, housing consumption declines very little as households age. In fact, longitudinal data show strong cohort effects: for a given age, later birth cohorts show an increase in housing consumption. Table 8.19 presents the German case. The bottom row represents the average floor-space consumption of a panel of households in the SOEP in the five years from 1983 through 1988. The lack of change replicates the result that German households, on average, do not decrease their housing consumption as they age. However, by comparing different cohorts at the same age—i.e., by comparing the entries on the seven diagonals for each of the seven age groups—we see that succeeding cohorts increased their housing consumption. The right-most column depicts the range of standard deviations for each age group. The cohort effects for the 55–75-year-old households are significant even though the households were traced within only a short five-year span of the German panel data.

I now turn to the evidence on living arrangement choices. I cast living arrangements into four categories. An elderly person lives "independently" if no

Table 8.18   **Housing Consumption (number of rooms)**

Age	United States			West Germany		
	Owners	Renters	Per Capita	Owners	Renters	Per Capita
50–54	5.2	3.7	1.9	4.6	3.4	1.6
55–59	5.0	3.3	2.0	4.6	3.3	1.7
60–64	4.8	3.1	2.1	4.5	2.9	2.1
65–69	4.6	2.9	2.2	4.2	2.8	2.3
70–74	4.6	2.7	2.3	4.2	2.6	2.2
75–79	4.4	2.7	2.3	4.1	2.5	2.2
80+	4.5	2.3	2.4	4.5	2.5	2.4

Sources: 1984 PSID; 1984 SOEP.

Note: Number of rooms excludes kitchen, bathrooms, and rooms smaller than 6 square meters (about 60 square feet).

Table 8.19   **Age and Cohort Effects in Housing Consumption (dwelling size, area in square meters)**

Cohort	Survey Year					Age	Standard Deviation
	1984	1985	1986	1987	1988		
1934–38					102.5	50–54	1.7–2.2
1933–37				101.1			
1932–36			100.5				
1931–35		99.4					
1930–34	101.6						
1929–33					98.7	55–59	2.0–2.2
1928–32				95.4			
1927–31			95.0				
1926–30		94.3					
1925–29	93.7						
1924–28					92.2	60–64	2.1–2.3
1923–27				92.4			
1922–26			91.4				
1921–25		91.5					
1920–24	90.5						
1919–23					87.4	65–69	2.3–2.7
1918–22				84.7			
1917–21			82.4				
1916–20		78.6					
1915–19	80.0						
1914–18					79.8	70–74	2.4–2.7
1913–17				76.7			
1912–16			76.1				
1911–15		73.3					
1910–14	75.2						
1909–13					71.2	75–79	2.8–3.1
1908–12				73.6			
1907–11			74.0				
1906–10		74.9					
1905–09	72.7						
1904–08					70.8	80+	3.4–4.4
1903–07				71.1			
1902–06			69.5				
1901–05		70.7					
1900–04	69.3						
All	93.3	93.4	93.5	93.4	93.5	50+	0.93

Source: SOEP, waves 1984–88.

other person lives in the household, except a spouse and minor children, and in "shared living arrangements" if at least one other person lives in the household, most frequently an adult child. For independent living arrangements, we distinguish the cases of a spouse present and absent. For shared living arrangements, we differentiate between "head" and "taken-in." In the first case, the elderly person is the head of household, while in the second case somebody else is head of household. Most frequently, an adult child has taken her or his parent in. Table 8.20 shows how frequently the different living arrangements were chosen by the elderly in the United States and West Germany, based again on comparable survey data from the PSID and the SOEP.

The most significant difference in living arrangement choices between the two countries is in the percentage of shared living arrangements. It is much higher in the United States. Almost one-third of the very old live with their adult children or others. This fraction is only one-fifth in Germany. Note that the percentage living alone is about comparable for the elderly aged 65 and above, while the percentage living as couples is substantially lower in the United States. This is a reflection of the much higher incidence of divorces in the United States. In 1986, the United States had about 22 divorces per 10,000 married women, West Germany only 8.3. Consequently, U.S. marital rates are about 10–12 percent lower than in West Germany for elderly aged 65 and above.

The data in both countries do not produce reliable estimates of institutionalization. They have thus been omitted from table 8.20. The PSID attempts to keep track of institutionalized sample persons with less than perfect success (Börsch-Supan 1990; Ellwood and Kane 1990). The SOEP starts in 1984 with a noninstitutionalized sample and therefore underestimates the percentage of elderly living in nursing homes. If at all, these panel studies reveal a decreasing

Table 8.20   **Living Arrangements of the Elderly (% of elderly population)**

	United States				West Germany			
	Independent		Shared		Independent		Shared	
Age	Couple	Alone	Head	Taken-In	Couple	Alone	Head	Taken-In
50–54	55.3	14.2	17.6	12.2	82.2	7.9	7.3	2.6
55–59	58.3	16.9	13.8	10.1	82.9	8.5	7.2	1.4
60–64	51.2	20.1	18.6	9.4	77.4	14.3	5.9	2.4
65–69	48.7	25.5	14.3	11.2	67.8	22.1	6.4	3.7
70–74	44.0	33.3	12.0	8.8	57.3	34.5	5.1	3.1
75–79	38.5	40.3	9.5	11.3	45.0	44.6	3.8	6.7
80+	18.6	46.6	9.0	23.5	31.4	47.8	4.8	16.0

Sources: 1984 PSID; 1988 SOEP.

Notes: Independent (Couple): No other adult except spouse in household. Independent (Alone): No other adult in household. Shared (Head): Elderly is head of household that contains another family unit. Shared (Taken-In): Elderly lives in household headed by another person.

proportion of elderly living with adult children and an increasing proportion living alone or in institutions (Börsch-Supan 1990; Ellwood and Kane 1990).

A similar trend is observed in the German SOEP panel for the choice between living alone and living with children; see table 8.21, set up in a fashion similar to table 8.19 on housing consumption. The longitudinal data reveal three effects. Going down each column, the pure age effect mirrors table 8.20 and shows the familiar fact that the proportion of elderly living with children increases with age. However, this effect is more than offset by a strong cohort effect. This effect is visible by following each diagonal, holding age constant. Younger German cohorts are much less inclined to live with their children than were the older ones. These cohort effects are statistically highly significant and dominate the aggregate effect in the bottom row of table 8.21: the proportion of the elderly in the SOEP survey who live in with their children decreases from 1984 to 1988.

8.5.3 Policy Implications

The different housing market policies in West Germany and the United States have the predicted impacts: higher homeownership rates in the United States, dramatically lower mobility rates and a lower proportion of shared living arrangements in West Germany. While it would be unreasonable to attribute all differences in observed housing and living arrangement choices by the elderly to the different housing market policies, the consistency of responses is striking.

Having realized the effectiveness of housing market policies, we should ask ourselves whether these policies make sense when the population is aging rapidly. I recognize several problems here. First, housing supply by intergenerational transfer is impeded because of the suppressed mobility of the elderly. Second, supply by new construction is distorted in the direction of too few, too large houses. Third, there are too few incentives, and even some economic disincentives, for family care and multigenerational living arrangements. The first point is caused by the homeownership subsidies in the United States and by the tenant protection legislation in West Germany. The second point relates mostly to the United States, again because of homeownership subsidies, while the third point is most relevant in West Germany with its compulsory health insurance system. In the following, I will comment on these points in more detail.

A first problem is that the elderly who consider moving into a smaller dwelling are discouraged to do so in both countries. In the United States, there is little incentive to give up valuable tax deductions unless reductions in dwelling size are compensated by quality improvements in dimensions other than size. The situation is complicated by the fact that the United States offers little attractive apartment housing for rent since the tax laws split the tenure choice along income lines, creating the well-known external effects that make rental housing so inferior in the United States.

Table 8.21   **Age and Cohort Effects in the Living Arrangement Choice (proportion of persons living in multigenerational households)**

Cohort	Survey Year 1984	1985	1986	1987	1988	Age	Standard Deviation
1919–23					2.3	65–69	1.1–1.4
1918–22				2.0			
1917–21			2.0				
1916–20		2.0					
1915–19	4.3						
1914–18					1.6	70–74	1.3–1.5
1913–17				2.0			
1912–16			2.3				
1911–15		2.7					
1910–14	5.6						
1909–13					4.2	75–79	1.3–1.6
1908–12				5.8			
1907–11			8.6				
1906–10		9.3					
1905–09	9.1						
1904–08					13.7	80+	1.4–2.2
1903–07				13.6			
1902–06			13.2				
1901–05		17.6					
1900–04	19.8						
All	7.54	5.95	5.20	4.83	4.72	65+	0.76

Source: SOEP, waves 1984–88, persons aged 65+.

Note: Multigenerational households are composite households consisting of elderly parents and their adult children.

In West Germany, where many more elderly live in rental housing, the rent adjustment provision of the tenant protection laws supports high initial rents for movers and large discounts for sitting tenants, so-called tenure discounts, creating windfall gains for the older and a large rental burden for the young. The size of the wedge between rents for flow and rents for stock supply appears inefficient, and a smoother adaptation of rents in times of demand pressures would be welfare improving. Let me stress that, if the elderly want to stay, they should do so. My point is that the numbers in table 8.17 indicate that there are elderly who would adjust their housing consumption downward were it not for the penalty of a large rent increase.

Homeownership subsidies in the United States and rent adjustment provisions in West Germany also distort the supply of new housing. By lowering the marginal price of land and dwellings, the tax deductions in the United States channel resources to large houses where the marginal room has little utility, thereby suppressing the supply of a larger number of smaller houses, which appears to be more appropriate in times of population aging. In West Germany, the rent adjustment clause, if binding, lowers expected returns of a prospective landlord and therefore reduces supply. The argument, however, is quite subtle, because not all of the wedge between spot market and long-term rent must be inefficient. Tenure discounts may be an efficient way to minimize maintenance and revolving costs in a manner similar to that in which seniority payments create efficient wage schedules. Since tenure discounts are also observed in completely unregulated markets, one may argue that the German rent adjustment provision is not binding and can be dropped without harm. This may be true in the steady state. However, the policy dilemma starts when increases in demand raise spot market rents. Now the rent adjustment provision becomes binding and suppresses supply at the expense of the newcomers, while protecting sitting tenants (and providing windfall gains to them). Population aging is an example where this is the case.[20]

Mobility-reducing policies impede the intergenerational transfer of housing, which represents an important mechanism of housing supply. Direct transfer alone—homes that are inherited—amounts to 28 percent of all owned homes in Germany.[21] Indirect transfer is much more common: in 1983, about 74 percent of all recent home buyers purchased existing homes in the United States. This percentage increased steadily to over 80 percent in 1989 (*Statistical Abstract*, various issues). Population aging implies a longer stay in the family home by the older generation, which leads to a relative shortage of housing for the younger generation.

The magnitude of this longevity-induced shortage effect is substantial, as is evident from the following back-of-the-envelope calculation. The current cohort of elderly aged 80 comprises about 350,000 persons in approximately 250,000 households. If a one-year increase in life expectancy implies that this cohort will stay one year longer in their current dwellings, an increased housing demand of 250,000 units is generated. Since average life expectancy has increased by 1.3 years in West Germany from 1981 to 1986, the annual additional demand due to population aging amounts to 65,000 dwelling units. This is about 28 percent of all new construction in 1986.[22]

In Germany, the prolonged duration of more elderly in their homes is unlikely to be offset by a decreasing demand of the younger generation. Hence, German housing markets will stay tight for the near future, unless more downgrading of dwelling size in old age and faster new construction is forcefully encouraged. Since population aging is slower in the United States and housing

---

20. It is important to stress that tenant protection per se—the prohibition of eviction and rent increases beyond market rents—is a social achievement particularly important for the elderly, who face higher psychic, and sometimes monetary, moving costs.

21. Computed from the 1988 wave of the SOEP.

22. In 1986, 225,000 dwelling units were constructed in West Germany (Statistisches Jahrbuch 1988).

markets there are currently not as tight as in Germany, similar problems are less pronounced in the United States.

Another area in which we identified distortions are living arrangement choices. In the United States, the extent of family care appears to be much higher than in West Germany, although the trend is in direction of a decreasing proportion of elderly living with adult children and an increasing proportion living alone and in institutions. Since living alone and living in an institution incur much higher social costs (induced health expenditures, stationary and ambulatory services for the elderly, etc.) than living with others, it appears wise to intercept some of the external effects by subsidizing home care. The case is strongest in West Germany, where current health insurance policies create an additional distortion by effectively subsidizing living alone.

If the current proportions of living arrangements are not reversing, the demand for social support services such as ambulatory care will increase dramatically. For the low-income elderly, the associated expenses have to be borne by welfare programs financed by general taxes. They are thus subject to the familiar problems of pay-as-you-go social insurance schemes in times of increasing dependency ratios.

8.6 Summary and Conclusions

What do we learn from a microeconomic, cross-national analysis about the interrelation between economic policy and population aging? A first and important point is the effectiveness of economic policy. Retirement decisions, savings behavior, and housing and living arrangement choices are very consistent with the incentives provided by economic policy in form of regulations, taxes, and subsidies in Germany and the United States. Examples are the response of retirement dates to pension schedules, the consistency of cross-national differences in savings with cross-national differences in retirement income and health insurance provisions, and the reaction of housing choices and mobility to homeownership subsidies and rental regulations.

Second, the analysis identifies several trouble spots where incentives set by economic policy work in the wrong direction in times of population aging. Germany has failed to respond quickly to the dangers of unsustainably high social security contributions. This is particularly worrisome in the light of social security benefits which are so large in old age that they induce forced savings among the well-to-do elderly. The United States has adjusted its social security system relatively earlier in spite of a less pronounced increase in the ratio of pensioners to workers. Both countries have fiscal disincentives for family care and multigenerational living arrangements. Providing positive incentives here could help to offset the shortage of family care generated by the demographics of a dwindling number of children per elderly.

References

Auerbach, Alan J., L. J. Kotlikoff, R. P. Hagemann, and G. Nicoletti. 1990. The economic dynamics of an aging population: The case of four OECD countries. *OECD Economic Studies,* no. 12 (Spring): 97–130.

Barro, Robert J. 1974. Are government bonds net wealth? *Journal of Political Economy* 82, no. 6: 1095–1117.

Behring, Karin, A. Börsch-Supan, and G. Goldrian. 1988. *Analyse und Prognose der Nachfrage nach Miet- und Eigentümerwohnungen in der Bundesrepublik Deutschland.* Berlin: Duncker und Humblot.

Börsch-Supan, Axel. 1985. Tenure choice and housing demand. In *U.S. and West German housing markets,* ed. K. Stahl and R. Struyk. Washington, D.C.: Urban Institute Press.

———. 1990. Elderly americans: A dynamic analysis of household dissolution and living arrangement transitions. In *Issues in the economics of aging,* ed. David Wise. Chicago: University of Chicago Press.

———. 1991a. The choice of living arrangements in Germany. Paper prepared for the European Population Conference, Paris, October.

———. 1991b. Implications of an aging population: Problems and policy options in West Germany and the United States. *Economic Policy* 12 (April): 103–39.

———. 1992a. Population aging, social security design, and early retirement. *Journal of Institutional and Theoretical Economics* 148:533–57.

———. 1992b. Saving and consumption patterns among the elderly: The German case. *Journal of Population Economics* 5:289–303.

Börsch-Supan, Axel, and Konrad Stahl. 1991a. Do dedicated savings programs increase aggregate savings and housing demand? *Journal of Public Economics* 44:265–97.

———. 1991b. Life cycle savings and consumption constraints. *Journal of Population Economics* 4:233–55.

Bundesminister für Arbeit und Sozialordnung. 1990. *Die Rentenreform 1992.* Bonn: Bundespresseamt.

Casmir, Bernd. 1989. *Staatliche Rentenversicherungssysteme im internationalen Vergleich.* Frankfurt: Lang.

Chesnais, Jean-Claude. 1987. Quand un peuple en devient deux: une Allemagne et l'autre. *Population et Societes* 209:1–4.

Ellwood, David, and Thomas Kane. 1990. An American way of aging. In *Issues in the economics of aging,* ed. David Wise, Chicago: University of Chicago Press.

Feinstein, J., and D. McFadden. 1988. The dynamics of housing demand by the elderly. In *Issues in the Economics of Aging,* ed. David Wise. Chicago: University of Chicago Press.

Feldstein, Martin. 1974. Social security, induced retirement, and aggregate capital accumulation. *Journal of Political Economy* 82:905–26.

Frerich, Johannes. 1987. *Sozialpolitik.* München: Oldenbourg.

Hagemann, Robert P, and Giuseppe Nicoletti. 1989. Population ageing: Economic effects and some policy implications for financing public pensions. *OECD Economic Studies* no. 12 (Spring): 51–96.

Hurd, Michael D. 1989. Issues and results from research on the elderly: Economic status, retirement, and savings. *Journal of Economic Literature* 21:637–56.

Jacobs, Klaus, Martin Kohli, and Martin Rein. 1987. Testing the industry-mix hypothesis of early exit. Discussion paper prepared for Wissenschaftszentrum Berlin.

Kessler, Denis. 1990. Presidential address at the fourth annual meeting of the European Society of Population Economics, Istanbul. *Journal of Population Economics,* in press.

Kotlikoff, Lawrence J., and Lawrence Summers. 1981. The role of intergenerational transfers in aggregate capital accumulation. *Journal of Political Economy* 89:706–32.

Kotlikoff, Lawrence J., and David A. Wise. 1987. Incentive effects of private pension plans. In *Issues in pension economics,* ed. Z. Bodie, J. Shoven, and D. Wise. Chicago: University of Chicago Press.

Lazear, Edward P., and Robert L. Moore. 1988. Pensions and turnover. In *Pensions in the U.S. economics,* ed. Z. Bodie, J. Shoven, and D. Wise. Chicago: University of Chicago Press.

Mayo, Stephen K., and Jörn Barnbrock. 1985. Rental housing subsidy programs in West Germany and the United States. In *U.S. and West German housing markets,* ed. K. Stahl and R. Struyk. Washington, D.C.: Urban Institute Press.

Organisation for Economic Cooperation and Development (OECD). 1988. *Aging populations: The social policy implications.* Paris: OECD.

Schmähl, Winfried. 1989. Labour force participation and social pension systems. In *Workers versus pensioners: Intergenerational justice in an ageing world,* ed. P. Johnson, C. Conrad, and D. Thomson. Manchester and New York: Manchester University Press.

Statistical abstract of the United States, various issues. Washington, D.C.: Government Printing Office.

Statistisches Jahrbuch für die Bundesrepublik Deutschland, various issues. Wiesbaden: Statistisches Bundesamt.

Stock, James H, and David A. Wise. 1990. In *Issues in the economics of aging,* ed. David Wise. Chicago: University of Chicago Press.

Venti, Steven F., and David A. Wise. 1987. Have IRAs increased U.S. savings? Evidence from consumer expenditure surveys. *Quarterly Journal of Economics,* in press.

———. 1990. But they don't want to reduce equity. In *Issues in the economics of aging,* ed. David Wise. Chicago: University of Chicago Press.

Wolff, Edward N. 1990. Methodological issues in the estimation of the size distribution of household wealth. *Journal of Econometrics* 43:179–95.

Comment   N. Gregory Mankiw

I learned a lot from reading this paper by Axel Börsch-Supan. It presents a large variety of facts about the behavior of the elderly in Germany and the United States as well as about some of the policies that influence that behavior. The facts are presented in the way that I like to consume them—simply, with a minimum of econometric processing.

In some ways, this is a hard paper to comment on. Börsch-Supan does not offer a single, grand theory that purports to explain all the differences between these two countries. In fact, he is so reserved in drawing conclusions, and so careful about presenting caveats, that there is little to argue about. So, in my comments, rather than being disagreeable, I would like to discuss those areas in which I see some important puzzles left unanswered.

N. Gregory Mankiw is professor of economics at Harvard University and a research associate of the National Bureau of Economic Research.

Saving Behavior of the Elderly

I would like to begin with a topic that has puzzled both microeconomists and macroeconomists for many years: the saving behavior of the elderly. It is now a well-known stylized fact that the elderly do not behave as Franco Modigliani said they should (Ando and Kennickell 1986). According to the life-cycle hypothesis, wealth should decline after retirement, and that just does not happen—at least not as quickly as the most basic version of the theory predicts.

There are various explanations of this failure of the life-cycle hypothesis, but none seems fully satisfactory. These explanations can be grouped into two broad categories: those that allow the elderly to be rational and those that assume some element of irrationality. In the rational category, there are two candidates. One is that the elderly have a bequest motive—altruistic, strategic, or otherwise. The second is that the elderly hold onto their wealth for reasons of precautionary saving—either because of uninsurable medical expenses or because of uncertainty about life span.

Both of these rational explanations seem hard to square with the evidence. As Börsch-Supan notes, the elderly without children do not seem to obey the life-cycle hypothesis any more than those with children. Since children are the most likely beneficiaries of a bequest motive, this fact casts doubt on the bequest explanation. The precautionary-saving explanation is hard to rule out with only U.S. data, but the German data seem move conclusive. According to Börsch-Supan, most of the risks that the U.S. elderly face are absent in Germany. The comprehensive health insurance system should eliminate the worry about large medical bills, and the high level of annuity income should insure against the uncertainty regarding life span. Yet the elderly in Germany do not listen to Franco Modigliani any more than do those in the United States. In fact, according to Börsch-Supan's numbers, a majority of the German elderly are consuming less than their annuity income; these elderly must be accumulating wealth rather than spending it.

One is, therefore, tempted to explain the behavior of the elderly by appealing to some sort of irrationality. Yet even that is not so easy. One possibility is that the elderly have excessively optimistic expectations about their own life span: admittedly, it is hard to accept one's own mortality. Such excessive optimism can explain lower consumption than is predicted by the life-cycle model with rational consumers. It cannot, however, explain consumption lower than annuity income. Even if a person plans to live to age 150, he should consume at least his annuity, since the annuity will continue as long as he does.

Börsch-Supan proposes another type of irrationality. Perhaps the elderly are excessively optimistic regarding marginal utility rather than life span. According to Börsch-Supan, the elderly save in the expectation of enjoying consumption during retirement, but then, because of deteriorating health, they are systematically surprised that the marginal utility of consumption is lower than expected.

I am not convinced by this story. Even if marginal utility does fall unexpectedly, the elderly should still consume their wealth—after all, you can't take it with you. Sure, they will just enjoy the consumption less, but unless the marginal utility of consumption falls to zero, it is still in the elderly's interest to spend their wealth as they age.

In the end, the failure of the elderly to dissave remains a puzzle. My own guess is that the resolution will come from a combination of bequest and precautionary-saving motives. If both motives are relevant, then the comparison between the elderly with children and those without children is ambiguous. Having children raises the bequest motive, but it also reduces the precautionary-saving motive, because children provide implicit insurance. The best thing that can be said about this explanation is that it is logically consistent and is not rejected by the data. As far as I know, however, there is no affirmative evidence to suggest that it is in fact the right explanation.

Saving and the Aging of Society

Let me now turn from the individual level to the societal level. In particular, how will the aging of society influence national saving? Börsch-Supan suggests that, since the elderly do not dissave, we should not expect national saving to fall as the elderly become a larger percentage of the population. I am not so sure.

There are two ways to examine the impact of demographic change on national saving. One way is to examine micro data on the saving of individuals and then to aggregate to get national saving. This is the approach that Börsch-Supan implicitly takes. The second way is to examine macro data—that is, to exploit the time-series and cross-country variation in demographic structure to examine how aging influences national saving.

In his Harvard dissertation, David Weil compared these two approaches and showed that they lead to strikingly different conclusions. Micro data show little dissaving by the elderly. Yet macro data show that nations with a large elderly population tend to have low saving rates.

Weil reconciles these two results by emphasizing the role of bequests. The failure of the elderly to dissave implies, as a matter of logic, that the elderly are dying with substantial wealth and thus leaving substantial bequests. Even if these bequests are accidental rather than the result of a bequest motive, they cannot be ignored, because somebody is receiving them. These recipients will presumably consume more in response. Thus, nations with a large elderly population save less not necessarily because the elderly dissave, but perhaps because the young consume more in response to the greater likelihood of receiving a bequest.

There are three reasons for believing this mechanism is important. First, there is substantial evidence (from Kotlikoff and Summers 1981, e.g.) that bequests are an important component of wealth accumulation, and it is hard to argue that those receiving the bequests should be unaffected by them. Second, there is the disparity between micro and macro data that Weil documents; I do not know of any better way to explain it. Third, there is some direct evidence. In his dissertation, Weil examines the consumption of individuals in the PSID; he finds that those who have recently received a bequest, or say they expect to receive a bequest, tend to consume more than those without any prospect for receiving a bequest (holding other things, such as income, constant). Moreover, the estimated magnitude of this effect is large enough to reconcile the micro and macro data.

The bottom line is that the aging of a society may well depress national saving, but not for the reasons given by the life-cycle model. Rather, as the elderly population grows and bequests become more common, the young may save less than they otherwise would.

Social Security and the Disincentive to Work

The last issue that I will address is the disincentive to work provided by the social security system. Börsch-Supan shows that this disincentive is substantial in both Germany and the United States. He suggests that it would be better if social security were "nondistortionary"—that is, if it did not influence the work incentive of the elderly.

Although I am generally sympathetic with this conclusion, I do have one reservation. It is my understanding that the disincentive to work is a feature not only of the German and U.S. systems, but of the public pension system in almost every industrial society. As economists, we usually follow the methodological precept that people do not systematically make mistakes. Similarly, if we observe some policy adopted in many countries, we might be tempted to think that there is some reason for it—maybe even a good reason.

In a recent paper, Xavier Sala-i-Martin has suggested that social security's work disincentive may be optimal. He argues that, because of depreciation, the elderly have low levels of human capital. Moreover, in the spirit of some recent work on economic growth, he argues that there are externalities to the average level of human capital. These two assumptions naturally lead to the conclusions that the working elderly depress an economy's productivity and that public policy should encourage the elderly to leave the labor force.

Although Sala-i-Martin's explanation of public pensions is ingenious, I am not persuaded by it, as I find it hard to believe that this externality is significant. Yet before I sign on with Börsch-Supan's conclusion that we should move to a nondistortionary system, I would like to see this issue addressed more fully. Perhaps the work disincentive is so universal because it is optimal. If it is not optimal, at least in some second-best sense, then it is puzzling that it is so common. In the absence of any explanation of why social security systems so universally discourage the elderly from working, I am reticent to conclude that existing policies must be undesirable.

References

Ando, Albert, and Arthur Kennickell. 1986. How much (or little) life cycle saving is there in micro data? In *Macroeconomics and finance: Essays in honor of Franco Modigliani,* ed. R. Dornbusch, S. Fischer, and J. Bossons. Cambridge: MIT Press.

Kotlikoff, Lawrence, and Lawrence Summers. 1981. The role of intergenerational transfers in aggregate capital accumulation. *Journal of Political Economy* 89:706–32.

Sala-i-Martin, Xavier. 1992. Pensions. Yale University.

Weil, David N. 1990. Age and saving in micro and macro data. Chapter in Ph.D. dissertation, Department of Economics, Harvard University.

9 Saving, Growth, and Aging in Taiwan

Angus S. Deaton and Christina H. Paxson

This paper examines issues of life-cycle saving, growth, and aging in Taiwan. We are mainly concerned with standard issues of life-cycle saving and their implications for the living standards of the elderly. We investigate whether saving appears to be motivated by life-cycle factors, how income growth has affected the profiles of income, consumption, and saving, and how changes in the demographic structure of Taiwan have influenced saving behavior. We use data from 15 consecutive household income and expenditure surveys, from 1976 through 1990. Although there is no panel element to these data, the large number of households surveyed (approximately 14,000 per year) and the large number of cross sections allows us to track cohorts of people through time and to observe the evolution of their levels of income, consumption, and saving.

Taiwan provides an excellent laboratory in which to study the determinants of household saving. First, as table 9.1 shows, the last four decades have seen both very rapid growth and very high saving rates. The annual growth of GNP per capita averaged 4.3 percent in the 1950s, 7.0 percent in the 1970s, and 6.7 percent in the 1980s, and although the oil price shocks of the early 1970s and 1980s were associated with periods of relatively slow growth, there is no evidence that per capita growth rates are beginning to slow. Indeed, growth rates in the latter half of the 1980s exceeded any in the previous three decades. The high saving rates are also documented in table 9.1. The national accounts data show that gross national saving as a fraction of GNP has increased over the past three decades, from an average of 18.7 percent in 1961–65 to over 32

Angus S. Deaton is the William Church Osborn Professor of Public Affairs and professor of economics and international affairs at Princeton University and a research associate of the National Bureau of Economic Research. Christina H. Paxson is associate professor of economics and public affairs at Princeton University and a research associate of the National Bureau of Economic Research.

The authors are grateful to Jonathan Skinner for useful comments, to Alec Levenson for assistance with the data, and to David Card and Gregory Chow for helpful discussions.

Table 9.1   Statistics on Income, Growth, Saving, and Population

Year	GNP per Capita (base = 1986)	Growth in GNP per Capita	Income per Household (base = 1986)		Gross Saving as a Percentage of GNP	Household Savings Rate		Population (millions)		Population Growth Rate
			National Accounts	Survey		National Accounts	Survey	National Accounts	Survey	
1961	25,408	–	–	–	18.4	–	–	11.149	–	–
1965	33,386	6.83	–	–	20.7	–	–	12.628	–	3.03
1970	47,710	7.14	143,088	–	25.7	–	–	14.676	–	2.38
1975	63,428	5.69	193,062	–	26.7	20.0	–	16.149	–	1.88
1978	84,316	9.49	250,100	248,854	34.4	20.7	14.1	17.136	16.482	1.92
1979	89,605	6.08	271,363	279,332	33.4	19.8	15.6	17.479	17.012	2.01
1980	92,098	2.74	288,934	288,173	32.3	17.9	17.1	17.805	17.694	1.86
1981	94,374	2.44	294,759	286,102	31.3	20.2	19.0	18.135	18.224	1.86
1982	96,944	2.69	294,322	287,190	30.1	20.1	16.7	18.458	18.645	1.78
1983	104,130	7.15	310,414	308,659	32.1	21.4	17.3	18.733	19.181	1.49
1984	114,903	9.84	326,692	331,271	33.8	22.9	16.2	19.013	19.494	1.49
1985	119,581	3.99	331,193	338,155	33.6	23.9	17.1	19.258	19.548	1.29
1986	137,992	14.32	341,728	359,387	38.5	28.5	18.6	19.455	19.916	1.02
1987	154,838	11.52	364,700	380,111	38.5	28.3	19.1	19.673	20.080	1.12
1988	164,229	5.89	404,138	423,080	34.5	23.6	20.5	19.904	20.169	1.18
1989	174,407	6.01	443,866	465,652	30.8	19.5	22.1	20.107	20.716	1.02
1990	180,053	3.19	478,296	507,242	29.2	20.0	23.3	20.353	20.958	1.22

Notes: All numbers are from National Accounts statistics (from Taiwanese Statistical Office) unless otherwise indicated. National Accounts household savings rate includes private institutions serving households. All money figures are in N.T. dollars, base year = 1986.

percent in 1976–90. Household saving represents a large fraction of national saving, and the national accounts data show that roughly 50 percent of national saving is done by households, even if we exclude the savings of private corporations. What is more, the household survey data that we use yield savings figures that are of comparable magnitude to those in the national accounts. This situation stands in sharp contrast to that in many developing countries, where survey data yield savings estimates that are much lower than those in the national accounts.

The second feature of Taiwan that is relevant to life-cycle saving is its rapid transition over the last several decades from high to low population growth; see again table 9.1. In the 1950s, Taiwan's rate of population growth averaged 4.13 percent per year, reflecting the influx of immigrants from mainland China and then a postwar baby boom. The rate declined slowly through the early and middle 1960s and fell sharply in the late 1960s and early 1970s. The overall decline in the rate of population growth masks two offsetting factors, both of which are important to our topic. Life expectancy has increased, and there has been a sharp drop in fertility. In 1961, a 60-year-old male had a life expectation of 13.92 years. By 1990, this expectation had increased to 17.93 years (Republic of China 1991). For females, comparable numbers are 17.85 and 20.51 years. The decline in population growth rates despite these increases reflect the behavior of fertility, which began to fall in the late 1960s. The total fertility rate fell from 6.1 in 1958 to 1.9 in 1985. An important implication of this decline is that Taiwanese who are currently young will, when old, have far fewer adult children to provide potential support than do those who are old now. In fact, the fraction of the elderly who live with their children is already beginning to decline (see Lo 1987), although this may be due more to an increase in wealth that makes independent living possible, rather than to a decline in the number of children who can potentially provide care.

High growth, declining fertility, and increasing life expectancy all have consequences for saving that are predictable by standard life-cycle theory, and it is these predictions that we examine in this paper. We first investigate whether the observed patterns in consumption and saving across different households can be fit into the life-cycle story. In particular, we examine the basic implication of a life-cycle model that savings should (at least eventually) decline with age. We also examine cohort effects in consumption and in saving. Those who are currently young in Taiwan have lifetime earnings that are many times larger than those of their parents and grandparents, and we test whether their consumption profiles are shifted in the appropriate way. We also look for the increased saving rates among the younger cohorts that might be expected in the face of rising life expectancy and falling numbers of children. We find reasonable conformity been the Taiwanese facts and the life-cycle theory; it is certainly possible to interpret the broad features of the data in life-cycle terms.

We also look at the familiar implications of the life-cycle model for the relationship between savings and productivity growth. High income growth across cohorts should yield high national savings rates, because younger savers have a much higher lifetime wealth level than do older dissavers, a mechanism that links growth to saving at the aggregate, but not at the individual, level. We find strong evidence of a link between growth and saving at the individual level, something that is not predicted by the theory. We also run a battery of standard excess sensitivity tests, which do not provide any evidence against the life-cycle story. Even so, we find a very marked coherence between the age profiles of consumption and income for different cohorts, a coherence that is consistent with the life-cycle but strongly suggests a more direct link between consumption and income. We find it hard to rationalize such a relationship in the Taiwanese context, so that the life-cycle model remains perhaps the most satisfactory account of our evidence.

9.1   The Survey Data

The data used in this paper come from a time series of household surveys, the Personal Income Distribution Surveys, collected in the Taiwan area of the Republic of China (ROC), or Taiwan for short, in the 15 calendar years 1976–90. In 1976 and 1977, the sample sizes are a little over 9,000 households, but from 1978 there are over 14,000 households in each survey. The number of persons covered varies from around 50,000 in the first two years to around 75,000 later. New samples are drawn each year, so that it is not possible to track individual households over time; instead, we shall track individual age *cohorts* through the successive surveys.

The survey design is described in Republic of China (1989). For income and consumption, data are collected both from interviews and from diaries. At the single interview, questions are asked about major items of income and expenditure in the past year, while the diaries, maintained throughout the year and regularly inspected by field workers, keep track of all items of income and expenditure. Only a "small number of households" keep the diaries; these households are also interviewed, and the results of comparing the two methods are "used to check and/or correct results of all interviews in the survey." The survey is a comprehensive one and collects information on household structure, on socioeconomic characteristics (including industry, occupation, and education), on household expenditures in some detail, and on the incomes by source of the household and of each of its members. All money amounts in this paper are in real N.T. dollars, base year = 1986.

Our impression from the work that we have done and from the results reported below is that the data are of good quality. One of the attractions of working with data from a high saving country is the ability to study saving at the household level. For many developing countries, it is difficult to find much reported saving in household survey data, even in those cases where national accounts data indicate that households as a whole are saving substantial amounts; see, for example, Visaria (1980) for several Asian countries, Paxson

(1992) for Thailand, and Deaton (1992a) for Côte d'Ivoire. The Taiwanese survey data do not have this problem, and the high national saving rates are reflected in the behavior of the individual households. Table 9.1 shows that, according to the national accounts, saving by households has varied around 20 percent of household income since 1975, while the figures from the surveys, although far from identical, are of the same order of magnitude. Given that saving is the difference between two large magnitudes, each estimated with error, given that the coverage of the surveys and the national accounts is different, and given the difficulties that are typically encountered in reconciling household and national accounts, we view the correspondence as remarkably close. For household incomes, which are also shown in table 9.1, the survey data are again close to those from the national accounts, with a maximum discrepancy of 5 percent.

Since we shall be concerned with saving within a life-cycle context, it is useful to look first at the demographic information in the surveys. Figure 9.1 shows the age-sex pyramids for each of the survey years; as with all of the summary statistics presented in the paper, numbers are weighted by the appropriate inflation factors so as to provide estimates of the underlying population. No inflation factors are available for the first two years, 1976 and 1977, for which the results are presented in unweighted form; evidence from the other years suggests that the unweighted data are unlikely to be misleading.

Note first that the surveys evidently fail to capture a substantial number of young males aged 20–25, presumably those in college or engaged in military service. In the last few years, 1988–90, a similar phenomenon is beginning to be evident for young females over a somewhat broader age range. This may again be related to college, and indeed more than half of college students in Taiwan are women; it may also reflect employment patterns among young women. In any case, these people, both male and female, are "missing" as a result of the survey design, and not because of any similar feature in the population.

Another feature of these survey demographics reflects a genuine peculiarity of the Taiwanese population. In all years, there is an excess of middle-aged to older men over women in the same age group; see the sex ratios by age in figure 9.2. In the first year, 1976, the number of males per 100 females is greater than 100, over the range of ages 40–65, reaching a peak of 140 at age 50. This peak ages one year per year, and by 1990, there are somewhat less than 140 65-year-old males for each 65-year-old female. These numbers are a consequence of the cohort of predominantly male "mainlanders" who came to Taiwan in 1949, and an unusually large fraction of whom have never married. These people differ in a number of other respects from the rest of the population; for example, many were soldiers, and a high proportion have government pensions (or pension rights), and so they provide a group whose life-cycle consumption and saving behavior can be expected to differ from that of other Taiwanese.

The changing shapes of the pyramids also shows very clearly the marked

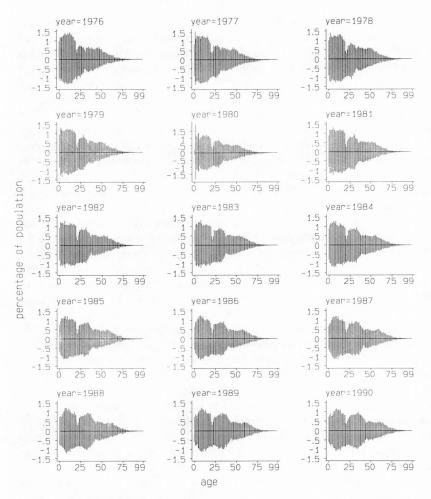

Fig. 9.1   Age-sex pyramids
Note: Positive values represent males. Negative values represent females.

(and remarkable) aging of the population over the 15-year period of our sample. Figure 9.3 shows, for each year, the fractions of the population older than each age. In 1976, .046 of the population were over 60; in 1990, the fraction was .092. The ratio of the elderly to their surviving children, although still high because of older fertility rates, will fall rapidly over time. For example, Hermalin, Ofstedal, and Li (1991) indicate that women aged 61–65 in 1990 had, on average, 5.1 children ever born in their lifetimes. The number of children ever born is expected to drop to 3.6 for those aged 46–50 in 1990 and to 2.4 for those aged 31–35 in 1990. Although numbers of children ever born is

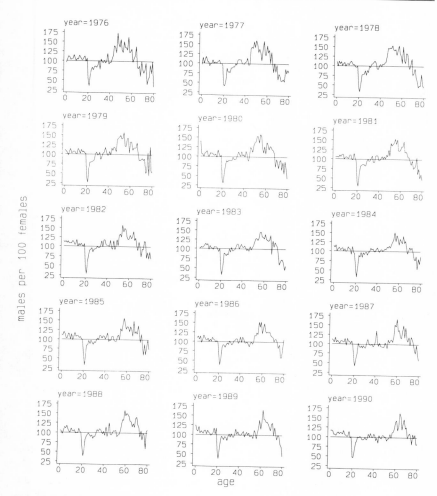

Fig. 9.2   Sex ratios

not the same as children surviving into their parent's old age, the evidence strongly suggests that many of the current generation of young adults cannot expect to avail themselves of the traditional Chinese pattern whereby elderly parents move into their son's home. This idea is supported by survey evidence from Chang (1987), which indicates that a growing fraction of currently young Taiwanese women do not expect to live with their sons when they are old. Absent state intervention in the form of social security (and although social security is being expanded in Taiwan, the coverage and amounts are still very small), the current generation of young workers has a strong incentive to save a larger fraction of their incomes than did their parents. One of our aims in this

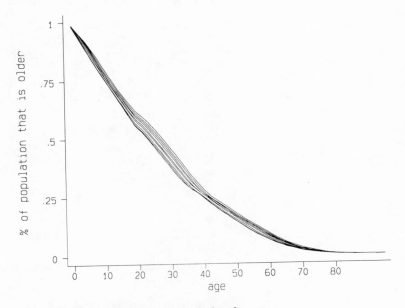

Fig. 9.3   Age distribution of the population, by year

paper is to see if we can find evidence of such an increase in life-cycle saving among the young and whether it can plausibly be attributed to the effects of the demographic transition.

9.2   Constructing Cohorts

For most of the interesting questions about saving and the life cycle, it is necessary to track individuals over time and to observe the changes in consumption, income, and saving as people age. Although we cannot track individual households in the data, we can track "cohorts" of households, with cohorts defined according to their year of birth. For each year of data, we average the variables of interest by age of individuals or age of household head and then track, not the same individuals, but the sample from the same cohort one year older in the next survey. In this way, we can follow cohort means for 15 years of each age cohort of households or individuals. We do this both at the level of the household, with age defined by the age of the head, and at the level of the person, again using age as the grouping variable. Where we have individual data, for example on earnings, the (sample weighted) cohort means of individuals by age provide unbiased estimates of mean earnings for the underlying population of that age. For other variables, which can be collected only at the household level, matters are a good deal less clear. Averaging by the age of the household head has the inevitable effect of confounding genuine changes in stable households with changes in both household formation and in headship. For example, since earnings (eventually) decline with age and since older men cease (by definition in these data) to be heads when they cease to be the main earner, households with older heads will be an increasingly selected sample of the population and will therefore display behavior that increasingly disguises actual patterns of household change over time. For example, households with older heads will be those whose head has unusually high earnings compared with others of his or her cohort, or those who have an unusual amount of wealth that enables the household to survive as an independent unit. As a consequence, and if, for argument's sake, savings rates are positively correlated with earnings, or are positively correlated with wealth (households who are predisposed to save are typically richer than those who are not), we may observe that, at high ages, household saving rates increase with the age of the head even though assets are typically being run down in old age.

The alternative, of averaging over individuals by age, although minimizing selectivity, is difficult, because so many variables are reported only at the household level, so that we have to impute individual consumption or incomes based on those of the household to which they belong. Old people who live with their children are therefore attributed some fraction of household income or consumption, an attribution that is essentially arbitrary when there is no information about intrahousehold allocation. These problems are not soluble, and they have to be kept continuously in mind when interpreting the results presented below.

Table 9.2 reports the numbers of households in five selected household cohorts, for each year of the survey data; table 9.3 records the same information for the numbers of people in the "individual" cohorts. To save space, we show numbers for only five cohorts, but we have constructed (and will use) the cohorts at each age, although in some cases it will be necessary to eliminate the youngest and the oldest groups. In total, the data allow us to calculate 1,031 household head age/year pairs for the household data and 1,161 age/year pairs for the individual data; only 75 of these are shown in each table. Cohorts are defined by year of birth, or more conveniently, by age in 1976. Hence, the first column of table 9.2 shows the sample representation of households headed by those born in 1956, who were age 20 in 1976 and 34 in 1990. The increase in numbers, from 26 households in 1976 to 640 households in 1990, shows not that the cohort of those born in 1956 is increasing, nor that the sample is incorrectly drawn, but that 34-year-olds are much more likely to be household heads than 20-year-olds. For the older cohorts, the variation in sample size is much less, and it is these middle years of household headship for which the averages are likely to be most accurate, both because there are more households in each average, and because selection problems are less severe.

Figure 9.4 shows how the cohort grouping can be used to show both the life-cycle pattern of family formation and the cohort effects of falling fertility. The age of the head of the household is plotted on the horizontal axis, while the

Table 9.2   Numbers of Households in Selected Household Cohorts (indicated by age of head in 1976)

Year	Cohort 1 (age 20)	Cohort 11 (age 30)	Cohort 21 (age 40)	Cohort 31 (age 50)	Cohort 41 (age 60)
1976	26	203	304	275	113
1977	35	274	280	237	71
1978	70	401	380	344	106
1979	133	352	383	300	88
1980	188	393	359	329	82
1981	261	375	372	318	87
1982	363	372	370	327	74
1983	394	364	376	278	71
1984	463	410	347	237	70
1985	519	400	296	242	48
1986	543	398	303	222	53
1987	563	367	281	191	65
1988	604	390	260	208	49
1989	636	364	256	184	41
1990	640	299	228	196	59

vertical axis shows the average number of children in the household; children are here defined according to the official survey definition, which is 20 years old or younger. The plotted points are connected when we are following the same cohort through time, but different cohorts are left unconnected. To avoid complete clutter, we show only every fifth cohort, so that the first line segment on the left-hand side of the figure shows the number of children in households headed by those who were age 20 in 1976; by the time these people are age 35 in 1990, they are well launched into their child-rearing years and have a little under two children per household. The second cohort, the 25-year-olds in 1976, overlap with the first cohort for 10 years, but take us another five years into the life cycle, since these people are age 40 in the last, 1990 survey. To the extent that these two cohorts and the next one overlap, the profiles of children by age have similar shapes, with the maximum number of children attained around age 40 and falling thereafter, as the oldest leave home and new children cease to be born. However, the falling fertility shows up in the profiles as pronounced vertical shifts, or cohort effects, as we move from one cohort to the next.

One way of turning these pictures into numbers is to fit to these means a polynomial in age together with a series of cohort dummies, one for each date of birth. For figure 9.4, we do this only for those older than age 19 and younger than age 61, so as to exclude those cohorts where there are few individuals in the means. The estimated cohort effects show that, apart from the first five groups, aged 20–24 in 1976, which we know to be unreliable both because of the sample design and because of selectivity, there is an average decline of 0.06 children per year, so over the 35-year age span, from heads aged 25 to

Table 9.3   **Numbers of Persons in Selected Person Cohorts (indicated by age in 1976)**

Year	Cohort 1 (age 20)	Cohort 11 (age 30)	Cohort 21 (age 40)	Cohort 31 (age 50)	Cohort 41 (age 60)
1976	788	521	608	461	249
1977	648	602	535	422	186
1978	1008	854	738	629	287
1979	1126	796	708	574	269
1980	1238	834	723	625	268
1981	1261	794	720	624	293
1982	1401	771	695	655	273
1983	1368	737	718	597	292
1984	1392	825	711	541	291
1985	1426	766	651	596	238
1986	1305	725	659	549	263
1987	1347	634	632	513	254
1988	1366	674	617	548	196
1989	1331	672	600	519	202
1990	1330	601	575	508	219

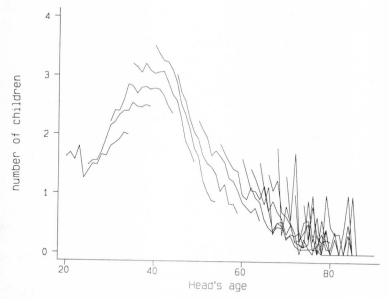

Fig. 9.4   Number of children in the household

heads aged 60, there has been a decline in number of children per household of 2.3, from 4.71 to 2.44 at the maximum of the profile. Of course, this measure is neither a measure of the decline in children ever born, nor of children available to parents in old age, but it nevertheless seems likely that for those in their mid-thirties now, there will be only half as many sons to look after them in old-age as there are now for those who are 70 years old.

The demographic transition is one remarkable fact about modern Taiwan; another is its rate of economic growth and the effects on the earnings of the different cohorts. Figure 9.5, which is constructed for individuals and not for households, shows the cohort earnings patterns for every fifth cohort, again starting with those who were 20 years old in 1976. Again we can make out the usual pattern of earnings with age, but superimposed is very rapid within-cohort growth, at least for some of the cohorts. For those aged 25 in 1976, real earnings have grown at the astonishing rate of 12 percent per year over the 15 years since. For older cohorts, the amount is less, falling with age and eventually becoming negative for the cohort aged 50 in 1976. The bias of earnings growth toward the young is plausibly attributable to the much higher levels of education among young cohorts and is consistent with evidence from the United States, where earnings functions frequently show a positive interaction between education and experience. In the United States, much of the growth in earnings among the young is associated with job changes and with the greater tendency of young workers to move from one job to another. The same phenomenon might well hold true in Taiwan, with young people moving into the new jobs created by the rapid rate of economic growth.

Figure 9.6 shows nonlabor income by age and by cohort. In a country with savings rates as high as those in Taiwan, total income behaves very differently from earnings, and the figure shows how asset income and transfers replace earnings with age, so that total income does not collapse with age nearly as rapidly as does earnings. Lo (1987) provides more detail on the composition of income of the elderly and on how it has changed over time.

9.3   A Life-Cycle Interpretation of Consumption and Saving

With the demographic and earnings environment described, we turn to consumption behavior and the extent to which it fits the standard life-cycle framework. We are particularly concerned with whether Taiwan's high saving ratio can be attributed to its high rate of growth through the traditional life-cycle mechanism, with younger, richer cohorts being responsible for the bulk of the saving. We also want to look for traces of the demographic transition in the behavior of younger cohorts and, in particular, to investigate whether they are saving not just large amounts because their earnings are high, but are actually saving at a higher rate than their predecessors.

The cohort data are ideally suited for examining these issues. There are a large number of cohorts, with younger cohorts very much richer in lifetime

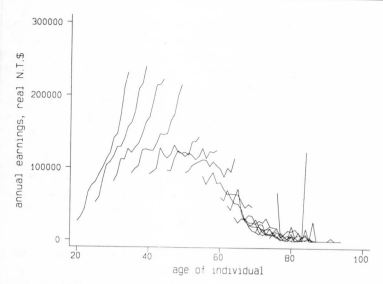

Fig. 9.5   Individual earnings, by age

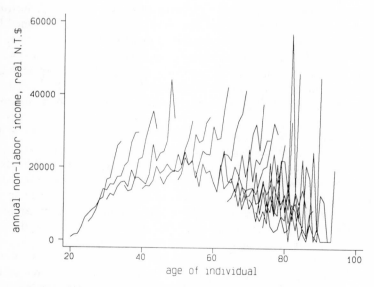

Fig. 9.6   Individual nonlabor income, by age

resources than their parents or grandparents. Even at 10 percent per annum real earnings growth, which is less than the 12 percent average experienced by the younger cohorts, 25-year-olds in Taiwan can expect real lifetime earnings that are nearly 11 times greater than those of 50-year-olds. At the same time, since the data run for 15 consecutive years, we observe behavior at the same age for a range of different cohorts, so that it is possible to separate cohort (wealth) effects from age (preference) effects. Indeed, as we shall show below, it is even possible to say something about the effects of common macroeconomic shocks, as represented by year effects.

With no income uncertainty, the life-cycle model predicts that consumption is a function of lifetime resources (earnings plus inherited assets), with the fraction of resources consumed being a function of age, as dictated by preferences and the life-cycle variation in household size and composition. We write

(1) $$c = g(a)W,$$

where W is the sum of assets and the discounted present value of current and expected future labor income, and $g(a)$ is some function of age a. Taking logs, we have

(2) $$\ln c = \ln g(a) + \ln W.$$

This equation holds at the level of the individual, but given its additive structure, it can be averaged over all households of the same age (as defined by head's age) in each year, so that the average of the logarithms of consumption for each age/year combination should be additively decomposable into a wealth term, which is constant within cohorts, and an age term. Equation (2) can then be estimated nonparametrically using the cohort data, by regressing the cohort averages of the logarithm of consumption against cohort dummies and age dummies.

The raw data on total household consumption are plotted in figure 9.7 in the same format as the earlier cohort diagrams; the figure shows the average of consumption, although it is the average of log consumption that will be used in the regressions. (Similar pictures for consumption per head, or consumption per adult equivalent, for various definitions of the latter, give very similar results.) Figure 9.7 shows a remarkable resemblance to figure 9.5, for earnings, a resemblance that will be explored further in the next section. Note again that, while there is a distinctly visible life-cycle pattern to consumption, rising with age and then falling, there is also a great deal of within-cohort consumption growth, especially for the younger cohorts. Clearly, old and young households are not sufficiently altruistically linked for their consumption to move in lockstep.

The results can be given an explicit life-cycle interpretation by estimating equation (2), and the results are given, not in numerical form, since there are 66 cohort effects and 51 age effects, but graphically in figure 9.8, where cohort

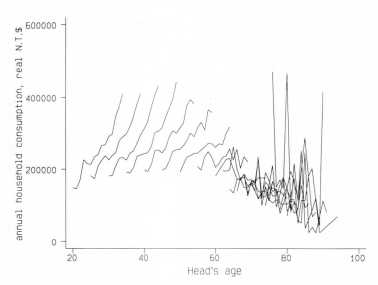

Fig. 9.7   Total household consumption, by age of household head

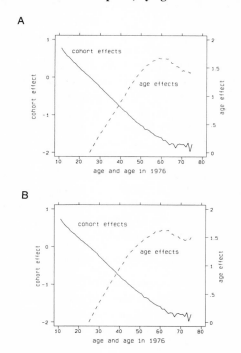

Fig. 9.8   Age and cohort effects in consumption
Note: Controls for numbers of adults and children are excluded from panel *A* and included in panel *B*.

effects (age in 1976) and age effects are shown together. In panel A equation (2) is estimated with age and cohort dummies only, while in panel B we show the age and cohort effects when the (average) numbers of adults and children are added as additional regressors. (Additional adults markedly increase consumption; additional children have little effect.) As predicted by the life-cycle model for a growing economy, the cohort effects decline steadily from younger to older cohorts; both graphs show that, at the same age, consumption increases at about 4 percent per cohort, so that, for example, the consumption at age 40 of someone born in 1950 is on average 3.4 times larger than the consumption at age of 40 of someone born in 1925. As is to be expected, the age effects depend to some extent on whether the household composition variables are explicitly included in the regressions. In either case, the age profile is much steeper than is typically seen in the United States, or even in other LDCs, flattening out only very gradually with age. In both panels, consumption falls with age only after age 60, although the decline is less pronounced in the bottom panel, where we control for the numbers of household members. Note again, however, that the selection effects should make us very skeptical about conclusions for households with elderly heads. While steep age-consumption profiles are unusual, they are certainly not inconsistent with the life-cycle model. In an economy growing as rapidly as Taiwan's, real interest rates are very high, especially in the large and rapidly developing small-business sector, so that there are strong intertemporal incentives to postpone consumption and for consumption to grow rapidly over time. Alternatively, it is possible that the Taiwanese are more patient than most other people, or that the Chinese veneration for the elderly extends to a perceived high marginal utility of consumption in old age.

One feature of figure 9.7 is not accounted for by either the age or the cohort effects in figure 9.8. This is the fact that the individual cohort "tracks" have similar shapes, so that, for example, almost all show a decline in consumption with age between the fourth and fifth observations. These are clearly caused by the presence of macroeconomic effects that impinge on all cohorts to a greater or lesser degree, but which are located in real time and which cannot be explained by cohort or age effects. The obvious extension to equation (2) is to allow for fixed-year effects, so that the consumption equation becomes

(3) $$\ln c_{at} = \ln g(a) + \ln W_b + \theta_t,$$

where θ_t is a year fixed effect, and the subscripts a, b, and t denote age, cohort, and time, respectively. Note that given age and time, cohort is determined; indeed we have been measuring b as age in 1976, which is $a - t + 1976$.

Equation (2) is an implication of the life-cycle model of consumption when there is no uncertainty, so that cohort wealth levels are never revised. Once uncertainty is admitted, wealth levels will be revised in response to macroeconomic shocks, so that the life-cycle model with uncertainty provides at least some basis for equation (3). However, the link between equation (3) and the model under uncertainty is not as clean as was the link with equation (2) under certainty, since the effects of a common macroeconomic shock on wealth levels ought to vary with age. While it is possible in principle to include interaction terms between year and cohort effects, unrestricted estimation would not be possible even with the current data. Nevertheless, the year effects are certainly present in the data, and it seems useful to estimate equation (3) as an approximation to the more general model, if only to ensure that the failure to accommodate the year effects does not contaminate the estimates of the age and cohort effects, with which the year dummies are strongly correlated.

The estimation of equation (3) requires some thought about the relationship between age, cohort, and year dummies. Write C, Y, and A for matrices of dummy variables of cohort, year, and age dummies; each matrix has 1,031 rows, the number of year/head's-age pairs, while the numbers of columns are 65 for cohorts (for those aged 11 in 1976 to those aged 75 in 1976), 15 for years, and 51 for ages (from age 25 to age 75). Note that we have truncated on age of head, eliminating those below 25 to avoid the "missing" males below that age group and those above 75 to avoid the very imprecisely estimated cohort means from households with very old heads. Of course, there are no heads of households in 1976 who were then 11 years old, but we do include one observation on that cohort, when they are 25-year-old heads of household in 1990. Equation (3) can be rewritten in terms of the dummy variable matrices as

$$(4) \qquad \ln c_{at} = \iota\beta + C\gamma + A\alpha + Y\psi + \varepsilon,$$

where ι is a vector of units, and the vectors α, γ, and ψ are parameters of age, cohort, and year effects. As usual, one category from each set of dummies must be excluded, and doing so presents no nonstandard issues of interpretation. However, the dependency between age, cohort, and year introduces a slightly less standard complication.

Let σ_n denote the (transpose of the) vector $(1, 2, 3, \ldots, n)$. Then, since cohort is age minus year plus a constant, the matrices of dummy variables satisfy the exact linear relationship

$$(5) \qquad C\sigma_{n_c} = A\sigma_{n_a} - Y\sigma_{n_y} + n_y\iota,$$

where n_c, n_a, and n_y are the numbers of cohorts, ages, and years. To see that the constant term in equation (5) equals n_y, note that the youngest cohort of people (aged 11 in 1976) will be the youngest age of 25 in the n_y^{th} year. As a result of the identity expressed by equation (5), the parameters in equation (4) are not identified, even after one category has been dropped from each set of dummies. In particular, if the vectors α, γ, β, and ψ are replaced by $\tilde{\alpha}$, $\tilde{\beta}$, $\tilde{\gamma}$, and $\tilde{\psi}$, where

$$(6) \qquad \tilde{\alpha} = \alpha - \kappa\sigma_{n_a}, \quad \tilde{\beta} = \beta - n_y\kappa,$$

$$\tilde{\gamma} = \gamma + \kappa\sigma_{n_c}, \quad \tilde{\psi} = \psi + \kappa\sigma_{n_y},$$

and κ is some arbitrary nonzero scalar, then, as is easily checked by substitution into equation (4), there is no consequence for the predicted value of consumption. The way that this works can readily be seen from the original cohort-consumption plots in figure 9.7. For the first cohort, suppose that there is no cohort effect, so that the first trace is the sum of age and year effects. Since the cohort ages one year at a time, adding equal amounts to year and age dummies will leave the trace unchanged. The trace for the second cohort starts from the same year but one year of age younger, so that the second trace will also be left unchanged if the second cohort effect is incremented by one, and so on through the cohorts according to equation (6). In effect, any trend in the data can be arbitrarily reinterpreted as a year trend or (since year equals age minus cohort plus a constant) as trends in ages and cohorts that are equal but of opposite sign. However, it is clear that the appropriate normalization is to require that the year effects sum to zero. As an example, consider a hypothetical case in which there are apparently no cohort or age effects, but where the logarithm of consumption increases by ψ per annum for all age groups. Consider what the cohort diagram figure 9.6 would look like in such a case. Each cohort trace would increase by ψ per year of age, but each cohort trace would start at the same horizontal level as the previous one, or equivalently, at a vertical shift of ψ below it. A steady growth in year effects simply means that consumption is growing with age and declining with cohort, and it is appropriate to attribute the effects to age and cohort, not time.

In the light of this discussion, we estimate equation (4) with the first age group, and the fifteenth cohort omitted, so that the reference group is that for a household headed by a 25-year-old in 1976. The 15-year dummies are constrained to be orthogonal to a time trend and to add to zero. The "base year" is thus a timeless average of all years, and any time trend is attributed to cohorts and ages, not to time.

Figure 9.9 shows the resulting age, cohort, and year effects, with (*bottom panels*) and without (*top panels*) the addition of the average adult and children variables. The figure also shows the same decomposition for the average of the logarithms of total income (earnings plus asset and other income) and for the "saving ratio," measured here as the difference of the logarithms of income and consumption. (For Taiwanese saving ratios, the approximation is not particularly accurate, but the logarithmic form is convenient, given that we are working with the logarithms of income and consumption.) The consumption profiles are not markedly different from those in the figure 9.8, even though the year effects are quite significant, with an associated F-value of 59.8 in the basic model and 81.5 in the model with adults and children. The corresponding F-values for age and cohort effects are, respectively, 408.8 and 373.1 in the basic model, and 437.0 and 60.4 in the extended model, and it is these effects that are our primary concern in examining life-cycle behavior. Conditional on cohort and age effects, adults increase income by about as much as they in-

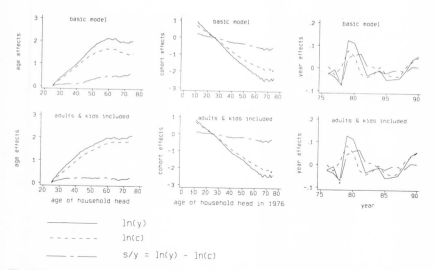

Fig. 9.9   **Age, cohort, and year effects in consumption, income, and saving rates, for household heads**

crease consumption and have little effect on household saving, while children decrease income with little effect on consumption and so decrease saving.

The cohort effects are larger the younger the cohort for consumption, for income, and for the *saving ratio,* so that, at the same age, those born later in calendar time are saving a higher fraction of their incomes. This is exactly what we might expect from the life-cycle model in the Taiwanese context in the face of rapidly declining fertility and rapidly rising life expectancy. Although the cohort differences in saving ratios are too large to be plausible in the model without the addition of numbers of adults and children, the extended model shows a flatter profile of savings rates across cohorts. For example, the saving cohort effects in the second plot in the bottom panel of figure 9.9 show a difference of -0.23 in ln (y/c) between the cohort aged 11 in 1976 (aged 25 in 1990) and the cohort 35 years older, aged 60 in 1990. The average value of ln (y/c) in 1990 for households headed by 25-year-olds was 0.276, a saving rate of 24 percent, so that the model predicts a saving rate of 4.5 percent for the older cohort at the same age, i.e., in 1955. As we saw above, this is exactly the comparison group for which the number of children has fallen by a half, and the increase in the saving rate is perhaps of the order of magnitude required to replace family by autarkic old-age insurance.

The age effects in the left-hand panels are not obviously consistent with the life-cycle story. The rising age-profile of consumption is matched by an even more rapidly rising age pattern of income, so that the saving rate, instead of being positive at young ages and negative later, shows a steady increase with age. If such a result is correct, an increase in the rate of growth of productivity would *decrease,* not increase, aggregate saving since it would redistribute income toward the young, who have the lowest saving propensity, at least provided cohort effects are eliminated, as would be expected when the demographic transition is complete. However, it is quite likely that the age effects on saving are contaminated by the selection processes for headship, certainly at old ages, and perhaps also at young ages. As already discussed, it is entirely plausible that those households headed by older people are those with an unusually high propensity to save, so that the right-hand panels in figure 9.9 are revealing only the selection effects, and not the true patterns of saving ratios. Nor can this problem be resolved by switching from a household to an individual basis, as is done in figure 9.10, which repeats figure 9.9, but with averages taken over individuals, not households. The problem is that here we are still looking at *household* incomes, consumption, and saving, only the household magnitudes have been attributed to individuals. The age effects on saving are now even more extreme, because the old individuals on the right of the diagram are now predominately located in households headed by younger adults, so that we lose the flattening of income, consumption, and savings profiles with age that is observed in the household-level data.

Our results can thus be interpreted in terms of a more-or-less standard life-cycle model, at least provided we are allowed to choose a desired consumption profile that rises rapidly with age, which indeed is theoretically plausible in the circumstances. Saving *rates* are systematically higher for the younger cohorts, and the effect is consistent with the increased need to provide for old age. And if we fail to observe any life-cycle profile in saving rates by age, there are statistical grounds that can perhaps explain what we see.

9.5 Alternative Explanations: Tracking and Growth

The ability to give a life-cycle interpretation to the data does not mean that the life-cycle model is in fact correct, and in this section we look at some more negative evidence. In particular, we consider whether there is evidence in these data that consumption "tracks" income by more than would be expected if the life-cycle model is correct, and we look more closely at the relationship between saving and growth.

Tracking has been found in other data; see particularly Carroll and Summers (1991) for the United States and Deaton (1992b) for Thailand and Côte d'Ivoire. However, in all these examples, the large mass of households accumulate little or nothing, and saving is used to buffer short-term fluctuations in income; in the absence of accumulation, consumption and income must move together in the long run. However, there is certainly no lack of accumulation by households in Taiwan, so that we should expect to observe a greater decoupling of consumption and income, even over long life-cycle spans. Taiwanese households have demonstrated their ability to accumulate enough assets to accomplish even "low-frequency" consumption smoothing. Although the evi-

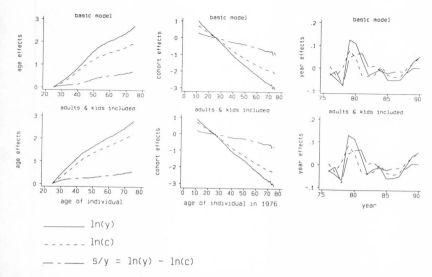

Fig. 9.10   Age, cohort, and year effects in consumption, income, and saving rates, for individuals

dence in the previous section is consistent with the life-cycle story, it does not immediately follow that much long-term smoothing is being done, since the preferred profile of consumption may not call for it. It is therefore necessary to look at the data in a different way.

Figure 9.11 shows the same data on consumption and income by age as in figure 9.5, but with a separate diagram for each cohort, and with income and consumption shown together. Once again, we see the marked differences in the shape of the profile between the younger and older cohorts, with much more rapid growth for younger households. We also see the growing saving ratio as a widening between consumption and income over time. But the most marked feature of figure 9.11 is the extraordinary coherence between the patterns of consumption and income for each of the cohorts. The shape of each changes with age, but they change together, with consumption tracking income, year by year, and age by age. Such a picture suggests a crude Keynesian consumption function, with consumption strongly linked to income. And yet we have seen in the previous section that the data, which are the same as those used here, are consistent with a life-cycle interpretation. The key to the reconciliation is the fact that in the earlier analysis, in figure 9.9, the cohort effects, the age effects, and the year effects have very similar shapes, across cohorts, age, and time, for both consumption and income. While this is consistent with the life-cycle model, only the coherence between income shocks and consumption shocks is directly predicted by it, although it could also be argued that in a rapidly growing economy, real returns will be high, so that optimal intertem-

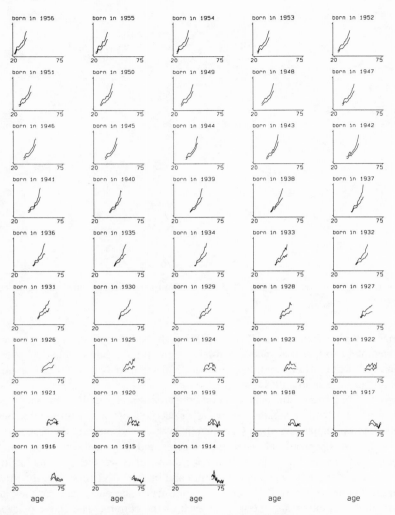

Fig. 9.11   Consumption and income, by age of household head

poral planning should generate rapid consumption growth to match rapid income growth. Even so, figure 9.11 is strongly suggestive of some simpler model embodying a much more direct link between consumption and income. That said, it is no simple matter to think of a coherent alternative. Liquidity constraints make very little sense in an environment in which so many people are saving so much. Nor do buffering models seem relevant here, whether with borrowing constraints as in Deaton (1991) or with precautionary saving and large shocks as in Carroll (1991). Both of these models work by supposing that people generally wish to accumulate little or nothing, but use saving to buffer consumption against short-term fluctuations in income. For such people, consumption tracks income because, in the long run, consumption is identical to income. That is not the case here. Perhaps the life-cycle model still provides the best theoretically consistent account of the facts.

Before accepting that position, consider the positive relationship between saving and growth, perhaps the most celebrated prediction of the life-cycle model. We have already seen that the estimated models do not clearly support this prediction in the Taiwanese case, since the saving rate appears to increase with age, although we cannot use this to reject the model because of the increasing selection of household heads with age. Even so, the *fact* that there is a connection between saving and growth seems hard to dispute. Taiwan, like Korea, Japan, Hong Kong, and Singapore, is among the most rapidly growing and highest saving economies in the world, and the cross-country relationship between saving and growth has been repeatedly documented. Furthermore, the productivity slowdown in the OECD countries has been accompanied by a reduction in national saving ratios, essentially without exception (see Modigliani 1990). However, there is still far from general acceptance that the *mechanism* is that of the life-cycle model, whereby slower growth redistributes national income away from younger, saving cohorts, to their lower-saving or dissaving elders. Indeed, for the United States, Bosworth, Burtless, and Sabelhaus (1991) have undertaken the very difficult task of interpreting the time-series evidence from the various Consumer Expenditure Surveys and have provided strong evidence that the decline in saving in the United States has been a decline that has affected all age groups; it is not the aggregation phenomenon that the life-cycle model requires. This evidence suggests that there is a mechanism linking growth and saving *within* cohorts, and it is this possibility in Taiwan to which we now turn.

The top panel of table 9.4 shows regressions of the "saving rate" (defined as before by the logarithm of the ratio of total income to consumption) against growth rates of earnings. These are run on the same averaged data displayed in the household diagrams above, with each observation corresponding to an age/year pair, and once again include only ages 25–75. As appropriate, averages are averages of the logarithms of the underlying household data, not the logarithms of averages, and all regressions are weighted by (the square root of) the number of households in the cohort average. The regression of the saving rate on the current rate of change of earnings, i.e., the growth of current earnings over last period's earnings, is *not* shown; it produces a strong positive coefficient, but such a result tells us little, since measurement error will induce a positive correlation between current saving and current income. Instead, the first line shows the regression of the saving rate on the first four lags of earnings growth; all the coefficients are positive and significantly different from zero. The second line explores the possibility that the relationship is between saving and current earnings growth, but using instrumental variables estimation to purge the measurement error. Since measurement error will induce a

Table 9.4   Saving Rates, Consumption Growth, and Earnings Growth

Effects Included	$d\ln e$	$d\ln e_{-1}$	$d\ln e_{-2}$	$d\ln e_{-3}$	$d\ln e_{-4}$	F-Test for Overidentification
		Saving Rate Regressions: $\ln y - \ln c$				
1. None		0.0793	0.1049	0.0888	0.0632	
		(8.3)	(9.2)	(7.7)	(5.8)	
	0.6995					10.75
	(1.6)					
2. Cohorts		0.0302	0.0483	0.0431	0.0321	
		(4.1)	(5.5)	(4.9)	(3.9)	
	0.2150					10.36
	(0.9)					
3. Cohorts and ages		0.0187	0.0421	0.0430	0.0329	
		(2.3)	(4.1)	(4.2)	(3.5)	
	0.2881					3.09
	(1.5)					
4. Cohorts, ages, and years		−0.0136	−0.0114	−0.0099	0.0075	
		(1.7)	(1.0)	(0.9)	(0.8)	
	0.0318					0.56
	(0.7)					
		Consumption Growth Regressions: $d\ln c$				
5. None			−0.0188	−0.0116	0.0064	
			(1.8)	(1.0)	(0.6)	
	−0.0354					2.37
	(0.3)					
6. Cohorts			−0.0307	−0.0260	−0.0062	
			(2.8)	(2.2)	(0.5)	
	0.0552					4.80
	(0.3)					
7. Cohorts and ages			−0.0158	−0.0033	0.0260	
			(1.4)	(0.3)	(2.1)	
	0.1510					4.16
	(1.1)					
8. Cohorts, ages, and years			−0.0005	0.0024	0.0071	
			(0.1)	(0.2)	(0.6)	
	0.0258					0.03
	(0.4)					

Notes: The regressions in the top panel have the cohort average of the individual "saving rates" $\ln(y/c)$ as the dependent variable, where y is total income and c is consumption. In the first regression, $\ln(y/c)$ is regressed on four lags of earnings growth $d\ln e$; in the second, saving growth is regressed on current earnings growth by instrumental variables, with the second through fourth lags of earnings growth as instruments. The regressions are repeated with the inclusion of cohort effects, cohort and age effects, and cohort, age, and year effects. The bottom panel repeats the regressions with consumption growth as the dependent variable. All consumption regressions, OLS and IVE, exclude the first lag of earnings growth. All regressions include the average numbers of adults and children, and all are weighted by the square root of the number of observations in each cohort. When computing the cohort averages of log earnings (used to construct earnings growth), the few households with no earnings are assigned a value of earnings equal to one.

Numbers in parentheses are t-values.

spurious correlation between successive lags of earnings growth, we use only the second and third lags as instruments. This regression shows no relationship between the saving rate and predictable earnings growth, and the overidentification test rejects the hypothesis that lagged growth rates affect saving rates only through their ability to predict current growth. (Indeed they have little ability to predict current earning growth.)

The rest of the top panel explores the same regressions but with the addition first of cohort dummies, then of cohort and age dummies, and finally of cohort, age, and year dummies. Given the relationships that exist between earnings growth, age, and cohorts, we would argue for including these dummies, but for excluding the year dummies, since the latter should be subsumed in the effects for which we are testing. Although the coefficients are smaller than in the first row, the positive association between lagged growth of earnings and saving rates remains, at least until the year effects are introduced. None of the results suggest that the effect is working through anticipated earnings growth. These results show a positive relationship between saving rates and growth, a relationship that is not an aggregation effect, but holds for specific cohorts over time. Tracking the same group of people as they age, we find that their saving rate is higher in the years following rapid earnings growth. Because this effect is from *lagged* earnings growth, it has nothing to do with the standard response of saving to transitory income, and it is not an effect that is predicted by life-cycle theory.

These effects of within-cohort growth on within-cohort savings are a good deal smaller than those that are typically predicted from the aggregation effects of life-cycle saving, or that are typically found in the cross-country or long time-span evidence. Those findings, and again see Modigliani (1990), typically show an effect of growth on savings of about two, so that a shift in earnings growth from 5 to 10 percent will generate an increase of 10 percentage points in the saving rate. If we take the results from the third row of table 9.4, the effect is 0.137, which is less than a tenth of the typical cross-country estimates. Even the first row estimates, which condition on neither cohort nor age effects, add up to only 0.33. Hence, while the within-cohort growth effects are present and while they cast doubt on the life-cycle model, they probably cannot account for a major share of the relationship between saving and growth in Taiwan.

The second panel of table 9.4 reports similar regressions, but with the dependent variable the rate of growth of consumption. These correspond closely to the standard "excess sensitivity" tests in the macroeconomic consumption literature; see, for example, Campbell and Mankiw (1991), who look for a relationship between consumption growth and anticipated growth in labor income. The only difference between the top and bottom panels, apart from the dependent variable, is that the first lag of earnings growth is excluded from the unrestricted regression; if consumption growth is correlated with unanticipated growth in earnings, as the life-cycle theory supposes, and if earnings are mismeasured, there will be a spurious correlation between consumption growth and lagged earnings growth that does not contradict the model. The results provide no evidence of excess sensitivity in Taiwan, although there are good reasons to question the power of the test. Lagged earnings growth has little predictive power for consumption growth in any of the regressions, but it also has little predictive power for current earnings growth. With little ability to anticipate earnings growth, we cannot tell whether the component of earnings growth that might be anticipated is or is not correlated with changes in consumption.

9.6 Summary and Conclusions

Where do these results leave us, and what is their implication for saving in Taiwan, particularly for retirement saving in a rapidly aging population? We have found it a good deal harder to find fault with the life-cycle theory than we supposed would be the case. Although consumption seems to move very closely with income, the Taiwanese save a great deal, and the comovement can be explained in terms of earnings shocks, which induce a short-run correlation between consumption and income, together with a taste for rapid consumption growth with age, which itself might be attributed to the intertemporal incentives generated by very high rates of return in a rapidly growing economy. We also find that younger cohorts have higher saving rates, as is to be expected given falling fertility and rising life expectancy. If we accept such a picture, we can attribute at least part of Taiwan's high saving ratio to farsighted young consumers preparing for a "modern" old age in which they will be thrown on their own resources, rather than on those of their married sons.

We are not entirely convinced that the picture is quite so simple, although we have no really coherent alternative to offer. The life-cycle explanation for the coherence between consumption and income seems farfetched compared with some simpler and more parsimonious story in which consumption is directly linked to income, although we also recognize that it is difficult to explain why people should behave in this way, especially in a high-saving economy where liquidity constraints are unlikely to be a problem. There is certainly no evidence of excess sensitivity in our results, though better and more powerful tests might yield different results. We also found evidence that saving responds to growth within cohorts, something that is consistent with the importance of habits in consumption. Even so, the effect is not nearly as large as that delivered by simple life-cycle stories and is small compared with other empirical evidence on the relationship. Our data do not show dissaving or even decreased saving among older households; indeed the estimated age effects in saving behavior increase steadily with age. Of course we recognize that this evidence is severely contaminated by the processes of household dissolution and combination as individuals age. Nevertheless, such results are hardly overwhelming evidence in favor of the life-cycle model. We therefore hesitate to endorse the position that the life-cycle model is alive and well and living in Taiwan, especially if such a position is taken to imply that there is no need for public action to supplement social security among those who will be old 25 years from now.

References

Bosworth, Barry, Gary Burtless, and John Sabelhaus. 1991. The decline in saving: Some microeconomic evidence. *Brookings Papers on Economic Activity* 1:183–256.

Campbell, John Y., and N. Greg Mankiw. 1991. The response of consumption to income: A cross-country investigation. *European Economic Review* 35:715–21.

Carroll, Christopher D. 1991. Buffer stock saving and the permanent income hypothesis. Washington, D.C.: Board of Governors of the Federal Reserve System. Circulated manuscript.

Carroll, Christopher D., and Lawrence H. Summers. 1991. Consumption growth parallels income growth: Some new evidence. In *National saving and economic performance,* ed. B. Douglas Bernheim and John Shoven. Chicago: University of Chicago Press.

Chang, Ming-cheng. 1987. Changing familial network and social welfare in Taiwan. In *Conference on economic development and social welfare in Taiwan,* vol. 2. Taipei: Institute of Economics, Academia Sinica.

Deaton, Angus S. 1991. Saving and liquidity constraints. *Econometrica* 59:1221–48.

———. 1992a. Saving and income smoothing in Côte d'Ivoire. *Journal of African Economies* 1:1–24.

———. 1992b. *Understanding consumption.* Oxford and New York: Oxford University Press.

Hermalin, Albert, Mary Beth Ofstedal, and Chi Li. 1991. The kin availability of the elderly in Taiwan: Who's available and where are they? Population Studies Center, University of Michigan. Circulated manuscript.

Lo, Joan Chi-chiung. 1987. The changing patterns of household structure and economic status of the elderly: 1976 to 1985. In *Conference on economic development and social welfare in Taiwan,* vol. 1. Taipei: Institute of Economics, Academia Sinica.

Modigliani, Franco. 1990. Recent declines in the savings rate: A life cycle perspective. Frisch Lecture, Sixth World Congress of the Econometric Society, Barcelona, August.

Paxson, Christina H. 1992. Using weather variability to estimate the response of savings to transitory income in Thailand. *American Economic Review* 82:15–33.

Republic of China. 1989. *Report on the survey of personal income distribution in Taiwan area of the Republic of China.* Taipei. Directorate-General of Budget, Accounting and Statistics, Executive Yuan.

———. 1991. *Statistical yearbook of the republic of China.* Taipei: Directorate-General of Budget, Accounting and Statistics, Executive Yuan.

Visaria, Pravin. 1980. Poverty and living standards in Asia. Living Standards Measurement Study Working Paper. Washington, D.C.: World Bank. Circulated manuscript.

Comment   Jonathan Skinner

Taiwan has enjoyed rapid per capita economic growth during the past 40 years. Saving rose dramatically, while fertility rates declined sharply. As Deaton and Paxson show, such large changes provide a natural "laboratory" to test nearly any theory of saving and consumption. The consistent aggregate growth allows its pure effect on consumption to be distinguished easily from the usual background noise of business cycles and age-related changes in income. Furthermore, they have the right data set to perform the analysis—a consistent, apparently reliable 15-year synthetic panel of survey data on families in Taiwan.

They develop what seems to be the only sensible way to distinguish among year effects, age effects, and cohort effects and use this method to show the strong impact of growth on the younger cohorts' consumption and saving decisions. They present evidence that they interpret as supporting the orthodox life-cycle model, but also present evidence that cannot be explained by any life-cycle model. In these comments, I will make two points. First, studying saving behavior in Taiwan, as Deaton and Paxson do, is an important exercise, precisely because it is a country that managed to more than double its personal saving rate during the 1960s. And second, the light such study casts on the life-cycle model is perhaps not as reassuring as Deaton and Paxson suggest. The life-cycle model has been an enormously successful paradigm of consumption behavior and has spawned a huge number of variants. Nearly any empirical phenomenon can fit somewhere under the "big tent" of these many variants. Hence the evidence presented does not convince me that "the" life-cycle hypothesis has adequate predictive power to explain the many variants of saving behavior in different countries.

It is useful to gain some perspective on the postwar history of income growth and saving in Taiwan (see Rabushka 1987; Hwan 1991). Figure 9C.1 shows aggregate real growth in GDP, and in national saving rates, for Taiwan between 1952 and 1989. Income growth has averaged 8.5 percent annually during the entire time period, with the sharpest decline during the oil price shock of the early 1970s.[1] Saving only increased during the mid-1960s, from an average rate of 9.9 percent of GDP during 1952–65 to 24.3 percent during 1970–89. Most of this increase was generated by personal (individual plus unincorporated business) saving; between 1952–65 and 1970–89, personal saving rose from 4.6 percent to 14.3 percent.

Why did the personal saving rate shift so dramatically during the 1960s? Domestic investment seemed to have remained stable during this period, but when foreign investment (particularly from the United States) was cut back in the 1960s, domestic personal saving took up the slack. Whatever the cause of

Jonathan Skinner is associate professor of economics at the University of Virginia and a research associate of the National Bureau of Economic Research.
1. This and subsequent calculations are based on *National Income in Taiwan Area of the Republic of China,* published by the Directorate of the Budget.

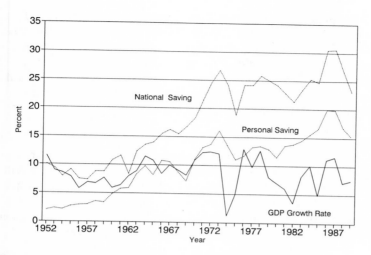

Fig. 9C.1   Saving and income growth, Taiwan: 1952–89

this shift in saving, it should be remembered in interpreting the Deaton-Paxson results that the habit of saving during the 1970s was still a recent phenomenon. Laggard saving during the 1950s and 1960s by the older generations in the Deaton-Paxson data could explain why they appeared to share little in the rapid aggregate growth occurring during the 1970s and 1980s.

Deaton and Paxson carefully document the dramatic changes in fertility rates during the period of analysis and suggest that such changes may in part be responsible for the rapid saving rates. They calculate that parents in their mid-thirties can expect to have only half the (average) number of male children as parents now in their seventies. With fewer children to support parents in their old age, the younger parents must substitute into financial wealth, thereby increasing saving as fertility declines.[2] One problem with such a hypothesis is that, in a general life-cycle–bequest model, the effect of fertility on saving rates is indeterminate: if parents are saving for bequests or inter vivos transfers, fewer children could mean less required saving. The timing of the fertility and saving changes is consistent with this alternative theoretical model: saving increased rapidly in the mid-1960s, just when the "baby-boom" parents would have been at an age typically consistent with rapid wealth accumulation (e.g., ages 35–50). That is, different variants of the life-cycle model could explain either a negative correlation between saving and fertility rates (as in Taiwan) or a positive correlation (as in the United States in recent years).

A "celebrated prediction" of the life-cycle model, the positive relationship

2. Paul David (1977) advances this hypothesis to explain high saving rates and declining fertility in the United States during the nineteenth century; also see Hammer (1986).

between saving and income growth, is also confirmed quite strongly in this analysis. While I have no quibble with the compelling empirical evidence, I do question whether the theoretical prediction is robust to relatively minor changes in the specification of the life-cycle model. In the Modigliani (1986) view, each cohort might be characterized as ψ percent richer, where ψ is the overall productivity growth rate, but the age-earning profiles are fixed over time. That is, log earnings at age a for cohort i is

$$y_{ai} = g(a) + i\psi,$$

where a is normalized to zero for the youngest age group, and $g(a)$ is the age-earning path for the benchmark cohort $i = 0$. In this case, the young are wealthier and hence save more, while the less wealthy old dissave less; on net, capital accumulation is positive and large in magnitude.

A different view comes from the Summers (1981) life-cycle model, in which a ψ percent cohort growth rate is realized by every worker;

$$y_{ai} = g^*(a) + (a + i)\psi,$$

where $g^*(a)$ is the age-earning profile in the absence of productivity growth for cohort $i = 0$. In the Modigliani case, the log annual growth in earnings, denoted $\dot{y}$, is given by $g(a) - g(a - 1)$; any productivity growth is enjoyed solely by the youngest cohort, who begins life with an initial wage ψ higher than those one year younger. By contrast, the Summers specification implies that

$$\dot{y} = g^*(a) - g^*(a - 1) + \psi,$$

so that the "rising tide raises all boats" or at least boats of all ages. This specification implies that age-earnings profiles should be quite steeply sloped during periods of rapid growth, which is certainly consistent with Deaton and Paxson's figure 9.5.

With this slightly different specification of earnings growth, the predicted correlation between saving and growth is easily reversed.[3] Current generations anticipate large increases in future earnings and want to spend some of that lifetime wealth today. In such a model (absent borrowing constraints), saving can easily plummet to zero in the presence of productivity growth. This is not to say that one model is superior to another, but rather that any correlation between saving and growth could find comfort in a life-cycle model.

Perhaps the most startling and noteworthy contribution of this paper is the finding that consumption tracks income, even when the individual is saving a large fraction of his income. I agree with the authors that this tracking behavior is hard for the standard life-cycle model or even a "buffer stock" model to explain. In fact, I would argue that the authors have found an economic rarity—an empirical phenomenon that every mutation of the life-cycle model rules out on theoretical grounds.

3. It is straightforward to perform such calculations using the model in Summers (1981).

References

David, Paul. 1977. Invention and accumulation in America's economic growth: A nineteenth-century parable. In *International Organization, National Policies, and Economic Development*, ed. K. Brunner and A. Meltzer. Amsterdam: North-Holland.

Hammer, Jeffrey. 1986. Children and savings in less developed countries. *Journal of Development Economics* 23:107–18.

Hwan, Y. Dolly. 1991. *The rise of a new world economic power: Postwar Taiwan.* New York: Greenwood.

Modigliani, Franco. 1986. Life cycle, individual thrift, and the wealth of nations. *American Economic Review* 76 (June): 297–313.

Rabushka, Alvin. 1987. *The new China: Comparative economic development in mainland China, Taiwan, and Hong Kong.* Boulder, Co.: Westview.

Summers, Lawrence. 1981. Capital taxation and accumulation in a life cycle growth model. *American Economic Review* 71 (September): 533–44.

VII   Long-Term Care

10 Forecasting Nursing Home Utilization of Elderly Americans

Andrew Dick, Alan M. Garber, and Thomas A. MaCurdy

Nursing home care accounts for most expenditures for long-term care, yet little is known about the risk that the elderly face of having a prolonged nursing home stay. The issue is of growing and fundamental importance: the design of policies to insure against the expenditures associated with institutionalization depends on the distribution of nursing home utilization. It is not sufficient to know the expected value of nursing home utilization, because many insurance plans have a fixed ceiling on the nursing home benefit and their risk of paying the maximum benefit is the likelihood that an enrollee's utilization will exceed the ceiling. Similarly, for public-private partnerships, in which private insurers might cover the first 12 or 24 months of nursing home care, while the federal government provides coverage above the private limit, the expenditures borne by insurers and by the federal government depend on the exact distribution of utilization. Insurers are not the only ones with an interest in nursing home utilization: before individuals can make an informed decision about purchasing long-term care insurance, saving to cover the costs of institutionalization, or changing living arrangements, they need to know how much nursing home care they are likely to use. To address these issues, this paper describes the likelihood and duration of nursing home admissions experienced by Americans after age 65. Our analysis generates predictions for a representative popu-

Andrew Dick is an instructor in the Public Policy Analysis Program in the Department of Political Science at the University of Rochester. Alan M. Garber is HSR&D Senior Research Associate of the Palo Alto Department of Veterans Affairs, associate professor of medicine at Stanford University, and a research associate of the National Bureau of Economic Research. Thomas A. MaCurdy is professor of economics at Stanford University and a research associate of the National Bureau of Economic Research.

This research was supported in part by grants R29 AG07651 and P01 AG05842 from the National Institute on Aging and by grant 12671 from the Robert Wood Johnson Foundation. Andrew Dick was supported by grant T32 HS00028 from the Agency for Health Care Policy and Research.

lation, not for one selected to be at high risk of institutionalization, and should therefore be of direct relevance to the design of long-term care policies.

The existing literature contains remarkably little information about either the number of times older Americans are admitted to nursing homes or their cumulative utilization of nursing home care. Much of the literature on the risk of institutionalization, for example, has used a variety of methods to assess the probability that an individual at a given age will enter a nursing home before dying (Palmore 1976; Vicente, Wiley, and Carrington 1979; Wingard, Jones, and Kaplan 1987; Branch and Jette 1982; McConnel 1984; Murtaugh, Kemper, and Spillman 1990). Other studies explore the duration of nursing home admissions (Keeler, Kane, and Solomon 1981; Lewis, Cretin, and Kane 1985; Spence and Wiener 1990), but not the number of admissions or overall utilization. The few studies that analyze overall utilization typically are based on nonrandom samples of the elderly (Liu, Coughlin, and McBride 1991).

Failure to address cumulative utilization in representative samples undoubtedly reflects the inadequacy of much existing data. No individual data sets have sufficiently complete longitudinal data to infer comprehensive measures of nursing home utilization for a nationally representative, random sample of elderly Americans. Ideally such a study would enroll a large number of elderly individuals, track them for several years, and obtain complete information on the number and timing of nursing home stays during the period of observation. Data sets such as the Longitudinal Study on Aging fail to track admission and discharge dates for every nursing home stay and have no means of determining the total number of days an individual spends in a nursing home. Data sources on institutional populations typically have good information about the duration of nursing home stays but cannot be used to determine either the risk of admission or the time subsequently spent in the community.

Perhaps the most natural method for determining patterns of nursing home utilization after a given age is to obtain complete retrospective data on prior nursing home use among a random sample of the elderly who are above that given age at the time of their death. However, it is very difficult to obtain such data, since it is rare to have both a representative sample and complete retrospective data. In the most prominent study of this kind, Kemper and Murtaugh (1991) used the 1986 National Mortality Followback Survey of next of kin to assess prior nursing home utilization of a sample of decedents. They employed a weighting scheme to reconstruct a random sample of the national population. Unfortunately, next of kin's recollections were the sole basis for estimating lifetime nursing home use. The information was recorded as one of four categories of use (less than 3 months, 3–12 months, 1–5 years, and more than 5 years). The memories of next of kin about prior utilization, particularly if it began several years before death or if the decedent had multiple nursing home admissions, may well be inaccurate. Furthermore, the study did not estimate number of admissions and other aspects of patterns of use. Thus, this otherwise well-designed study suffered from important data limitations.

The length of the period during which a person is at risk of entering a nursing home poses a related challenge to prospective data. A person who reaches age 65 faces a gradually increasing risk of entering a nursing home and may be at risk for 30 years. Yet most of the longitudinal data sources cover only one- to two-year windows. Retrospective studies based on time at death do not face this challenge, but obtaining accurate retrospective data for a period of many years, particularly for very old decedents, is often impossible.

Because of these challenges, there is no single data source for estimating the distribution of utilization of nursing home care for a random sample of Americans after the age of 65. In this paper, we overcome these challenges by combining data from two major data sets based on nationally representative samples of the elderly. To exploit the information from these data sources, which are longitudinal but cover short periods (a two-year window), we develop a transition probability model and an empirical framework that allows us to infer the relevant measures of utilization.

The empirical model is designed specifically to forecast the distribution of utilization for a cohort of 65-year-olds until their deaths, although with trivial changes it can be used to forecast utilization for any older cohort. Our interest is not only in predicting total nursing home utilization, but also the pattern of utilization; thus we estimate the likelihood of multiple admissions and determine the distribution of both the durations of nursing home admissions and the intervening episodes of community residence.

The transition probability model focuses on the two states that any living study subject can occupy at any time: community residence or nursing home residence. Our model treats hospital admissions as part of community residence. A spell in the community can terminate either in admission to the nursing home or in death; similarly, a nursing home admission can end either by discharge to the community or by death. Our model builds on transition probabilities, which are the monthly probabilities of a change in status, and exit probabilities, which are the conditional probabilities that if an exit occurs it will be to a particular state (death or change of residence). We account for demographic characteristics, for history of prior nursing home utilization, and for duration effects. We measure durations in months after the start of spells, with changes in age (rather than time) as the relevant metric. We thereby produce estimates capable of forecasting transitions at all ages 65 years and older, using only the data available from a two-year observation window provided by our major data sources. The estimated model enables us to perform simulations that characterize several aspects of nursing home utilization.

In the following section, we discuss the general empirical model underlying our approach. We next turn to a description of our data sets, the National Long-Term Care Survey (NLTCS) and the National Nursing Home Survey (NNHS). In the section following, we describe the implementation of the empirical model, the mechanisms used to deal with the multiple types of patients included in the two surveys, and the empirical results. We then turn to simulation results derived from the model, and close with a discussion of the implications of the analysis.

10.1   Empirical Framework

Our duration model incorporates three mutually exclusive states: residence in the community, residence in a nursing home, and death. Two sets of transition probabilities within and across states fully describe behavior in the model, one set for each state other than death, which represents the absorbing state. We structure the transitions in the model as follows. Persons who reside in the community face a probability each period of remaining in the community; the alternative event is exiting to a different state. Given an exit, one of two mutually exclusive events can occur: the individual either dies or enters a nursing home. We structure the transition probabilities for residence in a nursing home in an analogous manner. That is, we estimate the probability that an individual remains in the nursing home for the next month. If the person exits, we assess the probability that the exit is to the community, the alternative being death. Of course, as the absorbing state, death completes an individual's experience. Hence, we specify four basic probabilities to describe lifetime nursing home experiences. Given knowledge of these four probabilities, we can calculate the probability of observing various patterns of lifetime experiences. After introducing specifications for these probabilities, we describe a simulation procedure to summarize lifetime nursing home experiences.

10.1.1   Model Characterization

Define $P(i{\rightarrow}j) \equiv P(i{\rightarrow}j|X, H, \tau)$ as the probability that an individual transits from state i to state j in the next month, conditional on the values of X, H, and τ. X is a covariate vector made up of demographic characteristics; H is a vector of variables summarizing an individual's nursing home history prior to the start of the current spell in state i; and τ is the current number of consecutive months in state i. The primary covariate included in H is an indicator variable signifying whether the individual has had a nursing home admission between age 65 and the current age. In the duration model considered here, i and j take values representing each of the three states: community (C), nursing home (N), and death (D). Hospitalizations are included as part of state C. With three states, nine transition probabilities are required to fully characterize experiences in the model, i.e., the probabilities $P(i{\rightarrow}j)$ for i, j = C, N, D. For the trivial case of the absorbing state death, $P(D{\rightarrow}D) = 1$ always, so $P(D{\rightarrow}C) = P(D{\rightarrow}N) = 0$. Consequently, it is the remaining six transition probabilities that are of interest.

Consider the transition probabilities associated with residence in the community: $P(C{\rightarrow}j)$ for j = C, N, D. Because the sum of these three probabilities equals one, the specification of two probabilities provides a complete characterization. The quantity $1 - P(C{\rightarrow}C)$ is the probability that the individual exits the community in the next month. Given the event that a community spell ends, let $P(D|C\text{-Exit}) \equiv P(D|C\text{-Exit}, X, H, \tau)$ denote the probability that an individual dies; this probability explicitly conditions on exiting the community after a spell lasting τ months with history H for an individual with characteristics X. Thus, $1 - P(D|C\text{-Exit})$ represents the likelihood that the individual enters a nursing home given termination of a community spell. Specifying the quantities, $P(C{\rightarrow}C)$ and $P(D|C\text{-Exit})$ implies the following relationships among the three transition probabilities for community residents:

$$P(C{\rightarrow}C) = P(C{\rightarrow}C),$$

(1) $$P(C{\rightarrow}N) = [1 - P(C{\rightarrow}C)][1 - P(D|C\text{-Exit})],$$

$$P(C{\rightarrow}D) = [1 - P(C{\rightarrow}C)]P(D|C\text{-Exit}).$$

Because these quantities depend on an individual's current and recent history, they vary from month to month. Knowledge of $P(C{\rightarrow}C)$ and $P(D|C\text{-Exit})$ provides complete information regarding the experience of an elderly community resident in any month of his life.

Nursing home residence is characterized by an analogous pair of probabilities. The quantity $P(N{\rightarrow}N)$ is the transition probability that an individual remains in a nursing home for the next period, conditional on values of X, H, and τ; thus $1 - P(N{\rightarrow}N)$ is the probability that the individual leaves a nursing home in the next period. Given termination of a nursing home spell, let $P(D|N\text{-Exit})$ be the probability that an individual dies. From the two probabilities, $P(N{\rightarrow}N)$ and $P(D|N\text{-Exit})$, one can infer the three transition probabilities associated with nursing home residence via the formulae

$$P(N{\rightarrow}N) = P(N{\rightarrow}N),$$

(2) $$P(N{\rightarrow}C) = [1 - P(N{\rightarrow}N)][1 - P(D|N\text{-Exit})],$$

$$P(N{\rightarrow}D) = [1 - P(N{\rightarrow}N)]P(D|N\text{-Exit}).$$

Thus, knowledge of $P(N{\rightarrow}N)$ and $P(D|N\text{-Exit})$ provides complete information regarding experience at any time in the life of an elderly nursing home resident.

10.1.2   Formulating Duration Distributions

The specification of the transition probabilities $P(C{\rightarrow}C)$ and $P(N{\rightarrow}N)$ provides all the information needed to formulate duration distributions for nursing home and community spells, where spell duration refers to the number of continuous months in a state. Consider the distribution describing the length of stays in state i. With $P(i{\rightarrow}i) \equiv P(i{\rightarrow}i|X, H, \tau)$ representing the probability of remaining in state i at least another month, given continuous occupancy of τ months and given the values of X and H, the duration distribution for spells is given by

(3) $$f_i(\tau) = S_i(\tau - 1) [1 - P(i{\rightarrow}i)],$$

with

(4)
$$S_i(\tau - 1) = \prod_{t=1}^{\tau-1} P(i \rightarrow i).$$

The quantity $S_i(\tau - 1)$ is the survivor function, representing the probability that a spell lasts at least $\tau - 1$ months. Both X and H are fixed at the time of entry into the state; X includes such factors as gender and age, and H incorporates measures of prior experience. The probability that an exit occurs at τ, given that a spell has lasted at least $\tau - 1$ months, is defined as

(5)
$$h_i(\tau) = \frac{f_i(\tau)}{S_i(\tau - 1)} = 1 - P(i \rightarrow i).$$

Negative (positive) duration dependence exists if h increases (decreases) as a function of duration τ.

10.1.3   Analytically Characterizing Nursing Home Experiences

The above elements serve as building blocks for several approaches to summarizing lifetime nursing home experiences. First, one could compute the likelihood of observing any lifetime experience as an appropriate product of the transition probabilities in equations (1) and (2). Formula (3) shows how to calculate the probability of observing a spell of any length at any time in an individual's life. The likelihood of observing any sequence of spells can be calculated as the product of the probabilities of observing the given spells and the appropriate $P(D|i\text{-Exit})$.

Consider an individual who lives in the community at age 65, remains in the community for three months, and enters a nursing home for two months before dying. The probability of observing this pattern of lifetime experiences is

$$f_C(3) \, [1 - P(D|C\text{-Exit}, X, H, 3)] \, f_N(2) \, P(D|N\text{-Exit}, X, H, 2),$$

where the covariates X and H are properly updated to reflect changes with age and history. The same likelihood can be calculated via the six transition probabilities as

$$\left[\prod_{t=1}^{2} P(C \rightarrow C|X, H, t) \right] P(C \rightarrow N|X, H, 3)$$
$$\left[\prod_{t=1}^{1} P(N \rightarrow N|X, H, t) \right] P(N \rightarrow D|X, H, 2).$$

Summarizing the distribution of lifetime nursing home utilization within this framework requires computing the probability of observing every possible pattern of lifetime experiences and then calculating the cumulative duration of each state. For example, calculating the expected number of months of nursing home residence after a particular age requires a summation over probabilities associated with every possible pattern of experiences. Rather than proceeding with this cumbersome approach, we implement an alternative that uses a familiar simulation procedure to summarize lifetime experiences.

10.1.4   Simulating Nursing Home Experiences of the Elderly

We can simulate the lifetime experiences of an individual by randomly drawing discrete variables indicating a person's state of residence in each month, using the transition and exit probabilities to determine the values of these variables given the realized experiences to date. The simulation method that we employ makes use of predicted values of the probabilities of equations (1) and (2). For an individual with characteristics X, we construct predicted values of the four probabilities, $P(i{\rightarrow}i)$ and $P(D|i\text{-Exit})$ for $i = C$ and N, recomputing for each period as we update the values of X, H, and the current spell duration, τ. By evaluating these probabilities in every month of a lifetime we simulate a person's entire set of lifetime experiences.

Consider a 65-year-old male living in the community. Calculate the predicted probability that he will exit the state in the next month, and draw a random variable from a uniform distribution between zero and one. If the realization is greater than the predicted probability that the individual exits the community, assign him to the community state for another period, update τ, and repeat the process until a random variable is drawn such that he does exit the community. When an exit occurs, calculate the predicted probability that the man exits to death, and again draw a random variable. If the realization of the random variable is less than the predicted probability of death, assign the man to death for the period, completing his experience; otherwise, assign the man to the nursing home and repeat the process using predicted probabilities associated with nursing home residence. The simulation appropriately updates the values of the covariates, and hence the transition probabilities, as the individual ages.

Repeating the above procedure numerous times and recording sequences of monthly experiences for a large number of hypothetical individuals allows us to characterize the nursing home experiences for a population of 65-year-old males residing in the community. With suitable adjustments in the values of the covariates, the same procedure can be applied to simulate lifetime experiences for various populations.

10.1.5   Initial Conditions

Although our empirical model is designed to predict the distribution of nursing home utilization at ages 65 and older, a small number of 65-year-olds are already in nursing homes. A comprehensive description of nursing home utilization from age 65 to death must account for their nursing home experience. To incorporate utilization from this group in our forecasts, we include a distinct component of our empirical model that estimates the likelihood that an individual resides in an institution upon reaching age 65, and the distribution of the number of months that elapse from the date of the 65th birthday until death or discharge from the nursing home. Along with race and sex, these quantities constitute the initial conditions of our forecasting model. We estimate the probability of nursing home occupancy by directly calculating the proportion of our nationally representative sample that resides in a nursing home upon reaching age 65. We estimate the distribution of subsequent duration by calculating the empirical survivor function from our sample. This approach is equivalent to using nonparametric procedures to estimate the initial conditions.

10.2   The Data

To estimate the parameters of the empirical model, we require longitudinal data on individuals residing in the communities and on individuals residing in nursing homes. In developing the model, we assume that it is important to distinguish experiences that represent *recurrent* nursing home and community spells from initial spells. We do not expect persons residing in the community following a nursing home discharge, for example, to have the same survival or subsequent nursing home utilization as a person of the same age who was never in a nursing home. Insofar as second and higher-order spells differ from first spells, it is important to distinguish them in the modeling. This is only possible if the data permit this distinction.

This poses a significant challenge to our analysis, since as far as we know, no nationally representative data set offers a random population of individuals in second or higher-order spells in sufficient numbers and with sufficient information about them to carry out the analysis. Hence we combine data from two distinct data sets, the NLTCS and the NNHS, to estimate the parameters of the empirical model. We use the NLTCS to estimate components of our empirical model needed to describe community spells and their mode of termination. We use the NNHS for the corresponding analyses of nursing home admissions and forecast the patterns of utilization by applying the empirical model, which is estimated from the combined data.

10.2.1   The National Long-Term Care Survey

The NLTCS offers suitable data for the analysis of community spells because it includes a stratified random sample of spells over a two-year window for the entire population of elderly, along with information about nursing home entry. Other data sets have similar information on nursing home utilization, but offer either selected populations or inadequate spell information, making comparable analysis impossible. For example, the National Long-Term Care Demonstration enrolled only a sample of high-risk elderly suffering at least one "unmet need," and the National Nursing Home Survey enrolled only nursing home residents. Its population coverage makes the NLTCS appropriate for estimating community survival rates.

Although the NLTCS was designed to provide information on the need for long-term care services of the functionally impaired community-based elderly population, it also gathered information on other groups of elderly people. One of its goals was to discover characteristics that are associated with utilization of home-based long-term care, and so to anticipate future needs for other services for the chronically disabled elderly. To address these issues, the NLTCS identified and interviewed a sample of chronically disabled individuals who resided in the community. They also kept and reported critical information on the remaining segments of the elderly population.

The first survey was administered in 1982. From a randomly selected sample of 50,000 Medicare recipients in the (Medicare) Health Insurance Skeleton Eligibility Write-off (HISKEW) in 1982, about 6,000 community-dwelling disabled elderly were identified by a telephone screening process. Although this is the only population that was surveyed in 1982, another 2,000 elderly individuals were determined to be institutionalized. Another 5,000 individuals were identified who would turn age 65 by the 1984 follow-up interview date (the 1984 aged-in population). The remaining 25,000 screened-out were non-disabled and living in the community. Thus, although we only have detailed information on a limited subset of the elderly in 1982, we are able to identify the vital status and place of residence (community or nursing home) of all individuals included in the 1982 and 1984 files.

The 1984 NLTCS makes use of three detailed questionnaires: one administered to the 1984 community population, a second administered to the institutional population, and a third administered to the next of kin of those who died between the 1982 and 1984 interview dates. All of the 6,000 disabled community residents from 1982 were automatically reinterviewed regardless of their 1984 functional status, as were the 2,000 individuals in the 1982 institutional population. All of the aged-in cohort, and roughly half of those screened-out in 1982, were rescreened in 1984 following the same process as in 1982. Thus, the 1984 NLTCS contains detailed information on a broad community-based elderly population (of roughly 6,000), an institutionalized elderly population (of roughly 1,700), and a recently deceased elderly population (of roughly 2,500). In addition, information collected in the screening process is provided for the screened-out population—individuals who were not functionally impaired (roughly 14,000).

The weights we use are the 1984 final screener cross-sectional weights, which are calculated as the reciprocal of the probability of inclusion in the sample when the sample is stratified across characteristics such as age, gender, and race. Summing these weights produces a national cross-sectional estimate of the U.S. population above age 64. Thus, although some subgroups may be oversampled, by appropriate weighting we can generalize our results to the entire elderly population.

NLTCS Nursing Home Data

NLTCS is an incomplete data source, for the purposes of our analysis, because it has incomplete information about nursing home utilization for some subgroups. While the community and deceased questionnaires offer complete retrospective histories, the institutional questionnaire focuses only on the period between 1982 and the current interview period. Information concerning utilization prior to the 1982 interview date, such as admission and discharge dates and the number of prior admissions, was not collected. Thus the duration and number of previous nursing home and community spells is unknown. Furthermore, for spells beginning after 1982 but prior to the current admission, only the admission dates were collected, making it impossible to determine their durations. Consequently, the NLTCS cannot be used to compile complete nursing home histories for this important component of the elderly population. Although this does not impede our estimation of the likelihood of experiencing a first nursing home spell, it seriously impairs our ability to measure durations of nursing home spells.

We compiled information covering 2,774 nursing home episodes, of which 1,604 came from the 1984 institutional questionnaire and were therefore still in progress at the end of the study, or right-censored. Another 1,170 spells came from the remaining questionnaires. The information from the retrospective components of these questionnaires limits spell durations to less than 100 months. In addition, the deceased questionnaire, which allows us to calculate long spells if they end in death or just prior to death, includes a heavily used "Don't Know" category, further confounding our efforts to create a random sample of nursing home spells. As a result, while 5 percent of the 2,774 spells are longer than 100 months, all but two of them are censored, making it impossible to observe either the exact duration or outcome of long spells. Table 10.1 summarizes the nursing home spell information calculated from the NLTCS.

NLTCS Community Spell Data

We also use the NLTCS data to characterize duration and exit probabilities for the repeat community spells, or the community spells that follow nursing home discharges. Although the retrospective character of the NLTCS makes it possible to calculate spell data regarding experiences prior to the 1982 interview date, inclusion of repeat community spells initiated prior to the 1982 interview date would introduce a (positive) selection bias. The bias occurs because repeat community spells ending in discharge to death prior to the 1982 interview date are excluded, so probability of inclusion in the sample is enhanced for those with longer spells. Furthermore, since short spells ending prior to 1982 are included in the sample universe only if they do not end in death, we would underrepresent short repeat community spells that end in death. Thus, if we included pre-1982 experiences, our estimates of the probability of nursing home readmissions (i.e., the probability that a repeat community spell terminates in nursing home admission) would be biased upward. In

Table 10.1   **LTCS Nursing Home Spell Summary Statistics**

	Number of Observations	Mean	Standard Deviation	Minimum	Maximum
Institutional questionnaire					
Spell length (months)	1,601	34.53	36.82	1	229
Male = 1	1,601	0.23	0.42	0	1
White = 1	1,601	0.94	0.24	0	1
Age (months)	1,601	973.18	91.06	781	1,234
Other questionnaires					
Spell length (months)	1,169	5.24	10.04	1	112
Male = 1	1,169	0.33	0.47	0	1
White = 1	1,169	0.94	0.24	0	1
Age (months)	1,169	957.93	88.13	781	1,194
All spells					
Spell length (months)	2,770	22.17	32.17	1	229
Male = 1	2,770	0.27	0.45	0	1
White = 1	2,770	0.94	0.24	0	1
Age (months)	2,770	966.74	90.13	781	1,234
Censored = 1	2,770	0.58	0.49	0	1

order to avoid these selection biases, we include in our analysis only those community spells that begin between the two survey interview dates. Thus, we include all spells that commence after the 1982 interview date and conclude with exits either to death or to repeat nursing home admissions or are right-censored at the 1984 interview date. Many spells are therefore right-censored and it is impossible to characterize fully repeat community experiences of more than about 28 months. Table 10.2 summarizes the NLTCS data used to characterize the return community spells.

To measure the probabilities that an individual will enter a nursing home for the first time or will die, we use the information regarding these transitions between the 1982 and 1984 interview dates. Inclusion of nursing home admissions prior to the 1982 interview date would introduce selection biases analogous to those for repeat community spells discussed above. We drop all individuals who experienced first spells prior to the 1982 interview and an additional 254 individuals from the institutional questionnaire, for whom we cannot determine when the first spell occurred. Table 10.3 summarizes NLTCS data used to calculate community spells prior to a first nursing home episode after age 65.

10.2.2   The 1985 National Nursing Home Survey

The 1985 NNHS, which is a nationally representative data set developed to provide comprehensive information about nursing home services, offers extensive data about the lengths of nursing home spells, their modes of termination, and prior nursing home usage. Our analysis uses the discharged resident file of the NNHS, which provides a random sample of nursing home spells that

Table 10.2   LTCS Return Community Spell Summary Statistics

	Number of Observations	Mean	Standard Deviation	Minimum	Maximum
Spell length (months)	472	6.33	7.15	1	28
Male = 1	472	0.33	0.47	0	1
White = 1	472	0.94	0.23	0	1
Age (months)	472	965.24	87.15	788	1,190
Censored = 1	472	0.51	0.50	0	1

Table 10.3   NLTCS Summary Statistics for First Community Spells

	1984 Community Cohort	1984 Institutional Cohort	1984 Deceased Cohort	1984 Screened-out Cohort	Total
Total individuals	5,934	1,690	2,475	14,145	24,244
Individuals dropped					
Ambiguous history	0	254	0	0	0
Transition pre-1982 date	154	1,099	140	24	326
Inaccurate transition date	192	24	147	22	385
Total individuals remaining	5,588	313	2,188	14,099	22,188
Transitions with state changes	64	313	2,188	35	2,700
Censored spells	5,424	0	0	14,064	19,488
Transitions without state changes	161,547	5,870	31,837	389,500	588,754

	Mean	Standard Deviation	Minimum	Maximum
Observations per individual	23.99	7.15	1	33
Fraction with exit	0.12	0.33	0	1
Male = 1	0.41	0.49	0	1
White = 1	0.91	0.29	0	1
Age at 1982 interview date (months)	868.48	85.66	781	1,443

are completed within the 12 months prior to the survey date. All spells are noncensored, and outcomes for each spell are known. The file includes basic demographic characteristics, health status, place of residence prior to admission and after discharge, services received, and indications of the outcome of care. Weights associated with each observation are derived as the reciprocal of the probability of inclusion in the sample for each stratum along which the selection is based.

The discharged resident file includes information on 5,317 nursing home discharges. We compile information on 4,705 nursing home episodes beginning after age 65, of which 2,354 are first spells. The remaining 612 spells began prior to the individual's sixty-fifth birthday. Table 10.4 summarizes characteristics of the population included in the file. A comparison of tables 10.1 and 10.4 reveals the difficulties in utilizing the nursing home spell information from the NLTCS. The spell characteristics from both data sets for all spells are similar; however, the mean of the completed spells in the NLTCS is only slightly greater than 5 months, while the mean of the censored spells is more than 34 months.

10.2.3   Definition of Variables

All of our analyses incorporate demographic characteristics as covariates. The variable MALE is set to one for males and zero for females. The variable AGE refers to the age of the individual in months beyond his or her sixty-fifth birthday. The variable WHITE is set to one if the individual is white and zero otherwise.[1]

We account for history dependence by specifying the spell number of a particular state. We set the dichotomous dummy variable CM1 equal to one for those community spells that occur before a first nursing home admission, or for which the only prior nursing home admissions were completed before reaching age 65. The covariate PRE65 is set to one to account for differing experiences of those with completed nursing home spells prior to age 65. The dichotomous variable NH1 equals one for first nursing home admission and zero otherwise.

10.2.4   Initial Conditions

The NLTCS provides the nationally representative sample from which we calculate the quantities needed to infer initial conditions. This sample consists of a random selection (stratified and weighted) of individuals reaching age 65 between the 1982 interview data and the 1984 interview date. Although the NLTCS did not record information on these individuals in 1982, the individuals were screened in 1984 and, according to the result of the screen, either administered the institutional questionnaire, the community questionnaire, or their next of kin were administered the deceased questionnaire. For respondents not meeting the criteria for any of these survey instruments, the screening information was reported. Thus, we can identify the characteristics of each individual on his or her sixty-fifth birthday.

Few of these individuals had nursing home admissions prior to age 65. For

---

1. The NLTCS does not distinguish respondents of Hispanic origin. The NNHS contains a separate variable for Hispanic origin, but since Hispanic is not a racial classification, it categorizes some as white and some as black. Because there are few Hispanics in the NNHS and because the NLTCS data set does not identify them at all, we use the race variable that does not contain information regarding Hispanics. Thus, blacks, Asians, Pacific Islanders, and Native Americans, including Eskimos and Aleuts, make up the population in which WHITE equals zero.

Table 10.4   NNHS Nursing Home Spell Summary Statistics

	Number of Observations	Mean	Standard Deviation	Minimum	Maximum
First nursing home spells					
Spell length (months)	2,348	21.22	34.82	1	321
Male = 1	2,348	0.33	0.47	0	1
White = 1	2,348	0.93	0.25	0	1
Age (months)	2,348	979.87	90.77	781	1,298
End in death	2,348	0.48	0.50	0	1
Second nursing home spells					
Spell length (months)	1,012	19.93	30.63	1	239
Male = 1	1,012	0.32	0.47	0	1
White = 1	1,012	0.96	0.20	0	1
Age (months)	1,012	985.96	89.74	781	1,267
End in death	1,012	0.41	0.49	0	1
Third and above nursing home spells					
Spell length (months)	1,337	13.53	21.01	1	231
Male = 1	1,337	0.30	0.46	0	1
White = 1	1,337	0.94	0.24	0	1
Age (months)	1,337	988.34	91.27	781	1,221
End in death	1,337	0.15	0.36	0	1
All spells					
Spell length (months)	4,697	18.75	30.74	1	320
Male = 1	4,697	0.32	0.47	0	1
White = 1	4,697	0.94	0.24	0	1
Age (months)	4,697	983.59	90.75	781	1,298
End in death	4,697	0.37	0.48	0	1
Number of spells	4,697	2.15	1.76	1	22

those who had not completed the admission, we estimate the corresponding distribution of duration in the nursing home beyond the age of 65.

We construct weighted nonparametric estimates of the likelihood of every possible combination of covariates occurring. Because the weights convert the data to national totals by age, gender, and race, our procedure estimates initial covariate values for a nationally representative population. We draw our combinations of initial covariates using these estimates, thus reproducing the characteristics of a random sample of the entire 65-year-old U.S. population.

10.3   Empirical Specifications and Results

To implement the empirical formulation described in section 10.1, we need to specify two sets of transition probabilities, $P(i \rightarrow i)$, where $i = N, C$: the probabilities of remaining in either the community or a nursing home; and the exit probabilities $P(D|i\text{-Exit})$, giving the probabilities that the community or nursing home spells terminate in death. In this section, we first introduce empirical specifications for the transition probabilities $P(C \rightarrow C)$ and $P(N \rightarrow N)$.

We then introduce specifications for the exit probabilities $P(D|i\text{-exit})$ ($i = C$, N). Finally, we present the estimates that result from implementing these specifications.

10.3.1 Parameterizations of Transition Probabilities

The presence of duration dependence implies that $P(i \rightarrow i)$ varies with the number of continuous months in a state (τ). The empirical specification needs to be flexible enough to account for general types of duration dependence, which may be nonmonotonic. Return episodes in the community may show increasing duration dependence for small values of τ, as short stays (say in a hospital) end either in death or in return to a nursing home, and decreasingly thereafter. Eventually any spell will exhibit decreasing duration dependence for large values of τ, especially at very advanced ages. Standard empirical specifications typically do not accommodate nonmonotonic duration dependence, nor do they allow for interaction between the form of duration dependence and covariates X and H. To allow for such flexibility, we specify the following logistic model for the probabilities $P(i \rightarrow i)$:

$$(6) \qquad P(i \rightarrow i) = \frac{1}{1 + e^{Z_1 \beta + \theta(\tau, Z_2)}},$$

where Z_1 and Z_2 are vectors of variables included in X and H, β is a parameter vector, and the function $\theta(\tau, Z_2)$ captures the properties of duration dependence.

Spline models are an attractive approach for modeling duration effects, since they fit the data with a flexible and smooth function of duration. Implicit in conventional spline models, which fit polynomial functions to a series of intervals over duration, is a tradeoff between smoothness and goodness of fit. Fit can be improved by increasing the number of polynomial functions, but non-differentiability at the boundaries requires a sacrifice in smoothness. Limiting the number of intervals or the order of the polynomial functions yields a smoother curve but diminishes the capabilities of detecting complicated forms of duration dependence.

In our approach, we specify $\theta(\cdot)$ as the general function:

$$(7) \qquad \theta(\tau, X_2) = \sum_{j=1}^{K_\theta} [\Phi_{1j}(\tau) - \Phi_{2j}(\tau)] (\alpha_{0j} Z_2 + \alpha_{1j}\tau + \alpha_{2j}\tau^2 + \alpha_{3j}\tau^3).$$

K_θ represents the number of polynomial functions entered in the specification. The quantity $\Phi_{ij}(\tau)$ denotes the cumulative distribution function of a normal random variable having mean μ_{ij} and standard deviation σ_{ij}, and the coefficients α_{ij} represent parameter vectors. This "overlap-spline" specification allows the polynomial functions to be operative as the linear combination of cumulative normal functions (i.e., $\sum \Phi_{1j}(\tau) - \Phi_{2j}(\tau)$) takes nonzero values. Thus, each polynomial function begins and ends gradually, according to the properties of the cumulative normal. As the value of σ decreases, the polynomial has a more abrupt impact; as σ approaches zero, this specification approaches that of conventional spline models without equality constraints at interval boundaries. While our overlap-spline specifications do not require equality constraints, they do allow for several polynomials to be operative over an interval. Unlike conventional splines, they are also continuously differentiable at all points.

This specification of $\theta(\cdot)$ allows covariates in Z_2 to have different effects at different ages. Covariates in Z_1 from model (6) are similar to covariates in a typical proportional hazards model in that they simply shift the hazard rate up or down at all times.

To allow the experiences in first community spells and first nursing home spells to differ from subsequent spells, we estimate distinct transition probabilities for first and later episodes. The literature often refers to this form of history dependence as "occurrence dependence."

10.3.2   Parameterizations of Exit Probabilities

The probabilities $P(\text{D}|i\text{-Exit})$ are also likely to display history dependence. For example, if short nursing home spells are predominantly short recuperative episodes, they are more likely to end in return to the community. Longer spells, especially for the very old, may more frequently end in death. Therefore, the functional specification for the exit probabilities, like the transition probabilities, should be flexible enough to detect dependence on previous spell duration as well as interactions of characteristics, X, with duration. We adopt the specification

$$(8) \qquad P(\text{D}|i\text{-Exit}) = \frac{1}{1 + e^{-Z_1\gamma - \Gamma(\tau, Z_2)}},$$

where Z_1 and Z_2 are vectors of variables included in X and H, γ is a parameter vector, and the function $\Gamma(\tau, Z_2)$ captures dependence on the duration of the previous spell, τ. The function $\Gamma(\cdot)$ takes a form analogous to the overlap-spline function $\theta(\cdot)$:

$$(9) \qquad \Gamma(\tau, Z_2) = \sum_{j=1}^{K_\Gamma} [\Phi_{1j}(\tau) - \Phi_{2j}(\tau)] \, (Z_2\gamma_{2j}),$$

where $\Phi_{ij}(\tau)$ represents the cumulative normal distribution function, as before, and τ is the spell length of the previous spell. K_Γ represents the number of polynomial functions entered in the specification. If $\sigma_{ij} = 0$ for all i and j, the model can be interpreted as interacting a series of dummy variables in duration with the covariates in Z_2, where the values of the μ_{ij} terms determine the range over which the dummy variables apply. In this specification, the Z_2 variables can have different effects as duration changes for the spell just ended. For example, the model could detect relatively high mortality rates for the very old, given a short nursing home admission. This phenomenon would be reflected in the γ parameters. Our overlap-spline specification allows for the effect of the dummy variables to change gradually with time, according to the properties of the cumulative distribution functions, $\Phi_{ij}(\tau)$.

For the analysis reported below, we fix the values of K_θ, K_Γ, and of each μ_{ij} and σ_{ij}. We selected their values after extensive exploratory data analysis; the properties of the empirical hazard rates principally determine the formulation of the function $\theta(\cdot)$, and the properties of the empirical exit probabilities guided the formulation of the function $\Gamma(\cdot)$ (i.e., the values of the exit probabilities as a function of duration determine $\Gamma(\cdot)$).

10.3.3   Estimation of Community Transition Probabilities

We accommodate history dependence (distinct from duration dependence) in estimating $P(C{\rightarrow}C)$ by introducing the covariate CM1 in the specification (6). CM1 is a binary variable that indicates that the individual has had no nursing home experiences since age 65. Incorporating it into equation (6) allows the duration characteristics of first community spells (CM1 = 1) to differ from those of return community spells (CM1 = 0). We fully interact CM1 with all other variables to fully distinguish the characteristics of first and higher-order spells in the community. Because AGE and τ are exactly collinear for first community spells, we substitute AGE for τ when CM1 = 1 in equation (6) and estimate $P(C{\rightarrow}C|X, H, AGE)$ at each age. To avoid length-biased sampling when estimating the conditional exit probabilities, we include only those transitions that occur between interview dates in the NLTCS.

We estimate the parameters of $P(C{\rightarrow}C)$ in equation (6) using weighted maximum likelihood to account for the nonrandom sample design. After exploring a variety of specifications for equation (6), we adopted a formulation for CM1 spells with MALE, WHITE, and PRE65 in Z_1 and an intercept in Z_2. In this case, the best combination of smoothness and fit resulted in the overlap-spline parameters of $K_\theta = 1$ with (μ_{11}, σ_{11}) and (μ_{21}, σ_{21}) set to any combinations such that, for every observation in the data,

$$\Phi_{11} (AGE) - \Phi_{21} (AGE) = 1.$$

These values are not unique: any set of pairs of (μ_{11}, σ_{11}), with μ_{11} small enough, and (μ_{21}, σ_{21}), with μ_{21} large enough, will produce the same result. This is equivalent to dropping the overlap-spline terms altogether and entering an intercept, MALE, WHITE, PRE65, AGE, AGE^2, and AGE^3 in Z_1.

The specification for return community spells (CM1 = 0) includes MALE, WHITE, AGE, and AGE^2 in Z_1 and an intercept in Z_2.[2] Table 10.5 contains the coefficient estimates for the community spell duration model.

---

2. It also sets $K_\theta = 3$ with $(\mu_{11}, \sigma_{11}) = (-5, 0.5)$, $(\mu_{12}, \sigma_{12}) = (3, 1.0)$, $(\mu_{21}, \sigma_{21}) = (3, 1.0)$, $(\mu_{22}, \sigma_{22}) = (16, 2.0)$, $(\mu_{31}, \sigma_{31}) = (16, 2.0)$, and (μ_{32}, σ_{32}) set to any combination such that, for every observation in the data, $\Phi_{32}(\tau)$ equals zero for all τ. We also restrict $\alpha_{21} = \alpha_{22} = \alpha_{j3} = 0$ for $j = 1, 2,$ and 3, eliminating the linear and quadratic terms in duration for the second overlap-spline, the quadratic term in duration for the third overlap-spline, and the third-order term from all overlap-splines.

Table 10.5   Parameter Estimates of Community Spell Duration Probabilities

A. First Community Spells

	Coefficient	Standard Error
Z_1 Variables		
MALE	−0.40633	0.042886
WHITE	−0.04472	0.070229
PRE65	0.263979	0.450623
(prior nursing home)		

	Spline: All Months	
	Coefficient	Standard Error
Z_2 Variables		
Intercept	7.255503	0.117733
AGE	−0.01756	0.001858
AGE^2	0.000047	0.00001
AGE^3	−6.5E-08	1.60E-08

B. Return Community Spells

	Coefficient	Standard Error
Z_1 Variables		
AGE	−0.00045	0.005521
AGE^2	0.000005	0.000013
MALE	0.490293	0.279404
WHITE	0.308954	0.373481

	Spline					
	1–3 Months		3–16 Months		≥16 Months	
	Coefficient	Standard Error	Coefficient	Standard Error	Coefficient	Standard Error
Z_2 Variables						
Intercept	1.978263	1.316833	−4.22992	0.671357	−13.1521	3.154348
t	−3.76324	1.508056			0.420809	0.134577
t^2	0.652585	0.423117				

The results for first community spells indicate that duration dependence is monotonically decreasing and accelerating. That is, $P(C \rightarrow C | X, H, AGE)$ always decreases and at an increasing rate as AGE increases. Men have significantly shorter spells throughout, but neither race nor prior nursing home experience significantly alter spell lengths.

Second and higher-order community spells (CM1 = 0) display nonmonotonic duration dependence, rapidly increasing over the first few months, slowly increasing over the next year, and decreasing and accelerating for the remaining nine months. The age at which these spells are experienced has little impact on the form of duration dependence and the magnitude of $P(C \rightarrow C | X, H, \tau)$. The variable MALE is of borderline significance, reducing $P(C \rightarrow C | X, H, \tau)$ throughout τ at all ages. Individuals have only a 62 percent change of surviving in the community the first month, while the chance of surviving each of months 3 through 22 exceeds 95 percent.

10.3.4 Estimation of Nursing Home Transition Probabilities

We control for history dependence in a similar manner when estimating model (6) for nursing home residence. In order to allow estimates for first nursing home admissions (NH1 = 1) to vary from those of second and higher-order nursing home admissions (NH1 = 0), we interact the dummy variable NH1 with the other covariates. We also include measures of age. The final specification of equations (6) and (7) for nursing home spells includes MALE and WHITE in Z_1; an intercept, AGE, and AGE^2 in Z_2.[3] Table 10.6 contains the coefficient estimates of equations (6) and (7) for the nursing home spells.

First and repeat nursing home spells display the same general forms of duration dependence, sharply increasing over the first several months, then leveling off and slowly decreasing. The coefficient of MALE is significantly different from zero for both types of admissions, but it is almost 60 percent larger for first admissions. The decreased duration of nursing home stays for men is most pronounced for first admissions. The variable WHITE does not have a significant impact on the lengths of either first or subsequent admissions.

10.3.5 Estimation of Community Exit Probabilities

In estimating the probability that a community spell will end in death rather than in nursing home entry, we control for history dependence in several ways. First, in order to allow the characteristics of first community spell exits to

3. This specification sets the spline parameter to $K_0 = 3$ with, for NH1 = 1,

$$(\mu_{11}, \sigma_{11}) = (-5, 0.5), \quad (\mu_{21}, \sigma_{21}) = (4, 0.5),$$
$$(\mu_{12}, \sigma_{12}) = (4, 0.5), \quad (\mu_{22}, \sigma_{22}) = (20, 1.0), \text{ and}$$
$$(\mu_{13}, \sigma_{13}) = (20, 1.0),$$

and for NH1 = 0,

$$(\mu_{11}, \sigma_{11}) = (-5, 0.5), \quad (\mu_{21}, \sigma_{21}) = (4, 1.0),$$
$$(\mu_{12}, \sigma_{12}) = (4, 1.0), \quad (\mu_{22}, \sigma_{22}) = (22, 4.0), \text{ and}$$
$$(\mu_{13}, \sigma_{13}) = (22, 4.0),$$

and (μ_{23}, σ_{23}) is set to any combination such that, for every observation in the data, $\Phi_{23}(\tau)$ equals zero, for all types of nursing home spells. We restrict α_{23} to be zero for first nursing home spells, thus eliminating the quadratic term in the third spline for these spells. We also restrict α_{3j} to be zero for both types of nursing home spells, thus eliminating the third-order term in duration.

Table 10.6   **Parameter Estimates of Nursing Home Spell Duration Probabilities**

A. First Nursing Home Spells

	Coefficient	Standard Error
Z_1 Variables		
MALE	0.278368	0.072025
WHITE	0.003483	0.11065

	Spline					
	1–4 Months		4–20 Months		≥20 Months	
	Coefficient	Standard Error	Coefficient	Standard Error	Coefficient	Standard Error
Z_2 Variables						
AGE	−0.00087	0.001819	−0.00003	0.000023	0.000248	0.000213
AGE^2	4.75E-07	0.000004	6.23E-08	5.35E-08	−7.1E-08	5.19E-07
Intercept	0.101047	0.317329	−1.59763	0.473573	−4.11875	0.254231
t	−0.81425	0.296768	−0.17948	0.081135	0.00007	0.001238
t^2	0.056743	0.071692	0.004761	0.003546		

B. Second or Higher-Order Nursing Home Spells

	Coefficient	Standard Error
Z_1 Variables		
MALE	0.17539	0.068032
WHITE	0.090283	0.102742

	Spline					
	1–4 Months		4–22 Months		≥22 Months	
	Coefficient	Standard Error	Coefficient	Standard Error	Coefficient	Standard Error
Z_2 Variables						
AGE	−0.00057	0.001946	0.000006	0.00002	−0.00008	0.000237
AGE^2	0.000002	0.000005	1.11E-10	4.81E-08	8.92E-07	5.87E-07
Intercept	−0.75217	0.342505	−2.4842	0.476187	−3.60134	0.33752
t	−0.46025	0.285716	−0.03874	0.071455	−0.00492	0.006101
t^2	0.023516	0.069963	−0.00051	0.002806	0.000032	0.000033

differ from those of return community spells, we fully interact the dummy variable CM1. We also control for the duration of the current spell, τ, by introducing the function $\Gamma(\cdot)$ as discussed above. Finally, to determine how $P(D|C\text{-Exit})$ changes with age, we interact a quadratic polynomial in age with overlap-splines in duration of the previous spell.

The duration of first community spells (CM1 = 1) is always equal to the age of the individual; thus, we substitute AGE for τ and estimate $P(D|C\text{-Exit}, X, H, \text{AGE})$ for these observations. The final specification of models (8) and (9) for exits from community spells with CM1 = 1 includes MALE, WHITE, and PRE65 in Z_1 and an intercept, AGE, and AGE^2 in Z_2.[4] Because τ is replaced by AGE in the overlap-spline specification, we are allowing for different polynomials in AGE to be operative over different age intervals, determined by the properties of the overlap splines. We use this specification explicitly to allow exit characteristics to be different for the very old. For return community spell exits (CM1 = 0), the final specification of equations (8) and (9) includes WHITE in Z_1 and an intercept, MALE, AGE, and AGE^2 in Z_2.[5] The overlap-spline intervals are determined over the values of previous spell duration, τ. We fit separate polynomials in AGE over the two intervals determined by the overlap-spline properties, one for short previous spells and one for long previous spells. Table 10.7 contains the coefficient estimates of equations (8) and (9) for community spell exits.

The results, as displayed in table 10.8, indicate that most people at all ages die on their first community exit. Females are more likely than males, and whites are more likely than nonwhites, to enter nursing homes on termination of a first community spell. For men at age 65, there is about an 85 percent chance that a community spell will end in death; the probability is about 75 percent for females. The percentage of individuals who terminate community spells by entering nursing homes gradually increases with age, until it reaches a peak (at about age 85) of almost 30 percent for males and 53 percent for females. The probability then decreases sharply with age. The risk of entering a nursing home is greatest between the ages of 78 and 95, with more than 20 percent of male exits and more than 30 percent of female exits at each age.

Return community spell exits (CM1 = 0), as displayed in table 10.8, differ from first community exits. The likelihood that a community spell will end in death increases steadily through age. Long return community spells, defined as more than six months in the community, are much more likely to end in nursing home admissions at young ages, with fewer than 10 percent of 65-year-olds dying on exit, while almost 80 percent of men and 60 percent of women aged 95 die on exit. Mortality rates for short spells vary less with age, ranging from a low of around 60 percent dying at age 65 to about 65 percent dying at age 95. In other respects, the return community spells are similar to first spells; whites are more likely than blacks to enter nursing homes on exiting a return community spell. Females exiting long return community spells

---

4. This specification sets the spline parameter $K_\Gamma = 2$ with $(\mu_{11}, \sigma_{11}) = (-5, 0.5)$, $(\mu_{12}, \sigma_{12}) = (200, 10.0)$, $(\mu_{21}, \sigma_{21}) = (200, 10.0)$, and (μ_{22}, σ_{22}) set to any combination such that, for every observation in the data, $\Phi_{22}(\text{AGE})$ equals zero.

5. We set the spline parameter $K_\Gamma = 2$ with $(\mu_{11}, \sigma_{11}) = (-5, 0.5)$, $(\mu_{12}, \sigma_{12}) = (6, 0.5)$, $(\mu_{21}, \sigma_{21}) = (6, 0.5)$, and (μ_{22}, σ_{22}) set to any combination such that, for every observation in the data, $\Phi_{22}(\tau)$ equals zero.

Table 10.7   Parameter Estimates of Community Spell Exit Probabilities

A. First Community Exit Probabilities		
	Coefficient	Standard Error
Z_1 Variables		
MALE	−0.703840	0.095611
WHITE	0.482762	0.170774
PRE65 (prior nursing home)	2.491183	1.163058

	Spline			
	1–200 Months		≥200 Months	
	Coefficient	Standard Error	Coefficient	Standard Error
Z_2 Variables				
Intercept	−1.60232	0.19079	−3.87718	2.064165
AGE			0.024363	0.014405
AGE^2	0.000018	0.000006	−0.00005	0.000025

B. Return Community Exit Probabilities		
	Coefficient	Standard Error
Z_1 Variable		
WHITE	0.389739	0.2181

	Spline			
	1–6 Months		≥6 Months	
	Coefficient	Standard Error	Coefficient	Standard Error
Z_2 Variables				
MALE	0.2181	0.342772	−0.77631	0.931566
Intercept	−0.801	0.697308	2.682614	1.561231
τ	−0.00238	0.001887	−0.00906	0.005279

are more likely than males to enter nursing homes, but females exiting short return community spells are more likely than males to die.

10.3.6   Estimation of Nursing Home Exit Probabilities

The same structure serves to account for history dependence in nursing home exits. We allow first nursing home admissions (NH = 1) to have different exit characteristics from second and higher-order nursing home admissions (NH1 = 0) by fully interacting the dummy variable NH1. The final specifica-

Table 10.8   **Probability of Dying Given a Community Spell Exit**

A. Exit from First Community Spells

Age	Male	Female
70	0.853	0.742
75	0.828	0.704
80	0.778	0.634
85	0.702	0.538
90	0.702	0.539
95	0.766	0.618
100	0.863	0.757
105	0.944	0.892

B. Exit from Second or Higher-Order Community Spells

	Male		Female	
Age	Short Spell	Long Spell	Short Spell	Long Spell
70	0.547	0.394	0.600	0.225
75	0.627	0.223	0.677	0.114
80	0.677	0.213	0.722	0.108
85	0.698	0.353	0.742	0.196
90	0.695	0.701	0.739	0.512
95	0.665	0.956	0.712	0.906
100	0.608	0.998	0.658	0.995
105	0.517	1.000	0.571	1.000

tion is identical for both types of admissions and has WHITE in Z_1, and an intercept, MALE, AGE, and AGE^2 in Z_2. We set the overlap-spline parameters to distinguish between very short (less than three months) and other nursing home spells.[6] Table 10.9 contains the coefficient estimates of equations (8) and (9) for nursing home exits.

Table 10.10 contains results for exits from first nursing home spells. Most spells at early ages end in return to the community, while the probability of a spell ending in death increases monotonically with age. The probability that a nursing home spell will end in death increases rapidly with age for long nursing home spells. Although age is a significant determinant of the probability for long spells, it is not significant for short spells. The variable MALE is significant for short spells, but not for long spells; consequently, women are much more likely than men to return to the community when exiting short nursing home spells. The probability that a nursing home spell will end in death does not vary with race.

Table 10.10 also contains results for exits from second or higher-order nurs-

6. The overlap-spline parameters are $K_\Gamma = 2$, $(\mu_{11}, \sigma_{11}) = (-5, 0.5)$, $(\mu_{12}, \sigma_{12}) = (2.5, 0.5)$, $(\mu_{21}, \sigma_{21}) = (2.5, 0.5)$, and (μ_{22}, σ_{22}) is set to any combination such that, for every observation in the data, $\Phi_{22}(\tau)$ equals zero.

Table 10.9   **Parameter Estimates of Nursing Home Spell Exit Probabilities**

A. First Nursing Home Exit Probabilities

	Coefficient	Standard Error
Z_1 Variable		
WHITE	0.010358	0.200626

	Spline			
	1–2.5 Months		≥2.5 Months	
	Coefficient	Standard Error	Coefficient	Standard Error
Z_2 Variables				
MALE	−0.9564	0.246972	−0.10943	0.150629
Intercept	1.410593	0.477743	1.670388	0.383976
τ	−0.0004	0.004379	−0.00809	0.003043
τ^2	−2.2E-06	0.00001	0.000004	0.000006

B. Second or Higher-Order Nursing Home Exit Probabilities

	Coefficient	Standard Error
Z_1 Variable		
WHITE	0.013078	0.259445

	Spline			
	1–2.5 Months		≥2.5 Months	
	Coefficient	Standard Error	Coefficient	Standard Error
Z_2 Variables				
MALE	−0.49471	0.257421	0.029287	0.160889
Intercept	2.959729	0.753246	1.867464	0.424702
τ	−0.00763	0.006547	−0.00019	0.003156
τ^2	0.000006	0.000014	−8.8E-06	0.000007

ing home spells. For these spells, the probability of death increases monotonically with age for both short and long spells. Race remains insignificant, and gender is only of borderline significance for short spells, in which men have higher mortality rates.

10.4   Simulation Results

The assessment of alternative policies toward financing or delivering long-term care requires full characterization of the distribution of nursing home utilization. Measures of central tendency, such as the mean or median, are of

Table 10.10   **Probability of Dying Given a Nursing Home Spell Exit**

	A. Exit from First Nursing Home Spells			
	Male		Female	
Age	Short Spell	Long Spell	Short Spell	Long Spell
70	0.393	0.249	0.200	0.229
75	0.405	0.340	0.207	0.316
80	0.420	0.436	0.218	0.409
85	0.439	0.529	0.232	0.501
90	0.463	0.612	0.249	0.586
95	0.490	0.683	0.270	0.658
100	0.521	0.739	0.295	0.718
105	0.556	0.784	0.325	0.765

	B. Exit from Second or Higher-Order Nursing Home Spells			
	Male		Female	
Age	Short Spell	Long Spell	Short Spell	Long Spell
70	0.115	0.134	0.073	0.137
75	0.162	0.147	0.105	0.150
80	0.216	0.169	0.144	0.173
85	0.274	0.205	0.187	0.209
90	0.331	0.257	0.232	0.263
95	0.385	0.331	0.276	0.338
100	0.431	0.431	0.316	0.438
105	0.468	0.551	0.349	0.559

limited value in estimating utilization, since insurance is often concerned with providing protection against catastrophic events rather than covering expected utilization for the average enrollee. In some respects, then, it is as important to learn the likelihood that an individual will have a very lengthy nursing home admission as it is to know the expected value of utilization. These quantities can be obtained from our empirical analysis, but doing so requires simulations that construct the distributions of nursing home and community spells.

Our simulations follow the procedure described in section 10.1.4 and are based on random draws of 5,000 hypothetical individuals from the estimated distribution of initial covariate values. Key results from the simulation appear in table 10.11, which lists summary statistics for the simulation population, measures of nursing home utilization, and durations of community spells and survival.

Because we drew the simulated population from a distribution representing the composition of the U.S. 65-year-old population in 1984, the hypothetical population should be similar to the actual population. Forty-four percent of the simulated population are men, and 91 percent are white. Fewer than 0.4 percent had been discharged from a nursing home before reaching age 65, and

Table 10.11   Simulation Results

	Mean	1%	5%	10%	25%	Median	75%	90%	95%	99%
MALE = 1	0.44									
WHITE = 1	0.91									
PRE65 = 1 (prior nursing home)	0.0038									
Fraction residing in nursing home at 65th birthday	0.0062									
Fraction with at least one nursing home admission	0.35									
Number of nursing home admissions	0.53	0	0	0	0	0	1	2	2	4
Male	0.51	0	0	0	0	0	1	1	2	4
Female	0.54	0	0	0	0	0	1	2	2	4
Total nursing home utilization (months)	7.47	0	0	0	0	0	2	23	50	111
Male	5.80	0	0	0	0	0	2	17	37	87.28
Female	8.77	0	0	0	0	0	3	29.1	61	119.91
Nursing home utilization for those with at least one admission (months)	21.06	1	1	1	2	6	27	66	88.3	139
Male	16.11	1	1	1	1	4	20	50	70.5	127.5
Female	25.03	1	1	1	2	9	34	74.5	100.75	155.45
Time before first nursing home admission (months)	207.98	0	44	74.4	142.5	212	280	330.2	361	414.26
Male	191.58	0	37.5	60	127	195	261	312	336.5	381.1
Female	221.13	0	49	87.5	154	227	292.75	341.5	376	426.3

Spell length of first nursing home admissions (months)	14.45	1	1	1	1	3	14	48	69	135
Male	11.05	1	1	1	1	2	9	34	54.05	102.21
Female	17.19	1	1	1	1	3	18	57	83	136.35
Spell length of nonfirst nursing home admissions (months)	12.27	1	1	1	2	4	14	33	53.4	103.96
Male	11.11	1	1	1	1	4	12	27.8	53.6	98.52
Female	13.01	1	1	1	2	5	15	36	53.95	112.11
Time spent in community after first nursing home admission, for those with at least one nursing home admission (months)	11.92	0	0	0	0	1	25	33	53.4	103.96
Male	8.67	0	0	0	0	1	9.5	29	43	65.1
Female	14.53	0	0	0	0	1	27	39.5	60	102
Time from onset of first spell until death, for those with at least one nursing home admission (months)	32.98	1	1	1	3	18	49	91	114	172.25
Male	24.77	1	1	1	2	9	35	69	93.5	167
Female	39.55	1	1	1	5	28	61.5	100	132	187.12
Age at death (months after 65th birthday)	207.50	9	43	67	129	204	284	350	380	436
Male	186.14	6	38	61	115	183	252	317	352	394.07
Female	224.17	13	48.45	75	142.25	225	309	366.1	398	446

0.62 percent were residents in nursing homes on their sixty-fifth birthdays. Thus 99 percent of the simulated population had no prior nursing home admissions at age 65.

The distribution of age at death is similar to figures obtained from the 1984 life tables for the United States, particularly in the middle of the distribution. The median age at death from the life table and from the simulation is 82. The simulations tend to predict slightly lengthier survival than do the life-table figures for individuals in the lower half of the distribution (up to just over one year).

Perhaps the most common statistic used to describe nursing home utilization is the probability that an individual who reaches age 65 will *ever* enter a nursing home. The simulation reveals that 35 percent have at least one nursing home admission; this compares with figures in the literature ranging from 25 to 50 percent. Although a substantial minority (10 percent) have more than one admission, very few have large numbers of admissions; only 0.5 percent have more than four.

More important is the likelihood of a lengthy admission. Many of the people admitted to nursing homes spend little time there. Almost 25 percent of those with at least one admission spend only one month in nursing homes during their lifetime. Of the individuals with some nursing home utilization, only half have more than six months of accumulated nursing home residency. But a substantial minority have lengthy stays—nearly 25 percent of all women who enter a nursing home will spend three years there. Thus the distribution of nursing home utilization is highly skewed; most elderly persons never enter a nursing home, many enter for short times, and a substantial minority spend years in an institution. This minority accounts for a large fraction of nursing home utilization.

When nursing home admission occurs, it tends to be at advanced ages. For men, the median age at a first admission exceeds the median age of death; most community spells that terminate at young ages end in death, while nursing home admissions occur in the middle of the age distribution. The median age of first admission is about age 81 for men and age 84 for women; half of all individuals who enter nursing homes do so for the first time between the ages of 76 and 88.

Inasmuch as 42 percent of first nursing home admissions end in death, entering a nursing home signals a high mortality rate. However, if the admission terminates in discharge alive, the outlook is not grim, at least for women. Leaving the admission alive marks the onset of the first return community spell, which on average lasts slightly more than a year for women and less than nine months for men. Of those who have return community spells, females accumulate far more months of residency. Half of the females with return community spells experience at least two years in the community, while the corresponding value for males is around nine months. The large difference in male and female return community experiences persists throughout the distributions.

From an insurer's point of view, a potential subscriber with a history of health service utilization is likely to have above-average claims. In this respect, it is interesting to examine the utilization pattern of individuals with at least one prior admission. The simulations reveal that the mean duration of repeat nursing home admissions is longer than first admissions for men, but not for women. The upper percentiles of spell durations for women are substantially greater for first admissions than for repeat admissions. For men and women combined, fewer than 10 percent of repeat spells are more than three years long, while 10 percent of first spells are at least four years long. The skew in utilization revealed in these simulations suggests that there should be a strong role for insurance; a large percentage of people are at risk for very limited nursing home stays, but a nonnegligible minority will have lengthy admissions that could lead to catastrophic expenditures.

10.5   Conclusions

The elderly have a substantial risk of entering nursing homes. According to our analysis, most of the admissions are short, and multiple admissions are uncommon. Median nursing home utilization is only six months for those with at least one admission, and only 25 percent of 65-year-olds can expect to spend more than two months in a nursing home during the remainder of their lives.

We find that very heavy utilization is somewhat less likely than Kemper and Murtaugh (1991) reported in the only published study that attempts to measure cumulative nursing home utilization in a random sample of elderly Americans. They reported a similar lifetime risk of nursing home utilization for 65-year-olds—37 percent in their study, compared to 35 percent in ours. They also found, as we did, that about one-third of persons who have any admissions will spend less than three months in nursing homes. However, in their study, 21 percent of persons with a nursing home admission, compared to 28 percent in our study, spent 3–12 months in a nursing home. The differences in findings are most striking for persons institutionalized for several years; 12 percent of the patients with any nursing home utilization in our simulations, compared to 17 percent of their subjects, spent five or more years in a nursing home. Kemper and Murtaugh estimate that about 48 percent of people with any admissions will have at least one year of utilization, compared to our estimate of 40 percent. Their results may differ from ours because they are based on recall alone, which may be particularly inaccurate for long stays, while ours are based on direct measurements of length of stay from two nationally representative data sources. Like Kemper and Murtaugh, though, we find that few of the elderly have prolonged stays and that those who do account for most nursing home utilization. Thus there is a nonnegligible but small risk of "catastrophic" nursing home admissions and a very high likelihood of experiencing a brief admission.

Our projections do not take into account changes in mortality rates over time, changes in the organization and supply of institutional care, or behavioral responses to changes in financing. If long-term care insurance is purchased more frequently, or if government agencies begin to finance or supply long-term care, utilization is likely to change. We previously showed that for Medicare-financed nursing home admissions, the exhaustion of Medicare nursing home benefits leads to a sharp rise in the discharge rate, suggesting that utilization is responsive to price (Garber and MaCurdy 1991). Since insurance constitutes a subsidy to covered services, it is likely that the development of insurance would lead to increased utilization as compared with what we observe in these samples. Thus our estimates provide evidence for the belief that there is a substantial potential market for long-term care insurance. Changing social arrangements, economic factors, and the dissemination of insurance could promote even greater use of long-term care in the future.

References

Branch, L. G., and A. M. Jette. 1982. A prospective study of long-term care institutionalization among the elderly. *American Journal of Public Health* 72:1373–79.
Garber, A. M., and T. MaCurdy. 1991. Nursing home discharges and exhaustion of Medicare benefits. NBER Working Paper no. 3639. Cambridge, Mass.: National Bureau of Economic Research.
Keeler, E. B., R. L. Kane, and D. H. Solomon. 1981. Short- and long-term residents of nursing homes. *Medical Care* 19:363–69.
Kemper, P., and C. M. Murtaugh. 1991. Lifetime use of nursing home care. *New England Journal of Medicine* 324:595–600.
Lewis, M. A., S. Cretin, and R. L. Kane. 1985. The natural history of nursing home patients. *Gerontologist* 25:382–88.
Liu, K., T. Coughlin, and T. McBride. 1991. Predicting nursing-home admission and length of stay: A duration analysis. *Medical Care* 29:125–41.
McConnel, C. E. 1984. A note on the lifetime risk of nursing home residency. *Gerontologist* 24:193–98.
Murtaugh, C. M., P. Kemper, and B. C. Spillman. 1990. The risk of nursing home use in later life. *Medical Care* 28:952–62.
Palmore, E. 1976. Total chance of institutionalization among the aged. *Gerontologist* 16:504–7.
Spence, D. A., and J. M. Wiener. 1990. Nursing home length of stay patterns: Results from the 1985 National Nursing Home Survey. *Gerontologist* 30:16–20.
Vicente, L., J. A. Wiley, and R. A. Carrington. 1979. The risk of institutionalization before death. *Gerontologist* 19:361–67.
Wingard, D. L., D. W. Jones, and R. M. Kaplan. 1987. Institutional care utilization by the elderly: A critical review. *Gerontologist* 27:156–63.

11   Policy Options for Long-Term Care

David M. Cutler and Louise M. Sheiner

11.1 Introduction

Over the next 30 years, the ranks of the elderly are projected to increase 64 percent, well above the 20 percent projected for the population as a whole. The number of old elderly, those age 85 and over, is projected to increase even more, by 94 percent. This growth in the elderly population, coupled with likely increases in the costs of long-term care, has caused policymakers to focus attention on how to most efficiently provide and pay for long-term care.

The current system of long-term care financing relies largely on out-of-pocket spending by individuals and their families and on Medicaid. There is no entitlement program akin to Medicare that provides long-term care for the elderly. Many view the current system as unsatisfactory, primarily because in order to qualify for government assistance, individuals have to reduce their incomes and assets to welfare levels, and because of the perceived bias in the system away from home care and toward nursing homes.

Over the past decade, a number of proposed solutions have been advanced to increase coverage of long-term care. These solutions range from having Medicare provide for long-term care in the same way that acute-care benefits are provided, to increasing tax or other incentives for private long-term care insurance, to modifying the current system by increasing the level of income and assets a Medicaid recipient can keep, or to moving toward a system that recovers any public expenditures on long-term care from the individuals' es-

David M. Cutler is assistant professor of economics at Harvard University and a faculty research fellow at the National Bureau of Economic Research. Louise M. Sheiner is an economist at the Federal Reserve Board of Governors.

The authors are grateful to Doug Bernheim, Jonathan Feinstein, Billy Jack, Joe Newhouse, Jim Poterba, and David Wise for comments, and to the National Institute on Aging for financial support. The paper does not represent the views of the Board of Governors or the staff of the Federal Reserve System.

tates, rather than requiring spenddown before death (see Rivlin and Weiner 1988, for a discussion of a number of policy alternatives).

Both private and public approaches to increasing long-term care insurance are problematic, in at least two ways. First, long-term care is difficult to define, and the demand for long-term care, particularly for home care, is likely to be quite price elastic. Thus, any increases in long-term care insurance may lead to large increases in long-term care demand. Second, expanding long-term care insurance, particularly through the public sector, may have deleterious effects on savings of the young and old, if much of savings is because of precautionary motives.

This paper addresses the first of these problems. In particular, we try to answer three questions. First, how responsive is demand for nursing home care to price? Second, to the extent that governments choose to ration care, how efficient is that rationing? And third, as governments increase access to nursing homes, either by increasing supply or increasing demand subsidies, what happens to the amount of care the elderly receive in the community?

We use the price differential between Medicaid and the private market to measure government supply policy and the existence of a spenddown provision for state Medicaid funding to measure government demand policy. We then relate these two measures of state policy to access to nursing homes by the elderly, living arrangements in the community, and use of formal and informal care in the community.

Our conclusions are threefold. First, both demand- and supply-side policies affect the utilization of nursing home care by the elderly. States with spenddown allowances have greater rates of nursing home utilization than states without these provisions, as do states with smaller Medicaid price differentials. Second, state policies do affect the composition of the nursing home population, independent of the total utilization. As Medicaid payments increase relative to private market prices, poorer people have greater access to nursing home care. In states with a spenddown provision, there is some evidence that the sicker elderly are more likely to be admitted to a nursing home.

Third, the marginal source of care for persons in the community considering nursing home utilization appears to be support from children. One commonly expressed view is that the elderly admitted to nursing homes would otherwise live alone and without support. We find no evidence for this view. Rather, in states with more restrictive policies, the elderly live with their children more and receive more substantial help from their children. In addition, as demand subsidies increase or Medicaid underpayment amounts decline, the elderly are less likely to receive substantial help from their children on a day-to-day basis. We conclude from this that the moral hazard problem in subsidizing nursing home care is quite large and that subsidies toward institutionalization may provoke large inefficiencies.

The paper is structured as follows. We begin in the next section with a discussion of the policy goals and problems associated with long-term care, highlighting the issues of moral hazard in long-term care provision and the importance of long-term care insurance for private sector savings. Section 11.3 gives information about how different countries provide long-term care services. Contrary to public opinion, most countries do not provide long-term care as an entitlement in the same manner as they do acute medical care. Rather, almost all countries have some form of cost sharing in long-term care provision, many use a welfare method similar to the United States, and some consider children's income in determining long-term care subsidies. Section 11.4 provides a more detailed description of how long-term care is financed in the United States, focusing in particular on differences across states. We document substantial differences across states in the policies governments pursue toward long-term nursing home care. Sections 11.5 and 11.6 then use these cross-state differences to explain differences in the amount and type of long-term care services actually received by the elderly. Section 11.7 concludes.

11.2   Policy Issues for Long-Term Care

11.2.1   Rationales for Public Involvement

Governments in the United States are heavily involved in the financing of formal (i.e., paid) long-term care. In 1989, direct government expenditure on nursing homes was $24.3 billion, roughly 51 percent of total nursing home expenditures. The rationales for public provision of long-term care are quite similar to those that have been advanced for the public provision of social security (see Diamond 1977, for a discussion). First, if individuals are myopic or not sufficiently knowledgeable about long-term care risks, they might not save enough on their own.[1] In this case, social provision of long-term care might be justified, although there are a number of alternatives, including mandated saving, that may be more appropriate.

Perhaps more important, the need for long-term care is uncertain, because both longevity and future health status are uncertain. Thus, it is more efficient for people to purchase long-term care insurance than to save enough for the possibility of significant long-term care needs. Because of adverse selection problems or large variability in the cost of care, however, the market for private long-term care insurance may be quite inefficient; an advantage of public provision of long-term care insurance is that it provides efficient insurance by pooling the entire population into one risk pool (Cutler 1992).

---

1. In a 1984 survey, 79 percent of the elderly thought that Medicare paid for long-term care. In fact, Medicare pays very little for long-term care. Recent surveys indicate that between one-quarter and one-half of the elderly still have this view (Rivlin and Weiner 1988).

11.2.2   Problems with Public Provision of Long-Term Care

Public provision of long-term care shares many of the problems of private insurance, however. One of the most significant problems is moral hazard. Because long-term care services may have significant consumption value (for instance, people in nursing homes may be provided with meals, laundry, and other services that individuals without impairments often pay for), providing these services at a zero or low price might encourage overconsumption of long-term care.[2] People who would otherwise manage on their own, or rely on the help of their children, might choose to use publicly provided services were they available at a subsidized price.[3]

The potential for moral hazard in this market is a dominant concern because the size of the formal long-term care sector is so small. Only about 5 percent of the elderly are institutionalized at any point in time, and even among those 85 years old and older, only one-quarter are institutionalized at any point in time. Thus, substitution to formal long-term care by even a small share of those currently cared for informally could result in a large increase in long-term care demand.

If policymakers were able to ration efficiently (providing long-term care only to the most medically or financially needy, for example), then moral hazard need not be a problem. However, it is very difficult to define who needs long-term care. Indeed, even very specific rules are likely to result in a great deal of moral hazard. For instance, 66 percent of nursing home residents in 1985 had three or more limitations in their Activities of Daily Living (ADL) (Price, Rimkunas, and O'Shaughnessy 1990). Only 5 percent of community residents over 65 had three or more ADL limitations (Rowland et al. 1988). Since less than 5 percent of the elderly live in nursing homes, however, roughly 60 percent of the elderly with three or more ADL impairments live in the community. Thus, even using quite severe impairment measures to ration eligibility for nursing home care will not restrict the eligible population enough to eliminate significant moral hazard. Similarly, limiting publicly provided long-term care assistance to those without other sources of care (for instance, to those without children) is likely to be both inefficient and unfair.

Without other constraints, the moral hazard problems associated with long-term care insurance could lead to exorbitantly expensive public programs. The size of the public program is of concern for two reasons. First, regardless of

2. The Long-Term Care Survey, which we utilize below, also asked the elderly their view of nursing home care. Seven percent of the respondents disagreed with the statement, "People go to nursing homes only when there is no other place to live." Similarly, 22 percent disagreed that, "Nursing homes are lonely places to live in," and 30 percent agreed that, "There are lots of things to do in a nursing home to keep people busy." A large share of the elderly may thus be predisposed to enter a nursing home when they get older.

3. Nursing home utilization could increase with increased subsidies both because the elderly choose nursing homes and because children might not offer to take their parents in when subsidized nursing home care is available.

whether insurance is provided publicly or privately, induced overconsumption of long-term care services results in an inefficient use of society's resources. Second, when the program is publicly financed, the inefficiency is magnified by the deadweight loss associated with the taxation necessary to finance the program. Thus, most public programs rely on demand or supply constraints to limit the size of public programs. Indeed, one of the advantages of a public program over a private program is the ability to restrict the supply of nursing home beds.

A second problem with public provision of long-term care is its impact on saving. If potential long-term care expenses provide an important motivation for saving, then publicly provided long-term care may significantly reduce private saving. Precautionary savings motives have been highlighted by many as an important source of saving in the United States (Deaton 1989; Carroll and Summers 1991; Hubbard, Skinner, and Zeldes 1992).

The impact of public long-term care insurance on saving can be separated into two conceptually distinct effects. First, to the extent that individuals currently have to save for long-term care expenses even though the likelihood of actually needing long-term care is low,[4] the lack of public long-term care insurance may lead to more saving by the elderly. In this case, providing public insurance or improving access to private insurance for long-term care will lower private saving, even as it increases the welfare of the elderly. Second, public provision of long-term care services may further reduce saving relative to improved access to private long-term care insurance, because long-term care services are likely to be financed on a pay-as-you go basis.

Countering the effects on the amount of precautionary savings is the current system of means-tested public funding of long-term care.[5] All states in the United States have income and asset tests to determine Medicaid eligibility for publicly funded long-term care (described in more detail in section 11.4). This system of means-tested public insurance imposes a significant tax on savings by the elderly; with some probability, all of their savings will be spent on an item which the government would have provided had they not saved. While the unconditional probability of entering a nursing home for an extended period of time is low (so the incentive to reduce saving is also low), the probability of entering a nursing home may become less uncertain as a person ages. The tax effect of Medicaid provision may increase with age. If this effect is large, publicly provided long-term care insurance may increase saving among the elderly.

This paper does not provide empirical tests of the impact of government long-term care policies on saving. Many of the effects on saving should be the same as those of the public provision of Social Security benefits. Unlike Social

---

4. Kemper and Murtaugh (1991) estimate that 43 percent of the people who turn age 65 in 1990 will use a nursing home before they die.

5. This argument is the same as that advanced by Feldstein (1987) about the ambiguous effects on saving and welfare of means-testing social security.

Security, however, long-term care policies differ by state. In principle, then, the methodology we use to test the effects of government policies on moral hazard can also be used to test the effects on saving. We anticipate returning to this issue in future work. Before discussing the effects of state policies on nursing home use and living arrangements, however, we first discuss the long-term care financing mechanisms of other countries.

11.3 International Evidence on the Financing of Long-term Care[6]

Most developed countries provide government financing of a much larger share of acute medical care than does the United States. Australia, Canada, France, Sweden, and the United Kingdom, for example, all insure 100 percent of the population publicly, and other countries, such as Germany and the Netherlands, insure most of the population. Typically, such coverage is provided without private premiums and with small or no patient deductibles or copayments. The United States, in contrast, provides government insurance for less than 25 percent of its population.

Unlike the provision of acute medical care, however, long-term care provision in the United States is much more similar to that in other countries. Most countries impose some form of cost sharing for nursing home care, and many have spenddown features similar to those of the United States. Table 11.1 provides evidence on the types of financing employed by various countries. The table divides the countries into two groups: those that provide long-term care on a welfare basis (i.e., recipients of government subsidies need to meet certain income or asset requirements) and those that provide it on an entitlement basis. The first set of countries leaves a substantial share of long-term care financing to the individual. In Belgium and France, for example, the government pays for the medical component of long-term care, but individuals are responsible for room and board.[7] In Germany and the United States, the individual may be responsible for the entire cost of long-term care, and in Germany, children may also have to contribute to long-term care for their parents before the government pays for care.

In each of these countries, there are provisions for government payment of care for the poor elderly. In France and Germany, individuals qualify for public funding if either gross income or income net of medical expenses is below a given cutoff. All states in the United States have a gross income means test, and many, although not all, states have a net income means test as well. The process of qualifying for public funds because of high medical expenses is termed "spenddown" in the United States.

Thus, even in the "welfare" countries, many residents of long-term care

---

6. This discussion draws heavily on information in Doty (1988, 1990) and Schwab (1989).
7. On average, the French government pays approximately 14 percent of the cost of long-ter
are.

Table 11.1   **Payment for Long-Term Care in Different Countries**

Country	Institutionalization Rate (%)	Qualifications for Public Funding
Welfare basis for payment		
Belgium	6.3	Government pays medical component only; consumer pays residential component
France	6.3	Government pays medical component only; consumer pays residential component; means test for public funding of consumer share
Germany[a]	3.6–4.5	Consumer and children responsible for care; means test for public funds
United States	5.7	Consumer responsible for costs; means test (income and assets) for public funds; spenddown provision in many states
Entitlement basis for payment		
Australia	6.4	Consumer fee fixed at 87.5 percent of social security pension
Canada	8.7	Consumer pays maximum social security pension less a fixed amount
Denmark	7.0	Consumer pays social security pension plus share of other income (60–80 percent)
Netherlands	10.9	Skilled homes (AWBZ) covered under national health insurance with little cost sharing; spenddown provision for less medicalized facilities
Japan	3.9	Consumer pays 10 percent of cost
Sweden	8.7–10.5	Consumer pays social security pension plus share of other income (60–80 percent)
United Kingdom	4.1	National Health Service hospitals and Local Authority old-age homes paid by government; means test for private old-age homes

Note: The table shows the institutionalization rate and mechanisms for public assistance.

Sources: International descriptions are from Doty (1988, 1990), and Schwab (1988).

[a]Utilization rate does not count long-term care provided in general hospitals.

facilities receive some government assistance. For instance, in both France and Germany, roughly 50 percent of residents in nursing homes and old-age homes receive some public support. In the United States, public financing of institutional long-term care accounts for roughly 50 percent of all formal long-term care costs.

The second set of countries pays for at least part of long-term care as an entitlement rather than strictly on a welfare basis. Generally, the consumer's part of long-term care is fixed relative to income: either social security income (Australia and Canada) or total income (Denmark, Japan, and Sweden).[8] As a result, all elderly receive some amount of public funding. Even in countries that use an entitlement method to reimburse nursing home care, however, it is striking that all of the countries require significant cost sharing on the part of the individual. In many of these countries (Australia, Canada, and the United Kingdom, e.g.), there is little or no private payment required for acute medical care.[9]

Institutionalization rates vary from 3.5 to 6.5 percent of the elderly population for the welfare countries and from 4 to 11 percent of the elderly population for the entitlement countries, suggesting at least some link between more generous public funding of nursing homes and the share of the population that is institutionalized. The link, however, is difficult to test formally with only a few countries. Further, as Doty (1990) notes, some of this relation is misleading. In the Netherlands, for example, where the institutionalization rate is very high, about three-quarters of the population is in forms of care which are run under the welfare method rather than the entitlement method. In the United Kingdom, only 20 percent of the institutionalized elderly are in National Health Service hospitals (which are covered as inpatient care); most of the remainder have some cost sharing for long-term care. Indeed, a potentially more important policy in explaining international differences in nursing home utilization, which is not included here, is government restrictions on nursing home beds. The policy decisions of governments in setting nursing home bed capacity appear to be as important as cost-sharing provisions on the demand side in regulating nursing home use (Doty 1988).

The conclusion from table 11.1 is thus that many countries have very similar long-term care policies. Contrary to the financing of acute medical care, the United States is not a large outlier in its financing of long-term care. In fact, almost all countries require significant cost sharing, and many have means testing similar to the United States. To a great extent, this similarity in long-term care provision is due to the difficulty in identifying the group most in need of long-term care. Unlike acute care hospital admissions, the need for long-term

---

8. Prior to the early 1980s, many provinces in Canada had a spenddown system similar to the United States. With the provision of more central government financing of long-term care in the 1960s and 1970s, most provinces moved to an entitlement basis for payment (Kane and Kane 1985).

9. Although some services, such as private hospital rooms, are only available at private expense.

care is not necessarily indicated by a discrete event. Further, many elderly need help only with some tasks, so that institutionalization may not be the most appropriate site of care even for those with disabilities. Finally, the potential for moral hazard in long-term care is much greater than for acute medical care. Given these difficulties with long-term care provision, it is not surprising that countries have generally not chosen to include long-term care as a benefit provided by national health insurance.

The natural question from the international data is the extent to which these financial and supply decisions affect nursing home utilization and long-term care provision outside of nursing homes. Data to answer this question, however, are generally unavailable across countries. In the next sections, we examine U.S. data on state policies and the provision of long-term care to address these questions.

11.4   Long-Term Care Financing in the United States

In the United States, most assistance provided to the disabled elderly is informal and unpaid. Little information is available about the costs of that care. More information is available on formal long-term care. Formal care is financed partly by private payers and partly by government. Table 11.2 presents a breakdown of sources of payment for formal care. In 1989, Medicaid paid directly for 43 percent of nursing home costs. However, this number underestimates the impact of the Medicaid program on nursing home expenditures, because an additional 18 percent of nursing home expenditures are financed by the incomes of residents on Medicaid who are also receiving Medicaid assistance. Thus, over 61 percent of nursing home expenditures are paid by Medicaid or by residents on Medicaid. Out-of-pocket expenditures by wholly private-pay patients[10] account for only 26 percent of nursing home expenditures. Medicare pays for only 7.5 percent of nursing home spending, and the remaining 5 percent of spending is from insurance and other sources.

Medicaid is thus the dominant government program for nursing home care. State Medicaid policies differ considerably, however. States participating in the Medicaid program have leeway to decide the groups that are eligible and the payment structure for these services. We describe these state policies in the remainder of this section.

11.4.1   State Differences in Medicaid Eligibility

The Federal Medicaid program requires states with Medicaid programs[11] to provide Medicaid to "categorically eligible" individuals. For the elderly in

10. Actually, some of the other out-of-pocket expenditures are contributed by people on Medicare who are paying their deductible or copayment.

11. All states currently have Medicaid programs. However, Arizona's program only recently moved from being a "demonstration project" to a certified Medicaid program. Long-term care in Arizona was not provided through the state's Medicaid demonstration project until January 1, 1989, and is therefore not discussed here.

Table 11.2   Sources of Payment for Nursing Homes, 1989

Source	Payment (billion $)	Percentage of Total
Medicaid	20.7	43.1
Medicare	3.6	7.5
Out-of-pocket expenditures	21.3	44.4
Nursing home residents on Medicaid	8.7	18.1
Nursing home residents not on Medicaid	12.6	26.3
Private insurance	0.5	1.0
Other	1.9	4.0
Total	47.9	100.0

Source: Lazenby and Letsch (1990).

most states, categorical eligibility is defined as countable income (income less $20 per month) below the maximum Supplemental Security Income (SSI) benefit in the state. Because SSI benefits for individuals who are institutionalized are very low (a maximum of $30 per month in 1988), only individuals with very low incomes can receive categorical coverage from Medicaid while in an institution. Indeed, while 80 percent of the noninstitutionalized Medicaid recipients qualify under categorical eligibility, only 22 percent of the institutionalized Medicaid recipients qualify based on categorical eligibility.[12]

A small set of states—those that had more restrictive cash assistance programs for the elderly before SSI was enacted—are allowed to use these more restrictive criteria in place of the categorical eligibility rules. These states are termed "209(b)" states, the designation of the waiver option for this group. Currently, 14 states determine Medicaid eligibility using this option.

In addition to categorical eligibility, states are permitted to cover certain optional groups of people. All states (except Arizona) cover at least one of these optional groups. For the elderly, these options are generally of two forms. The first is a "medically needy" program. Under this system, individuals are allowed to subtract their medical expenses from their income before applying the Medicaid income test.[13] In 1987, 36 states had a medically needy program for at least some component of the population, but not all of the programs applied to the elderly. Two states (Georgia and Texas) did not cover the elderly at all, six states (Arkansas, Florida, Iowa, Louisiana, New Jersey, and Oklahoma) covered the elderly but excluded long-term care,[14] and one state (New

12. In 1986, out of 6.2 million Medicaid recipients, 4.1 million received cash assistance. Out of 1.5 million Medicaid recipients in intermediate care facilities (ICFs) or skilled nursing facilities (SNFs), only 330,000 received cash assistance (Carpenter 1988).

13. The maximum income allowed under this option is 133 percent of the state's maximum AFDC payment for a family of the same size.

14. Medicaid also pays the hospital deductible, physician copayment, and other expenses such as prescription drugs for recipients. These six states covered only those services for the elderly.

Hampshire) covered skilled nursing facilities but not intermediate care facilities. In addition, three states with 209(b) programs (Indiana, Missouri, and Ohio) were required to allow individuals to subtract their medical expenses from their income before applying the income test, making the plan effectively similar to a medically needy program.[15]

Table 11.3 shows the composition of states with medically needy programs in 1987. The first column indicates whether the state had a medically needy program or the equivalent for long-term care.[16] The second and third columns report the income and asset tests[17] that are applied for Medicaid coverage. In 1987, maximum monthly income was on the order of $400 to $500, and maximum assets were approximately $2,000.

The second optional group that states can cover are people with incomes higher than the SSI limits. States are permitted to choose an income limit up to 300 percent of the state SSI benefit as an income eligibility standard—in effect superseding the categorical eligibility criterion.[18] In 1988, 19 states used this option; these states are also detailed in table 11.3. These higher income limits averaged about $1,000 per month in 1987.

Once eligibility is determined, individuals are expected to spend most of their income to pay for their nursing home bills. Medicaid will only pay the difference between the Medicaid rate and the individual's required contribution. The amount of income that individuals are allowed to keep varies slightly across states, but in general is quite low, ranging between $30 and $75 in 1991. Hence, for most individuals receiving Medicaid, the price of nursing home care is their full income.

11.4.2 Modeling State Policies: Demand and Supply Factors

To examine the effect of state policies on nursing home utilization and community support, we relate long-term care receipt to differences in state policies. Only a limited amount of existing work deals with public policies affecting nursing home utilization. Liu, Coughlin, and McBride (1991) estimate hazard models for nursing home admission, including the number of beds per 1,000 elderly and the Medicaid nursing home reimbursement rate as explanatory variables. They conclude that increased bed supply increases the probability of nursing home use, and that increased Medicaid payment rates lowers the probability of nursing home use. They interpret this latter finding as a negative demand elasticity for nursing home care, if the Medicaid payment rate is correlated with the private market price.

---

15. The other 11 "209(b)" states already have a medically needy program for the elderly.

16. Two of the 30 states (Oregon and Tennessee) began their medically needy programs for the elderly in 1986, after our micro data end. For our empirical work, we thus have 28 states with medically needy programs or the equivalent.

17. The asset tests exclude the value of an owned home.

18. The special SSI income limit may be on either gross income or on income net of the $20 disregard. We do not distinguish between these two cases.

Table 11.3   **Eligibility Criteria for Long-Term Care, 1987**

State	Program	Medically Needy Income Standard ($)	Medically Needy Asset Standard ($)	Special SSI Limits ($)
Alabama	No			853
Alaska	No			1,020
Arizona				
Arkansas	No			1,020
California	Yes	570	1,800	
Colorado	No			1,020
Connecticut	Yes	478	1,600	
Delaware	No			632
District of Columbia	Yes	382	2,600	
Florida	No			881
Georgia	No			937
Hawaii	Yes	320	1,800	
Idaho	No			1,020
Illinois	Yes	292	1,800	
Indiana	Yes[a]	356	1,500	
Iowa	No			1,020
Kansas	Yes	361	1,800	
Kentucky	Yes	212	1,800	
Louisiana	No			1,020
Maine	Yes	420	1,800	
Maryland	Yes	354	2,500	
Massachusetts	Yes	475	2,000	
Michigan	Yes	390	1,800	
Minnesota	Yes	410	3,750	
Mississippi	No			1,020
Missouri	Yes[a]	360	1,000	
Montana	Yes	360	1,800	
Nebraska	Yes	383	1,600	
Nevada	No			734
New Hampshire	No[b]			848
New Jersey	No			1,020
New Mexico	No			871
New York	Yes	437	3,000	
North Carolina	Yes	253	1,500	
North Dakota	Yes	365	3,000	
Ohio	Yes[a]	308	1,500	
Oklahoma	No			1,020
Oregon	Yes	375	1,800	
Pennsylvania	Yes	395	2,400	
Rhode Island	Yes	512	4,000	
South Carolina	No			1,020
South Dakota	No			1,020
Tennessee	Yes	170	1,800	
Texas	No			659
Utah	Yes	309	1,800	

Table 11.3   (continued)

State	Program	Medically Needy		Special SSI Limits ($)
		Income Standard ($)	Asset Standard ($)	
Vermont	Yes	432	1,800	
Virginia	Yes	345	1,800	
Washington	Yes	388	1,800	
West Virginia	Yes	220	1,800	
Wisconsin	Yes	463	1,800	
Wyoming	No			1,020

Source: Carpenter (1988); Neuschler and Gill (1986).

Note: Resource standards are for single people.

[a]State has a 209(b) program which bases eligibility on income net of medical spending.

[b]State covers skilled nursing facilities but not intermediate care facilities.

Garber and MaCurdy (1991) provide evidence that Medicare payment rules affect the duration of nursing home admissions. If a nursing home admission qualifies for Medicare payment, Medicare pays for all of the first 20 days, imposes a copayment for days 21–100, and pays nothing beyond 100 days. Using the variation in prices associated with the 100-day Medicare termination, Garber and MaCurdy estimate a fivefold increase in the nursing home discharge date in the period around 100 days after admission.

Newman et al. (1990) examine the effect of nursing home vacancy rates and the presence of formal and informal care on nursing home admissions. They find that increased vacancy rates increase nursing home utilization, but find only mixed evidence on the substitution of formal and informal care for nursing home care. While informal care appears substitutable for nursing home care, individuals with paid caregivers are more likely to experience nursing home admissions than those without.

In our empirical work, we have tried to find policy variables that capture both exogenous demand and supply for nursing home care. Because states choose whether to implement these policies, it is impossible to be sure that they are truly exogenous. It may be that states with higher demand for nursing home care are more likely to provide greater subsidies and encourage supply. Because we include so many demographic and financial characteristics of the individuals, however, it seems unlikely that unmeasured demand accounts for our results about the effects of state policies.

The measure of demand we use is the presence of a medically needy program. This measures the ability of some higher-income individuals to qualify for Medicaid on the basis of large medical care expenses. Although the income eligibility criteria vary across states, this variation is relatively small compared with the difference between being able to deduct medical expenses from income and having a fixed pre-medical-expense income cap.

Measuring supply is trickier. In the past, many states restricted the supply of nursing home beds. This was done both explicitly, by requiring nursing homes to apply for Certificates of Need before increasing the number of nursing home beds, and implicitly, by maintaining a low Medicaid payment rate relative to private rates. Because nursing home occupancy rates are generally quite high (the national average was about 95 percent in 1982) and most nursing homes maintain waiting lists (Norton 1992), it is often argued that the supply constraints are binding.

If supply is not completely exogenous, however, it is inappropriate to use the number of beds per elderly as an explanatory variable in an equation predicting nursing home usage.[19] We thus do not use a measure of bed supply in the equations. One variable which may affect nursing home supply, however, is the Medicaid underpayment amount, the difference between the private market price and the Medicaid per diem. The underpayment amount may have a number of effects on nursing home utilization. First, construction of nursing homes may be lower in states where Medicaid compensation is low. Second, nursing homes have a greater incentive to wait for private-pay or low-cost (low-need) patients in states with low Medicaid reimbursement.

Medicaid underpayments may also change the quality of nursing homes, thus affecting the demand for care. The direction of this effect is unclear, however. If there is an unlimited supply of Medicaid patients at any quality level, higher Medicaid compensation may be associated with a lower quality of care (Scanlon 1980; Gertler 1989). The higher the Medicaid compensation rate, the less nursing homes care about private patients and thus the lower their quality. Alternatively, if there is a limited supply of Medicaid patients or if nursing homes act partly on an altruistic basis (increases in revenue are spent on increases in quality rather than greater profits), higher Medicaid payments may lead to higher quality and thus greater nursing home demand. Indeed, there is some anecdotal evidence that states with low Medicaid compensation rates have low quality. Low payment rates have been blamed for the poor condition of nursing homes in California and Texas, for example (Little 1992).

We use the underpayment amount in 1987, the earliest year for which data are available; we suspect that the relative payment levels across states are reasonably constant over time. Although this variable may pick up both demand and supply factors, the results below suggest that it generally proxies for supply effects.

---

19. We considered two variables as possible instruments for bed supply. First, we tried the share of Medicaid expenditures that are paid by the federal government. However, because this share is a nonlinear function of per capita income in a state, it is correlated with income and hence with demand for nursing home care. Empirically, the higher the federal share, the higher the bed supply. The second variable we considered was the approval rate of Certificate of Need applications (measured in dollars of construction proposed). Although this variable is positively related to bed supply, it might also be correlated with demand, because states with high demand may approve a larger share of construction proposals.

If supply is constrained, then increasing demand by expanding Medicaid eligibility will affect the composition but not the total number of nursing home residents. Because nursing homes generally have leeway to select who gets admitted to nursing homes and who does not and because most nursing homes are for-profit businesses, nursing homes may not ration care efficiently, but may rather choose to admit those patients with the highest incomes and the lowest expected costs. Previous studies have found evidence that nursing homes do indeed discriminate against patients with significant caretaking needs (Ettner 1991; U.S. General Accounting Office 1990; Norton 1992). This is particularly true in states where the Medicaid payment is independent of the patient case mix. We thus examine how the state policies affect the composition of nursing home utilization in addition to the aggregate utilization rate.

Finally, we also include as a policy variable the existence of a home care waiver. Under Medicaid, states that wish to provide Medicaid funding for home care services must apply to the federal government for a waiver. Since such waivers were relatively new during the period of our data, we suspect they will have little effect on nursing home utilization.

Table 11.4 shows summary statistics for the measures of state policy. We use data from the 45 states for which all data are available.[20] Panel A of the table reports summary statistics on state policies. About 55 percent of the states have medically needy programs or the equivalent. Medicaid underpayments average about $10 per day, or roughly 22 percent of the average cost of a nursing home. The variation in the underpayment amount is also large. Minnesota pays for Medicaid use of nursing homes at the private market rate, while Colorado has an underpayment of approximately $25 per day relative to private market prices.

Panel B of the table shows cross correlations of the state policies. Measures of state generosity are positively correlated. States with a medically needy program are likely to have lower underpayments (i.e., the Medicaid rate is closer to the private rate) and are also more likely to have home care waivers. One natural hypothesis—that states with generous supply policies implement more restrictive demand controls—is not supported by the data. Rather, the results suggest that states that are more generous along the supply margin are also more generous with demand subsidies.

11.5   Determinants of Nursing Home Utilization

In this section, we examine the effect of state factors on utilization of nursing homes. We focus both on total nursing home use and on use among differ-

---

20. Unfortunately, data on underpayment amounts are not available for the District of Columbia, Illinois, New Jersey, New York, and Rhode Island.

Table 11.4   **Summary Statistics on State Nursing Home Policies**

A. Summary Statistics

Variable	Mean	Standard Deviation	Minimum	Maximum
Medically needy	.55	.50	0	1
Medicaid underpayment (dollars per day)	10.0	4.6	0	25
Home care waiver	.47	.50	0	1

B. Cross Correlations

	Medically Needy	Medicaid Underpayment	Home Care Waiver
Medically needy	1.000		
Medicaid underpayment	−.103	1.000	
Home care waiver	.250	.122	1.000

Note: The table shows the means and correlations between the state policy variables. All statistics use the 45 states for which data on all variables are available.

ent components of the population. We begin with a summary of the micro data and then present equations for the determinants of nursing home use.

11.5.1 National Long-Term Care Survey

The primary micro data we employ is the National Long-Term Care Survey (NLTCS). The NLTCS is a panel of the disabled elderly from 1982 to 1984. The survey selected individuals in 1982 with some chronic impairment in Activities of Daily Living (ADLs) or Instrumental Activities of Daily Living (IADLs) who were living in the community in 1982.[21] Individuals meeting the criterion (6,088 total) were given extensive interviews about health and demographic factors. While the sample is a random sample of the disabled elderly population, there is little reason to believe that the selection on disability status biases our results. Indeed, the NLTCS has been used by a number of researchers to study medical influences on nursing home admissions (Hanley et al. 1990; Liu et al. 1991), the probability of spenddown to receive Medicaid (Liu and Manton 1989; Liu, Doty, and Manton 1990), the transition of the elderly among states of disability (Liu, Manton, and Liu 1990; Manton 1988),

---

21. There are nine potential ADLS: eating, getting in or out of bed, getting in or out of chairs, walking around inside, going outside, dressing, bathing, using the toilet, and controlling bowel movements or urination. There are seven potential IADLs: preparing meals, doing laundry, doing light housework, shopping for groceries, keeping track of bills and handling cash, taking medicine, and making telephone calls.

Additional respondents were added to the survey in 1984, to make it more representative of the nation at that time. Since there is no information for these people on health or living status in 1982, we do not include them in the sample.

and discrimination between Medicaid and non-Medicaid patients in nursing home admissions (Ettner 1991).

The NLTCS reinterviewed these individuals in 1984, obtaining 5,795 complete responses. The 1984 reinterview had three components: a community questionnaire for those not institutionalized (4,182 persons), a separate questionnaire for those institutionalized (414 persons), and a questionnaire answered by the next of kin for those who had died (1,199 persons).

Total nursing home utilization is the sum of utilization for the three types of people. Since everyone in the nursing home in 1984 was admitted in the preceding two years, this group automatically counts as nursing home users. Determining use among the other two groups is more difficult. We use two selection criteria. First, we include people who reported entering (or whose next of kin reported that the person entered) a nursing home after the survey month in 1982. Second, we included people who reported having been in a nursing home before the 1984 survey but who had never been in a nursing home prior to the 1982 survey, even if the person did not know the specific date of nursing home entry. While this undoubtedly underestimates the extent of nursing home utilization, there is no other alternative given these data.

To provide some evidence on the types of nursing home use, table 11.5 shows the distribution of nursing home use by status in 1984. All told, almost 15 percent of the people were admitted to a nursing home between 1982 and 1984. As the third column shows, however, the distribution of nursing home stays appears bifurcated between short-term stayers (those who return to the community shortly or die) and long-term stayers (those still in the nursing home or who die without returning to the community). About 4.5 percent of the community residents in 1984 had used a nursing home in the intervening two years, and over 20 percent of those who were dead in 1984 used a nursing home prior to death. These two groups thus account for about one-half of nursing home spells over the two-year period. Past research has emphasized the size of this short-stay population in evaluating the importance of Medicaid spenddown for nursing home residents (Liu and Manton 1989).

To control for individual determinants of nursing home use, we use a variety of demographic characteristics drawn from past studies.[22] The characteristics are of three types. First, we include demographic information on the individual: sex, age, race (white or nonwhite), number of children (number truncated to five), and an indicator for not being married. Past research has suggested that older individuals are more likely to enter a nursing home, as are women and whites (Garber and MaCurdy 1989). People without children are also more likely to enter a nursing home, as are people who are not married (Wan and Weissert 1981).

Second, we use financial data: income of the disabled person and spouse (if

---

22. See Hanley et al. (1990) and Garber and MaCurdy (1989) for more discussion of these factors.

Table 11.5   Characteristics of Nursing Home Use by Status, 1984

| | Sample Population | | Nursing Home Use | |
	Number	Percentage of Total	Percentage with Some Use	Percentage of Total Use
Status in 1984				
In community	4,182	72.2	4.5	21.9
In nursing home	414	7.1	100.0	48.2
Dead	1,199	20.7	21.4	29.9
Total	5,795	100.0	14.8	100.0

married), whether the person owns a home, and total dividend and interest income (which is also included in total income). We interpret the coefficient on dividend and interest income as a measure of wealth, independent of income flow. Past research has suggested that individuals with lower incomes are more likely to be admitted to a nursing home (Cohen, Tell, and Wallick 1986), although private-pay patients may have above average income (Scanlon 1980). Home owners appear substantially less likely to enter a nursing home (Garber and MaCurdy 1990). Asset income is generally positively related to nursing home admission (Hanley et al. 1990).

Finally, we use a number of indicators of health status: the number of times the person was in the hospital in the year prior to the survey, whether the person has any IADLs, the number of ADLs the person has,[23] the number of prior times the person has been in the nursing home, whether the person has ever had a stroke, and whether the person has ever had a broken hip. Past research has suggested that the probability of nursing home admission increases with measures of functional disability and poor physical or mental health (Cohen et al. 1986; Shapiro and Tate 1988).

Table 11.6 shows summary statistics for the individual characteristics. From the sample of 45 states discussed above, we omit people without adequate income data.[24] The resulting sample is 4,374 persons. The average age is almost 77 years, and the sample is dominated by women (two-thirds of the sample) and whites. Average income is just over $8,000, with about $700 in dividend and interest income. About 58 percent of the people own their own house, an estimate close to that in Sheiner and Weil (1991). Finally, the group is less healthy than the elderly population at large. The average number of hospital visits in the past year is over one-half, with an average of one-tenth of a stay in a nursing home. Over 7 percent of the population has had a stroke, and over 2 percent a broken hip.

23. This specification for IADLs and ADLs is similar to that in Hanley et al. (1990).
24. We excluded persons if they refused to answer questions about Social Security income, pension income, or other annuity income for themselves or their spouse.

Table 11.6   **Summary Statistics for Individual Characteristics**

Variable	Mean
Demographics	
Male	37.1%
Age	77
White	86.6%
Number of children	2.4
Financial status	
Total income	$8,036
Home owner	58.2%
Dividend/interest income	$691
Health status	
Hospital use	.573
Any IADLs	89.8%
Number of ADLs	1.88
Prior nursing home use	.093
Stroke	7.1%
Broken hip	2.0%

Note: Each row is based on 4,374 observations for which all data are available.

11.5.2   Factors Affecting Aggregate Nursing Home Utilization

To examine the determinants of nursing home utilization, we estimate logit models for any nursing home use over the two-year interval. The dependent variable is the log odds of the probability that a person was admitted to a nursing home between 1982 and 1984. The independent variables are the individual and state factors noted above. Denoting the probability of nursing home use as p_i^{nh}, the probability of no use $p_i^{no\ use}$ ($= 1 - p_i^{nh}$), and the individual characteristics as $\mathbf{X}_i$, the equation we estimate is of the form:

$$(1) \qquad \log(p_i^{nh}) - \log(p_i^{no\ use}) = \mathbf{X}_i \times \boldsymbol{\beta} + \gamma_1 \times \text{MEDNEED}_j + \gamma_2 \times \text{UNDPAY}_j + \varepsilon_i,$$

where i denotes the individual and j is the state in which the individual resides.

Our explanatory variables are all from the 1982 survey. If patient characteristics change over time (such as marital or health status), one might want to allow for these changes. An alternative approach is thus to use data from 1984 as the explanatory variables.[25] Unfortunately, data on changes in demographic status are not generally available for those who were dead in 1984. Further, the data do not permit us to examine the timing of health status changes and nurs-

---

25. Alternatively, one might specify a hazard model of nursing home entry and incorporate the nursing home admissions of those who subsequently died. Since there are no data on individual characteristics between 1982 and 1984, however, the hazard models could not allow for time variation in the individual characteristics. We thus use the simpler logit formulation.

ing home use for those who are alive in 1984. We thus use the 1982 data to measure individual characteristics.

Table 11.7 reports estimates of the probability of nursing home use as a function of the state and individual characteristics. The first three columns report the results with the state policy variables included individually; the last two columns include the state policies jointly. In all of the equations, the individual characteristics are very important in explaining nursing home use. Older people are more likely to enter a nursing home, as are whites and people with fewer children. Given health and demographic characteristics, men are less likely to enter a nursing home than are women, although this result is not statistically significant.[26] Being married has no effect on the probability of nursing home entry conditional on health and demographic factors.

Richer people are less likely to enter a nursing home than are poor people, as are people who own a house, although only the latter finding is statistically significant. In equations without the health and demographic characteristics (not reported), richer people are statistically significantly less likely to enter a nursing home than are poorer people, with a coefficient twice as large as the reported coefficients.[27] This finding suggests that at least some of the explanatory power of income in predicting medical care use is related to underlying health or attitudes toward nursing homes, rather than an exogenous effect of income. People with greater dividend and interest income are more likely to enter a nursing home, although this result is also not statistically significant. The dichotomy between home ownership and financial wealth suggests that the two are not substitutable in the nursing home decision.

Almost all of the health status measures are significantly related to nursing home use, in the expected direction. Individuals with IADLs are more likely to enter a nursing home than are those without, as are individuals with greater numbers of ADLs. Having had a stroke is also positively and statistically significantly related to subsequent use. Prior nursing home use or having suffered a broken hip are associated with greater nursing home use, although these results are not statistically significant.

The coefficients on the state policy variables support the hypothesis that these policies are important determinants of nursing home use. The presence of a medically needy program is positively related to nursing home use (col. [1]). To evaluate the magnitude of the coefficient (and the state policies throughout the paper), we evaluate the change in the probability of nursing home use for a "typical" elderly individual.[28] The estimates imply that adding

26. Hanley et al. (1990) reach similar conclusions about the relative entry probability of men and women.
27. With just the financial variables included in the equation, the coefficient on income is −.027 (.010).
28. The individual is female, aged 75–79, white, with two children, and married. Total family income is $8,000, with $700 of dividend and interest income. The person owns her own home. The person had one hospital visit in the past year, at least one IADL, and two ADLs. The person had not suffered a stroke or broken hip.

Table 11.7   **Predictions of Nursing Home Use by the Elderly—Dependent Variable: Any Use of Nursing Home, 1982–84**

Independent Variable	Equation				
	(1)	(2)	(3)	(4)	(5)
State policy					
Medically needy	.199**	–	–	.261**	.249**
	(.093)			(.095)	(.096)
Medicaid underpayment	–	−.032**	–	−.034**	−.036**
		(.010)		(.011)	(.011)
Home care waiver	–	–	−.094	−.094	−.095
			(.090)	(.092)	(.092)
Demographics					
Male	−.086	−.088	−.082	−.092	−.155
	(.109)	(.109)	(.109)	(.109)	(.110)
Age 70–74	.434**	.441**	.443**	.431**	.434**
	(.179)	(.179)	(.178)	(.179)	(.179)
Age 75–79	.764**	.764**	.761**	.760**	.723**
	(.172)	(.172)	(.172)	(.172)	(.173)
Age 80–84	1.010**	1.007**	1.015**	.997**	.958**
	(.173)	(.173)	(.173)	(.173)	(.174)
Age 85+	1.225**	1.227**	1.233**	1.206**	1.141**
	(.174)	(.174)	(.174)	(.175)	(.176)
White	.773**	.771**	.803**	.738**	.750**
	(.163)	(.163)	(.163)	(.164)	(.164)
Number of children	−.169**	−.175**	−.172**	−.174**	−.173**
	(.026)	(.026)	(.026)	(.027)	(.027)
Not married	.055	.068	.065	.061	.056
	(.126)	(.126)	(.126)	(.126)	(.127)
Financial status					
Total income	−.013	−.009	−.010	−.011	−.011
	(.011)	(.011)	(.011)	(.011)	(.011)
Home owner	−.255**	−.296**	−.277**	−.282**	−.290**
	(.099)	(.099)	(.098)	(.099)	(.100)
Dividend/interest income	.024	.020	.021	.023	.024
	(.021)	(.021)	(.021)	(.021)	(.021)
Health status					
Hospital use	.062	.058	.059	.063	.036
	(.044)	(.044)	(.044)	(.044)	(.045)
Any IADLs	1.032**	1.065**	1.044**	1.056**	1.038**
	(.258)	(.258)	(.258)	(.259)	(.259)
Number of ADLs	.111**	.108**	.107**	.113**	.099**
	(.022)	(.022)	(.022)	(.022)	(.023)
Prior nursing home use	.103	.109	.108	.106	.115
	(.076)	(.077)	(.078)	(.077)	(.079)
Stroke	.393**	.415**	.405**	.411*	.392**
	(.154)	(.154)	(.154)	(.154)	(.155)
Broken hip	.111	.081	.109	.086	.154
	(.269)	(.271)	(.269)	(.270)	(.271)
Dead in 1984	–	–	–	–	.460**
					(.105)

(*continued*)

Table 11.7   (continued)

Independent Variable	Equation				
	(1)	(2)	(3)	(4)	(5)
Change in probability of use (percentage points)					
Medically needy	2.49	–	–	3.31	2.92
Medicaid underpayment	–	−1.71	–	−1.71	−1.64
Home care waiver	–	–	−1.16	−1.05	−.99
Number of observations	4,374	4,374	4,374	4,374	4,374
Log likelihood	−1,651	−1,649	−1,653	−1,645	−1,635

Note: The table reports logit equations for the probability of nursing home use as a function of demographics, financial and health status, and state policy variables. Standard errors are in parentheses.

*Indicates that variable is statistically different from zero at 10 percent level.

**Indicates that variable is statistically different from zero at 5 percent level.

a medically needy program increases the probability of nursing home use by about 2.5 percentage points over the two-year period. Since about 15 percent of the disabled elderly entered a nursing home over the two-year period, this change is over 15 percent of the mean utilization rate, a reasonably large effect. This finding suggests both that nursing home demand increases when more people are eligible for the subsidy and that either bed supply is not effectively constrained or state bed supply policy is responsive to anticipated increases in demand. To the extent that bed supply is a constraint on utilization, however, the coefficient on the medically needy variable is then an underestimate of the true effect on demand.

The Medicaid underpayment rate is negatively and statistically significantly related to nursing home use (col. [2]). A one standard deviation increase in the Medicaid underpayment amount ($4.6 per day) lowers the probability of nursing home utilization by about 1.7 percentage points. Finally, the existence of a home care waiver program has no effect on nursing home use (col. [3]). Because home care waivers do not predict nursing home utilization, we drop this policy variable from the remainder of the analysis.

Column (4) shows the results with all three state policy measures included in the equation. The coefficients are roughly the same, indicating that the medically needy and Medicaid underpayment amounts both affect utilization. Evidently, the policy effects are not just picking up some unmeasured aspect of demand that is correlated with both policy variables.

Column (5) includes a measure of ex post health status—whether the person was dead in 1984—to account for unobserved variation in underlying health. As table 11.5 indicated, individuals are substantially more likely to have used a nursing home between 1982 and 1984. Controlling for individual characteristics, people who are dead in 1984 are substantially more likely to have used a nursing home. The coefficients on the policy variables, however, are essentially unchanged in this specification. To the extent we can control for patient heterogeneity, therefore, such heterogeneity does not appear to explain our results.

We also experimented with a variety of other predictors of nursing home use. One important measure is an indicator of senility. Garber and MaCurdy (1989) show that elderly displaying signs of senility are much more likely to use a nursing home than those without these signs. Adding an indicator for senility did predict nursing home use,[29] but had little effect on the coefficients on state policy. Since not all people were given the same test for senility, we do not report these results.

In addition, we estimated equations including state factors such as the number of days of snow in the major city in the state. Areas with more snow are likely to be less hospitable for disabled elderly attempting to live in the community. The measure of the amount of snow was positively and statistically significantly related to nursing home use in the absence of the state policy variables. Including the policy variables, however, substantially reduced the coefficient on the amount of snow, and the resulting estimate was statistically insignificantly different from zero.[30] The coefficients on the medically needy variable were smaller in this specification, with a larger standard error, while the coefficient on the Medicaid underpayment was essentially unchanged. States seem to choose to have medically needy programs when the value of nursing home care is high.

11.5.3   State Policies and Nursing Home Composition

The effects of state policies on the composition of nursing home residents may be as large as those on the total number of admissions. In particular, when states have medically needy programs, it is likely that middle income and disabled individuals will have a greater demand for nursing home care. If nursing home bed supply does not increase as much as demand, then lower income individuals are likely to find access to nursing home care more difficult.

Similarly, Medicaid underpayments could also affect the mix of patients. When nursing home payment is limited, nursing homes could choose to ration according to a "first-come, first-served" rule. In this case, there is no reason to expect that supply constraints would affect the mix of patients. However, if nursing homes ration their beds in order to maximize profits, it is likely that poorer and sicker individuals will have their access to nursing home beds reduced more severely than will other individuals.

To examine this issue in more detail, we distinguish people along two di-

---

29. The coefficient on an indicator for senility is .517 (.137).
30. Without policy controls, the coefficient on days of snow was .0083 (.0024). With the bed supply included, the coefficient on snow days declined to .0047 (.0031).

mensions: financial status (income below \$5,000 or above \$10,000)[31] and health status (more than two ADLs).[32] We then interact these variables with the state policies. Our equation is of the form

$$
\begin{aligned}
\log(p_i^{hh}) - \log(p_i^{no\ use}) = \mathbf{X}_i * \boldsymbol{\beta} + \gamma_2 \times UNDPAY_j + (\gamma_1 + \delta_1 \\
\times LOWINC_i + \delta_2 \times HIGHINC_i + \delta_3 \times HIGHADL_i) \\
\times MEDNEED_j + \varepsilon_i.
\end{aligned}
$$

(2)

Interaction terms (the coefficients δ) which are not statistically distinguishable from zero would indicate that the policies have uniform effects on the elderly. Conversely, interaction terms that are different from zero indicate that some groups are more affected by state policies than others, and that the composition of nursing home users varies with changes in state policies.

Table 11.8 shows the estimates of these interaction equations. We begin with the equation in column (5) of table 11.7, although without the home care measure. The first column of table 11.8 examines the interactions with the medically needy policy variable. The upper panel of the table reports the coefficients on the interaction terms δ_k. The second panel reports the coefficients on the state policy variables γ_k. The other independent variables are included in the equation but are omitted from the table for convenience.

The last panel reports the change in the probability of nursing home use for five typical people. The first three vary by income: low income (\$4,000 in family income), middle income (\$8,000 in family income), and high income (\$12,000 in family income). The last two differ in the number of ADLs: low ADLs (one ADL) and high ADLs (three ADLs).[33] The entry in each row is the change in the probability of nursing home use for that group resulting from the addition of a medically needy program.

Being in a state with a medically needy program increases the likelihood of nursing home utilization for middle- and high-income individuals, but not for low-income individuals. The estimates suggest that medically needy programs increase the probability of nursing home use by over 2 percentage points for middle- and upper-income individuals, but reduce it only slightly, by 0.21 percentage points, for low-income individuals. Clearly, there is an aggregate expansion in nursing home beds in states with a medically needy program.

The coefficient on the interaction between the medically needy variable with the disability dummy variable is positive and large, but insignificantly different from zero. The increased probability of nursing home use due to the medically needy program is 2.1 percentage points for individuals with fewer than 2 disabilities, but 5.5 percentage points for those with more ADLs. This potentially

31. In 1982, the poverty rate was \$4,626 for single elderly and \$5,836 for couples. The low-income indicator is thus close to a measure of poverty among the elderly.

32. We experimented with a variety of other measures as well, including the other financial and health status measures. The results with these two variables were the most consistent of the equations.

33. In each case, we keep the other characteristics the same as in table 11.7.

Table 11.8   **Interactions of State Policies in Nursing Home Use—Dependent Variable: Use of Nursing Home, 1982–84**

Independent Variable	Equation		
	(1)	(2)	(3)
Interaction terms			
Income < $5,000	−.222	–	.077
	(.140)		(.195)
Income ≥ $10,000	.089	–	.125
	(.170)		(.241)
ADLs > 2	.230	–	.232
	(.160)		(.181)
Medicaid underpayment			
Income < $5,000	–	−.033**	−.037**
		(.011)	(.015)
Income ≥ $10,000	–	.013	.007
		(.014)	(.019)
ADLs > 2	–	.010	.000
		(.015)	(.017)
State policy			
Medically needy	.203	.197**	.047
	(.134)	(.095)	(.162)
Medicaid underpayment	−.039**	−.035**	−.029**
	(.014)	(.013)	(.015)
Change in probability of use (percentage points)			
Medically needy			
Low income	−.21	–	1.19
Middle income	2.25	–	.53
High income	3.15	–	1.94
Low ADLs	2.13	–	.50
High ADLs	5.49	–	3.60
Medicaid underpayment			
Low income	–	−2.49	−2.47
Middle income	–	−1.61	−1.39
High income	–	−1.03	−1.03
Low ADLs	–	−1.51	−1.32
High ADLs	–	−1.36	−1.49
Individual controls	Yes	Yes	Yes
Number of observations	4,374	4,374	4,374
Log likelihood	−1,633	−1,630	−1,629

Note: The table reports logit equations for nursing home use. Each column interacts the state policies with income and the number of ADLs. Standard errors are in parentheses.

*Indicates that variable is statistically different from zero at 10 percent level.

**Indicates that variable is statistically different from zero at 5 percent level.

suggests that medically needy programs offer a greater subsidy to the more disabled relative to the less disabled.

Column (2) of table 11.8 examines the interactions of income and ADLs with the Medicaid underpayment variable. In states with a greater Medicaid underpayment, the poor suffer much larger decreases in access than do middle- or high-income individuals. The effect is large and statistically significant. A one standard deviation increase in Medicaid underpayment results in a 2.5 percentage decline in nursing home utilization for those with low incomes, a 1.6 decline for those with middle incomes, and a 1 percentage point decline for high-income individuals. This is consistent with the hypothesis that nursing homes discriminate in filling their beds. On the other hand, we find no evidence of discrimination against individuals with more disabilities. The impact of the Medicaid underpayment variable is essentially independent of health status.

Column (3) of table 11.8 includes the interactions with both state policies. These equations need to be interpreted with some caution because of the high correlation between the different interaction terms. The standard errors in column (3) are much larger than in the previous two columns. Including the medically needy interactions does little to the coefficients on the Medicaid underpayment interactions. The estimates still suggest large discrepancies between the utilization of nursing homes by the poor and by those with higher incomes.

In contrast, the interactions between the medically needy variable and income become smaller. In column (3), both high- and low-income people appear to utilize nursing homes more in the presence of a medically needy program. Evidently, some of the explanatory power of the medically needy variable in column (1) comes from its correlation with the Medicaid underpayment. There is still evidence that people with more ADLs are more likely to be admitted to a nursing home in states with a medically needy program. The estimates suggest a differential of about 3 percentage points, although this result is not statistically significantly different from zero.

11.6   What is the Marginal Source of Community Care?

Because the elderly live either in nursing homes or in the community, it is clear that when nursing home utilization increases, community living decreases. In this section, we try to determine whether one form of community living is more responsive to state policies than others. The substitution of different types of community care for nursing home care is fundamental to concerns about moral hazard in nursing home provision. If nursing homes are viewed by the elderly or their children as a last resort, then improving access to nursing homes might reduce the number of elderly who are living alone without other sources of care. On the other hand, if nursing homes are not viewed in this dire light, then improving access might lead many elderly who currently receive informal help from family and friends to seek nursing home care. This could result in either an extremely expensive program or, if nursing home supply is severely restricted, long queues and potentially inefficient nursing home rationing.

11.6.1   Community Living Responses to State Policies

The upper panel of table 11.9 shows living arrangements of the elderly in 1984. We divide living arrangements into three types: living in a nursing home (9.0 percent), living alone or with a spouse only, which we term receiving no help (62.7 percent), and living with children or others (28.2 percent).[34] The last category predominantly involves children (about two-thirds of the cases), with the remainder involving siblings, "other relatives," and "other nonrelatives."[35] The fact that nursing home use is so low, even among the disabled elderly, is the source of much of the moral hazard concern. Even policies that lower the share of people in the community by a small amount will increase aggregate institutionalization rates substantially. On the other hand, the fact that almost two-thirds of the elderly live alone or with a spouse only has led some to suggest that adequate long-term care is lacking for many of the elderly.

There are two ways for community living to respond to state policies. The first is the "mathematical" response that must occur when nursing home use responds to state variables—as more people live in a nursing home, fewer people will live in the community. The community response may be greater than this response, however, if people in the community change their behavior in anticipation of future nursing home access. For instance, in states with large bed supplies, children may not bother to have their parents move in with them when the parents begin to need help, anticipating than when severe disability occurs, the parents will enter a nursing home. Similarly, children anticipating difficulty in procuring nursing home access for their parents may react to the onset of disability by making alternative arrangements right away. In this case, increases in nursing home access would lead to increased probabilities of living alone, rather than reductions in this probability.

To examine the substitution of nursing home and community living arrangements, we estimate equations for the probability of the elderly being in each living arrangement. We model living status as a multinomial choice, a natural extension of our earlier logit models for nursing home use. Letting $p_i^{\text{no help}}$ be the probability of living without help and p_i^{kid} be the probability of living with children or others, we assume that:

---

34. These living arrangements need not be mutually exclusive. Some individuals will live both with a spouse and with children, for example. To facilitate the empirical work, however, we have defined people who live with any other people to be in the third category. The results are similar if we use broader definitions of the living arrangements and estimate logit models for each type of living arrangement separately.

35. We have experimented with separating children from the other groups and found similar results. We group them together here both because the amount of nonchild living arrangements are relatively small and because we suspect errors in some of the records (e.g., some people report living with grandchildren but do not mention living with children).

Table 11.9   Measures of Living Status and Help Received

Measure	Number	Percent
Living Status in 1984		
In nursing home	414	9.0%
No help	2882	62.7%
With children or others	1298	28.2%
Total	4596	100%
Use of Helpers in 1984		
Some paid help	1043	22.7%
Substantial paid help	404	8.8%
Some help from children	1799	39.1%
Substantial help from children	963	21.0%
Total	4596	100%

Correlation of Paid Help and Help From Children

	Some Help From Children	
Some Paid Help	No	Yes
No	60%	40%
	[76%]	[79%]
Yes	63%	37%
	[24%]	[21%]

Note: The table shows the living status of the elderly and use of helpers in 1984. In the last panel, the first number in each cell is the percentage of people in that row who are in that column. The second number (in brackets) is the percentage of people in each column who are in that row.

$$
(3) \quad
\begin{aligned}
\log(p_i^{nh}) - \log(p_i^{no\ help}) &= \mathbf{X}_i \times \boldsymbol{\beta}^{nh} + \gamma_1^{nh} \times \text{MEDNEED}_j + \gamma_2^{nh} \\
&\times \text{UNDPAY}_j + \varepsilon_i^{nh}, \\
\log(p_i^{kid}) - \log(p_i^{no\ help}) &= \mathbf{X}_i \times \boldsymbol{\beta}^{kid} + \gamma_1^{kid} \\
&\times \text{MEDNEED}_j + \gamma_2^{kid} \times \text{UNDPAY}_j + \varepsilon_i^{kid}.
\end{aligned}
$$

We use the same set of individual characteristics as in the earlier equations, except we omit the measure of home ownership, since this is likely to be endogenous to the chosen living arrangement.[36] Presumably, individual demographic, financial, and health status are less influenced by living status than is the home ownership decision. All of the variables in the regression are measured as of 1982.

Table 11.10 presents estimates of the determinants of living arrangements, including all three policy variables. The coefficients on the individual charac-

36. Since our sample is of people alive in 1984, we omit the indicator for death over the two years.

Table 11.10   **Living Status of Elderly—Dependent Variables: Living Status in 1984 (probability relative to no help)**

	Entire Sample			Nonmarried Sample		
Independent Variable	Nursing Home (1)	Children or Other (2)	p-Value (1)=(2)	Nursing Home (3)	Children or Other (4)	p-Value (3)=(4)
State policy						
Medically needy	.070	.029	.769	.020	−.020	[.799]
	(.134)	(.087)		(.153)	(.103)	
Medicaid	−.017	.018*	.029	−.021	.020*	[.018]
underpayment	(.015)	(.010)		(.017)	(.012)	
Demographics						
Male	−.043	.206**		.225	.206	
	(.164)	(.103)		(.197)	(.132)	
Age 70–74	.537**	−.204		.693**	.019	
	(.267)	(.130)		(.326)	(.166)	
Age 75–79	.853**	−.051		.751**	.071	
	(.261)	(.131)		(.319)	(.162)	
Age 80–84	1.134**	−.091		1.067**	.080	
	(.260)	(.139)		(.312)	(.166)	
Age 85+	1.657**	.526**		1.538**	.627**	
	(.264)	(.144)		(.310)	(.169)	
White	.524**	−.790**		.545**	−.739**	
	(.251)	(.116)		(.278)	(.135)	
Number of children	−.149**	.164**		−.163**	.116*	
	(.039)	(.023)		(.044)	(.027)	
Not married	.776**	1.405**		−	−	
	(.179)	(.117)				
Financial status						
Total income	−.027	−.023**		−.044**	−.040**	
	(.017)	(.011)		(.021)	(.015)	
Dividend interest	.017	−.027		.075*	−.017	
income	(.032)	(.029)		(.043)	(.040)	
Health status						
Hospital use	.065	−.044		.114	−.012	
	(.073)	(.052)		(.093)	(.065)	
Any IADLs	1.329**	.027		1.404**	.347*	
	(.426)	(.148)		(.471)	(.185)	
Number of ADLs	.205**	.139**		.241**	.186**	
	(.033)	(.023)		(.040)	(.028)	
Prior nursing home	.141	.105		.104	.087	
use	(.098)	(.094)		(.098)	(.094)	
Stroke	.576**	.190		.567**	.204	
	(.230)	(.181)		(.284)	(.225)	
Broken hip	.055	−.296		−.137	−.335	
	(.350)	(.305)		(.408)	(.333)	

(*continued*)

Table 11.10   (continued)

| | Change in Probability (percentage points) | | | | | |
| | Entire Sample | | | Nonmarried Sample | | |
	Nursing Home	No Help	Children or Other	Nursing Home	No Help	Children or Other
Medically needy	.48	−.70	.22	.28	.23	−.51
Medicaid underpayment	−.59	−.27	.86	−1.31	−1.12	2.44
Number of observations		3,477			2,112	
Log likelihood		−2,610			−1,880	

Note: The table reports logit equations for the probability of different living arrangements as a function of demographics, financial and health status, and state policy variables. No help is defined as living with a spouse only or living alone. Standard errors are in parentheses.

*Indicates that variable is statistically different from zero at 10 percent level.

**Indicates that variable is statistically different from zero at 5 percent level.

teristics indicate that older and sicker people are relatively more likely to live in nursing homes than without help. There is some evidence (but less uniform) that these people are also more likely to live with their children or others as well. Having more children significantly increases the probability of living with them and decreases the probability of living in a nursing home.

Unmarried people are substantially more likely to live in a nursing home or with others than are married people. This contrasts with table 11.7, where there was no increase in the probability of any nursing home use for these people. The primary difference between the measure of nursing home use here and that in table 11.7 is that the "any use" measure in table 11.7 includes many more shorter-duration stays than the point-in-time measure in table 11.10. At a single point in time, many more people in a nursing home will have been in for a long time, even if the share of stays which are of short duration is large. Apparently, unmarried people are much more likely to have long-duration rather than short-duration nursing home stays. Higher-income people are significantly less likely to live with children or others, perhaps because they are more likely to have paid help, or because their children are less likely to invite them in, given that they can afford paid help.

The first row of table 11.10 examines the effects on living status of being in a medically needy state. Unlike the findings in table 11.7, the elderly are no more likely to live in a nursing home in a medically needy state than in a non–medically needy state. As noted above, this measure of nursing home use is weighted toward longer durations than the "any use" variable used in table 11.7.

One possible interpretation of the different effects of the medically needy variable is that the medically needy program increases demand more for short nursing home stays than for long nursing home stays. In medically needy states, individuals need only spend current income on nursing home care (assuming they meet the asset test). In non–medically needy states, however, if a person's income is too high for Medicaid but lower than the nursing home price, they must sell their assets (such as their house) in order to afford nursing home care. People who anticipate returning to the community after a short nursing home stay may be less willing to do this than people anticipating living in the nursing home until they die. Alternatively, because there are fewer individuals in a nursing home in 1984 than individuals who used a nursing home between 1982 and 1984, it may be harder to pick up the effects of the medically needy program.

The second row of table 11.10 reports the effects of the Medicaid underpayment on living status. As in table 11.7, the lower the Medicaid underpayment, the more likely is living in a nursing home. The coefficient on living in a nursing home is not significantly different from the probability of receiving no help but is significantly different from the probability of no help or living with children. In addition, the lower the underpayment, the greater the probability of living with one's children. Reducing the underpayment by one standard deviation raises the probability of living in a nursing home by 0.6 percentage points, lowers the probability of living with children by 0.9 percentage points, and actually raises the probability of living without help by 0.3 percentage points. Evidently, there is some additional change in living status away from children and toward living alone in states with smaller underpayment amounts.

Columns (3) and (4) of table 11.10 repeat these regressions for a sample of nonmarried elderly. The results are quite similar, and the effect of the Medicaid underpayment is even stronger. Lowering the Medicaid underpayment by one standard deviation raises the probability of living in a nursing home by 1.3 percentage points, lowers the probability of living with children by 2.4 percentage points, and raises the probability of living with no help by 1.1 percentage points. Thus, there is some evidence that increasing access to nursing homes by reducing the Medicaid underpayment amount would not only encourage individuals to live in nursing homes rather than with their children, but would also encourage individuals to live alone rather than with their children.

The finding that individuals living in states with low Medicaid underpayments are less likely to live with their children is consistent with the moral hazard interpretation. However, the result may also be due to differences in underlying health status. Because the people living with their children may be sicker or more disabled than those living alone, they may be more likely to demand nursing home care when access is increased. Because we include so many health status variables in the regression, this interpretation seems unlikely to be correct.

A second question about these results concerns the interpretation of the coefficient on living with children. Because we are looking at net flows rather than gross flows, we may miss some response to state policies. For example, if reducing the Medicaid underpayment caused individuals living alone to move into the nursing home, but also caused individuals living with their children to live alone, one would observe an increased probability of nursing home use, a reduced probability of living with children, and possibly no change in the probability of living alone. Unfortunately, we have no way to sort out gross and net flows with our data.

As with the earlier equations, it is important to consider the interactions of the state policies with personal characteristics, to evaluate the effects of these factors on people with different incomes and health statuses. Table 11.11 presents the results of these interactions, and table 11.12 reports point estimates of the change in living arrangements for five typical individuals, using the results from equation (3) in table 11.11.

The coefficients on the medically needy variable are difficult to interpret. The estimates suggest that the poor are more likely to live with their children than are the middle- or high-income elderly. This might be consistent with the hypothesis that the poor's access to nursing home care is reduced in medically needy states, except that the poor are also more likely to be in a nursing home. Similarly, while the rich are more likely to be in nursing homes in medically needy states, they are no less likely to live with their children. Finally, the interaction between the medically needy variable and the number of ADLs indicates that, in medically needy states, it is harder for the sick to gain access to nursing homes. This is opposite to the result in table 11.8.

The interactions with Medicaid underpayment are more consistent with the earlier results. In states with high underpayments, the poor's access to nursing homes is limited more than is the access of middle- and high-income individuals. As before, the marginal source of care appears to be children. When Medicaid underpayment increases by one standard deviation, the probability of living with children increases 1.4 percentage points for the poor, 0.6 percentage points for the middle-income group, and 0.3 percentage points for the high-income group. This finding is consistent with nursing homes discriminating against poorer individuals when underpayments are higher. As in the previous equations, we find no evidence of an interaction between Medicaid underpayment and ADLs.

11.6.2   Helper Response to State Policies

Living with one's children or others is not the only way of receiving community care. As shown in table 11.9, many of the elderly living in the community have helpers for at least some tasks (22.7 percent), and even more receive some help from their children (39.1 percent).[37] The NLTCS also asks questions about

---

37. People living in nursing homes are defined as receiving no paid help and no help from children.

Table 11.11   **Interaction of State Policies in Living Status Equations—Dependent Variable: Living Status in 1984**

	Equation					
	(1)		(2)		(3)	
Independent Variable	Nursing Home	Children or Others	Nursing Home	Children or Others	Nursing Home	Children or Others
Interaction terms						
Medically needy						
Income < $5,000	.207	.448**	–	–	.436	.358**
	(.200)	(.134)			(.275)	(.184)
Income ≥ $10,000	.113	.100	–	–	.315	.135
	(.258)	(.175)			(.367)	(.446)
ADLs > 2	−.300	.162	–	–	−.357	.101
	(.235)	(.164)			(.265)	(.186)
Medicaid underpayment						
Income < $5,000	–	–	−.003	.028**	−.025	.011
			(.015)	(.010)	(.021)	(.013)
Income ≥ $10,000	–	–	.002	−.001	−.016	−.009
			(.021)	(.014)	(.029)	(.019)
ADLs > 2	–	–	−.004	.017	.012	.013
			(.022)	(.015)	(.025)	(.017)
State policy						
Medically needy	.113	−.222*	.068	.062	−.026	−.157
	(.197)	(.121)	(.135)	(.088)	(.235)	(.151)
Medicaid underpayment	−.016	.020**	−.014	.003	−.006	.014
	(.015)	(.010)	(.018)	(.012)	(.020)	(.013)
Individual controls	Yes		Yes		Yes	
Number of observations	3,477		3,477		3,477	
Log likelihood	−2,603		−2,605		−2,601	

*Indicates that variable is statistically different from zero at 10 percent level.
**Indicates that variable is statistically different from zero at 5 percent level.

how many days of help each source provided in the week preceding the survey. We define substantial help as help of three days or more in the previous week. Almost 9 percent of people receive substantial paid help, and 21 percent receive substantial help from children.

While many people living with their children receive substantial help from them (70 percent), this is not always the case. Further, some people living alone or with a spouse receive substantial help from their children (6 percent). The measure of help from children is thus an independent measure of the provision of informal community care.

The bottom panel of table 11.9 presents the correlations between paid help and help from children. The two forms of community care do not appear to be substitutes. For example, 37 percent of those receiving paid help also receive help from children. In contrast, 40 percent of those not receiving paid help

Table 11.12   **Interactions of State Policies in Living Status—Dependent Variable: Living Status in 1984**

Independent Variable	Nursing Home (1)	No Help (2)	Children or Others (3)
Change in probability (percentage points)			
Medically needy			
Low income	2.94	−4.72	1.78
Middle income	−.07	1.42	−1.35
High income	1.96	−1.57	−.38
Low ADLs	−.07	1.33	−1.26
High ADLs	−3.10	3.27	−.17
Medicaid underpayment			
Low income	−.97	−.42	1.39
Middle income	−.26	−.37	.63
High income	−.59	.34	.25
Low ADLs	−.21	−.37	.58
High ADLs	.09	−1.42	1.32

Note: The table reports the predicted change in living status from a one standard deviation increase in bed supply or underpayment rates, or adding a medically needy program, on the probability of any nursing home use. The estimates are based on equation (3) of table 11.11.

receive help from children. Similarly, those elderly receiving help from children are no less likely to receive paid help than those not receiving help from children.

To examine the responsiveness of the probabilities of receiving paid help and help from children to state policies, we estimate logit model for each type of help. We estimate the equations separately since there is no natural link between the different measures of help. Table 11.13 presents the results.

Generally the elderly who receive help have the same characteristics as those who are likely to be in nursing homes. Older and sicker people have substantially increased probabilities of receiving both types of help. Having more children is associated with a lower probability of receiving paid help, but a higher probability of receiving help from children. Higher-income people are more likely to use paid help, but less likely to receive help from their children.[38]

Again, we find that children are the marginal source of community care. We find no significant effect of state policies on the use of paid help, but large effects on the probability of receiving substantial help from children. In states with medically needy programs, the elderly are 0.9 percentage points less likely to receive any help from their children and 2.1 percentage points less likely to receive substantial help. Similarly, increasing the Medicaid underpayment amount by one standard deviation is associated with a 0.5 percentage point increase in the probability of receiving any help from children and a 2.1 percentage point increase in the probability of receiving substantial help.

---

38. This finding contradicts the finding in Bernheim, Shleifer, and Summers (1985) that children of rich parents are more attentive to them.

Table 11.13   **Use of Helpers by Elderly—Dependent Variable: Use of Help in 1984**

Independent Variable	Paid Help		Help from Children	
	Any (1)	Substantial (2)	Any (3)	Substantial (4)
State policy				
Medically needy	.056	−.047	−.043	−.271**
	(.088)	(.136)	(.082)	(.097)
Medicaid underpayment	−.006	.003	.006	.041**
	(.010)	(.015)	(.009)	(.011)
Demographics				
Male	−.324**	−.085*	−.447**	−.227*
	(.104)	(.162)	(.097)	(.122)
Age 70–74	.255*	.278	.160	.089
	(.137)	(.241)	(.124)	(.164)
Age 75–79	.412**	.631**	.319**	.355**
	(.139)	(.234)	(.127)	(.160)
Age 80–84	.573**	.787**	.610**	.667**
	(.143)	(.237)	(.133)	(.161)
Age 85+	.395**	.810**	.786**	1.200**
	(.154)	(.247)	(.141)	(.163)
White	.248*	.329	.039	−.185
	(.135)	(.219)	(.121)	(.132)
Number of children	−.179**	−.096**	.507**	.375**
	(.025)	(.038)	(.024)	(.026)
Not married	.388**	.440**	.881**	1.144**
	(.111)	(.175)	(.106)	(.137)
Financial status				
Total income	.027**	.028**	−.010	−.023*
	(.009)	(.012)	(.010)	(.014)
Dividend/interest income	−.019	−.018	−.008	−.022
	(.018)	(.026)	(.023)	(.036)
Health status				
Hospital use	.106**	.095	.013	−.036
	(.048)	(.072)	(.048)	(.058)
Any IADLs	.312**	.184	.847**	.862**
	(.160)	(.269)	(.151)	(.226)
Number of ADLs	.085**	.151**	.033	.107**
	(.022)	(.033)	(.022)	(.024)
Prior nursing home use	.031	.003	−.111	−.102
	(.055)	(.079)	(.100)	(.119)
Stroke	.143	.063	.230	.400**
	(.174)	(.254)	(.170)	(.183)
Broken hip	−.154	−.077	−.434	−.425
	(.274)	(.391)	(.281)	(.334)
Change in probability (percentage points)				
Medically needy	1.01	−.32	−.85	−2.12
Medically underpayment	−.48	.09	.51	1.79
Number of observations	3,477	3,477	3,477	3,477
Log likelihood	−1,736	−881	−1,890	−1,447

(*continued*)

Table 11.13   (continued)

Note: The table reports logit equations for the probability of use of helpers as a function of demographics, financial and health status, and state policy variables. Substantial use is defined as utilization of more than three days in the preceding week. Standard errors are in parentheses.
*Indicates that variable is statistically different from zero at 10 percent level.
**Indicates that variable is statistically different from zero at 5 percent level.

To test the effects of state policies on different types of people, we again interact the state policies with income and the number of ADLs. We consider only the equations for substantial help from children, since the largest effects are found for this measure. The results are presented in table 11.14.

Being in a medically needy state reduces the probability of receiving help from children for all the elderly. The lowest income group is the least affected, however, and the high-income group is the most affected. This is consistent with the interpretation that the demand for nursing home care is increased more for the higher-income groups than for the lower-income groups. We also find that children's help is reduced relatively more for those with fewer disabilities, although this effect is not statistically significant.

The Medicaid underpayment amount has the expected effects on the different elderly groups. Increasing the Medicaid underpayment barely affects the amount of help high-income people receive, but has large effects on amount of help lower- and middle-income individuals receive. Once again, this is consistent with a story of discrimination against low-income individuals. Similarly, the point estimates suggest some discrimination against those with many ADLs, although the effect is small and statistically insignificant.

Column (3) of table 11.14 includes all the interactions. The coefficients are similar to the regression when the interactions are included individually. The estimates suggest large differences by age, with the medically needy variable substantially affecting care provided by children of high-income elderly and the Medicaid underpayment amount affecting care provided by children of low-income elderly. The results in table 11.14 thus strongly confirm the moral hazard interpretation of the aggregate results.

11.7   Conclusions

Government policies have a substantial effect on the utilization of nursing homes by the elderly. Policies such as the ability to spend down income and receive government support and the relative payment levels of Medicaid programs affect both the overall rate of nursing home utilization and the distribution of elderly who are institutionalized. In states with more liberal spenddown rules, the richer elderly are more likely to utilize a nursing home than are the poorer elderly. Similarly, in states with larger price differentials, the poor elderly receive substantially less nursing home utilization.

Table 11.14   **Interaction of State Policies in Substantial Help from Children—Dependent Variable: Substantial Help from Children in 1984**

Independent Variable	Equation		
	(1)	(2)	(3)
Interaction terms			
Medically needy			
Income < $5,000	.099	–	.064
	(.147)		(.202)
Income ≥ $10,000	−.382*	–	−.226
	(.233)		(.308)
ADLs > 2	.235	–	.194
	(.178)		(.202)
Medicaid underpayment			
Income < $5,000	–	.009	.007
		(.011)	(.014)
Income ≥ $10,000	–	−.032*	−.021
		(.017)	(.023)
ADLs > 2	–	.017	.008
		(.016)	(.018)
State policy			
Medically needy	−.340**	−.260**	−.323*
	(.136)	(.098)	(.171)
Medicaid underpayment	.042**	.037**	.040**
	(.011)	(.013)	(.015)
Change in probability (percentage points)			
Medically needy			
Low income	−2.03	–	−2.20
Middle income	−2.66	–	−2.53
High income	−4.71	–	−3.30
Low ADLs	−2.48	–	−2.38
High ADLs	−.97	–	−1.24
Medicaid underpayment			
Low income	–	2.19	2.20
Middle income	–	1.61	1.76
High income	–	.18	.68
Low ADLs	–	1.52	1.66
High ADLs	–	2.87	2.42
Individual Controls	Yes	Yes	Yes
Number of Observations	3,477	3,477	3,477
Log Likelihood	−1,444	−1,445	−1,444

Note: The table reports coefficients from interaction terms in logit equations for substantial help from children. The sample is elderly alive in 1984. Standard errors are in parentheses.

*Indicates that variable is statistically different from zero at 10 percent level.

**Indicates that variable is statistically different from zero at 5 percent level.

The marginal source of community care for people in a nursing home appears to be care from children and others. Estimates suggest that all of the elderly admitted to nursing homes when policies change formerly lived with their children or with others. In addition, changes in state policies affect the share of elderly who receive substantial help from their children on a regular basis. The view that the marginal nursing home admission is an elderly person living alone and without other means of support does not appear true in our data. Rather, the fact that moral hazard in nursing home admissions appears to be pervasive suggests that governments are justified in only cautiously expanding the set of people eligible for public funding of nursing home care.

These results are particularly important because the distribution of the elderly population is likely to change substantially over the next half century. Between 1990 and 2020, the percentage of women aged 85 and over without any living children is projected to fall from 22 percent to 10 percent (Wolfe et al. 1991; Advisory Council on Social Security 1991). A number of people have suggested that the coming decrease in childless elderly will substantially reduce demand for nursing home care (Rivlin and Weiner 1988). Indeed, the results presented earlier indicate that people with more children are substantially less likely to use a nursing home than those with fewer children. As the number of childless elderly falls, however, the moral hazard risk will increase. To the extent that nursing homes are substitutes for care from children, a reduction in the share of childless elderly reduces the "deserving" elderly population relative to the total population. In future years, subsidies to nursing home care may have more of an effect on care provided by children, and less of an effect on the childless elderly.

Indeed, these results suggest exploring policies targeted only to the childless elderly, rather than to the entire elderly community. For the childless group, nursing home demand is high and the loss from moral hazard is low. It is interesting, in this light, that the German system of long-term care explicitly counts income of children as resources to be spent on the elderly. The results here suggest greater exploration of this type of program in the United States, as well.

References

Advisory Council on Social Security. 1991. Income security and health care: Economic implications 1991–2020. Washington, D.C.: Advisory Council on Social Security.
Bernheim, B. Douglas, Andrei Shleifer, and Lawrence H. Summers. 1985. The strategic bequest motive. *Journal of Political Economy* 93:1046–76.
Carpenter, Letty. 1988. Medicaid eligibility for persons in nursing homes. *Health Care Financing Review* 10 (Winter): 67–77.
Carroll, Christopher D., and Lawrence H. Summers. 1991. Consumption growth parallels income growth: Some new evidence. In *National saving and economic perfor-*

mance, ed. B. Douglas Bernheim and John B. Shoven, 305–43. Chicago: University of Chicago Press.

Cohen, Marc A., Eileen J. Tell, and Stanley S. Wallack. 1986. Client-related risk factors of nursing home entry among elderly adults. *Journal of Gerontology* 24:785–92.

Cutler, David M. 1992. Why doesn't the market fully insure long-term care? Harvard University, June. Mimeograph.

Deaton, Angus. 1989. Saving in developing countries: Theory and review. Paper prepared for the First Annual World Bank Conference on Economic Growth, Washington, D.C.: World Bank.

Diamond, Peter. 1977. A framework for social security analysis. *Journal of Public Economics* 8:295–98.

Doty, Pamela. 1988. Long-term care in international perspective. *Health Care Financing Review* (annual suppl.): 145–55.

———. 1990. A comparison of long-term care financing in the U.S. and other developed nations—dispelling some myths. *Generations* 14, (Spring): 10–14.

Ettner, Susan. 1991. Do elderly Medicaid patients experience reduced access to nursing home care? Harvard Medical School. Mimeograph.

Feldstein, Martin. 1987. Should Social Security benefits be means tested? *Journal of Political Economy* 95:468–84.

Garber, Alan M., and Thomas MaCurdy. 1990. Predicting nursing home utilization among the high-risk elderly. In *Issues in the Economics of Aging,* ed. D. Wise, 173–200. Chicago: University of Chicago Press.

———. 1991. Nursing home discharges and exhaustion of Medicare benefits. NBER Working Paper no. 3639. Cambridge, Mass.: National Bureau of Economic Research, March.

General Accounting Office. 1990. Nursing homes: admission problems for Medicaid recipients and attempts to solve them. GAO/HRD-90-135, September.

Gertler, Paul J. 1989. Subsidies, quality, and the regulation of nursing homes. *Journal of Public Economics* 38 (February): 33–53.

Hanley, Raymond J., Maria B. Alecxih, Joshua M. Wiener, and David L. Kennell. 1990. Predicting elderly nursing home admissions. *Research on Aging* 1 (June): 199–228.

Hubbard, R. Glenn, Jonathan Skinner, and Stephen P. Zeldes. 1992. Precautionary saving and social insurance. The Wharton School, University of Pennsylvania. Mimeograph.

Kane, Robert A., and Rosalie L. Kane. 1985. *A will and a way: What the United States can learn from Canada about caring for the elderly.* New York: Columbia University Press.

Kemper, Peter, and Christopher M. Murtaugh. 1991. Lifetime use of nursing home care. *New England Journal of Medicine* 324:595–600.

Lazenby, Helen, and Suzanne Letsch. 1990. National health expenditures, 1989. *Health Care Financing Review* 2 (Winter): 1991.

Little, Jane Sneddon. 1992. Lessons from variations in state Medicaid expenditures. *New England Economic Review,* Federal Reserve Bank of Boston (January/February): 43–66.

Liu, Korbin, Teresa Coughlin, and Timothy McBride. 1991. Predicting nursing-home admission and length of stay. *Medical Care* 29:125–41.

Liu, Korbin, Pamela Doty, and Kenneth G. Manton. 1990. Medicaid spenddown in nursing homes. *Gerontologist* 30:7–15.

Liu, Korbin, and Kenneth G. Manton. 1989. The effect of nursing home use on Medicaid eligibility. *Gerontologist* 29:59–66.

Liu, Korbin, Kenneth G. Manton, and Barbara Marzetta Liu. 1990. Morbidity, disability, and long-term care of the elderly: Implications for insurance financing. *Milbank Quarterly* 63:445–92.

Manton, Kenneth G. 1988. A longitudinal study of functional change and mortality in the United States. *Gerontologist* 43:S153–S161.

Neuschler, Edward, and Claire Gill. 1986. Medicaid eligibility for the elderly in need of long-term care. Congressional Research Service Publication no. 86-26, Washington, D.C.: CRS.

Newman, Sandra J., Raymond Struyk, Paul Wright, and Michelle Rice. 1990. Overwhelming odds: Caregiving and the risk of institutionalization. *Journal of Gerontology* 5:S173–83.

Norton, Edward C. 1992. Towards a theory of nursing home admissions. Harvard Medical School, March. Mimeograph.

Price, Richard, Richard Rimkunas, and Carol O'Shaughnessy. 1990. Characteristics of nursing home residents and proposals for reforming coverage of nursing home care. Congressional Research Service Report, September 24.

Rivlin, Alice M., and Joshua M. Weiner. 1988. *Caring for the disabled elderly: Who will pay?*, Washington, D.C.: Brookings Institution.

Rowland, D., B. Neuman, A. Salganicoff, and L. Taghavi. 1988. Defining the functionally impaired elderly population. Washington, D.C.: AARP Policy Institute, November.

Scanlon, William. 1980. A theory of the nursing home market. *Inquiry* 17: (Spring): 25–41.

Schwab, Teresa. 1989. *Caring for an aging world.* New York: McGraw-Hill.

Shapiro, Evelyn, and Robert Tate. 1988. Who is really at risk of institutionalization? *Gerontologist* 28:237–45.

Sheiner, Louise M., and David N. Weil. 1992. The housing wealth of the aged. NBER Working Paper no. 4115. Cambridge, Mass.: National Bureau of Economic Research.

Wan, Thomas T. H., and William G. Weissert. 1981. Social support networks, patients status, and institutionalization. *Research on Aging* 3:240–56.

Wolfe, D., V. Freedman, B. Soldo, and E. Stephen. 1991. Intergenerational transfers: A question of perspective. Washington, D.C. Population Studies Center, Urban Institute. Mimeograph.

Comment on Chapters 10 and 11   Jonathan Feinstein

The papers by David Cutler and Louise Sheiner and by Andrew Dick, Alan Garber, and Thomas MaCurdy examine several different aspects of long-term care. The two papers address interesting and related issues, but they do so in very different ways, reflecting the different styles of the authors. Since both papers are concerned with policy-relevant issues, it is useful, in evaluating the contributions of each paper, to keep in mind the broad socioeconomic facts and policy alternatives which frame the current debate about long-term care in the United States. In what follows I first very briefly describe this larger context. I then discuss each paper in greater detail. Finally, I conclude my discussion by returning to the broader context, suggesting some general orientations which may help guide future research in this area.

Jonathan Feinstein is associate professor of economics at the Yale School of Organization and Management and a research associate of the National Bureau of Economic Research.

Overview of the Socioeconomic Context

As is described in some detail in earlier papers in this volume, the United States is faced with an aging population: there are increasing numbers of elderly, and the life expectancy of each elderly person is steadily increasing, in recent decades at the rate of nearly two years every decade.[1] As life expectancy increases among the elderly, we can expect that the number of years a typical elderly person spends while afflicted with significant impairments of daily living will at least remain constant, and may well increase. In addition, many elderly experience and can be expected to continue to experience periods of limitation interspersed with periods of relative health, a life pattern which is of especial concern to Dick, Garber, and MaCurdy in their paper. As has also been well documented by earlier papers at this conference, the elderly are also consuming an increasing share of national expenditures, especially because of increases in their health-care costs.

In considering appropriate policy responses to these statistics, three issues strike me as especially salient. First, we must consider options for long-term care as part of the larger set of issues concerning elderly living arrangements. Though long-term care is most commonly pictured as arising within a life history in which an elderly person lives in his or her own home and moves to a nursing home when significantly impaired, in fact the actual pattern of mobility is often more complex than this, encompassing movements in and out of hospitals, the provision of at-home care by family members, paid at-home care, retirement communities, and life care facilities. Any policy which affects any one of these living and health-care options implicitly affects the others as well.

Second, many issues of long-term care involve other family members. On the one hand, family members may be the main alternative source of care to nursing home care or residence in a life care facility. On the other hand, of that portion of long-term care expenditures which are financed out-of-pocket, most are implicitly being taken from a later bequest. Hence the incentives, abilities, and opportunity costs-of-time of family members are important aspects of many long-term care debates.

Third, much more attention needs to be paid to political economy arguments in assessing current long-term care configurations and the usefulness of proposed policies. Well-entrenched nursing home, hospital, and other interest groups can exert a powerful impact on policies and outcomes. I return to each of these points several times in the subsequent discussion, and in my concluding comments.

Detailed Discussion of Dick, Garber, and MaCurdy

The paper by Dick, Garber, and MaCurdy specifies a careful econometric model of transitions into and out of nursing homes, estimates the model, and

---

1. As Jim Vaupel and Burt Singer have emphasized in some of these earlier papers, great uncertainty attaches to the actual increase in the dependency ratio and life expectancy over the next 100 years or more.

uses the estimates to simulate the distribution of cumulative nursing home utilization. In discussing the paper, I will first argue that the results may be of broader usefulness than the authors appear to realize and will then review the paper's methodology and results, suggesting some possible weaknesses.

In their paper, Dick, Garber, and MaCurdy argue that the distribution (not just the mean or per capita level) of individual cumulative nursing home utilization over the life span contains important information for policy. They also point out that, if appropriate data were available, calculating this distribution would be relatively straightforward. Perhaps the best data for this exercise would be the complete set of nursing home records on each of a random sample of deceased individuals. Unfortunately, such data is not available. As an alternative, the authors adopt an indirect approach, combining data from the National Nursing Home Survey and the National Long-Term Care Survey to estimate a complete Markov transition model of entry into and out of nursing homes over the life span, and then using their estimates to reconstruct an estimate of the cumulative distribution of nursing home utilization. This is a clever approach and yields some very useful estimates and projections.

The authors present their model as being almost entirely motivated by the desire to recover the distribution of cumulative utilization. While I agree that this distribution is important for policy, it is worth asking whether the more detailed estimates of this paper, including the estimates of transitions in and out of nursing homes, of the durations of first and subsequent nursing home spells and first and subsequent (what they call return) community spells, and of exit probabilities, have independent interest. It seems to me that these various estimates do have interest, for at least three reasons. First, the elderly experience significant mobility costs. As a ballpark figure, about one-half of all moves by the elderly result in serious physical or psychological deterioration, involving disorientation and loss of attachment. Such costs arise not only when the elderly move to a nursing home, but also in a move from a nursing facility to a home or hospital, and in most other kinds of moves. Since each move has a cost, the overall welfare of an elderly person who experiences a given cumulative amount of nursing home care will differ depending on whether that care arose in one long stay or two or more shorter stays. Thus if policy is designed around considerations of welfare, the pattern of moves is relevant.

Second, the kinds of living arrangements which are appropriate for the elderly upon discharge from a nursing home depend in part on how long the elderly can be expected to stay in the community before either dying or moving back to a nursing home. Again, the Dick, Garber, and MaCurdy estimates can provide evidence on this issue.

Finally, should a viable long-term care insurance market emerge, the contracts sold in this market could conceivably be structured so as to change rates or renegotiate the terms of insurance following a first nursing home stay, in a fashion analogous to the way automobile insurance is updated following an accident. If such contracts were written, information about multiple spells would be important for calibrating insurance rates and evaluating the welfare consequences of a given insurance package.

Although the Dick, Garber, and MaCurdy estimates are of considerable interest, it seems to me that the most interesting part of these estimates is also the most difficult to estimate with the data they use. Their estimates of nursing home spell durations and exit probabilities are only of mild interest: for the most part these estimates simply confirm the findings of earlier work, including the raw data tables in the National Nursing Home Survey compendium itself. In contrast, their estimates of the duration and outcome of first community spells is somewhat new, and their estimates of the duration and outcome of return community spells is to my knowledge the first of its kind. However, these latter two sets of estimates are more problematic than the former.

Regarding initial community spells, note the following. Most of these spells are quite long. Unfortunately, however, the data which Dick, Garber, and MaCurdy use to estimate these spells cover only a 28-month window (from 1982 to 1984), which is why the majority of these spells which are ongoing as of 1982 are still ongoing (and thus censored) as of 1984. As a result, to get an adequate estimate of the duration of first community spells, the authors must rely extensively on retrospective data, which is inherently less reliable. Further, since retrospective data is being relied on more for the longer spells than the shorter, one must worry about possible biases creeping into the estimate of the duration distribution.

Return community spells are typically short, and therefore censoring is less of a problem in estimating a duration distribution for these. However, there are fewer than 500 return spells recorded in the data; while this quantity is undoubtedly enough to estimate exit probabilities and crude duration probabilities, it is probably not enough to precisely estimate a detailed duration distribution, particularly once covariates are taken account of.

I will mention two further issues related to the Dick, Garber, and MaCurdy results. First, because data on hospitalizations is not recorded in the data being used, the empirical results do not incorporate hospitalization spells into the analysis; this is unfortunate, since many transitions into and out of nursing homes come from hospitals, particularly those which end in death. If hospitalization data were available over the 1982–84 time period, it could presumably be folded into the analysis.

Second, the authors use a flexible spline procedure to control for duration dependence and some covariates. This is a nice procedure, well explained in the paper and presumably quite flexible. However, one thing the authors do not do is provide a tight characterization of the statistical properties of these splines. In particular, they do not provide any sensitivity analysis which might indicate why they chose the number of spline terms they did, and they do not provide any theorem or statement of how their spline families might converge toward a more fully nonparametric analysis (that is, they do not show that the collection of splines they are using could in the limit generate a legitimate nonparametric analysis).

Toward the end of the Dick, Garber, and MaCurdy paper, useful simulations are presented which summarize the findings of the paper for predicting cumulative nursing home utilization. I believe even more could be done here. For example, the authors could shed interesting light on the "end of life" controversy, by computing what proportion of total utilization happens in the last year or two of life. They might also be able to say something about how morbidity may be expected to change in response to an increase in life expectancy. Overall, this is a useful, interesting, and well-executed paper.

Detailed Discussion of Cutler and Sheiner

The paper by Cutler and Sheiner is stylistically opposite to the work of Dick, Garber, and MaCurdy. Where Dick, Garber, and MaCurdy focus on one specific issue, Cutler and Sheiner explore a wide range of topics, often in novel and interesting ways. While Dick, Garber, and MaCurdy devote a good deal of attention to econometric modeling, Cutler and Sheiner fit rather simple models and instead emphasize institutional detail. In my discussion of the Cutler and Sheiner work, I will first voice some reservations about certain of their premises. Then I will discuss their results, suggesting that these are highly suggestive and potentially quite valuable, but not fully convincing as currently developed.

In the beginning of their paper, Cutler and Sheiner argue that moral hazard is an important issue in nursing home entry and policy development. I find their argument about moral hazard somewhat implausible; accordingly, I will briefly criticize their discussion and suggest some alternative considerations.

Cutler and Sheiner seem to be suggesting that elderly individuals may choose to enter a nursing home unnecessarily whenever financial (and lifestyle) considerations make this an attractive option; based on this view, Cutler and Sheiner argue throughout the paper that financial reimbursement for nursing home care is susceptible to abuse and must be carefully monitored.

In fact, there is not much direct evidence that the elderly themselves unnecessarily enter nursing homes (I consider the evidence in this paper largely indirect; see below). On the contrary, there are several pieces of evidence which indicate that the elderly do not and should not desire to enter a nursing home except when absolutely necessary. First, as I mentioned in the context of the Dick, Garber, and MaCurdy paper, the elderly experience high mobility costs and will rarely move if they can avoid it. Second, recent work has revealed that nursing homes are rather undesirable places to be. For example, a number of recent articles have publicized the fact that anywhere from 20 to 50 percent of all nursing home residents are physically restrained at some point during their stay in the nursing home (see the general discussion in Burton et al. 1992)—hardly an enticement to entry! Further, inspections of nursing homes in California and elsewhere have frequently uncovered substandard health conditions and poor living conditions. While not all nursing homes are unpleasant, it is hard to believe that most elderly would willingly move to one unless it seems necessary. Taking all of these arguments into account, I believe it is hard to argue that the elderly enter nursing homes for their "entertainment" value, as is stated early in the paper. In fact, the only group of elderly for which unnecessary entry seems even remotely plausible are the extreme poor (who would have nursing home stays subsidized by Medicaid), who are not by and large the target of most of the policy debates (such as those about cost sharing) relevant to the material in this paper.

To the extent that moral hazard among the elderly is a problem, states have established preadmission screening guidelines (see Jackson, Eichorn, and Blackman 1992); these guidelines do vary significantly across states and would be a natural set of variables to include in the models of this paper.

If moral hazard is a problem, it is probably not associated with the elderly themselves, but with two related groups. One group are nursing home operators. As Cutler and Sheiner remark, several recent studies, including one by Edward Norton, have shown that, when a vacant bed opens up, nursing homes will often pass over Medicaid or indigent patients for a significant period of time in the hope of attracting a private-pay patient. The other group are the elderly's family relatives, especially children, who must care for the elderly who remain in the community. Of course, if moral hazard by either of these two groups leads to excessive entry into nursing homes, this problem should be addressed; doing so, however, would require more complex models than those developed in this paper (involving game theory or multiperson decision theory rather than single-person decision theory).

Cutler and Sheiner present interesting evidence on the way in which long-term care costs are financed in various developed countries. They argue, I think persuasively, that in most countries these costs are usually shared between the elderly person's household and either insurance or state funds, in contrast to acute care costs, which in most countries are nearly wholly insurance or state financed.

I have three comments about this evidence. First, in thinking about the differences between long-term care and acute care, it occurs to me that differences in the stage of life at which these costs are incurred may go some way toward explaining why different kinds of insurance may be optimal. Acute care may be required at almost any stage in the life cycle, but is often needed when a person is younger, has dependents, and therefore has considerable demands on his or her financial resources (this of course is not entirely true, since some modest fraction of costs are spent in the last year or two of life and a significant amount of costs are spent on individuals over aged 65). Because of these differences, I would expect acute care costs to be almost wholly insured. In contrast, long-term care occurs predominantly at the end of life, when, other than for bequests, an individual may have only moderate needs (again, this is not wholly true, since the individual may have a living spouse). Thus long-term care costs may not need to be insured to the same degree as acute care costs. This argument is essentially one about the form of the utility function at different stages of the life cycle. If it is correct, it suggests two things: first, that long-term care should not be fully insured, and second, that children may be an important beneficiary of any insurance which is offered.

My second comment is simply that long-term care insurance contracts could be formally modeled using the sort of set-up first developed by Laffont and Tirole, in which cost sharing emerges as the equilibrium solution. My final comment on long-term care insurance is that such insurance is beginning to emerge, spurred on by state programs (see the article in the *New York Times,* May 3, 1992). It would be of considerable interest to explore the form this insurance is taking, and the role of state governments in promoting it.

I now turn to a short discussion of Cutler and Sheiner's results. Cutler and Sheiner focus on the variation across states in nursing home beds per capita, in the eligibility requirements for reimbursement for nursing home costs, and in the difference between Medicaid reimbursement rates and actual nursing home costs. They use data from the National Long-Term Care Survey to estimate logit models of the likelihood of a person of given characteristics entering a nursing home and, later in the paper, use this data to estimate multinomial logit models of a broader range of care arrangements, including nursing home care, paid at-home care, and family at-home care.

I found the results presented in this paper extremely interesting, in large part because they raise a host of relevant new issues. Especially interesting are the attempt to link state policies to nursing home entry decisions, the effort to study the interaction between state policies and such socioeconomic variables as income, and the multinomial logit models which estimate the relationship between nursing home utilization and home health care.

However, there are a number of serious problems with how the models have been specified, which lead me to believe that the results are only suggestive and not conclusive. One problem relates to one of the key variables in the study, the number of nursing beds per 1,000 population. At first glance, it is hard to understand why such a variable should be included in a model of nursing home entry, and it is especially hard to interpret the result that entry is more likely when this variable is larger. Obviously, if more nursing home beds are available in a state, an individual will be more likely to enter a nursing home bed, since these beds are in general occupied. In fact, if nursing home beds were always occupied, I am not sure there would be any behavioral interpretation for this variable. Since there is some slight vacancy rate (but it is truly slight), which may vary across states with the number of beds per capita, it is possible for this variable's coefficient to have a behavioral interpretation. Nonetheless, it is the price of nursing home utilization which will determine occupancy, and this poses problems for the specification used, for several reasons. First, nursing home price is not itself included in these models—the closest thing is the differential between price and Medicaid reimbursement rates, which is not quite the same. Second, even in the same state, different individuals will face different prices, depending on their eligibility; as far as I can tell, this problem is not directly addressed, though the models which interact state variables with income may do a reasonable job of capturing this effect. Finally, not all nursing homes charge the same price—presumably, price varies with quality; data which matched individuals to specific nursing homes would thus be considerably more useful.

A second problem with the models is that they implicitly attribute all variations in nursing home utilization across states to the three measured state policy variables. I believe this is quite misleading. There are many unmeasured characteristics of states which may explain both the choice of state variables and individual behavior. Because these characteristics are not included in the model, they may lead to biased estimates of the coefficients on characteristics which are included.

Let me be slightly more precise about this last point. Support that there is a characteristic h which varies across states; for example, h might be the percentage of the population which is urban, the liberal–conservative ranking of the state, or any other characteristic which is likely to affect the need for and attitude toward nursing homes. In state j, h is distributed in the population according to the density function $g_j(h)$. Individual i in state j has characteristic h_i, which is, again, drawn from distribution $g_{j(i)}(h)$. The variable h can exert two distinct kinds of effects. On the one hand, for individual i, h_i may affect the likelihood that i enters a nursing home. On the other hand, in the aggregate the voters in a state may choose a nursing home policy to reflect their preferences; if, for example, $g_j(h)$ has median $\bar{g}_j$, nursing home policy in state j may be a function of $\bar{g}_j$, following the median voter rule.

These two points can be made more precise as follows. First, suppose that the correct formulation of nursing home entry decisions is that

$$Y_i^* = X_i\beta + s_{j(i)}\gamma + h_i,$$

$$Y_i = 1 \text{ (enter)} \quad \text{if } Y_i^* \geq 0,$$

$$Y_i = 0 \quad \text{else,}$$

where X_i are the individual's characteristics and $s_{j(i)}$ are the state policies in the state in which i resides. Cutler and Sheiner have omitted the term h_i. Further, they have implicitly assumed that the expectation of h_i is zero or constant across all states. In fact, however, since g_j varies across states, the expectation of h_i will also vary. As a result, this model is misspecified. Since it is a logit model, it is easy to show that the standard theorems related to misspecified maximum likelihood models apply and that in general all coefficient estimates will be biased. The biases will be especially severe for γ, since $s_{j(i)}$ presumably depends on $\bar{h}_{j(i)}$, which is correlated with h_i.

Second, a more complete model would specify the determination of the state policy rules, s_j, jointly with individuals' decisions about nursing home entry. These two equations would be linked by the distribution $g(h)$, which is (it is hoped) exogenous and which is therefore a better candidate for the variation in nursing home practices across states.

Having made all of these criticisms, I must emphasize that the results of Cutler and Sheiner are very interesting, because they raise new issues, many of which are important in the debate about long-term care. It is my hope that in further work some of the shortcomings I have identified can be addressed.

Concluding Comments

In conclusion, let me return to the broad picture of long-term care statistics and policy and make a few general remarks. First, in evaluating alternative long-term care policy options, it must be recognized that any policy directed at some one option implicitly affects all the other alternatives. Thus, for example, a nursing home spenddown rule which protects elderly assets can implicitly affect the home health-care and life care industries. Ultimately, I hope researchers will be able to estimate models which incorporate the full range of living arrangements and health-care options, leading to estimates of the substitutibility among these options.

Second, political economy can offer an important perspective on long-term care. A good example of the power of interest groups to influence policy has been the recent struggle in Florida between retirement communities and nursing homes. Inhabitants of retirement communities have "aged in place" and now wish to construct modest nursing home facilities. Their attempt to do so has been stymied (at least as of this writing) by the Florida nursing home industry, which probably fears the competition which might result from a less regulated environment.

References

Burton, Lynda C., Pearl S. German, Barry W. Rovner, Larry J. Brant, and Rebecca D. Clark. 1992. Mental illness and the use of restraints in nursing homes. *Gerontologist* 32 (2): 164–70.

Jackson, Mary E., Ann Eichorn, and Donald Blackman. 1992. Efficacy of nursing home preadmission screening. *Gerontologist* 32 (1): 51–57.

New York Times. 1992. Medicaid plan promotes nursing-home insurance. Sunday, May 3.

Contributors

B. Douglas Bernheim
Department of Economics
Princeton, University
Princeton, NJ 08544

Axel Börsch-Supan
Department of Economics
University of Mannheim
Postfach 10 34 62
D-68131 Mannheim 1
Germany

David M. Cutler
President's Council of Economic
    Advisers
Old Executive Office Building, Room
    311
Washington, DC 20500

Angus S. Deaton
221 Bendheim Hall
Woodrow Wilson School
Princeton University
Princeton, NJ 08544

Peter Diamond
Department of Economics
Massachusetts Institute of Technology
50 Memorial Drive, Room E52-344
Cambridge, MA 02139

Andrew Dick
Public Policy Analysis Program
Department of Political Science
University of Rochester
Rochester, NY 14627

Jonathan Feinstein
Yale School of Organization and
    Management
Yale University
Box 1A
New Haven, CT 06520

Alan M. Garber
National Bureau of Economic Research
204 Junipero Serra Boulevard
Stanford, CA 94305

Michael D. Hurd
Department of Economics
SUNY, Stony Brook
Stony Brook, NY 11794

Edward P. Lazear
Graduate School of Business
Stanford University
Stanford, CA 94305

Robin L. Lumsdaine
Department of Economics
Princeton University
Princeton, NJ 08544

Hans Lundström
Statistics Sweden
Stockholm
Sweden S-11581

Thomas A. MaCurdy
Department of Economics
Stanford University
Stanford, CA 94305

N. Gregory Mankiw
Department of Economics
Littauer 223
Harvard University
Cambridge, MA 02138

Kenneth G. Manton
Center for Demographic Studies
Duke University
2117 Campus Drive
Durham, NC 27706

Daniel McFadden
Department of Economics
655 Evans Hall
University of California, Berkeley
Berkeley, CA 94707

Christina H. Paxson
Department of Economics
Princeton University
219 Bendheim Hall
Princeton, NJ 08544

James M. Poterba
Center for Advanced Study in the
    Behavioral Sciences
202 Junipero Serra Boulevard
Stanford, CA 94305

John Rust
Department of Economics
Social Science Building
University of Wisconsin
1180 Observatory Drive
Madison, WI 53706

Louise M. Sheiner
Federal Reserve System
Board of Governors
Stop 83
Washington, DC 20551

John B. Shoven
Department of Economics
Stanford University
Encina Hall
Stanford, CA 94305

Burton H. Singer
Department of Epidemiology and Public
    Health
Yale University
60 College Street
New Haven, CT 06510

Jonathan Skinner
Department of Economics
Rouss Hall
University of Virginia
Charlottesville, VA 22901

James P. Smith
Rand Corporation
1700 Main Street
Santa Monica, CA 90407

Eric Stallard
Center for Demographic Studies
Duke University
2117 Campus Drive
Durham, NC 27706

James H. Stock
Kennedy School of Government
Harvard University
79 Kennedy Street
Cambridge, MA 02138

Michael D. Topper
Department of Economics
College of William and Mary
Williamsburg, VA 23185

James W. Vaupel
Odense University Medical School
Winsløwparken 17,1
DK-5000 Odense C
Denmark

Steven F. Venti
Department of Economics
301 Rockefeller Center
Dartmouth College
Hanover, NH 03755

David A. Wise
National Bureau of Economic Research
1050 Massachusetts Avenue
Cambridge, MA 02138

Author Index

Advisory Council on Social Security, 34, 35t, 36t, 432
Ahlburg, D. A., 63, 80
Ai, C., 270, 279
Akerlof, G., 97
Alho, J. M., 73
Ando, Albert, 326
Andrews, Emily, 133
Ashby, J., 81
Attanasio, Orazio, 146, 149
Auerbach, Alan J., 145, 146, 148, 149, 164n10, 291, 312
Ausink, John A., 184

Bagwell, Kyle, 153n3, 174
Barnbrock, Jörn, 314
Barro, Robert J., 153n3, 163n8, 164n9, 174, 306
Becker, Gary S., 153n3, 163, 174
Behring, Karin, 315
Berkman, L., 49
Berkovec, J., 218–19
Bernheim, B. Douglas, 153n3, 170, 172, 173, 174, 175, 176, 428n38
Bishop, Y. M., 47
Blackburn, H., 41
Blackman, Donald, 439
Borjas, George, 154n4
Börsch-Supan, A., 251, 291, 302, 306, 309n13, 311, 314, 315, 319, 320
Boskin, Michael, 226
Bosworth, Barry, 170, 353
Bourgeois-Pichat, J., 81

Branch, L. G., 366
Brody, J. A., 81
Buchanan, James M., 175
Bulow, Jeremy, 184
Burtless, Gary, 170, 353
Burton, Lynda C., 438

Campbell, A. J., 70
Campbell, John Y., 355
Carnes, B. A., 81
Carpenter, Letty, 404n12, 406–7t
Carrington, R. A., 366
Carroll, Christopher, 145, 149, 350, 352, 399
Casmir, Bernd, 295, 297tw
Cassel, C.-M., 74
Cassel, C., 81
Central Council for Savings Promotion, 172
Chang, Ming-cheng, 337
Chesnais, Jean-Claude, 292–93n2
Christiano, Lawrence J., 145
Clarke, R. D., 81
Coale, A. J., 82
Cohen, Marc A., 412
Comfort, A., 81
Consulting Panel on Social Security, 226
Cook, Leah M., 145
Corder, L. S., 67
Coughlin, Teresa, 366, 405
Cox, Donald, 159n6
Crapo, I. M., 81
Cretin, S., 366
Cutler, David M., 397

Darby, Michael, 227
Daula, Thomas V., 211
David, Paul, 359n2
Dawber, T. R., 53
Deaton, Angus, 335, 350, 352, 399
Demeny, P., 79
Diamond, Peter A., 96, 97, 175n1, 227, 397
Doty, Pamela, 400n6, 401t, 402, 410
Dowd, J. E., 51
Drexler, H., 70

Eichorn, Ann, 439
Ellwood, David, 319, 320
Epstein, F. H., 62
Ettner, Susan, 409, 411

Feenberg, Daniel, 116n5, 170
Feinstein, J., 279
Feldman, J. J., 61
Feldstein, Martin, 164nn9,10, 165, 306, 308, 316, 399n5
Fienberg, S. E., 47
Fiore, M. C., 61
Forman, S. H., 82
Frank, J. W., 62
Frerich, Johannes, 297t
Fries, J. F., 79, 80, 81
Frydman, H., 50

Gale, Douglas, 175
Gale, William G., 116n5
Gambill, B. A., 86
Garber, A. M., 394, 407, 411, 412, 417
Gavrilov, L. A., 81
Gavrilova, N. S., 81
Gertler, Paul J., 408
Gill, Claire, 406–7t
Goldberger, A. I., 42
Goldrian, G., 315
Gompertz, B., 81
Gowan, A. E., 79, 81
Grand, A., 70
Gray, R. G., 81
Green, L. W., 81
Guralnik, J. M., 63, 79, 81

Hagemann, Robert P., 291
Haines, P. S., 61, 74
Hall, Robert E., 152, 173
Hammer, Jeffrey, 359n2
Hanley, Raymond J., 410, 411n22, 412, 414n26
Hashimoto, Masanori, 166

Hatsopoulos, George N., 170–71, 173
Haub, C., 229
Hausman, Jerry A., 118n7, 227
Hayashi, Fumio, 164n9
Hayflick, L., 81
Hebel, J. Richard, 139n1
Hendershott, Patric, 170
Henderson, J., 252
Henry, N. W., 47
Hermalin, Albert, 336
Hewitt Associates, 106, 115n4
Higuchi, Yoshio, 166
Holland, P. W., 47
Horiuchi, S., 82
Hubbard, R. Glenn, 399
Hurd, Michael D., 227, 270, 295, 307, 308
Hwan, Y. Dolly, 358

Ioannides, Y., 252

Jackson, Mary E., 439
Jacobs, Klaus, 296
Jette, A. M., 366
Jones, D. W., 366
Jorgenson, Dale W., 165n11, 166, 173

Kahn, R. L., 81
Kane, R. A., 402n8
Kane, R. L., 366, 402n8
Kane, Thomas, 319, 320
Kannisto, V., 82
Kaplan, R. M., 366
Katz, Lawrence F., 150
Keeler, E. B., 366
Kemper, Peter, 366, 393, 399n4
Kennickell, Arthur, 326
Kessler, Denis, 313
Keyfitz, N., 81
Kiefer, J., 47
King, R., 164n10
Kisker, E. E., 82
Kohli, Martin, 296
Kohn, R. R., 81
Kopcke, Richard W., 145
Kotlikoff, Laurence, 145, 146, 148, 149, 164n10, 170, 184, 227, 296, 313, 327
Krugman, Paul R., 170–71, 173
Kusko, Andrea, 132
Kuzma, J. W., 70

Lazarsfeld, P. F., 47
Lazear, Edward P., 154, 184, 301
Lazenby, Helen, 404t

Letsch, Suzanne, 404t
Levine, S., 81
Lewis, M. A., 366
Li, Chi, 336
Lindsted, K. D., 70
Lipsitz, L. A., 42
Little, Jane S., 408
Liu, Korbin, 366, 405, 410, 411
Lo, Joan Chi-chiung, 333, 342
Lohman, P. H. M., 81
Lucas, Robert E., 213
Lumsdaine, R., 184, 185n1, 194, 198, 207, 213

McBride, T., 366
McClellan, Mark, 139n1
McConnel, C. E., 366
McFadden, Daniel, 227, 279, 316
MaCurdy, Thomas A., 394, 407, 411, 412, 417
Mankiw, N. Gregory, 227, 245, 286, 355
Manton, K. G., 43, 44, 46, 47, 49, 50, 52, 66, 67, 79, 81, 86, 91, 410, 411
Marschak, T., 213
Mayo, Stephen K., 314
Mazess, R. B., 82
Medvedev, Z., 43
Mincer, Jacob, 166
Mirrlees, J. A., 175n1
Modigliani, Franco, 353, 355, 360
Moffitt, Robert A., 211
Moore, Robert L., 301
Munnell, Alicia, 145
Murphy, Kevin, 150
Murtaugh, C. M., 366, 393, 399n4
Myers, G. C., 41, 73, 81

National Center for Health Statistics, 41
Neaton, J. D., 62
Neuschler, Edward, 406–7t
Newhouse, Joseph, 139n1
Newman, Sandra J., 407
New York Times, 440
Nicoletti, Giuseppe, 291
Norton, Edward C., 408, 409

Ofstedal, Mary Beth, 336
Oliver, M. F., 62
Olshansky, S. J., 81
Organization for Economic Cooperation and Development (OECD), 291
O'Shaughnessy, Carol, 398
Owen, J. M., 81

Pachon, Alvaro, 165n11, 166
Palmer, Brian, 229
Palmore, E., 366
Parish, S. E., 81
Patterson, R. E., 61, 74
Paxson, Christina, 334–35
Pearl, R., 81
Pearson, K., 81
Peek, Joe, 170
Permutt, Thomas, 139n1
Peto, R., 81
Phelan, C., 217, 218, 219
Popkin, B. M., 61, 74
Poterba, James M., 22, 81, 118n7, 132, 170–71, 173, 227, 265, 287
Price, Richard, 398

Rabushka, Alvin, 358
Ravnskov, U., 62
Ray, Debraj, 174
Rein, Martin, 296
Republic of China, 333, 334
Rimkunas, Richard, 398
Rivlin, Alice M., 396, 397n1, 432
Rosen, K., 227
Rosen, S., 265
Rosenfeld, A., 81
Rosenwaike, I., 82
Rowe, J. W., 81
Rowland, D., 398
Russell, L., 227
Rust, John, 213, 217, 218, 219
Ryder, N. B., 81

Sabelhaus, John, 170, 353
Sacher, G. A., 81
Sala-i-Martin, Xavier, 163n8
Sankaranarayanan, K., 81
Sarndal, C.-E., 74
Scanlon, William, 408, 412
Schatzkin, A., 81
Schmähl, Winfried, 303
Schneider, E. L., 63, 79, 81
Scholz, John Karl, 116n5
Schwab, Teresa, 400n6, 401t
Shapiro, Evelyn, 412
Shefrin, Hersh M., 172
Sheiner, Louise M., 412
Sheshinski, E., 96, 97
Shleifer, Andrei, 153n3, 428n38
Shoven, John, 170, 173, 226, 227
Shryock, H. S., 82
Siegel, J. S., 82

Sims, Christopher, 287n1
Singer, B. H., 43, 49, 50
Skinner, Jonathan, 116n5, 121, 170, 270, 399
Slemrod, Joel, 170
Smeeding, T., 281
Smith, D., 227
Soldo, B. J., 81
Solomon, D. H., 366
Spence, D. A., 366
Spencer, G., 41, 57, 70, 73, 82, 229
Spilerman, S., 50
Spillman, B. C., 366
Stahl, Konrad, 306, 309n13
Stallard, E., 43, 46, 50, 52, 67, 79, 86
Stark, Oded, 175
Stern, N., 97
Stern, Steven, 215, 218–19
Stock, J., 183, 184, 185n1, 209, 213, 301
Summers, Lawrence H., 22, 81, 121, 145, 149,
    152, 153n3, 170, 227, 313, 327, 350,
    360, 399, 428n38

Tate, Robert, 412
Tell, Eileen J., 412
Thaler, Richard H., 172
Tolley, H. D., 47, 49, 79
Tonstad, S., 70
Topel, R., 265
Tsevat, J., 73

U.S. Bureau of the Census, 18, 19t, 20, 22t,
    24f
U.S. Congress: Congressional Research Ser-
    vice, 205n4; Joint Committee on Taxa-
    tion, 169
U.S. Department of Commerce, 229, 237,
    245, 281
U.S. Department of Health and Human Ser-
    vices, 19n3

U.S. General Accounting Office (GAO),
    108n1, 111, 112t, 113, 115n4, 133, 409
U.S. Health Insurance Institute, 205n3
U.S. Social Security Administration, 14n2,
    15t, 22t, 67

Vaupel, J. W., 46, 63, 79, 80, 81, 86
Venti, Steven F., 116n5, 122n8, 125, 139, 173,
    279, 306, 316
Vicente, L., 366
Visaria, Pravin, 334

Wade, A., 41, 73
Wallick, Stanley S., 412
Wan, Thomas T. H., 411
Weil, David, 227, 245, 286, 412
Weissert, William G., 411
Welch, Finis, 150
Weyl, H., 47
Wiener, Joshua M., 366, 396, 397n1, 432
Wilcox, David, 132
Wiley, J. A., 366
Williams, T. F., 74
Wingard, D. L., 366
Wise, David A., 116n5, 122n8, 125, 139, 173,
    183, 184, 185n1, 209, 213, 279, 296,
    301, 306, 316
Wolfe, D., 432
Wolff, Edward N., 308
Wolfowitz, J., 47
Woodbury, M. A., 44, 47, 49, 50, 51, 52, 81
Wretman, J. H., 74

Yanagishita, M., 63, 79
Yashin, A. I., 43, 46

Zeldes, Stephen P., 399

Subject Index

Age distribution: comparison of savings rates in Japan and United States using, 147–50; effect of changes in population, 14–18, 33–34; effect on allocation of government spending, 25–26, 33–34; estimates of over–65 (1900–1940), 237; of income and housing assets, 245–61; of income and housing consumption, 252–54; model of forecast of nursing home use by, 367–72; projections of U.S. population by age (1900–2100), 229–35; Taiwan, 335–38

Aging population: budgetary pressure from, 25–26; comparison of Germany and United States, 292–93; double aging in Germany, 293–95; effect of changing risk factor on forecasts for, 100–102; effect on existing government spending programs, 25–26, 33–34, 36–37; forecasts (2035–2040), 99–100, 225–26; forecasts based on disability variables in dynamic mortality model, 62–73; impact of predictions for size and composition, 225–29; projections, 229, 236–37

Altruism (intergenerational), 154–59

Bequests: as factor in saving behavior: Germany and United States, 327; volume: Germany and United States, 313

Bias: in estimates of age distribution of over–65 population, 237

Capital gains taxation (Germany and United States), 305

Capital markets (Germany and United States), 305–6

Community living: effect of state policy on use of helpers for elderly, 426–30; for elderly people: response to state policy, 420–30; model with policy variables of substitution by elderly of nursing home or, 421–30; residence duration model, 367–88

Consumption: effect of bequest expectation on, 327–28; of elderly: Germany and United States, 307–13; of housing among elderly people in Germany and United States, 315–23; of housing by age: United States, 256–61; housing equity extraction among very old for, 279–83; income-tracking of younger and older cohorts: Taiwan, 350–56, 360; predictions using life-cycle model: Taiwan, 342–50

Current Population Survey (CPS), 107

Data sources: determinants of nursing home utilization, 409–12; forecasts of nursing home use among elderly, 367, 372–77; housing market in response to demographic swings, 237–45; 401(k) plan eligibility and participation, 107; for life expectancy analysis, 82, 86; for mortality model, 53–57; pension plan provisions and retirement decisions, 184, 190; saving, growth, and aging in Taiwan, 334–35; savings behavior among aged, 307; for U.S. population projections, 14. *See also* Household cohorts.

Deferred compensation plans. *See* 401(k) saving plans
Demographic factors: characteristics in model of determinants of nursing home use, 411–13; effect on housing market growth, 278–79; in explanation of differences in Japan/U.S. savings rates, 147–50; industrialized countries and Germany, 292–95; projected changes in structure, 14–18; Taiwan, 335–37. *See also* Aging population; Household cohorts; Population
Departure rates: under firm window of retirement option: predicted and actual, 194–96, 198–205; life-cycle for men and women: firm level, 190; predicted and actual: option value and stochastic dynamic programming models, 198–208; retirement age: at firm level, 191–94
Dependency ratio: Germany and industrialized countries, 293–94; predicted future U. S., 225–26
Disabilities: forecasts of cohort changes in dynamic physiology-based mortality model, 66–72; Grade of Membership concept to identify profiles of, 42, 43, 47–49; measures used in Grade of Membership analysis for mortality model, 53–57; model of distribution in population, 47–49; as predictor of mortality, 70
Dissaving (Germany), 326–27
Double aging. *See* Aging population

Earnings. *See* Income
Economic performance, Taiwan, 331–32
Economic Recovery Tax Act (1981), United States, 105
Education spending, future, 23–25
Elderly people: assistance to disabled in United States, 403; behavior under life-cycle hypothesis, 326–27; child-dependent in Taiwan, 333; dissaving: Germany, 326–27; effect of state policy in community living choices, 420–30; effect of state policy on use of helpers in community, 426–30; forecast model of age distribution use of nursing homes, 367–94; free riding, 159–62; health care and long-term care: industrialized countries, 400–403; home ownership, mobility and housing consumption: Germany and United States, 314–20; housing equity, 227–29; independent living in Taiwan, 333; independent or child-

dependent living: Taiwan, 333; labor force participation: Germany and United States, 299–304; model of projections of U. S. elderly population, 229, 236–37; model of substitution between community living or nursing home with variables related to policy, 421–30; old-age dependency ratios: industrialized countries and Germany, 293–95; projecting future health status, 42–72; welfare implications of housing prices for oldest old, 279–83

Fertility rates: industrialized OECD countries, 293–94; Taiwan, 333
Force of mortality: at ages 85, 90, and 95 in Sweden, 83–84, 91; hazard in model of mortality, 43–45; limited-life-span and mortality-reduction paradigms, 80–82; pattern of reduction in Sweden, 85–91
Forecasts: generated from dynamic physiology-based mortality model, 46–48, 53–73; of housing market, 274–79; of over–65 population in United States, 99–101; of response to change in risk factors, 101; of U. S. population (1900–2100), 229–35; of U. S. population (1990–2080), 14–18; uncertainty in population, 98–100. *See also* Predictions
401(k) saving plans: characteristics, 111–14; effect on saving behavior, 122–31, 139–41; eligibility and participation in, 106–13, 132; employer matching of employee contributions, 113–14; employer provision of, 106; potential effect on elderly households, 105; probability of contribution of given amount, 107; as saving instrument, 176–78; as substitute for individual retirement accounts, 114–21, 129–32

GoM. *See* Grade of Membership (GoM) concept
Government programs: effect of demographic changes on, 13–14; estimates of cost to maintain 1986 levels, 20–25; expected payments in United States (1986), 18–20, 29–33; housing markets: Germany and United States, 314, 320; projections of expected payments, 18–25, 34–37; transfer program descriptions, 27–28. *See also* Public policy, state-level
Government spending: current and projected, 34–36; estimated costs of maintaining

government program outlays, 13–14; for nursing homes, 397

Grade of Membership (GoM) concept, 42, 43, 47–49, 53–57, 73–74

Hazard or intensity of death. *See* Force of mortality

Health care: projected costs related to life expectancy of elderly, 98; scenario projections of future spending, 35–36. *See also* Medicaid program; Medicare program

Health insurance systems: effect on housing decisions of elderly: Germany and United States, 315; financing in industrialized countries: Europe and Canada, 400–403; Germany and United States, 306. *See also* Long-term care

Health models, 101–2

Helpers (as aids to elderly), 426–30

Household cohorts: construction for saving and life-cycle analysis: Taiwan, 338–42; evidence for consumption tracking income: Taiwan, 350–56, 360; in life-cycle interpretation of consumption and saving: Taiwan, 342–50

Households: aging of German, 293; effect of tax-deferred saving plans on other forms of saving, 114–21; elderly: Germany, 293; participation and balances in 401(k) saving plans and IRAs, 107–13, 132; potential effect of 401(k) plans on elderly, 105; savings: Taiwan, 331–33; savings and wealth: Germany and United States, 307–12; substitutability of IRAs and 401(k)s, 114–22, 129–30; test of savings effects of 401(k) plans, 122–31

Housing: age distribution of housing assets, 245–61; ownership, mobility, and consumption: Germany and United States, 315–20; real user cost under expectations models, 245–50

Housing equity: of elderly, 227–29; extraction among very old, 279–83

Housing market: consumption profiles (1940, 1960, 1970, 1980), 257–61; different models of demand and supply functions, 251–74, 286–87; government intervention in Germany and United States, 314–15; impact of changing demographics on, 227–29; impact of demographic changes on, 227; projections of prices, supply and demand, 274–79, 286; rental: Germany and United States, 314–15

Income: age distribution of, 245, 251–61; annuity income in Germany, 307–13; sources: Germany and United States, 307–13; taxation in Germany and United States, 304–5; tax treatment while receiving public pension: Germany and United States, 299

Income, retirement: differences in levels: Germany and United States, 295–99; increase relative to labor income in Germany and United States, 300

Individual retirement accounts (IRAs): participation and balances in, 107–11, 116–17; as substitute for 401(k) saving plans, 114–21, 129–32; volume of contributions, 105, 116–20

Insurance. *See* Health insurance systems; Long-term care; Unemployment insurance

Intergenerational considerations: altruism in saving model, 154–59; effect of preferences on levels of savings, 174; effect of public policy on housing transfers, 322–23; estimates of saving with, 154–62; in housing demand model, 279–84, 288; transfers in savings model, 145–62; undersaving by elderly in savings model, 159–62

Investment, impact of saving, 175–76

Labor force participation: age 65 and over: Germany and United States, 299–304; retiree/worker ratio: Germany, 294; trends in OECD countries, 299–300

Lexis maps, 86–89

Life–cycle hypothesis: age-wealth profiles: Germany and United States, 311–12; behavior of elderly under, 326–27; of consumption and saving: Taiwan, 342–50; implications in Taiwan, 331–34

Life expectancy: current and long-term in industrialized countries, 79–81, 293–94; forecast of remaining life expectancy in Sweden, 89–91; forecasts for over-65 population in United States, 99–100; forecasts from dynamic physiology-based mortality model, 66–73; Germany, 293–94; limited-life-span paradigm, 81–82; oldest-old mortality rates in Sweden, 89–90; Taiwan, 333

Living status, elderly: determinants dependent on public policy, 421–26; housing and living arrangements: Germany and United

Living status, elderly (*continued*)
States, 315–23. *See also* Community living; Elderly people; Housing; Housing market; Intergenerational considerations; Nursing homes
Long-term care: current financing, 395; degrees of financing in industrialized countries, 400–403; financing in United States, 403–9; insurance to provide for possibility of long-term care, 397; model of demand and supply factors in market for, 405–9; proposals to increase coverage, 395–96; public provision, 397–98. *See also* Community living; Living status, elderly; Medicaid program; Medicare program; Nursing homes

Malnutrition, 74
Mapping of demographic rates, 86–88
Medicaid program: effect on incentive to save, 175; effect on use of nursing homes, 417–20; estimates of future payments, 22–26; long-term care financing by, 395, 399, 403; state program eligibility differences, 403–7
Medicare program: effect on decision to retire, 185, 205–7; effect on incentive to save, 175; estimates of future payments, 21–26; payment rules for nursing home care, 407
Moral hazard (long-term care), 396, 398, 403, 420–21, 438–39
Mortality: disability as predictor of, 70; dynamic model using physiological influences as variables, 42–53, 95; level of, 83. *See also* Force of mortality
Mortality rates: current and long-term in industrialized countries, 79–81; data from Statistics Sweden, 82; evidence of reduction in Sweden, 83–91; life expectancy at current: industrialized countries, 79–80; modeling to forecast, 100–101
Mortality-reduction paradigm, 81–82
● Mortality risk factors: effect of variation on population forecasts, 99–102; forecast of change using health models, 101–2

National Long-Term Care Survey (NLTCS), 50, 53, 410–11
Nursing homes: Medicaid payments for costs of, 403; model to forecast age distribu-
tion of use, 367–72; model with policy variables of substitution by elderly of community living or, 421–30; simulation of elderly experiences in, 371–72, 388–94
Nursing home use: composition of users, 417–20; duration model, 367–88; factors affecting aggregate use in model of, 413–17; model and estimates, 368–88

Option value model: comparison of parameter estimates with stochastic dynamic programming model, 198–207; description, 194–97, 208–9; related to retirement age decisions: Germany and United States, 301–2; of retirement: predictive validity, 183–85

Pension plans, private: effect on time frame of decision to retire, 185–90; in Germany and United States, 295–303
Population: age composition, 225–26; forecast uncertainty, 98–102; predicted peak U.S., 225–26; projections (1990–2080), 14–18; projections by age of U.S. (1900–2100), 229–35; Taiwan, 331–33. *See also* Aging population; Demographic factors
Predictions: of health status of elderly, 42–72; of life expectancy: implications for public policy, 3; of nursing home use by elderly people, 413–17; of retirement: comparison of decision model outcomes, 194–207, 213–14; of retirement: option value model, 194–208, 213–14; of retirement: stochastic dynamic programming model, 194–208, 213–14; similarities and divergence of option value and stochastic dynamic programming models, 214–19; validity of option value and stochastic dynamic programming models, 184–85. *See also* Forecasts
Preferences: as reflection of savings rate differences, 153–65; effect on levels of saving of intergenerational, 174; effect on saving of intergenerational, 174–76; effect on saving behavior in Japan and United States, 143–44; as reason for decline in U.S. saving, 170–72; for saving, 177–78; in saving behavior, 122–31
Prices: forecasts of housing, 279–80, 286–88; welfare implications of changes in housing, 279–83

Prices. *See also* Housing equity; Housing market

Profit-sharing plans, 133

Public pension systems. *See* Social security systems

Public policy: designed to stimulate rate of saving, 176; effect of changing mortality risk determinants on, 98; effect on living arrangements of elderly, 322–23; for housing market: Germany and United States, 315–23; hypothetical role in changing saving behavior, 173; implications of life expectancy predictions for, 3; influence on housing market: Germany and United States, 314; long-term care programs in industrialized countries, 400–403; problems of proposed long-term care program, 398–99; response of retirement behavior to: Germany and United States, 303–4

Public policy, state-level: effect on nursing home use and community support, 405, 407–9; effect on user composition in nursing homes, 417–20; Medicaid eligibility differences, 22–23, 403–6; response of community resources to elderly living requirements, 420–30

Retirement age: in Germany and United States, 295–301; option value model to analyze decision for, 301–2; predictions using stochastic dynamic programming model, 197; simulated average: Germany, 302–3

Retirement decision: factors in consideration of, 185–90; firm motivation to provide options, 221; incentives in Germany and United States, 295, 298–99; life-cycle departure rates at firm level, 190–94; option value model of postponing, 194–97; predictions of option value and stochastic dynamic programming models, 194–208; two models testing validity of predictions of, 184–85, 213–15. *See also* Departure rates; Taxation; Window of retirement

Revenue Act (1978), 106

Risk factors: in dynamic model of mortality with physiological variables, 53–74; effect of changes on population forecasts, 100–102; effect of improvements on mortality rates, 41–42; forecasts from dynamic mortality model, 57–66; mortality

as function of histories of, 3. *See also* Mortality risk factors

Samaritan's dilemma, 175

Saving accounts, tax-deferred, 105. *See also* 401(k) saving plans

Saving behavior: bequests in, 327–28; under consumption-tracking-income theory: Taiwan, 350–56, 360; effect of interest rate differences: Japan and United States, 150–52; household: Germany and United States, 304–12; of 401(k) and non-401(k) contributors, 122–31; of 401(k)-eligible families and IRS contributors, 120–21

Savings: behavioral theory of household saving, 172–76; decline in U.S. national, 169–70; different options: Germany and United States, 306; 401(k) as component of retirement, 132; life-cycle hypothesis of household saving in Taiwan, 342–59; model in intergenerational context, 145–50; model in intergenerational context with social welfare function, 154–59; neoclassical reasons for low, 173–76; preferences in Japan and United States affects levels of, 143–44; rates in Japan and United States: context of world economy, 146–47; subsidy incentives in Germany, 304–5; tax-advantages savings plans as substitute for other, 114–21; test of effect of 401(k) plans on, 122–31. *See also* Wealth

Savings rates: differences reflect different tastes or preferences, 153–65; explanations for decline in U.S., 169–71; Germany and United States, 304–5; in Japan and United States (1960–89), 146–48

Senescence (in dynamic physiology-based mortality model), 42–46, 66

Social Security Administration, United States: effect on incentive to save, 175; estimates of future payments, 21–26, 34–35; as factor in time frame for retirement, 188–89; population projection data, 14, 34

Social security systems: disincentives to work: Germany and United States, 328; effect on incentives to save in Japan and United States, 175; effect on motives to save, 175; pay-as-you go method: Germany and United States, 295–96; reform in Germany and United States, 298–99; retirement income: Germany and United

Social security systems (*continued*)
States, 295–300, 306; simulated average
retirement age and contribution rates,
302–3; Taiwan, 337; tax treatment of
earnings while receiving public pension:
Germany and United States, 299. *See
also* Pension plans, private
Stochastic dynamic programming model: comparison of parameter estimates with option value model, 198–207; description,
197, 209–12; of retirement: predictive validity, 184–85
Subsidies: housing markets in Germany and
United States, 314–15, 320–21; incentives for saving behavior: Germany,
304–5; rental housing: Germany and
United States, 314–15, 320–23
Survey of Consumer Finances (SCF), 107
Survey of Income and Program Participation
(SIPP), 107

Taxation: of capital income affects levels of
saving, 173–74; of 401(k) savings plan,
106; of income and capital gains: Germany and United States, 304–5; of labor
earnings for pension recipients: Germany
and United States, 299
Tax Reform Act (1986): provisions for IRAs
under, 105, 111, 116–18, 132; provisions
related to 401(k) contributions, 106

Time process: in mortality model with physiological variables, 44–53, 73
Transfers, intergenerational, 145–62

Uncertainty: in growth and health changes of
elderly population, 73–74; in life-cycle
model of consumption: Taiwan, 346–48;
in population forecasts, 98–100; potential
effect on retirement decision: option
value and stochastic dynamic programming models, 215–18
Undersaving: free riding by elderly in saving
model in intergenerational context,
159–62; saving model in intergenerational context with social welfare consideration, 154–59
Unemployment insurance, 175

Wealth: bequests as component of accumulation, 327; tangible and intangible household: Germany and United States, 307–
12. *See also* Savings
Welfare: estimates of future payments, 23–25;
implications of housing price changes
for, 279–83
Window of retirement: at firm level: effect on
decision to retire, 189–90, 194; Germany
and United States, 296–97; option value
model describes actual behavior, 302. *See
also* Retirement decision